Profiles of 341 Syri
in the history of the

Naziq al- 22 who ripped off her veil, picked up a rifle, and ran to join the battle of Maysaloun against French invaders in July 1920.

Faris al-Khury, the Syrian statesman who participated in the founding of the UN in 1945. Khury was the first and only Christian to serve as prime minister of a Muslim country.

Shukri al-Quwatli, the esteemed father of Syrian independence in 1946— called by many the George Washington of Syria.

Husni Za'im, a military man who, with the backing of the CIA, seized power in a coup d'etat in 1949—the first modern day coup in the Arab world.

Hafez al-Asad, the son of a notable from an isolated mountain town who became president. The government he founded is one of the longest-lived in modern history.

Syria has been subjected to more trial since the armistice (in 1918) than any other Near Eastern country. All is not lost, however, there is room for hope. The territory we have been left with, greater than the area covered by Belgium, Holland, and Switzerland put together, is a vast playing field for our young people and for their entrepreneurial spirit. The Syrian soil is fertile, we produce cereals, cotton, fruit. We have oil. Our artisans are some of the most ingenious in the world. Our people are sober, tough, dutiful and hard-working. Syrians are found all over the world, and everywhere they occupy important positions. The spiritual forces of our country are intact. The past and the future are ours. We have every reason to believe that Syria will survive.

—Syrian Prime Minister Jamil Mardam Bey
at independence in April 1946.

Quick Reference
Profiles by Last Name

Quick Reference

Profiles by Chapter

Officers

Arts & Letters

Journalists

The Bridge between the Cultures Series from Cune Press

A Pen of Damascus Steel by Ali Farzat
Is Syria Next? by Carsten Wieland
The Road from Damascus by Scott C. Davis
Searching Jenin by Ramzy Baroud

Coming Soon
Light in the Palace by Scott C. Davis
Jerusalem Heat by Annette Peizer

To Abdul-Salam Haykal, with gratitude.

Steel & Silk

Men & Women Who Shaped Syria 1900 - 2000

By Sami Moubayed

 Cune

Steel & Silk:
Men and Women who Shaped Syria 1900–2000
Cune Press, Seattle 2006
© 2006 by Sami Moubayed
All Rights Reserved
Paperback ISBN 10 digit 1885942419 (13 digit 978-1885942418) $29.95
Hardback ISBN 10 digit 1885942400 (13 digit 978-1885942401) $44.95

Library of Congress CIP information:

Moubayed, Sami M.
Steel & Silk : Men and Women Who Shaped Syria 1900-2000 / Sami Moubayed.
p. cm. -- (Bridge between the cultures)
Includes bibliographical references and index.
ISBN 1-885942-40-0 (hardback : alk. paper) -- ISBN 1-885942-41-9 (pbk. : alk. paper)
1. Syria--Biography--Dictionaries--English. I. Title: Steel and Silk. II. Title. III. Bridge Between the Cultures Series
CT1916. M68 2004
920.05691--dc22
2004015477

Cune Press
PO Box 31024
Seattle, WA 98103
Tel (206) 782-0136
www.cunepress.com
Copies of *Steel & Silk* can be purchased from your local independent bookstore,
from www.cunepress.com, or by calling 1-800-445-8032.
Errata: corrections of fact will be posted online at:
www.cunepress.com/errata

Thanks to Mamoun Sakkal (www.sakkal.com) for calligraphy.
Thanks to the Salaam Cultural Museum for its support.

Contents

Definitions & Abbreviations

Listed below are translations of names that appear in Arabic throughout the text, along with phrases and terms that also appear repeatedly and for many readers will require explanation. (Other newspapers are given graphic representation in Journalists.)

Names of Periodicals

Al-Ahram: The Pyramid
Al-Akhbar: The News
Akher Daqiqa: The Last Minute
Alif Ba'e: A, B
Al-Arus: The Bride
Al-`Asi: The Orontes
Al-Asima: The Capital
Al-Ayyam: The Days
Al-Baath: The Revival
Barada: For the River Barada in Damascus.
Dimashq: Damascus
Ad-Domari: The Lamplighter
Al-Dunya: The World
Fata al-Arab: The Arab Youth
Al-Fayha: Damascus
Al-Hawadeth: The Events
Al-Inshaa: The Creation
Al-Islah: The Reform
Al-Iqtisad wa Annaqel: Economy and Transport
Al-Kifah: The Struggle
Lisan al-Arab: The Arab Tongue
Al-Manar: The Light
Al-Manar al-Jadid: The New Light
Mir'at al-Sharq: Mirror of the East
Al-Mudhik al-Mubki: Laughing and Crying
Al-Nahhar: The Morning
Al-Naqid: The Critic
Al-Nas: The People
Al-Nasir: The Victory
Al-Nidal: The Struggle
Noor al-Fayha: The Light of Damascus
Al-Nuqqad: The Critics
Al-Qabas: The Firebrand
Al-Ra'e al-Am: Public Opinion
Al-Safir: The Ambassador
Al-Sha'b: The People
Al-Shahr: The Month
Al-Sham: Damascus
Al-Shati' al-Souri: The Syrian Coast
As-Shira: The Sail
Al-Souri al-Jadid: The New Syrian
Souriyya al-Jadida: The New Syria
Tabibak: Your Doctor
Al-Tahrir al-Arabi: Arab Liberation
Al-Thawra: The Revolution
Tishreen: October
Al-Wihda al-Arabiyya: Arab Unity
Usbu' al-Arabi: The Arab Week

Political Terms

Arab Mountain. Used in reference to the Druze Mountain in southern Syria. It is not used frequently in non-Arabic books and sources but is a common term in Syria.

Civil Rights. Refers to the civil rights of Syrian politicians that were abolished by the Revolutionary Command Council (RCC) in 1963. The terminated rights included: the right to vote, the right to hold public office, the right to receive a salary or pension from the state, and the right to work in a community (being religious or social), a syndicate (i.e. professional organization), or any academic institution. "Civil rights" also include the right to own property and work in the media, either as a publisher or a journalist, and the right to hold medals, ranks, titles, and decorations from the Syrian Republic.

Al-Fatat Society. Translated as "young and new." Al-Fatat is the secret society founded by Arab nationalists in Ottoman Syria in 1911.

Al-Gharra Society. Translated as "glorious." Al-Gharra is the charity society founded by Sheikh Ali al-Daqr in 1924 to cater to the education of Muslim children in Damascus.

Intifada. Means "uprising" in reference to the two uprisings that took place in Palestine in 1987 and in 2000.

Al-Tamaddun al-Islami Society
The Society of Islamic Urbanization.

ACRONYMS

ALM: Arab Liberation Movement. The party created by General Adib al-Shishakli in 1953. It preached pan-Arabism, Arab unity, women's. emancipation, and limited socialist reform. It lost all political weight when Shishakli was toppled in 1954.

AUB: American University of Beirut.

BCW: Beirut College for Women.

CUP: Committee for Union and Progress. Founded by young Ottoman officers who aimed to reform the Empire. They siezed power in 1908 and deposed Sultan Abdulhamid II in 1909. The CUP began as a reform movement but soon became a dictatorship, prompting the Arabs to declare a revolt against the CUP in 1916.

DCC: Damascus Chamber of Commerce.

DFLP: Democratic Front for the Liberation of Palestine.

IPS: Institute of Palestinian Studies. Established in Beirut in 1963. A pioneer in the translation of Israeli Hebrew sources. Established a school for the teaching of modern Hebrew, a Center for Hebrew Studies, and a monthly digest in Arabic of translations from the Hebrew press.

MAN: Movement of Arab Nationalists. Loyal to Gamal Abd al-Nasser of Egypt. In July 1963, tried and failed to sieze power in Syria with the help of Nasserist officers in the Syrian Army.

MBC: Middle East Broadcasting Channel. The pioneering Saudi Arabian satellite channel that achieved popularity in the Arab World during the early 1990s, long before the Doha-based Aljazeera Channel.

NPF: National Progressive Front. Founded by President Hafez al-Asad, after he came to power in 1970, as a coalition of socialist parties in parliament operating under the umbrella of the ruling Baath Party.

PLO: Palestinian Liberation Organization.

PFLP: Popular Front for the Liberation of Palestine.

RCC: Revolutionary Command Council. Created after the Military Committee of the Baath Party siezed power in Syria in March 1963. It became the supreme authority in Syria in 1963-1970, and ceased to operate when Hafez al-Asad came to power in 1970.

SANA: Syrian Arab News Agency.

SSNP: Syrian Social Nationalist Party. A party pledging unification of Greater Syria created by the Lebanese philosopher Antune Sa'ada in 1932.

UAR: United Arab Republic. The UAR was created by Syria and Egypt in 1958 and dissolved by Syria in 1961.

UN: United Nations.

UNDP: United Nations Development Program.

NOTE ON PARTIES:

The name "People's Party" can refer either to the 1925 Shahbandar People's Party or to the 1950s party of the same name that was associated with Rushdi al-Kikhiya and Nazim al-Qudsi.

PHOTO CREDITS: (See page 594.)

Acknowledgements

I would like to thank the institutions that helped me conduct my research in the Arab world and Europe. They are the Jaffett Library at the American University of Beirut (AUB), the Syrian Culture Club (SCC) at AUB, the Arab Language Assemblage in Syria, the Syrian Arab News Agency (SANA), the Asad National Library, the BBC World Service archives in London, the Arab Documentation Center at the University of Exeter, the London School of Economics (LSE), the School of Oriental and African Studies (SOAS) at the University of London, the British Library in London, the Public Records Office (PRO) in London, the Damascus Chamber of Commerce (DCC), and the Historical Documentation Center in Damascus.

The list of people who have assisted this project from its inception and offered their suggestions, corrections, and encouragement, is a long one. To all those who helped me in the completion of this work, I am grateful. Mr Abdul-Salam Haykal, Ms Thuraya Ismail, Assistant Professor Joshua Landis, Mr Jamal Mansour, Dr Kevin Martin read the book at various stages of composition and edited some of the manuscripts, while Dr Nicolas Chahine, Mr Salahuddine Habal, Mr Ridwan al-Atasi, Mrs Colette Khury, Ms Alia Mansour, Mr Sahban Abd Rabbo, Dr Mahmud Nofal, Mr Nazir Sinan, and the late Dr Munir al-Ajlani, and Mr Abd al-Ghani al-Itri, were also generous with their time, helping me with my research and in gathering documents for the work. Vice-President Abd al-Halim Khaddam, former Defense Minister Mustapha Tlas, and former Prime Ministers Dr Abdel Raouf al-Kassem and General Abd al-Rahman Khlayfawi took the time to see me for interviews and offered their insight on the work and on Syria in the twentieth century.

I thank Scott C. Davis of Cune Press for his support. Thanks also to many in the US who helped: John Anderson, Lorna Burden, Barbara Bodden, Melissa Flesch, Professor Thomas Gage, Janet Holt, Richard F. Johnson, Peggy Strawhorn Kass, Annette Peizer, Christina Velasquez, Dan Watkins, Meghan Bush Whitmore, Richard Wood. Needless to say, any faults, misconceptions, or omissions in this book are strictly my own.

Most important, I would like to thank my mother and father who have encouraged my interest in Syrian history from my early days, and who have support my education and all of my book projects.

On Arabic

For lay readers, the representation of Arabic words in English is an inexact science—the source of unnecessary confusion. Words that have a consistent spelling in Arabic may be transliterated several different ways in English—which often leads the lay reader to think that two different Arabic words are involved. In years past, for example, adherents of the Prophet were "Moslems," even though today we refer to "Muslims." To put it rather simply, from the gentle tone of Victorian travel narratives compared to the more gritty attitude of contemporary Western news reporting, a reader might judge that Moslems are a fair-minded hospitable people whereas Muslims are unpredictable and dangerous. In truth, the Arabic word is the same. Only the transliteration varies.

Many sounds that are represented in Arabic by characters such as Aayn ع have no exact correspondence to the Latin characters used in English. In some texts, the Aayn will be represented as "aa," and in others as "a'a." In order to make our text less intimidating to lay readers, I have for the most part dropped the apostrophe. So I refer to the newspaper *Inshaa*, rather than *Insha'a*.

There are also different conventions for transliteration. For example, the English prefer to transliterate the letter Sheen ش using "sh" where, in French, an "ch" is preferred. Hence our use of *"Inshaa"* for the newspaper—even though it carries the French transliteration of *"Inchaa"* on its masthead. Also, this explains our last minute effort to correct the transliteration of the name of the esteemed Administrator Nicolas Shahine to Nicolas Chahine. Mr Chahine argued that most of his family speaks French as a second language and English only as a third language—so they prefer the French transliteration.

Perhaps the greatest source of confusion for lay readers is the use of the article in front of many names—and the varied spellings of the article. Most Arabic names that take an article use the proper "al-" or "el-" (as in the Egyptian newspaper *Al-Ahram, The Pyramid*). However, in actual speech the article is slurred when the word that follows begins with certain consonants (called "solar letters"), and so the article can be spelled differently in English. For example, the satirical newspaper that figured in Syria's Damascus Spring is transliterated *"Ad-Domari"* (the Lamplighter) and the small Lebanese newspaper that broke the Iran Contra scandal is spelled *"As-Shira."* Although the spoken transliteration is most often used, the "al-" is also correct. And often you will see a name represented both ways. I have used both forms, preferring the "al-" in bibliographic listings and the spoken version in the body of the book.

In many cases the transliterations used in this book will seem unfamiliar to non-specialists. For the most part, I have forsaken modern journalistic practice to use transliterations that are most common in historical works on the period such as Patrick Seale's *Asad: the Struggle for the Middle East* and Philip Khoury's *Syria and the French Mandate.*

Occasionally, I will transliterate the name of a post World War II figure in an old fashioned way (the way his father's and grandfather's names would have been spelled in their day) to show the continuity from one generation to the next. In the case of individuals who are extremely well known public figures, I have had to relent. I refer to King Hussein of Jordan, for example, and hope that the reader will still grasp the point that he is the descendant of Sharif Husayn of Mecca.

Author's Note

I took up this book project because no serious attempt since 1957 has been made to create a comprehensive biographical dictionary for Syria. The first "who's who" in Syria was written by the late journalist George Faris in 1946 to commemorate the end of the French Mandate. The book was released in 1949 with the idea that it would be updated periodically. When Syria and Egypt merged to form the United Arab Republic (UAR) in 1958, President Gamal Abd al-Nasser of Egypt put a stop to the project. In the late 1990s, a few biographical dictionaries appeared in Syria, but they were too subjective and weak in historical research to serve as proper reference sources on Syria.

The idea to write this book first came to mind in 1997, while I was doing research for my first book *The Politics of Damascus 1920-1946*. I realized that writers would benefit immensely from a reference to Syrian lives in the years 1900-2000. I began working on this book three years later. This is the first book in English to deal with Syria from the reign of Sultan Abdulhamid II, whose final years in power were 1900-1909, to the era of President Bashar al-Asad, who came to power in 2000.

Few people today understand what Syria went through during these past 100 years. Most Westerners know little about Syria prior to the Arab-Israeli Conflict in 1948, whereas Arabs in general and Syrians in particular are interested mainly in the past 30 years under the late President Hafez al-Asad. I have written about the men and women who contributed to the country that exists today, in the first few years of the 21st century.

To make a project of this size feasible, I have excluded religious leaders and businessmen. I also excluded those who worked strictly in legal affairs and the sciences. Instead I have concentrated on the following fields: officers, administrators, national activists, politicians, academics or educators, journalists, diplomats, and men and women of arts and letters.

My objective in writing this book was to include a comprehensive list of men and women who I believed were influential in the shaping of Syria. Technically, *Steel & Silk* is not a who's who of modern Syria. In other words, it does not attempt to be complete. Neither does it cover everyone who reached a senior post in the past 100 years, nor does it include all those who became famous in their respective fields. It does not concentrate on the notables. Neither does it focus on the leaders of post-1963 Syria. The profiles in this work do not thoroughly represent everyone who passed through Syrian history in the past 100 years. I offer my apologies to the many distinguished Syrians not included. I also extend regrets for my narration of flaws, foibles, failures, and folly. I have avoided the impulse to white-wash my subjects because, in the end, to do so is no honor. Every human being has imperfections, and it's necessary to note these before a reader is willing to give full credit to an individual's virtues or accomplishments.

My method of research was to conduct face-to-face interviews. I supplemented information gleaned from interviews with earlier biographical dictionaries in Arabic, newspapers from the past century, and books in both Arabic and English. For some profiles, I also relied on official documents that I found at the Public Records Office in London, the American University of Beirut, and various institutions in Damascus. While I was writing *Steel & Silk*, some subjects (for example ex-President Nazim al-Qudsi and ex-Prime Minister Ma'mun al-Kuzbari) died before giving me a promised interview. Others died right after I met with them (Ambassador Rafic Jouejati, the politician Abd al-Wahab Homad, and the journalist Abd al-Ghani al-Itri). The contributions of the latter group were instrumental to the completion of this work, since they are central figures in Syrian life from the 1930s until 2003.

All of my subjects endured a barrage of communication from me, aside from direct interviews. They answered dozens of questions delivered by email, post mail, phone, and fax.

I have found that many of the existing Arabic biographical reference works are inconsistent and unreliable. I have attempted to verify information using other published sources and my own interviews whenever possible. Unfortunately, the memories of friends, colleagues, and family are not exact and often contradict one another, even on simple matters of fact. The current text of this book is far more accurate than its predecessors. Still, I am aware of its shortcomings, and ask readers to assist me in improving future editions by forwarding documentary proof of errors and inaccuracies to me or to the publisher.

Finally, I must add that I am an admirer of many of the personalities in this book, while I am a sharp critic of others. Some will forever be hailed for their deeds while others will forever be cursed. Collectively, however, the men and women in this book are responsible for the Syria that exists today. *Steel & Silk* is an effort to give them their due place in the history of Syria and the history of the Middle East as a whole.

—Sami Moubayed
Damascus, May 2005

Preface

The Book, for Lay Readers

Steel & Silk was designed to be a reference work, an historical record, and part of the larger body of scholarly fact and analysis. Typically such works are dry and tedious to the lay reader.

But a funny thing happened. The small army of fact checkers and proof readers working on this book couldn't put it down. The text contained a human drama that was cinematic in its scope. Readers were reminded of a vast sprawling Dostoyevsky novel, with utterly black-hearted scoundrels, stooges, yes men—as well as feisty women who picked up rifles and fought for independence; wise leaders who were betrayed and murdered by their supposed protectors; and brave captains of underground revolt who were captured and hung on public scaffolds by stiff-uniformed foreign troops.

In fact, *Steel & Silk* has what Dostoyevsky novels are most known for: a plot that links a vast number of characters. The theme that runs through the 341 Syrian lives depicted here is the story of a people who yearned for independence under the Ottomans, achieved it after World War I, and then were keel-hauled by the French and British in Paris in 1919.

This is the story of a people who, when real independence arrived in 1946, quickly learned that a small state required a patron and protector to survive. Again and again they petitioned the United States to resume the role it had played during World War I, the role of an impartial broker and former colony that validated the aspirations of a people clawing their way out from under 400 years of foreign occupation.

This is the story of an innocent citizenry seeking to learn the lessons of the Enlightenment. Instead, France and the United States taught Syria that military might trumps democracy every time. In 1920, French artillery blasted away Syria's first national government. In 1945 Syrian diplomats participated in founding the United Nations in San Francisco and beseeched their fellow diplomats for help in creating an independent democracy. A month later, French warplanes responded by bombing the Parliament in Damascus and killing 600 civilians. In 1949, when Syria was once again independent and holding free elections, the CIA engineered the Arab world's first military coup in Syria and later participated in two other coups.

The story told by *Steel & Silk* takes the reader to the very edge of the cliff and then, at the moment when the hero is teetering on the brink—this book abruptly ends. Will Syria survive the violence in neighboring Iraq? Will Syria open its economy wide enough to unleash the entrepreneurial abilities of its people? Will Syria emerge as a native democracy that takes the best Western ideas and practices and gives them meaning within an Oriental context? *Steel & Silk* asks us to look to the next few years of unfolding history for the resolution of its themes.

Steel & Silk is an invaluable resource for scholars, journalists, and researchers. And this is a book for lay readers as well. The lives depicted in this volume—the aspiration, longing, and heartbreak—speak to us. The grit, the fact, the detail tell us of a specific past. Yet they also demonstrate the difficult science and the dark art of civic life—a science and an art that blesses and curses every human being on this planet.

The Syrian Nation

Syria is an ancient land that has been included in many different empires over the centuries. In "modern times," Syria was part of Alexander's Greek Empire, then the Roman-Byzantine Empire, then the Islamic Empire, and, finally, the Ottoman Empire. For three or four thousand years before World War I, Syria and neighboring lands were organized locally by their cities, tribes, and geographic enclaves—and organized broadly by the empire that held sway at the time. In 1914, if you asked a Syrian where he was from, it's likely that he would say, Beirut or Damascus or Alexandretta. Or he might say, Jebel Shouf, Jebel Druze, Jebel Nusayri. Syrians defined themselves by the nearest city, or by a nearby *jebel* (mountain). They also defined themselves by family or village or tribe—villages and tribes normally included people of similar race, religion, and language.

The governing system of empire, when transferred to an organizational chart, looks loose and sloppy to Western observers. At the turn of the last century, Western writers joked that the Ottoman Empire was the "sick man of Europe." But now scholars are beginning to appreciate the unparalleled ability of the Ottoman Empire to accommodate local differences and to mediate between competing groups.

Measured against the concept of empire, the nation is a highly organized political and economic entity. It requires local custom and culture to give way to a larger identity. The process of forging a nation is seldom pretty. Always, there is tension between the national concept and local allegiance, and frequently there is violence as the sharp edges of local culture and custom are ground off by the weight of national ambition. Yet the first nations that were successful in enticing or coercing their indigenous populations into cooperation in the national project were rewarded with enormous wealth. In the national system that emerged in the 1800s, just a few nations controlled 85% of the earth's surface area.

At the close of World War I, Britain and France imposed the concept of "nation" on Syria and other Arab lands. This concept aroused the aspirations of every tribal, ethnic, geographic, and religious group included within Syria's borders. Appeals to patriotism and the demonizing of a common Israeli enemy did little to induce voluntary consent for any one national government among people who, over the preceding 4,000 years, had sworn loyalty to family, to tribe, or to the city or mountain region of their birth. After independence in 1946, coups were frequent and, until the Baath took power in 1963, no government lasted longer than a year or two. Still, historians and Syrians themselves do not agree on the degree of centrifugal force present in Syria—then or now. Was the curtailment of human rights and democratic practices required to prevent fragmentation? Or was the threat of chaos merely a pretext invented or inflated by those who wished to assert the authority of the state? Either way this argument plays out, it's clear that the result of the European national system—as applied to Syria—was seventeen years of short-lived governments followed by a strict security regime that has lasted for more than four decades.

Syria suffered the drawbacks of nationhood, yet the prime benefit of this status—the opportunity to dominate vast territories, to colonize them, to loot their resources—was not available to it. The best that a nation such as Syria could hope for was to efficiently cultivate the resources within its boundaries. Unfortunately, this opportunity was also taken from Syria, at least in part, when foreign powers stole jewels from the Syrian crown.

After the French seized power in 1920, they hoped to leverage their traditionally close relationship with Beirut's Christians into a permanent presence in the Levant. They quickly carved western territory out of Syria, labeled it "Lebanon," and put Christians from Beirut and nearby Mount Lebanon in charge—sowing the seeds of the Lebanese Civil war fifty years later. In 1939, the French gave away a choice portion of the Syrian coast to Turkey in exchange for Turkey's neutrality in World War II. Most recently, in 1967 Israel (viewed in Syria as a vehicle for the projection of Western power) seized the Golan Heights in southern Syria.

After an unbroken string of territorial losses, it's understandable that Syrians would look on nationhood as an instrument of Western control rather than as a vehicle for expanding their power and enabling their commercial interests.

After independence in 1946, many Syrians and other Arabs were attracted by the ideal of pan-Arabism—the notion of a broader Arab nation made more emotional sense than tight national borders and the definition of "nation" itself that had been imposed by Britain and France. The experiment of uniting Syria with Nasser's Egypt in 1958 followed a similar logic. After the failure of union with Egypt, the Baath Party devoted itself to implementing the pan-Arab ideal within Syria, while using the pan-Arab concept to guide their diplomacy.

It's true that the Baath military government that has dominated Syria since 1963 truncated the country's political culture and put an end to its vibrant free press. Certainly there were excesses, incompetence, and corruption during the last forty-plus years of one party rule. But these difficult years mirror comparable periods of development in the evolution of all other nations. Under Baath rule, roads, water, electricity, and public education were delivered to poor country districts for the first time. Land reform was made permanent. And the principle was established that Syrians, even those of humble origin, could aspire to the most important positions in society and government.

In three years, Syria's oil will run out. The only alternative source of wealth is the ingenuity, talent, and dedication of Syrians inside the country and the many who have left to establish lives abroad. The future will bring power sharing, free elections, and a market economy—or chaos. The recent Baath Party Congress put Pan-Arabism on the back burner. Syrians are now facing the proposition that their fate is tied to that of their nation—however arbitrary and illogical its boundaries.

It's my hope that *Steel & Silk* will do its part to assist Syrians from many different backgrounds who seek a national consensus that they can use to forge a new Syrian nation. I hope this volume will restore links to people, political parties, independent newspapers, and cultural traditions that have been forgotten over the years. I hope that this book will inspire the young—a third of the Syrian population is under the age of twenty—to forgo selfish interests on behalf of the common good. I'd like them to know about people such as General Yusuf al-Azma who gave a heart-rending speech as he prepared to meet the French army in July 1920 with Syrian independence hanging in the balance. Although conceding that his death and the deaths of many of his citizen-soldiers were a forgone conclusion, al-Azma nevertheless declared, "The Syrian people will not die!"

The Author

I first met Sami Moubayed in a pizza place in London's Bayswater district one night in February 2002. I knew him by reputation as a writer, political commentator, and scholar. Since that night, I have gotten to know Sami well. He is completely literate in Arabic and English. He has had a first rate education in arts and humanities at the American University of Beirut and at the University of Exeter in Britain. Yet he is also an astute businessman who places service and honor above sharp dealing. Certainly, he has his flaws. Sometimes, without thinking, he lapses into an overbearing manner that, to me, is pure Medieval nobility. Some of his public debates with other Syrian intellectuals are crazy-fierce—a breath-taking display of fact, logic, intuition, instinct, and rock-like loyalty to the names of men long dead: amazing, yet far too intense for my taste.

Still, Sami has an astonishing unself-conscious love of things intellectual. Such guileless wonderment at words, ideas, and repartee is in short supply in the West where thinkers feel the need to adopt a cynical pose and where intellectuality tends to be a fashion statement or a career move. Sami revels in the complexities of history and history-in-the-making. He exults in intellectual exchange as a pleasure in its own right. I've spent hours with Sami, putting the world together and then taking it apart again. We debate Syrian politics and economics. I can never win, but I keep trying anyway. His intellect and training are excellent. Still, what distinguishes Sami is something simple: his love of ideas.

Sami's intellectual style is good entertainment, yet it's also helped me, and it's helped Syria. Take, for example, the US smear attacks on Syria that began on May 13, 2003—following the US invasion of Iraq. My book on Syria, *The Road from Damascus,* was arousing some interest, and I ended up as a guest on Fox News. They asked me to debate a professional talk show guest from the Heritage Foundation who had appeared on every major talk show and was paid a salary from conservative interests just to stay available to the media and to think about the world from a conservative point of view.

I was definitely outgunned. And Fox had a reputation of using liberals to wipe the floor. Also, Syria is a deep subject. I had only studied this country for 16 years. What did I really know about Syria, especially its politics and economics?

Then it struck me. I'd have no trouble talking about Syria if I were sitting in a Damascus coffee house with Sami Moubayed. Why do a talk show host and a conservative think-tanker have to be more intimidating than Sami? Now I understood: This was my opportunity to play Sami Moubayed while some other poor guy got to play the ignorant American. "I'm ready!" I told the producer. "I can do this!"

The interview went well. What worries me now is that the next time I'm on TV I may face an armed opponent. That's because *Steel & Silk* will make the personalities, the facts, and the broad themes of Syrian history readily available. This book will give Americans and all Westerners access to Syria.

Syrian Culture

I first visited Syria in 1987. I spent nearly three months traveling alone in the country, riding rickety country buses, drinking tea with the secret police, sleeping on concrete floors in the homes of hospitable Syrians who had spontaneously invited a stranger to stay the night.

In March 2003, in the run up to the Iraq War, the US embassy ordered Americans to leave, and nearly all Europeans left as well. I suppose that Damascus, as an international city, was the Syrian location that would be most understanding of an American under these strained circumstances. But I wanted to get beyond the Damascus bubble, to travel among ordinary Syrians, and to find out what they were thinking. So I headed out into the countryside, traveling at night to save time. I waited in the bus stations in dingy lounges filled with smoke and decorated with sullen Saudi travelers who, I guessed, were not members of the royal family. Every time I boarded a bus, I had to show my passport—so all the passengers learned that I was an American. On one ride, the secret policeman who checked our documents seemed personally insulted by the US invasion and offered some crude advice for President Bush. Others, however, spoke quietly about the need for change and the impossibility of ordinary men and women unseating a government such as Saddam's. The buses were small and the seats were hard—as they had been in 1987. Now, however, the buses had televisions mounted in front above the aisle. As we careened through the darkness, the TVs showed the bombing of Baghdad, the hunt for a downed American flyer in the reeds on the banks of the Euphrates, and the mangled bodies after a cruise missile landed on a Baghdad souk. The images were in living color.

Syrians were overtly anti-American. At least they disagreed with our foreign policy. Even though my countrymen were spilling Iraqi blood a few miles away, however, I was never challenged or threatened. Other than the one angry secret policeman, I was never treated rudely.

In my travels around Syria, I have met many Syrians who expressed incisive intellect and broad culture. Still, I'm won over by less dazzling qualities that are even more pervasive: nearly all Syrians express simple goodness, charm, allegiance, warmth, and courtesy.

The Syrians I admire have a whimsical medieval quality about them. Syria grew more slowly and over a longer period of time than America. A tradition of the "strong individual" emerged in the US. Certainly there were strong families as well. Yet America missed out on an essential intervening stage where village communities lived for centuries close to the earth, in balance with their surroundings, and pursued group strategies for coaxing a living from the soil.

Perhaps this is the reason that Syrian society is free of a whole range of problems that plague the US. Street crime in Syria is nearly non-existent, even though the Syrian criminal justice system is not extreme. No teen drugs, gangs, weapons. No school shootings. Little or no homelessness. Scarcely any old age homes. Syrian families and communities are large and enduring. They regulate society far more effectively than an impersonal legal system ever could. They create a stage and give a role to every member of every family. In Syria you may be loved or hated but beyond doubt you are known. You own a place in a family and a community and this gives you a reason to protect and enhance your reputation. In Syria, men and women participate in the common artistic endeavour of weaving and decorating a social fabric whose origins stretch far into the past.

You can accuse Syrian families of being too strong, too dominated by men. To a certain extent this is true of Syria and all other Mediterranean cultures. Yet those who read Steel & Silk will learn that a women's suffrage law was proposed in the independent Syrian parliament in 1918, two years before a similar measure passed into law in the United States. Today, Syria is changing and evolving. The aspirations of Syrian women who want to break free from the will of their male relatives is largely supported by government and by law. Syrian woman compose slightly more than fifty percent of the work force. Women's rights are equal to those in the United States and ahead of those in some European nations. Many Syrian women tell me that their families have reached the perfect balance of individual freedom and family closeness.

These days I visit Syria once or twice a year. I bring friends from America to travel among the villages, to see the monuments, and to meet the people. I'm writing another book. I can't stay away from this place where camaraderie, innocence, rich artistic temperament, an embracing family and community life, and pure intellectual exchange are found on every street corner.

American Readers

Steel & Silk gives Americans the opportunity to penetrate the stereotypes that prevail in the American media, to remove the haze of false accusation, and to see Syrian society in one sharply defined perspective. This book can prevent us from inadvertently harming a nation that has long sought our friendship. But there is more. Syria is a traditional society that is emerging into the modern world in an idiosyncratic way. Syrians are far from perfect. Yet they have something to teach us about the value of balancing individual careers and quick-paced free-flowing society with the restful and stable presence of family and community. Syrians have developed techniques for defending the best traditions of the past against the worst excesses of the present. And *Steel & Silk* provides a distinct point of access. It's my hope that American readers will have the wisdom to use this book well.

—Scott C. Davis,
Cune Press, Seattle

Steel & Silk

The first graduating class of the Syrian Air Force, 1947.

Fawzi al-Quawiqji, commander of the Army of Deliverance, during the Arab-Israeli War of 1948.

A group of Syrian officers at the warfront in Palestine in May 1948. To the far left of the photo is General Jamil Ramadan, who became director of military police and deputy chief-of-staff in the post-1948 era.

General Wadih al-Muqabari, who became commander of the Syrian Air Force in 1956-1963, pictured with an American airplane, Harvard AT-6. This airplane was originally used for training, but transferred into a war plane for emergency use in the Arab-Israeli War of 1948. During the war, 16 training planes were transformed into war planes and used in combat.

OFFICERS

The people listed in this chapter are Syrian military officers who held senior posts in three official armies: The Ottoman Army 1916-1918, the French Army (Army of the Levant) in 1920-1946, and the Syrian Army, created after Syria gained independence from France in 1946. This chapter also includes coup d'etat leaders, along with officers who became ministers and directors of the air force, the army, and political intelligence.

The National Bloc was a coalition of Syrian urban notables who comprised the leading anti-French movement in Syria. They sought to terminate the French Mandate (1920-1946) through diplomatic rather than military means.

Six wars punctuate the biographies of Syrian officers: World War I in 1914-1918, the Arab-Israeli War of 1948, the Six Day War against Israel in 1967, the Arab-Israeli War of 1973, known as the October War, and the war against Israel during its invasion of Lebanon in 1982. Most recently, in 1991 the Syrian army fought alongside the United States in Operation Desert Storm to liberate Kuwait from the Iraqi Army of Saddam Hussein.

In addition, Syrian officers joined in two rebellions, one against the Ottoman Army in 1916-1918, and the other against the French Mandate in 1920-1927. They were victorious against the Ottomans, but were defeated by the French in what is regarded as the greatest battle in modern Syrian history. The battle of Maysaloun took place on July 24, 1920, when Syrian forces met and engaged the invading French Army. The Syrians were defeated, and Syria's minister of war, Yusuf al-Azma, was killed in combat.

Alwan, Jassem
(1928-)

Jassem Alwan studied at the Homs Military Academy and joined the Syrian Army in 1946. In the 1950s, he joined the movement of Arab nationalism headed by President Gamal Abd al-Nasser of Egypt. During the union years with Egypt (1958-1961), Alwan established himself as one of the most prominent Nasserists in the Syrian Army. He served as commander of the Qatana military base on the outskirts of Damascus.

When a military coup dissolved the union in 1961, Alwan opposed the post-Nasser government of President Nazim al-Qudsi. He felt guilty that on the night of the coup (September 28) he had not been at his base, but rather on a military mission in Damascus. Had he not been away, Alwan believed he could have prevented the overthrow of the Nasser government in Syria. In 1962, Alwan tried to launch a coup against the Qudsi government, but it failed. In collaboration with the Military Committee of the Baath Party, Alwan succeeded in ousting the Qudsi administration in March 1963 and pledged to restore the United Arab Republic (UAR). To his dismay, however, he discovered that the Military Committee had no intention of sharing power with him, nor did it intend to restore Nasser as president of Syria.

In April 1963, Alwan began plotting for another coup with members of the Movement of Arab Nationalists (MAN), a radical Nasserist organization headed by Jihad Dahi and Hani al-Hindi. On July 18, 1963, Alwan launched his coup, but it was crushed by Interior Minister Amin al-Hafez. With submachine gun in hand, Hafez opened fire on a group of Alwan's best men, who had laid siege to the Damascus radio station. In the stampede, many civilians were killed. Nasser made a radio announcement, condemning the suppression of Alwan's coup and saying, "No union with the Baathists!"

Alwan was arrested, brought to court, and sentenced to death for treason. He remained in jail for one year, but was then released through the intervention of Nasser, President Tito of Yugoslavia, President Houarie Boumedienne of Algeria, and President Abd al-Salam Aref of Iraq. Nasser gave Alwan asylum in Egypt, but twenty-four rebels who had taken part in the failed coup were hauled before military courts in Syria, declared guilty of treason, and executed. Alwan continued to oppose the Baathist regime from abroad and eventually joined a coalition of Syrian dissidents funded by Iraqi dictator Saddam Hussein. The coalition included none other than his former archenemy, General Amin al-Hafez, who had been overthrown in 1966 and sentenced to execution in 1967, though he escaped before the sentence could be carried out.

Alwan's status in Egypt was shaken when, in 1991, Egypt's President Husni Mubarak went to war against Saddam Hussein. Iraqi money stopped reaching the Syrian dissidents in exile, and Alwan's diplomatic passport and honored status in Egypt were repealed. Jassem Alwan remained in Cairo, however, until General Mustapha Tlas, Syria's ex-minister of defense, intervened on his behalf and permitted his return to Syria in April 2005.

Sources:
Seale, Patrick. *Asad: Struggle for the Middle East* (1988).
Van Dam, Nicolas. *The Struggle for Power in Syria* (1996).
Al-Hayat (April 22, 2005).

al-Asad, Hafez (1930-2000): see "Politicians"

al-Ashi, Suhayl
(1918-)

A product of Damascus, Suhayl al-Ashi studied at the Homs Military Academy and graduated in 1939. That same year he joined the French-created Army of the Levant. After Syrian independence in 1946, he moved into the Syrian Army. On February 20, 1946, he became military assistant to President Shukri al-Quwatli. Ashi became very close to the Syrian president and served as his confidant, advisor, and aide-de-camp during the 1940s.

On March 29, 1949, General Husni al-Za'im seized power in Syria and arrested both Quwatli and Ashi. Shortly thereafter, Quwatli was released and exiled to Egypt, though Ashi remained in prison for twenty days. Za'im then released Ashi and appointed him director of police. He accepted the post but supported the coup that ousted Za'im on August 14, 1949.

Adib al-Shishakli, the new strongman of Syria, sent Ashi to France for advanced military training at the Ecole Superieure de Guerre. When Ashi returned in 1951, he became commander of the Syrian Air Force. In February 1954, Shishakli was overthrown by military coup, and Ashi became director of the Homs Military Academy. He then became commander of the 3rd Armored Division and allied himself once again with Quwatli, who had returned from exile in Cairo to be reelected president in September 1955. During the Suez Canal War of 1956, Quwatli delegated Ashi to meet with King Hussein of Jordan, and to plan for a joint Syrian-Jordanian offensive on Israel during the British-French-Israeli attack on Egypt. President Gamal Abd al-Nasser of Egypt called off the plan, however, when US President Dwight Eisenhower intervened on Egypt's behalf and secured a cease-fire.

In 1957, Suhayl al-Ashi joined a group of fellow officers opposed to Quwatli's alliance with the USSR and its socialist allies in the Eastern Bloc. Chief of Staff Afif al-Bizreh, who was closely allied to the Communist Party, accused Ashi and his colleagues of being CIA agents and dismissed them from the Syrian Army. Intelligence reports claimed that Kermit Roosevelt, the CIA officer responsible for intelligence gathering in the Middle East, and Howard Stone, his representative in Damascus, met with Ashi sometime in 1957 and discussed the possibility of a coup. It is believed that Ashi refused to join the conspiracy due to his personal friendship with President Quwatli.

For the remainder of the 1950s, Ashi engaged in commercial activity. In 1958, Syria and Egypt merged to form the United Arab Republic (UAR). Ashi voiced his disapproval of the UAR as it followed a hard-line, pro-USSR foreign policy. He supported the coup that overthrew the UAR in September 1961 and allied himself with Syria's new president, Nazim al-Qudsi, who appointed Ashi ambassador to Morocco in February 1962 and ambassador to Tunisia in July 1962. When the Baath Party came to power in March 1963, Ashi was forced out of the diplomatic service.

In 1999, Suhayl al-Ashi published his memoirs entitled, *Fajr al-Istiqlal fi Souriyya (Dawn of Independence in Syria)*. The autobiography included a detailed account of his political career, including his relationship with President Quwatli.

Sources:
Rathmell, Andrew. *Secret War in the Middle East*, London 1995.
Ashi, Suhayl. *Fajr al-Istiqlal fi Souriyya*, Beirut 1999.
Interview with General Suhayl al-Ashi (June 14, 2002).

Aslan, Ali
(1933-)

General Ali Aslan studied at the Homs Military Academy. He allied himself with General Hafez al-Asad, an air force pilot, who became commander of the Syrian Air Force in 1963. While rivalries over leadership rocked Syria in the 1960s, Aslan remained loyal to Asad and continued to support him when he became president of the republic in 1971.

As a reward for his loyalty, Asad appointed Aslan commander of the 5th Infantry Division and commissioned him to fight in the Arab-Israeli War of 1973. In the early war hours, Aslan's troops broke through the Israeli's three-columned defensive line and drove the Israeli forces out of southern and central Golan. In 1975, Asad noted Aslan's courage and appointed him deputy to Chief of Staff Hikmat al-Shihabi.

When Shihabi retired from office in 1998, Ali Aslan replaced him as chief of staff. He negotiated military treaties with Japan and several countries in Eastern Europe, constantly calling for an arms buildup. After Ariel Sharon became Israeli prime minister in 2001, Aslan also warned against a sudden outbreak of war with Israel. Thus, Aslan established himself as a hard-liner, enforcing military conscription on Syrian youth, and canceling military exemptions that had been freely granted by his predecessor.

In June 2000, Aslan was promoted to the Central Committee of the Baath Party and developed a close relationship with Syria's new president, Bashar al-Asad. Two years later, however, in January 2002, Asad retired Ali Aslan from the Syrian Army and appointed him military advisor at the Presidential Palace.

Sources:
Al-Ahram (February 7, 2002).
Batatu, Hanna. *Syria's Peasantry: The Descendants of Its Lesser Rural Notables and Their Politics* (2000).
Seale, Patrick. *Asad: Struggle for the Middle East* (1988).

al-Atasi, Faysal
(1916-1999)

Faysal al-Atasi was born into a prominent political family in Homs and studied at the Homs Military Academy. He pursued a military career and rose in rank to become director of Syrian Army affairs in August 1949. The following year, Deputy Chief of Staff Adib al-Shishakli appointed him commander of the Lattakia garrison.

When Shishakli became president in June 1953, he moved Atasi to the garrison of Aleppo, giving him military control over the Syrian heartland. Aleppo, Syria's second largest city, was boiling with anti-Shishakli sentiment at the time, so Shishakli charged Atasi with controlling political activity in Aleppo.

In December 1953, however, Atasi clashed with his former mentor and, along with the officers Mustapha Hamdun and Amin Abu Assaf, began plotting for a military coup d'etat. Atasi declared his opposition to Shishakli's dictatorship and criticized the one-party state he had created. He also criticized Shishakli's arrest of leading politicians and his closure of newspapers and political parties.

In February 1954, Atasi, Hamdun, and Assaf launched a military insurrection aimed at restoring civilian rule to Syria. Under Atasi's orders, armed men occupied the city of Aleppo, arrested the governor, took over the broadcasting station, and declared autonomy from Shishakli's central government in Damascus. Several hundred of Shishakli's best men were rounded up and imprisoned in Aleppo. Adib al-Shishakli resigned from office on February 23, 1954, and Atasi's uncle, Hashim al-Atasi, who had been in the presidential office prior to Shishakli's assumption in 1951, was restored to the presidency. From here, however, Faysal al-Atasi's role came to a rapid end. He quarreled with his fellow officers on ideological matters and retired from the Syrian Army in 1955.

Sources:
Seale, Patrick. *Struggle for Syria* (1961).

al-Atasi, Lu'ayy (1926-2003): see "Politicians"

Atfeh, Abdullah
(1897-1976)

Abdullah Atfeh studied at the Ottoman Military Academy in Istanbul and received advanced military training in France. He served as an officer in the Ottoman Army, but in 1916 joined the rebel army of Sharif Husayn, who was leading a military uprising from the Arabian Desert against the Ottoman Turks.

Until the Ottoman Empire was defeated in October 1918, Atfeh served as a commander in the Arab Army. He then allied himself with King Faysal I, the new ruler of Syria, and became an officer in the newly created Syrian Army. He took part in the battle of Maysaloun on July 24, 1920, when France defeated the army and occupied Syria. After the French proclaimed their mandate over Syria in July 1920, they dethroned Faysal, dissolved the Syrian Army, and arrested or exiled all officers who had been loyal to the ex-king. Atfeh went to Jordan for one year but returned when the French issued a general amnesty in 1921.

After his return to Syria, Atfeh joined the French-created Army of the Levant and advanced steadily in military rank. During World War II, the French appointed him commander of their troops on the Syrian coast. In May 1945, when the French Army advanced on Damascus, Atfeh mutinied and ordered his troops to take up arms against their French superiors. When Syria achieved independence from the French in April 1946, Atfeh rallied around President Shukri al-Quwatli and became chief of staff of the new Syrian Army in 1947. Quwatli charged him with transferring the allegiance of the Army of the Levant from France to the Syrian Republic. This was not an easy task. Many of the men had spent the better part of their lives working with the French, living under their protection, and receiving military training from them.

On May 14, 1948, the British Mandate in Palestine ended—an event that determined the timing of the 1948 Arab-Israeli War. On their first foray into Palestine, Syrian forces were driven back by the Jews—an event that caused an uproar in Syria. It is often thought that, in 1948, Abdullah Atfeh became minister of defense in the cabinet of Prime Minister Jamil Mardam Bey, commanded the Syrian Army in the Arab-Israeli War, and was responsible for their poor showing on the battlefield. In actuality, Atfeh never became minister of defense under President Quwatli. Jamil Mardam assumed the position himself after he fired Ahmed al-Sharabati from the post at the beginning of the war. For his part, Atfeh was relieved of his duties as chief of staff in favor of Husni al-Za'im. Thus, there were only a few days at the onset of the war that Atfeh commanded the Syrian Army and Sharabati served as minister of defense.

Politicians in Syria accused Atfeh and al-Sharabati of mismanaging the war and of profiteering at the army's expense by purchasing outdated weapons. Politicians demanded that they be brought to court on corruption charges. Seven months after the war began, Atfeh shouldered the blame for the defeat when he stepped down from office in disgrace and retired (temporarily) from public life.

On March 29, 1949, the Quwatli regime was overthrown by General Husni al-Za'im, and the new president revived Atfeh's career by using him as a military advisor. When Za'im was toppled and killed in August 1949, Atfeh allied himself with the politicians that replaced him and became director of state affairs (with duties similar to those of a military governor) for an interim period of one week. In November 1949, Syria's new president, Hashim al-Atasi, appointed Atfeh minister of defense for three months. Afterward, Abdullah Atfeh retired completely from public life.

Sources:
Babil, Nasuh. *Sahafa wa Siyasa fi Souriyya* (1988).
Hawrani, Akram. *Muzakarat Akram al-Hawrani* (2000).
Moubayed, Sami. *Damascus Between Democracy and Dictatorship* (2000).
Seale, Patrick. *Struggle for Syria* (1961).

al-Ayyubi, Shukri
(1851-1922)

Shukri al-Ayyubi studied at the Ottoman Military Academy in Istanbul and graduated with high honors in 1870. He taught at the same academy, befriended leading Ottoman officers in Istanbul, and rose to become one of the most prominent officers in the Military Academy. Sultan Abdulhamid II rewarded Ayyubi's services by giving him the princely title of pasha.

In 1905, Ayyubi joined other Arab loyalists in the Empire and founded the Ottoman-Arab Brotherhood Society in Istanbul. In 1908, however, a coup took place in Istanbul, bringing to power a group of radical young officers named the Committee for Union and Progress (CUP). Some of them had been Ayyubi's students, but once firmly in power, they dismissed many Arab officials (including Ayyubi) and replaced them with Ottoman Turks. Turkish became the official language of the courts, schools, and civil service of the Arab provinces in the Empire. Ayyubi joined the political underground, devoted himself to toppling the CUP, and was arrested for his views in 1916.

In 1917, Ayyubi became an officer in the rebel Arab Army of Sharif Husayn, who was leading a military uprising against the Ottoman Empire from the Arabian Desert. The CUP accused Ayyubi of treason, confiscated his property, and sentenced him to death in absentia. Later that year, while on a secret mission to Damascus to raise funds for the Arab warriors in Mecca, Ayyubi was arrested and sentenced to life in prison. He served for one year at the notorious Khan Pasha prison in Damascus, but Husayn's Arab army released him when they liberated Syria in October 1918.

Syria's new ruler, King Faysal I, appointed Ayyubi royal envoy to Beirut and gave him authority to govern in the name of the newly created Syrian throne. Faysal declared that the jurisdiction of the Arab government reached as far as Beirut, the coast, and Mount Lebanon. He also gave Ayyubi authority over the Maronite district of Baabda and asked him to administer it along with its governor, Habib Pasha al-Sa'ad. This infuriated the Maronites of Lebanon and the French who had their eyes on a French Mandate in the Middle East. The Maronites refused to recognize Ayyubi's authority over their territory.

For their part, the French declared that Beirut and Mount Lebanon were destined to become parts of their mandate in the region and could not be governed by

Ayyubi or Faysal. Faysal recalled Ayyubi to Syria shortly afterward and appointed him governor of Aleppo. Ayyubi kept this post even after the French occupied Syria in July 1920 and deposed Faysal. Later Shukri al-Ayyubi became a friend of French High Commissioner Henri Gouraud.

Sources:
Commins, David. *Historical Dictionary of Modern Syria* (1996).
Khury, Colette. *Awrak Faris al-Khury* (1989).
Zamir, Meir. *The Formation of Modern Lebanon* (1985).

al-Azma, Yusuf
(1883-1920)

Of notable Damascene heritage, Yusuf al-Azma studied at the Ottoman Military Academy in Istanbul and graduated with high honors in 1906. He pursued advanced military training in Germany for two years, returning to Istanbul in 1909 to join the Ottoman Army and was immediately appointed Ottoman military delegate in Cairo.

When World War I broke out in 1914, Azma was commissioned to the front and appointed commander of the 25th Ottoman Brigade in Bulgaria. He was transferred back to Istanbul after a short time to serve as military assistant to the Ottoman general, Anwar Pasha. When the war ended in 1918, Azma returned to his native Damascus and became private chamberlain to King Faysal I, the new leader of Syria.

In January 1919, Faysal appointed him military delegate to Beirut, then minister of war in the cabinet of Prime Minister Rida al-Rikabi. General Azma created the Syrian Army from almost nothing. Within only six months, Azma had gathered the remains of Ottoman ammunition, mobilized an active defense force, raised funds for an arms build-up, and laid the infrastructure and hierarchy of the modern Syrian Army. On January 26, 1920, King Faysal appointed him commander-in-chief of the Syrian Army. By mid-1920, his army was estimated at ten thousand men, mostly volunteers from Bedouin tribes. At the time, there was no forced military conscription in Syria and no official school for military training.

On July 14, 1920, the French government issued an ultimatum to King Faysal, ordering him to dissolve the Syrian Army and prepare for the implementation of the French Mandate over Syria and Lebanon. The French demanded that Faysal arrest anti-French politicians and reshuffle the Rikabi cabinet to include French allies. The French troops occupied the Syrian coast, took over Beirut and Lattakia, and began advancing toward Damascus. Azma refused to surrender, pleading with King Faysal for a chance to prove that his army could fight and survive.

On July 20, the French forces advanced into the Syrian heartland, causing an uproar in Damascus and forcing King Faysal to mobilize for war. Azma toured all parts of Syria and drafted an additional 3,000 men. When he ordered his army, estimated now at around 13,000 troops, to go to war, only 3,000 showed up for battle. On July 24, 1920, Azma's troops clashed with the invading French Army, and he was killed in combat at the infamous Battle of Maysaloun.

Yusuf al-Azma.

Azma is revered for his heroism at the Battle of Maysaloun, yet it was one of the worst defeats in Syria's modern history. Azma's men had only 270 rounds of ammunition apiece. Many rifles were rusted leftovers from the Ottoman Army and incapable of firing, while other guns had been used in the Arab revolt of World War I. In the first hours of battle, ammunition ran out completely, and the French were able to penetrate the Syrian line. French General Henri Gouraud, who had fought at Maysaloun, gave a short description of the battle in his memoirs, *La France en Syria*. ". . . the battle ended at 11:00 AM with the defeat of the Arab Army," wrote Gouraud, "leaving behind 15 cannons, 40 rifles, and a general who had graduated from Craig Academy named Yusuf Bey al-Azma. He died a courageous soldier's death in battle." Yusuf al-Azma was the only officer killed in the Battle of Maysaloun. His name has been immortalized in Syrian history.

Sources:
Commins, David. *Historical Dictionary of Modern Syria* (1996).
Gouraud, Henri. *La France en Syrie* (1922).
Hakim, Yusuf. *Souriyya wa al-Ahd al-Faysali* (1986).
Husari, Sati. *Yawm Maysaloun* (1947).
Moubayed, Sami. *The Politics of Damascus 1920-1946* (1999).
Qassab Hasan, Najat. *Saniou al-Jalaa fi Souriyya* (1999).
Russell, Malcolm. *The First Modern Arab State: Syria under Faysal I* (1987).
Sultan, Ali. *Tareekh Souriyya 1908-1918* (1987).

Bannud, Anwar
(1908-1979)

Anwar Bannud was born in Aleppo and studied at the Military Academy in Damascus. He joined the French-created Army of the Levant in 1925 and became director of the Homs Military Academy in 1944. After the French invaded Damascus in May 1945, Bannud played an instrumental role in rousing nationalist sympathies among young cadets, calling on them to mutiny against their French superiors.

When Syria gained independence from France in 1946, Bannud joined the newly created Syrian Army. He took part in the Arab-Israeli War of 1948 and became a commanding officer in the Army of Deliverance, an outfit funded by Saudi Arabia and led by the Syrian officer Fawzi al-Qawuqji. On May 13, 1948, Bannud led the first armored Syrian squadron into Palestine. His troops occupied the Samakh region in the early hours of war but were forced back in defeat when the Zionists received reinforcements. Bannud managed to occupy the Bridge of the Daughters of Jacob, as well as the settlements of Mishmar Hayarden and Mishmar Hagolan. On October 26, 1948, Qawuqji resigned from office and Bannud replaced him as commander of the Army of Deliverance.

Bannud was highly critical of the civilian regime of Shukri al-Quwatli, accusing its leaders of leading the officers into war with an ill-prepared army. He supported Chief of Staff Husni al-Za'im when Za'im seized power in March 1949, overthrowing Quwatli. On July 1, 1949, Bannud became deputy to Chief of Staff Za'im, who by now was also serving as president of the republic. However, Bannud argued with Za'im over Za'im's dictatorial ruling style and helped orchestrate a coup that brought Za'im down on August 14, 1949.

Although Bannud had allied himself with the coup mastermind, Sami al-Hinnawi, Bannud then supported another coup, launched this time by General Adib al-Shishakli, an old friend of Bannud from the Arab-Israeli War of 1948. Shishakli's coup ousted Hinnawi in December 1949. On December 19 of that year, Shishakli appointed Bannud chief of staff of the Syrian Army.

A charismatic and popular officer, Bannud commanded a devoted following among young men within the military. Fearing Bannud's popularity, Shishakli discharged him on April 23, 1951, and appointed him military attaché to Ankara (a purely ceremonial post). Rather than fighting to retain his power, Bannud traveled to Turkey. In February 1954, when Adib al-Shishakli was deposed by military coup, Anwar Bannud found himself out of favor with the new Syrian government.

Sources:
Abd al-Karim, Ahmad. *Hasad* (1994).
Faris, George. *Man Hum fi al-Alam al-Arabi?* (1957).

al-Bizreh, Afif
(1914-1994)

Afif al-Bizreh was born in Sidon in modern north Lebanon and studied at the Military Academy in Damascus. In 1940, he pursued advanced military training in Paris and while in France was exposed to the popular political theory of communism. Bizreh met several French communists and developed a radical Marxist philosophy, but never officially became a member of the Communist Party.

Nevertheless, by the mid-1950s, Bizreh was advocating the creation of a socialist state in Syria and preaching communist views to fellow officers. He joined the revolt of Rashid Ali Kaylani against the British in Iraq in 1941. In 1945, Bizreh was arrested for anti-French activity in Syria and deported to Beirut. He escaped from prison a few weeks later and resumed his military career.

When Syria achieved independence from the French Mandate in April 1946, Bizreh became an instructor of topography at the Homs Military Academy. He volunteered to fight in the Arab-Israeli War of 1948 and befriended Chief of Staff Husni al-Za'im, who came to power in March 1949. Za'im created a senior officer delegation to negotiate an armistice with Israel following the 1948 war. Bizreh was appointed to the committee that signed the armistice agreement with the Israelis in July 1949. When Za'im was ousted from power and killed, Bizreh went to France where he studied geography. In 1953, he returned to Syria to take part in politics as a member of the underground that sought to topple the regime of General Adib al-Shishakli.

In the late 1950s, Bizreh joined the movement of Arab nationalism headed by Egyptian President Nasser and praised Nasser's alliance with the USSR. In August 1957, President Shukri al-Quwatli, an ally of Nasser who was also creating an alliance with the USSR, appointed Bizreh chief of staff of the Syrian Army. His appointment was aimed at appeasing Nasser, who complained that former Chief of Staff Tawfiq Nizam al-Din was doing little to advance the interests of Arab nationalism in the Syrian Army. Under Nasser's patronage, Bizreh worked relentlessly to spread Arab nationalism in the armed forces and promote officers who were loyal to Nasser.

Shortly after coming to power, Bizreh accused a group of officers of plotting against the regime of President Quwatli. Bizreh discharged them collectively from office on the charge of spying for the CIA in order to damage Syria's friendship with the Kremlin. Bizreh also clashed with the civilian leaders who opposed Nasser, mainly Defense Minister Khalid al-Azm. Moreover, he forced Prime Minister Sabri al-Asali to follow a radical pro-Nasser policy or suffer arrest for his views.

General Bizreh headed a military tribunal in 1957 that brought Nasser's main opponents in Syria to trial. Among the accused were the parliamentary deputies Munir al-Ajlani, Adnan al-Atasi, Sami Kabbara, and Mika'il Ilyan. He accused them of receiving funds from anti-Nasser governments in the Arab world—including those of King Hussein of Jordan, Prime Minister Nuri al-Sa'id of Iraq, and President Kamil Sham'un of Lebanon—to topple the pro-Nasser government in Damascus. In a highly publicized trial at the amphitheater of Damascus University, Bizreh revealed the details of what came to be known as the "Iraqi Conspiracy."

The "Iraqi Conspiracy" alleged that a group of exiled Syrians were to receive training in Lebanon and funding from Iraq in order to invade Syria, arrest Prime Minister Asali, and assassinate Chief of Intelligence Abd al-Hamid Sarraj, the socialist leader Akram al-Hawrani, the Communist Party leader Khalid Bakdash, and Afif al-Bizreh. The conspirators would then present an ultimatum to Quwatli, demanding that he sever his relations with the USSR and Nasser or step down from office. Bizreh sentenced the coup masterminds to death, but commuted their sentences after the intervention of Arab countries, Great Britain, and President Quwatli. After the court hearings, Bizreh became a frequent guest in Moscow and formulated long-term loans and arms purchases with the USSR. Bizreh also lobbied for goodwill relations with the Eastern Bloc in Europe and repeatedly clashed with pro-American statesmen in Syria.

In January 1958, acting on his own initiative, Bizreh led a group of officers to Cairo, where they pleaded with Nasser for the unification of Syria and Egypt. When some officers showed reservations about backing Bizreh's call, he is reported to have said, "Men, there are two roads before you, one leads to Cairo and the other leads to Mezzeh." Bizreh was referring to the infamous dungeon at Mezzeh on the outskirts of Damascus, where all the anti-Nasser elements had been imprisoned from 1955 to 1958.

In Cairo, Bizreh participated in the union talks between Quwatli and Nasser that resulted in the signing of the union charter on February 1, 1958. He then began preparing himself for a senior post in the United Arab Republic (UAR), having his eyes set on becoming military governor of Syria. Nasser, however, had other plans and appointed his friend, Egyptian General Abd al-Hakim Amer, as governor of Syria. When Bizreh complained, he was dismissed from office in June 1959. Then, fearing the rising influence of the Communist Party, Nasser outlawed the party and dismissed Bizreh's men from the Syrian Army.

Bizreh went to Beirut and issued a political declaration, accusing Nasser of establishing a dictatorship. He called on officers in the Syrian Army to topple the very same UAR that they had created. Once this was done, Bizreh said, civil liberties would be restored and a "new union" would be established with separate parliamentary governments in Cairo and Damascus. This was the first signal that trouble was brewing in the UAR, since one of its creators was now calling for its destruction.

On September 28, 1961, the ex-general supported a coup headed by Colonel Abd al-Karim al-Nehlawi that brought down the UAR. Due to his record as a troublemaker, however, Bizreh was declined a post in the new regime of President Nazim al-Qudsi. In 1962, he authored *al-Nasseriyya fi Jumlat al-Istimar al-Hadeeth* (*Nasserism in the Line of Modern Imperialism*), a book expressing his anti-Nasser views. On March 8, 1963, the Baath Party came to power in Syria and pledged to restore the UAR. The Revolutionary Command Council (RCC) terminated Bizreh's civil rights, and as a result, he fled Syria into exile, returning in 1965 when the political situation relaxed. In 1991, he gave an interview saying, "Nobody (but us the officers) wanted union. The politicians did not want union. Not even Gamal Abd al-Nasser wanted union!"

Afif al-Bizreh died on January 28, 1994.

Sources:

Azm, Khalid. *Muzakarat Khalid al-Azm* (1973).
Bizreh, Afif. *Al-Nasseriyya fi Jumlat al-Istimar al-Hadeeth* (1962).
Commins, David. *Historical Dictionary of Modern Syria* 1996.
Juma, Sami. *Awrak Min Daftar al-Watan* (2001).
Moubayed, Sami. *Damascus Between Democracy and Dictatorship* (2000).
Rathmell, Andrew. *Secret War in the Middle East* (1995).
Seale, Patrick. *The Struggle for Syria* (1965).
Torrey, Gordon. *Syrian Politics and the Military* (1964).
Interview with Afif Bizreh in *al-Manaber* Magazine (March 1989).

al-Hafez, Amin (1925-): see "Politicians"

Hamdun, Mustapha
(1923-)

Mustapha Hamdun was born in Hama and studied at the Homs Military Academy. He was a relative and political ally of the socialist leader Akram al-Hawrani. Hamdun joined the Syrian Army and allied himself with the socialist movement spearheaded by Hawrani in the late 1940s.

At the end of 1952, Hawrani clashed with President Adib al-Shishakli and went to Lebanon. While in exile, he rallied Hamdun's support for the creation of an anti-Shishakli movement. Hamdun pledged full cooperation and in February 1954 collaborated with a group of disgruntled officers, headed by Faysal al-Atasi, in bringing down the Shishakli regime. Hamdun led the occupation of major cities in Syria and captured the national radio station in Damascus where he personally read a communiqué announcing the fall of "the dictator Adib al-Shishakli."

During the second half of the 1950s, Hamdun and Hawrani joined the movement of Arab nationalism led by President Gamal Abd al-Nasser of Egypt. In January 1958, Hamdun was part of an officers' delegation that went to Cairo and pleaded for Syria's immediate unification with Nasser's Egypt. Through his military attaché in Damascus, Nasser demanded from Hamdun the names of loyal officers in the Syrian Army who could protect the union government. Hamdun gave the names of his Baath comrades, but rather than rely on their loyalty, Nasser curbed their power and transferred them to Cairo, fearing that they would make trouble if left in Syria.

When the union was established in February 1958, Hamdun was appointed minister of social affairs while Hawrani became vice president of the United Arab Republic (UAR). In October 1958, Nasser appointed Hamdun minister of agricultural reform. In 1960, Nasser carred out a vast land redistributino program in Syria. Years later (July 1983), Hamdun gave an interview to the Lebanese magazine, *al-Hawadeth,* where he explained, "I did not approve the land redistribution." Hamdun responded to Nasser's redistribution move by resigning from office, along with Hawrani. In 1961, the UAR was overthrown by a military coup. Hamdun and Hawrani supported the post-Nasser government of President Nazim al-Qudsi.

From 1961 to 1963, Mustapha Hamdun served as a deputy in parliament. In 1962, Hawrani resigned from the Baath Party and resurrected his Arab Socialist Party (which had been active in the early 1940s). Hamdun joined the party but kept a low profile in political events during the early Baathist era. He remained influential, though, when his comrade and friend, Amin al-Hafez, came to power in 1963. Hamdun fled Syria when Hafez was overthrown and arrested in February 1966. Hamdun lived briefly in exile in Lebanon, then moved to Iraq where the Baath Party founder, Michel Aflaq, resided as a guest of Iraqi President Saddam Hussein. Hamdun quarreled with Aflaq over collaboration with Saddam and was pardoned by President Hafez al-Asad in 1998. At the age of seventy-one, Hamdun returned to Syria after thirty years of exile.

In March 1972, Asad created the National Progressive Front (NPF), a coalition of socialist parties that operated in parliament under the umbrella of the Baath Party. The Arab Socialist Party, which helped to establish the NPF, served as one of the NPF's principal allies in the next thirty years of the Asad presidency. In 2001, the Arab Socialist Party's secretary-general, Abd al-Ghani Qannut, another one-time Hawrani protégé, died while in office. Party elections were held in June 2001, and Hamdun was elected secretary-general. He made a deal with Ahmad Qannut, the son of the party's ex-leader who sought a position in the party for himself, and appointed him to its central committee.

But Ahmad al-Ahmad, a veteran partisan, as well as other members of the party, were angered at Hamdun's election, claiming that it was illegitimate. They petitioned a court in Damascus to disqualify the elections. Vice President Zuhayr Masharka intervened and agreed with them, thereby forcing Hamdun to step down. At the time of writing, Mustapha Hamdun lives in political retirement in Syria.

Sources:

Samman, Mutih. *Watan wa Askar* (1995).
Seale, Patrick. *The Struggle for Syria* (1961).
Torrey, Gordon. *Syrian Politics and the Military* (1964).
The Daily Star (February 19, 2001).
Zissar, Eyal. "Bashar al-Asad and his regime-Between Continuity and Change" published in *L' Orient*, Vol. 45, (June 2004), pp.239-256.
Al-Nahhar (June 16, 1998).

al-Harriri, Ziyad
(1930-)

Ziyad al-Harriri studied at the Homs Military Academy and enlisted in the Syrian Army in 1954. In the 1950s, he became involved in the movement of Arab nationalism that was headed by President Gamal Abd al-Nasser of Egypt. He supported Syria's merger with Egypt to form the United Arab Republic (UAR) in 1958 and fought against the coup that dissolved the UAR regime in 1961.

From 1961 to 1963, Harriri vigorously opposed the civilian regime of President Nazim al-Qudsi and vowed to work toward restoration of the UAR. He attracted a significant following in the armed forces, and many disgruntled officers of the Nasserist movement pledged to support him. Harririworked with the Military Committee of the Baath Party, which included Hafez al-Asad, Abd al-Karim al-Jundi, Mohammad Umran, and Salah Jadid, and worked for Qudsi's downfall.

In mid-1962, the Baath officers of the Military Committee made Harriri an offer. "If we succeed (in a coup d'etat)," they told him, "you can become Chief of Staff. If we fail, you can disown us." Harriri, who was serving as commander of the forces on Syria's front-line with Israel, agreed to take part in the conspiracy. He had recently argued with Prime Minister Khalid al-Azm, a longtime opponent of officers meddling in political affairs. As a result, Azm was planning to discharge Harriri from his duties and appoint him military attaché to Baghdad.

On March 8, 1963, the officer junta of the Military Committee of the Baath Party overthrew the existing regime and established a government under Baath Party control. Harriri, who had occupied Damascus in the coup, became a member of the Revolutionary Command Council (RCC) and assumed the duties of chief of staff as promised, replacing ex-General Abd al-Karim Zahr al-Din. Harriri mistakenly believed that, once in power, the Military Committee would stand back and let him become the new military strongman of Syria. The Baath Party officers who led the coup, however, propped up Lu'ayy al-Atasi as president of the RCC and made Salah al-Bitar, the Baath Party co-founder, prime minister of Syria. Harriri soon realized that they did not intend to give him credit for his role in the revolution. He also learned that they were attempting to purge his supporters from the Syrian Army.

On July 18, 1963, a group of Nasserist officers tried to seize power from the Baath Party, but their coup was crushed by Interior Minister Amin al-Hafez. The Baath Party suspected Harriri of involvement in the conspiracy and fired thirty of his best men from the Syrian Army on July 1963. Harriri, who happened to be in Algeria on a visit, was then discharged from his post as chief of staff and appointed to the ceremonial position of military attaché to Washington. Ziyad al-Harriri turned down the post, retired from politics, and moved to France in self-imposed exile.

Sources:
Seale, Patrick. *Asad: The Struggle for the Middle East* (1988).
Van Dam, Nicolas. *The Struggle for Power in Syria* (1996).

Hatum, Saleem
(1928-1967)

A native of the Arab Mountain, Saleem Hatum studied at the Homs Military Academy, then joined the Baath Party of Michel Aflaq and became an officer in the Syrian Army. Hatum helped launch the March 8, 1963 revolution that brought the Baath Party to power.

As a reward for his services, Hatum was appointed to the Military Committee of the Party, which included strongmen like Hafez al-Asad and Salah Jadid. The Military Committee was the de facto ruling body of Syria from 1963 to 1966, challenging the authority of Aflaq and President Amin al-Hafez.

On February 23, 1966, however, Asad and Jadid launched a second coup, ousting the first Baath government of Amin al-Hafez, and Saleem Hatum was ordered to arrest the president. Jadid knew that Hatum was ruthless and would be perfect for the job. Hatum led a commando force to Amin al-Hafez's private residence. When Hafez resisted with force, Hatum raked his villa with tank fire. Shooting continued throughout the Syrian capital, and eventually Hatum arrested Amin al-Hafez. But the arrest came only after badly wounding Hafez and his children, causing his daughter to lose an eye. In the battle, fifty people were killed.

Hatum expected a reward for his services, but was given nothing by Asad and Jadid. He kept his post on the expanded Military Committee, but was not appointed to the prestigious and powerful Regional Command. Unlike other officers, he was also given no position in government or in the Syrian Army. Instead, he was ordered to command a garrison guarding Syrian Radio. In 1965, he was appointed to the special court created to try and execute Elie Cohen, the Israeli spy operating in Syria.

In reality, Asad and Jadid feared Hatum's authority. They accused him of being a reckless officer and blamed him for the fifty deaths on February 23, claiming that they had ordered him to arrest Amin al-Hafez, not to conduct a bloodbath in Damascus. Responding to what he perceived as poor treatment at the hands of Asad and Jadid, Hatum contacted other angry officers, ironically the same officers loyal to the deposed Hafez and exiled Michel Aflaq. Primary among these men were Dr Munir al-Razzaz, the ex-secretary-general of the National Command, who had stayed behind in Syria, and Major General Fahd al-Sha'ir, the ex-deputy chief of staff.

They planned a coup for June 1, 1966, but Hatum rescheduled it for September 3. In August, however, one of the co-conspirators, Colonel Talal Abu Asali, attended a party for officers from the Syrian Army, some of whom were loyal to Salah Jadid. After too many drinks, Abu Asali began to curse Jadid and pledge revenge. The next morning, Chief of Staff Ahmad Suwaydani arrested Asali and the other officers suspected of supporting him. Ironically, Hatum was so far above suspicion that he was made head of the investigative committee. Before the inquiry began, he whispered in the ears of his arrested co-conspirators, "I will kill anyone who talks!"

Salah Jadid became suspicious and soon dissolved Hatum's committee, setting up a new one chaired by the ruthless Abd al-Karim al-Jundi, the director of Syrian Intelligence, who was schooled in the dark art of torture. Jundi applied heavy torture to the accused, and on August 20, 1966, one of them confessed that Fahd al-Sha'ir was planning a coup (without mentioning Saleem Hatum), in collaboration with Munif al-Razzaz. Sha'ir went into hiding, while Jundi cracked down on the Druze community (of which Hatum was a member), arresting over two hundred men, including many officers.

Resentment ran so high in the Arab Mountain that, on September 8, 1966, Jadid went to Suwayda, capital of the Mountain, to calm things down. He was accompanied by President Nur al-Din al-Atasi and Jamil Shayya, the only Druze member of the Regional Command. Saleem Hatum ordered Talal Abu Asali to take control of the city with a squadron of tanks. Then, while Jadid, Atasi, and Shayya were assembled at Baath Party headquarters in Suwayda, Hatum broke in, gun in hand, and threatened to kill them all. Druze elders begged him not to harm the three men, since they were guests of the Druze community. (According to Arab tradition, guests are under the protection of their hosts.) Instead, Hatum had them arrested.

Hatum's glory did not last long, however, since Jadid, Atasi, and Shayya had left Defense Minister Hafez al-Asad behind in Damascus. Asad ordered Hatum to immediately lay down his arms. When Hatum refused, Asad sent air force jets to bomb the Citadel of Suwayda and ordered the 70th Armored Brigade to quell the mutiny in the Arab Mountain. Jadid, Atasi, and their colleague, Shayya, were saved, but at the price of demonstrating to Asad that his military guaranteed the safety of the government.

Before he could be arrested, Hatum fled south to Jordan where King Hussein, an opponent of the Jadid regime, gave Hatum asylum, along with Talal Abu Asali. In Damascus, Asad dismissed more than four hundred officers suspected of loyalty to Hatum. This was the biggest shake-up in the history of the Syrian Army. In March 1967, a military court headed by Asad's ally, Mustapha Tlas, sentenced Hatum, Abu Asali, and Sha'ir to death for treason. The executions were never carried out, however, and later that summer Syria went to war against Israel.

On June 6, 1967, Hatum foolishly announced that he would return to Syria to join the battle against Israel, despite the death sentence looming over his head. He mistakenly believed that Jadid would not dare arrest or execute him now that his regime had been defeated in war. He hoped that the Syrian government would now be more tolerant of the opposition. On the other hand, he seemed to have calculated that the regime had become so weak that it would fall before it had time to kill him. Upon setting foot in Syria, he was arrested and brought before military court, headed by Tlas. At 4:00 AM, Hatum's death sentence was confirmed.

Nearly forty years later, Tlas looked back at the Hatum trial and said, "I personally took the decision to execute him because he had lost the correct path by conspiring with Jordan. One of those executed with him was a very close friend of mine from Homs. I informed Defense Minister Hafez (al-Asad) and the following day, at 12 pm, I got President Nur al-Din al-Atasi to sign the execution warrant. We had executed him without presidential approval and yet, the decree needed the President's signature. Atasi had not been informed."

Saleem Hatum was shot at dawn on June 26, 1967. He was only thirty-nine years old, but is remembered for being one of the most ruthless officers to ever rule Syria.

Sources:
Batatu, Hanna. *Syria's Peasantry: the Descendants of its Lesser Rural Notables and their Politics* (2000).
Seale, Patrick. *Asad: Struggle for the Middle East* (1988).
Van Dam, Nicolas. *The Struggle for Power in Syria* (1996).
Interview with General Mustapha Tlas (May 8, 2005).

Haydar, Ali
(1932-)

Ali Haydar was born in the village of Hallet Ara, in the province of Jableh. As a schoolboy, he joined the Baath Party of Michel Aflaq and studied at the Homs Military Academy.

In 1963, the Baath Party came to power in Syria, and in 1968, Haydar became commander of the Special Forces, an elite unit of the Syrian Army trained for "special missions." He allied himself with Defense Minister Hafez al-Asad, who came to power in November 1970. Haydar provided military support for Asad's Corrective Movement—the coup that arrested the civilian president, Nur al-Din al-Atasi, and Baath Party strongman Salah Jadid.

Ironically, Asad had saved these two men four years earlier when Saleem Hatum had attempted to overthrow the government. Haydar maintained his post in the Special Forces, and in the 1970s and 1980s, emerged as one of Asad's most trusted and reliable officers. Haydar's men swelled in numbers to 15,000, becoming the backbone of the Asad government. They were highly paid, highly trained, and highly endorsed by the president—rivaled in strength only by the Defense Companies of Asad's brother, Rifaat. The Special Forces got involved in the Lebanese Civil War (1975-1991), engaging in battle against the PLO of Yasser Arafat.

In 1982, Israeli Defense Minister Ariel Sharon invaded Beirut, and Haydar's men engaged in combat with the invading Israeli Army. They grew to paramount influence in Lebanon and were mainly stationed in Bhamdun and Tripoli. In Damascus, they occupied strategic positions in al-Qutayfa, a position twenty-four miles northeast of Damascus, in Mount Qasiyoun overlooking the Syrian capital, and in the coastal city of Tartus. They stood on permanent alert to protect the Asad government against domestic or foreign threats.

In November 1983, Hafez al-Asad fell ill, and his brother, Rifaat al-Asad, began plotting a coup. Haydar had been close to Rifaat, but when the latter approached him to take part in the coup, Haydar curtly refused. He reportedly said, "I recognize no leader in this country other than Hafez al-Asad! What I have of power and prestige I owe to him. I am a soldier in his service and a slave to his beck and call. While I am alive, I bear obedience to him and will not fall away from him."

Haydar's vow of loyalty to Asad further endeared him to the bedridden president. In March 1984, when Rifaat attempted his coup, he was confronted on the streets of Damascus by the forces of Ali Haydar. The confrontation nearly left Syria in bloody civil war and was only halted by President Asad himself, who foiled the coup and sent his brother into exile.

In 1988, Ali Haydar suffered an aneurysm and ceased military activity. He resumed his duties in the 1990s and was categorically opposed to peace negotiations with Israel after the Madrid Peace Conference. In the summer of 1994, Haydar was arrested under direct orders from Asad, for reasons that remained unclear until today. Among other things, he was accused of opposing the peace talks taking place between Asad's envoys and the Israelis in Washington.

But Ali Haydar was never brought to court nor humiliated in public. He briefly remained in dignified captivity and was then released and retired from the

Special Forces. He continued to occupy a leading role in the Baath Party and serve in the Syrian Army until Asad's death in June 2000.

Sources:
Batatu, Hanna. *Syria's Peasantry* (1999).
Seale, Patrick. *Asad: Struggle for the Middle East* (1988).

al-Hinnawi, Sami
(1896-1950)

Sami al-Hinnawi studied at the Ottoman Military Academy in Istanbul, graduated with distinction in 1914, and joined the Ottoman Army in World War I. He defected from service in 1916 to become a member of the Arab underground that worked to topple the Ottoman Empire.

Hinnawi became an officer in the rebel army of Sharif Husayn, who was leading an Arab Revolt against the Ottoman Turks from Mecca. When the Ottoman Empire was defeated in 1918, Hinnawi joined the Arab Army of King Faysal I, the new ruler of Syria.

In 1920, the French Mandate was proclaimed in Syria and Lebanon, and Hinnawi joined the French-created Army of the Levant. When the mandate was abolished in April 1946, Hinnawi enlisted in the Syrian Army and became sympathetic to the ideology of the Syrian Social Nationalist Party (SSNP), a paramilitary group aimed at uniting the Levant within the historical boundaries of Greater Syria. Sami al-Hinnawi fought in the Arab-Israeli War of 1948 where he became a close friend and ally of Syria's chief of staff, Husni al-Za'im.

On March 29, 1949, Hinnawi helped General Za'im seize power in Syria and overthrow the civilian leader, Shukri al-Quwatli. They accused Quwatli of having purchased inferior arms for the Syrian Army in the War of 1948 and accused the president of poor leadership. During the four-month era of Husni al-Za'im, Hinnawi was considered second-in-command in Syria. He distanced himself from the new leader, however, following Za'im's clash with the Lebanese philosopher, Antune Sa'ada, who was founder and president of the SSNP.

In June 1949, Sa'ada took refuge in Syria to escape a death sentence in Beirut. Za'im received him with open arms and promised to support him in his desire to overthrow Lebanese President Bshara al-Khury and Prime Minister Riyad al-Sulh. These Lebanese leaders had refused to recognize Za'im's Syrian government out of loyalty to deposed President Quwatli. In exchange for Za'im's assistance, Sa'ada pledged to set up an SSNP regime in Beirut that would back the ambitions of Za'im and his government. While Sa'ada was preparing for his insurrection, however, Za'im contacted his opponents in Lebanon and secretly agreed to extradite the SSNP leader in exchange for Lebanese support of his government. On July 8,

Za'im abducted Sa'ada and handed him over to Lebanese authorities. Sa'ada was tried for treason and executed.

Sa'ada's death infuriated Hinnawi, who then rallied other angry officers and ousted Za'im later that summer. On August 14, 1949, in accordance with Hinnawi's orders, Za'im was executed by firing squad along with Prime Minister Muhsen al-Barazi (who had negotiated the treacherous deal with Lebanese Prime Minister Riyad al-Sulh). The coup was funded by the anti-Za'im monarchy in Iraq and was carried out by SSNP officers in the Syrian Army.

Sami al-Hinnawi.

General Hinnawi then declared that the era of military intervention in politics was over. Claiming to have no ambition in seizing power for himself, he invited the longtime civilian leader, Hashim al-Atasi, to become president of the republic. In return, Atasi appointed Hinnawi chief of staff of the Syrian Army. Atasi and Hinnawi desired to see Syria merge with neighboring Iraq in order to bring about greater Arab unity. The two received a senior Iraqi delegation composed of King Faysal II and Crown Prince Abd al-Illah to negotiate the terms of a Syrian-Iraqi union. It was decided that both countries would unite in military, economic, cultural, and educational affairs, while maintaining independent leadership in Damascus and Baghdad.

Shortly before the agreement was finalized, General Adib al-Shishakli, a declared opponent of the proposed union, came to power in Syria. He promised to put an end to Hashemite ambitions. Under Shishakli's orders, Hinnawi was arrested on December 19, 1949, whereas Atasi was permitted to remain in office, provided that he abandon the Iraqi union project. Atasi complied. Hinnawi was deported to the notorious Mezzeh prison until the following September when he was released and exiled to Lebanon.

Hinnawi was not beyond the reach of his enemies, however, and the family of the late Muhsen al-Barazi (Za'im's prime minister, executed on Hinnawi's order) had a long memory. On October 31, 1950, Hersho al-Barazi (a cousin of late Prime Minister Barazi), hunted down Sami al-Hinnawi in Beirut and shot him to death.

Sources:

Azm, Khalid. *Muzakarat Khalid al-Azm* (1973).
Drewry, James. *An Analysis of the 1949 coups d'etat in Syria* (1960).
Encyclopedia of the Modern Middle East, Vol II (1996). Article by
Abdul Karim Rafeq.
Fansa, Nazir. *137 Hazat Souriyya: Ayyam al-Za'im Husni al-Za'im* (1982).
Fansa, Bashir. *al-Nakbat wa al-Mughamarat* (1997).
Hawrani, Akram. *Muzakarat Akram al-Hawrani* (2000).
Moubayed, Sami. *Damascus Between Democracy and Dictatorship* (2000).
Seale, Patrick. *The Struggle for Syria* (1961).
Torrey, Gordon. *Syrian Politics and the Military* (1964).

Jadid, Ghassan
(1920-1957)

Ghassan Jadid studied at the Homs Military Academy and joined the Syrian Social Nationalist Party (SSNP) at the age of eighteen. He enlisted in the French-created Army of the Levant and was stationed in Tripoli (northern Lebanon) in 1945. Meanwhile, Jadid worked with the Lebanese nationalist, Abd al-Hamid Karameh, in the Lebanese underground resistance movement against the French.

When Jadid's French superiors found out about his revolutionary activities, they court-martialed him for disobeying orders. Jadid mutinied against the French, declaring an all-out war against the mandate authority. He attempted to seize power in Homs by arresting French officers stationed there. But his revolt was crushed by the French, and a French military tribunal sentenced him to life imprisonment. President Shukri al-Quwatli issued a general amnesty and released him when the French Mandate in Syria ended on April 17, 1946.

Then Jadid became an instructor at the Homs Military Academy. In 1948, he volunteered for service in the Arab-Israeli War. He served as a commanding officer in Jaysh al-Inqadh or Arab Liberation Army (ALA), a volunteer pan-Arab force created under an Arab League mandate to assist the Palestinians in defending Palestine against the Yashuv. Fawzi al-Qawuqji was the military commander of the ALA. It was supposed to be funded and armed by all the nations of the Arab League, but in actuality, Syria bore the main costs. At the end of the 1948 war, Taha al-Hashimi, the political liaison between the Arab League and ALA, accused Ghassan Jadid and Qawuqji of conspiring with the SSNP to overthrow the Lebanese and Syrian governments in order to create a greater Syria.

At this point, Ghassan Jadid had returned to Homs to continue his career as a military instructor. In November 1951, Adib al-Shishakli, a longtime friend and SSNP party comrade, came to power in Syria and appointed him director of the Homs Military Academy. In his new post, Jadid utilized his talent as an orator to preach SSNP ideology and recruit SSNP members into the armed forces. From

1951 to 1954, he gained influence within the Syrian Army and befriended the country's leading decision-makers. Even after a military coup toppled Adib al-Shishakli in February 1954, Jadid remained at his post. His widespread popularity alarmed many officers, including the Deputy Chief of Staff Adnan al-Malki, who began to plot his downfall.

Ghassan Jadid.

In April 1955, under orders from SSNP President George Abd al-Masih, a group of SSNP officers assassinated Malki in Damascus. Although it was the SSNP president who had a personal grudge against Malki, the ordeal nonetheless tainted the entire SSNP leadership. Immediately, Ghassan Jadid was accused of involvement in the affair, and a warrant was issued for his arrest, along with Abd al-Masih and other SSNP leaders. Jadid denied the charges, claiming that Abd al-Masih had ordered the killing for personal reasons and that the party was neither informed nor involved in the assassination. A military court interrogated Jadid in Syria and sentenced him to death for the murder of Malki. Lebanese President Kamil Sham'un gave him asylum in Beirut and used the SSNP to campaign against Syrian officers whom he claimed were trying to topple his regime.

While in Beirut, Jadid took part in a failed coup against the Syrian government. This insurrection was funded by Iraq and aimed to overthrow the regime of President Shukri al-Quwatli in 1956. Involved in the conspiracy were the Syrian politicians Munir al-Ajlani, Mikh'ail Ilyan, Adnan al-Atasi, and the SSNP leader Sa'id Takkiddine.

Initially, Prime Minister Nuri al-Sa'id of Iraq had asked ex-President Shishakli to launch a coup in Syria. In 1956, Shishakli came to Beirut in order to discuss with Jadid the political conditions in Syria. Shishakli then backed out of the conspiracy, claiming that a coup at such a time would be risky. His refusal to participate forced Jadid and his comrades to take action on their own.

A Syrian military court sentenced Jadid to death in absentia for working with a foreign power to foment civil war in Syria. Jadid continued to live in Lebanon. On February 19, 1957, Ghassan Jadid was assassinated at the gates of SSNP headquarters in Ras Beirut by agents of Abd al-Hamid al-Sarraj, the director of Syrian Intelligence.

Sources:
BBC Archives. "The Damascus Trial" on February 2, 1957.
Dayeh, Jean. *Ghassan Jadid* (1990).
Encyclopedia of the Modern Middle East, Vol II (1996). Article by Charles U. Zenzie.

Khalidi, Ghassan. *Al-Hizb al-Qawmi wa Qadiyyat al-Malki* (2000).

Jadid, Salah (1926-1993): see "Politicians"

Jamil, Naji
(1930-)

Naji Jamil was born in the Dayr al-Zur province, studied at the Homs Military Academy, and later pursued advanced aviation training in Great Britain. He returned to Damascus in the early 1950s and joined the Baath Party of Michel Aflaq and Salah al-Bitar. In 1957, through the party and military apparatus, he met Hafez al-Asad, another officer in the Syrian Air Force, and they became good friends.

When the Baath Party came to power in March 1963, Asad became commander of the Air Force while Naji Jamil became the head of the Military Police. Jamil sided with Asad in the inter-party strife that rocked Syria during the mid-1960s. They shared many common enemies in Syria, most notably Baath Party strongman Mohammad Umran, who Jamil despised, and who was close to Michel Aflaq and President Amin al-Hafez. Once again, Jamil supported Asad when Asad launched a coup in February 1966, toppling the regime of President Hafez and arresting General Umran. Asad became minister of defense in the new government and Jamil became chief of the Air Force.

For the third time in his career, Jamil supported Asad when the latter seized power once and for all on November 16, 1970, when he ousted the regime of President Nur al-Din al-Atasi and Salah Jadid. Jamil helped orchestrate this "Correction Movement" with Asad's close associates, General Mustapha Tlas and General Mohammad al-Khuly. In reward for his services, Jamil was appointed head of the Bureau of State Security and commander of the Syrian Air Force. He served on the Syrian-Egyptian Armed Forces Supreme Council in August 1973 and as air defense commander during the Arab-Israeli War of 1973.

In 1975, Jamil became Asad's intermediary to the Lebanese Civil War. Along with Chief of Staff Hikmat al-Shihabi and Foreign Minister Abd al-Halim Khaddam, Jamil made numerous visits to Beirut during the early war months to try and reach a compromise between the warring factions, specifically the Lebanese state, embodied by President Sulayman Franjiyyieh, and the warring militias of Yasser Arafat and Pierre Gemayel.

With the reputation as a peacemaker in the Lebanese Civil War, Jamil went on to lobby for Asad throughout the Arab world after Anwar al-Sadat visited Jerusalem in 1977. Jamil met with numerous Arab leaders to drum up support against Sadat's peace plan. In October 1978, Jamil went to Cairo to meet with Sadat himself and lecture him on Arab nationalism and the need to keep his separate peace from undercutting the Palestinians and Syria.

In 1978, Jamil also became deputy to Mustapha Tlas, the minister of defense and Asad's right-hand man. In March of that year, Jamil was suddenly retired from his military post, but he retained his post on the National Command of the Baath Party. According to Seale's book, *Asad*, Jamil's sudden retirement was due to a clash with Rifaat al-Asad, the president's younger brother, who was the number two man in Syria. Jamil was replaced by General Mohammad al-Khuly as commander of the Syrian Air Force Intelligence. Jamil eventually made his peace with Rifaat, but this cost him what remained of his political career.

Jamil was forced out of the Regional Command on August 1, 1984, when Hafez al-Asad began to purge Rifaat's men from power. Thereafter, Naji Jamil ceased all political activity, but he is still considered one of the strongest and ablest officers to emerge in Syria during the era of Hafez al-Asad.

Sources:
Encyclopedia of the Modern Middle East vol. II. Entry by
Charles U. Zenzie p. 934
Seale, Patrick. *Asad: Struggle for the Middle East* (1988).

al-Jundi, Abd al-Karim
(1932-1969)

Abd al-Karim al-Jundi studied at the Homs Military Academy and joined the Baath Party in 1952, at the age of twenty. In the mid-1950s, he joined the movement of Arab nationalism that was headed by President Gamal Abd al-Nasser of Egypt. He also supported Syria's merger with Egypt that formed the United Arab Republic (UAR) in 1958.

In 1960, Jundi and four other Baathists, Hafez al-Asad, Salah Jadid, Ahmad al-Meer, and Mohammad Umran co-founded the Military Committee of the Baath Party. It had one purpose: to protect the union leadership.

When a military coup d'etat dissolved the UAR in September 1961, the committee vowed revenge. Syria's new president, Nazim al-Qudsi, discharged many of the committee's officers from the Syrian Army for their Nasserist views. On March 8, 1963, the Military Committee launched a coup and overthrew the civilian regime of President Nazim al-Qudsi. They were influenced by a coup that Baath Party officers had orchestrated in Iraq on February 8, 1963, where the Iraqi dictator, Abd al-Karim Qasim, had been killed. The officers distributed posts accordingly among themselves. Jundi was appointed to the Revolutionary Command Council (RCC) and became a member of the Party's Regional Command.

In 1964, Jundi became minister of agriculture in the cabinet of Prime Minister Salah al-Bitar. Two years later, he became director of the General Intelligence Bureau. Jundi reigned in an atmosphere of terror and was given carte blanche to use the military apparatus for wide-scale repression. During the Jundi years, arbitrary arrests and torture, unknown since the days of Abd al-Hamid Sarraj (1954-1961), once again became commonplace. Having accumulated many enemies, Jundi feared for his life and withdrew into seclusion.

In 1968, he began to plot the overthrow of Salah Jadid and Hafez al-Asad, his two former associates in the Military Committee. Asad noticed Jundi's political maneuverings and recommended to President Nur al-Din al-Atasi that he dismiss Jundi. Then Asad arrested the officers who were loyal to Jundi and fired two of his most vocal advocates, the editors of the state-run dailies, *al-Thawra* and *al-Baath*. Unable to face arrest and interrogation, Abd al-Karim al-Jundi committed suicide on March 2, 1969. He was thirty-seven years old.

Sources:
Batatu, Hanna. *Syria's Peasantry: The Descendants of Its Lesser Rural Notables and Their Politics* (2000).
Seale, Patrick. *Asad: Struggle for the Middle East* (1988).

Kanaan, Ghazi
(1933-)

Ghazi Kanaan was from a small village in the Syrian mountains. He studied at the Homs Military Academy and steadily rose in rank, becoming head of intelligence in Homs. In 1982, President Hafez al-Asad appointed him director of Syrian Intelligence in Lebanon. He was welcomed to Beirut, where the Lebanese Civil War had unleashed a wave of terror and violence in the streets.

Kanaan escaped an assassination attempt carried out by Hizbullah, the Shiite militia group that was to become Syria's foremost ally in Lebanon. He helped broker Syria's alliance with warring Lebanese militias, most notably with Amal, the Shiite movement of Nabih Berri, and the militia of the Druze leader Walid Jumblatt. Kanaan worked relentlessly under orders from President Hafez al-Asad to dissolve the May 17, 1984 Agreement between Lebanese President Amin Gemayel and Israel, brokered through US mediator George Shultz.

Kanaan also worked closely with Vice President Abd al-Halim Khaddam, who orchestrated the Tripartite Agreement between Berri, Jumblatt, and the Maronite warlord, Elie Hobeika, in December 1985. The new agreement was aimed at bridging the gap between the warring militias and to void, once and for all, the May 17 Agreement. Kanaan helped Hobeika defect from the vehemently anti-Syrian Lebanese Forces and Hobeika became a trusted ally of Damascus. Kanaan rewarded Hobeika for his loyalty by appointing him a minister in several cabinets when the war ended in 1991.

In October 1990, Kanaan played an instrumental role in creating an alliance between Syria and Samir Gagegea, another commander of the Lebanese Forces, when Syrian forces invaded East Beirut to topple the unconstitutional military cabinet of Prime Minister Michel Aoun, Syria's top enemy in Lebanon. The defeat of Aoun, sanctioned by the United States in exchange for Syrian assistance in the 1991 Gulf War, signaled an end to the Lebanese Civil War.

Under the post-war regime of President Elias Hrawi, Kanaan became the "kingmaker" of Lebanese politics; without him, nothing could get done in Beirut. He supported Hrawi against his enemies, then lobbied for his reelection in 1995 and pushed for the election of General Emile Lahhoud as president of Lebanon in 1998. When he was called back to Damascus in October 2002, President Lahhoud awarded Kanaan the Cedar Medal of the Commodore, Excellence Class. Kanaan became director of the Political Security Department of Syrian Intelligence. One journalist observing his departure from Beirut in 2002 remarked, "Few major events in the history of this nation over the past 20 years took place without being shaped in some way by his presence."

Syria's supremacy and control over the complex web of Lebanese politics from 1976 to 2000 can single-handedly be attributed to three men: Hafez al-Asad, Abd al-Halim Khaddam, and Ghazi Kanaan. In 2004, Kanaan became minister of interior in the cabinet of Prime Minister Mohammad Naji al-Itri.

Sources:
Batatu, Hanna. *Syria's Peasantry* (1999).

Kaylani, Haitham
(1926-)

Haitham Kaylani studied at the Homs Military Academy, where he graduated in 1945. He underwent advanced military training at the Air Force Academy in Paris and joined the Syrian Army following independence in 1946. In 1949, he became military assistant to General Husni al-Za'im during Za'im's four-month stint as president of Syria.

On August 14, 1949, Kaylani was on duty when Za'im was overthrown and executed by General Sami al-Hinnawi. Kaylani, however, did not participate in this coup nor any other counter coups in Syria during the 1950s. He steadily rose in rank to become chief of the Air Force in 1957 and supported Syria's merger with Egypt to form the United Arab Republic (UAR) in 1958. During the UAR years, he was stationed in Cairo as director of the office of Sidqi Mahmud, the chief of the Egyptian Air Force. In September 1961, after the dissolution of the UAR, Kaylani returned to Syria where he became secretary-general of the Ministry of Information.

In July 1962, Syria filed an official complaint against Nasser, claiming that he was interfering in her affairs and trying to persuade officers in the Syrian Army to rebel against the post-Nasser order. The Arab League called for roundtable talks between Syria and Egypt to be held in the Lebanese town of Shtura on the Syrian-Lebanese border. Syria's new president, Nazim al-Qudsi, appointed Kaylani to the Syrian delegation. The talks ended abruptly, however, when the Egyptian delegation walked out before the Arab League issued a verdict condemning Egypt for her accusations against Syria.

Also in 1962, Kaylani was appointed ambassador to Algeria. Kaylani was charged with asking President Ahmad Ben Bella to mediate between Syria and Gamal Abd al-Nasser, who had severed relations with Damascus following the coup of 1961. Although the Syrians had dissolved the UAR, they tried to maintain cordial relations with Nasser's Egypt from 1961 to 1963.

In 1963, the Baath Party came to power in Damascus, and Syria's new president, Amin al-Hafez, appointed Kaylani ambassador to Morocco. One year later, he was transferred back to Damascus and appointed senior inspector at the Ministry of Foreign Affairs. In 1968, he became secretary-general of the Ministry. In 1971, President Hafez al-Asad appointed Kaylani as Syria's ambassador to East Germany. While serving in Berlin, he obtained a doctorate in history. In 1973, he was appointed Syria's permanent ambassador to the United Nations (UN). He held this post until 1975 when he was summoned back to Syria and appointed secretary-general of the Ministry of Foreign Affairs. In 1976, shortly after assuming his duties, he clashed with Foreign Minister Abd al-Halim Khaddam over Syria's intervention in Lebanon. Khaddam was in favor of full-scale intervention in the Lebanse Civil War while Kaylani wanted diplomatic, rather than military, intervention. Kaylani was overruled.

Then, in 1984, Kaylani became senior consultant at the Arab League in Tunis. He served as editor-in-chief of the League's publication, Shu'un Arabiyya (Arab Affairs), until 1998. He then returned to Syria and joined the Arab Center for Strategic Studies in Damascus, becoming editor-in-chief of its periodical, Shu'un Stratigiyya (Strategic Affairs). He has since maintained his post with the periodical and served as assistant to Ali Nasser Mohammad, the ex-president of North Yemen, who lives in Syria.

Kaylani spent the remainder of the 1990s writing books, lecturing at academic institutes and working with NGOs in Syria and the Arab world. His most memorable works are Al-Ahamiyya al-Stratigiyya wa al-Askariyya Lil Jumhuriyya al-Arabiyya al-Mutahida (The Strategic and Military Importance of the United Arab Republic), and Dirasa fi al-Askariyya al-Israeliyya (Study in Israeli Militarism). In 1991, he published his book, Al-Istratijiyya al-Harbiyya Lilhurub al-Arabiyya 1948-1988 (War Strategy of the Arab Wars 1948-1988). Other publications include, Turkiyya wa al-Arab (Turkey and the Arabs), and Al-Taswiyya al-Silmiyya Lilsira' al-Arabi al-Israeli (Peace Settlement of the Arab-Israeli Conflict), both of which were published in 1996.

One of Haitham Kaylani's most memorable books is his latest, published in 1999 and entitled, *Al-Irhab You'asis Dawla: Namuzaj Israel* (*Terrorism Founds a State: The Israeli Example*).

Sources:
Interview with Dr Haitham Kaylani (July 16, 2002).

al-Khlayfawi, Abd al-Rahman (1927-): see "Politicians"

al-Khuly, Mohammad
(1937-)

Mohammad al-Khuly studied at the Homs Military Academy and joined the Baath Party of Michel Aflaq. In 1963, the Military Committee of the Baath Party came to power in Syria, and Khuly became deputy commander of Air Force Intelligence.

Khuly also acted as deputy to Hafez al-Asad, the commander of the Syrian Air Force. He allied himself with Asad when Asad launched a coup in February 1966 and ousted the regime of President Amin al-Hafez. Four years later, he participated in a coup that brought Asad to power on November 16, 1970.

Khuly was charged with arresting top officials in the regime of President Nur al-Din al-Atasi. Asad gave him eight hours to do the job; Khuly did it in two, without shedding a drop of blood. In reward for his loyalty, Khuly was promoted to commander of Air Force Intelligence, a critical post he held until 1987. From 1971 to 1987, he was also chairman of the Presidential Intelligence Committee, reporting directly to Asad on security affairs. Mohammad al-Khuly became one of the closest officers to Asad during the 1970s and 1980s, thereby becoming one of the most powerful men in Syria. He was among the very few who had constant access to the president.

During his tenure at Air Force Intelligence, on April 17, 1986, the famous (or infamous) Hindawi Affair took place at Heathrow Airport in London. Nizar Hindawi, a Jordanian living in London, planted a suitcase bomb (1.5 kilograms of explosives) in the luggage of his Irish girlfriend who was boarding an El Al airplane headed for Tel Aviv. The bomb was expected to explode in the air, but it was intercepted by Israeli security. Subsequently, Hindawi disappeared, only to show up shortly afterward and surrender to British police.

According to Patrick Seale, the biographer of Hafez al-Asad, during his brief disappearance, Hindawi fled to the Syrian Embassy in Belgrave Square and sought the assistance of Syrian Ambassador Dr Lutfallah Haydar. Following an interrogation, Hindawi confessed that he had been dragged into the conspiracy by Colonel Haytham Sa'id, one of the senior officers in Khuly's Air Force Intelligence, whom he had met in January 1986. In court, however, Hindawi disavowed his previous statements, claiming that Syria was not responsible. On the contrary, he charged that it was entirely planned by Israel to portray Syria as a state sponsor of terrorism.

Hindawi was sentenced to forty-five years in prison, the longest term given to date at the Old Bailey in London. Hours after the verdict was issued, British Prime Minister Margaret Thatcher cut off diplomatic relations with Syria, calling on Great Britain's allies to do the same, and accusing Damascus of conducting international terrorism. The United States and Canada responded by recalling their ambassadors from Syria, while the European community adopted limited sanctions.

It was widely believed that the motive behind the Hindawi Affair was pure revenge, since only two months earlier Israel had forced down an executive jet carrying Syrian officials from Libya to Damascus. President Asad had not been informed of the plot, and it was carried out by Khuly, through Sa'id. No evidence ever surfaced proving that the conspirators had acted on any orders given by

Mohammad al-Khuly.

Asad. Khuly denied involvement as well, and was backed by Jacques Chirac, then Prime Minister of France. Chirac said in an interview with the *Washington Times* on November 10, 1986, that he and German Chancellor Helmut Kohl believed that "the Hindawi plot was a provocation designed to embarrass Syria and destabilize the Asad government."

In October 1987, Asad himself gave an interview to *Time Magazine,* denying involvement in the Hindawi Affair and claiming that it had been engineered by Israel. As a result of the Hindawi Affair, Mohammad al-Khuly was transferred to the less powerful post of deputy commander of the Air Force. On paper, this was a demotion, but Khuly continued to wield much power and lost none of his privileges or authority. He held this post

until 1994 when he returned to his previous job. By then, Syria's relations with Great Britain had returned to normal after Asad participated in Operation Desert Storm to liberate Kuwait from Iraqi occupation.

In 1998, having reached pension age, Mohammad al-Khuly retired from the Syrian Army. He has been in political and military retirement ever since, but is considered one of the most powerful officers to rule Syria during the thirty-year era of Hafez al-Asad.

Hanna Batatu, the Palestinian academic who wrote a book on Asad's Syria, says that Mohammad al-Khuly was, "deep in Asad's confidence" and "unwavering in his loyalty to him." Batatu adds, quoting a source on Khuly, "he is clever and cultured" and a "man with a horizon" unlike many of the officers that ruled Syria from 1963 onwards.

Sources:
Batatu, Hanna. *Syria's Peasantry* (1999).
Seale, Patrick. *Abu Nidal: A Gun for Hire* (1995).
Seale, Patrick. *Asad: Struggle for the Middle East* (1988).

al-Kuzbari, Haydar
(1920-1996)

Haydar al-Kuzbari was born and raised in Damascus. He joined the French-sponsored Army of the Levant and, when independence was proclaimed in April 1946, he was transferred to the Syrian Army. He rose steadily in rank, taking no part in the coups and countercoups that rocked Syria from 1946 to 1958.

When Syria and Egypt merged to form the United Arab Republic (UAR) in 1958, Kuzbari became commander of Syria's eastern border with Iraq. In 1960, he was appointed director of tribal affairs in the UAR and charged with monitoring the security of President Gamal Abd al-Nasser during his periodic visits to Syria.

Kuzbari lost faith in Nasser's leadership, however, and resented the dominance of Egyptian officials over all aspects of Syria's military, social, and political life. He teamed up with a group of similarly frustrated officers, known as the Damascus Coalition. They orchestrated a coup on September 28, 1961, declaring Syria's secession from the UAR. The Damascus Coalition expelled all Egyptian officers from Syria and Kuzbari personally deported Marshal Abd al-Hakim Amer, Nasser's right-hand man, to Cairo. In response, Nasser dispatched a contingent of armed parachuters to the coastal city of Lattakia. The Egyptians, however, were apprehended and arrested upon landing. Seven people were killed and eight injured, including Labor Minister Akram al-Dayri, who was fired at by Kuzbari himself.

No sooner had the officers of the Damascus Coalition assumed control of Syria than arguments broke out within the coalition itself. Some advocated the return of ex-President Shukri al-Quwatli,

Haydar al-Kuzbari.

who had orchestrated the UAR and left office in 1958. Kuzbari, however, vetoed his return, claiming he had been too much in favor of Nasser from 1955 to 1958. In his argument with his fellow officers, Kuzbari said, "This (the return of Quwatli) is cowardliness. Did we sacrifice our blood for the return of Quwatli?"

Kuzbari then argued over the appointment of a new prime minister for Syria. He also clashed with the coup mastermind, Abd al-Karim al-Nehlawi, and objected to his interference in the day-to-day affairs of the state. For one month, a struggle for power prevailed between Nehlawi and Kuzbari, with each trying to discredit the other within the decision-making circles of the Syrian Army.

In November 1961, Kuzbari was arrested on Nehlawi's orders and sent to the notorious Mezzeh prison. He was released shortly thereafter, kept under house arrest, and retired from the army. In March 1963, his civil rights were terminated by the Baath Party government that pledged to restore the UAR. The Revolutionary Command Council (RCC) accused Kuzbari and the entire Damascus Coalition of having obstructed the dream of Arab unity. The RCC arrested Kuzbari, but soon released him.

Then, in July 1963, Jassem Alwan, an officer working on the Egyptian payroll, tried to seize power in Syria. Interior Minister Amin al-Hafez cracked down on the armed movement and arrested all opponents of the Baath Party, including (once again) Kuzbari and many officers in the Damascus Coalition. Haydar al-Kuzbari, however, was eventually released and went into political retirement. He died in 1996.

Sources:
Encyclopedia of the Modern Middle East, Vol II (1996). Entry by Charles U. Zenzie.
Samman, Mutih. *Watan wa Askar* (1995).
Zahr al-Din, Abd al-Karim. *Muzakarati an Fatrat al-Infisal fi Souriyya* (1968).

al-Mahmud, Iyad
(1950-)

Iyad al-Mahmud was born in the coastal city of Tartus. He studied at the Homs Military Academy and then obtained a degree in political science from the Lebanese University. He was first appointed consul at the Syrian Embassy in Cairo.

When President Anwar al-Sadat of Egypt signed a peace treaty with Israel in 1978, President Hafez al-Asad recalled Mahmud to Damascus. In February 1979, Asad appointed him minister to the Syrian Embassy in Iran, immediately following the Islamic Revolution that overthrew the regime of Shah Rida Pehlavi. Mahmud established contact with Ayatollah al-Khomeini and served as a liaison officer between the Iranian cleric and President Hafez al-Asad. In 1980, Asad appointed Mahmud consul and chargé d'affaires in Tehran. Also in 1980, the Iranian government offered Syria, through Mahmud, the equivalent of one billion dollars worth of oil.

When the Iran-Iraq War broke out in 1980, Syria did not offer Iran any military assistance because Asad believed that the war was a conspiracy to sideline both Iraq and Iran from the Arab-Israeli conflict. Mahmud became an intermediary between Asad and Khomeini, communicating back and forth between Damascus and Tehran. Asad wanted to find an alternative to Egypt following the imbalance in Arab power created by Sadat's 1978 Camp David Accord with Israel. With Egypt and her large army out of the fight with Israel, Asad needed an alternative and relied heavily on Iran to serve as this substitute. Asad embraced a political alliance with Tehran but refused to help its leaders in their war against Iraq.

In 1984, Mahmud's relation with the Iranians began to falter when he intervened with Shiite militias in Lebanon to release David Dodge, president of the American University of Beirut (AUB), who had been taken hostage in the Lebanese Civil War. Mahmud secured Dodge's release and brought him to Damascus, from where he was returned to the United States. The event caused arguments among several of the Iranian revolutionaries who had orchestrated Dodge's kidnapping. Also in 1984, eight Yugoslav citizens were kidnapped in northern Iraq by the Islamic Kurdish Movement and taken as hostages to Iran. Mahmud secured their release, thereby opening up more diplomatic channels between Syria and Washington.

On November 2, 1986, while leaving the Syrian Embassy in Tehran, a group of armed men opened fire on Mahmud's automobile. Although Mahmud fired back and wounded one person, Mahmud was ultimately wounded and kidnapped. Asad attempted to locate him, but failed to do so.

When the Iranian government demonstrated only mild interest in the crisis, Asad publicized the ordeal to the press, thereby pressuring Tehran to acknowledge that Mahmud had been kidnapped on Iranian soil. The mullahs of Iran claimed, however, that Israeli agents had abducted him. Three days later, the clerics secured his release. Western observers, including Asad's biographer, Patrick Seale, claimed that Mahmud had been kidnapped because he had revealed the secrets of the Irangate Affair, a US political scandal that came out in 1987 which involved senior members of the Reagan administration. The US government had secretly sold weapons to Iran in 1985 in exchange for hostages held in Lebanon by pro-Iranian militias.

Asad recalled Mahmud from Iran and transferred him to Beirut where he became director of Syrian state security in Lebanon from 1986 until 2000. From 1988 through 1990, Mahmud opened channels of communication with the Maronite warlord, Samir Gagegea, who was fighting a war against General Michel

Aoun, the interim prime minister of Lebanon. Mahmud also communicated with other political groups in Lebanon from Maronite and Muslims circles, helping end the Civil War and resulting in the Taif Accord of October 1989.

Iyad al-Mahmud retired from office following Asad's death in June 2000.

Sources:
Seale, Patrick. *Asad: Struggle for the Middle East* (1988).

al-Malki, Adnan
(1918-1955)

Adnan al-Malki was born and raised in Damascus. He studied at the Homs Military Academy and joined the Syrian Army.

In 1951, Malki was troubled when President Adib al-Shishakli outlawed most political parties. In preparation for a confrontation with Shishakli, Malki urged Akram al-Hawrani's Arab Socialist Party to unite with the Baath Party—a step taken at the end of 1952 when they formed the *Hizb al-Baath al-Arabi al-Ishtiraki* or Baath Arab Socialist Party. Then, in 1953, Malki met with President Shishakli and presented the Syrian leader with a list of demands that included the release of all political prisoners, an end to one-party rule, and the restoration of political parties that had been outlawed two years earlier.

Shishakli responded by arresting Malki and persecuting those who had agreed with his demands. In jail, Malki met with a group of arrested officers, mostly members of the Baath Party. These were men, like him, who believed in Arab nationalism and harbored socialist views. Although Malki never became a member of the Baath Party, he was close to its military leadership, and his brother, Riyad, was a veteran Baathist. In 1954, following the downfall of Shishakli, Malki was released from prison and reinstated into the armed forces. The Baath Party supported his rise to power, and in 1955 he was appointed deputy to Chief of Staff Shawkat Shuqayr.

Between 1954 and 1955, Adnan al-Malki enjoyed unprecedented popularity and was viewed as a natural leader by the Damascene officers in the Syrian Army. Unlike Shuqayr, who was from Lebanon, Malki was a native of Damascus and was politically allied to the strongest left-wing party in Syria. He was young, charismatic, belonged to a well-to-do Sunni family, and was a firm believer in the policies of Arab nationalism. Malki also became a member of the popular movement of Arab nationalism that was headed by President Gamal Abd al-Nasser of Egypt.

Unfortunately, Malki's popularity alienated many politicians in Syria, including Ghassan Jadid, a member of the Syrian Social Nationalist Party (SSNP), and the SSNP President George Abd al-Masih. Both parties were opposed to Nasser's pan-Arab approach and feared his spreading influence in the armed forces. If Arab nationalism spread, they argued, it would counterbalance the SSNP ideology. Abd al-Masih tried to discredit Malki by claiming that he was a sectarian officer who practiced favoritism toward fellow Sunni officers in the Syrian Army. In turn, Malki often threatened to extradite Abd al-Masih to Lebanon, where a death sentence awaited him for the 1951 murder of Lebanese Prime Minister Riyad al-Sulh. Malki also argued with Jadid, who was very popular in the armed forces and often contested Malki's leadership.

Adnan al-Malki.

On April 22, 1955, while attending a football match in Damascus, Adnan al-Malki was shot dead by two members of the SSNP. One of the assassins immediately committed suicide while the other was arrested and confessed to the killing, acting on direct orders from George Abd al-Masih. Following the assassination, the SSNP was banned in Syria and its leadership was sent into exile or arrested. The party remained outlawed due to the Malki affair until 2005.

The military regime of the Baath Party that came to power in 1963 honored Adnan al-Malki's legacy by naming a luxurious neighborhood after him and erecting a large statue of him in central Damascus.

Sources:
Azm, Khalid. *Muzakarat Khalid al-Azm* (1973).
Commins, David. *Historical Dictionary of Modern Syria* (1996).
Hawrani, Akram. *Muzkarat Akram al-Hawrani* (2000).
Moubayed, Sami. *Damascus Between Democracy and Dictatorship* (2000).
Seale, Patrick. *The Struggle for Syria* (1961).
Torrey, Gordon. *Syrian Politics and the Military* (1964).

Maloian, Hrant
(1896-?)

Hrant Maloian was an Armenian from Aleppo. He studied at the Ottoman Military Academy and graduated in 1916. A professional soldier, he did not leave the Ottoman ranks despite the boiling anti-Ottoman sentiment. He remained loyal to his commanding officers until the Ottoman Empire fell in November 1918.

Maloian then moved to Damascus, allied himself with the post-Ottoman regime of King Faysal I, and served as an officer in the newly formed Syrian Army.

In July 1920, the French took over Syria and dissolved the Syrian Army, setting up the Army of the Levant instead. Maloian joined the newly created army, but then allied himself with the nationalist movement brewing against the French. In 1928, he befriended members of the National Bloc. In August 1945, President Shukri al-Quwatli, a veteran of the National Bloc, appointed Maloian director of police and public security—the highest post ever held by an Armenian in Syria.

Popularly called "Hrant Bey," Maloian held office during the Arab-Israeli War of 1948, charged with keeping the country under strict control in the face of the defeat at the war front. He proclaimed martial law, imposed a curfew on all citizens, and outlawed all parades and riots. Maloian took over the police force at a time when it was characterized by widespread insubordination and chaos, and he managed to transform it into a disciplined force. In 1943, the police force totaled 5,200 troops. By the time Maloian left office in 1949 they numbered 9,751. He obtained generous funding from Quwatli to enlarge the force and crack down on corruption in the police department. During Maloian's era, four hundred senior police officers were either court-martialed or jailed for corruption and insubordination.

In September 1946, Maloian used his impressive police force to crack down on Sulayman al-Murshed, the chieftain who claimed to have divine powers and was leading a separatist movement based out of the Syrian Mountain against the Quwatli regime. Maloian dispatched one thousand armed men to the Mountain, had Murshed arrested, brought him to trial, and presided over his execution in November 1946. Maloian retired from the force in August 1949 and spent the remainder of his years working as a private businessman and an agent for British Airways in Damascus.

Toward the end of his life, Hrant Maloian moved to the USA where he died in California.

Sources:
Faris, George. *Man Hum fi al-Alam al-Arabi?* (1957).
Landis, Joshua. *Nationalism and the Politics of Za'ama* (1997).

al-Meer, Ahmad
(1922-)

Ahmad al-Meer studied at the Homs Military Academy and joined the Baath Party in the early 1950s. He joined the movement of Arab nationalism that was headed by President Gamal Abd al-Nasser of Egypt and supported the merger of Syria and Egypt to form the United Arab Republic (UAR) in 1958. As part of the exchange program between Syria and Egypt, Meer was stationed in Cairo during the union years.

In 1959, Meer founded the Military Committee of the Baath Party, a secret society that aimed at preserving the UAR. The committee was composed of other like-minded officers serving in Egypt, including Hafez al-Asad, Salah Jadid, Abd al-Karim al-Jundi, and its president, Mohammad Umran. When the UAR was dissolved by a military coup in September 1961, these men vowed revenge and pledged to oust the post-union government of President Nazim al-Qudsi. Meer and his comrades were persecuted for their pro-Nasserist loyalties and forced out of the Syrian Army.

In 1962, Meer and his associates began plotting Qudsi's downfall. The young party members were influenced by the coup that took place in Iraq on February 8, 1963, and led to the killing of General Abd al-Karim Qasim. It was carried out by a group of Baath Party officers. Meer hoped that he and his comrades could do the same thing in Syria. On March 8, 1963, they launched a coup that toppled the Qudsi government. They arrested the president and exiled his prime minister, Khalid al-Azm, to Lebanon. They then created the Revolutionary Command Council (RCC) to preside over state affairs, with Meer as its top leader. Meer became one of the RCC's earliest members and was also voted onto the Regional Command of the Baath Party.

In the wake of Syria's second major war with Israel in 1967, Ahmad al-Meer was stationed on the Golan Heights as commander of the Syrian Army there. The Israeli Army surprised him with an offensive on June 5 that led to his evacuation of the Golan Heights. He returned in disgrace to Syria, where he was blamed for the defeat and for failing to hold back the Israelis. Subsequently, Meer was discharged from the Syrian Army. Some members of the Baath demanded that he be court-martialed, but Baath Party strongman Salah Jadid refused. Instead, Meer was sent off as Syria's ambassador to Spain. Ahmad al-Meer held this post from 1968 to 1970, then retired when Hafez al-Asad came to power in November 1970.

Sources:
Batatu, Hanna. *Syria's Peasantry: The Descendants of Its Lesser Rural Notables and Their Politics* (2000).
Seale, Patrick. *Asad: The Struggle for the Middle East* (1988).

al-Nehlawi, Abd al-Karim
(1926-)

Abd al-Karim al-Nehlawi was born and raised in Damascus. He studied at the Homs Military Academy and pursued a career as an officer in the Syrian Army.

In 1958, Syria and Egypt merged to form the United Arab Republic (UAR) and Nehlawi became deputy director of officer affairs in the UAR. His direct superior

Abd al-Karim al-Nehlawi.

was an Egyptian officer with whom Nehlawi had differences. Nehlawi allied himself with a group of Syrian officers who were displeased with the UAR and who complained of being ranked as inferior to their Egyptian counterparts.

In January 1961, Nehlawi and his fellow officers began planning for a coup to restore Syria's pre-1958 independent status. Nehlawi spearheaded the movement funded by urban merchants from Damascus, Aleppo, Homs, Hama, and Lattakia. These merchants had suffered nationalization of their enterprises under Gamal Abd al-Nasser's socialist decrees in July 1961. Secret channels of communication were opened with King Hussein of Jordan, a prime opponent of Nasser, and King Saud of Saudi Arabia, Nasser's rival over pan-Arab leadership.

On September 28, 1961, this group, dubbed the Damascus Coalition, launched a coup d'etat in Syria and declared the dissolution of the UAR. Under Nehlawi's orders, all Egyptian officers stationed in Syria, including Nasser's right-hand man, Abd al-Hakim Amer, were deported to Egypt and all Syrians stationed in Egypt were called back home. All those holding office under Nasser were asked to renounce their loyalty to the UAR or suffer arrest. Nasser attempted a counter-attack by sending Egyptian parachuters into Lattakia, but Nehlawi had them arrested without a shot being fired in defense of the union.

By noon, Nasser's regime was declared over and Nehlawi called for parliamentary elections, claiming to have no presidential ambitions. Instead, in December 1961, he supported the election of Nazim al-Qudsi, a declared anti-Egyptian statesman, as president of Syria. Shortly after assuming office, however, President Qudsi began to curb Nehlawi's powers, claiming that military officers should not meddle in political affairs. Qudsi appointed Ma'ruf al-Dawalibi, an open opponent of military intervention in political affairs, as prime minister and dismissed many of Nehlawi's allies from government.

Upset at being marginalized and ignored by the politicians, Nehlawi decided to strike back. On March 28, 1962, he launched a second coup. He arrested President Qudsi, Prime Minister Dawalibi, and his comrades in the Damascus Coalition, accusing them of selling out to the civilian leadership.

Chief of Staff Abd al-Karim Zahr al-Din called for a military meeting in Homs on April 1 when he and forty-one other officers declared a countercoup against Nehlawi. Zahr al-Din's forces defied Nehlawi's orders, released the prisoners, and discharged Nehlawi from the Syrian Army. Nehlawi was later pardoned by

President Qudsi and dispatched as Syria's ambassador to Rome—the traditional exile for troublemakers.

On January 10, 1963, while on a brief visit to Syria, he tried launching a third coup, but failed at garnering much support. When the Baath Party came to power on March 8, 1963, Abd al-Karim al-Nehlawi's civil rights were canceled and he ceased all political activity.

Sources:

Azm, Khalid. *Muzakarat* (1973).
Commins, David. *Historical Dictionary of Modern Syria* (1996).
Hawrani, Akram. *Muzakarat Akram al-Hawrani* (2000).
Samman, Mutih. *Watan wa Askar* (1995).
Zahr al-Din, Abd al-Karim. *Muzakarati an Fatrat al-Infisal fi Souriyya* (1968).

al-Nfuri, Amin
(1921-)

Amin al-Nfuri studied at the Homs Military Academy and received advanced military training in Paris. He graduated in 1952 and served briefly in Iraq.

In August 1957, Nfuri was summoned back home and appointed deputy to Chief of Staff Afif al-Bizreh, a seasoned officer who brought Nfuri under his patronage and introduced him to the rising generation of Arab nationalists in the armed forces. Nfuri joined the Arab movement headed by President Gamal Abd al-Nasser of Egypt, and in January 1958, was part of an officer delegation that went to Cairo to plead for Syria's unification with Egypt.

In February 1958, the United Arab Republic (UAR) was created and Nasser appointed Nfuri minister of transport. But Nfuri lost faith in Nasser's leadership shortly thereafter and supported a coup that ousted the UAR in September 1961. Nfuri then allied himself with Nazim al-Qudsi, who became president of the Syrian Republic in December 1961, and was appointed minister of agricultural reforms. Nfuri was entrusted with revoking the massive land redistribution that was imposed by Nasser from 1958 to 1961.

In July 1962, Syria filed an official complaint against Nasser, claiming that he was interfering in her affairs and trying to persuade officers in the Syrian Army to rebel against the post-Nasser order. The Arab League called for roundtable talks to be held between Syria and Egypt in the Lebanese town of Shtura on the Syrian-Lebanese border. Qudsi appointed Nfuri to the Syrian delegation. The talks ended abruptly, however, when the Egyptian delegation walked out before the Arab League issued a verdict condemning Egypt for her accusations against Syria.

From 1961 to 1963, Nfuri served as a deputy in parliament. His reforms never got past the drawing board, however, for the Qudsi government was overthrown by military coup in March 1963. The Military Committee of the Baath Party seized power in Syria and pledged to restore the UAR. They created a Revolutionary Command Council (RCC) to govern Syria and went on to punish all those who had worked against the UAR. The RCC fired Nfuri from his job and terminated his civil rights. He was also briefly arrested, then subsequently retired from any further political activity.

In 1970, Amin al-Nfuri published his classic work, *Istratijiyyat al-Harb Did Israel wa al-Amal al-Arab al-Muwahhad* (*Strategy of War Against Israel and Joint Arab Action*).

Sources:
Azm, Khalid. *Muzakarat Khalid al-Azm* (1973).
Barada (March 24, 1963).
Hawrani, Akram. *Muzakarat Akram al-Hawrani* (2000).
Seale, Patrick. *The Struggle for Syria* (1961).

al-Omari, Subhi
(1898-1973)

Subhi al-Omari was born in Damascus and studied at the Ottoman Military Academy in Istanbul. He joined the Ottoman Army when World War I broke out in 1914 and fought against the British in Gaza.

Omari then defected from the Ottoman Army and joined the Arab underground in 1916, becoming an officer in the rebel Arab Army of Sharif Husayn, serving as commander of a machine gun platoon. He was sentenced to death by a military court and forced to remain in Mecca, leading the life of an outlaw until 1918 when the Ottoman Empire was defeated in World War I. He returned to Damascus and joined the Arab administration of King Faysal I, the new ruler of Syria, becoming an officer in the Syrian Army from 1918 to 1920.

On July 24, 1920, Omari went to battle with General Yusuf al-Azma, the minister of war, against the French Army. Omari fought in the infamous Battle of Maysaloun, where the Syrian Army was defeated and the French Mandate was proclaimed over Syria and Lebanon. The French occupied Damascus on July 25, dethroned Faysal, dissolved his army, and sentenced Omari to death. Omari fled to Amman and became military advisor to Prince Abdullah, the Emir of Transjordan. In the newly created Emirate of Transjordan, Omari established the Arab Legion in Amman with British General John Glubb and the Syrian officer Mahmud al-Hindi, who was also escaping a death sentence from the French in Syria.

In 1928, Omari was invited to Baghdad where Faysal I, who had now become king of Iraq, appointed him advisor to the throne. Omari joined the Iraqi Army and served Faysal until his death in 1933. Omari also served under Faysal's son, King Ghazi I (1933-1939), and King Faysal II, who became king of Iraq in 1939.

In 1938, Omari reached the rank of lieutenant colonel in the Iraqi Army and became commander of the Hashemite Cavalry Brigade. Omari took up arms against the British Army in Iraq, commanding a unit at the town of Abu Ghurayb. As a result, he was expelled from the Iraqi Army and had his citizenship revoked. He was then exiled to Syria, only to be arrested by the British and incarcerated in a prison in Sidon (Lebanon). He was freed in 1943 and went to Damascus where he became director of supplies and chief of police under President Shukri al-Quwatli. In 1949, Omari became a deputy in parliament. He also served on the Constitutional Assembly that drafted a new constitution for Syria.

In the second half of the 1950s, however, Omari became increasingly alienated from the rising movement of socialism, headed by President Gamal Abd al-Nasser of Egypt. Omari resented Syria's alliance with Nasser's Egypt and the USSR, preferring instead an alliance with Great Britain, France, and the USA. He joined a group of like-minded politicians and sought to bring down the pro-Nasser government of President Shukri al-Quwatli.

The group recruited armed men, trained in Lebanon by the anti-Nasser government of Kamil Sham'un. The goal was to occupy Damascus, dismiss all pro-Nasser officials, and force Quwatli to change his pro-Egypt and pro-USSR policies. If Quwatli declined, then he would be asked to resign from the presidency. Prime Minister Sabri al-Asali would also be dismissed, and Munir al-Ajlani would create a pro-Hashemite cabinet in which Omari would become minister of defense. While invading Damascus, went the plan, the armed troops would assassinate the socialist Nasserist leaders of Syria: Akram al-Hawrani of the Baath Party, Chief of Staff Afif al-Bizreh, Director of Intelligence Abd al-Hamid Sarraj, and Khalid Bakdash, president of the Syrian Communist Party.

From Baghdad, Iraqi Crown Prince Abd al-Illah and Prime Minister Nuri al-Sa'id funded the plan. Involved in the conspiracy were Munir al-Ajlani, a longtime ally of the Hashemites, Sami Kabbara, publisher of the al-Nidal newspaper, and Adnan al-Atasi, a founding member of the pro-Hashemite People's Party. Sarraj foiled the plot prior to its implementation and had all of its leaders, including Omari, imprisoned and charged with high treason. For the third time in his career, Subhi al-Omari was tried and sentenced to death. But his sentence was commuted to life in prison and, once again, he evaded execution. He remained in prison when Syria and Egypt merged to form the United Arab Republic (UAR) in 1958. In 1960, he was moved from prison to Alexandria where he was placed under house arrest. There he remained until the UAR was dissolved by military coup in September 1961.

Omari wrote three books on his early military experience: al-Maarik al-Ula:

al-Tareeq ila Dimashq (*The First Battles: the Road to Damascus*), covering the Arab Revolt of Sharif Husayn 1916-1918; *Lawrence: al-Haqiqa wa al-Ukzuba* (*Lawrence: the Truth and the Lie*), on the British general, T.E. Lawrence, who fought alongside the Arabs in World War I; and the classic, *Maysaloun: Nihayat Ahd* (*Maysaloun: the End of an Era*). These writings were collectively combined into a three-volume book, *Awrak al-Thawra al-Arabiyya* (*The Arab Revolt Papers*), and published in Great Britain in 1991.

Among Subhi al-Omari's other publications is a book entitled, *Lawrence Kama Ariftahu* (*Lawrence As I Knew Him*), published in Beirut in 1969.

Sources:
BBC Archives. "The Damascus Trial" February 26, 1957.
Omari, Subhi. *Awrak al-Thawra al-Arabiyya* (1991).
Omari, Subhi. *Lawrence Kama Ariftahu* (1969).

al-Qawuqji, Fawzi
(1887-1977)

Fawzi al-Qawuqji was a perpetual rebel who participated in almost every major Arab revolt during the first half of the twentieth century. He was born in Tripoli (north Lebanon) and studied at the Ottoman Military Academy in Istanbul.

Qawuqji served in the Ottoman Army, but deserted to join the rebel Arab Army of Sharif Husayn in 1916. Husayn was working to expel the Ottoman Turks from Syria. When the Ottoman Empire was defeated in 1918, Qawuqji joined the army of King Faysal I, the new leader of Syria. When the French occupied Syria in July 1920, they dethroned Faysal and dissolved the Arab Army. Qawuqji fought the invading forces, but when occupation became inevitable, he joined the French-created Army of the Levant and became commander of a cavalry near Hama.

In July 1925, Qawuqji was highly impressed with a military uprising launched from the Arab Mountain by Sultan al-Atrash against the French Mandate. In August 1925, he secretly went to Damascus to meet with Dr Abd al-Rahman Shahbandar, a leading nationalist, to discuss expanding the revolt to other districts of Syria. When Shahbandar agreed, Qawuqji began planning for the Hama Revolt. He raised funds from the elite of Hama, who were religiously conservative and believed in a holy war (jihad) against the French. His revolt was mainly funded by the Hama notables Najib al-Barazi and Tawfiq al-Shishakli. Qawuqji used his position in the Army of the Levant to secure French maps that gave detailed locations of French military installations throughout Syria.

On October 4, 1925, Qawuqji's troops caught the French off-guard and invaded Hama. They easily disarmed the small contingent of French troops and headed toward the Serail, the government headquarters in Hama where High

Commission staff worked. The building was destroyed and its archives burned. Qawuqji also ordered the destruction of the French-sponsored Bureau of Taxation and the Land Registration Office. In the process, he also disarmed French police and shot those who refused to lay down their arms.

The French high commissioner, General Maurice Sarrail, struck back. He destroyed 144 homes in Hama, arrested 355 locals, and sentenced Qawuqji to death in absentia on the charge of high treason against the French Mandate. In response to the widespread persecution of Frenchmen and destruction of property in Hama, Sarrail bombarded Damascus on October 8 and threatened Qawuqji's allies with public execution. In 1927, the revolt was crushed and its leaders were forced to flee to Iraq or Jordan. The uprising left 6,000 people dead and another 1,000 homeless. In Hama alone, damage was estimated at £200,000.

Following the French suppression of the Great Syrian Revolt in the mid-1920s, Qawuqji fled to Saudi Arabia with Sultan Pasha, where he served as military advisor to Saudi Arabia. In 1932, he fell out with King Abd al-Aziz, who had him arrested and then expelled. Qawuqji went to live in Iraq where he held the post of lecturer at the Military Academy in Baghdad. He decamped to Palestine in 1936 to lead guerrilla operations against the British and Zionist militias. He allied himself with the Mufti of Jerusalem Amin al-Husayni and led an armed band of 700 Arab fighters until 1937 when this revolt, too, was crushed. He then traveled the Arab world, returning to Baghdad in 1941. At this point he joined Rashid Ali al-Kaylani's movement against the British and fought fiercely against the Transjordanian Arab Legion, which entered Iraq in alliance with the British to restore the Hashemite family to the throne.

When Qawuqji was seriously injured on the battlefield, he made his way to Germany for treatment, where he married a German woman, was arrested and jailed for a short period of time, and where he remained until 1947. In that year, Qawuqji made a daring return to Syria through France and Palestine, where he was nearly apprehended by the British.

In 1948, the Arab League chose Qawuqji to create and lead an army of Arab volunteers for an all-out offensive in Palestine. The Army of Deliverance, as it was called, engaged in combat alongside the national Arab armies in the Arab-Israeli War of 1948. It was funded by King Abd al-Aziz of Saudi Arabia. When the Arab armies conceded defeat in 1948, Qawuqji retired from public life.

Fawzi al-Qawuqji's memoirs were published in 1975 by Dr Khayriyyah Qasmiyyah, a history professor at Damascus University.

Sources:
Commins, David. *Historical Dictionary of Modern Syria* (1996).
Qasmiyya, Khayriyyah. *Muzakarat Fawzi al-Qawuqji* (1975).

Ramadan, Jamil
(1901-1954)

Jamil Ramadan was born in Damascus and studied at the Homs Military Academy during the years of the French Mandate. After graduation he joined the French-sponsored Army of the Levant.

When Syria achieved independence in 1946, Ramadan joined the newly created Syrian Army. He fought in the Arab-Israeli War of 1948 and was among the commanding officers who fought in Mishmar Hayarden, a Jewish settlement first occupied, then relinquished, by the Syrian Army. Like all other officers in the Syrian Army, he was embittered by the Syrian defeat, but refused to take part in the conspiracies against President Shukri al-Quwatli by his chief of staff, General Husni al-Za'im. Quwatli was an elected president, Ramadan argued, and the officers were not entitled to interfere in political affairs. Therefore, Ramadan did not join in the coup d'etat that overthrew Quwatli on March 29, 1949. Afterward, however, he worked with the Za'im regime as a professional officer, rising to become director of military police and then director of the Syrian Deuxieme Bureau.

Ramadan did not resist the coup that ousted and killed Za'im in August 1949, but it is unclear if he was actually involved in the putsch orchestrated by General Sami al-Hinnawi, a fellow officer from the War of 1948.

In 1949-1950, the Syrian Army and the People's Party came into conflict over the issue of unification with neighboring Iraq. Ramadan refused to get involved politically and maintained his status as a military professional. He opposed the coup that overthrew Hinnawi in December 1949. This strained his relations with General Adib al-Shishakli, the mastermind of the coup and a fellow veteran of the 1948 war. Ramadan quarreled with Shishakli over the latter's meddling in political affairs, and as a result, was forced to retire from the Syrian Army when Shishakli became president in 1953.

Jamil Ramadan became ill and died while visiting Lebanon on June 29, 1954, four months after Adib al-Shishakli was toppled from power in Syria.

Sources:
Interview with Ghassan Ramadan (October 1, 2001).

al-Rikabi, Rida (1864-1943): see "Politicians"

Safa, Mohammad
(1908-1968)

Mohammad Safa was born and raised in Aleppo and studied at the Homs Military Academy. He joined the Syrian Army and fought in the Arab-Israeli War of 1948.

Vehemently opposed to the regime of President Shukri al-Quwatli, Safa claimed that Akram al-Hawrani had encouraged Quwatli to launch a coup during the War of 1948, one year before Chief of Staff Husni al-Za'im launched his own coup that overthrew Quwatli in 1949. In 1951, Safa allied himself with President Adib al-Shishakli and was appointed military attaché to Washington. One year later, he quarreled with Shishakli and was dismissed from office.

Safa was a hard-line supporter of the Hashemite family who had ruled the Arab world since 1914, and he longed for Syria's unification with the Hashemite governments in Amman and Baghdad. Shishakli, on the other hand, wanted to sever Syria's ties with the Hashemites and establish himself as a pan-Arab leader. Safa tried to block his ambitions. Consequently, Safa was dismissed from the army and sentenced to death on the charge of high treason. He fled to Baghdad where, with Iraqi funds, he created the first anti-Shishakli movement in exile in October 1953. It was modeled on the Revolutionary Command Council that had come to power in Egypt in 1952.

Safa portrayed himself as the "Gamal Abd al-Nasser of Damascus" and called his coalition the Free Officer Movement of Syria. He coordinated sabotage against the Shishakli regime, funded other rebel movements within Syria, and established an anti-Shishakli newspaper in Iraq. He also channeled funds to the anti-Shishakli movement in Lebanon and encouraged officers in the Syrian Army to join his Free Officer Movement.

In February 1954, Safa took part in the insurrection that overthrew the Shishakli regime and restored civilian rule to Syria. To his dismay, however, the post-Shishakli leader, Hashim al-Atasi (1954-1955), welcomed Safa back to Syria but did not readmit him into the Syrian Army. Safa's history as a troublemaker during the Shishakli years made authorities fear him. He unleashed his anger against Chief of Staff Shawkat Shuqayr, claiming that it was Shuqayr who influenced Atasi to refuse readmitting Safa into the Syrian Army. Shuqayr snapped back, accusing Safa of wanting to replace him as chief of staff and of having future ambitions at the presidency.

Safa tried to rally a group of disgruntled officers around him to topple Shuqayr, but Shuqayr struck back. He discharged the officers from the Syrian Army and brought sixty of them before military courts on charges of conspiracy. To avoid arrest, Safa returned to Iraq and lived in Baghdad until the Hashemite dynasty was overthrown by military coup in July 1958.

In 1956, Safa supported a coup attempt funded by Iraq and aimed at toppling the civilian president, Shukri al-Quwatli, who was anti-Hashemite. The coup, engineered by Prime Minister Nuri al-Sa'id of Iraq, planned to restore Adib al-Shishakli to power using Iraqi financing. Once Shishakli was back in power in Damascus, Sa'id would abandon his earlier hostilities toward Iraq and rule with pro-Iraqi officers like Mohammad Safa. Eventually, these officers would create union between Syria and Iraq under the Hashemite crown.

Shishakli came to Lebanon to meet with Safa and other officers to discuss the coup. However, he concluded that conditions were not right for a military movement and that the coup had a high risk of failure. As a result, the coup was altered to include other politicians. But, before the plan was executed, Abd al-Hamid Sarraj, the director of general intelligence in Syria, uncovered the plot. The coup leaders in Syria were brought before a military tribunal and sentenced to death on charges of treason. Shishakli was also sentenced to death, while Safa was charged with conspiring with a foreign country to commit crimes in Syria. Mohammad Safa was sentenced in absentia to fifteen years of hard labor.

Sources:
BBC Archives. "The Damascus Trial" February 26, 1957.
Rathmell, Andrew. *Secret War in the Middle East* (1995).

Sarraj, Abd al-Hamid (1925-): see "Politicians"

Selu, Fawzi (1905-1972): see "Politicians"

Shakkur, Yusuf
(1926-)

Yusuf Shakkur of Homs studied at the Homs Military Academy, then enlisted in the Syrian Army and took advanced military courses at the Soviet Voroshilov Academy in the USSR. Upon completing his studies, Shakkur served as consul in Venezuela and Brazil from 1961 to 1964.

In March 1963, the Baath Party came to power in Syria and Shakkur became commander of army artillery in the Security Forces. He also became commander of the southwestern front, but was not involved in the coups and countercoups that prevailed within the Baath Party from 1966 to 1970. He served as commander of the Security Forces from 1964 to 1967 and chief of army headquarters during the Arab-Israeli War of 1967.

Shakkur allied himself with Defense Minister Hafez al-Asad, who was struggling for control of the Baath Party and the state from Salah Jadid, the de facto ruler of Syria. After the War of 1967, Asad appointed his leading ally, Mustapha Tlas, as chief of staff of the Syrian Army. Tlas appointed Shakkur as his deputy in 1968. When Tlas became minister of defense in 1972, Shakkur replaced him as chief of staff. He remained in power until 1974 when his deputy, General Hikmat al-Shihabi, replaced him. Yusuf Shakkur remained a military strategist and consultant in Syria, reemerging in 1996 as a member of the Syrian delegation to the peace talks with Israel administered by Ambassador Muwafaq al-Allaf.

In 1999, Shakkur accompanied Foreign Minister Farouk al-Shara to the peace negotiations with Israeli Prime Minister Ehud Barak, held first in Washington at the White House, and then in Shepherdstown, West Virginia. Yusuf Shakkur served as a military advisor on security details, but his role ended when the Syrian-Israeli negotiations ended in failure in 2000.

Sources:
Encyclopedia of the Modern Middle East, Vol IV (1996). Entry by George Irani.
The International Who's Who in the Arab World (1987-1988).

al-Shihabi, Hikmat
(1931-)

Hikmat al-Shihabi was born in the village of al-Bab, north of Aleppo. He studied at the Homs Military Academy and underwent advanced military training in the United States. He returned to Syria and joined the Baath Party of Michel Aflaq and Salah al-Bitar.

Shihabi befriended Baath Party strongman, Hafez al-Asad, who came to power in November 1970 and appointed Shihabi chief of military intelligence and deputy to Chief of Staff Yusuf Shakkur. Shihabi played an instrumental role in preventing the involvement of Syrian troops in the events of September 1970 in Jordan, when King Hussein ordered his army to purge the Palestinian Liberation Organization (PLO) and its leader, Yasser Arafat, from Amman.

In August 1973, Shihabi served on the Syrian-Egyptian Armed Forces Supreme Council. This was the body that planned and executed the Syrian-Egyptian War against Israel in October 1973.

From April to May 1974, Shakkur became Asad's emissary to the Disengagement Agreement with Israel brokered by US Secretary of State Henry Kissinger. In his book, *Asad: Struggle for the Middle East,* Patrick Seale estimates that Shakkur logged 130 hours of face-to-face talks in drafting the Disengagement Agreement, and no fewer than twenty-six trips of shuttle diplomacy. These talks were headed by Israeli Chief of Staff Moshe Dayan and led to the return to Syria of the Qunaitra, the principal town in the Golan Heights. Also in 1974, Shakkur retired from office as chief of staff (he was replaced by Shihabi). Shakkur became a confidant of Asad and served as his special envoy to the Arab world.

In 1975 and 1976, Shakkur traveled to Lebanon to broker a cease-fire between the Palestinian militias of Yasser Arafat and the militias of the Phalange Party of Pierre Gemayel. Shihabi conducted diplomatic visits to Beirut and met frequently with Arafat, Gemayel, and President Sulayman Franjiyyieh, but his efforts failed to contain the violence. In 1976, Shihabi pacified the Maronite leadership and promised support in their war against the Palestinian Liberation Organization (PLO). In turn, they journeyed to Damascus and requested that Asad involve the

Syrian Army in the Lebanese War.

The alliance corroded when Asad clashed with Gemayel's son, Bashir, who was elected president in 1982 and vowed to expel both the PLO and the Syrian Army from Lebanon. Shihabi served once again as an intermediary between Asad and Gemayel. Unable to restore the relationship between the two leaders, he helped broker a new alliance between Syria and Muslim leaders Sa'eb Salam, Rashid Karameh, and the Druze warlord, Walid Jumblatt, who rose to power and became a close friend of Shihabi after the death of his father, Kamal Jumblatt, in 1976.

When President Anwar al-Sadat of Egypt went to Israel in 1978, Shihabi headed to Moscow where he complained to the Soviet leaders about Egypt's separate peace with Israel and requested more arms for the Syrian Army, claiming that Syria's traditional Egyptian ally was no longer part of the Arab-Israeli conflict.

At home, Chief of Staff Shihabi took no part in daily politics, but restricted his duties to military affairs. In November 1983, Asad suffered a heart attack and appointed Shihabi to a six-man team that administered state affairs while Asad recovered. That same year, Shihabi clashed with Asad's younger brother, Rifaat, who tried to seize power in Damascus.

In 1994, following a visit by US President Bill Clinton to Syria that was designed to advance the Syrian-Israeli peace negotiations, Asad agreed to send a senior Syrian officer to meet with Israeli Chief of Staff Ehud Barak in Washington. Yitzhak Rabin, the Israeli prime minister, had agreed to concede the Golan Heights, the Syrian territory occupied by the Israeli Defense Forces (IDF) in 1967, in exchange for a peace treaty and normalization of relations with Syria. The mission was entrusted to Shihabi, who visited the White House in December 1994, not only in his capacity as chief of staff, but also as one of the most senior political decision-makers in Syria.

The Shihabi-Barak meeting was the first one-on-one encounter between a senior Syrian and Israeli official. Barak described him as "focused and highly intelligent," but added that the talks "failed to meet both our expectations." The negotiations were spoiled by Israel's insistence on discussing normalization before the signing of a peace treaty. The meeting was a steppingstone, however, for further talks held under the auspices of President Clinton in 1996.

In January 1998, having reached an advanced age, Hikmat al-Shihabi retired from the Syrian Army. He had served for twenty-four years as chief of staff. He is considered one of the most influential officers of the thirty-year presidency of Hafez al-Asad.

Sources:
Bergman, Ahron. Tahri, Jihan. *The Fifty Years War* (1998).
Rabinovich, Itamar. *The Brink of Peace* (1997).
Seale, Patrick. *Asad: the Struggle for the Middle East* (1988).

The International Who's Who in the Arab World (1987-1988).

Tlas, Mustapha. *Mirat Hayati* (1995).

Ziser, Eyal. *Asad's Legacy* (2000).

al-Shishakli, Adib (1909-1964): see "Politicians"

Shuqayr, Shawkat
(1912-1982)

Shawkat Shuqayr was born into a notable family in the village of Shouf on Mount Lebanon. He studied at the Homs Military Academy and joined the French-created Army of the Levant in 1932. He was stationed in Syria and served until independence in 1946.

Shuqayr, who was in Damascus when the French left the Middle East, did not return to his native Mount Lebanon at that time. Instead, he remained in Syria and in 1947 joined the newly formed Syrian Army. He rose in rank within the armed forces and befriended military strongman Adib al-Shishakli in 1950.

In July 1953, Shishakli dismissed the puppet regime of President Fawzi Selu that Shishakli had propped up in November 1951 and appointed himself president of the republic. In turn, Shuqayr was appointed chief of staff of the Syrian Army. The Syrian troops, mostly Sunni Muslims, received Shuqayr's appointment with strong reservations since he belonged to a religious minority. As his origins were from Mount Lebanon, and not Syria, Shuqayr was viewed as an imported officer, not qualified to serve as a popular and local military leader. While many viewed these traits with concern, Shishakli saw them as an asset, knowing that Shuqayr would have no power to topple the regime, if he so desired. Shishakli defended his position saying, "Shuqayr has no past and no future. Nobody follows him in the first place because he is a Lebanese Druze!"

Chief of Staff Shuqayr's support was further eroded in December 1953 when Shishakli declared an all-out war against the Druze community of Syria, accusing the Druze of plotting an insurrection. After he discovered a vast stockpile of ammunition in their villages, Shishakli arrested the rebel leaders and conducted an air raid on the Arab Mountain. Shuqayr was criticized for seeing his co-religionists being slain and doing nothing to stop the genocide.

In February 1954, an insurrection broke out against Shishakli from within the armed forces. The insurrection received full support from the chief of staff and the Druze community. Shishakli was ousted and sent into exile. Hashim al-Atasi, a civilian leader, became president of the republic. In reward for his alliance with the revolution, Atasi reappointed Shuqayr as chief of staff.

In a bid to create confusion, however, two of Shishakli's supporters kidnapped General Shuqayr and issued orders in his name to the armed forces, asking them to refrain from supporting the Atasi government and fight for Shishakli's comeback instead. Their ploy was foiled, however, and they were sent into exile while Shuqayr was released and reinstated to his military post. Shuqayr received the highest military decoration for his services in the armed forces.

In April 1954, members of the Syrian Social Nationalist Party (SSNP) assassinated General Shuqayr's deputy, Colonel Adnan al-Malki. In response, President Atasi outlawed the SSNP and Shuqayr was charged with purging the armed forces of all SSNP elements. Atasi appointed Abd al-Hamid Sarraj, a ruthless officer, as chief of intelligence to assist him. In the process, several officers were forced from service for their ideological beliefs. Despite many complaints from the public, Shuqayr remained in power until President Hashim al-Atasi was replaced by Shukri al-Quwatli in September 1955.

In 1956, Quwatli retired Shuqayr from the Syrian Army and replaced him with the strictly professional and politically independent officer, General Tawfiq Nizam al-Din. In 1957, Shuqayr returned to his native Lebanon and allied himself with the Druze leader Kamal Jumblatt. One year later, in 1958, Jumblatt joined forces with a group of Muslim leaders to launch an uprising against the pro-United States regime of Lebanese President Kamil Sham'un. The Lebanese president's hostility to the Arab nationalist movement of President Gamal Abd al-Nasser of Egypt disturbed Jumblatt, Shuqayr, and the Sunni leaders Sa'eb Salam and Abd al-Hamid Karameh. They accused Sham'un of being an agent of the United States and Great Britain.

Although they failed to remove Sham'un from office, Shawkat Shuqayr stayed in Lebanon until the beginning of the second Civil War in 1975. He returned to Syria and lived in Damascus until his death in 1982. His son, Ayman Shuqayr, continued to work in politics and served as a deputy in the Lebanese Parliament and an ally of the Druze leader Walid Jumblatt.

Sources:
Abd al-Karim, Ahmad. *Hasad* (1994).
Encyclopedia of the Modern Middle East, Vol IV (1996). Entry by Charles U. Zenzie.
Moubayed, Sami. *Damascus Between Democracy and Dictatorship* (2000).
Samman, Mutih. *Watan wa Askar* (1995).
Seale, Patrick. *The Struggle for Syria* (1961).
Torrey, Gordon. *Syrian Politics and the Military* (1964).

Suwaydani, Ahmad
(1932-1994)

Ahmad Suwaydani, from the town of Hawran in southern Syria, studied at the Homs Military Academy. He joined the Baath Party of Michel Aflaq, and following the party's assumption to power in 1963, became chief of military intelligence. He was also appointed to the Baath Party's Regional Command and was voted into its Central and Military Committees.

Along with Air Force Commander Hafez al-Asad, Suwaydani helped fund and arm Fateh, a rising guerrilla movement headed by Yasser Arafat, that aimed at liberating Palestine through combat rather than diplomacy. Suwaydani and Asad believed in armed resistance to occupation and supplied Arafat with arms (at times without informing other members of the party leadership). Suwaydani met frequently with Arafat and Salah Khalaf (Abu Iyad), and helped them raise money for their cause from other countries in the Middle East.

In 1965, Suwaydani also became director of military personnel. Then, in 1966, he allied himself with military strongman Salah Jadid, who overthrew the Baath Party founders and propped up Nur al-Din al-Atasi as president of the republic. Jadid, the de facto ruler of Syria, appointed Suwaydani as chief of staff in 1966.

Suwaydani held office during the Arab-Israeli War of 1967 and clashed with his former ally, Asad, who since 1966 had become minister of defense. Asad accused Suwaydani, along with Jadid, of poor leadership at the war front and blamed them for the defeat of 1967. The war also affected Suwaydani's relationship with Jadid. After the defeat, Jadid began accusing Suwaydani of planning a coup against him. In February 1968, Jadid discharged Suwaydani from office and dismissed many of his followers from the Syrian Army.

Asad's right-hand man, Mustapha Tlas, replaced Suwaydani as chief of staff. Infuriated by the changes, Suwaydani began planning for revenge in August 1968. Jadid ordered his arrest, but Suwaydani fled to Baghdad where he joined Michel Aflaq in leading the opposition to Salah Jadid, Nur al-Din al-Atasi, and Hafez al-Asad.

In July 1968, Suwaydani was arrested at the Damascus Airport when his plane, flying from Baghdad to Cairo, was forced into an emergency landing in Syria. Plane officials were obliged to report the names of passengers to ground control. Immediately, officers boarded the plane and apprehended Suwaydani. A purge of his loyalists soon followed in the Syrian Army.

In 1970, Asad came to power and kept Suwaydani behind bars, fearing that if released, he might try to seize power once again. Ahmad Suwaydani was released from jail in February 1994 and died shortly thereafter.

Sources:

Batatu, Hanna. *Syria's Peasantry: The Descendants of Its Lesser Rural Notables and Their Politics* (2000).
Encyclopedia of the Modern Middle East, Vol IV (1996). Entry by Charles U. Zenzie.
Seale, Patrick. *Asad: Struggle for the Middle East* (1988).

Van Dam, Nicolas. *The Struggle for Power in Syria* (1996).

al-Tawil, Mohammad Rabah
(1925-1992)

Mohammad Rabah al-Tawil hailed from the coastal city of Lattakia and studied at the Homs Military Academy. He joined the Baath Party of Michel Aflaq and Salah al-Bitar and allied himself with the party's Military Committee that was secretly formed in 1960.

The Baath Party leaders included Hafez al-Asad, Salah Jadid, Abd al-Karim al-Jundi, and Mohammad Umran. These men pledged to restore the Syrian-Egyptian union that had been created in 1958 and dissolved in 1961. In March 1963, the four men came to power in Syria and appointed Tawil to the Military Committee. He was voted into the Baath Party's Central Committee and became a member of its Regional Command. In 1964, Chief of Staff Salah Jadid appointed him commander of Syrian Army headquarters in Damascus. In 1965, he became commander of the Qatana military camp on the outskirts of the capital and minister of social affairs and labor in the cabinet of Prime Minister Salah al-Bitar.

In February 1966, Jadid seized power in Syria and toppled the regime of President Amin al-Hafez and Prime Minister Salah al-Bitar. Tawil allied himself with Jadid and in 1967 became minister of interior in the cabinet of Prime Minister Yusuf al-Zu'ayyin. Tawil and Abd al-Karim al-Jundi, the director of general intelligence, effectively created a police state in Syria. They outlawed political parties and regulated political affiliations at Damascus University, in trade unions, and throughout professional syndicates. Journalists, politicians, professors, students, and merchants were all required to report to one of the many intelligence bureaus that were set up throughout Syria.

Under Jadid's leadership, Tawil was also responsible for maintaining security following the Syrian defeat in the Arab-Israeli War of 1967. He did not hesitate to arrest, deport, and torture all who were suspected of mischief. The mercantile class of Damascus shut down in symbolic protest to his measures. Tawil responded by leading his troops to the old marketplace with submachine gun in hand, where they shattered the shop windows of all closed businesses. When President Hafez al-Asad came to power in 1970, he arrested both Salah Jadid and Mohammad Rabah al-Tawil.

Sources:
Seale, Patrick. *Asad: the Struggle for the Middle East* (1988).
Tlas, Mustapha. *Mirat Hayati* (1995).

Tlas, Mustapha
(1932-)

Mustapha Tlas studied at the Homs Military Academy and joined the Baath Party of Michel Aflaq and Salah al-Bitar in 1947. He enlisted in the Syrian Army and befriended Hafez al-Asad, an air force officer two years his senior, who was also a member of the Baath. The friendship between the two men, which lasted a lifetime, began on November 1, 1951.

Asad and Tlas shared political views and ambitious dreams—Asad wanted to become a doctor while Tlas hoped to study literature and philosophy at the Sorbonne in Paris. In 1958, they supported the merger of Syria and Egypt into the United Arab Republic (UAR) and were stationed in Cairo. Both men were firm believers in the policies of Arab nationalism preached by the UAR President Gamal Abd al-Nasser.

In 1961, the UAR was overthrown in Damascus and Egyptian authorities arrested both Asad and Tlas. The Egyptians feared that both men were working to overturn the Nasser government from within Egypt. Asad remained in jail while Tlas was allowed to return to Syria. He returned by sea, bringing back with him Asad's wife and baby daughter, Bushra. Eventually, Asad also returned to Damascus since no evidence existed concerning his involvement in a conspiracy. Back home, however, they were discharged from the army for opposing the coup that brought down the UAR. Briefly, Tlas took a civilian job at the Ministry of Supply.

Eventually, in 1963, the Baath Party came to power in Syria through a military coup. Asad, who had co-planned the coup, became commander of the Syrian Air Force. He reinstated Tlas, who by now had become his trusted friend and companion, into the Syrian Army and appointed him commander of the 5th Armored Brigade. Tlas also became a member of the ruling Military Committee of the Baath Party.

In April 1964, the Muslim Brotherhood tried to seize power in Syria and declared a holy war against the Baath government. President Amin al-Hafez cracked down on the movement and arrested hundreds of activists who were affiliated with the Brotherhood. President Hafez created a military tribunal to bring the Brotherhood to justice and appointed Tlas as its president. In September 1965, Tlas became a member in the Revolutionary Command Council (RCC).

Mustapha Tlas.

Mustapha Tlas allied himself with Asad in 1966 when the latter launched a coup that overthrew the regime of Baath Party founders Michel Aflaq and Salah al-Bitar. Tlas arrested the commander of the Homs garrison, who was loyal to the National Command of Aflaq, and helped round up Aflaq's loyalists in Hama. In February 1966, Aflaq and Bitar were forced to flee Syria, and a new regime was created, with Hafez al-Asad as minister of defense.

In 1966-1967, Baath Party strongman Saleem Hatum tried and failed to launch a coup in Syria. Tlas headed the military committee that tried Hatum for conspiracy and found him guilty in March 1967. Tlas found him guilty and had him executed in June 1967, without informing President Atasi, yet after obtaining permission from Asad, who then appointed Tlas commander of the troop reserve on the frontline in the Syrian Army and president of the High Security Court in Syria. Tlas held this post during the Arab-Israeli War of 1967. In 1968 Tlas was promoted in military rank and appointed deputy to Defense Minister Asad. President Nur al-Din al-Atasi appointed him chief of staff of the Syrian Army after the Arab-Israeli War of 1967.

From 1969 to 1970, Asad and Tlas quarreled with President Atasi and Salah Jadid, the military strongman of Syria, over ideological differences and the distribution of power within the government. Asad blamed them of poor leadership at the war front in 1967, while Atasi and Jadid accused Asad and Tlas of trying to oust the existing regime. On November 13, 1970, Atasi and Jadid called for a Baath Party meeting and decided to rid themselves of both Asad and Tlas. Jadid planned to dismiss them from the Syrian Army and have them arrested. Asad retaliated rapidly, striking first by launching his own coup and having both Atasi and Jadid arrested.

When Hafez al-Asad became president in March 1971, Tlas was promoted to deputy commander-in-chief of the Syrian Army. Asad was a lieutenant-general (*fariq* in Arabic), a rank which he held when he became president, and which no other officer could surpass. To distinguish Tlas from other major-generals below him, Asad created a new rank especially for him, making him an *imad*. This military rank was held exclusively by Tlas until Chief of Staff Hikmat Shihabi also became *imad* in the mid-1970s. In March 1972, Tlas was appointed minister of defense and deputy prime minister for military affairs. Both positions were renewed under every government Asad presided over until his death in 2000.

In 1970, after a gridlock in relations that had prevailed during the Atasi years and well into Asad's rise to power, Tlas was dispatched to Jordan to build bridges with King Hussein, who was fighting a bloody war since September 1970 against the Palestinian forces of Yasser Arafat. Syria had sided with the Palestinians. Tlas offered Arafat's guerillas military sanctuaries overlooking the Jordan Valley, lobbying with the king to accept the arrangement as a means of diffusing tensions between the warring factions. As a temporary solution to the crisis, Hussein agreed with the plan, but the guerillas refused, eventually moving on to Lebanon.

Tlas also served as a deputy in the first parliament under President Asad from February to December 1971. In 1972, Tlas signed a military cooperation agreement with the USSR. He co-planned the Arab-Israeli War of 1973 and served on the senior Syrian-Egyptian Military Committee. In 1975, Asad dispatched him to help facilitate a cease-fire between the Phalange Party in Lebanon and the forces of Palestinian leader Yasser Arafat. When Asad became ill in 1983, Tlas was appointed to a six-man delegation that oversaw state affairs on Asad's behalf. In 1984, Tlas sided with Asad in a domestic confrontation with Asad's younger brother, Rifaat, who tried in vain to seize power.

When Asad died in 2000, Tlas supported the election of his eldest son, Bashar, as president of the republic. Tlas served as a confidant of the new president, and in December 2001 was reappointed minister of defense in the cabinet of Prime Minister Mohammad Mustapha Miro. In September 2003, he was appointed to the cabinet of Prime Minister Naji al-Itri.

During his career, Tlas wrote numerous books on poetry, literature, history, and politics. Among his published books are *al-Rasul al-Arabi wa Fan al-Harb* (*The Arab Prophet and the Art of War*), published in 1972; *Afaq al-Istratijiyya al-Suhiyouniyya* (*Horizons of Zionist Strategy*), published in 1987; and *Rad Ala al-Shaytan* (*Responding to the Devil*), published in 1990. He also wrote several books about Arab nationalism, including *al-Thawra al-Arabiyya al-Qubra* (*The Great Arab Revolt*), published in 1978; *al-Thawra al-Jaza'iriyya* (*The Algerian Revolution*), published in 1982; and *al-Thawra al-Filistiniyya 1965-1987* (*The Palestinian Revolution*), published in 1989. His memoirs, *Mir'at Hayati* (*Mirror of My Life*), were published in 1995. In 2003, he published a highly controversial book on the failed coup of Rifaat al-Asad, which took place in 1984 and led to Asad's banishment from Syria.

On May 11, 2004, Mustapha Tlas retired from the Syrian Army after fifty-two years of service, and from his position as head of the Ministry of Defense, a post he held for thirty-two years. In June 2005, Mustapha Tlas resigned from his job in the Central and National Committees of the Baath Party. He currently devotes his time to research and writing.

Sources:
Seale, Patrick. *Asad: the Struggle for the Middle East* (1988).
Tlas, Mustapha. *Mirat Hayati* (1995).
Interview with General Mustapha Tlas (November 16, 2002, May 8, 2005).

al-Ulshi, Jamil (1883-1951): see "Politicians"

Umran, Mohammad (1922-1972): see "Politicians"

Zahr al-Din, Abd al-Karim
(1919-)

Abd al-Karim Zahr al-Din was born to a prominent Druze family in the Arab Mountain and studied at the Homs Military Academy. He graduated in 1937 and joined the Syrian Army, becoming a general in 1960. During the years of the Syrian-Egyptian union (1958-1961), he was appointed director of supply in the armed forces.

Zahr al-Din allied with a movement of young officers, headed by Colonel Abd al-Karim al-Nehlawi, who were striving to overthrow the United Arab Republic (UAR). They opposed the dictatorship imposed on Syria by President Gamal Abd al-Nasser of Egypt and were critical of the one-party state he had established in 1958. Nasser had annoyed officers in Syria by making them subordinate to their Egyptian counterparts, and by making Cairo, rather than Damascus, the central city of the UAR.

As planned, the officers staged a coup on September 28, 1961 and dissolved the UAR, appointing themselves as the temporary military governors of Syria. Due to their youthfulness and military rank, however, they could not assume full control of Syria and had to share power with established politicians and older officers from the Syrian Army. As a result, they appointed seasoned politician Ma'ruf al-Dawalibi as prime minister and Abd al-Karim Zahr al-Din as chief of staff.

In December 1961, Nazim al-Qudsi, a declared opponent of Nasser, was elected president of the republic. Zahr al-Din allied himself with the new president and they began to curb Nasserist influence in Syria. He dismissed many Nasserists from the Syrian Army and promoted those who were loyal to the post-union order. Along with Qudsi and his new prime minister, Ma'ruf al-Dawalib, Zahr al-Din tried to contain the influence of Abd al-Karim al-Nehlawi and the officers who had orchestrated the coup of 1961. Qudsi and Dawalibi believed in a professional army where officers were not involved in political affairs, and the two strove to achieve that in Syria.

On March 28, 1962, Nehlawi struck back and launched another coup, arresting Qudsi, Dawalibi, and their entire administration. Nehlawi charged them with misusing their constitutional powers and destroying the ambition and morale of the Syrian Army. Zahr al-Din, who evaded arrest, called for a general conference in Homs on April 1 and refused to endorse Nehlawi's coup. He mobilized the armed forces against Nehlawi, released Qudsi from prison, and defeated the rebels. Zahr al-Din then dismissed all of Nehlawi's supporters from the Syrian Army and sent the coup mastermind into exile as minister to Indonesia (a purely ceremonial post).

Qudsi thanked Zahr al-Din for his loyalty, reappointed him chief of staff in April 1962, granted him more powers, and appointed him acting minister of defense in the cabinet of Prime Minister Khalid al-Azm.

Enjoying his newfound authority, Zahr al-Din wanted more power and planned a coup in order to seize power for himself. Having rallied many officers in 1962, and possessing the complete confidence of the president, Zahr al-Din believed no one would suspect his activity. He thought he would be able to topple the regime without shedding a drop of blood, and without facing any serious resistance. The coup was scheduled for March 1963, and it was to be orchestrated by his friend, the veteran nationalist Farid Zayn al-Din. It was planned that, once firmly in power, Zahr al-Din would become president and Zayn al-Din would become prime minister.

But, on March 8, 1963, the Baath Party came to power in Syria and pledged to restore the Syrian-Egyptian union. The Baath leaders arrested all officials in the Qudsi government, including Zahr al-Din, and dismissed him from the Syrian Army. When word of the Baath revolt broke out, Zahr al-Din dressed in full military uniform and went to military headquarters, thinking that his revolutionaries had advanced on Damascus and seized power in his name. He was surprised to see himself being taken to the Mezzeh prison rather than the Presidential Palace. The Revolutionary Command Council (RCC) terminated his civil rights, then released him from prison and exiled him to Lebanon.

Abd al-Karim Zahr al-Din lived in the mountain resort of Aley until the Israelis invaded Lebanon in 1982 and forced him to return to Syria. In 1968, he published his autobiography entitled, *Muzakarati an Fatrat al-Infisal (My Memoirs on the Secession Period)*.

Sources:
Azm, Khalid. *Muzakarat* (1973).
Samman, Mutih. *Watan wa Askar* (1995).
Zahr al-Din, Abd al-Karim. *Muzakarati an Fatrat al-Infisal fi Souriyya* (1968).

al-Za'im, Husni (1894-1949): see "Politicians"

Lattakia in Ottoman times.

The Syrian police force in 1929.

Car accident in Damascus in the 1930s.

ADMINISTRATORS

The people listed in this chapter are civil servants who held senior posts in government. This chapter also includes technical ministers (technocrats) who were not politicians, along with economists, bankers, and public servants who assumed senior civil service jobs in the Arab world.

One of the pleasures of life in Damascus in the first decades of the last century was the riverside outdoor cafe. (Caption: "Jardin Soufanieh," Soufanieh Garden).

Syrian administrators served in the Ottoman government until 1918. They worked for an independent Syrian government for a year-and-a-half after the fall of the Ottomans. This period was very active, since administrators had to translate the entire bureaucracy, civil service, and government administration of Ottoman Turkish into Arabic. From 1920 until independence in 1946, these administrators served a Syrian government under the authority of the French. Following independence, they served independent Syrian governments except during the period of union with Nassar's Egypt from 1958 to 1961. Since 1963, Syria has been governed by the Baath Party.

al-Abid, Ahmad Izzat
(1849-1924)

Alternate spelling: Ahmad Izzat Abed.

Ahmad Izzat al-Abid was born in Damascus to a wealthy family of Ottoman aristocracy. His father, Hawlu Pasha al-Abid, was an affluent businessman who owned huge shares in the profitable Suez Canal Company in Egypt. Ahmad Izzat studied with private tutors in Beirut and began his professional career as an inspector at the Ministry of Justice in Istanbul.

In 1879, Abid founded the pro-Ottoman daily newspaper *Dimashq (Damascus)* and became a benefactor to local citizens, offering them money and protection in exchange for their allegiance. Abid served as editor-in-chief of *Dimashq* until he became a judge in the Ottoman Court of Appeals in 1894. That same year, Abu al-Huda Sayyadi, an advisor at the imperial court, introduced Abid to Sultan Abdulhamid II, who appointed him aide-de-camp at his office in Istanbul. Abid became private advisor to the sultan and influenced him in pursuing a pan-Islamic policy in the early years of the twentieth century.

Ahmad Izzat al-Abid.

Abid lobbied for bringing electricity to Damascus (a project that was completed in 1903), the construction of the Victoria Hotel (the largest hotel in Damascus), and the creation of the Hijaz Railway connecting Damascus to Medina. He is most remembered for the Hijaz Railway—completed in 1908 through donations from Muslims living in the Syrian provinces of the Ottoman Empire. Abid was also instrumental in distributing posts to Arab subjects, especially in the judicial arena, and in giving Arab subjects in the imperial court a greater voice in Syrian society.

In reward for his services, Abdulhamid bestowed upon Abid the princely title of pasha and appointed his eldest son, Mohammad Ali, as Ottoman ambassador to the United States in 1908. In the pre-war era, Ahmad Izzat Pasha was the most influential Arab in Ottoman circles, prompting him to finance the writing of his biography entitled, *Abqariyyat Shamiyya fi al-Siyasa wa al-Idara (Damascene Geniuses in Politics and Administration).*

In July 1908, however, the Committee for Union and Progress (CUP), a coalition of hard-line military officers, staged a coup in Istanbul. They curbed Abdulhamid's powers, forcing him to reinstate the constitution of 1876 and dismiss a number of high-ranking Syrian notables from his administration. Many leaders who were closely associated with Abdulhamid's rule, like Abid and his son Mohammad Ali, were fired from their posts and forced into exile in Egypt. A delegation of CUP officers invited Abid to return to Istanbul and offered him the title of senator, provided that he would contribute 100,000 Turkish coins to the CUP treasury. Abid refused, but offered instead to donate an amount of 20,000 Turkish coins to the military establishment in the Ottoman Empire.

The CUP advised the new sultan, Mohammad Rashad V, to issue a decree confiscating Abid's property in the empire, but Rashad refused. Abid owned so much property that everyone in Istanbul preferred to pacify him rather than have him angry. Therefore, Abid's property was not confiscated and he remained in Egypt until World War I ended in 1918. The Ottoman sultan invited him back to a defeated empire and appointed him grand vizier, charged with negotiating the terms of the Ottoman surrender. Abid attended the Versailles Conference and hammered out the armistice treaty with the United States, France, and Great Britain. The Versailles Treaty was signed on June 28, 1919, and Ahmad Izzat al-Abid resigned from political activity.

Sources:

Commins, David. *Historical Dictionary of Modern Syria* (1996).

Itri, Abd al-Ghani. *Alam wa Mubdioun* (1999).

Khoury, Philip. *Urban Notables and Arab Nationalism* (1983).

FO 371/1848 file 58138 Devey to Mallet (December 9, 1913).

al-Attar, Najah
(1933-)

Najah al-Attar was born and raised in Damascus. Her father was one of the nationalist leaders who took part in the Syrian Revolt of 1925-1927 against the French Mandate in Syria. She studied at Damascus University, graduating in 1954, and obtained her graduate and postgraduate degrees in Arabic literature from the University of Edinburgh in Great Britain.

Al-Attar became a schoolteacher in Damascus in 1960. In 1969, she was chosen to be the director of composition and literature translation at the Ministry of Culture. Four years later, on August 7, 1976, President Hafez al-Asad appointed Attar Minister of Culture and National Guidance in the cabinet of Prime Minister Abd al-Rahman al-Khlayfawi. She was the first woman to serve as a government minister in Syria. She promoted cultural exhibitions, shows, and theatrical performances during her twenty-four years as minister. In 1995, she co-founded the National Symphonic Orchestra and initiated the construction of the Syrian Opera House. She encouraged the concerts of Maestro Sulhi al-Wadi and called on Syrian artists living abroad to return home and work in Syria.

In 1983, French President Francoise Mitterrand gave Attar the Medal of Honor of the French Republic. She held office in Syria throughout four different cabinets and was dismissed under Prime Minister Mohammad Mustapha Miro in March 2000. Among her published works are *As'ilat al-Hayat* (*Questions of Life*), *Kalimat Mulawanah* (*Colored Words*), *Hemingway, Isbania wa al-Thiran* (*Hemingway, Spain, and the Bulls*), and *Al-Fikr al-Thawri Bayn Azar wa October* (*Revolutionist Theory Between March and October*). Two of her works, *Man Yazkor Tilk Al-Ayyam?* (*Who Remembers Those Days?*), and *Adab al-Harb* (*Literature of War*) were co-written with the renowned Syrian novelist Hanna Mina.

In 2002, after the September 11, 2001 terrorist attacks on Washington and New York, President Bashar al-Asad appointed Najah al-Attar director of the Center for the Dialogue of Civilizations, an academic foundation which conducts research, holds debates, and publishes articles on global political issues in the post-9/11 order. In 2003, she became a board member of Kalamoun University, one of the oldest private Syrian universities, located in the town of Dayr Atiyyeh.

As of this writing, Najah al-Attar is president of the board of trustees at the Syrian Virtual University (SVU), a pioneering project that introduced online education to Syria.

Sources:
Nuwayhed, Nadia. *Nisaa Min Biladi* (2000).

al-Azm, Fawzi
(1880-1934)

Fawzi al-Azm grew up in one of the most influential political families in the Ottoman Empire. Due to his various enterprises and landownings, Azm enjoyed a strong power base in Damascus and commanded considerable influence in other districts of the Ottoman Empire.

In 1881, al-Azm met Sultan Abdulhamid II, and in 1882 he became head of the Administrative Council in Damascus. Eight years later, in 1900, Azm was appointed Minister of Religious Affairs, one of the most sensitive and influential posts in Ottoman Syria. Azm was charged with supervising Islamic education, administering mosque affairs, and dealing with Islamic societies in the Ottoman Empire. He also became special advisor to Abdulhamid II and director of public works for the Hijaz Railway.

In July 1908, however, the Committee for Union and Progress (CUP), a coalition of hard-line military officers, staged a coup in Istanbul. They curbed Abdulhamid's powers, forcing him to reinstate the constitution of 1876 and to dismiss a number of high-ranking Syrian notables from his administration. Many leaders closely associated with Abdulhamid's rule, like Azm, were fired from their posts and forced into political retirement. The officers distrusted the notability and saw them as an upper class coalition of amateurs who put personal financial gain above the advancement of the Ottoman Empire.

In April 1912, however, Azm patched up his differences with the CUP and was elected into the Ottoman Parliament. Along with Abd al-Rahman al-Yusuf, another Arab aristocrat in the imperial court, Azm lobbied against the leaders of the pan-Arab movement who were emerging in the Syrian provinces of the empire. Particularly, Azm worked against the Ottoman Party of Decentralization, an opposition movement in exile from Syria headed by Rafic al-Azm, a prominent Arab intellectual. Fawzi al-Azm accused members of the Party of Decentralization of being agents of the United States and Great Britain.

In 1918, the Ottoman Empire was defeated and the Istanbul government was forced to evacuate troops from Syria. Fawzi al-Azm shifted his allegiance to the Arabs, becoming private advisor to Syria's new ruler, King Faysal I. Azm also became a deputy for Damascus in the Syrian National Congress, the equivalent of a modern parliament that declared independence from the Ottoman Empire and crowned Faysal as king of Syria.

From November 11, 1919, until March 8, 1920, Fawzi al-Azm served as president of the Syrian National Congress, but he ceased all political activity when the French Mandate was implemented over Syria in 1920 and spent the remainder of his years in political retirement. His son, Khalid al-Azm, commenced a political career in French Mandate Syria and became prime minister on several occasions from 1940 to 1963.

Sources:
Commins, David. *Historical Dictionary of Modern Syria* (1996).
Farfur, Abd al-Latif. *Alam Dimashq* (1987).
Khoury, Philip. *Urban Notables and Arab Nationalism* (1983).
FO 371/1002 file 28562 Devey to Lowther (July 12, 1910).
FO 371/1002 file 39460 Devey to Lowther (October 11, 1910).

Barakat, Awad
(1913-2005)

Awad Barakat studied law and political science at the Sorbonne in Paris. He began his career as a lawyer in Damascus, but in 1938 returned to Europe to complete his graduate studies in law before returning permanently to Damascus in 1945.

Barakat joined the Ministry of Finance and became director of inspection and budgeting in 1946. In 1948, he became director of financial studies and statistics. Two years later, in 1950, Barakat was promoted to director of financial affairs. In 1953, President Adib al-Shishakli appointed him to the Syrian delegation at the International Monetary Fund (IMF) in New York.

In March 1956, Barakat became deputy to Dr Izzat Tarabulsi, the governor of the Central Bank of Syria. Tarabulsi and Barakat spent the next five years conducting economic research and publishing works on the monetary policies of Syria. Barakat was opposed to the unification of Syria and Egypt in 1958, warning against the socialist policies of President Gamal Abd al-Nasser, claiming that they would prove disastrous for Syria. In July 1961, he lobbied in vain against the nationalization of factories and confiscation of lands by Nasser in Syria.

When union was dissolved in September 1961, Awad Barakat rallied around Syria's new president, Nazim al-Qudsi, who promised to revoke all socialist measures imposed on Syria in the union years. Barakat became a member of the first post-Nasser Syrian Parliament, and on September 29, he was appointed Minister of National Economy and Industry in the cabinet of Prime Minister Ma'mun al-Kuzbari. At the time, *Time Magazine* wrote, "Able, French-trained Economics Minister Awad Barakat said he would press forward with land redistribution, 'with certain modifications,' and retain intact 'social benefits' instituted by the previous regime, including compulsory profit sharing in private industry."

Barakat's tenure was renewed by Prime Minister Izzat al-Nuss in November and terminated on December 23, 1961, when Nuss's caretaker cabinet resigned. In March 1963, the Baath Party came to power in Syria and pledged to restore Syria's union with Egypt. Due to his anti-Nasser record, Awad Barakat was forced out of government, and he retired from all political activity. He died in February 2005.

Sources:

Adil, Fou'ad. *Qissat Souriyya bayn al-Intidab wa al-Intikhab 1942-1962* (2001).
Barada (March 24, 1963).
BBC Archives (January 1, 1962-January 1, 1963).
Kourani, As'ad. *Zikrayat wa Khawater* (2000).
Samman, Mutih. *Watan wa Askar* (1995).
Time Magazine, "Welcome" (October 20, 1961).

Chahine, Nicolas
(1859-1932)

Nicolas Chahine was born and raised in Damascus, where he studied languages. He joined the Ottoman civil service and was appointed to the translation department in Damascus.

In 1875, Chahine joined the Ottoman Police and in 1915 became director of judiciary police in Syria. During World War I, he served as deputy to Police Force

Nicholas Chahine.

Commander Hamdi al-Jallad. In 1916, Chahine was accused of harboring pan-Arab sympathies and was fired from his post by Jamal Pasha, the military governor of Syria. Chahine had never become a member of the Arab underground, but was arrested and brought before a military tribunal in Aley on the charge of treason. He was declared innocent, however, and set free. But he stayed out of the limelight until the Ottoman Empire collapsed in 1918.

Once free, Nicolas Chahine was restored to the police force during the era of King Faysal I, the new ruler of Syria, and kept his job when the French Mandate was proclaimed in July 1920. In 1925, an uprising erupted against the mandate authority from the Arab Mountain in Syria, and Police Commander Hamdi al-Jallad failed to crush it. As a result, he was retired from his job and Chahine replaced him as police commander. Chahine held this position until the Druze revolt was crushed in 1928, and then he retired from the force in the era of Prime Minister Taj al-Din al-Hasani.

Sources:
Interview with Dr Nicolas Chahine (April 11, 2001).

al-Hakim, Yusuf
(1879-1969)

Yusuf al-Hakim was born in Lattakia to a prominent Greek Orthodox family and studied at American missionary schools in his native city. He studied law in Istanbul and began his career as an attorney in Ottoman courts in 1904. He maintained a neutral stance during World War I and did not join the Arab underground or the rebel Arab Army headed by Sharif Husayn, the Prince of Mecca.

Furthermore, Hakim did not take part in the pro-Ottoman movement headed by Arabs who wanted to preserve the Ottoman Empire. In 1918, following the defeat of the empire, Hakim became a deputy for Tripoli in the Syrian National Congress, the equivalent of a modern parliament, that was convened by the country's notables to decide on the future of post-Ottoman Syria. He also became deputy to Congress President Hashim al-Atasi. In March 1920, King Faysal I, the new ruler of Syria, appointed him minister of agriculture, commerce, and public works in the cabinet of Prime Minister Rida al-Rikabi.

When the French occupied Syria and toppled Faysal in July 1920, a new cabinet was created under Dr Ala al-Din Droubi. Hakim held the same portfolios of agriculture, transportation, and commerce under Droubi. Hakim then became president of the Court of Appeal in Syria. In February 1926, the French appointed Hakim's longtime friend Ahmad Nami, a Beirut-born Ottoman aristocrat, as prime minister of Syria. In the absence of a presidential office, Nami served as head of state.

Hakim knew Nami from the days of the Ottoman Empire when both men were ranking freemasons. Nami appointed Hakim minister of justice for a five-month term before making him minister of agriculture and commerce in December 1926. Hakim also served as Nami's trusted advisor and encouraged Nami to make his claim for the Syrian throne when the French toyed with the idea of reestablishing a monarchy in Syria. Nami and Hakim met with French High Commissioner Henri de Jouvenel and proposed that the mandate be replaced with a treaty of friendship between Syria and Lebanon that would last for thirty years. Meanwhile, France would have all the economic, political, and military privileges it wanted in Syria. In exchange, France would grant Syria the right to a national army, unity of Syrian lands, and entry into the League of Nations. Syria also demanded financial compensation for those citizens whose homes had been destroyed in the fighting of 1925-1927 and asked that France issue a general amnesty to permit the return of Syrian exiles. The plan, although approved by de Jouvenel, was rejected in Paris and never got off the drawing board.

Hakim resigned from political activity when Nami left office in February 1928. Hakim then devoted the remainder of his years to his legal practice in Damascus. Following the French evacuation from Syria in April 1946, Hakim maintained his job in the Syrian judiciary. He wrote a series of books that became classics on modern Syrian history. They include *Beirut wa Lubnan fi Ahd Bani Uthman (Beirut and Lebanon in the Era of the Ottoman)*, published in Beirut in 1964, *Souriyya wa al-Imbaratoriyya al-Uthmaniyya (Syria and the Ottoman Empire)*, *Souriyya wa al-Ahd al-Faysali (Syria and the Faysalian Era)*, and *Souriyya wa al-Intidab al-Faransi (Syria and the French Mandate)*.

Yusuf al-Hakim's books are some of the most well-established works on Syria under King Faysal (1918-1920) and under the French Mandate (1920-1946).

Sources:
Hakim, Yusuf. *Souriyya wa al-Ahd al-Faysali* (1961).
Hakim, Yusuf. *Souriyya wa al-Intidab al-Faransi* (1961).

al-Halabi, Mohammad Izz al-Din
(1889-?)

Mohammad Izz al-Din al-Halabi was a product of the Arab Mountain and studied at the Ottoman Military Academy in Istanbul. He joined the Ottoman Army and allied himself with leading Ottoman officers who appointed Halabi chamberlain to Sultan Mohammad Rashad V.

When Sultan Abdulhamid II was overthrown in 1908, Halabi was transferred to the Military Court of Istanbul and appointed judge in 1916. In 1918, following the Ottoman Empire's defeat in World War I, Halabi joined the Syrian Army. He fought at the Battle of Maysaloun on July 24, 1920. This battle led to the occupation of Damascus and the implementation of the French Mandate over Syria. The Syrian Army was dissolved and Halabi returned to the Arab Mountain. He befriended French officers stationed in the Mountain, and in 1921, Halabi was appointed secretary-general of the Arab Mountain. In 1923, he became director of education in the Mountain. In 1925, the Druze launched an uprising against the French headed by the veteran Druze leader Sultan al-Atrash.

Halabi defected from government service and joined the Syrian underground, becoming a senior commander in the rebel leadership. When the revolt was crushed in 1927, the French sentenced Halabi to death, and he fled to Amman, becoming military advisor to Prince Abdullah, the Emir of Transjordan. Halabi remained in exile for the next nine years, returning under the general amnesty of 1936. In 1943, he ran for parliament on an independent ticket and won, serving as a deputy for his native Arab Mountain until 1947. He allied himself with President Shukri al-Quwatli, who was on bad terms with the Atrash family and challenged their authority over the Mountain in the mid-1940s. Halabi founded the People's Party of the Arab Mountain to promote his cause, which was funded by Quwatli and King Abd al-Aziz of Saudi Arabia.

In 1947, violent clashes took place in the Mountain, between the People's Party and the Atrash family, leading to many deaths and prompting Sultan al-Atrash to take up arms against Halabi and his men. A cease-fire was mediated by the Lebanese Druze leader Kamal Jumblatt and Prince Adil Arslan. Halabi was forced to silence his opposition when Quwatli was overthrown in 1949.

Sources:
Faris, George. *Man Hum fi al-Alam al-Arabi?* (1957).

al-Hanbali, Shaker
(1876-1958)

Shaker al-Hanbali studied at the Muluki Academy in Istanbul and joined the Ottoman civil service in Damascus. From 1900 to 1918, Hanbali served at the municipalities of Aley, Homs, and Beirut. In 1917, he became mayor of Hama.

In 1918, the Ottoman Empire was defeated in World War I, and Hanbali allied himself with King Faysal I, the new ruler of Syria. In the four-day interlude between the departure of the Ottoman Turks and the arrival of the Arab Army, Hanbali created a preliminary government with a group of Syrian notables in Damascus, headed by Prince Sa'id al-Jaza'iri. From 1918 to 1919, Hanbali served as political advisor to Faysal's prime minister, Rida al-Rikabi, where he also became director (bureau chief) of correspondence in Rikabi's government. When Hashim al-Atasi became prime minister, Hanbali served as his political advisor from May to July 1920. But that same year, the French Mandate was proclaimed over Syria, forcing Hanbali to abandon his ties to Faysal and ally himself with the mandate authority.

From 1923 to 1925, Hanbali served as a parliamentary deputy in Damascus and deputy to the Damascus assembly president, Badih Mu'ayyad al-Azm. Hanbali was critical of the military uprising against the French in 1925, launched by the Druze leader Sultan al-Atrash. Hanbali claimed that the revolt would cost the lives of hundreds of innocent Syrians. When the insurrection was partially crushed in June 1926, Hanbali became minister of education and justice in the cabinet of Prime Minister Ahmad Nami. Hanbali tried in vain to persuade the French to issue a general amnesty in order to allow those who had taken up arms against the mandate to return to Syria.

In August 1930, Hanbali became minister of justice in the cabinet of Prime

Minister Taj al-Din al-Hasani, France's number one ally in Syria. Hanbali held this post until the Syrian Republic was created in 1932. Then he taught political administration and law at Damascus University, and in 1936 founded the *al-Hadara* newspaper. Hanbali devoted the remainder of his life to political journalism.

Shaker al-Hanbali wrote many books on modern history and Islam, including *Al-Qawanin al-Idariyya (Administrative Laws)*, published in 1936, *Usul al-Idara al-Islamiyya (Origins of Islamic Administration)*, also published in 1936, and *Usul al-Fikr al-Islami (Origins of Islamic Thought)*, published in 1947.

Sources:
Faris, George. *Man Hum fi al-Alam al-Arabi?* (1957).
Khoury, Philip. *Syria and the French Mandate* (1987).

Homsi, Edmond
(1901-1972)

Edmond Homsi studied sociology and political science at Jesuit University in Lebanon and the American University of Beirut (AUB). He pursued his graduate and postgraduate studies in banking and finance at Oxford University and returned to Syria in 1922 to become aide-de-camp to Prime Minister Subhi Barakat.

In 1928, Homsi co-founded the National Bloc, the leading anti-French movement, with Hashim al-Atasi. The movement aimed at liberating Syria from French control through diplomatic rather than armed resistance. In February 1936, in a bid at appeasing the National Bloc, Prime Minister Ata al-Ayyubi appointed Homsi minister of finance, a post he kept until December 1936. In March 1936, while serving as a cabinet minister, Homsi became a member of the Bloc delegation that traveled to Paris to negotiate an end to the French Mandate.

The Bloc delegation formulated a treaty of independence that guaranteed complete Syrian emancipation within the framework of a twenty-five year period. When the Bloc returned from Paris in September 1936, Homsi became a deputy in a Syrian parliament dominated by the National Bloc. He held office until the Bloc regime fell in 1939.

In February 1946, President Shukri al-Quwatli appointed Homsi minister of finance in the National Bloc cabinet of Prime Minister Saadallah al-Jabiri. Homsi negotiated an end to Syria's monetary reliance on France, which ended the concessions that had been granted to the French-owned Banque de Syrie in 1920. In October 1946, Homsi became Syria's ambassador to the United Kingdom. In February 1950, Atasi made him ambassador to Belgium, a position he kept until 1955.

Homsi then returned to Syria and became president of the Aleppo Chamber of Commerce. In the second half of the 1950s, he was opposed to Syria's alliance with President Gamal Abd al-Nasser of Egypt. Nasser's socialism, if implemented in Syria, Homsi argued, would prove disastrous to Syria's free-market economy. He lobbied against the merger of Syria and Egypt in 1958 and accused Nasser of imposing a dictatorship on Syria.

Consequently, Homsi was completely marginalized during the union years (1958-1961), and he supported the military coup that overthrew union in September 1961. When the union government fell, Homsi signed the secession declaration with a group of anti-Nasser politicians. The declaration was a hand-written document that accused Nasser of having destroyed Syria's democratic system and free-market economy.

Edmond Homsi willingly retired from politics when the Baath Party came to power in 1963.

Sources:
Faris, George. *Man Hum fi al-Alam al-Arabi?* (1957).
Khoury, Philip. *Syria and the French Mandate* (1987).

al-Imadi, Mohammad
(1930-)

Mohammad al-Imadi studied economics at Damascus University, graduating with an MA in 1953. He obtained his PhD from the University of New York in 1960 and then returned to Syria and became a professor of economics at Damascus University.

In 1964, Imadi was appointed assistant secretary-general of the Ministry of Economy. In 1972, he became assistant minister of planning in the cabinet of Prime Minister Mahmud al-Ayyubi. In September 1973, President Hafez al-Asad appointed him minister of economy in the second Ayyubi cabinet. All told, Imadi held office for seven years under three different cabinets, resigning for health reasons in January 1980.

From 1977 to 1981, Imadi served as a deputy in parliament. He moved to Kuwait and became president of the Arab Bank from 1980 to 1985. In April 1985, Imadi returned to Syria and once again became minister of economy under Prime Minister Abdel Raouf al-Kassem. His post was renewed by Prime Minister Mahmud al-Zu'bi in November 1987 and by Prime Minister Mohammad Mustapha Miro in March 2000. Imadi was unable, however, to decentralize the economy or to reduce unemployment, which reached 9.5% in 1999. But he succeeded in advancing the public sector, canceling many of Syria's debts, and encouraging foreign investment in Syria in the early 1990s.

SST

In July 2000, President Bashar al-Asad came to power and promised to reform Syria's stagnant economy. Asad authorized the establishment of private banks in December 2000, thereby ending a thirty-eight year state monopoly over the banking sector. He also called for banking secrecy laws and a monetary stock exchange. He promised to reduce taxes, and he increased wages in the public sector.

Mohammad al-Imadi was charged with implementing Asad's reforms. He backed the new state policies, but was reluctant to allow the existence of private banks in Syria, arguing that reform of the state-owned Central Bank of Syria should come first. He also called for Syria to join the World Trade Organization (WTO), claiming that WTO membership would terminate the burden of taxes on local industries, thereby improving the quality of Syrian goods for export. Imadi argued that WTO membership would also provide Syrian consumers with higher quality local goods and a wider variety of products to choose from. He acknowledged that WTO membership would have negative side effects, pointing out that once European goods entered the Syrian market, many local manufacturers would be put out of business.

Mohammad al-Imadi was retired from office before a decision was taken on WTO membership. In December 2001, Prime Minister Miro created a new cabinet and appointed Dr Ghassan al-Rifaii, a World Bank economist, as minister of economy.

Sources:
The Daily Star (January 9, 2001).
The International Who's Who in the Arab World (1987-1988).
Syrian Arab News Agency (SANA).

al-Jabi, Rushdi
(1905-?)

Rushdi al-Jabi studied medicine at the American University of Beirut (AUB) and began his career by opening a clinic in Sudan. He rose to fame in the 1920s and became director of two prominent hospitals in Khartoum.

In August 1933, along with a group of fifty radical Arab nationalists, Jabi founded the League of National Action in the Lebanese Mountain town of Quarna'il. He served as chairman of the founding conference of the league. It was a pioneering organization established by a second generation of Arab politicians whose ages were between twenty-five and thirty and bent on eradicating the region of foreign influence. Unlike other political establishments dominated by landowners and Ottoman-trained politicians, the League of National Action was composed of professors, lawyers, and civil servants who were not living off of their family estates, but rather leading career-focused lives. All the league members had studied in Europe, the United States, or American universities in the Middle East.

The League of National Action achieved high acclaim in 1933, but died out in 1935 with the early death of its founder and charismatic leader, Abd al-Razzaq al-Dandashi. Jabi helped administer the league's political affairs and served as editor of its publication, *al-Amal al-Quawmi (National Action)*. He returned to Syria in 1927 and opened a medical clinic in Damascus, becoming an inspector at the Department of Health in Damascus. Jabi joined the National Bloc, the leading anti-French movement in Syria, and was arrested by the French for taking part in the Damascus underground. He also became a leader of the Syrian Boy Scouts and served as a member of their executive committee until the scouts were outlawed by the military regime of the Baath Party in 1963.

In 1938, Jabi fled to Amman, evading a twenty-year prison sentence for his activities in the League of National Action, and worked in Amman as a doctor until a general amnesty was issued in 1942. In 1944, President Shukri al-Quwatli, a member of the National Bloc, appointed Jabi director of health in Lattakia. He held this post until 1948 when he became director of Health in Aleppo. In 1949, he became secretary-general of the Ministry of Health. He retired from the civil service in February 1951 and went to Lebanon where he became a professor at the School of Medicine at AUB. In 1962, Rushdi al-Jabi became director of the Palestinian Refugee Agency in Lebanon and held this post until 1964.

Sources:
Bawab, Sulayman. *Mawsuat Alam Souriyya fi al-Qarn al-Ishreen* (1999).
Faris, George. *Man Hum Fi al-`Alam al-Arabi* (1957).

al-Jallad, Hamdi
(1883-1975)

Hamdi Jallad studied military affairs and public administration in Damascus and Istanbul. He joined the Hijaz Railway and became director of the railway's project committee in 1910. In 1913, he was appointed chief of police in Beirut.

Jallad drifted through different administrative posts in Ottoman Syria, becoming prefect of Akkar, Salt, Nablus, and Jenin. While in office, World War I broke out and the Ottoman defeat became certain. Jallad recalculated his alliances and established secret channels with the Arab leadership in Mecca. He joined the Arab Army of Sharif Husayn and smuggled arms and funds from the Arab Mountain to the Arabian Desert where the rebels were based. One Arab rebel was arrested while carrying arms, was tortured in Damascus, and relinquished the names of his accomplices, mentioning Hamdi al-Jallad. Thus, the Ottomans fired Jallad from his post and arrested him on the charge of high treason. Jallad went to prison, but managed to escape when the Ottoman Empire collapsed in 1918.

Returning to Damascus with the Allied forces that liberated the Syrian capital, Jallad became director of police in post-Ottoman Syria and head of the Damascus Municipality. He led the committee that crowned Faysal I as king of Syria on March 8, 1920, and maintained his post at the Municipality of Damascus in 1920 when the French Mandate was proclaimed over Syria. In 1925, a Druze uprising broke out in the Arab Mountain. When Jallad refused to crush the rebellion, he was retired from service by the French high commissioner, General Henri Gouraud. Subsequently, Hamdi al-Jallad was accused by the French of misuse of public office and embezzlement, but he was never convicted of those charges, and he spent the remainder of his years in retirement.

Sources:
Faris, George. *Man Hum fi al-Alam al-Arabi?* (1957).
Khoury, Philip. *Syria and the French Mandate* (1987).

Mahasin, As'ad
(1913-)

As'ad Mahasin studied international law at the Sorbonne in Paris. His father was Sa'id Mahasin, a former minister of justice in the 1920s. The young Mahasin practiced law at his father's office and taught at Damascus University.

In July 1953, President Adib al-Shishakli appointed Mahasin minister of justice and deputy to Foreign Minister Khalil Mardam Bey. Mahasin held office until Shishakli was overthrown in 1954 and returned to his legal practice. In 1955, President Hashim al-Atasi appointed Mahasin ambassador to France, a job he held until Syria and Egypt merged to form the United Arab Republic (UAR) in 1958. He was categorically opposed to the UAR and spoke out against the police state of Gamal Abd al-Nasser. He argued that Nasser's dictatorship would prove fatal for Syria and would destroy the country's democratic system and free-market economy. Thus, he supported the coup that toppled the UAR in September 1961, and he signed the secession declaration, a handwritten document that accused Nasser of having imposed a dictatorship over Syria.

Mahasin hailed Syria's new president, Nazim al-Qudsi, who promised to revoke Nasser's socialism. Mahasin became minister of foreign affairs in the cabinet of Prime Minister Khalid al-Azm. In July 1962, Syria filed an official complaint against Nasser, claiming that he was interfering in Syrian affairs and trying to get officers in the Syrian Army to rebel against the post-Nasser order. The Arab League called for round table talks between Syria and Egypt, which were held in the Lebanese town of Shtura on the Syrian-Lebanese border.

Qudsi appointed Mahasin as chairman of the Syrian delegation to the talks, but the summit was ruined when the Egyptian team walked out before the Arab League issued a verdict condemning Egypt for her accusations against Syria. In March 1963, however, the Baath Party came to power in Syria and dismissed Qudsi, Azm, and Mahasin from office. At this time, As'ad Mahasin's civil rights were terminated and he was forced to retire from political activity.

Sources:
Faris, George. *Man Hum fi al-Alam al-Arabi?* (1957).
Samman, Mutih. *Watan wa Askar* (1995).

Malek, Hanna
(1900-1992)

Hanna Malek was born in the town of Rashayya (modern Lebanon). His father was Abdullah Malek, an attorney who had served in the post-Ottoman Parliament under King Faysal I from 1918 to 1920. Malek studied law at Damascus University and completed his graduate studies at the American University of Beirut (AUB). He began his career as a judge in June 1925.

Ihsan al-Sharif, a prominent attorney and politician, offered Malek membership in the People's Party, the first political party created in French Mandate Syria and headed by Dr Abd al-Rahman Shahbandar, an AUB graduate like Malek who had been minister of foreign affairs from 1918 to 1920. The People's Party promoted the creation of a constitutional government in a free and unified Syria that would include Palestine, Jordan, and parts of Lebanon. But Malek refused to join, claiming that as a judge, he should be politically independent.

In September 1926, Malek became a judge in the Mixed Courts of Damascus. He investigated and dealt with famous cases in Syrian history, such as the assassination attempt on Prime Minister Jamil Mardam Bey in 1938, the kidnapping of Governor Tawfiq Shamiyya in the Jazeera district along the Euphrates River, and the arrest of the pro-Shahbandar politician Zaki al-Khatib. In 1938, Malek became prosecutor in the Court of Cassation, and in 1943 was appointed judge in the Higher Court of Justice. In 1949, Justice Minister Munir al-Ajlani made Malek president of the Higher Judiciary Council in Syria. On January 14, 1951, he became attorney general of Syria. He held this post during the regime of President Adib al-Shishakli (1951-1954). But when Sabri al-Asali, an attorney

Hanna Malek.

and a former classmate and friend, became prime minister, he appointed Malek secretary-general of the Cabinet of Ministers. In December 1955, Malek's position was renewed by Prime Minister Sa'id al-Ghazzi.

When Syria and Egypt merged to form the United Arab Republic (UAR) in 1958, President Gamal Abd al-Nasser of Egypt dissolved the office of prime minister and transferred its duties to the presidency. As a result, Malek became secretary-general of the presidency. From the beginning, however, he clashed with the socialist leader Akram al-Hawrani, who had helped create union in 1958. Hawrani coveted the post for himself, but instead had been given the ceremonial post of vice president of the UAR. He lobbied with Egyptian authorities to have Malek dismissed, and Nasser agreed, retiring Malek from service on February 17, 1959.

Malek devoted the remainder of his years to his legal practice and to the legal affairs of the Greek Orthodox Church in Damascus. He published numerous legal books and one political work entitled, *al-Dawla, wa al-Qawmiyya, wa al-Deen, wa al-Wihda* (*The State, Nationalism, Religion, and Unity*), published in 1986.

Hanna Malek's memoirs, *Muzakarat Hanna Malek*, is due for release in 2006.

Sources:
Al-Inshaa (January 17, 1945).
Faris, George. *Man Hum fi al-`Alam al-Arabi?* (1957).
Malek, Hanna. *Mzakarat Hanna Malek* (2006).

al-Nehlawi, Fayek
(1914-1976)

Fayek al-Nehlawi studied law at Damascus University and began his career as a lawyer and a journalist, writing under a pen name for several Egyptian and Lebanese newspapers. He became a member of the editorial board of the nationalist newspaper *al-Qabas* and wrote important political editorials for three years. In 1943, at the young age of twenty-nine, he was appointed secretary-general of parliament by Speaker Faris al-Khury.

Nehlawi became a close advisor to President Shukri al-Quwatli and his two consecutive prime ministers, Faris al-Khury and Saadallah al-Jabiri. In March 1949, when a military coup took place in Syria, toppling Quwatli and Khury, Syria's new leader, Husni al-Za'im, dissolved parliament and ordered Quwatli into exile in Alexandria. In April 1949, Nehlawi, a fervent supporter of Quwatli, defied state orders and accompanied the ex-president to the Damascus Airport. Soon after, Za'im ordered Nehlawi's arrest, but he fled to Beirut until Za'im was overthrown and the parliament was reinstated on August 14, 1949.

In February 1958, Syria and Egypt merged to form the United Arab Republic

(UAR) and Nehlawi became secretary-general of the joint Syrian-Egyptian Chamber in Cairo. In September 1961, following the dissolution of the UAR, Nehlawi allied himself with Syria's new president, Nazim al-Qudsi, and was once again appointed secretary-general of parliament. He was also close to the new strongman of Syria, Abd al-Karim al Nehlawi.

Fayek al-Nehlawi (right) with President Adib al-Shishakli when the latter was sworn in as President of Syria in 1953.

Nehlawi remained in office until the Baath Party came to power in March 1963. The Military Committee of the Baath Party dissolved parliament and replaced it with the Revolutionary Command Council (RCC). In 1969, Fayek al-Nehlawi moved to Beirut where he managed a family business hotel until his death in May 1976.

Sources:

Faris, George. *Man Hum fi al-Alam al-Arabi?* (1957).

Moubayed, Sami. *The Politics of Damascus 1920-1946* (1999).

Information supplied by Dr Tamim Nehlawi (July 16, 2002).

Nizam al-Din, Abd al-Baqi
(1905-?)

Abd al-Baqi Nizam al-Din was born in the town of Quamishli. In 1930, he joined the National Bloc, the leading anti-French movement in Syria, and became director of the Bloc's Quamishli office. In 1946, independence was achieved and the National Bloc was dissolved and renamed the National Party.

Nizam al-Din joined the new party and became director of its Quamishli office as well. He clashed with President Shukri al-Quwatli, the de facto leader of the National Party, and resigned from the party in 1947. Nizam al-Din then joined the opposition and co-founded the People's Party, a movement that aimed to bring down the Quwatli regime. He ran for parliament on a People's Party ticket in 1947 and won. In 1949, he was voted onto the Constitutional Assembly to draft the first post-Quwatli constitution. In December 1949, the independent prime minister, Khalid al-Azm, appointed him minister of agriculture, a position he kept until Azm made him minister of justice in March 1951.

As a deputy in parliament, Nizam al-Din briefly allied himself with Akram al-Hawrani, leader of the Arab Socialist Party, and Mustapha al-Sibaii, leader of the Syrian Muslim Brotherhood. Together, these men created a Republican Front to oppose a proposed Syrian-Egyptian union advocated by President Hashim al-Atasi and his prime minister, Nazim al-Qudsi.

When the People's Party began demanding union with Iraq, Nizam al-Din terminated his membership in the party and became a political independent. He claimed that union with Iraq would threaten Syria's republican regime and replace it with a Hashemite monarchy. In December 1949, Syria's military strongman, Adib al-Shishakli, launched a mini-coup in the Syrian Army, creating a cabinet crisis. President Atasi asked Nizam al-Din to form a government, but after consultations in late December 1949, he failed at reaching a suitable cabinet.

When Shishakli came to power in November 1951, Nizam al-Din retired from political life, and did not return to the limelight until Shishakli was overthrown in February 1954. In December 1954, Prime Minister Sabri al-Asali made Nizam al-Din minister of public works and telecommunications. Shukri al-Quwatli returned to the presidency in 1955, and in a bid at appeasing the opposition, appointed Nizam al-Din as minister of health and education in the cabinet of Prime Minister Sa'id al-Ghazzi.

In 1956, Nizam al-Din became minister of health once again under Prime Minister Asali. In December of that year, however, he resigned from office in protest of the state's pro-USSR foreign policy. He was also opposed to Syria's alliance with the socialist regime in Egypt and argued that Gamal Abd al-Nasser should not be allowed to dictate state policy on Syria. In 1958, Abd al-Baqi Nizam al-Din resigned from office when the United Arab Republic (UAR) was created. He remained categorically opposed to Nasser and the USSR during the years of the UAR (1958-1961). He supported the coup that ousted the UAR in 1961 and retired from political activity when the Baath Party came to power in March 1963.

Sources:
Faris, George. *Man Hum fi al-Alam al-Arabi?* (1957).

al-Qasim, Nihad
(1905-1970)

Nihad al-Qasim studied law at Damascus University and opened a legal practice in Damascus. In 1951, he co-founded the Government Inspection Bureau and served as its director until 1954.

The Government Inspection Bureau was an official institute charged with monitoring the accounts and activities of various state agencies. In 1954, Qasim became minister of education and agriculture in the cabinet of the independent prime minister, Sa'id al-Ghazzi. In July 1954, Qasim became acting president of Damascus University. He kept this post until November 1954.

In 1955, Qasim returned to his job at the Government Inspection Bureau and joined the movement of Arab nationalism headed by President Gamal Abd al-Nasser of Egypt. He lobbied extensively in favor of Nasser and supported Syria's merger with Egypt to form the United Arab Republic (UAR) in 1958. During the union years (1958-1961), Qasim was one of the most prominent members of the Nasserist bloc in Syria. In October 1958, Nasser appointed Qasim minister of justice, a position he was to hold until the UAR was dissolved in September 1961.

But after union failed, Qasim clashed with President Nazim al-Qudsi, who came to power in 1962. In consequence of their disagreements, Qasim fled to Lebanon. In Beirut, he co-founded the United Front, a coalition of Arab nationalists who were still committed to Nasser and wanted to restore the UAR. In March 1963, the Military Committee of the Baath Party came to power in Syria and pledged to restore the UAR. President Qudsi and his prime minister, Khalid al-Azm, were dismissed from office and banished from Syria.

Qasim's pro-Nasser record paid off and he was appointed deputy to Prime Minister Salah al-Bitar and minister of justice in the first Baath cabinet. Two months later, he realized that the Baath had no intention of restoring the UAR, so he resigned from office. He clashed with Prime Minister Bitar over the crackdown on political freedoms, the creation of a one-party state, and the closure of independent newspapers. Jassem Alwan, a Nasserist officer, tried to seize power in July 1963, but his coup was foiled by Baath Party strongman Amin al-Hafez. Nihad al-Qasim was accused of being involved in the attempted coup. He was imprisoned for six months, then released into exile in Lebanon.

Sources:
Faris, George. *Man Hum fi al-Alam al-Arabi?* (1957).
Itri, Abd al-Ghani. *Alam wa Mubdioun* (1999).

al-Qasmi, Zafer
(1913-1984)
Alternative spelling: Zafer al-Quasmi
Zafer al-Qasmi studied law at Damascus University and opened a legal practice in Damascus with the young attorney Sabri al-Asali. In 1936, Asali joined the National Bloc, the leading anti-French movement in Syria, and made Qasmi a member of its Damascus office.

The two men were involved in mass politics during the 1930s and became hard-line loyalists of President Shukri al-Quwatli in 1943. Following independence from France in 1946, Qasmi became a member in the National Party, the offset of the National Bloc led by Quwatli and Asali. But Qasmi spent 1946 to 1950 working in his legal practice in Damascus, steering clear from political activity.

When General Adib al-Shishakli came to power in 1951, however, Qasmi publicly called for his overthrow, labeling his regime during a university lecture as, "an un-constitutional and illegal dictatorship." He was arrested, then released when Shishakli was overthrown in 1954. From 1955 to 1958, Qasmi once again rose to prominence when his allies, Shukri al-Quwatli and Sabri al-Asali, returned to power and became president and prime minister respectively.

Though Qasmi supported the creation of the United Arab Republic (UAR) in 1958, he nonetheless signed the secession manifesto that dissolved it in 1961, asserting that Syria's union with Egypt had been ill-planned, and that Nasser's socialism had been catastrophic to Syria. But when the Baath Party government came to power in 1963, Qasmi's civil rights were terminated and he was sent into exile to Saudi Arabia where he served as legal advisor to the Saudi's Ministry of Economy and Foreign Trade.

In 1969, Zafer al-Qasmi moved to Beirut to teach at the Lebanese University, a position he kept until the Lebanese Civil War broke out in 1975. From 1963 to 1975, he published a number of works including *Adwa' ala al-Lugha wa al-Adab (Light on Language and Literature), Nazarat fi al-Sh'ir al-Islami wa al-Umawi (Vision into Islamic and Umayyad poetry),* and a book on the history of Maktab Anbar, Syria's elite high school.

In 1965, Qasmi also published a number of documents from the Syrian revolt of 1925, taken from Sabri al-Asali, his one-time patron and a participant in the 1925 revolt. In 1975, Qasmi moved to Paris in self-imposed exile, where he remained until his death in 1984.

In 1982, Zafer al-Qasmi published his last book entitled, *Al-Jihad wa al-Huquq al-Dawliyya al-Amma fi al-Islam (Holy War and International Law in Islam).*

Sources:
Itri, Abd al-Ghani. *Abqariyyat wa Alam* (1996).

Raslan, Abd al-Hasib
(1901-?)

Abd al-Hasib Raslan was born in Homs and studied pharmacy at the American University of Beirut (AUB). He administered his family's various enterprises throughout the early 1930s and began his public career in 1932 as secretary of the Chamber of Agriculture in Homs.

In 1934, Raslan became president of the Homs Chamber of Industry and Commerce, a post he kept until 1948. During the years of the French Mandate (1920-1948), he financed the nationalist movement in Homs and joined the National Bloc, the leading anti-French movement in Syria. Raslan was influenced by his mentor and uncle, Mazhar Raslan, a co-founder of the Bloc and one frequently asked to serve as government minister in the 1930s. Raslan was elected board member of the Banque Liban et Syrie and appointed to the executive committee of the Syrian Ministry of Economy in 1945.

In 1949, Raslan was elected a Homs deputy at the Constitutional Assembly, entrusted with drafting a new constitution for Syria. In 1954, he was elected to parliament on an independent ticket. In September 1954, he became minister of interior in the caretaker government of Prime Minister Said al-Ghazzi. In June 1956, the new prime minister, Sabri al-Asali, appointed him minister of defense. But Raslan resigned his post in 1957 to protest the meddling of senior military officers in political affairs, claiming that their job was to defend Syria and not take part in decision-making.

When parliament met to vote on union with Egypt in February 1958, Abd al-Hasib Raslan spoke out against union. He criticized Gamal Abd al-Nasser's socialism and warned that union would damage Syria's political and economic life. He retired from political life in 1958.

Sources:
Faris, George. *Man Hum fi al-Alam al-Arabi?* (1957).

al-Sawwaf, Husni
(1906-1985)

Husni al-Sawwaf studied business administration at the American University of Beirut (AUB) and graduated in 1925. He pursued postgraduate studies at the University of Pennsylvania, and upon graduation began teaching at the AUB Business Department. From 1925 to 1927, al-Sawwaf held administrative posts at the comptroller's office at AUB. Then he taught at AUB from October 1927 until February 1945.

In 1945, Husni al-Sawwaf was called back to Syria by Prime Minister Faris al-Khury and appointed to the Syrian Embassy in Washington. Along with Ambassador Constantine Zurayk, Sawwaf administered Syria's diplomatic mission in the United States until 1949. During these years, the US administration of President Harry Truman abruptly shifted to an anti-Arab foreign policy, and both men tried without success to gain President Truman's support during the Arab-Israeli War of 1948.

Sawwaf remained at his post until General Husni al-Za'im came to power in March 1949. Then he was summoned home once again and was appointed secretary-general of the Ministry of Economy. He kept this post until 1955, when he returned to his original job as a professor at AUB.

In 1959, Gamal Abd al-Nasser appointed Sawwaf governor of the Central Bank of Syria. On March 8, 1960, Nasser made him minister of economy in the

United Arab Republic (UAR). Sawwaf held this job until the UAR was dissolved in September 1961, returning to his job as governor of the Central Bank in Syria until the Baath Party government retired him in 1963.

Then Husni al-Sawwaf moved to Beirut, where he established a consulting office on economic matters, and where he remained in self-imposed exile until the Lebanese Civil War broke out in 1975. President Hafez al-Asad welcomed him back to Syria and even considered reappointing him to the Central Bank, but Sawwaf declined for health reasons.

Sources:
Faris, George. *Man Hum fi al-Alam al-Arabi?* (1957).
Interview with Dr Wahid al-Sawwaf (May 26, 2001).

al-Shallah, Bader al-Din
(1908-1999)

Bader al-Din al-Shallah was born and raised in Damascus. His father, Saleem al-Shallah, was a wealthy merchant who had funded the nationalist movement during the years of the French Mandate (1920-1946). Running a successful dried apricot business in Damascus, the young Shallah was an active supporter of the National Bloc, the leading anti-French movement in Syria.

Shallah was also close to the Bloc's Damascus leaders, Shukri al-Quwatli and Sabri al-Asali. Shallah became a member of the Damascus Chamber of Commerce in 1928 and was voted onto its board of directors in 1947. During this time, he joined the Grand Masonic Lodge of Syria and was a prominent benefactor to poor neighborhoods in Damascus. In the 1940s, he served as a member of the Damascus Municipality and dean of the Islamic Arab Institute.

In 1954, members of the Damascus Chamber of Commerce lobbied against the socialist policies of the Baath Party. In his memoirs, Baath Party leader Akram al-Hawrani wrote that Bader al-Din al-Shallah and Chamber President Musallam al-Sioufi met with President Hashim al-Atasi on June 16, 1954, and asked that the Baath Party be declined any ministerial post in the all-party cabinet of Prime Minister Sabri al-Asali. The party's socialist ideology, the merchants argued, was in opposition to the mercantile interests in Damascus. Atasi complied with their request and didn't appoint the Baath Party leader Salah al-Bitar as government minister.

Bader al-Din al-Shallah (r) with Presiden Hafez al-Asad.

From 1954 to 1962, Shallah lobbied further against the Baath and clashed with its leadership following their rise to power in 1963. In 1970, however, he made his peace with President Hafez al-Asad and supported his rise to power. In 1982, the Muslim Brotherhood tried to seize power in Syria and declared a holy war against the Asad government. Shallah used his considerable influence to prevent the anti-Asad movement from spreading to Damascus. He personally intervened with local merchants and pleaded that they stay out of the conflict and refrain from backing the Brotherhood.

When the uprising was crushed, Shallah was appointed president of the Damascus Chamber of Commerce. His son, Rateb al-Shallah, assumed the post from after him, and the elder Shallah continued to serve as honorary president of the chamber until his passing in 1999.

Bader al-Din al-Shallah published three autobiographies: *Al-Tareekh wa al-Zikra (History and Reminiscence)*, published in 1991, *Min Hasad Al-Ayyam (From the Harvest of Days)*, published in 1996, and *Alsira al-Tijariyya (The Commercial Story)*, published in both English and Arabic in 1997.

Sources:
The International Who's Who in the Arab World (1987-1988).
Hawrani, Akram. *Muzakarat Akram al-Hawrani* (2000).
Shallah, Bader al-Din. *Al-Tareekh wa al-Zikra* (1991).
Shallah, Bader al-Din. *Min Hasad Al-Ayyam* (1996).
Shallah, Bader al-Din. *Alsira al-Tijariyya* (1997).
Seale, Patrick. *Asad: Struggle for the Middle East* (1988).

Shatila, Khalid
(1910-1983)

Khalid Shatila studied law at Damascus University, obtained a graduate degree in education, and a doctorate in sociology. He began his career as an instructor of philosophy in Aleppo, and in 1946 he became director of higher education at the Ministry of Education in Syria.

Later, Shatila became dean of the faculty of education at Damascus University. In 1947, President Shukri al-Quwatli appointed him chargé d'affaires at the Syrian Embassy in Belgium. In 1954, President Hashim al-Atasi appointed him secretary-general of the Presidential Palace. One year later, however, Quwatli returned to power, and appointed Shatila ambassador to Spain. In 1958, he resigned from his diplomatic post to teach comparative education at Damascus University. In 1961, he became a senior consultant at the Ministry of Education.

Khalid Shatila left Syria in April 1963 and joined UNESCO, serving as director of its mission in Mali. He spent the remainder of his years between Lebanon and

Europe. Among his published books is *al-Zawaj Ind al-Muslimun Fi Souriyya* (*Marriage Among Muslims in Syria*).

Sources:
Faris, George. *Man Hum fi al-Alam al-Arabi?* (1957).
Bawab, Sulayman. *Mawsuat Alam Souriyya fi al-Qarn al-Ishreen,* Vol III (1999).

al-Shatti, Iyad
(1940-)

Iyad al-Shatti studied medicine at Damascus University and continued his medical studies at the Case Western Reserve University in Cleveland, Ohio, graduating in 1969. His father, Ahmad Shawkat al-Shatti, was a veteran educator in Syria who had co-founded Damascus University in 1923.

Iyad al-Shatti taught at the American University of Beirut (AUB) from 1971 to 1978 and then moved back to Syria to practice and teach medicine at Damascus University. In 1986, Shatti became dean of the Medical School in Damascus. In 1987, President Hafez al-Asad appointed him minister of health in the cabinet of Prime Minister Mahmud al-Zu'bi. In 1990, Shatti became president of the Regional Office at the World Health Organization (WHO) in Geneva, becoming the first Arab to attain such a senior position in the WHO. His government post was renewed under the cabinet of Prime Minister Mohammad Mustapha Miro in March 2000, then again in December 2001.

In 1996, Iyad al-Shatti introduced the concept of "health villages" to Syria. Medical representatives were dispatched to rural districts of Syria to spread health awareness, improve the health environment, upgrade agriculture, and work on sanitation. The Ministry of Health commenced on a media campaign to promote healthier lifestyles, encourage citizens to eat better, smoke less, and be vaccinated against diseases. By 2002, five health villages had been established in Syria, and Shatti currently plans to establish 1,500 others. During his tenure as minister, Shatti also founded a School of Public Health at Damascus University and a School of Quality Management. He was reappointed minister of health in the cabinet of Prime Minister Naji al-Itri in September 2003, keeping this post until October 2004.

Dr Iyad Shatti served at the Ministry of Health for twenty-seven years, longer than any other health minister in Syrian history.

Sources:
Syrian Arab News Agency (SANA).
Interview with Dr Iyad al-Shatti (July 25, 2001).

al-Shayeb, Fou'ad
(1911-1970)

Fou'ad al-Shayeb studied law at Damascus University and began his career by writing for local newspapers and running a legal practice in Damascus. From 1935 to 1939, he wrote articles for the Damascus daily *Fata al-Arab* (*The Arab Youth*). He also submitted articles frequently to the Beirut daily *al-Nida* (*The Appeal*), run by the Lebanese journalist Kazem al-Sulh. In 1940, he moved to Baghdad to teach Arabic literature at local high schools. He also wrote for the Baghdad daily *al-Bilad* (*The Country*).

When Shukri al-Quwatli became president in August 1943, Shayeb was summoned back to Syria and appointed media advisor to the Presidential Palace. Shortly afterward, Quwatli made him director of press, news, and information, a post he was to hold well after Quwatli left the presidency in 1949. During his six-year tenure with the Quwatli regime, Shayeb helped elevate the president's image in Syria's published media, saw to it that all activities received front page coverage in all major Syrian newspapers, and encouraged Quwatli to constantly seek the limelight. Shayeb made it a habit to publish Quwatli's photograph on page one of Syria's main newspapers, an uncommon act in previous years.

In May 1951, Shayeb became director of press, news, and information at the Presidential Palace, playing a critical role in bolstering and brandishing the public image of President Adib al-Shishakli, the new military strongman of Syria. He relied heavily on the radio, which had become popular in recent years, and he encouraged Shishakli to make weekly addresses to the Syrian people. Shayeb was mainly influenced by the "Fireside Chats" of US President Franklin D. Roosevelt that were delivered weekly over the radio during World War II and managed to enhance Roosevelt's popularity throughout America.

In 1954, Shishakli made Shayeb director of Syria's National Radio. From 1961 to 1963, Shayeb became director of national guidance at the Ministry of Culture. In 1962, Shayeb began work at the literary weekly *al-Maarifa* (*Knowledge*) and served as editor-in-chief until 1967. He was commissioned into the Arab League and appointed director of the league's bureau in Argentina, keeping this post until his death in 1970.

Fou'ad al-Shayeb published several books including *Awrak Muwazaf* (*Papers of a Civil Servant*), *Liman Tuqra al-Tubul* (*For Whom the Drums Beat*), and *Jumhuriyatuna* (*Our Republic*). In 1944, he published his classic, *Tareekh al-Jurh* (*History of Scar*), a collection of eleven short stories.

Sources:
Faris, George. *Man Hum Fi al-`Alam al-Arabi* (1957).
Farfur, Abd al-Latif. *Alam Dimashq* (1987).
Itri, Abd al-Ghani. *Abqariyyat wa Alam* (1996).

Kayyali, Sami. *Al-Adab al-Arabi al-Mouasir fi Souriyya 1850-1950* (1968).

al-Shihabi, Mustapha
(1893-1968)

Prince Mustapha al-Shihabi was born in the village of Hasbayya, which is today part of Lebanon, to a notable family. He studied agriculture in Paris and moved to Istanbul in 1915 for a career at the Ottoman Ministry of Agriculture.

As a youth, Shihabi was influenced by his brother, the nationalist leader Aref al-Shihabi, who was executed for his views by the Ottoman Turks in 1916. During World War I, Shihabi joined the Arab underground in Damascus and was a member of al-Ahd, a coalition of young Arabs working for the liberation of all Arab territories from Ottoman control. In 1918, following the defeat of the Ottoman Empire, Shihabi became director of the Ministry of Agriculture and in 1925 became director of government property in Damascus. In 1928, he joined the National Bloc, the leading anti-French movement in Syria, and served on its executive committee. In 1934, Shihabi became director of national economy in Syria. Two years later, he became secretary-general of the Ministry of Education and held office until February 1936. Then he became minister of education in the cabinet of Prime Minister Ata al-Ayyubi.

In March 1936, Prime Minister Ayyubi delegated Shihabi to accompany the National Bloc to independence talks in France. When the Bloc came to power in December 1936, President Hashim al-Atasi appointed Shihabi governor of Aleppo. But he was retired from office when Atasi left the presidency in 1939.

In January 1943, Shihabi became minister of finance in the cabinet of Prime Minister Jamil al-Ulshi. On March 22, 1943, however, Shihabi resigned in disagreement with the prime minister because of Ulshi's pro-French views. From March to August 1943, Shihabi became minister of finance, economy, and supply in the independent cabinet of Prime Minister Ata al-Ayyubi.

From 1939 to 1943, Shihabi allied himself with the Bloc leader Shukri al-Quwatli, who became President in 1943, and appointed Shihabi governor of Lattakia. He was charged with administering the Alawite Mountain and containing a popular uprising led by the chieftain Sulayman al-Murshed. Shihabi served in Lattakia for two years. Once he succeeded in containing Murshed's movement, Shihabi was brought back to Damascus and appointed secretary-general of the Cabinet of Ministers. In 1946, following independence from France, he became governor of Aleppo once again, and in 1948 was reappointed governor of Lattakia.

In March 1949, a military coup took place in Damascus and General Husni al-Za'im, President Quwatli's chief of staff, toppled the Quwatli regime and had the president arrested. The new leader arrested most officials associated with Shukri al-Quwatli, but declined to arrest Mustapha al-Shihabi. Instead, the two men became friends and Shihabi was appointed minister of justice in April 1949. But he fell from grace when Za'im was overthrown in August 1949. Shihabi emerged once again, however, under the regime of General Adib al-Shishakli (1951-1954), as Syria's first ambassador to Egypt. He served as Shishakli's link to President Mohammad Najib, and then to President Gamal Abd al-Nasser following their rise to power in 1952.

Shihabi returned to Syria when the Shishakli regime was overthrown in 1954 and was elected vice president of the prestigious Arab Language Assemblage—the highest international scientific authority in the field of Arab language and literature. He wrote several technical books including *Alzira'aa al-Amaliyya Hadeetha* (*Modern, Practical Agriculture*), published in 1935, and *Dictionaire Francais-Arabe des Termes Agrioles*, a French-Arabic dictionary of agricultural terms published in 1943. His political works include *Al-Mustalahat al-Ilmiyya fi al-Lugha al-Arabiyya* (*Scientific Terminology in Arabic Language*), published in 1955, *Al-Qawmiyya al-Arabiyya* (*Arab Nationalism*), published in 1961, and *Sadd Aswan al-Ali* (*The Aswan High Dam*), co-written and edited by the Egyptian politician Usmat Abd al-Majid.

In 1959, Prince Mustapha al-Shihabi became president of the Arab Language Assemblage and kept his post until his death in 1968.

Sources:
Itri, Abd al-Ghani. *Abqariyyat* (1997).
Kayyali, Sami. *Al-Adab al-Arabi al-Mouasir fi Souriyya 1850-1950* (1968).

Sihnawi, Jean
(1903-1975)

Jean Sihnawi was born in Damascus. He studied medicine in Beirut for one year and then dropped out to pursue a commercial career with his father. He worked as a merchant in Damascus and eventually became president of the Damascus Chamber of Commerce.

In 1930, Sihnawi joined the National Bloc, the leading anti-French movement in Syria, and became a financer of its activities. Sihnawi believed in the Bloc's cause—to liberate Syria from French control through diplomacy rather than armed resistance. In April 1941, five years before the end of the French Mandate, Sihnawi became minister of finance in the independent cabinet of Prime Minister Khalid al-Azm. From 1942 to 1946, Sihnawi served as director of Syrian Airways. He took no part in day-to-day politics during the final years of the French Mandate, but he allied himself with President Shukri al-Quwatli, the National Bloc leader who had become president of the republic in 1943.

In January 1949, Sihnawi became minister of economy in the cabinet of Khalid al-Azm. But Sihnawi was forced from office by the military regime of President Husni al-Za'im, who ousted Quwatli and Azm in March 1949. During the 1950s, Sihnawi served as president of the Syrian Higher Monetary Committee. He was opposed to the rising socialist trend in Syria and spoke out against the merger of Syria and Egypt. He argued that the leadership of Egyptian President Gamal Abd al-Nasser, along with his dictatorial policies and socialist vision, would be catastrophic for Syria's free market economy and liberal political system.

When the two countries merged to form the United Arab Republic (UAR) in 1958, Sihnawi withdrew from public life for several years. He supported the coup that overthrew the UAR in September 1961 and served as a deputy in parliament until the Baath Party came to power in March 1963.

On March 28, 1962, a coup was launched in Syria by Colonel Abd al-Karim al-Nehlawi. He arrested President Nazim al-Qudsi and Jean Sihnawi, accusing them of misusing public office and persecuting the officers of the Syrian Army. Along with other deputies and ministers, Sihnawi remained in prison until a counter-coup took place on April 2 and restored the Qudsi government.

Sources:
As'ed, Shakir. *Al-Barlaman al-Souri fi Tatawurhu al-Tareekhi* (2002).
Bawab, Sulayman. *Mawsuat Alam Souriyya fi al-Qarn al-Ishreen,* Vol III (1999).
Faris, George. *Man Hum fi al-`Alam al-Arabi?* (1957).
Samman, Mutih. *Watan wa Askar* (1995).

al-Tarabulsi, Izzat
(1913-2000)

Izzat al-Tarabulsi studied law and political science in Paris. He practiced law from 1934 to 1938, then began to teach at Damascus University. In 1939, he became a judge at the real estate court and opened a legal practice in Damascus. In 1947, he left the Faculty of Law at Damascus University and worked briefly at the Ministry of Finance as manager of public revenue before becoming manager of the Lattakia port in 1950.

In 1951, Tarabulsi was appointed director of the Customs Department, then secretary-general of the Ministry of Finance. In 1955, he became governor of the Central Bank of Syria. In 1958, Syria and Egypt merged to form the United Arab Republic (UAR), and Izzat al-Tarabulsi was retired from office. Tarabulsi was opposed to the economic policies of Nasser during the UAR years (1958-1961) and supported the coup d'etat that dissolved union in September 1961.

In 1962, wanting a non-partisan to assume power, President Nazim al-Qudsi toyed with the idea of calling on Tarabulsi to form an economic reform government. The idea never materialized, but in September 1962, Tarabulsi was appointed minister of national economy in the cabinet of Prime Minister Khalid al-Azm. In February 1963, he became acting minister of finance as well. Tarabulsi was also appointed part of a senior economic committee drafted by President Qudsi to formulate economic reforms for post-union Syria. Tarabulsi came to office with the aim of reviving Syria's dislocated industry. In 1960, Nasser had nationalized all factories and transferred their administration to the state with the aim of redistributing wealth.

Izzat al-Tarabulsi.

Tarabulsi passed several laws designed to eradicate the socialist stamp imposed on Syria during the union years. He proposed that all enterprise and factories confiscated by Nasser be restored to their rightful owners, and that industrialists, landowners, and businessmen be financially compensated for losses incurred during union. The project was warmly received among Syrian industrialists, some of whom had declared bankruptcy in the union years.

The plan never got past the drawing board, however, for in March 1963 the Baath Party came to power in Syria and established a socialist state based on Nasser's model in Cairo. Both Azm and Tarabulsi were dismissed from office and exiled to Lebanon. Tarabulsi settled in Beirut and became director of Banque Liban et d' Outre Mer (BLOM). He wrote several books on Syria from the date of his exile in March 1963 until his death in December 2000. Among his works are *Agriculture in Syria,* written in French, *Dirasat fi al-Maliyya al-Amma (Lessons in General Finance),* co-written with former Syrian minister Awad Barakat, and his classic, *General Guidelines for Economic and Political Policies in Syria.*

Sources:
Azm, Khalid. *Muzakarat* (1973).
Faris, George. *Man Hum fi al-Alam al-Arabi?* (1957).
Samman, Mutih. *Watan wa Askar* (1995).

The entourage of Abd al-Rahman Pasha al-Yusuf heading for Mecca in 1911.

Members of al-Fatat, the most popular opposition party in Ottoman Syria, founded in Paris in 1911. This group photo was taken in Dummar, a resort near Damascus. Front row (seated on floor from left to right): Tawfiq al-Hayyani, Prince Fayez al-Shihabi, Rafiq al-Tamimi, Awni Abd al-Hadi, Dr Ahmad Qadri, Muen al-Madi, Tawfiq al-Yazagi, Dr Said Talab.

Middle row, standing from left to right: Wasfi al-Atasi, Ahmad Muraywed, Shukri al-Quwatli (future president of Syria), Bahjat al-Shihabi, Saleem al-Attar, Zaki al-Tamimi, Husni al-Barazi (future prime minister of Syria). Back row (from left to right): Adil al-Azma, Rushdi al-Husami, Riyad al-Sulh (future prime minister of Lebanon), Saadallah al-Jabiri (future prime minister of Syria), Afif al-Sulh, Izzat Darwaza.

Dr Abd al-Rahman Shahbandar in 1923 at the Arwad Island Prison, off the Syrian coast near Tartus.

In 1920, after the French deposed the Hashemite king of Syria, Faysal I, Shabandar had remained in Europe and lobbied Western governments for Syrian independence and also for the creation of an independent pan-Arab nation under Hashemite governance.

Shahbandar returned to Syria in 1922 under an amnesty and made contact with US diplomats, who were sympathetic to the Arab cause. Then the French accused Shabandar of engaging in an "American plot" to topple the French Mandate and sentenced him to twenty years. A second French amnesty set him free a year later.

POLITICIANS

The historical figures mentioned in this chapter were actively involved in the political life of Syria, including presidents, prime ministers, cabinet ministers,

(continued on page 127)

Jamal Pasha (second from left) met with Sharif Ali-Haydar (left), an envoy of Sharif Husayn, during World War I in 1916. Jamal Pasha hoped to prevent an Arab rebellion.

On June 10, 1916 Sharif Husayn declared the Arab Revolt.

The victorious Arab Army entering Damascus on October 1, 1918. The field commander was Husayn's son Prince Faysal (who worked closely with the British Colonel T. E. Lawrence of "Lawrence of Arabia" fame). What the Arab Army won in the field, however, it lost in Paris following the war.

Faysal with Lawrence in Paris, 1919.

Syrians welcome Faysal to Aleppo in October 1918. (In the background is the Hotel Baron, the favorite lodging place of T. E. Lawrence.) Faysal served as King of Syria until deposed by the French in 1920. Faysal later was installed by the British as King of Iraq.

(Right.) The last portrait of Faysal as King of Syria. (Far right.) A young woman, Naziq al-Abid, who joined the Syrian army and distinguished herself, defending Faysal's throne and Syrian independence against French cannons in the Battle of Maysaloun on July 24, 1920. (See National Activists.)

School children demonstrate during 1932 parliamentary elections (when Mohammad Ali al-Abid was president). Earlier, the French had passed a treaty of friendship with Syria. This treaty was vetoed by the National Bloc whose leaders asked their supporters to take to the streets. The disturbances reflected the power struggle between the National Bloc's Hashim al-Atasi and pro-French Prime Minister Haqqi al-Azm.

Syrian women protest the 1939 French decision to give a choice portion of the Syrian coast (the Sanjak of Alexandretta), including the port of Alexandretta and the historic Christian city of Antioch, to Turkey in exchange for Turkey's aggreement not to enter World War II on the side of Germany. For the previous four hundred years, Alexandretta had served as the port for Aleppo, Syria's primary trading city. Opinion polls established the strong preference of residents to remain part of Syria. Following the turnover, most residents fled to Syria, including numerous Christians. One result is that the "Patriarchs of Antioch" of several Christian denominations are today located, not in Antioch, but in Damascus.

Girl Scouts parading in Damascus to celebrate the Iraqi Revolution that ousted King Faysal II on July 14, 1958. (Faysal was the grandson of Faysal I who had served as the King of Syria following World War I.)

President Gamal Abd al-Nasser of Egypt in January 1958 meeting with a group of Syrian officers who came to Cairo to plead for Syria's merger with Egypt. He is shaking hands with Syria's Chief-of-Staff Afif al-Bizreh. To the left stands Nasser's right-hand-man Marshal Abd al-Hakim Amer and next to him is General Amin al-Hafez, who became president of Syria after the Baath revolution in March 1963.

Eleanor Roosevelt signing the guestbook at the Presidential Palace in Damascus in March 1953. This is during the era of President Adib al-Shishakli. Although Shishakli was a military strongman, he was the first Syrian president to be visited by three famous Americans: John Foster Dulles, Roosevelt, and Helen Keller. Standing next to Roosevelt is Abdullah al-Khani (see Diplomats), the director of protocol at the presidency.

parliamentarians, and political party leaders. Some of the individuals were not decision-makers, but they assumed senior government and party positions for long periods of time and therefore deserve to be mentioned.

This section does not include every person who assumed a senior government post in Syria over the past one hundred years, since many people quickly rose to power and just as quickly lost it, thereby leaving no lasting mark on Syrian political history.

Until the end of World War I in 1918, Syrian politicians served in the Ottoman government based in Istanbul. For nineteen months after the fall of the Ottomans, Syria was an independent monarchy. During this time (October 1918 - July 1920), politicians served the royal Hashemite court of King Faysal I, which was based in Damascus. From 1920 until 1946, Syrian politicians served in parliament and held other offices under the French. After independence in 1946, there were eight different governments until the Baath Party took power in a coup in 1963. Baath rule before

Parliament in Damascus, early 1950s. The Syrian Eagle (top of building) was adopted as a national symbol in 1945.

1970 is divided into two parts: the early years (1963-1966), and the radical regime of Salah Jadid (1966-1970). In 1970, Hafez al-Asad emerged as the uncontested Baath leader in the Corrective Movement, and in 2000 his son Bashar succeeded him.

The politicians of Syria faced numerous coups from 1946 onward. In all, there were nine successful coups from 1946 to 1970. There were eight failed coups during the same period, two carried out by the CIA from 1955 through 1958. The last coup attempt was by Rifaat al-Asad in 1984.

One surprising episode was the union with Egypt from 1958 to 1961. During the years of union, land reform and other socialist measures favored by the left were introduced to Syria. Egyptian President Gamal Abd al-Naser was an ally of the Soviet Union during these Cold War years, and the union cemented Syria's own alliance with the Soviets.

al-Abid, Mohammad Ali
(1868-1939)

Mohammad Ali al-Abid was born in Istanbul to a prominent Arab family in the Ottoman Empire. His father, Izzat Pasha al-Abid, was private advisor to Sultan Abdulhamid II and was considered one of the most influential Arabs in the imperial court at Istanbul. The young Abid studied law in Istanbul and began his career in the Ottoman Ministry of Foreign Affairs.

In January 1908, Sultan Abdulhamid appointed Abid Ottoman ambassador to the United States. He moved to Washington, serving until a coup took place in Istanbul later that summer, bringing a group of Ottoman officers known as the Committee of Union and Progress (CUP) to power. The officers fired all of the Sultan's associates, sending the Abid family into exile, and forcing Abdulhamid to relinquish all of his powers in 1909. Izzat Pasha and his son Mohammad Ali were exiled to Paris, where they remained until the Ottoman Empire collapsed in 1918.

The Abid family returned to Damascus in 1919, retired from political activity, and administered their various enterprises throughout the Arab world. Among other things, the Abid family owned the large Victoria Hotel in Damascus, and held shares in the British-owned Suez Canal Company in Egypt.

In 1928, Abid allied himself with the National Bloc, the leading anti-French movement in Syria, and became a friend of its president, Hashim al-Atasi. In 1930, under Atasi's urging, Abid made significant donations to the nationalist movement and provided subsidies to the National Bloc newspaper, *al-Ayyam*. In

Mohammad Ali al-Abid.

November 1931, the French called for national elections and Abid became a parliamentary deputy for Damascus. He then announced his candidacy for the presidency. He campaigned against his friend, Hashim al-Atasi, and won, becoming Syria's first president on July 11, 1932. The National Bloc recognized Abid as their leader and pledged to uphold his government. In August 1932, however, Abid appointed two French sympathizers, Haqqi al-Azm and Subhi Barakat, as prime minister and speaker of parliament respectively, thereby angering hard-line elements in the Bloc.

In 1933, he ratified an agreement with France that granted Paris long-term administrative rights over the Alawite and Arab Mountains, two regions that the French had declared autonomous in 1920. In exchange, France agreed to grant Syria a limited degree of autonomy. Abid argued that liberating parts of Syria would be better than keeping the entire country under occupation. The Bloc responded by calling for a nationwide strike and asking for the resignation of the president. Abid called on Taj al-Din al-Hasani, an unpopular yet smart politician, to create a cabinet and solve the prevailing crisis, causing further uproar in Bloc ranks.

The National Bloc kept all of Syria on strike for sixty days, crippling the economy, causing hundreds of deaths, and damaging the president's image in local and international circles. In 1936, after two months of hostility, France agreed to listen to nationalist worries and receive a Bloc delegation in Paris. By doing so, the French were effectively recognizing the parliamentary opposition to the Abid government and destroying what remained of Abid's credibility in Europe. In September 1936, the Bloc declared victory, having secured an agreement with France that guaranteed the complete independence of all Syrian lands in twenty-five years. Complete independence, the treaty claimed, would be achieved in 1961 (it actually took place fifteen years earlier in 1946).

In defeat, President Mohammad Ali al-Abid resigned from office, taking the blame for having failed to obtain such a concession from the French. He moved to Paris where he lived in self-imposed exile until his death in 1939. He was buried in Damascus at a state funeral attended by his immediate successor, President Hashim al-Atasi.

Sources:
Commins, David. *Historical Dictionary of Modern Syria* (1996).
Hakim, Yusuf. *Souriyya wa al-Intidab al-Faransi* (1966).
Itri, Abd al-Ghani. *Alam wa Mubdioun* (1999).
Khoury, Philip. *Syria and the French Mandate* (1987).
Khoury, Philip. *Urban Notables and Arab Nationalism* (1983).

Abu Ghuddah, Abd al-Fattah
(1917-1997)

Abd al-Fattah Abu Ghuddah was born and raised in Aleppo. He studied at the Academy of Islamic Studies in Aleppo and received advanced training in psychology and education at the al-Azhar Mosque in Egypt. During his years in Cairo (1944-1950), Abu Ghuddah met Sheikh Hasan al-Banna, the charismatic spiritual leader of the Egyptian Muslim Brotherhood. Under the sheikh's guidance, Abu Ghuddah joined the Egyptian Brotherhood.

Upon returning to Syria, Abu Ghuddah became a member in the Syrian Muslim Brotherhood and rose to prominence within Islamic circles in Aleppo. He became an instructor at the Academy in Aleppo, and in 1960, became an instructor of theology at Damascus University.

In 1962, Abu Ghuddah nominated himself for parliament, and following his victory, President Nazim al-Qudsi appointed him Mufti of Aleppo. He was opposed to the authoritarian policies of the Brotherhood leader, Issam al-Attar, claiming that he was unrestrained in his authority and consulted no one on political affairs. In 1962, Attar stepped down from the party leadership and Abu Ghuddah replaced him as superintendent general of the Muslim Brotherhood.

In 1966, he criticized the coup that brought Baath Party strongman Salah Jadid to power, appearing at Friday sermons to warn Syrians against the dangers of Jadid's "dictatorship." He rallied scholars around him, calling on them to boycott the state and voice their opposition to Jadid's "violent measures." He spoke out and wrote extensively asking for Jadid's downfall, claiming that he did not represent the people.

As a result, Abu Ghuddah was arrested and incarcerated in the remote Palmyra prison where he spent eleven months in captivity. In 1967, Jadid released all political prisoners in the wake of Syria's war with Israel. Abu Ghuddah was exiled to Saudi Arabia, where he taught at King Saud University. He also served as a visiting lecturer at the Um Durman Institute in Sudan.

Abu Ghuddah was opposed to the militarization of the Muslim Brotherhood, a group that emerged in the 1970s and 1980s in Egypt and Syria. In 1995, President Asad welcomed Abu Ghuddah back home on the condition that he refrain from political activity. At the age of eighty, the elderly sheikh returned to Syria and spent the remainder of his days in Aleppo. After Abd al-Fattah Abu Ghuddah's death in February 1997, Asad offered his condolences to the Abu Ghuddah family in what was seen as the first rapprochement between the Syrian president and the Muslim Brotherhood.

Sources:

Batatu, Hanna. *Syria's Peasantry: the Descendants of its Lesser Rural Notables and their Politics* (2000).
Bawab, Sulayman. *Mawsuat Alam Souriyya fi al-Qarn al-Ishreen*, Vol I (1999).
Ziser, Eyal. *Asad's Legacy* (2000).

Aflaq, Michel
(1901-1989)

Michel Aflaq was born to a Greek Orthodox family in Damascus. He studied history at the Sorbonne in Paris from 1928-1932 and returned to Syria to teach at the al-Tajheez School, an all-male public high school.

During his studies in France, Aflaq witnessed the evolution of the French Communist Party. He was attracted to its call for a classless society, equal distribution of wealth, and free education. On returning to Syria, Aflaq began to preach similar ideas in Damascus. Salah al-Bitar, another schoolteacher who had recently returned to Syria from studies at the Sorbonne, shared Aflaq's pan-Arabist and (many would argue) socialist vision. Sharing a similar vision, having studied together in France, and teaching at the same high school, Aflaq and Bitar found much to unite them. As early as 1943, they began to lead a group of socialist thinkers in Damascus, meeting with them on a regular basis at the Havana Café to exchange views and talk politics. In the summer of 1943, Michel Aflaq nominated himself for parliament as an independent deputy for Damascus, but he lost the election.

Michel Aflaq.

In April 1947, Aflaq and Bitar co-founded the Baath Party, preaching Arab unity, liberation from colonial rule, and social justice. The two men claimed that all of Syria's problems were the result of two things: the French occupation of Syria from 1920 to 1946 and the dominance of the Syrian urban elite over the country's social, political, and economic establishments. The peasants should rise up against the landowners, went their argument, and regain their rights as free citizens, as should workers in factories, professionals in the civil service, and officers in the armed forces. Aflaq and Bitar found an eager and receptive audience in young students, especially those from poor families in the Syrian countryside who were attracted to the socialist vision of both men. By the late 1940s, their influence had spread in Damascus and began to infiltrate Aleppo, Homs, Hama, and the Syrian Mountains.

Aflaq became the party's mentor and ideologue while Bitar took charge of conducting day-to-day politics. The second half of the 1950s witnessed an increasing number of Syrian youth, mainly cadets in the armed forces, joining the Baath Party. The two men gave free lessons on Baath ideology and founded a political daily newspaper called *al-Baath (Rebirth)*. Aflaq's first chance to test his party's popularity came during the Arab-Israeli War of 1948. Following an early Syrian defeat at the warfront, he called on party members to mobilize against the regime of President Shukri al-Quwatli, an urban landowner, claiming that it was corrupt, capitalistic, and responsible for the army's failure. Aflaq personally led marches and protest strikes against Quwatli, calling on him to resign from office. He wrote daily articles in *al-Baath*, criticizing the president and his prime minister, Jamil Mardam Bey, accusing them of purchasing arms at inflated prices and pocketing the difference. When his words became too strong, Mardam Bey closed his newspaper and had Aflaq arrested.

In April 1949, a military coup took place in Syria, toppling the regime of President Quwatli. Syria's new president, Husni al-Za'im, outlawed all political parties and arrested their leaders, claiming that Syria was still not ready for a multi-party democratic system. Za'im ordered Aflaq's arrest at the notorious Mezzeh prison, where he was forced to sign a pledge renouncing the Baath Party doctrine and promising to refrain from future political conduct.

When Za'im was overthrown by a military coup in August 1949, a group of civilian politicians came to power and elected Hashim al-Atasi, a veteran leader of the nationalist movement, as president of the republic. Atasi created a government of national unity and distributed posts to all parties in Syria, making Aflaq, as a representative of the Baath Party, minister of education. It was the first and last time he assumed any public office. Aflaq ran for parliament that same year, however, and along with Salah al-Bitar, suffered a defeat at the polls. Aflaq served as minister from August to December 1949. In 1951, another military regime came to power, headed by General Adib al-Shishakli. Aflaq extended his support to the new government, believing that Shishakli would appoint him minister, since the two men shared a common vision on imperialism and Arab nationalism. He was surprised, however, to see Shishakli outlaw all political parties, including the Baath, just as Za'im had done in 1949.

In protest, Aflaq and Bitar emigrated to Lebanon where they formed an opposition party to the Syrian government. In December 1952, while still in Beirut, they merged their party with the Arab Socialist Party of Akram al-Hawrani, a charismatic leader and a fiery orator who commanded paramount influence within Syria's rural districts. Hawrani was an early socialist whom Syria's poor regarded as a spiritual godfather. And having him on the Baath leadership, Aflaq believed, would enhance the party's presence in rural Syria. The three men remained in exile, coordinating opposition activities with other exiled politicians until a military coup toppled Adib al-Shishakli in February 1954 when civilian rule was restored in Syria.

In 1957, the Communist Party began increasing its power in Syria and began to pose a serious threat to the Baath leaders. To save their doctrine from collapse, the three leaders turned to Gamal Abd al-Nasser of Egypt, pleading for him to unite Egypt with Syria in order to save Syria from communist influence. Aflaq believed that if such a union between the two countries were to materialize, he would become *the* ideological mentor of the new republic, preaching Arabism to Egypt. He knew that since Nasser did not believe in political ideologies, he would put an end to the Communist Party, just as he had done with the Egyptian Communist Party in 1952.

Union was, in fact, created on February 1, 1958, but Aflaq received no position in the United Arab Republic (UAR). His colleague, Salah al-Bitar, however, became minister of national guidance in a union cabinet headed by Nasser himself, while Akram al-Hawrani became vice president of the republic. Aflaq, Bitar, and Hawrani co-authored a classic Baath booklet commemorating the union entitled, *Itihad Souriyya was Misr (Unity between Syria and Egypt),* published in 1958. That same year, he also wrote his classic *Ma'rakat al-Masir al-Wahid (Battle for One Destiny).*

Shortly after the establishment of union, however, Aflaq became increasingly critical of Nasser's authoritarian rule, claiming that the Egyptian leader had imposed a dictatorship over Syria and was no different from local dictators like Husni al-Za'im and Adib al-Shishakli. Finally, Aflaq, Bitar, and Hawrani lost faith in Nasser's leadership and moved into the opposition in 1960. In 1958, they had not even thought that Nasser would exclude them from the union that they had created. They supported the coup that brought down Nasser's government in Syria on September 28, 1961.

On March 8, 1963, the Military Committee of the Baath Party came to power in Damascus. It was composed of a group of young Baath officers (and a few outside the Baath Party) who opposed Aflaq's decision to break from the UAR. They outlawed all parties other than the Baath, closed newspapers, declared martial law, and exiled or arrested their opponents. The committee members were Hafez al-Asad, Abd al-Karim al-Jundi, Salah Jadid, and Mohammad Umran. All of them ostensibly were strong supporters of Nasser and wanted to restore him as president of the UAR. This was true although Nasser had outlawed all parties during the UAR, including the Baath, and appointed many of its members in Cairo, to keep them away from decision-making in Damascus. The officers distributed military posts among themselves, appointing Salah al-Bitar as prime minister, and Amin al-Hafez, a Baath officer who was an ally of Aflaq, as president of the republic.

Akram al-Hawrani, whose relations with the officer junta had soured, was expelled from the party and sent into exile. Michel Aflaq, however, was kept at his post as secretary-general of the Baath. Although he did not get along with the young officers, Aflaq went along with their policies, knowing perfectly well that, without army backing, he had no hope of assuming power. Theoretically, he now held the strongest post in Syria. The officers appointed him to the Revolutionary Command Council and made him chairman. For their part, the Baath officers, although opposed to Aflaq's actions, needed his name to enjoy pan-Arab and international legitimacy for the regime they set about creating. To the broader Arab public, Aflaq still personified the Baath and its true principals of Arab nationalism. Real power, however, lay in the hands of the Military Committee.

By the mid-1960s, however, the Baath Party was to divide, with an officer coalition on one front, and the civilian leadership of Aflaq on the other. The officers resented Aflaq's sophisticated approach to matters, while he despised their heavy-handed interference in state affairs. Aflaq shunned the officers' militarization of Syria, arguing that they had established a dictatorship, and called for more political freedoms.

A new generation of radical socialists who wanted to overthrow the existing order and establish themselves as alternative leaders challenged his position as the party's senior ideologue. In February 1966, the officers launched a second coup, relieving Salah al-Bitar of his duties, arresting President Amin al-Hafez, and banishing Aflaq from Syria, with orders never to return. The coup masterminds were Salah Jadid and Air Force Commander Hafez al-Asad.

Aflaq took up residence in Beirut, living in exile until 1968, when the Baath Party leadership in Iraq invited him to live in Baghdad upon reassuming power in Iraq. President Hasan al-Bakr appointed him secretary-general of the Iraqi Baath Party and spiritual godfather to the Iraqi regime. In September 1970, Aflaq clashed with the Iraqi leadership for failing to assist the Palestinians in their war with King Hussein of Jordan. Aflaq lobbied extensively for the Palestinian Liberation Organization (PLO) and its leader Yasser Arafat, prodding the Iraqi government for armed Iraqi intervention in Jordan to save the Palestinian commandos from a bloodbath. Bakr, however, refused to involve his troops in battle, and in disgust, Aflaq returned to a self-imposed exile in Lebanon and began to criticize the Baath government in Baghdad.

When the Lebanese Civil War broke out in Beirut in 1975, Aflaq made peace with the Iraqis and returned to Baghdad whereupon he embarked on publishing and writing on Baath ideology, but refrained from taking an active part in politics. Among his published works in the early 1970s are *Nuqtat al-Bidayya* (*The Starting Point*), a book about the Arab-Israeli War of 1967, published in 1971, *Al-Baath wa al-Wihda* (*The Baath and Unity*), published in 1972, and *Al-Baath wa al-Ishtirakiyya* (*The Baath and Socialism*), published in 1973. In 1975, he published his classic, *Al-Nidal did Tashweeh Harakat al-Thawra al-Arabiyya* (*The Struggle Against Distorting the Movement of Arab Revolution*).

In 1979, Aflaq befriended Iraq's new president, Saddam Hussein, and regained some of his previous influence over day-to-day politics in Baghdad. During the Iran-Iraq War (1980-1988), the Iranian mullahs of Tehran used Aflaq's presence in Baghdad to launch accusations against Saddam of being under the influence of Aflaq, whom they labeled "a Christian infidel."

When Aflaq died on June 24, 1989, Saddam Hussein claimed that, prior to his death, Aflaq had converted to Islam. When Saddam's regime was overthrown in March 2003, a group of Iraqi citizens, who were angry after many years of brutal dictatorship, attacked Aflaq's home in Baghdad, destroyed it, and burned his books. Michel Aflaq's grave was demolished and a statue of him in Baghdad was draped with the US flag before being destroyed by the mob.

Sources:

Aflaq, Michel. *Ma'rakat al-Masir al-Wahid* (1958).

Batatu, Hanna. *Syria's Peasantry: the Descendants of its Lesser Rural Notables and their Politics* (2000).

Commins, David. *Historical Dictionary of Modern Syria* (1996).

Devlin, John. *The Baath Party: a History from its Origins to 1966* (1976).

Elias, Joseph. *Aflaq wa al-Baath (Aflaq and the Baath)* (1991).

Hawrani, Akram. *Muzakarat Akram al-Hawrani* (2000).

Karkout, Zoukan. *Aflaq: al-Kitabat al-Ula ma Diarasa Jadida Li Sirat Hayatihi* (1993).

Mardini, Zuhayr. *Al-Ustaz: Qissat Hayat Michel Aflaq* (1988).

Moubayed, Sami. *Damascus Between Democracy and Dictatorship* (2000).

Seale, Patrick. *Asad: The Struggle for the Middle East* (1988).

Seale, Patrick. *The Struggle for Syria* (1961).

Ahmad, Ahmad Iskandar
(1944-1983)

Ahmad Iskandar Ahmad was born in Homs and studied Arabic literature at Cairo University in Egypt. He joined the Baath Party of Michel Aflaq and Salah al-Bitar and returned to Syria in 1963, shortly after the party came to power through a military coup. He worked as a journalist in the two state-run newspapers, *al-Thawra* and *al-Baath*. In 1966, Ahmad became editor-in-chief of both papers and was also appointed director of the Syrian Arab News Agency (SANA).

Ahmad then allied himself with Defense Minister Hafez al-Asad, who came to power in November 1970 and became president in March 1971. During the Arab-Israeli War of 1973, he wrote patriotic editorials in Syrian newspapers that caught the attention of President Asad, who appointed him minister of information in the cabinet of Prime Minister Mahmud al-Ayyubi on September 1, 1974.

Ahmad Iskandar Ahmad rose to an elevated standing in the 1970s. He was among the privileged few who had constant access to the president. He became Asad's friend, consultant, publicist, and image-maker. Ahmad was responsible for the massive propaganda campaign that helped engineer Asad's larger-than-life image in the late 1970s and early 1980s. It was his idea to have life-size pictures of the president plastered throughout the streets of Syria. Ahmad also ordered that statues of the president decorate every official building and to stand at the gates of every city throughout Syria. The president's picture became front-page material in daily newspapers and all his activities—which had become a national obsession—were covered in minute detail throughout the Syrian media. In many cases, according to Asad's biographer, Patrick Seale, Ahmad Iskandar Ahmad helped to boost Asad's image in a manner similar to what Mohammad Hasanein

Haykal did for President Gamal Abd al-Nasser's image in Egypt. Seale wrote, "the key to his (Ahmad's) success was his ability to catch the trend of Asad's thinking and prepare opinion for changes of policy."

In April 1975, Ahmad visited Lebanon and met President Sulayman Franjiyyieh in an attempt at controlling the civil disturbances that led to the Civil War. Along with then-Foreign Minister Abd al-Halim Khaddam, Ahmad struggled in vain to broker a cease-fire between the Maronite militias of Bashir Gemayel and the Palestinian forces of Yasser Arafat. In October 1978, he met with Tariq Aziz, the deputy prime minister of Iraq, in an attempt to resolve the festering hostility between the Baath Party governments in Damascus and Baghdad.

Ahmad Iskandar Ahmad's illustrious career abruptly ended, however, upon his death caused by brain cancer on December 29, 1983.

Sources:
Seale, Patrick. *Asad: Struggle for the Middle East* (1988).

al-Ajlani, Munir
(1912-2004)

Munir al-Ajlani studied law at the Sorbonne in Paris and obtained a degree in literature and linguistics. Upon completing his postgraduate degree in international law, he returned to Damascus to pursue a legal practice. He wrote frequently for the Damascus daily *al-Qabas* (*The Firebrand*) and founded his own newspaper, *al-Nidal* (*The Struggle*), with the attorney, Sami Kabbara.

In 1934, Ajlani joined the National Bloc, the leading anti-French movement in Syria, and in 1936 ran for parliament on the Bloc ticket. He nominated himself for parliament again in 1943, 1947, 1949, and 1954, winning each time. Once in parliament, Ajlani joined with Sayf al-Din al-Ma'mun, another prominent lawyer, and co-founded the National Youth, a paramilitary youth force modeled upon the Brown Shirts in Germany and the Black Shirts in Italy.

The National Youth aimed at protecting locals from French aggression and mobilizing support for the National Bloc. Its leaders were a group of young men who wanted to introduce the concept of disciplined and armed resistance to occupation. As long as the French were not permitting the creation of a Syrian Army, Ajlani claimed, the National Youth would have to serve as an alternative. He believed in the concept of mass politics and created a powerful network of young men to engage in marches, strikes, and rallies. National Youth members donned armbands showing a torch-bearing hand, similar to the infamous swastika that was being promoted in Nazi Germany at the time. Among the party's co-founders were the university professor Ahmad al-Samman, the National Bloc leader Fakhri al-Barudi, and the journalists Munir and Najib al-Rayyes. The

National Youth remained in charge of Syrian mass politics from 1936 to 1946 and was disbanded by its own leadership when the French occupation of Syria ended in 1946.

In 1939, Turkey annexed the Sanjak of Alexanderetta, territory in northern Syria that had once formed part of Ottoman-ruled Syria. Ajlani resigned from office to protest the National Bloc's inability to prevent the annexation. He became a member of the opposition, headed by Dr Abd al-Rahman Shahbandar, and engaged in anti-Bloc activity throughout the 1930s.

Munir al-Ajlani.

When agents of the French killed Shahbandar in 1940, Ajlani allied himself with Sheikh Taj al-Din al-Hasani, a hard-line opponent of the National Bloc. Ajlani married his daughter, Inaam, and when Hasani became president of the republic in 1941, he appointed him secretary-general of the Presidential Palace. The following year, Hasani appointed Ajlani minister of youth affairs in the cabinet of Prime Minister Husni al-Barazi. Hasani created the position exclusively for his son-in-law, and it was abolished when he left office in 1943 to become minister of social affairs.

In January 1943, President Hasani died and Ajlani returned to the fold of the National Bloc orbit. In October 1947, Prime Minister Jamil Mardam Bey, a National Bloc leader, appointed him minister of education. That same year, he was also voted into the Arab Language Assemblage, the highest international scientific authority in the field of Arab language and literature.

In the 1940s, Ajlani befriended King Abdullah of Jordan and called for union between Syria and the Hashemite governments in Baghdad and Amman. He advocated the Hashemite cause, and in 1949 Syria's new president, Husni al-Za'im, accused him of being an agent for Abdullah. Ajlani was arrested and the *al-Nidal* newspaper, for which he frequently wrote, was closed. When Za'im was ousted in August 1949, Ajlani was released by Syria's new leader, Hashim al-Atasi, and voted into the Constitutional Assembly that formulated a new constitution for Syria. In 1950, General Adib al-Shishakli, the de facto ruler of Syria, brought Ajlani to trial on the charge of attempting to topple Syria's republican regime and replace it with a Hashemite monarchy. Ajlani went to court and was declared innocent of the charges. When Shishakli came to power in 1951, Ajlani joined the opposition to his regime and was once again arrested for his views. He was released from jail when Shishakli was overthrown in February 1954. In November of that year, Ajlani became president of Damascus University, and in September 1955, became minister of justice in the independent cabinet of Prime Minister Sa'id al-Ghazi.

In the second half of the 1950s, however, Ajlani became increasingly alienated from the rising movement of socialism, headed by President Gamal Abd al-Nasser of Egypt. Ajlani joined a group of disgruntled politicians and sought to bring down the pro-Nasser and pro-USSR government of President Shukri al-Quwatli, who had returned to office in 1955. It was planned that a group of armed men, trained in Lebanon (by the anti-Nasser government of Kamil Sham'un) and funded by Hashemite Iraq, would occupy Damascus, dismiss all pro-Nasser officials, and force Quwatli to change his pro-Egypt and pro-USSR policies. Once all Nasserist elements were dismissed, Syria would unite with Hashemite Iraq. Prime Minister Sabri al-Asali would be dismissed, and Munir al-Ajlani would create a pro-Hashemite cabinet where Subhi al-Omari, an ex-officer in the Hashemite Army of the Arabian Desert, would become minister of defense.

The plan was funded from Baghdad by Crown Prince Abd al-Illah and Prime Minister Nuri al-Sa'id. Involved in the conspiracy were the Druze leader Hasan al-Atrash, a long-time ally of the Hashemites, Sami Kabbara, publisher of the *al-Nidal* newspaper, along with Adnan al-Atasi and his cousin Faydi al-Atasi, founding members of the pro-Hashemite People's Party. They had no intention, however, of ousting President Quwatli. He would be asked to endorse their measures and to keep his ceremonial post as president. If he refused, then he would be asked to step down. They had no intention of arresting or humiliating the man, since they recognized him to be the founding father of the independent Syrian state in 1946. Abd al-Hamid Sarraj, the pro-Nasser director of intelligence, foiled the plot prior to its implementation and had all of its leaders, including Ajlani, imprisoned and charged with high treason.

Munir al-Ajlani was fired from his post at Damascus University and expelled from the Arab Language Assemblage. He refused to hire an attorney and defended himself in court, receiving a standing ovation from an audience of Damascus University students who came to support their former professor. His defense proved futile, however, and a military tribunal sentenced him to death on the charge of treason. Three Arab leaders, King Faysal II of Iraq, King Hussein of Jordan, and President Kamil Sham'un of Lebanon, intervened on his behalf, and as a result, Ajlani's sentence was commuted to life imprisonment. During his imprisonment, Syria and Egypt merged to form the United Arab Republic (UAR), and the Hashemite monarchy in Baghdad, which had supported his career, was overthrown by military coup in July 1958. Ajlani was released from jail in 1961, following the dissolution of the UAR, but he refrained from any political activity.

When the Baath Party came to power in March 1963, its leaders pledged to restore the UAR and Ajlani was once again forced to flee Damascus. He went to Saudi Arabia and served as a private advisor to King Saud and his brother, King Faysal Ibn Abd al-Aziz. He also taught law at Riyadh University and became editor-in-chief of *al-Majala al-Arabiyya* (*The Arab Magazine*). Among his published works are *Tareekh al-Mamlaka al-Arabiyya al-Saudiyya* (*History of the Kingdom of Saudi Arabia*), and *Majmu'at Khitabat* (*Collection of Speeches*). He passed on in Saudi Arabia in 2004. His last visit to Syria was in 1963.

When asked by an interviewer about the "Iraq conspiracy" in 2000, forty-four years later, Munir al-Ajlani took a long pause and replied, "We were young—maybe we overdid it!"

Sources:
Babil, Nasuh. *Sahafa wa Siyasa fi Souriyya* (1987).
BBC Archives. "The Damascus Trial" February 26, 1957.
Khoury, Philip. *Syria and the French Mandate* (1987).
Moubayed, Sami. *Damascus Between Democracy and Dictatorship* (2000).
Moubayed, Sami. *The Politics of Damascus 1920-1946* (1999).
Rathmell, Andrew. *Secret War in the Middle East* (1995).
Interview with Dr Munir al-Ajlani (Beirut August 13, 1999; September 4, 1999).

Antaki, Naim
(1903-1971)

Naim Antaki, a Greek Orthodox Christian, studied law at the American University of Beirut (AUB) and opened a legal practice in his native Aleppo. He rose to fame for his skills as an attorney and became president of the Syndicate of Lawyers in 1936.

In 1932, Antaki became a member of the National Bloc, the leading anti-French movement in Syria. He attended the Bloc's founding conference in Beirut and allied himself to its president, Hashim al-Atasi. In 1936, Antaki accompanied Atasi on a diplomatic visit to Paris, where they negotiated the future of Syrian independence with the French government of Prime Minister Leon Blum. The two parties decided that Syria would become independent over a twenty-five year period in exchange for economic, military, and political concessions to France. The Syrian delegation, in turn, offered to support France if a war were to break out in Europe, as well as use of its air space and territory. The Bloc leadership returned to Syria in 1936 and elected Atasi as president of the republic. Antaki became secretary of the Ministry of Foreign Affairs, at the same time serving as director of the Bloc's Aleppo office. Antaki kept both posts until Atasi resigned from office in 1939, following France's failure to ratify the Treaty of 1936. He then became minister of foreign affairs and public works in the cabinet of Prime Minister Ata al-Ayyubi, holding office from March to August 1943.

In August 1943, Antaki ran for parliament on a Bloc ticket and won. He allied himself with the Bloc government of President Shukri al-Quwatli (1943-1949), and in 1945, Prime Minister Faris al-Khury appointed him on Syria's mission to the United Nations' founding conference in San Francisco. The Syrian delegation was to meet with member states in the Security Council and lobby support for the evacuation of French troops from Syria. In 1946, Antaki became deputy to Faris al-Khury, the president of the UN mission. Khury created a new government in April 1945 and appointed him minister of finance and public works.

In December 1946, following independence from France, Prime Minister Saadallah al-Jabiri appointed Antaki as Syria's first post-mandate minister of foreign affairs. During the Arab-Israeli War of 1948, Faris al-Khury summoned him back to the UN to attend the General Assembly sessions on Palestine. Following the War of 1948, Naim Antaki retired from politics and devoted the remainder of his years to his legal practice. He died in Beirut on December 15, 1971.

Sources:
Faris, George. *Man Hum fi al-`Alam al-Arabi?* (1957).
Hakim, Yusuf. *Souriyya wa al-Intidab al-Faransi* (1966).
Khoury, Philip. *Syria and the French Mandate* (1987).
Moubayed, Sami. *The Politics of Damascus 1920-1946* (1999).

Arslan, Adil
(1882-1954)

Prince Adil Arslan was born in the town of Aley on Mount Lebanon to an aristocratic Druze family closely allied to the Ottoman Empire. Arslan established himself as a dedicated supporter of the Ottomans, speaking out against the Arab Revolt that broke out in 1916, and refusing to follow the pan-Arab movement that was developing in the Arabian Desert.

When the Ottoman Empire collapsed in 1918, however, Arslan shifted his allegiance to the Hashemite family and became private advisor to King Faysal I, the new leader of Syria. He also served as advisor to Faysal's prime minister, Rida al-Rikabi, from October 1918 to January 1920. In July 1920, the French occupied Syria, overthrew the Faysal regime, and forced Arslan into exile. He fled to Amman and became political advisor to Prince Abdullah, the prince (later king) of the newly-established State of TransJordan. The British, who were the de facto rulers of Jordan, exiled him to Europe, claiming that the French government objected to his presence in Jordan.

In 1924, Prince Arslan co-founded the Syria-Palestine Congress, a grouping of Arab nationalists in exile who worked relentlessly to bolster Hashemite influence in the Middle East and Europe. The congress was based in Cairo and had an office in Geneva. It was funded and chaired by Prince Michel Lutfallah, a Lebanese banker who handled the financial fortunes of the Hashemite family. The Syrian-Palestinian Congress was vehemently pro-Hashemite, asking for the liberation of all Arab territories once under Ottoman control, and the creation of an Arab kingdom to be headed either by King Faysal or his brother, Prince Abdullah. He allied himself with Shukri al-Quwatli, another Syrian exile, and the two men toured Europe to raise financial and political support for the Hashemite cause. In future years, starting with the 1930s, both Arslan and Quwatli were to lose faith in the Hashemite family and would work to undermine their influence in Syria.

In 1931, Arslan was expelled from Egypt for his alleged anti-Italian activities. He moved to Baghdad and once again became advisor to King Faysal, who had become king of Iraq in 1921. In Iraq, Arslan built considerable commercial interests as the representative of a large British firm. In 1925, the Hashemite kingdom in Mecca was overthrown by King Abd al-Aziz who established the modern Kingdom of Saudi Arabia. Quwatli, who was close to the Saudi royals, introduced Arslan to the new king and Arslan befriended him, thereby immediately falling from grace in Amman and Baghdad. When forced to choose between King Abd al-Aziz and Prince Abdullah, who were vehement enemies, Arslan chose Abd al-Aziz. Both Quwatli and Arslan had grown disenchanted with the Hashemites and criticized their solid friendship with the British, accusing them of being too soft on British influence in the Arab world. Arslan moved to Jerusalem, where he worked with its mufti, Amin al-Husayni, another outspoken opponent of the Hashemites, in arousing anti-Hashemite sentiment and orchestrating anti-French and anti-British propaganda.

Arslan returned to Syria under a general French amnesty in 1936. He joined the National Bloc, the leading anti-French movement in Syria, and became minister of education in the cabinet of Prime Minister Jamil Mardam Bey. In October 1937, he became ambassador to Turkey and served as a liaison officer between President Hashim al-Atasi and Turkish President Kemal Ataturk. Arslan met frequently with Ataturk, prior to his death in 1938, to talk the Turkish leader out of annexing the Sanjak of Alexanderetta, territory in northern Syria that had once been part of the Ottoman Empire. When Ataturk died, his successor Ismet Innunu annexed the Sanjak in July 1939. Damascus closed the Syrian embassy in Ankara and recalled Arslan to Syria.

Arslan allied himself with Shukri al-Quwatli, who became president in 1943, and appointed him private advisor at the Presidential Palace. In September 1946, Husni Sabah, the president of Damascus University, resigned from office and Arslan became acting president. He held office until September 1947. From 1947 through 1949, he served as a deputy in the Syrian Parliament.

Prince Adil Arslan emerged during the Arab-Israeli War of 1948 as an ally of Chief of Staff Husni al-Za'im. In March 1949, Za'im came to power in Damascus and appointed Arslan as minister of foreign affairs. Syria's new president established secret channels with Israel and tried to negotiate a peace treaty with Prime Minister David Ben Gurion. He offered Israel a comprehensive peace deal in which embassies would be opened and relations would be normalized in exchange for American political and military aid to Syria. When a deal was almost ready after weeks of secret talks, Za'im called on Arslan and delegated him to meet with Israeli Foreign Minister Moshe Sharett to finalize the agreement. Arslan had not been informed of the talks and resigned from office in protest.

Arslan spent the remainder of his life in political seclusion, unable to regain power due to the stigma of his alliance with Husni al-Za'im. Future governments in Syria criticized the Za'im regime and accused all those who had worked with him of having contributed to the militarization of Syrian politics.

Prior to his death in 1954, Arslan published a book entitled, *Muzakarat al-Ameer Adil Arslan an Ahd al-Za'im Husni al-Za'im* (*Memoirs of Prince Adil Arslan on the Era of General Husni al-Za'im*). In his memoirs, Arslan attempted to justify his collaboration with Za'im as having been aimed at preventing Za'im from any excesses and deviations rather than in Arslan's personal pursuit of power. He was harshly critical of Za'im and shed light on the first-ever round of Syrian-Israeli talks of 1949, claiming that he was not involved in the behind-the-scenes discussions with Ben Gurion. Adil Arslan's other book, *Muzakarat al-Ameer Adil Arslan* (*Memoirs of Prince Adil Arslan*), is a four-volume work covering the various stages of his career, compiled by the Syrian academic Yusuf al-Ibish.

Sources:
Arslan, Adil. *Muzakarat al-Ameer Adil Arslan an Ahd al-Za'im Husni al-Za'im* (1954).
Arslan, Adil. *Muzakarat al-Ameer Adil Arslan* (1972).
Commins, David. *Historical Dictionary of Modern Syria* (1996).
FO 371/2142 vol 20849, May 6, 1937.
Ismail, Thuraya. *Myths and Realities* (2002).
Moubayed, Sami. *Damascus Between Democracy and Dictatorship* (2000).

al-Arsuzi, Zaki
(1908-1968)

Zaki al-Arsuzi was born into a notable Alawite family in the province of Alexanderetta, fertile territory in northern Syria (now part of Turkey). He studied philosophy at the Sorbonne in Paris, and after graduation, returned to teach at local high schools in his native Antioch in 1931.

In August 1933, along with a group of fifty radical Arab nationalists, Arsuzi founded the League of National Action in the Lebanese mountain town of Quarna'il. The League was a pioneering organization established by a second generation of Arab politicians, aged between twenty-five and thirty at the time, who were determined on ridding the Arab region from foreign influence. Unlike other political establishments that were dominated by landowners and Ottoman-trained politicians, the League of National Action was comprised of young professionals: professors, lawyers, and civil servants who were not living off their family estates but rather leading career-focused lives. They all had Western educations, having studied in Europe, the United States, or American universities in the Middle East. The League of National Action achieved high acclaim in 1933 but petered out with the early death of its founder and charismatic leader, Abd al-Razzaq al-Dandashi, in 1935. Between the years 1932 to 1939, Arsuzi served as president of the League of National Action branch office in Antioch.

In 1939, Zaki al-Arsuzi's anti-French activities became more intense when Paris decided to give Turkey the right to annex the Sanjak of Alexanderetta in return for Turkish support of France in its upcoming war against Nazi Germany. Arsuzi spearheaded the anti-French movement in Antioch and instigated violent marches protesting the Franco-Turkish deal. The French responded by closing the League office in Antioch and ordering his arrest.

When Turkey annexed Alexanderetta in July 1939, Arsuzi fled the Sanjak to Iraq where he briefly taught in schools. He then moved to Damascus and taught philosophy in its high schools. His ideas greatly resembled those of the Damascus schoolteacher, Michel Aflaq. Both men sought to overthrow the existing order of Syria's landowning elite and replace it with a socialist state. They called for an end to European control of the Arab world, preached pan-Arabism, and advocated a secular, socialist, and classless society.

In 1947, Aflaq joined Salah al-Bitar, another schoolteacher, to found the Baath Party. Arsuzi protested, claiming that the ideas were his and that the two men had "stolen" his views. The struggle between the two men continued for the next ten years. By the mid-1950s, due to the lack of steel in his character, Aflaq began to lose popularity within conservative circles of the Baath Party, while Arsuzi's following gradually increased in the armed forces and within the increasingly leftist intellectual circles as well.

Two of his most prominent followers were Wahib al-Ghanim, a prominent doctor, and Hafez al-Asad, an air force pilot. Arsuzi spent the 1950s and early 1960s teaching at high schools while promoting his own version of the Baath Party. Arsuzi's Baath Party was utopian and more radical than that of Aflaq and Bitar. The two men were willing to settle for a semi-socialist state with mild policies of Arab nationalism, whilst Arsuzi adopted an "all or nothing" approach.

In March 1963, the Military Committee of the Baath Party, of which Asad was a member, came to power in Syria and appointed Aflaq as ideological mentor of the Baath Party government. Asad and his allies did not call on Arsuzi to serve as mentor, fearing that this would anger Aflaq's numerous civilian associates in Syria and the Arab world. In order to earn credit, Arsuzi's students needed Aflaq's name, which, to the entire Arab world, personified the image of the Baath. The aging Arsuzi, however, did not object.

In 1966, an internal Baath Party coup took place in which Aflaq and his team were overthrown by a group of officers and exiled from Syria. Two of Arsuzi's students, Hafez al-Asad and Salah Jadid, created a new regime and hailed him as the true ideologue of the Baath Party. From 1966 until his death in 1968, Arsuzi served as ideological mentor to both Asad and Jadid. He did not live long enough, however, to see the two men quarrel and to witness Asad's rise to power in 1970.

After becoming president in 1971, Asad declared that Arsuzi was "one of the greatest Syrians of his day and the first to conceive of the Baath as a political movement." During his career, Zaki al-Arsuzi published several philosophical, historical, and political works. Among his most acclaimed books are *Al-Umma al-Arabiyya* (*The Arab World*) and *Mashakiluna al-Qawmiyya* (*Our Nationalist Problems*), both published in Damascus in 1958.

Sources:
Arsuzi, Zaki. *Mashakiluna al-Qawmiyya* (1958).
Commins, David. *Historical Dictionary of Modern Syria* (1996).

al-Asad, Bashar
(1965-)

Bashar al-Asad was born and raised in Damascus. His father, Hafez al-Asad, launched a coup in November 1970 and became president of the republic in March 1971, when the young Asad was only five years old. Asad studied medicine at Damascus University and specialized in ophthalmology at St. Mary's Hospital in the United Kingdom.

In January 1994, just three months short of completing his residency, the young Asad returned to Syria to attend the funeral of his brother, Basil, who had died in a car accident. Basil, who was being groomed for the presidency, had been an active officer in the Syrian Army and a close confidant of his father. One month after Basil's death, President Asad called on the young doctor to assume the responsibilities of his late brother.

From 1994 until 2000, Dr Asad led an anti-corruption campaign in Syria that led to the firing of Prime Minister Mahmud al-Zu'bi, Minister of Transportation Mufid Abd al-Karim, and Saleem Yassin, the deputy prime minister for economic affairs. Other bureaucrats who had used public office to amass riches were also fired from the civil service and brought to trial on charges of corruption.

In March 2000, Bashar al-Asad helped engineer the ousting of the cabinet of Prime Minister Zu'bi, which had been in office since 1987, blaming it for Syria's economic depression. Asad then handpicked the governor of Aleppo, Mohammad

Mustapha Miro, a reportedly hard-working civil servant, for the premiership and helped choose the new ministers for what was described as "a cabinet of economic reform."

In the one year prior to his father's death, Asad toured Arab capitals to familiarize himself with their leaderships. He visited Saudi Arabia, Oman, Kuwait, Lebanon, and Jordan. President Asad put him in charge of the Lebanese "portfolio," a sensitive task that included handling all negotiations, deals, and relations with neighboring Lebanon and its politicians. In the West, Dr Asad paid a visit to President Jacque Jacques Chirac of France and received red-carpet treatment at the Elysee Palace.

Domestically, Dr Asad embarked on a campaign to increase his popularity among citizens at home, becoming highly accessible in public and paying surprise visits to numerous cities, including Aleppo, to mingle with the public and listen to their worries. Asad pledged to modernize Syria, and in March 1999, introduced the Internet. One year later, in February 2000, he authorized cellular phones in Syria.

On June 10, 2000, President Hafez al-Asad died in Damascus. Immediately, his followers rallied around Bashar al-Asad, promoting him in military rank and appointing him commander-in-chief of the Syrian Army. A few hours following the president's death, the Syrian Parliament met and amended Article 83 of the Constitution, lowering the age limit to assume the presidency and thereby enabling Dr Asad to run for presidential office. By law, a presidential candidate had to be forty years old and Asad was only thirty-four. The amendment was approved, and on July 17, 2000, Bashar al-Asad was sworn in as president of the republic. He was the youngest person to become the president of Syria since the republic was created in 1932.

President Asad immediately began work in earnest on his reform campaign; loosening bureaucratic laws, raising salaries by 25% in 2000 and by 20% in 2002. The new president issued a general amnesty, releasing 700 prisoners from the outlawed Muslim Brotherhood, some of whom had spent up to twenty years in prison for their attempts to topple his father's government in 1982. From 2000 to 2005, Asad released an additional 900 prisoners and closed down the notorious and very symbolic Mezzah prison first built by the French, and which had housed political dissidents since the 1940s. Asad's first two years in office were marked by two dominating topics in foreign affairs: the presence of Syrian troops in Lebanon and the al-Aqsa Intifada (uprising) in the occupied Palestinian territories that began in September 2000.

In November 2000, the Maronite patriarch of Lebanon, Mar Nasrallah Boutros Sfeir, began to speak out against the 35,000 Syrian troops stationed in Lebanon, demanding that they withdraw from Lebanon as stipulated by the Taif Accord of October 1989. The issue, a virtual taboo almost unheard of during the late Asad's

Bashar al-Asad.

lifetime, became a pressing subject in Lebanon and Syria as well. At first, Asad tried to ignore it, but when the anti-Syrian movement increased, he began to redeploy his troops in June 2001, April 2002, and February 2003.

Asad also tried to appease Christian complaints by allowing for the return to Lebanon of ex-President Amin Gemayel, who had been in self-imposed exile since 1988. In March 2002, Asad made another gesture of goodwill toward the disgruntled Lebanese by paying a surprise visit to Beirut, becoming the first Syrian president to do so since 1956. He visited Beirut once again in the end of March 2002 to attend an Arab League summit.

In addition, President Asad kept a visible distance from the Lebanese parliamentary elections in November 2000, where many of Syria's primary allies, including Prime Minister Saleem al-Hoss, Beirut chief Tammam Salam, and Syria's war-time ally, Elie Hobeika, suffered humiliating defeats at the polls. Asad also refrained from taking part in the on-going feuds between President Emile Lahhoud and Prime Minister Rafic al-Harriri, dismissing them as domestic issues that concerned Lebanon alone and had nothing to do with Syria.

President Asad tried to show that, during his term, Syria would handle Lebanese affairs in a manner distinctly different from the past. This was made clear in his inauguration where he acknowledged, "We consider our relationship with Lebanon an example of a relationship that should exist between two brotherly countries. But this example is not yet perfect and still needs great efforts in order to be ideal and to achieve the joint interests of both countries in a way that responds to their respective ambitions."

On September 28, 2000, the Palestinian Intifada broke out at the Aqsa Mosque in Jerusalem. The Palestinians revolted against Israel, protesting a provocative visit carried out by Ariel Sharon to the Aqsa Mosque, a holy site to all Muslims. Asad backed the Palestinians by channeling funds to the occupied territories and extending political support to several of the Palestinian resistance movements based in Damascus. Most notable among Asad's allies were Hamas and Islamic Jihad, two resistance movements that had carried out dozens of attacks in Israel since September 2000 and had political and media bases in Damascus.

In Lebanon, Asad was allied with the Islamic resistance of Hizbullah, a Shiite guerrilla force that had originally received wholehearted support from the late President Asad. In May 2000, Hizbullah had liberated occupied South Lebanon.

Syria's miscalculation in backing the renewal of the mandate of Lebanese President Emile Lahhoud in 2004 angered the international community. Backed by the USA and France, the United Nations passed resolution 1559 that called on Syria to withdraw its troops from Lebanon.

The assassination of Lebanon's prime minister, Rafic al-Harriri, on February 14, 2005, further exacerbated anti-Syrian sentiment in Lebanon, where the masses took to the streets and called on the Syrian Army to leave. Without evidence, members of the opposition accused Syria of having assassinated Harriri because, late in 2004, he had quarreled with Damascus over the renewal of Lahhoud's presidency. He had resigned from office and was replaced, with the approval of Syria, with the pro-Syrian prime minister, Omar Karameh. In response to the accusations, an estimated one million pro-Syrian demonstrators, headed by Hizbullah's leader, Hasan Nasrallah, paraded in Beirut in favor of Damascus and Bashar al-Asad. On March 5, 2005, Asad gave a speech before parliament announcing his army's withdrawal from Lebanon, in compliance with resolution 1559. The last of the Syrian troops, who had first entered Lebanon in 1976, completely evacuated the country on April 26, 2005.

At home, Asad's alliance with the Popular Front for the Liberation of Palestine (PFLP), the Democratic Front for the Liberation of Palestine (DFLP), Hamas, and Islamic Jihad strained his relationship with the United States. US President George W. Bush, who came to power in 2001, declared that all of these groups were "terrorist" organizations, but Asad defended them as "freedom fighters" and constantly drew parallels between the Palestinian resistance to Israel and the French resistance to Nazi occupation in World War II.

Israel responded to Syria's alliance with the Palestinian resistance and Hizbullah by launching an air raid on a Syrian radar station in Lebanon in April 2001. Asad, however, continued to back the Lebanese guerrillas in South Lebanon and refused to expel the Palestinian resistance from Syria, despite heavy pressure from Washington.

In September 2001, Asad demonstrated solidarity with the US following the terrorist attacks on Washington and New York City that were carried out by the Saudi-born terrorist Osama Bin Laden. Asad pledged to be part of the international coalition against terrorism. Syria, he claimed in numerous press interviews, had suffered from Islamic fundamentalism and terrorism in the early 1980s when the Muslim Brotherhood had tried to topple the government and, therefore, would be the first to stand up to Islamic fundamentalism and terrorism. In October 2001, as a result of her cooperation in the war on terrorism, Syria was voted in for a two-year term as one of the ten rotating members of the Security Council at the UN.

At home, during the first fourteen months of his presidency, Bashar al-Asad proved to be a moderate liberal who quietly overturned more than forty years of socialist nationalization legislation. Asad passed laws allowing for political publications other than those run by the ruling Baath Party. He also authorized the opening of private banks, thereby ending a state monopoly over the banking sector that dated back to 1963. Furthermore, Asad permitted the privatization of secondary and higher education.

For the first time in Syrian history, private universities were permitted in Syria. In 2002, three schools were opened: Kalamoun University, the Higher Institute of Business Administration (HIBA), and Syrian Virtual University (SVU). Kalamoun University was located in a small town near Damascus. The university offers a modern education in all fields, including international relations, diplomacy, and political science, which, until 2002, had been restricted to the Baath-administered Department of Political Science at Damascus University. HIBA provides a university education, at all levels, in business studies. Meanwhile, the SVU introduced Syrian students to online academic programs in affiliation with leading US universities such as Harvard and Georgetown.

President Bashar al-Asad has also worked for the return of Syrian expatriates, creating a Ministry for Expatriate Affairs dedicated to this end in December 2001. He promised his people to "wait and see, I will work so hard so that every Arab comes to wish he were a Syrian!"

Sources:
President Bashar al-Asad's inaugural speech given at the Syrian
Parliament on July 17, 2000.

al-Asad, Hafez
(1930-2000)

Hafez al-Asad was born in the village of Qirdaha in the Syrian Mountains and raised in the coastal city of Lattakia. He entered the Air Force Academy in Aleppo and graduated in 1955.

In 1947, while still a student, Asad became a member of the Baath Party of Michel Aflaq and Salah al-Bitar. It was a party that preached Arab nationalism, unity, and called for the establishment of a socialist state in Syria. He also joined the movement of Arab nationalism that President Gamal Abd al-Nasser of Egypt headed in the 1950s.

When Syria and Egypt merged to form the United Arab Republic (UAR) in February 1958, Captain Asad was stationed in Egypt as part of an exchange program between the armies of both countries. During his years in Cairo, Asad and four other officers, Major Salah Jadid, Major Ahmad al-Meer, Lieutenant Colonel Mohammad Umran, and Captain Abd al-Karim al-Jundi, founded the Military Committee of the Baath Party. It was a secret junta of young officers ostensibly aimed at preserving the UAR and steering Syria toward a hard-line policy of Arab nationalism.

On September 28, 1961, the UAR was dissolved by a military coup launched by officers in the Syrian Army, and Asad was arrested in Egypt. Authorities in Cairo feared that he, too, was involved in the conspiracy against the UAR. Investigations proved him not guilty, and he was deported to Syria in 1962, having spent forty-four days in prison.

At home, the new administration of Nazim al-Qudsi, fearing Asad's overt unionist tendencies, had him discharged from the Syrian Army. For a short period in 1962, Asad was assigned to (but never attended) a civilian job at the Department of Maritime Transportation at the Ministry of Economy. He then began plotting with the other members of the Military Committee on launching a coup to seize power from President Qudsi. The party members were influenced by the coup that took place in Iraq on February 8, 1963 and led to the killing of General Abd al-Karim Qasim. It was carried out by a group of Baath Party officers, and Asad hoped that he and his comrades could do the same in Syria. On March 8, 1963, he played an instrumental role in overthrowing the regime of President Qudsi. Asad captured the Dumayr air base east of Damascus where the entire air force was stationed. Collectively, the officers reinstated themselves in the Syrian Army. Asad was promoted from captain to lieutenant general, appointed commander of the Dumayr air base, and also became a member of the Revolutionary Command Council (RCC).

For the next three years, internal strife characterized the Baath Party government of President Amin al-Hafez. Two factions developed within the party, one revolving around the president and the party founders, Michel Aflaq and Salah al-Bitar, and the other around the military wing of Asad and his ally, Salah Jadid. Aflaq and Bitar wanted to demilitarize the state while Asad and Jadid wanted to impose Arabism on foreign affairs and socialism on domestic politics. In later years, Asad recalled saying, "We came to distrust their commitment to the Baathist ideals we had grown up with. We felt they had been trading slogans." As a result of his alliance with Jadid, Asad was appointed commander of the Syrian Air Force and promoted to major general in December 1964.

On February 23, 1966, the latter faction overpowered the first when Asad and Jadid launched a second coup d'etat and arrested President Amin al-Hafez. The party founders, Michel Aflaq and Salah al-Bitar, were exiled from Syria and the civilian, Baathist Dr Nur al-Din al-Atasi, was appointed president of the republic. Real power, however, was centralized in the hands of Asad and Jadid and their respective officer factions. The latter became deputy secretary-general of the Baath Party and Asad became minister of defense.

From here, further problems rocked the Baath Party government. A rivalry over leadership developed between Asad and Jadid, and the Arab-Israeli War of

1967 aggravated the conflict between them. Asad blamed Jadid for the defeat, while Jadid accused him of wanting to overthrow the regime. Asad slowly began to challenge Jadid's authority by dismissing pro-Jadid officers from the armed forces and replacing them with his own loyalists. In the process, Mustapha Tlas, a loyal friend from the Air Force Academy, became chief of staff. Asad also dismissed the editors of Syria's two newspapers, *al-Thawra* and *al-Baath*, for their allegiance to Jadid and replaced them with more reliable figures who would serve his interests. On November 16, 1970, Asad launched what he labeled a "Correction Movement," overthrowing both Atasi and Jadid and sending them to the notorious Mezzeh prison in Damascus, where they remained until their deaths in the 1990s.

For the next four months, Asad ruled Syria through the post of prime minister and appointed Ahmad al-Khatib, a civilian member of the Baath Party, as ceremonial head of state. In his slow and meticulous manner, Asad gradually affirmed his grip on the affairs of state, then called for a plebiscite to elect him to the post of president of the republic in March 1971. His ascendancy was welcomed within Syria, coming after a period characterized by intra-Baath strife, coups and counter-coups under former presidents Amin al-Hafez (1963-1966) and Nur al-Din al-Atasi (1966-1970).

Asad appointed General Abd al-Rahman Khlayfawi, a veteran Baathist, to form a government and strove to create jobs for the unemployed. Some of his earliest measures were a wage increase, a pension for workers, and an extensive program of infrastructure including the construction of roads, hospitals, and dams, all of which created thousands of jobs for the unemployed throughout the 1970s.

Asad launched the Arab-Israeli War of 1973, in collaboration with President Anwar al-Sadat of Egypt, which helped boost both mens' images among their compatriots and elevated their regional and international stature. The Sinai Peninsula (occupied by Israel in 1967) was restored to Egypt and Qunaitra, the principal village in the occupied Golan Heights (also occupied in 1967), was restored to Syria.

In foreign policy, Asad's era was marked by a shift toward Saudi Arabia in the mid-1970s, bridging the gap created during the years of Salah Jadid. To show his good faith toward King Faysal of Saudi Arabia, Asad closed an anti-Saudi radio station in Damascus that had defamed the Saudi royals since the 1960s. His alliance with Saudi Arabia coincided with a complete break with Egypt following President Sadat's visit to Jerusalem in 1977, and the signing of the Camp David Peace Accord with Israel in 1978. Asad remained on bad terms with Egypt until he allied himself with Sadat's successor, President Husni Mubarak, following the Persian Gulf War of 1991.

His long-time relationship with King Hussein of Jordan was troubled and uneasy. In September 1970, he clashed with Hussein when the latter launched a war on the Palestinian Liberation Organization (PLO) that was based in Amman. Asad refused to engage his own air force in combat but Syrian tanks did cross the border into Jordan, bearing the PLO insignia. They supplied the Palestinian fighters with arms and ammunition, then returned to Syria, reportedly under pressure from the USSR and President Nasser of Egypt. Asad then invited PLO Chairman Yasser Arafat to set up base in Damascus in 1971-1973. In a letter to the Syrian government, Arafat wrote, "I shall never forget how our eminent brother Abu Sulayman (as Asad was popularly called in Arabic in the 1970s and 1980s), infused new vig- or in us, and despite all the objections emanating here and there, gave us some arms and person- ally directed us to preserve our course." Arafat then moved to Lebanon to launch a war against Israel from the Lebanese-Israeli border.

Hafez al-Asad.

In October 1973, Asad's relations with Amman plummeted when King Hussein refused to take part in the Syrian-Egyptian offensive against Israel. Not only did Hussein refuse, but he also admitted in an interview with BBC years later that he went to Israel in secret, days before the war began, to warn Prime Minister Golda Meir against the Syrian-Egyptian offensive. This led to a permanent distrust between Asad and Hussein. In the 1980s, Syria accused Hussein of funding the Muslim Brotherhood, who were bent on toppling the Baath government. In 1994, Syria accused the king of dividing Arab ranks by signing a separate peace deal with Israel.

Asad took the initiative toward mending relations with Jordan by attending Hussein's funeral in February 1999 and supporting the ascent of his son, King Abdullah II, to the throne in Amman. To show his goodwill toward the new monarch, Asad signed a treaty with Abdullah II that offered to relieve Jordan's prolonged and chronic water shortage. In 1999, he began to pump 750 cubic meters of drinking water per day from the southern town of Daraa to Jordan and signed other economic and political deals with the new king.

Most of Hafez al-Asad's career, however, was focused on the Lebanese Civil War that broke out in Beirut in April 1975. He traveled to Lebanon once in 1975 to meet President Sulayman Franjiyyieh, and relied on his foreign minister, Abd al-Halim Khaddam, to deputize on his behalf in working for a cease-fire during the early war years. On June 1, 1976, Asad ordered his troops into Lebanon to fight the PLO of Yasser Arafat. The Syrian Army stormed through Lebanon and turned the tide in the Lebanese Civil War. Asad allied himself with the Maronite leader Pierre Gemayel, whose militia, the Phalange Party, had led a street war against Arafat and wanted to expel the PLO from Beirut. Asad accused Arafat, whom he had protected in Amman, of trying to destabilize Lebanon, and under no circumstances could Syria afford having a destabilized regime in Beirut. This would be a security problem for Syria. Asad also feared that a wild and uncontrolled Lebanon, under the leadership of Yasser Arafat, would allow Israel to launch a new war in the Middle East (which happened in the summer of 1982). He fought against Arafat in the 1970s, and then accused him of trying to destabilize Syria as well by funding an Islamic uprising in Hama.

In June 1982, however, the festering relations between Asad and his former allies reached the breaking point when the Phalange leader, Bashir Gemayel (the president-elect of Lebanon), overtly allied himself with Israel and both supported and facilitated General Ariel Sharon's invasion of Beirut. The Israeli Army encircled both the PLO and Syrian Army in West Beirut, and drove the Syrians into the Beqqa Valley. In August 1982, Asad withdrew his troops from Beirut under a US-brokered agreement negotiated by US envoy Philip Habib. Having relied on Syria to weaken the PLO, Gemayel now wanted to get rid of the Syrian Army as well, and establish Maronite hegemony while discarding Lebanon's Arab Muslim identity. Gemayel was killed in September 1982 and his brother, Amin Gemayel, was elected president instead. Gemayel shocked the Arab world and signed a peace deal with the Israeli government of Menahem Begin on May 17, 1983.

To counterbalance the Phalange-Israeli alliance, Asad allied himself with the Maronite leader Elie Hobeika (a former Israeli-trained military and intelligence leader of the Phalange), the Shiite leader Nabih Berri, and the Druze leader Walid Jumblatt. All of them had warring militias of their own and they journeyed to Damascus in December 1985 to bury the hatchet and join in Asad's battle to bring down Gemayel's May 17 Agreement with Israel.

In March 1989, Prime Minister Michel Aoun, a declared anti-Syrian statesman who had been appointed by Gemayel before the latter's departure from office in 1988, declared a "War of Liberation" against the Syrian Army in Lebanon. The war lasted until October 1990, when Syria was able to overpower Aoun and send him into exile in France. The Syrian Army restored calm by disarming the warring militias, and Asad propped up the pro-Syrian statesman, Elias Hrawi, as president of Lebanon. Aoun's expulsion from Beirut marked Asad's ultimate triumph in the Lebanese Civil War. The Syrian president had called for a peace conference in Saudi Arabia in October 1989, where Lebanese politicians gathered and agreed to end the war and redistribute power between Maronites and Muslims on a more equal basis.

Asad then funded and supported the Hizbullah guerrillas in their war of liberation against Israel, which was still occupying all of South Lebanon when the civil war ended in 1990. On May 24, 2000, less then one month before his death, Asad witnessed the evacuation of Israeli troops from South Lebanon, an achievement that Arab political circles largely attributed to him.

During his thirty-year tenure as president of Syria, Hafez al-Asad became a tactical ally of Iran and a vehement enemy of President Saddam Hussein of Iraq. Baghdad's welcome of Asad's enemies, ex-President Amin al-Hafez and Baath founder Michel Aflaq in 1966, led to permanent animosity between the Syrian and Iraqi wings of the ruling Baath Party. Increased alienation developed after the Iran-Iraq War (1980-1988). During this conflict, Syria backed the Iranians against the Iraqi president.

When the Iranian Revolution took place in February 1979, Asad supported the rise of Ayatollah Khomeini and antagonized the leaders of Iraq. Iran showed appreciation for Asad's alliance. It funded and supported the Hizbullah guerrillas in South Lebanon, who were reliable allies and proxies of Asad in his war against Israel. His alliance with the Khomeini regime stemmed primarily from his hatred of the earlier regime of Shah Mohammad Rida Pehlavi (who was a staunch ally of Israel). Khomeini also needed a regional power to support his war with Saddam Hussein. This Iranian-Syrian honeymoon carried on in the 1980s and 1990s, and continued even after Asad's death in 2000.

Asad ruled in the midst of public optimism throughout the 1970s. In 1984, he suffered a heavy stroke and his doctors doubted whether he would survive. His brother, Rifaat al-Asad, a key figure in the government and commander of a state-sponsored militia, tried to seize power in Damascus. The officers of the Baath Party, who had risen to power with Asad in 1970, split in two factions: one rallying around Rifaat and the other around the ailing president. In February 1984, Syria seemed on the verge of a bloody civil war, with armed troops stationed on the corners of every street throughout Damascus. On March 30, 1984, Rifaat ordered his troops into the Syrian capital, with clear orders to seize power. Patrick Seale, the British author who met Asad several times to write his book, *Asad: the Struggle for the Middle East*, described the situation, saying, "Had the two sides come to blows in the capital, the destruction would have been very great and the regime's image irreparably tarnished—that is, if it survived at all." Asad dressed in full-military uniform, and accompanied only his eldest son, Basil, drove through Damascus to confront his rebellious brother. When the two men came face-to-face, Asad said, "You want to overthrow the regime? Here I am, I am the regime!"

On May 28, with the help of his allies in the Kremlin, Asad dispatched seventy senior officers in the Syrian Army (including Rifaat) for a cooling-off period in the USSR. One by one, Asad called on the loyal ones to return, and kept Rifaat abroad. He remained in exile in Spain until 1993, when Asad called him back home to attend the funeral of his mother.

From the 1990s onward, Asad increased his economic liberalization and permitted marginal freedoms. The government encouraged foreign investments, while it loosened—and in some cases lifted altogether—regulations on commerce. The dissolution of the USSR in December 1991 left Asad without an international ally. His reliance on the USSR for more than twenty years had dictated his foreign policy and forced him to confront the United States.

In 1979, the Carter administration declared Syria a sponsor of international terrorism, but Asad—a noted tactician—avoided US sanctions by playing cat-and-mouse with Washington. He was a declared opponent of the United States, but, at times, he did not mind working with the Americans to achieve what he believed was in Syria's best national interest. In the 1980s, he helped rescue US hostages in Iran and Lebanon, and in 1991, allied Syria with the Bush administration to liberate Kuwait from Iraqi occupation. Following the Gulf War, the United States, a long-time enemy, became a potential ally for Syria. Asad's involvement in Operation Desert Storm, and his participation in the Madrid Peace Conference with Israel in October-November 1991, were all signals that he wanted to cooperate with the administration of President George Bush.

In 1996, the Syrian-Israeli talks went into effect (under US auspices), with Syrian Chief of Staff Hikmat Shihabi meeting his Israeli counterpart, Ehud Barak, at the White House. From 1996 until his death in 2000, Asad held his position demanding the complete return of the Golan Heights that were occupied by Israel in 1967 in exchange for a peace deal and normalized relations with Israel. Hafez al-Asad died not having achieved a settlement on the Golan and was labeled by Syrian historians, unlike King Hussein, Anwar al-Sadat, and Yasser Arafat, as "the man who did not sign."

In January 1994, Asad suffered the harshest setback of his career. His son, Basil al-Asad, being groomed for the presidency since 1992, died in a car crash. In his place, Asad summoned his second son, Bashar al-Asad, an ophthalmologist undergoing his medical residency in London, to assume the duties of his late brother.

By 1998, Dr Bashar al-Asad was the second-in-command of Syria. Then President Asad handed Bashar the "Lebanese portfolio," which until then had been administered by Vice President Abd al-Halim Khaddam, and promoted him within the military establishment. In March 2000, Asad took his son's advice and appointed Mohammad Mustapha Miro, a civil servant who had worked as governor of Aleppo, as prime minister of Syria. One month later, the father and son launched an anti-corruption campaign aimed at rooting out corrupt officials from the state apparatus. Under Dr Asad's influence, the president ordered the discharge of ex-Prime Minister Mahmud al-Zu'bi from the Baath Party, bringing him before court on the charges of gross embezzlement and "destroying the national economy." Other figures to fall in the stampede were Zu'bi's deputy for economic affairs, Saleem Yassin, and Minister of Transportation Mufid Abd al-Karim.

Asad then retired most of his long-time companions who had accompanied him since 1970. Chief of Staff Hikmat Shihabi, Commander of the Special Forces Ali Haydar, Chief of Military Intelligence Ali Duba, Commander of the Republic Guard Adnan Makhlouf, and Commander of Air Force Intelligence Mohammad al-Khuly all lost their jobs in the six years that preceded Asad's death. Hafez al-Asad died on June 10, 2000, only four months short of celebrating his thirtieth year in power. His son, Bashar al-Asad, was elected president in July 2000.

A striking description of Hafez al-Asad is given by former US President Richard Nixon, who, after meeting him in 1974, said that he was "very impressed" with the Syrian leader. He added that Asad was a "tough negotiator but he has a great deal of mystique, tremendous stamina, and a lot of charm. All in all he is a man of substance, and at his age (then forty-four), he will be a leader to be reckoned with in this part of the world. This man really has elements of genius—without any question!"

Sources:
Bergman, Ahron. Tahri, Jihan. *The Fifty Years War* (1998).
Nixon, Richard. *The Memoirs of Richard Nixon* (2nd ed. 1990).
Seale, Patrick. *Asad: the Struggle for the Middle East* (1988).
Tlas, Mustapha. *Mirat Hayati* (1995).
Ziser, Eyal. *Asad's Legacy* (2000).

al-Asad, Rifaat
(1937-)

Rifaat al-Asad was born in the village of Qurdaha in the Syrian Mountains. He grew up under the towering influence of his stern brother, Hafez al-Asad, who was seven years his senior. In 1952, Rifaat joined the Baath Party of Michel Aflaq and Salah al-Bitar, influenced to do so by his brother, who had become a member in 1947.

Rifaat began his compulsory military service during the years of the Syrian-Egyptian union (1958-1961). During the post-union government (1961-1963) he worked at the Ministry of Interior. In March 1963, the Military Committee of the Baath Party (of which Asad was also a member) seized power in Syria, and Rifaat joined the Homs Military Academy. Upon graduation, he served by his brother's side when Asad became commander of the Syrian Air Force.

In February 1966, Rifaat took an active part in the force headed by Baath Party strongman Saleem Hatum when the latter raided the residence of President Amin al-Hafez. Rifaat helped defeat President Hafez, thereby toppling the first Baath government (1963-1966). Under the regime of President Nur al-Din al-Atasi (1966-1970), he was given control of a crack unit of forces, created by the Military Committee to defend the regime, and once commanded by ex-Defense Minister Mohammad Umran.

Syria was marked during the late 1960s by a power struggle between Hafez al-Asad and Salah Jadid, the de facto ruler of Syria, on one front, and on a more junior level, between Rifaat and Jadid's director of intelligence, Abd al-Karim al-Jundi. Hostilities erupted when Rifaat learned that Jundi was planning to assassinate his brother. He convinced Asad that unless they arrest Jundi, or destroy him, their futures and very own survival was at stake.

From February 25-28, 1969, the Asad brothers carried out a semi-coup in Damascus. Tanks rolled into the center of town, and the editors of *al-Thawra* and *al-Baath*, who were loyal to Jundi and Salah Jadid, were arrested. Then, Rifaat arrested many of Jundi's best men as they drove into the Ministry of Defense gas station to fill up their automobiles. Rifaat won the battle when Jundi committed suicide on March 2, 1969 to avoid arrest or humiliation by the Asad brothers. Then, on November 17, 1970, Asad launched his own coup, arresting President Atasi and Salah Jadid. During the coup, Rifaat was put in charge of the security of Damascus.

During the Asad presidency, Rifaat al-Asad became commander of the Defense Companies, an elite force of 55,000 troops, created to maintain the security of the government. They became the best armed, best trained, and best paid forces in Syria. They had their own armor, artillery, air defense, and a fleet of helicopters— literally, an independent army unconnected in any way with the Syrian Army.

In April 1975, Rifaat was elected to the Regional Command of the Baath Party, and given responsibility for youth affairs in Syria. Rifaat became famous for providing scholarships to university students, and sponsoring courses in military affairs and parachute training for boys and girls. Parachute training would earn students extra points in their high school exit exams, and enable them easier acceptance at Syrian University. He created a magazine called *al-Fursan* (*The Knights*) that promoted youth development, and he also founded the League of Higher Graduates to unite Syrians with university degrees. It became a forum where educated men and women could meet and discuss political and public affairs.

He also lived extravagantly. He married four times, traveled abroad frequently, and developed a taste for Western culture.

In 1979, the Asad government came to blows with the Muslim Brotherhood when one of the Brotherhood's members, Adnan Uqla, ordered the slaughter of several Baathist cadets in Aleppo. This culminated in a cycle of violence that had been brewing throughout Syria, and in December 1979, Rifaat addressed the Baath Party's Regional Congress and said that it was time to respond with force.

Anyone not with the government, he argued, should be considered an outlaw. Absolute loyalty was needed for survival. "Stalin," he was famous for saying, "had sacrificed ten million people to preserve the Bolshevik Revolution, and Syria should do the same as well to preserve the Baath Party Revolution of 1963." The Brotherhood had promised to topple the Baath order, and so he swore "to fight a hundred wars, demolish a million strongholds, and sacrifice a million martyrs" to preserve the government.

Rifaat was given free rein in crushing the Islamic uprising between 1979 and 1982, which culminated in a bloody war in Hama. In 1983, he sent female paratroopers into the Syrian capital, with orders to rip the veils off women on the streets. This was an unsuccessful attempt to break the "fundamentalism" overtaking Damascus in the early 1980s. The paratroopers caused such an uproar that it forced Asad to publicly condemn this tactic.

Rifaat became the second-in-command of Syria, and did the government a great favor by crushing the rebellion in Hama. He effectively ruled Syria with his brother, inspiring supreme loyalty among his followers, and spreading fear among his enemies. He created a wide array of alliances, with Crown Prince Abdullah of Saudi Arabia, Yasser Arafat, and King Hasan II of Morocco.

When Asad fell ill in November 1983, it seemed as if Rifaat's moment had come and he began to act as an heir apparent, seeing himself as the only loyal and worthy successor to Hafez al-Asad. Rifaat began to rally the support of his generals, arousing the extreme displeasure of the president. In February 1984, Asad began to strike back, ordering the arrest of one of Rifaat's minions, his security aide Colonel Salim Barakat. Asad then sent a message to Rifaat through his other brother, Jamil, saying, "I am your older brother to whom you owe obedience. Do not forget that I am the man who made you!" In March 1984, Asad appointed Rifaat vice president of the republic, with no official duties. This, in fact, was no promotion, but it aimed at curbing Rifaat's powers with a purely political post where he would be under the watchful eye of the president. His security job, as head of the Defense Companies, was transferred to Colonel Mohammad Ghanim.

On March 30, 1984, Rifaat struck back, ordering his troops into Damascus with clear orders to seize power. They were stationed at strategic points throughout Damascus and its vicinity, points where it would be easy to shell the city. Rifaat's forces were confronted by Asad's loyalists, men like Ali Haydar of the Special Forces, and Adnan Makhlouf of the Presidential Guard. Patrick Seale, Asad's biographer, wrote in *Asad: Struggle for the Middle East,* "Had the two sides come to blows in the capital, the destruction would have been very great and the regime's image irreparably tarnished—that is, if it survived at all." He adds, "He [Asad] had deliberately allowed Rifaat enough rope to hang himself."

Asad was dressed in full military uniform and accompanied by his eldest son, Basil. He drove without guards through the capital to confront Rifaat at his military headquarters.

"You want to overthrow the regime?" Hafez Asad asked. "Here I am . . . I am the regime!" The Asad brothers argued among themselves, in the presence of their elderly mother. The president then offered his brother a way out, promising to respect his dignity, uphold his interests, and safe passage to an exile of his choice. He would not be arrested or killed, as had been the punishment for rebellious officers in Syria since 1949.

Before leaving Syria, Rifaat gave a large banquet for his friends in Damascus. It is the best testimony on his behalf of the events of 1984 that nearly left Syria on the brink of civil war. "My brother doesn't seem to like me anymore," Rifaat said. "When he sees me, he frowns. But I am not an American agent and I am not a Saudi agent. I have not plotted against my country . . . Had I been foolish, I could have destroyed the whole city, but I love this place. My men have been here for eighteen years. The people are used to us. They like us, and now these commandos (in reference to Asad's men who defied him) want to drive us out!"

Later in private, Rifaat went on to criticize Syria's involvement in the Lebanese Civil War and its dependence on the USSR, preferring instead an alliance with the United States. He was also critical of Syria's long-lasting feud with Arafat and Asad's friendship with Iran, claiming that this was giving Syria a bad reputation in the Western world as an ally of a "terrorist state." Hafez Asad endured this behavior until, on May 28, 1984, he dispatched a plane to Moscow, filled with his most senior officers (Rifaat included) for a cooling-off period. One by one, he recalled them to Syria and left Rifaat alone in banishment. Rifaat went to Switzerland, then Spain, and spent the remainder of the 1980s and 1990s leading a very public and lavis life, best described as royalty in exile. Hafez al-Asad never criticized Rifaat in public.

Rifaat returned to Syria in 1992 at the wish of his dying mother but refrained from any political activity. His influence had waned in Damascus, since his Defense Companies had long been dismembered and transferred into the Syrian Army. Many of his associates had either been fired, arrested, or exiled. He remained popular among those who had relied on him for a livelihood in the 1970s and 1980s. In 1994, he consoled Asad when his son, Basil, died in a car accident. Later that same year, however, he was discharged from his post in the Syrian Army but continued to officially hold the position of vice president, a purely ceremonial post.

Rifaat returned to exile. In 1999, his supporters were involved in a gun battle with government forces in the coastal city of Lattakia. He set up an independent satellite station in London in September 1997, called Arab News Network (ANN) and used it to criticize the government in Damascus for its crackdown on his troops in Lattakia in September 1999. He also founded his own party in Europe, headed by his son Dr Somar al-Asad, calling for political change in Syria. Somar began to issue manifestos, criticizing the government of his uncle, and met with leading officials opposed to Asad, including Arafat in Gaza.

When Hafez al-Asad died on June 10, 2000, his brother issued an official communiqué on ANN, mourning the late Syrian leader and claiming himself to be the rightful heir to the Syrian presidency. He declared a three-day mourning period on ANN, calling on Syrians to help him retrieve his rightful place in Syria, and bring about a democratic government. But his calls fell on deaf ears. Acting President Abd al-Halim Khaddam ordered Rifaat's arrest if he tried to attend the president's funeral on June 13.

Rifaat remained critical of the post-Hafez al-Asad order until Bashar al-Asad gave his inauguration speech on July 17, 2000, promising reforms in Syria. Shortly thereafter, Rifaat al-Asad declared support for his nephew, and has since declined any public appearance or statement.

Sources:
Batatu, Hanna. *Syria's Peasantry* (1999).
Seale, Patrick. *Asad: Struggle for the Middle East* (1988).

al-Asali, Faysal
(1919-1980)

Faysal al-Asali was born and raised in a family of prosperous Damascene landowners. He studied law at Damascus University and began his career by joining the National Bloc, the leading anti-French movement in Syria.

In 1941, the twenty-one-year-old Bloc stalwart founded the Social Cooperative Party, a paramilitary organization composed of young men with revolutionary views on social equality who wanted to liberate Syria from the French Mandate that was imposed in 1920. He mobilized its small forces in 1943 to lobby for Shukri al-Quwatli's election to the presidency. In many cases, his propaganda worked, for he was a charismatic orator whose rallies and public speeches became much-anticipated events in Damascus.

That same year, al-Asali became an inspector at the Ministry of Supply and was appointed assistant to President Quwatli. He became Quwatli's man in the traditional quarters of town, charged with organizing parades and marches, and eliciting support for the Quwatli regime in different neighborhoods of Damascus. In 1947, Asali won a seat in parliament on a Social Cooperative Party ticket.

During the Arab-Israeli War of 1948, Faysal al-Asali spoke out in parliament against the military officers who served in the war, accusing them of corruption and of profiteering at the country's expense. In response, the officers accused Shukri al-Quwatli of poor leadership. Asali specifically targeted the chief of staff, Husni al-Za'im, and recommended that he be dismissed from office. When Za'im came to power in March 1949, overthrowing the Quwatli regime, his first order was to have Asali arrested. Four months later, however, Za'im was overthrown by a group of officers and Asali was released from prison.

Al-Asali remained in obscurity from 1949 to 1954 and returned to activity only when Quwatli was reelected president in September 1955. Asali reemerged as a staunch supporter of the veteran leader, running on his list for parliament and becoming a deputy for Damascus. He remained by Quwatli's side from 1955 until the latter retired from politics in 1958.

When the Baath Party came to power in March 1963, Shukri al-Quwatli moved to Lebanon and Faysal al-Asali went to Saudi Arabia, where at Quwatli's request, the House of Saud extended him red carpet treatment as an honored guest.

Sources:
Seale, Patrick. *The Struggle for Power in Syria* (1961).

al-Asali, Sabri
(1903-1976)

Sabri al-Asali was the product of a wealthy, landowning family in Damascus. He studied law at Damascus University and graduated in 1925. He grew up under the influence of his uncle Shukri al-Asali, an attorney who had led the Damascus underground from 1908 to 1914, serving meanwhile as a deputy in the Ottoman Parliament until his execution by Ottoman authorities in May 1916.

The young Asali joined the Syrian revolt of the Arab Mountain in 1925, launched against the French Mandate regime in Syria, and mobilized support for the Druze fighters within his Damascus neighborhood. He also donated money to the Damascus underground and helped smuggle arms, funds, and medical equipment to its secret hideouts in the Ghuta orchards on the outskirts of Damascus. As a result, the French had him exiled to Saudi Arabia, where at the age of twenty-three, he became special advisor to King Abd al-Aziz. During his years in Riyadh, Asali befriended Shukri al-Quwatli, another exiled national-ist, and established a political alliance that was to last for the next forty years. A general amnesty allowed both men back home in 1932, and Quwatli moved into business while Asali opened a legal practice.

In August 1933, al-Asali became a founding member of the League of National Action in Quarna'il (Mount Lebanon), a movement aimed at uniting Arab intellectuals into one political force that would help liberate the region from European colonialism. The movement rose to overnight fame in Syria and Lebanon, calling for economic integration of all Arab countries once the French and British Mandates were terminated. The League included promising young men who were to become future leaders in Syria. Among its earliest members were the noted historian and professor Constantine Zurayk, the philosopher Zaki al-Arsuzi, the politician Munir al-Ajlani, and the diplomat Farid Zayn al-Din. Asali was elected secretary-general of the League of National Action and wrote frequently for its publication, *al-Amal al-Quawmi (National Action)*.

In 1936, Shukri al-Quwatli became vice president of the National Bloc, the leading anti-French movement in Syria, and brought Asali into Bloc ranks. Asali resigned from the League of National Action and ran for parliament on a Bloc ticket in 1936. He won again in 1943, 1947, 1954, and 1962. In March 1945, Quwatli, now president of the republic, appointed Asali minister of interior, a post he held until becoming minister of justice and education in August 1945. In September 1945, Prime Minister Saadallah al-Jabiri once again appointed him minister of justice and education. In April 1946, Asali became minister of interior in the first post-French Mandate government of Jabiri, keeping his post until November 1946. Meanwhile, the National Bloc was dissolved, and in its place, the National Party was created by former Bloc members, with Sabri al-Asali as secretary-general and Shukri al-Quwatli as its spiritual godfather. Asali declared that his party would work to uphold democratic principles, an independent foreign policy, and would be opposed to the unification of the Arab world under the Hashemite crown.

In 1945, Sabri al-Asali attended the founding conference of the Arab League in Cairo. In August 1948, Prime Minister Jamil Mardam Bey appointed him, for the fourth time in his career, minister of interior, and he became responsible for preserving security during the domestic turmoil in reaction to the Arab-Israeli War of 1948. He contained strikes, parades, and cracked down on socialist parties that were calling for the resignation of President Quwatli. Many anti-Quwatli demonstrators were arrested, under Asali's orders, including Michel Aflaq, leader of the Baath Party, who was apprehended for accusing Prime Minister Jamil Mardam Bey of corruption and embezzlement. When violence spread throughout Syria, Asali dispatched the army to the streets and pledged to arrest anyone working against the government in times of war. In 1948, several attempts were made on his life. At one point, he narrowly escaped a hand grenade hurled at him by unknown assassins.

In March 1949, Chief of Staff Husni al-Za'im came to power in Syria and toppled the Quwatli regime. The National Party, along with all other parties, was dissolved and President Quwatli was arrested. Asali refused to recognize or work with the new regime, and as a result, he was placed under house arrest by Syria's new leader. He remained confined to his home until Za'im was overthrown by military coup in August 1949.

Sabri al-Asali remained in obscurity during the four-month era of Husni al-Za'im and the four-year era of President Adib al-Shishakli (1951-1954). During

Sabri al-Asali.

the Shishakli years, Asali moved into the opposition, working with a group of exiled politicians in Iraq to overthrow the military regime and restore a civilian leadership to Syria. He allied himself with the Homs-based opposition of ex-President Hashim al-Atasi and was briefly arrested for his activities by President Shishakli.

In February 1954, Shishakli was overthrown by military coup, and Atasi replaced him as president of the republic, calling on Asali to form a civilian government. During his tenure as prime minister, the Syrian Social Nationalist Party (SSNP) assassinated the deputy chief of staff, Colonel Adnan al-Malki. The murder caused much strife in military circles, forcing Asali to outlaw the SSNP and arrest its entire political leadership. He allied himself with the military officers, who were the de facto rulers of Syria, fearing that otherwise they would force him to resign from office. In June 1956, Asali's alliance with the officers secured his nomination for a second term in the premiership.

In the 1950s, Gamal Abd al-Nasser began to preach the popular views of Arab nationalism and anti-imperialist politics. This garnered much support in Syria, especially among the officer class. Asali declared his support for Nasser's policies, and promoted officials with similar views within the state apparatus and in the Syrian Army. By 1955, Asali had become one of the leading advocates of Gamal Abd al-Nasser in Syria. That same year, to further bolster his image, he visited Shukri al-Quwatli in Egypt, where he had been in exile since 1949, and secured his return to Syria. He then encouraged him to run for presidential office in September 1955 and spearheaded the pro-Quwatli movement in Damascus. When Quwatli became president, he asked Asali to form a government. Together they formed the strongest pro-Nasser coalition in Syria.

Quwatli had allied himself with Nasser when the latter came to power in 1952 and voiced his support for the Egyptian leader's views on Arab nationalism. Asali played an instrumental role in spreading Nasserist propaganda during the Suez War of 1956, and one year later, journeyed to Cairo to plead that Egypt unite with Syria under Nasser's leadership. He established diplomatic relations with Nasser's allies in Eastern Europe and allied himself with the pro-Nasser officers in the Syrian Army: Chief of Intelligence Abd al-Hamid Sarraj and Chief of Staff Afif al-Bizreh. Asali even appointed Salah al-Bitar, a socialist with Nasserist views, as minister of foreign affairs and delegated him to negotiate a Syrian-Egyptian union with Nasser in January 1958. When the framework for union was ready, Asali and Quwatli went to Egypt to finalize the agreement with President Nasser. Syria and Egypt merged to form the United Arab Republic (UAR), under Nasser's terms, on February 1, 1958, and Asali became vice president of the UAR.

Asali's opponents, however, rallied against him and revealed documents implicating him of receiving illegal funds from the Iraqi government from 1951 to 1954. They accused him of having been on the payroll of a foreign country and forced him to resign from office in 1959.

Like many Syrians, al-Asali's enthusiasm for Nasser and pan-Arab unity had waned by 1960 and he began to criticize the union government, claiming that Nasser was no different from earlier dictators like Husni al-Za'im and Adib al-Shishakli. He accused Nasser of having ruined the country's free market economy and multi-party system.

In September 1961, al-Asali praised the coup that ousted the UAR and allied himself with the coup mastermind, General Abd al-Karim al-Nehlawi. Asali signed the secession declaration, a document drafted by a group of politicians that accused Nasser of being a dictator and blamed him for the dissolution of the UAR. It accused Nasser of "distorting the idea of Arab nationalism" and said that, during the union years, he had "strangled political and democratic life" in Syria. Asali did not return to any government post, but became a member of parliament in 1962.

In March 1963, the Military Committee of the Baath Party came to power and pledged to restore the UAR. The officers cracked down on all those who had worked with the post-Nasser government of President Nazim al-Qudsi (1961-1963), arresting some politicians and sending the rest into exile. Sabri al-Asali had his civil rights terminated, his property confiscated, and his National Party outlawed. He retired from political activity and died in Damascus on April 13, 1976.

Sources:

Azm, Khalid. *Muzakarat* (1973).
Faris, George. *Man Hum fi al-`Alam al-Arabi?* (1957).
Hawrani, Akram. *Muzakarat Akram al-Hawrani* (2000).
Itri, Abd al-Ghani. *Abqariyyat* (1997).
Khoury, Philip. *Syria and the French Mandate* (1987).
Moubayed, Sami. *Damascus Between Democracy and Dictatorship* (2000).
Rathmell, Andrew. *Secret War in the Middle East* (1995).
Seale, Patrick. *The Struggle for Power in Syria* (1961).
Torrey, Gordon. *Syrian Politics and the Military* (1964).

al-Atasi, Adnan
(1904-1969)

Adnan al-Atasi came from a prominent political family in Homs, a city located in the Syrian heartland. He studied law at Damascus University and obtained a PhD in international law from the University of Geneva.

Atasi's father was the nationalist leader Hashim al-Atasi, who had headed the nationalist movement against the French Mandate (1920-1946) and served as president of the republic in 1936-1939, 1949-1951, and 1954-1955. Upon completing his studies, the young Atasi joined the National Bloc, the leading anti-French movement in Syria that his father had founded in 1928. In 1930, Dr Atasi became assistant professor of law at Damascus University.

In August 1933, Atasi helped found the League of National Action in Quarna'il (Mount Lebanon), a movement aimed at uniting Arab intellectuals into one political force that would help liberate the region from European colonialism. The League gained instant fame in Syria and Lebanon and called for economic integration of all Arab countries once the French and British Mandates were terminated. Among the League's earliest members were the professor Constantine Zurayk, the philosopher Zaki al-Arsuzi, the politician Sabri al-Asali, and the diplomat Farid Zayn al-Din.

Adnan al-Atasi became a deputy for Homs in parliament in 1947 and 1954. In 1943, he lobbied for the election of Shukri al-Quwatli, a protégé of his father, as president of the republic and ran for parliament on Quwatli's electoral list. In 1945, Quwatli appointed him Syria's first minister to France. He also became non-resident minister to Belgium, Italy, Spain, and Switzerland. Atasi played an instrumental role in negotiating the final stages of French withdrawal from Syria and in maintaining cordial relations with Paris in the post-mandate era. In December 1946, he became minister of justice and public works in the cabinet of Prime Minister Saadallah al-Jabiri.

In 1947, Adnan al-Atasi co-founded the People's Party with a group of Aleppine and Homsi notables. It was a party aimed at maintaining Syria's democratic system, breaking the centralization of power practiced by the politicians of Damascus, and establishing union with Iraq and Jordan. The royal Hashemite houses in Amman and Baghdad funded the party and the pro-Hashemite lawyer,

Nazim al-Qudsi, and politician, Rushdi al-Kikhiya, handled its day-to-day affairs.

Atasi represented Syria in the Arab League Conference in Egypt, convened to discuss the Arab-Israeli War of 1948. In 1949, the People's Party was briefly outlawed during the military regime of Husni al-Za'im and then banned once again during the military era of President Adib al-Shishakli (1951-1954). Atasi clashed with Shishakli, who had ousted his father in 1951 and had set up a dictatorship in Syria. Atasi was arrested for his views, then released when Shishakli was overthrown in 1954.

Adnan al-Atasi.

In the second half of the 1950s, Adnan al-Atasi became disillusioned with the rising influence of Gamal Abd al-Nasser and conspired to promote a union with Hashemite Iraq. He was joined by Munir al-Ajlani, his cousin Faydi al-Atasi, Hasan al-Atrash, and Sami Kabbara. (See Munir al-Ajlani profile, page 136.)

Atasi and his comrades were imprisoned, charged with high treason, and brought before a military tribunal in one of the most publicized trials in Syrian history. He was accused of having orchestrated the movement and of receiving funds from Iraq. Chief of Staff Bizreh, who was serving as military judge, sentenced Atasi to death but, due to external pleas, and in deference to his father's reputation, the sentence was commuted to life imprisonment.

Adnan al-Atasi remained in prison from 1956 until 1960. During his sentence, Syria and Egypt merged to form the United Arab Republic (UAR) in February 1958, and the Hashemite family that had funded his conspiracy in Syria was overthrown by military coup d'etat in July 1958. Before leaving office in February 1958, President Quwatli intervened on his behalf, but the new leaders of Syria refused to set Atasi free.

In 1960, UAR President Nasser transferred the prisoners from jail to house arrest and had them exiled to Alexandria. Atasi was released from house arrest when the UAR regime was overthrown in September 1961. He traveled to Lebanon, then Turkey and Jordan, and did not return to Syria during the regime of President Nazim al-Qudsi.

Adnan al-Atasi died in exile in Beirut on September 7, 1969. Among his published works are *Al-Huquq al-Dusturiyya (Constitutional Rights)*, *Al-Fikr al-Siyasi al-Mu'asser fi Souriyya (Contemporary Political Thought in Syria)*, and *Al-Dimocratiyya al-Taqadumiyya wa al-Ishtirakiyya al-Thawriyya (Progressive Democracy and Revolutionary Socialism)*, published in 1965.

Sources:
BBC Archives. "The Damascus Trial" February 26, 1957.
Itri, Abd al-Ghani. *Hadeeth al-Abqariyyat* (2000).
Interview with Ridwan al-Atasi (November 11, 2001).

al-Atasi, Faydi
(1898-1982)

As a youth from a political family in Homs, Faydi al-Atasi was influenced by his uncle Hashim al-Atasi, a veteran nationalist who led the nationalist movement against the French Mandate (1920-1946) and served as president in 1936-1939, 1949-1951, and 1954-1955. Faydi al-Atasi studied law at Damascus University and began his career as an attorney, then as a civil servant in his native Homs.

In September 1941, Atasi allied himself with the pro-French President Taj al-Din al-Hasani and became minister of education in the cabinet of Prime Minister Hasan al-Hakim. One year later, the independent Prime Minister Ata al-Ayyubi appointed him minister of social affairs, justice, and education in a cabinet that lasted until August 1943.

When Syria achieved independence in April 1946, Atasi allied himself with the regime of President Shukri al-Quwatli, a protégé of his uncle Hashim, who came to power in 1943. In 1947, he became minister of public works and a Homs deputy in parliament. Also in 1947, Faydi al-Atasi co-founded the People's Party with a group of Aleppine and Homsi notables. It was a party aimed at maintaining Syria's democratic system, breaking the centralization of power practiced by the politicians of Damascus, and establishing union with Iraq and Jordan. The royal Hashemite houses in Amman and Baghdad funded the party, and pro-Hashemite lawyer, Nazim al-Qudsi, and the politician, Rushdi al-Kikhiya, handled its daily affairs.

In March 1949, General Husni al-Za'im came to power in Syria. In a quick reversal of alliances, Atasi hailed the new regime and abandoned ex-President Shukri al-Quwatli. In turn, Za'im invited him to form a government. Za'im hoped that Atasi would have enough popularity to legitimize his military rule and secure the support of traditional leaderships. The proposed Atasi cabinet never materialized, however, due to a disagreement between Za'im and Atasi over the latter's pro-Hashemite views. Atasi wanted strong relations with Jordan and Iraq while Za'im wanted to strengthen ties with Saudi Arabia and Egypt (two staunch enemies of the Hashemite family). As a result, Atasi turned down the offer but accepted the Ministry of Education in a cabinet created by Za'im himself. Za'im, however, clashed with the Hashemite royals in Baghdad and Amman, accusing them of wanting to occupy Syria, and broke off relations with both kingdoms within the first ten days of his rule. In protest, Atasi resigned from office, and Za'im responded by having him imprisoned.

When the Za'im regime was overthrown on August 14, 1949, the nationalist leader Hashim al-Atasi became head of state and appointed his nephew, Faydi, as minister of finance. The young Atasi kept this post until December 1949, where Prime Minister Nazim al-Qudsi appointed him minister of defense and national economy. The Qudsi cabinet lasted for two days and resigned due to disagreement on foreign policy between Qudsi and his ministers. In December 1949, the independent Khalid al-Azm formed a government and appointed Atasi as minister of justice, a position he kept until May 1950. During this time, he was voted into the Constitutional Assembly that drafted a new constitution for Syria.

From August to November 1951, Atasi served as minister of foreign affairs in the cabinet of Prime Minister Hasan al-Hakim. He criticized the regime of Syria's second military dictator, General Adib al-Shishakli, and was arrested in January 1954. One month later, Atasi was released when a coup toppled Shishakli. From

March to May 1954, he served as foreign minister under Prime Minister Sabri al-Asali. From October 1954 to February 1955, Atasi held the same post under Prime Minister Faris al-Khury. During his tenure as minister, Faydi al-Atasi clashed with President Gamal Abd al-Nasser of Egypt, who was contesting the leadership of the Hashemite family in the Middle East. Nasser tried bringing Syria into the anti-Hashemite coalition that was spearheaded by Egypt, and Atasi refused, claiming that it was to Syria's benefit to ally with Iraq and the United States rather than Egypt and the USSR.

In the second half of the 1950s, Atasi became increasingly distrustful of Nasser's socialism. Along with Adnan al-Atasi (his cousin), Munir al-Ajlani, Hasan al-Atrash, and Sami Kabbara, Atasi sought to bring down the regime of al-Quwatli through a Hashemite-backed conspiracy (see Munir al-Ajlani, page 136.) The plot was foiled and Faydi al-Atasi was wanted for high treason.

But Atasi managed to escape to Lebanon before a warrant was issued for his arrest. In January 1957, however, a military tribunal declared him innocent of the charge and he was welcomed back to Damascus to resume his parliamentary activity. No longer wishing to paint himself as an anti-Nasserite, he voted in favor of the Syrian-Egyptian union in February 1958.

When union was dissolved in 1961, Atasi allied himself with the post-Nasser government of President Nazim al-Qudsi and became a deputy for Homs in parliament. In 1962, Faydi al-Atasi became director of the committee for external relations in parliament, and held this post until the Baath Party came to power in March 1963. The Revolutionary Command Council (RCC) terminated his civil rights in 1963, in reprimand for his alliance with the post-union secessionist regime.

Sources:
Babil, Nasuh. *Sahafa wa Siyassa fi Souriyya* (1987).
BBC Archives. "The Damascus Trial" February 26, 1957.
FO 371/7540/E10944 (Man to Attlee September 3, 1949).
Hakim, Hasan. *Muzakarati* (1965).
Itri, Abd al-Ghani. *Hadeeth al-Abqariyyat* (2000).
Seale, Patrick. *The Struggle for Syria* (1961).

al-Atasi, Gamal
(1922-2000)

Gamal al-Atasi grew up in a prominent political family of Homs and studied medicine at Damascus University, where he graduated in 1947 with a PhD in clinical psychology.

Atasi joined the Baath Party of Michel Aflaq and became one of the party's earliest ideologues—the one who created the Baath Party motto: "One united Arab nation with an eternal message." Atasi helped lay out the party's constitution and served as senior editor for the party's daily newspaper, *al-Baath*. He opened a clinic in Homs, and became one of the most active party members from 1950 to 1958. He subsequently joined the movement of Arab nationalism that was headed by President Gamal Abd al-Nasser of Egypt and supported Syria's merger with Egypt to form the United Arab Republic (UAR) in 1958. During the union years (1958-1961), Atasi served as editor-in-chief of the pro-Nasser daily, *al-Jamahir (The Masses)*, and wrote, lectured, and worked in favor of the Egyptian leader. When a military coup ousted the Nasser government in Syria on September 28, 1961, Atasi shifted into the opposition, declaring that his official program would be to restore the UAR and retrieve power from Syria's new president, Nazim al-Qudsi.

Atasi clashed with the post-UAR regime of President Nazim al-Qudsi and became a political outcast from 1961 to 1963. In March 1963, however, the Military Committee of the Baath Party came to power in Syria and pledged to restore the UAR. He rallied around the Baath leaders and became minister of information in the cabinet of Prime Minister Salah al-Bitar. He was also voted into the party's Revolutionary Command Council. Atasi readily worked with Bitar and Aflaq, believing that they would reestablish union with Nasser. When it became clear that union was not on the Baath Party agenda, especially after the bloody clash between the Baathists and Nasserists in July 1963, Atasi resigned from office and set up his own political organ, the Arab Socialist Union. It was a hard-line grouping of Arab nationalists who wanted to restore the UAR and reappoint Nasser as president of Syria.

In 1970, Gamal al-Atasi welcomed the ascent of President Hafez al-Asad in Syria. In March 1972, Asad formed the National Progressive Front (NPF), a coalition of socialist parties working under auspices of the Baath, and invited Atasi to join. The veteran socialist was handpicked by Asad as part of the thirteen-man committee, charged with administering the NPF's political affairs. A year later, Atasi broke with the NPF and set up the Arab Socialist Democratic Union, an association which never entered parliament and remained outlawed as a political party.

For the next thirty years, Atasi preached pan-Arabism and worked for the continuation of Nasserist influence in Syria. He established himself as a political philosopher, with his own views on Arabism and socialism, and commanded widespread respect in Syria, despite his increasingly hostile attitude toward the Asad government. Atasi died shortly before Asad's own death in 2000 and was given a semi-official funeral at the president's orders. The friction between the two became clear in the 1980s, yet Asad respected Atasi and honored him as a man of principle, vision, and character.

Among Dr Atasi's published works are *Tareekh al-Ishtirakiyya al-Aurobiyya* (*The History of European Socialism*), *Al-Ishtirakiyya: Madiha wa Hadirha* (*Socialism: Its Past and Future*), *Fikr Karl Marx* (*The Thought of Karl Marx*), and *Gamal Abd al-Nasser wa al-Tajruba al-Thawriyya* (*Gamal Abd al-Nasser: The Revolutionary Experience*). In 1974, Gamal al-Atasi wrote a classic work with Michel Aflaq and Munif al-Razzaz called, *Makalat fi al-Ishtirakiyya* (*Articles on Socialism*).

Sources:
Atasi, Basil. *Tareekh al-Usra al-Atasiyya* (1998).
Atasi, Jamal. *Wada'an Jamal al-Atasi* (2000).
Uthman, Hashim. *Al-Ahzab al-Siyasiyya fi Souriyya: al-Siriyya wa al-Mu'lana* (2001).

al-Atasi, Hashim
(1873-1960)

Hashim al-Atasi studied public administration at the Muluki Academy in Istanbul, an elite university reserved for the Ottoman aristocracy, and graduated in 1894. From 1894 to 1898, he worked as a civil servant in the Ottoman Empire, serving in Beirut. From 1898 to 1913, he became prefect of several towns including Baalbak, Acre, and Jaffa (which included what was the then-small suburb of Tel Aviv). In 1913, he became governor of Hama, and from 1914 to 1918, the governor of two Ottoman towns in Anatolia.

Atasi took no part in nationalist politics, however, and was neither a supporter of the Ottoman Empire nor a member of the Arab underground. The Ottoman Empire collapsed in October 1918 and was succeeded in Syria by the regime of Faysal I. Atasi became governor of his native Homs and was then elected chairman of the Syrian National Congress, the equivalent of a modern parliament. On March 8, 1920, the congress crowned Faysal I as the first king of Syria. On May 3, 1920, Faysal appointed Atasi prime minister. Atasi then appointed the statesman, Abd al-Rahman Shahbandar, who had led the nationalist movement against the Ottoman Empire during World War I, as foreign minister. He delegated Shahbandar to formulate alliances between Syria and Europe, to prevent the implementation of a French Mandate over Syria as stated by the Sykes-Picot Agreement of 1916.

During Atasi's tenure as premier, French High Commissioner Henri Gouraud presented Faysal with an ultimatum, demanding the surrender of Aleppo to the French Army, the dismantling of the Syrian Army, the adaptation of the French franc in Syria, and the dissolution of the Atasi government. Shahbandar's efforts to talk Gouraud into a compromise proved futile, and Atasi's cabinet was dissolved on July 24, 1920, when the French defeated the Syrian Army at the

Battle of Maysaloun and imposed their mandate over Syria.

In October 1927, Hashim al-Atasi met with a group of urban notables and founded the National Bloc. This party was to lead the nationalist movement in Syria for the next twenty years. The Bloc was a political movement focused on liberating Syria from the French Mandate through diplomatic rather than violent resistance. Its founders were a group of landowners, lawyers, civil servants, and Ottoman-trained professionals from Damascus, Aleppo, Homs, Hama, and Lattakia. Atasi was elected permanent president of the National Bloc. In 1928, he was also elected president of the Constitutional Assembly, and charged with laying out Syria's first republican constitution. In 1928 and 1932, he became a deputy for Homs in parliament. That same year, he ran for presidential office but lost the first round of elections and dropped out of the second, throwing his endorsement over to the independent Mohammad Ali al-Abid, who became president in the summer of 1932.

Atasi initially supported the Abid government but grew distant from the new president when Abid appointed two French stooges, Haqqi al-Azm as prime minister and Subhi Barakat as speaker of parliament. In 1934, Abid negotiated a treaty with France that promised gradual independence from the mandate but kept the Syrian Mountains under French control. Atasi criticized the treaty, arguing that no independence would be recognized unless it encompassed all of Syria's territory. He called for a sixty day strike to protest Abid's proposed treaty. The Bloc mobilized massive street-wide support for Atasi's call and had all businesses closed down, crippling the economy and embarrassing Abid before the international community. French police killed hundreds of Syrians daily and the Syrian economy was severly disrupted.

In defeat, the French government agreed to recognize the National Bloc leaders as the sole representatives of the Syrian people and invited Hashim al-Atasi for diplomatic talks in Paris. On March 22, 1936, he traveled to France with a senior Bloc delegation, and over a six-month period, managed to formulate a Franco-Syrian treaty of independence. Atasi's treaty guaranteed emancipation over a twenty-five year period, with full incorporation of previously autonomous territories into greater Syria. In return, Syria pledged to support France in times of war, offer the use of Syrian air space, and allow the French to maintain military bases on Syrian territory. Other political, cultural, and economic agreements were made and Atasi returned to Syria in triumph on September 27, 1936. Hailed as a national hero, he was elected president of the republic by a majority vote in November 1936.

Hashim al-Atasi's rise to power coincided with French reluctance in granting the reforms promised to Syria. Among other things, France had promised to reduce its intervention in domestic politics and cut back on its troops, personnel, and military bases in Syria. In Europe, Adolph Hitler had just emerged as the new leader of Germany and was beginning to pose a serious threat to other European nations, especially France. Paris feared that if it relinquished its colonies in the Middle East, it would be outflanked in a European war. As a result, France decided not to ratify the treaty of 1936. Riots erupted in Syria's main cities, accusing the Bloc leaders of failing to deliver on their promises. Atasi attempted to explain that it was the French who had breached the agreement, but public discontent was high, and the masses rejected the explanation, calling for Prime Minister Jamil Mardam Bey's resignation.

Adding to President Atasi's worries was the return to Syria of the Bloc's prime opponent, Abd al-Rahman Shahbandar. After spending ten years in exile, Shahbandar aimed to regain his popularity and did so by criticizing the government of Atasi's prime minister, Jamil Mardam Bey. Shahbandar struck at the entire National Bloc leadership, accusing them of weakness and claiming that their treaty, whether ratified or not, was not what the Syrian people wanted. In 1939, Turkey annexed the Sanjak of Alexanderetta, territory in northern Syria that had once belonged to the Ottoman Empire. Atasi resigned from office on July 7, 1939, in protest of the annexation, which took place through French endorsement.

The ex-president retired to his native Homs and spent one year in seclusion. Following his resignation, France was occupied by Nazi Germany in 1940 and then liberated by the Allies and the Free French movement of General Charles de Gaulle in 1944. In an attempt to appease Syria, de Gaulle promised independence and visited Syria to elicit support for France. He visited Hashim al-Atasi in Homs and invited him back to the presidency, assuring the veteran leader that France wanted to turn a new page in her relations with Syria. Atasi rejected these claims, however, maintaining that his recent experience showed that France could not be trusted in her promises of independence. Rather than renominate himself, Atasi endorsed the election of Shukri al-Quwatli, a well-established Damascus leader who had risen to fame under President Atasi's patronage.

Hashim al-Atasi took no active part in the final struggle for independence, but supported the Quwatli regime, which lasted from 1943 to 1949. In 1947, while Syria was facing a prolonged cabinet crisis, President Quwatli called on Atasi to form a government of national unity. Due to a tense political atmosphere, however, and increasing anti-Quwatli sentiment within political circles, Atasi failed to come up with a suitable solution. He also quarreled with President Quwatli over presidential authority and demanded that the president's powers must be reduced if he were

Hashim al-Atasi.

to assume the prime minister's office—a suggestion Quwatli refused.

In March 1949, the Quwatli regime was overthrown by Chief of Staff Husni al-Za'im, who headed a military cabinet for four months before he was over-thrown in August 1949. Following the military coup that brought down the Za'im regime, leading politicians called on the ageing Atasi to create a national unity government that would supervise state elections. Atasi complied and formed a cabinet that included representatives of all parties, including the leftist Baath Party of Michel Aflaq, whom he appointed minister of education. Atasi served as prime minister from August to December 1949. Then a parliamentary majority nominated him for a second term as president.

Atasi's second term in office was even more turbulent than his first. He came into conflict with the politicians of Damascus for supporting the interests of the Aleppo notability and their desire to unite with Iraq. He supported the People's Party of Aleppo and appointed its leader, Nazim al-Qudsi, as prime minister. The party was fervently pro-Iraq with the declared aim of immediate union with Baghdad. One of the Atasi administration's most memorable tasks, performed by his prime minister, Khalid al-Azm, was the closure of Syria's border with Lebanon to prevent the influx of Lebanese goods into Syria.

From 1949 to 1951, Atasi began talks with the Iraqi government over the union issue. Atasi received senior Iraqi leaders in Damascus, including Crown Prince Abd al-Illah and King Faysal II. This angered Syria's new military strong-man, Adib al-Shishakli, who claimed that the Hashemite family of Baghdad shall have no authority whatsoever over Damascus. Shishakli demanded a change in course, yet Atasi remained adamant and refused to submit to military pres-sure. In response, Shishakli arrested Atasi's chief of staff, Sami al-Hinnawi, a People's Party sympathizer, and several other pro-Iraqi officers in the Syrian Army. Shishakli then demanded that one of his right hand men, Colonel Fawzi Selu, be appointed minister of defense, to ensure that pro-Iraqi influence in Syria remained under control. Fearing the consequences of a head-on clash with the military, Atasi reluctantly accepted the demands.

In December 1951, however, President Atasi asked Ma'ruf al-Dawalibi, anoth-er member of the People's Party, to form a cabinet. Dawalibi accepted the post but refused to give the Ministry of Defense to Fawzi Selu. As a result, Shishakli launched another coup, arresting the prime minister and all members of the People's Party. All ministers and pro-Hashemite statesmen were also arrested and parliament was dissolved. On December 24, 1951, President Atasi presented his resignation to the disbanded parliament, the true representatives of the people, but, in protest, refused to submit his resignation to Shishakli, who Atasi thought had no legitimate claim to authority.

During the years of Adib al-Shishakli's reign (1951-1954), Atasi spearhead-ed the opposition, claiming that the Shishakli regime was unconstitutional.

He rallied the support of disgruntled officers, pro-Hashemite politicians, and members of all outlawed political parties, and called for a national uprising. In February 1954, Shishakli responded by arresting Atasi's son, Adnan, and placing the veteran statesman under house arrest. The officers mutinied, political leaders mobilized against the regime, and an armed uprising exploded in the Arab Mountain.

On February 24, 1954, the regime of Adib al-Shishakli was finally overthrown. Six days later, on March 1, Atasi returned to Damascus to reassume his duties as president. He restored the cabinet of Ma'ruf al-Dawalibi, who had been in office before Shishakli's coup in 1951, and restored all pre-Shishakli ambassadors, ministers, and parliamentarians to office. In his attempts to restore the pre-Shishakli government and entire political class, it was as if he tried to deny the four-year Shishakli era had ever taken place.

In what remained of his term, the eighty-year-old Atasi tried to curb the influence of military officers and worked relentlessly against the leftist current that was brewing in Syria, characterized by socialist ideology, pro-Soviet sympathies, and blind adherence to the policies of the socialist leader of Egypt, Gamal Abd al-Nasser. Atasi defied President Nasser and worked in vain to keep Syria out of his socialist orbit. Unlike most Arab leaders, Atasi believed that Nasser was too young and inexperienced to lead the Arab world. The Syrian president cracked down on Nasserist elements and clashed with his own pro-Nasser prime minister, Sabri al-Asali, accusing him of wanting to transform Syria into an Egyptian satellite.

In 1955, President Atasi was tempted to accept the Baghdad Pact, an Anglo-American agreement aimed at containing communism in the region, but Nasserist elements in the Syrian Army prevented Atasi from doing so. He then rallied in support of Hashemite Iraq, whose leaders were competing with Nasser over pan-Arab leadership, and became allied to Iraqi Prime Minister Nuri al-Sa'id. Atasi then dissolved the cabinet of Asali and appointed Faris al-Khury, a moderate statesman, as prime minister. Atasi dispatched Khury to Egypt to object to Egyptian hegemony over Arab affairs.

President Hashim al-Atasi ended his term in September 1955 and retired from political life. In 1956, his son, Adnan, was involved in an Iraqi-funded conspiracy that tried to topple the pro-Nasser regime of President Shukri al-Quwatli. Adnan was brought to court and sentenced to death on the charge of treason. In deference to his father, however, his sentence was commuted to life imprisonment.

It was believed that the officers who administered the military tribunal were exceptionally harsh with Atasi's son out of spite for his father who had challenged their authority during his years in power (1949-1951 and 1954-1955). The former president, in a defiant gesture to the military, refused to visit Adnan in prison as a symbolic manifestation of his disdain over the increased militarization of

Syrian politics.

Hashim al-Atasi died during the union years with Egypt on December 6, 1960.

Sources:
Azm, Khalid. *Muzakarat* (1973).
Faris, George. *Man Hum fi al-`Alam al-Arabi?* (1949).
Hawrani, Akram. *Muzakarat Akram al-Hawrani* (2000).
Itri, Abd al-Ghani. *Abqariyyat wa Alam* (1996).
Kayyali, Abd al-Rahman. *Al-Marahil fi al-Intidab al-Faransi 1926-1938,* (1958-1960).
Khoury, Philip. *Syria and the French Mandate* (1987).
Moubayed, Sami. *Damascus Between Democracy and Dictatorship* (2000).
Moubayed, Sami. *The Politics of Damascus 1920-1946* (1999).
Qassab Hasan, Najat. *Saniou al-Jalaa fi Souriyya* (1999).
Rathmell, Andrew. *Secret War in the Middle East* (1995).
Seale, Patrick. *The Struggle for Power in Syria* (1961).
Torrey, Gordon. *Syrian Politics and the Military* (1964).
Interview with Mr Ridwan al-Atasi (Damascus November 12, 2002).

al-Atasi, Lu'ayy
(1926-2003)

Son of a prominent political family in Homs, Lu'ayy al-Atasi studied at the Homs Military Academy. He began his career as an officer in the Arab-Israeli War of 1948. He rose in rank within the Syrian Army, becoming chief of military protocol under President Hashim al-Atasi in 1954.

In 1956, Atasi became assistant military attaché at the Syrian Embassy in Egypt. He joined the movement of Arab nationalism headed by President Gamal Abd al-Nasser of Egypt. He was a strong advocate of a Syrian union with Egypt in 1958 and criticized the military coup d'etat that dissolved union in 1961.

In 1962, an attempted coup was made against the post-union government by officers loyal to Gamal Abd el-Nasser. Atasi tried to mediate between the officers and the new rulers of Syria, but he failed. He then became military attaché to the Syrian Embassy in Washington. Later that year he was called back to Syria to give testimony at the court of the coup masterminds. An ally of the Nasserists, Atasi refused to condemn the officers, which angered the post-union authorities, and as a result, they had Atasi arrested and deported to the Mezzah prison.

On March 8, 1963, the Military Committee of the Baath Party came to power in Syria. The Baath officers overthrew the regime of President Nazim al-Qudsi and pledged to restore union with Gamal Abd al-Nasser's Egypt. The officers released

Lu'ayy al-Atasi from prison and appointed him to the nine-man delegation created to preside over state affairs. On March 23, due to his experience and senior military rank, Atasi was declared president of the Revolutionary Command Council and vested with limited presidential powers. In theory, he had the power to assign ministers, declare war, and issue economic legislation.

In reality, however, Atasi was nothing but a figurehead, a puppet president, since real power lay in the hands of the Military Committee of the Baath Party. Since he had no power base and posed no serious threat to the officers, he seemed perfect for the job. Atasi remained at his ceremonial post until July 27, 1963, when he resigned and was replaced by Amin al-Hafez, who appointed himself president of the republic. Lu'ayy al-Atasi then gave up all political activity and moved to his native Homs, where he lived until his death in November 2003.

Sources:
Atasi, Basil. *Tareekh al-Usra al-Atasiyya* (1998).
Bawab, Sulayman. *Mawsuat Alam Souriyya fi al-Qarn al-Ishreen*, Vol I (1999).
Seale, Patrick. *Asad: Struggle for the Middle East* (1988).
Van Dam, Nicolas. *The Struggle for Power in Syria* (1996).

al-Atasi, Nur al-Din
(1930-1992)

Nur al-Din al-Atasi studied medicine at Damascus University and joined the Baath Party of Michel Aflaq and Salah al-Bitar. He was a firm believer in the radical policies of pan-Arabism as preached by Egyptian President Gamal Abd al-Nasser.

In 1951, in his capacity as a student leader, Atasi worked with the Baath in opposing the military dictatorship of President Adib al-Shishakli. In May 1952, Atasi was arrested and deported to the Palmyra prison. In April 1953, he was transferred to the infamous Mezzeh prison, where he went on a hunger strike, forcing Shishakli to release him from prison in May 1953.

In 1954, following the outbreak of the Algerian Revolution, Dr Atasi traveled to Algiers and donated his medical services to the Algerian resistance of Houari Boumedienne. When the revolution ended in 1962, Atasi returned to Syria, having established himself as an Arab nationalist.

In 1963, the Baath Party came to power in Syria and President Amin al-Hafez appointed Atasi minister of interior in the cabinet of Prime Minister Salah al-Bitar. Atasi came to office in August 1963 and remained at his post until May 1964. From October 1964 to September 1965, he was named deputy to Prime Minister Bitar and appointed to the party's Revolutionary Command Council.

Politically, Atasi was favorable to many members of the Baath, for he came from a prestigious family, endorsed economic reforms along socialist lines, and believed in the theory of popular resistance movements. By 1965, he had allied himself with the military wing of the Baath Party that opposed Michel Aflaq,

Salah al-Bitar, and President Amin al-Hafez. His primary allies were Salah Jadid and Air Force Commander Hafez al-Asad. His alliance paid off when, in February 1966, Jadid and Asad launched a coup and exiled Aflaq, Bitar, and Hafez from Syria.

Jadid, shunning the spotlight and favoring to rule Syria behind the scenes, appointed Atasi as president of the republic and secretary-general of the Baath Party. Asad became minister of defense, while Jadid chose the less public post of deputy secretary-general of the party.

Nur al-Din al-Atasi.

Atasi appointed two medical doctors like himself, in key positions, making Ibrahim Makhous his foreign minister and Yusuf al-Zu'ayyin his prime minister. All three of them had served as voluntary medics with Atasi in Algeria. The Atasi-Zu'ayyin-Makhous alliance prompted the Beirut daily *L'Orient* to write, "Syria is being ruled by three doctors. She must be sick." Eventually, however, the Atasi-Jadid-Asad alliance began to fall apart, with Asad becoming increasingly disenchanted with the hard-line policies of Atasi and Jadid.

In September 1966, Atasi faced an uprising in the Arab Mountain orchestrated by a Baath Party officer named Saleem Hatum. Atasi dismissed most of Hatum's men from office and caused an uproar in the Druze district. He then journeyed to Suwayda to appease the Druze locals, but was confronted by Hatum, who arrested him at gunpoint. Asad intervened from Damascus, sending airplanes to the Arab Mountain and threatening to bombard the district if Atasi was not set free. Asad managed to free the president and preserve his government for the next four years.

Atasi and Jadid clashed with Asad during the Arab-Israeli War of 1967, with each party attempting to blame the other for the defeat. In November 16, 1970, however, Asad launched his own coup and had both Atasi and Jadid arrested. Atasi had expected a military coup and planned to dismiss Asad and Chief of Staff Mustapha Tlas, but Asad struck first. The ex-president remained in prison from 1970 until 1980 when he was transferred to a small residence in the Qusur neighborhood of Damascus where General Mohammad al-Khuly, the air force commander, requested that Atasi sign a pledge renouncing his political views. Atasi refused, and as a result, was returned to Mezzeh prison. In 1992, he was released from Mezzeh because of poor health and sent for treatment in Paris at the expense of the French government. But Nur al-Din al-Atasi died shortly thereafter.

Sources:

Atasi, Basil. *Tareekh al-Usra al-Atasiyya* (1998).

Seale, Patrick. *Asad: Struggle for the Middle East* (1988).

Tlas, Mustapha. *Mirat Hayati* (1995).

al-Atrash, Hasan
(1905-1977)

Born in the Arab Mountain to a family of Druze aristocracy, Prince Hasan al-Atrash received his schooling at the hands of private tutors and did not obtain a university degree.

Atrash administered his family estates from 1919 to 1924, then joined the Druze uprising against the French Mandate in Syria launched in 1925 by Sultan al-Atrash. He led armed bands in sporadic attacks on French garrisons and inflicted heavy losses on French forces in the Arab Mountain. When the French Army suppressed the revolt in 1927, he was sentenced to death and fled to Amman, where he served in the court of Prince Abdullah, the Emir of Transjordan.

Atrash returned to Syria when the French issued a general amnesty in 1928 and joined the National Bloc, the leading anti-French movement in Syria. It was composed of Syrian notables who strove to expel the French through diplomatic rather than armed resistance. In 1936, the National Bloc came to power in Syria and the Bloc founder Hashim al-Atasi became president of the republic. He appointed Atrash as governor of the Arab Mountain, a post he held until April 1942, when he became minister of defense in the cabinet of Prime Minister Husni al-Barazi. He held office as minister until January 1943.

In 1943, Prince Hasan al-Atrash ran for parliament on a National Bloc ticket and won. He was voted into parliament again in 1947, and once more in 1954. On May 29, 1945, the French bombarded Damascus. Atrash retaliated by arresting French officers in the Arab Mountain, offering their release on the condition that the air raid on the Syrian capital cease. He clashed with the National Bloc government of President Shukri al-Quwatli (1943-1949) and resigned from Bloc ranks claiming that Quwatli was practicing favoritism toward the Damascenes and ignoring the needs of the Druze community. Atrash resigned from his post in 1947.

In November 1949, Atrash became a member of the Constitutional Assembly that drafted a new constitution for Syria. One year later, in September 1950, he became a deputy in parliament. In November 1951, however, a coup d'etat took place in Syria, bringing President Adib al-Shishakli to power. Shishakli came to office with a hostile attitude toward the Atrash clan, claiming that they were allies of the Hashemite royals in Amman and Baghdad and were striving to change the republican regime of Syria and replace it with a monarchy. He repeatedly clashed with the Atrash family, and in 1953, placed the veteran leader Sultan al-Atrash under house arrest. He then arrested Prince Hasan and other Druze notables, accusing them of plotting against the regime. Atrash spent one year in prison and was released when Shishakli was overthrown in 1954.

In reward for his anti-Shishakli policies, Hasan al-Atrash was appointed minister of agriculture in the first post-Shishakli cabinet of Prime Minister Sabri al-Asali. He held office from March to May 1954, then became director of the Hijaz Railway, based in Damascus. In October 1954, he became a deputy in the first post-Shishakli parliament. He also became minister of state under Prime Minister Sa'id al-Ghazi from September 1955 to June 1956.

Atrash, along with Adnan and Faydi al-Atasi, Munir al-Ajlani, and Sami Kabbara was involved in the anti-Nasserist conspiracy of the 1950s (see Munir al-Ajlani, page 136.) All except Atrash were imprisoned and charged with high treason. Atrash had used his paramount influence to garner support for the rebels in the Arab Mountain and channeled funds for their activities from Baghdad. Atrash was sentenced to death in absentia on the charge of intriguing with a foreign country to attack Syria and initiate a civil war. Hasan al-Atrash fled into exile and lived abroad until the Syrian-Egyptian union was dissolved in September 1961.

Sources:
BBC Archives. "The Damascus Trial" February 26, 1957.
Faris, George. *Man Hum fi al-`Alam al-Arabi?* (1957).
Landis, Joshua. *Nationalism and the Politics of Za'ama* (1997).

al-Atrash, Mansur
(1926-)

Mansur al-Atrash grew up in the most influential family in the Druze community of Arab Mountain. His father, Sultan Pasha al-Atrash, had led a national uprising against the French Army in 1925 and was revered throughout Syria as a national hero. The young Atrash studied political science at the American University of Beirut (AUB) and graduated in 1948. He then obtained a law degree from the Sorbonne in Paris.

In April 1947, Atrash helped found the Baath Party, along with Michel Aflaq and Salah al-Bitar, and became an active member of its political office. He wrote for the party daily, *al-Baath,* and took part in marches, strikes, and parades in the 1940s and 1950s. In 1951, General Adib al-Shishakli established a military dictatorship in Syria, and Atrash joined the underground that was working to bring him down. He was arrested twice, once in 1952 for throwing explosives at Shishakli's residence in Damascus, and the other in May 1953, at the height of the anti-Shishakli uprising. To appease the pasha, Shishakli released his son shortly afterward, but Sultan al-Atrash refused to tone down his criticism of the Shishakli regime, saying, "I didn't ask Shishakli for the freedom of my son. I asked him for the freedom of my country."

Shishakli had clashed with the Baath Party in 1953 and sent Aflaq and Bitar into exile in Lebanon. He then antagonized the Druze community by claiming that they wanted to topple his republican regime. He accused the Druze leaders of wanting to impose a Hashemite monarchy in Syria and of being on the payroll of the Hashemite royals in Amman and Baghdad. Shishakli arrested many Druze leaders, bombarded the Arab Mountain, and placed Atrash's father, Sultan Pasha, under house arrest. Mansur joined the anti-Shishakli movement in Homs and channeled arms to the Druze underground. He was instrumental in bringing down the Shishakli regime in February 1954. He also served as a deputy in parliament from 1954 to 1958. In 1956, he was offered

Mansur al-Atrash.

a government post in the cabinet of Prime Minister Sa'id al-Ghazi, but turned it down because the Baath Party leadership did not support the government's political composition.

In the 1950s, Mansur al-Atrash joined the movement of Arab nationalism that was headed by President Gamal Abd al-Nasser of Egypt. He supported Syria's merger with Egypt in 1958 and criticized the coup that toppled the union government in 1961. During union, he frequently wrote for the pro-Nasser daily, *al-Jamahir (The People)*. In March 1962, Prime Minister Bashir al-Azma called on the Baath Party to assume six cabinet posts, offering Atrash one of them, but he turned it down, claiming that he was ideologically opposed to the post-UAR regime. In September 1962, Prime Minister Khalid al-Azm appointed Atrash minister of social affairs without consulting him beforehand, and once again Atrash turned down the post.

In March 1963, the Military Committee of the Baath Party came to power and pledged to restore the UAR. Atrash supported the Baath takeover and allied himself with Syria's new president, Amin al-Hafez. He was appointed minister of social affairs and labor in the cabinet of Prime Minister Salah al-Bitar and held this post until May 1964. He also became a member of the presidential council, delegated with administering the state's day-to-day affairs, from May 1964 to October 1965.

On September 1, 1965, Atrash was appointed chairman of the Revolutionary Command Council (RCC), a government body that doubled as a modern parliament. The political posts that were occupied by the civilians were ceremonial, as Atrash was later to recall. He said, "the officers let us do the talking although, as we later discovered, they had agreed beforehand among themselves what the decisions would be."

Atrash retained his post until February 14, 1966. One week later, on February 23, an internal Baath Party coup took place and overthrew the administration of President Amin al-Hafez. Mansur al-Atrash was arrested, along with President Amin al-Hafez, and detained at the Mezzeh prison until 1967. While in jail, Atrash was visited by Hafez al-Asad, who came to inquire on his health and discuss the latest political developments in Syria.

During the Arab-Israeli War of 1967, days after Israel occupied the Golan Heights, President Nur al-Din al-Atasi released all political prisoners. Atrash claimed, "It was not agreeable to know that we owed our freedom to defeat." Abd al-Karim al-Jundi, the director of Syrian Intelligence, tried to have him arrested on the charge that he was involved in a coup attempt with Baath Party strongman Saleem Hatum. Mansur al-Atrash fled to Lebanon and remained in Beirut until Jundi died in April 1969. He retired from political life and spent the remainder of his years in seclusion in Syria.

Sources:
Seale, Patrick. *Asad: Struggle for the Middle East* (1988).
The International Who's Who in the Arab World (1987-1988).
Interview with Mansur al-Atrash (Damascus February 16, 2003).

al-Attar, Issam
(1925-)

Born and raised in Damascus, Issam al-Attar studied theology in Damascus and joined the Muslim Brotherhood in 1947. He befriended Sheikh Mustafa al-Siba'i, the Brotherhood leader in Syria, and succeeded him as superintendent general of the Brotherhood in 1957.

Al-Attar was opposed to the unification of Syria and Egypt that formed the United Arab Republic (UAR) in 1958. He claimed that the police measures of President Gamal Abd al-Nasser of Egypt would prove catastrophic for Syria's democratic system. Attar had criticized the Egyptian leader for his 1954 war on the Egyptian Muslim Brotherhood, claiming that once firmly in power in Syria, he would outlaw the Syrian Brotherhood as well. He was arrested on numerous occasions in the union years (1958-1961) and supported the coup that overthrew the UAR regime in September 1961. He rallied around Syria's new president, Nazim al-Qudsi, who restored a multi-party system to Syria and allowed the Brotherhood to operate once again.

In December 1961, Attar won a seat in parliament as a Brotherhood candidate, becoming a deputy from Damascus. In March 1963, however, the Baath Party came to power in Syria and outlawed all political parties (except its own). The Military Committee of the Baath Party closed the Brotherhood office, along with its newspapers, and arrested or exiled its members. Attar was briefly arrested, then released in 1963. One year later, while returning from the hajj pilgrimage in Saudi Arabia, authorities denied him entry to Syria and he went to Beirut.

In 1964, the outlawed Brotherhood launched a war against the Baath Party government of President Amin al-Hafez, and Attar supported their efforts from his exile in Lebanon through manifestos, speeches, and funds. The revolt was suppressed, however, and Amin al-Hafez requested that President Charles Helou hand over Attar and other wanted members of the Brotherhood to Syria. Attar fled Lebanon to Europe in 1966, where, in his own words, he led a "wandering life" because "all Arab countries closed their doors to me." He resided in West Germany and became director of the Islamic Center in Berlin. In 1979, when the Muslim Brotherhood began their second revolt against the Baath Party, Attar condemned the attacks, claiming that they would lead to nothing but destruction on both fronts. From 1979 to 1982, Attar called for an end to the armed conflict, but he had long ago lost his influence among the militant ranks and his call was ignored by the new, young, militant generation of Brotherhood leaders. President Hafez al-Asad appreciated his moderate stance, however, and invited him back to Damascus in 1992, on the condition that he give up political activity. Issam al-Attar turned down the offer, and at the time of this writing, still lives in Germany in political retirement. His Bilal Mosque in Aachen remains an attractive venue for Muslim activists in Europe.

During his career in politics, Attar has had few allies in Syria. This applied both to the era of civilian rule and the Baath Party years. Khalid al-Azm, a prime minister of the 1940s and 1950s, describes Issam al-Attar in his memoirs:

"I knew of no man whose aims or the feelings he harbors were as unfathomable. With a sweet smile on his lips, and rubbing his hands, he speaks to you in a soft voice and with all humility. Suddenly, he flares up, shakes his hands, and with his voice set in a higher pitch and fury in his eyes, he bursts into threats and impending denunciations from pulpits and mosques. When he realizes you are unaffected and attach no weight to his words, he quiets down, his expressions relax and the gentle smile reappears on his face."

Sources:
Al-Hayat (February 18, 1980).
Azm, Khalid. Muzakarat (1973).
Batatu, Hanna. Syria's Peasantry: the Descendants of its
Lesser Rural Notables and their Politics (2000).
Commins, David. Historical Dictionary of Modern Syria (1996).

al-Ayyubi, Ata
(1877-1951)

Ata al-Ayyubi, of a prominent political family in Damascus, studied public administration in Istanbul and began his professional career in the Ottoman civil service.

In 1908, Ayyubi became governor of Lattakia. He took no part in the Ottoman-Arab conflict during the years 1916 through 1918 but returned to live in Damascus when the Ottoman Empire fell in October 1918. In the four-day interlude between the departure of the Turks and the arrival of the Arab Army of Sharif Husayn, he created a preliminary government with a group of Syrian notables in Damascus, headed by Prince Sa'id al-Jaza'iri, an Algerian who was living in Damascus.

In July 1920, Prime Minister Ala al-Din Droubi appointed Ayyubi minister of interior. He held office in the wake of the French occupation of Syria. He established links with local nationalists and smuggled arms and funds to Saleh al-Ali, leader of the revolt on the Syrian coast, and Ibrahim Hananu, leader of the Aleppo Revolt. In Lattakia, he turned a blind eye to the activities of Omar al-Bitar, refusing in his capacity as minister, to arrest the rebels, thus facilitating their ambushes on French garrisons. In August 1920, a group of armed men tried to kill Ayyubi in the town of Hawran in southern Syria. They accused him of treason for accepting office under the French Mandate. The assassination attempt, however, failed to convince him to step down. Ayyubi remained at his post until 1922. Then he became minister of justice in the pro-French cabinet of Prime Minister Subhi Barakat, keeping his post until a national uprising took place against the French Mandate in 1925.

In 1928, Ayyubi allied himself with the National Bloc, the leading anti-French movement in Syria, but did not become an official member. The Bloc called for the liberation of Syria through diplomatic rather than armed resistance. Meanwhile, Ayyubi remained on cordial relations with French authorities. During the 1930s, he served as an intermediary between both sides. In March 1934, he became minister of justice in the pro-French cabinet of Prime Minister Taj al-Din al-Hasani.

In 1936, relations between the Bloc and the French sharply deteriorated and Bloc leaders called on the nation to go on strike. The strike crippled commercial life and hundreds of Syrian demonstrators were arrested or beaten by the French Army. The ordeal lasted sixty days and embarrassed France before the international community. Fearing that the sixty day strike would spread to French colonies in North Africa, the French government promised to address Syrian grievances and invited a senior Bloc delegation for independence talks in Paris. While the Bloc discussed Syria's future, the pro-French cabinet of Prime Minister Taj al-Din al-Hasani was dissolved and French High Commissioner Comte Henri de Martel asked Ata al-Ayyubi to form an independent government. The new prime minister managed to form a coalition cabinet that included elements from the National Bloc and the pro-French movement. When the Bloc returned from France in September 1936, Ayyubi resigned from office, having served for ten months as prime minister.

In March 1943, Ayyubi became head of an interim cabinet to preside over presidential and parliamentary elections after the death of President Taj al-Din al-Hasani. Ata al-Ayyubi held office as prime minister, minister of foreign affairs, interior, and defense, resigning only when Shukri al-Quwatli was elected president in August 1943.

Ata al-Ayyubi.

Sources:

Itri, Abd al-Ghani. *Hadeeth al-Abqariyyat* (2000).

Khoury, Philip. *Syria and the French Mandate* (1987).

Moubayed, Sami. *The Politics of Damascus 1920-1946* (1999).

al-Azm, Abd al-Rahman
(1916-)

Abd al-Rahman al-Azm was born to one of the largest and wealthiest landowning families in Hama, a city on the Orontos River. He studied law at the American University of Beirut (AUB) and obtained a PhD in international law from the Jesuit University in Lebanon.

In 1947, Azm nominated himself as an independent for parliament and became a deputy for Hama. In December 1949, Prime Minister Khalid al-Azm appointed him minister of finance in a non-partisan government, a post he held until May 1950. Also in November 1949, he was voted into the Constitutional Assembly that drafted a new constitution for Syria and served as a deputy for Hama in parliament.

In March 1951, Prime Minister Khalid al-Azm created a new government and asked his young relative to serve a second time as minister of finance. On November 28, 1951, Azm became minister of finance (for the third time in his life) in the cabinet of the new prime minister, Ma'ruf Dawalibi, Azm's successor. But, the next day, November 29, General Adib al-Shishakli launched a coup, dissolving the cabinet and arresting all ministers.

Azm served briefly in prison and was released in 1952. He joined the opposition to the Shishakli regime and helped oust him in February 1954. In March 1954, he became minister of finance in the cabinet of Prime Minister Sabri al-Asali and held office until May 1954. From 1954 to 1958, Azm held office as a deputy in the Syrian Parliament. In January 1956, President Shukri al-Quwatli appointed him ambassador to Egypt, six months before the Suez Canal War broke out. He joined the movement of Arab nationalism that was headed by President Gamal Abd al-Nasser of Egypt and supported Syria's merger with Egypt to form the United Arab Republic (UAR) in February 1958. He took part in union talks with President Shukri al-Quwatli that were held in Cairo and resulted in the signing of the union charter on February 1, 1958. When the UAR was formed, Nasser appointed Azm ambassador to Spain, and in 1960 he became the UAR ambassador to Japan. Azm returned to Syria when the union government was dissolved (by military coup) in September 1961 and became ambassador to the United Kingdom.

In March 1963, the Military Committee of the Baath Party came to power and retired all officials who held office during the regime of President Nazim al-Qudsi (1961-1963). The Baath Party dismissed Abd al-Rahman al-Azm from office and terminated his civil rights, forcing him to flee to Lebanon and then Switzerland, where he lives at the time of this writing, forty years later.

Sources:
Azm, Khalid. *Muzakarat* (1973).
Faris, George. *Man Hum fi al-`Alam al-Arabi?* (1957).
Hawrani, Akram. *Muzakarat Akram al-Hawrani* (2000).
Samman, Mutih. *Watan wa Askar* (1995).
Seale, Patrick. *The Struggle for Syria* (1961).

al-Azm, Haqqi
(1864-1955)

A native of Damascus, but raised in Istanbul by a family of Ottoman-Arab aristocrats, Haqqi al-Azm's ancestors had been the traditional governors of Damascus in Ottoman Syria, commanding widespread authority in the Ottoman Empire. Azm studied at the Military Academy in Istanbul but pursued a career in the Ottoman civil service.

In 1900, the young Azm became involved in Ottoman politics, establishing himself as an enthusiastic supporter of Sultan Abdulhamid II. He encouraged the Sultan's pan-Islamic views and his reliance on Arab advisors at the imperial courts. In 1908, however, the Young Turk coup took place in Istanbul, bringing a group of youthful, hard-line, and disgruntled Ottoman officers to power. This group, called the Committee for Union and Progress (CUP), forced Abdulhamid to dismiss his Arab advisors and replace them with Turkish ones, claiming that the Arab notables could not be trusted since they had no sincere loyalty to the Ottoman Empire or to Ottomanism. They made Ottoman Turkish, rather than Arabic, the official language of schools, courts, and government offices in the Arab provinces of the empire and centralized authority in Istanbul. In 1910, Azm became inspector general of the Ministry of Religious Affairs, only to be dismissed in 1911 (for his loyalties to ex-Sultan Abdulhamid) and replaced by a Turkish official.

Haqqi al-Azm.

Azm clashed with the CUP, accusing its leaders of practicing favoritism. He moved to Egypt where he met other like-minded Arab men displeased with the post-Abdulhamid regime. Along with other exiled nationalists, Azm formed the Ottoman Party of Administrative Decentralization in January 1913. It attracted Syrians from different backgrounds and brought to Egyptian circles the nationalist movement that was brewing in the Middle East. Azm served as the party's secretary while his cousin, Rafic al-Azm, became its president.

It was through this party that the first demands of complete Arab emancipation were made. The Azm cousins transformed the movement-in-exile into an influential party and were accused by authorities in Istanbul of being agents for the United States. Azm remained at odds with the Ottoman Empire until its defeat in 1918, at the end of World War I. Azm also clashed with the post-Ottoman administration of King Faysal I, claiming that having a Bedouin from the Arabian Desert rule Syria was "barbaric." He believed that, although the CUP was unfit to rule Syria, so were the Hashemite royals of the Arabian Desert, who had led a military uprising against the Ottomans from 1916 to 1918. Rather, Azm preferred that the Syrians themselves, through Ottoman-trained notables like himself, be given authority to run their country on their own in a republic, rather than a monarchy.

In 1919, Haqqi al-Azm moved to Paris and befriended senior French statesmen. He marketed himself as a potential ally of France and promised to endorse French colonial ambitions in Syria and Lebanon. When the French proclaimed their mandate over Syria in July 1920, Azm became director of the Consultation Bureau under Prime Minister Jamil al-Ulshi (from September to November 1920).

In December 1920, the mandate divided Syria into quasi-independent states, appointing Azm as governor of the state of Damascus. His administration was infamous for its inefficiency, corruption, and nepotism. He failed to secure a popular base of support among Syrians. Resentment against Azm increased in August 1921 when the French arrested the resistance leader, Ibrahim Hananu, and brought him to court on the charge of treason. The public accused Azm of weakness for failing to secure Hananu's release. When Azm did try to intervene on behalf of the resistance, the French dismissed him in June 1922.

In December 1924, Azm was restored to a one-year term in his earlier post as director of the Consultation Bureau. In 1930, he founded the Reform Party in Damascus, aimed at achieving political reform and administrative changes. The party did not have a popular base, however, and was limited to the allies and relatives of Haqqi Bey. He became a member of parliament in 1932.

Once in parliament, Azm nominated himself for presidential office. He lost the race, however, but, as consolation for his efforts, the French appointed him prime minister in the administration of President Mohammad Ali al-Abid. He assumed his duties on June 11, 1932, also becoming minister of interior until March 3, 1934. In 1933, Prime Minister Azm signed a proposed Franco-Syrian treaty, offering minor freedoms and a promise of gradual independence in exchange for keeping the Arab Mountain and the mountains surrounding Lattakia separate from the rest of Syria. The treaty came under sharp criticism from the National Bloc, the leading anti-French movement in Syria, and was criticized throughout nationalist circles. National Bloc leaders petitioned Abid to dismiss Azm from office. When he refused, countrywide protests took place, calling for the downfall of the prime minister. Facing mounting pressure, Abid called on Azm to step down in March 1934, but reappointed him director of the Consultation Bureau.

Azm remained at this post until Abid retired from office in 1936. Azm spent the remainder of his years divided between Istanbul, Damascus, and Cairo. In 1941, Haqqi al-Azm founded a weekly magazine entitled, *al-Shura (Consultation)*, and served as its editor-in-chief until his death in 1955.

Sources:
Caplan, Neil. *Futile Diplomacy,* Vol I (1983).
Commins, David. *Historical Dictionary of Modern Syria* (1996).
Khoury, Philip. *Urban Notables and Arab Nationalism* (1983).

al-Azm, Khalid
(1903-1965)

Khalid al-Azm was from one of the most prominent political families in Syria. His father, Fawzi Pasha al-Azm, was a wealthy Ottoman aristocrat who had served as minister of religious affairs in the Ottoman Empire, while his ancestors were the traditional nineteenth-century governors of Syria. Khalid al-Azm studied law at Damascus University and graduated in 1923.

In 1925, Azm became a member in the Municipality of Damascus and administered his family's various estates throughout Syria. In the mid-1930s, he befriended the leaders of the National Bloc, the leading anti-French movement in Syria, and became a close associate of its chief, Shukri al-Quwatli. He financed several Bloc enterprises and served as manager of the National Cement Company.

In April 1941, wanting to strike a balance between nationalist aspirations and French interests in the Middle East, the French appointed him prime minister, vested with presidential powers. Azm appointed himself minister of interior as well. It was believed that Azm would have enough moderation to protect French interests in Syria, and legitimacy to appeal to the Syrian nationalists. His government, although not dominated by the National Bloc, was nevertheless supported wholeheartedly by the Bloc president, Hashim al-Atasi. Azm appointed the Bloc vice president, Nasib al-Bakri, as minister of economy and public works. Azm held office in the midst of World War II, and was replaced in September 1941 by the French loyalist, Taj al-Din al-Hasani.

In January 1943, President Hasani died while in office and Azm's long-time friend, Shukri al-Quwatli, was elected president. Azm served as a deputy for Damascus in parliament (1943-1947), and his election was repeated in 1947-1949, 1949-1951, 1954-1958, and 1962-1963. In August 1943, Azm became minister of finance and supply in the National Bloc government of Prime Minister Saadallah al-Jabiri. In April 1946, he became minister of justice and economy.

Azm quarreled with Quwatli, however, and accused him of leading a one-man show. He resigned from office in September 1945 and became the self-appointed opposition leader to the Quwatli regime. The Syrian press wrote that Azm's opposition was a result of his personal desire for power and his scheme to denigrate Quwatli and replace him at the presidency. In 1947, his relationship with Quwatli was further strained when the latter nominated himself for a second term as president and amended the constitution to allow his reelection. Azm created a parliamentary bloc aimed at vetoing the bill for reelection. Quwatli responded by dispatching him as Syria's ambassador to France. Reluctantly, Azm accepted and served in Paris for one year,

Khalid al-Azm.

where he was given the task of purchasing arms for the newly created Syrian Army. He spent his time in Paris visiting private companies willing to sell arms to Syria, the first shipment of which arrived in 1948. France remained Syria's number one supplier of arms until Azm conducted another arms deal with the USSR in 1956. While he was in Paris, Quwatli was reelected for a second term at the presidency.

In May 1948, Azm was recalled to Syria and charged with creating a non-partisan cabinet. Quwatli had faced a sharp cabinet crisis and needed an independent to appease the different political parties. Azm came to power and promised to help solve many economic problems Syria had faced since its independence from France in 1946. He also served as minister of national defense and foreign affairs. He allied himself with France and the United States, promising to boost Syria's economy through financial loans from both countries. In September 1948, while holding office, he frequently traveled to New York to attend the General Assembly meetings on the Arab-Israeli conflict in Palestine. Azm and Quwatli managed to set aside their differences and presided over Syria during the Arab-Israeli War of 1948. He clashed with the military officers at the warfront and accused Chief of Staff Husni al-Za'im of poor command, recommending his dismissal from office to President Quwatli. On March 29, 1949, Za'im launched a military coup in Damascus and had both Azm and Quwatli arrested and imprisoned at the notorious Mezzeh prison.

In August 1949, less than five months after coming to office, Za'im was executed by a disgruntled group of officers, and civilian rule was restored to Syria. Khalid al-Azm made his comeback by becoming a deputy for Damascus in parliament and assuming the post of minister of finance. He was also voted into the Constitutional Assembly, charged with laying out a new constitution for Syria. In June 1950, President Hashim al-Atasi appointed him prime minister, putting him in charge of economic reforms and curtailing the influence of army officers within the state apparatus. One of Azm's most memorable legislative acts was the economic boycott of Lebanon in 1950, when Azm closed the border with Lebanon in an attempt to increase the quality of Syrian goods and halt the vast importation of Lebanese goods.

Azm headed three cabinets from 1950 to 1951, and clashed continuously with the armed forces, the socialists, and the People's Party, an opposition party that was working for union with Hashemite Iraq. The armed forces despised Azm for refusing to appoint an officer as minister of defense in any of his cabinets and for his insistence that the prime minister himself occupy the portfolio of defense. The People's Party clashed with his anti-Hashemite views, while the socialists viewed him as a hard-line capitalist and wealthy aristocrat who was out to enslave the country's working class.

Khalid al-Azm retired from public life from 1951 to 1954 in protest over the police measures taken by Syria's new military leader, President Adib al-Shishakli. He returned to the spotlight in the post-Shishakli era as a candidate for the presidency, running against Shukri al-Quwatli in 1955. Azm lost the election, retired briefly, and then reemerged in November 1956 as minister of defense in the independent cabinet of Prime Minister Sabri al-Asali. Azm played an instrumental, perhaps single-handed, role in establishing Syria's alliance with the USSR. Azm visited Moscow frequently and arranged several long-term loans and economic deals with the Kremlin. The US media, infuriated at his actions, coined him "the red millionaire," and this term was used interchangeably with his name by the Syrian press in the 1950s.

Azm did not care to refute the accusations leveled at him, claiming that he would solidify ties with any country willing to offer assistance to Syria. Despite his pro-Soviet policy, he was not in favor of Gamal Abd al-Nasser, the socialist leader of Egypt, who had emerged as the USSR's number one ally in the Arab world. When Nasser and Quwatli merged Syria and Egypt to form the United Arab Republic (UAR) in 1958, Azm voted against union, but a parliamentary majority overruled his vote, under pressure from Nasserist officers in the Syrian Army. He spoke out against Nasser's socialism, claiming that the Egyptian leader would destroy Syria's democratic system and free market economy, and called on Syrians to think twice before inviting a foreigner to rule them.

During the union years (1958-1961), Khalid al-Azm moved to Lebanon and played no part in Syrian-Egyptian affairs. He returned to Syria when the union was ousted in September 1961 and attended a conference of political parties in Damascus, where he accused the Nasser government of having been no different from the French Mandate that ruled Syria from 1920 to 1946. Azm helped draft the secession declaration, a written document that accused Nasser of having established a ruthless dictatorship in Syria. The document accused Nasser of "distorting the idea of Arab nationalism," adding that during the union years, he had "strangled political and democratic life" in Syria.

Azm once again ran for presidential office in December 1961 but the military officers, who were the de facto rulers of Syria, vetoed his candidacy. The officers remembered his anti-military stance in the post-1948 era, and many of them were still loyal to Nasser and could not tolerate a hard-line, anti-Nasser politician like Azm. To avoid conflict, he withdrew his candidacy and supported the election of Nazim al-Qudsi, another anti-Nasser statesmen, as president of the republic. Meanwhile, Azm was elected a deputy for Damascus in parliament.

On March 28, 1962, a coup was launched in Syria by Colonel Abd al-Karim al-Nehlawi. He arrested Qudsi and Azm, accusing them of misusing public office and persecuting the officers in the Syrian Army. A counter-coup took place on April 2, headed by Chief of Staff Abd al-Karim Zahr al-Din, who released both men from jail and discharged Nehlawi from the army. In September 1962, Qudsi asked Azm to form a government, hoping that he would be able to control the complex and tense situation in Syria. For the sixth time in his career, Khalid al-Azm came to office as prime minister. A troubled relationship with Qudsi over how to deal with the Nasserist threat was soothed by ex-President Quwatli, who had mediated between both men and advised them to root out Nasserism from the Syrian Army and re-appoint loyal officers discharged in 1958 in order to preserve the post-UAR order.

Azm came to office with the aim of reviving Syria's dislocated industries. In 1960, Nasser had nationalized all factories and transferred their administration to the state, with the aim of redistributing wealth among the workers. Azm passed several laws intended to terminate the socialist stamp imposed on Syria during the union years. He proposed that all enterprise and factories confiscated by Nasser be restored to their rightful owners and that industrialists, landowners, and businessmen be financially compensated for losses incurred during union. Syrian industrialists, some of whom had declared bankruptcy from 1958 to 1961, warmly welcomed the prospect.

But the plan never got past the drawing board. In March 1963, the Baath Party came to power in Syria and established a socialist state based on Nasser's model in Cairo. The Baath Party ordered the arrest of President Qudsi and Prime Minister Azm. Qudsi fled to Amman, Jordan while Azm took refuge at the Turkish Embassy in Damascus. Azm then fled to Lebanon and took up permanent residence in Beirut. Back in Syria, his civil rights were canceled and the government confiscated his vast landownings. He lived in bankruptcy, and in 1964 suffered heart problems, but checked out of the Italian hospital in Beirut because he was unable to pay his hospital bills.

Khalid al-Azm died and was buried in Beirut on November 18, 1965, after writing a three-volume memoir of his career, *Muzakarat Khalid al-Azm (Memoirs of Khalid al-Azm)*. Most noteworthy in his memoirs is Azm's animosity toward the officers who toppled him four times: in 1949, 1958, 1962, and 1963. His wife published the memoirs posthumously in 1973. The book has become a benchmark read on pre-1963 Syrian politics.

Sources:
Azm, Khalid. *Muzakarat* (1973).
Hawrani, Akram. *Muzakarat Akram al-Hawrani* (2000).
Itri, Abd al-Ghani *Abqariyyat* (1997).
Moubayed, Sami. *Damascus Between Democracy and Dictatorship* (2000).
Moubayed, Sami. *The Politics of Damascus 1920-1946* (1999).
Rathmell, Andrew. *Secret War in the Middle East* (1995).
Samman, Mutih. *Watan wa Askar* (1995).
Seale, Patrick. *The Struggle for Power in Syria* (1961).
Torrey, Gordon. *Syrian Politics and the Military* (1964).
Zahr al-Din, Abd al-Karim. *Muzakarati an Fatrat al-Infisal fi Souriyya* (1968).

al-Azma, Adil
(1886-1952)

From a prominent and wealthy Damascus family, Adil al-Azma studied public administration in Istanbul and began his career in 1911 as an instructor at the Sultanate School of Beirut. When World War I broke out in 1914, he was drafted into the Ottoman Army, and served until the Ottoman Empire fell in October 1918.

Al-Azma returned to Syria in 1919 and co-founded the Istiqlal Party with Shukri al-Quwatli. It was the first modern party in post-Ottoman Syria preaching pan-Arabism, anti-British solidarity, and demanding the creation of an Arab kingdom under the Hashemite crown. In 1922, he met a group of American diplomats in Damascus, sounding them out on local complaints with the French Mandate that was imposed on Syria in July 1920. French authorities accused him of working for the United States to obstruct French interests in the Middle East. He served one year in jail, and upon his release, was exiled to Amman, where he became political advisor to Prince Abdullah, the Emir of Transjordan.

In 1923, Adil al-Azma joined the Syrian-Palestinian Congress of Prince Michel Lutfallah, a grouping of Arab nationalists in exile, and worked relentlessly to bolster Hashemite influence in the Middle East. In 1925, he channeled arms and funds from Prince Abdullah's court to the Arab rebels in the Arab Mountain, who were launching a military insurrection against the French. In consequence, Azma was further blacklisted by the mandate regime. He also became a member in the Royal Jordanian Executive Bureau, holding this post until President Hashim al-Atasi, leader of the nationalist movement, came to power in 1936, issuing a general amnesty and recalling Azma to Syria.

When the Atasi administration fell in 1939, Azma moved to Baghdad, taught at local high schools and wrote articles on Arabism. He returned to Syria when his longtime friend, Shukri al-Quwatli, became president in August 1943. In 1945, Azma became governor of Lattakia. He held office in the coastal city at a time when Sulayman al-Murshed, a village chief living in the Lattakia vicinity, was amassing a rebel army in order to oust the Quwatli regime. Using funds from the French, Murshed proclaimed his divinity and ordered the villagers to rally to his support. When the French evacuated Syria in 1946, Azma had a police force attack Murshed's village and arrest him on the charge of treason and heresy. He lobbied with Quwatli to have him executed in his native village, but Quwatli refused, ordering his execution instead in Damascus.

From 1948 to 1949, Azma served as governor of Aleppo, and was fired from his post when General Husni al-Za'im came to power in March 1949, toppling the Quwatli regime. Azma was marginalized during the four-month era of Za'im and returned to political life when the general was overthrown in August 1949, becoming minister of state in the cabinet of Prime Minister Hashim al-Atasi.

Adil al-Azma retired from politics in 1950 and died in 1952. In 1990, Dr Khayriyyah Qasmiyyah, a historian at Damascus University, collected his memoirs and private papers into a book entitled, *Awrak Nabih wa Adil al-Azma* (*The*

Papers of Nabih and Adil al-Azma).

Sources:
Faris, George. *Man Hum fi al-`Alam al-Arabi?* (1957).
Khoury, Philip. *Syria and the French Mandate* (1987).
Qasmiyyah, Khayriyyah. *Awrak Nabih wa Adil al-Azma* (1990).

al-Azma, Bashir
(1910-1992)

Born to a prominent Damascene family, Bashir al-Azma studied medicine at Damascus University and graduated in 1934. He pursued his medical residency in Paris and moved back to Syria to become a professor at Damascus University.

In 1958, Syria and Egypt merged to form the United Arab Republic (UAR) and Azma was appointed minister of health in the UAR. During the union years, he also served as president of the Doctors' Syndicate in Syria. When union was dissolved in September 1961, Azma returned to his clinic in Damascus, and retained his post at the Doctors' Syndicate. On October 2, 1961, he joined a group of politicians in drafting the "secession declaration." The document accused President Gamal Abd al-Nasser of Egypt of "distorting the idea of Arab nationalism" and claiming that, during the union years, Nasser had "strangled political and democratic life" in Syria.

On March 16, 1962, following a prolonged cabinet crisis, President Nazim al-Qudsi asked Azma to form a national unity government. The officers, who were the de facto rulers of Syria, accepted Azma because of his professionalism, knowing that he would not interfere in their affairs while in office. Prime Minister Azma came to power with two objectives: to appease the officer class that had orchestrated the secession, and to curb the influence of Nasser in Syria. He struck at Nasser's men within the civilian leadership, firing them en masse, and filed an official complaint to the Arab League, protesting Nasser's interference in Syrian politics. He then declared that the constitution of 1950, having been abrogated by Nasser in 1958, would be restored.

The socialists, who were still in favor of Nasser, criticized Azma's measures and threatened to strike back if Azma did not cease his anti-Nasser campaign. To appease them, Azma appointed two members of the Baath Party, a socialist party that was pro-Nasser, as ministers. He resigned from office six months after becoming prime minister on September 17, 1962.

Bashir al-Azma.

He remained in government, however, and served as

deputy to Prime Minister Khalid al-Azm.

In March 1963, the Baath Party came to power in Syria and pledged to restore the UAR and punish all politicians who had taken part in the post-Nasser government. Dr Azma was dismissed from office and retired from politics, devoting his remaining years to his medical practice. He died in 1992. The Revolutionary Command Council (RCC) of the Baath Party terminated his civil rights. In 1991, Bashir al-Azma published his memoirs entitled, *Jeel al-Hazema Bayn al-Wihda wa al-Infisal* (*The Generation of Defeat Between Union and the Secession*).

Sources:

Azma, Bashir. *Jeel al-Hazeema Bayn al-Wihda wa al-Infisal* (1991).
Itri, Abd al-Ghani. *Hadeeth an al-Abqariyyat* (2000).
Samman, Mutih. *Watan wa Askar* (1995).
Zahr al-Din, Abd al-Karim. *Muzakarati an Fatrat al-Infisal fi Souriyya* (1968).

al-Azma, Nabih
(1886-1971)

From a noted Arab family in Damascus, Nabih al-Azma studied at the Ottoman Military Academy in Istanbul and graduated in 1907. He enlisted in the Ottoman Army and engaged in combat during World War I, serving in the Suez Canal, Gaza, and Tripoli.

In October 1918, the Ottoman Empire fell and Azma was discharged from service. He returned to Damascus and enlisted in the Arab Army of King Faysal I, the new ruler of Syria. In 1919, Faysal appointed Azma director of royal affairs in Syria. In 1920, he became chief of police in Aleppo. On July 24, 1920, the French proclaimed their mandate over Syria. King Faysal I was expelled and the Syrian Army, headed by Nabih's uncle Yusuf al-Azma, was defeated. Yusuf al-Azma, the minister of war under Faysal, was killed in combat, and this had a monumental effect on the young Azma. He fled Syria on July 25 and took up residence in Jordan. In 1922, Prince Abdullah, the Emir of Transjordan, appointed him Mayor of Amman. He also became mayor of Karak, then governor of Ajlun, and finally minister of interior in Jordan in 1925. In 1927, Azma became director of police and public security in Amman.

During his years in the Hashemite Kingdom, Nabih al-Azma established ties with Syrian nationalists in exile and was involved in the activities of the Syrian underground, of which his brother, Adil, was a leading member. The British authorities in Jordan pressured Abdullah to have him arrested, and as a result, Azma fled Amman and took up residence in Mecca. He served as political consultant to Prince Ali, the elder brother of Faysal and Abdullah. He then moved to Jerusalem, joining other Arab nationalists and establishing the Istiqlal Party, a pan-Arab organization calling for the liberation of all Arab territories from European control and the creation of a Hashemite kingdom in Arabia. In 1936, he returned to Damascus and allied himself with the National Bloc regime of President Hashim al-Atasi. He was appointed governor of the Sanjak of Alexanderetta, territory lying on the Syrian-Turkish border.

From 1936 to 1939, Azma formed the Arab Committee for the Defense of Palestine. It was a voluntary team of Syrian notables who were funding and supporting the anti-Jewish uprising in Jerusalem. In 1940, Azma was arrested by the French on the charge of treason and sentenced to forty years of hard labor. Shortly afterward, however, he was released by the moderate administration of French President Charles de Gaulle, having spent only nineteen months in jail. He left Syria and lived in Turkey until independence was achieved in 1946.

That year, Azma co-founded the National Party with a group of veteran politicians in Syria. It was a coalition of well-known urbanites who were allies of Saudi Arabia, opponents of the Hashemite bloc, and in favor of an alliance with Europe and the United States. Among its prominent members were Lutfi al-Haffar, Faris al-Khury, Jamil Mardam Bey, and Sabri al-Asali. Azma allied himself with President Shukri al-Quwatli, who had come to power in 1943, and became minister of defense. In March 1949, a coup was launched in Damascus by General Husni al-Za'im. The conspirators arrested President Quwatli and relieved all of his allies of their duties.

When Za'im was, in turn, ousted by military coup in August 1949, Azma returned to the spotlight as a veteran leader, but assumed no government post in the regime of President Hashim al-Atasi. In the 1950s, he joined the movement of Arab nationalism that was headed by President Gamal Abd al-Nasser of Egypt and supported Syria's merger with Egypt to form the United Arab Republic in 1958. In 1990, Nabih al-Azma's memoirs and private papers were published in a book entitled, *Awrak Nabih wa Adil al-Azma* (*The Papers of Nabih and Adil al-Azma*), compiled by the historian, Dr Khayriyyah Qasmiyyah.

Sources:
Faris, George. *Man Hum fi al-`Alam al-Arabi?* (1957).
Khoury, Philip. *Syria and the French Mandate* (1987).
Qasmiyya, Khayriyyah. *Awrak Nabih wa Adil al-Azma* (1990).

Bakdash, Khalid
(1912-1995)

Khalid Bakdash studied law at Damascus University and became an early member of the Syrian Communist Party. He dropped out of the university before obtaining his diploma, however, due to persecution by the French Mandate authorities.

A committed Marxist, Bakdash steadily rose in rank and reputation to become secretary-general of the Syrian Communist Party in 1934. Meanwhile, he joined the National Bloc in Damascus, the leading nationalist movement that was working against the French Mandate, and preached its independence cause. That same year, Bakdash translated the works of Karl Marx into Arabic, bringing to Syrian libraries the first Arabic version of *The Communist Manifesto*. In 1936, Bakdash accompanied National Bloc President Hashim al-Atasi to independence talks in Paris, serving as secretary to the National Bloc delegation. He went to Moscow in 1939 and studied the communist writings of Vladimir Lenin and Leon Trotsky at the International Communist College, returning to Syria in 1946.

Bakdash returned to Damascus in the wake of independence from France. President Shukri al-Quwatli strongly believed in political pluralism, thus granting Bakdash carte blanche to preach and write as he pleased. Throughout the 1940s, the communists were able to penetrate the urban intelligentsia in Damascus, Aleppo, Lattakia, Homs, and Hama. They were especially popular among university students and Sunni women of Damascus, who were attracted to their liberal views and the communist emancipation of women.

The increasing influence of the communists eventually alarmed the US administration of President Harry Truman, who authorized a CIA-supported coup in March 1949, bringing General Husni al-Za'im to power in Syria. The new ruler arrested Quwatli and cracked down on all communists. He closed the communist newspapers, revoked the party license, and arrested hundreds of communist activists. By late April 1949, four hundred Syrian communists, including Bakdash, were imprisoned. In the post-Za'im era, Bakdash regained his popularity, and in 1954, became the first communist leader to gain parliamentary office in the Arab world.

Once again, increased communist influence prompted other parties to work against Bakdash and his allies. Michel Aflaq and Salah al-Bitar, leaders of the Baath Party, were alarmed by the state's official shift toward the communist bloc, and spearheaded Syria's anti-communist campaign. In early June 1955, Prime Minister Sa'id al-Ghazzi dispatched a high-level parliamentary delegation, headed by Bakdash, to the Soviet Union to improve relations between Damascus and Moscow. By August 1955, diplomatic relations with Romania had been established and an arms deal between Syria and Czechoslovakia was negotiated.

Under the influence of Bakdash, Syria signed long-term arms deals with Moscow, established cultural ties with the Russians, and became a recipient of significant soft-term loans from the Kremlin. In 1956, Bakdash accompanied President Quwatli on the first visit by a Syrian head of state to Moscow, aimed at lobbying support for Egypt in her war against Great Britain, France, and Israel. Aflaq and Bitar began to mobilize against Bakdash, fearing that he would counter-balance their influence. In 1958, Bitar went to Cairo to plead for union with Egypt. He knew that Nasser, although an ally of the USSR, did not believe in a multi-party system, and this was clear from his crackdown on all political parties in Egypt from 1952 to 1958. When Syria and Egypt merged to form the United Arab Republic (UAR) in 1958, the Communist Party was outlawed, its leadership was persecuted, and Khalid Bakdash was forced into exile in Prague.

Throughout the UAR years (1958-1961), he remained in Eastern Europe, observing and condemning the wide-scale arrests that his followers suffered under Nasser's police state. In September 1961, a coup d'etat toppled the Nasser government in Syria, dissolving the UAR. Bakdash supported the new administration of President Nazim al-Qudsi but was surprised to see his party outlawed once again under the new regime. Like Nasser before him, Qudsi feared Bakdash's return and banned him from Syria from 1961 to 1963, despite a declaration of recognition and support by Bakdash for the post-Nasser regime. Syria's new chief of staff, Abd al-Karim Zahr al-Din, remarked to *Time Magazine*, "He (Bakdash) is welcome, but he will be hanged on arrival!" Bakdash gambled and took the risk in 1962, only to be turned away at Damascus Airport. In March 1963, the Baath Party came to power and also extended the ban, fearing that his influence would spread once again, as it did in the 1950s. The Military Committee of the Baath Party pledged to restore the UAR and vowed to have Bakdash arrested, accusing him of having fueled the anti-Nasser coup of 1961. His civil rights were terminated and the party's official newspaper was closed.

Bakdash traveled between Eastern Europe and Lebanon, not returning to Syria until the radical military wing of the Baath Party came to power in February 1966. During his exile (1958-1966), he devoted his efforts to writing about the communist cause in the Middle East. Among his published works in the 1960s are *Fi Sabil Huriyyat al-Sha`b al-Wihdawiyya wa al-Dimocratiyya (In Pursuit of a People's Unionist and Democratic Freedoms)*, *Al-Hizb al-Shiou'ii fi Souriyya wa Lubnan (The Communist Party in Syria and Lebanon)*, *Al-Alaqat bayn al-Duwal al-Arabiyya wa all Itihad al-Sovieti (Relations Between the Arab Countries and the USSR)*, and *Al-Sira' fi Sabil al-Ishtirakiyya (Struggle in Pursuit of Socialism)*.

The military regime of Salah Jadid welcomed Bakdash back to Syria in 1966 but made it clear that no meetings, speeches, or activities would be tolerated. Jadid needed the endorsement of the USSR for his regime and saw no better way to do that other than bringing Bakdash back after eight years in exile. The communist veteran suffered a sharp decline in popularity due to his compliance to the Jadid regime, and he resigned from the Communist Party leadership in 1968.

Bakdash reassumed the helm upon the overthrow of Jadid and Hafez al-Asad came to power in 1970. Asad struck an alliance with Bakdash, allowing the Communist Party to reactivate itself within socialist ranks but forbad Bakdash's active engagement in mass politics. On March 7, 1972, Asad along with Bakdash founded the National Progressive Front (NPF), a coalition of socialist parties functioning under the umbrella of the Baath.

Under the NPF, however, the Communist Party was forbidden to issue its own publication, stage political rallies, or recruit members from Syrian universities. Khalid Bakdash became a committee member of the NPF, representing the Communist Party until his death in 1995. His wife, Wisal Farha, replaced him as secretary-general of the Communist Party.

Sources:
Azm, Khalid. *Muzakarat Khalid al-Azm* (1973).
Commins, David. *Historical Dictionary of Modern Syria*, (1996).
Fansa, Bashir. *Al-Naqbat wa al-Mughamarat* (1997).
Hawrani, Akram. *Muzakarat Akram al-Hawrani* (2000).
Moubayed, Sami. *Damascus Between Democracy and Dictatorship* (2000).
Rathmell, Andrew. *Secret War in the Middle East* (1995).
Samman, Mutih. *Watan wa Askar* (1995).
Seale, Patrick. *The Struggle for Syria* (1961).
Time Magazine, "Welcome…" (October 20, 1961)
Torrey, Gordon. *Syrian Politics and the Military* (1964).
Uthman, Hashim. *Al-Ahzab al-Siyasiyya fi Souriyya: al-Siriyya wa al-Mu'lana* (2001).

al-Bakri, Fawzi
(1887-1960)

Fawzi al-Bakri, born and raised in Damascus, was the scion of a family of Arab-Ottoman notability. His father, Ata Pasha al-Bakri, was one of the most prominent Arabs in the imperial court in Istanbul. Ata and his sons Fawzi and Nasib were politically allied to Sultan Abdulhamid II, but fell from grace when the Sultan was ousted by military coup in 1908. The Bakri family criticized the young Ottoman officers who came to power, shifting into the opposition headed by well-known Syrians demanding the replacement of Ottomanism with Arabism.

In 1911, Bakri co-founded the al-Fatat Society, a secret party that called for the overthrow of the Ottoman Empire. In August 1914, at the outbreak of World War I, Bakri was conscripted into the Ottoman Army and stationed in Mecca, where he became a loyalist to Sharif Husayn, the Prince of Mecca. In 1915, he recruited Husayn's son, Faysal, into the secret society. In June 1916, Husayn launched a military uprising against the Ottoman Empire. Bakri spent 1916 to 1918 in Arabia, working as a link between the Hashemite family in Mecca and the Damascus underground. The Ottoman Empire was defeated in 1918, and that same year, Bakri became advisor to King Faysal I, the new ruler of Syria. In 1919, Bakri co-founded the Istiqlal Party, the first official party in post-Ottoman Syria. Istiqlal preached an Arab identity and aimed at uniting all liberated Arab territories under the Hashemite crown. From 1918 to 1920, Bakri served as a deputy for Damascus on the Syrian National Congress, the equivalent of a modern parliament.

When the French occupied Syria in July 1920, King Faysal fled to Europe and Bakri returned to Mecca, where he served once again as consultant to Sharif Husayn, who by then had become King of the Hijaz (now known as Saudi Arabia). In November 1920, Husayn appointed Bakri minister of interior in the Kingdom of the Hijaz. He held this post until Prince Abd al-Aziz Ibn Saud occupied the Hijaz in 1925.

Bakri returned to Damascus in 1925 and joined the People's Party, the first modern party in French Mandate Syria. Bakri allied himself with the leader of the People's Party, Abd al-Rahman Shahbandar, the leading statesman of the 1920s, and helped lead the Druze uprising of 1925. Bakri took up arms with Sultan al-Atrash and led armed attacks against the French Army in the Arab Mountain. In 1927, the French Army crushed the revolt and a French military tribunal sentenced Bakri to death. He fled to Amman and worked with Prince Abdullah until the French issued a general amnesty, allowing Fawzi al-Bakri to return to Syria in 1932.

Sources:
Dawn, Ernest. *From Ottomanism to Arabism: Essays on The Origins of Arab Nationalism* (1973).
Tlas, Mustapha. *Al-Thawra al-Arabiyya al-Kubra* (1987).
Zayd, Prince. *Muzakarat al-Ameer Zayd* (1990).

al-Bakri, Nasib
(1888-1966)

Nasib al-Bakri was born and raised in Damascus by a prominent Arab-Ottoman family. His father, Ata Pasha al-Bakri, was among the most important Arabs in the imperial court of Istanbul. Along with his father and his brother, Fawzi, Nasib was politically allied to Sultan Abdulhamid II, but fell out of favor when the Sultan was overthrown by the 1908 military coup. After criticizing the young Ottoman officers who came to power, the Bakri family shifted their allegiance to the opposition headed by Syrian notables demanding that Ottomanism be replaced by Arabism.

In 1911, Nasib al-Bakri co-founded the al-Fatat Society, a clandestine group devoted to the overthrow of the Ottoman Empire. In 1916, Bakri became a loyalist to Sharif Husayn, the Prince of Mecca, who was leading an armed uprising against the Ottomans from the Arabian Desert. Bakri spent 1916 to 1918 in Arabia, working as a link between the Hashemite family in Mecca and the Damascus underground.

The Ottoman Empire was defeated in 1918, and along with his brother, Fawzi, Bakri became advisor to King Faysal I, the new ruler of Syria. In 1919, Bakri co-founded the Istiqlal Party, an offshoot of the al-Fatat Society, the first offi-cial registered party in post-Ottoman Syria. The party preached an Arab identity and aimed at uniting all liberated Arab territories under the Hashemite crown. From 1918 to 1920, Bakri served as a deputy for Damascus in the Syrian National Congress, the equivalent of a modern parliament.

Bakri was forced to flee Damascus when the French Mandate was proclaimed over Syria in July 1920. He went to Amman and served as advisor to Prince Abdullah, Faysal's older brother, from 1921 to 1923. When the French issued a general amnesty in 1923, Bakri returned to Syria and joined the People's Party of Abd al-Rahman Shahbandar. It was the first modern party in French Mandate Syria, aimed at terminating the mandate, establishing a democratic system, and orienting the country's foreign policy toward the Hashemite families in Amman, Mecca, and Baghdad.

In 1925, Nasib al-Bakri joined the Syrian revolt of the Arab Mountain, headed by Shahbandar and the Druze leader Sultan al-Atrash. Shahbandar offered the revolt his political leadership while Bakri served as a commanding officer of the Druze rebel army. He led armed attacks in the Arab Mountain, set ablaze lead-ing government offices, and held many Frenchmen hostage. He was sentenced to death by a French Military Tribunal and forced to flee to Amman, returning to Syria when the French issued an amnesty in 1927.

While in exile, Bakri was hailed as one of the most charismatic and brave lead-ers of the Syrian resistance. Returning to Syria, he co-founded the National Bloc with Hashim al-Atasi in 1928. The party's aim was to liberate Syria from the French through diplomatic rather than armed resistance. In 1928, he held office for three months on the Constitutional Assembly that drafted the first republi-can constitution for Syria. In 1930, Atasi appointed Bakri vice president of the National Bloc. In 1932, Bakri ran for parliament on a National Bloc ticket and became a deputy for Damascus. He nominated himself for parliament again in 1936, 1943, and 1947, winning every round. When the National Bloc came to power in 1936, and Hashim al-Atasi became president of the republic, Bakri took over Bloc leadership and broke with his former patron, Abd al-Rahman Shahbandar, who shifted into the opposition. In 1937, President Atasi appointed Bakri governor of the Arab Mountain. In February 1939, he became minister of justice in the short-lived cabinet of Prime Minister Lutfi al-Haffar. In April 1941, the independent prime minister, Khalid al-Azm, appointed him minister of national economy and agriculture.

When Syria achieved independence in 1946, Nasib al-Bakri joined the People's Party of Nazim al-Qudsi and Rushdi al-Kikhiya. It was a pro-Western party that called for Arab unity. In 1951, President Atasi appointed him minister to Saudi Arabia, but due to ideological disagreements with the House of Saud (he was pro-Hashemite), Bakri declined the position. Instead, Atasi appointed him ambassador to the Hashemite Kingdom of Jordan. He resigned from office when General Adib al-Shishakli came to power in 1953.

When Shishakli was toppled by military coup, Bakri became president of the People's Party in Damascus. He created a committee to run its political affairs, with Tawfiq al-Mahayni as secretary and Hashim al-Nehlawi as treasurer. Both of them, however, were unknown names in Syria, forcing Bakri to call on more prominent citizens like Dr Munir al-Sadat and Jaafar al-Hasani into the party leadership. Despite these and other efforts, Nasib al-Bakri still was unable to secure a power base for his party in the Syrian capital, and resigned its leadership in April 1957.

Sources:
Commins, David. *Historical Dictionary of Modern Syria* (1996).
Dawn, Ernest. *From Ottomanism to Arabism: Essays on The Origins of Arab Nationalism* (1973).
Itri, Abd al-Ghani. *Alam wa Mubdioun* (1999).
Khoury, Philip. *Syria and the French Mandate* (1987).
Rayyes, Munir. *Al-Kitab al-Zahabi lil Thawrat al-Wataniyya fi al-Sharq al-Arabi* (1966).
Shahbandar, Abd al-Rahman. *Al-Thawra al-Wataniyya al-Souriyya* (1933).
Tlas, Mustapha. *Al-Thawra al-Arabiyya al-Kubra* (1987).
Uthman, Hashim. *Al-Ahzab al-Siyasiyya fi Souriyya: al-Siriyya wa al-Mu'lana* (2001).
Zayd, Prince. *Muzakarat al-Ameer Zayd* (1990).

Barakat, Subhi
(1883-1939)

Subhi Barakat was a native of the city of Antioch in the Sanjak of Alexanderetta, fertile territory on the Syrian-Turkish border that is currently part of Turkey. He began his career by administering his vast estates in the Sanjak. Due to his wealth, Barakat emerged as a local leader of Antioch in the 1910s.

When the Ottoman Empire was defeated in 1918, Barakat became a deputy for Antioch in the Syrian National Congress, the equivalent of a modern parliament that declared independence and crowned Faysal I as King of Syria. Barakat led an armed uprising against the French troops that had landed in his hometown in 1919, and he funded attacks on French troops along the Syrian coastline and in the neighboring mountains. His movement grew into a revolt that was dubbed "the revolt of Antioch." Barakat coordinated armed acts against French troops with the resistance leader, Saleh al-Ali, and the Aleppine leader, Ibrahim Hananu. In 1920, following the complete French occupation of Syria, Barakat made his peace with the mandate authority and promised cooperation in exchange for political office. The French gladly complied and appointed him president of the Syrian Federal Council on June 28, 1922, vested with presidential powers.

The French created the Federal Council to preside over all security, culture, and foreign affairs of the three recently-formed states of Damascus, Aleppo, and the Alawite Mountain. While in office, Subhi Barakat founded the Syrian Union Party, a coalition of notables with the goal of formulating an independence treaty with France, admitting Syria into the League of Nations, and discarding the broad Arab identity in favor of a Syrian identity. He chose his ministers with care, selecting them from among respected citizens, all the while trying to market himself as a dedicated nationalist. He appointed Dr Rida al-Sa'id, the president of Damascus University, as minister of education,

Subhi Barakat.

the civil servant Ata al-Ayyubi as minister of interior, and the businessman Mohammad Ali al-Abid, a former Ottoman ambassador in the United States, as minister of finance.

Barakat's era, however, was marred by economic dislocation, commercial and agricultural stagnation, and record levels of unemployment. As a result, Barakat was indirectly blamed for his country's suffering and he lost all form of public support. His image was further tarnished when the French, bent on crushing a military uprising against the mandate, bombed Damascus in October 1925, inflicting heavy civilian casualties. Not long after, on December 21, 1925, Barakat's government collapsed.

In 1932, Subhi Barakat was elected to parliament and served as deputy of Antioch until 1936. He then ran for presidential office, and despite popular support from the Syrian Union Party, lost the election. The French compensated Barakat for his defeat, appointing him speaker of parliament in the administration of President Mohammad Ali al-Abid on June 11, 1932.

From here, however, Barakat's political career came to a rapid end. He proved inefficient in his new post and lost all French endorsement. He then tried to build bridges with the National Bloc, the leading anti-French movement, but was shunned by the nationalists for his pro-French record. In 1933, Barakat voted against a French-sponsored treaty in parliament that gave Syria a limited degree of autonomy. In response, the French relieved him of his duties on November 25, 1932. He applied for membership in the National Bloc, but his request was turned down by the Bloc president, Hashim al-Atasi.

Facing increased political isolation, Barakat moved to Turkey and applied for Turkish citizenship. In 1939, the Sanjak of Alexanderetta was annexed to Turkey and his native Antioch became part of the Turkish Republic. Subhi Barakat nominated himself as a deputy for Antioch in the Turkish Parliament and won, serving briefly until his death in 1939.

Sources:
Hakim, Yusuf. *Souriyya wa al-Intidab al-Faransi* (1966).
Khoury, Philip. *Syria and the French Mandate* (1987).
Moubayed, Sami. *The Politics of Damascus 1920-1946* (1999).
Shambrook, Peter. *French Imperialism in Syria 1927-1936* (1998).

al-Barazi, Husni
(1893-?)

Husni al-Barazi was born in the city of Hama in western Syria to a family of prominent and wealthy landowners. He studied law at the Ottoman Academy of Law in Istanbul and ran his vast estates and plantations in Hama.

In 1916, Barazi joined the Syrian underground and became a member of the al-Ahd Party, an early resistance movement in Ottoman Syria. When the Ottoman Empire was defeated in 1918, he allied himself with King Faysal I, the new ruler of Syria, and became governor of the Sanjak of Alexanderetta, territory on the Syrian-Turkish border, from 1918 to 1920. In 1920, the French occupied Syria and Barazi became part of the Hama underground, joining the Istiqlal Party that worked for the liberation of Syria from the French Mandate.

In April 1926, Barazi became minister of interior in the pro-French cabinet of Prime Minister Ahmad Nami. He joined ranks with two other officials, Education Minister Faris al-Khury and Public Works Minister Lutfi al-Haffar, in opposing French-imposed policies in the new cabinet. Three months later, the French high commissioner fired all three men from their posts, then had them arrested. Barazi joined the anti-French movement during the 1920s and was allied to Abd al-Rahman Shahbandar, the leading anti-French statesman of his generation. In October 1927, Barazi co-founded the National Bloc, the first organized anti-French movement, with a group of urban notables headed by Hashim al-Atasi.

In 1928, Barazi held office for three months on the Constitutional Assembly that drafted the first republican constitution for Syria. In May 1934, he became minister of education in the pro-French cabinet of Prime Minister Taj al-Din al-Hasani. His collaboration with a pro-French regime damaged his reputation within the National Bloc, where he was asked to either resign from office or from the Bloc leadership. He resigned from the National Bloc and allied himself with Prime Minister Hasani and other pro-French officials in Damascus. In 1941, Hasani became president of the republic, and rewarded Barazi by appointing him prime minister on April 18, 1942. Barazi clashed with the president, however, over the distribution of power and accused Hasani of attempting to curb his constitutional powers. On January 8, 1943, Hasani forced him to resign from office. He ran for parliament as an independent in 1943 and 1949, winning both times.

In 1948, Husni al-Barazi was the only deputy in parliament who publicly supported the UN partition for Palestine, proposing the creation of an independent and small Jewish state in the Middle East. He argued that the Arabs could not possibly fight off the Jews, and accepting them would be far better than dragging the region into a never-ending confrontation. He briefly served as governor of Aleppo in 1948 and befriended the Syrian chief of staff, Husni al-Za'im, who came to power in March 1949 and appointed Barazi advisor at the Presidential Palace. In April 1949, Za'im made himself military governor of Syria and appointed Barazi as his deputy. He remained in office until Za'im was overthrown in August 1949, after which he was once again was elected into the Constitutional Assembly.

Husni al-Barazi.

Barazi teamed up with Nazir Fansa, Husni al-Za'im's brother-in-law, and founded an Aleppo-based newspaper, *al-Nass*. The newspaper was vehemently opposed to communism, preached pro-British and pro-American views, and criticized the socialist government of Gamal Abd al-Nasser that had come to power in Egypt in 1952. It was politically close to the pro-American regime in Turkey, headed by President Jalal Bayar and Prime Minister Adnan Menderes.

Due to his anti-Nasser views, Barazi clashed with the pro-Nasser administration in Damascus. In July 1955, Abd al-Hamid Sarraj, the director of Syrian Intelligence, arrested six officers on the charges of plotting a coup and accused Barazi of masterminding the plot. Husni al-Barazi fled to Lebanon before a warrant was issued for his arrest and his newspaper, *al-Nass*, was closed down.

Sources:
Haffar, Salma. *Lutfi al-Haffar 1885-1968* (1997).

Moubayed, Sami. *The Politics of Damascus 1920-1946* (1999).

Rathmell, Andrew. *Secret War in the Middle East* (1995).

Spears, Edward. *Fulfillment of a Mission* (1977).

al-Barazi, Muhsen
(1904-1949)

Muhsen al-Barazi was a native of Hama, a city in western Syria lying on the Orontos River. He studied law at the University of Lyon and graduated in 1930.

In August 1933, Barazi became a founding member of the League of National Action in Quarna'il (Mount Lebanon), a movement aimed at uniting Arab intellectuals into one political force that would help liberate the region from European colonialism. The League rose to overnight fame in Syria and Lebanon, calling for economic integration of all Arab countries once the French and British Mandates were abolished. The League included passionate young men who were to become leaders in Syria. Among its earliest members were the noted historian and professor Constantine Zurayk, the philosopher Zaki al-Arsuzi, the politician Sabri al-Asali, and the diplomat Farid Zayn al-Din.

In addition to his political activity, Barazi was a professor of law at Damascus University. In April 1941, he became minister of education in the independent cabinet of Prime Minister Khalid al-Azm. In August 1943, he became private aide-de-camp to President Shukri al-Quwatli. When independence was achieved in April 1946, he became Quwatli's speechwriter, confidant, legal consultant, and special envoy to the Arab world. During the Arab-Israeli War of 1948, Barazi conducted shuttle diplomacy on Quwatli's behalf, journeying from one Arab capital to the next, and lobbying support for the Arab cause in Europe. In March 1949, however, a coup d'etat took place in Syria, launched by General Husni al-Za'im, toppling Shukri al-Quwatli and all his associates.

Unlike all other members of Quwatli's team, Dr Barazi was not fired, but rather was retained at his post at the Presidential Palace, becoming advisor to Husni al-Za'im. With time, Za'im's reliance on the French-trained politician increased, and on June 25, 1949, he appointed Barazi prime minister. Za'im charged Barazi with polishing Za'im's image in the Arab world and conducting a peace treaty with Israel. Barazi was delegated to commence talks with his Israeli counterpart, Prime Minister David Ben Gurion, and formulate a solution to several outstanding points, such as the Palestinian refugee problem, access to the waters of Lake Tiberias, and the feasibility of a Za'im-Ben Gurion summit. On Arab affairs, Barazi took

Muhsen al-Barazi.

advantage of his warm relations with Saudi Arabia, Jordan, Egypt, and Lebanon (all of which were made during the Quwatli years) to secure Arab recognition for the Za'im regime.

In July 1949, Barazi negotiated a deal with Lebanese Prime Minister Riyad al-Sulh that obliged Za'im to hand over Antune Sa'ada, a Lebanese fugitive wanted for high treason in Lebanon, in exchange for full-fledged Lebanese support for the Za'im regime. Sa'ada had taken asylum in Syria following a foiled coup attempt by his party, the Syrian Social Nationalist Party (SSNP), to seize power in Beirut. Barazi finalized the hand-over of Sa'ada to Beirut, where authorities had him executed on July 8, 1949. That same afternoon, Barazi signed several long-term economic treaties with Sulh, ushering the dawn of a new era between both countries.

This prompted a group of SSNP officers in the Syrian Army to begin planning for Barazi's downfall. On August 6, the new prime minister, who was being described by opposition papers as "an evil genius", was approached by Israeli Foreign Minister Moshe Sharett to arrange a date for peace talks between the two parties. Barazi agreed, saying, "I am probably committing political suicide, and even taking a calculated risk of assassination in the hope of getting American assistance to get my country on its feet." He then addressed the US attaché in Syria and solemnly said, "Your country must not let me down!" Barazi never had time to conclude talks with Israel, however, for he was executed, along with Za'im, by disgruntled army officers on August 14, 1949. In 1953, the Lebanese journalist Kamel Mroweh published a collection of Muhsen al-Barazi's private papers in the Beirut-based *al-Hayat,* and in 1994, the historian Khayriyyah Qasmiyyah collected them into one book entitled, *Muzakarat Muhsen al-Barazi (Memoirs of Muhsen al-Barazi).*

Sources:
Arslan, Adil. *Muzakarat al-Ameer Adil Arslan an al-Za'im Husni al-Za'im* (1954).
Babil, Nasuh. *Sahafa wa Siyassa fi Souriyya* (1987).
Moubayed, Sami. *Damascus Between Democracy and Dictatorship* (2000).
Qasmiyyah, Khayriyyah. *Muzakarat Muhsen al-Barazi* (1994).
Rathmell, Andrew. *Secret War in the Middle East* (1995).
Seale, Patrick. *The Struggle for Power in Syria* (1961).

al-Barazi, Najib
(1882-1967)

Najib al-Barazi was born in Syria to a family of traditional landowners. He was considered the wealthiest man in Hama at the turn of the twentieth century. His wealth brought him high acclaim in local districts and he emerged during the final years of the Ottoman Empire as the uncontested leader of Hama.

Barazi criticized the revolution of 1908, which brought a group of young officers to power in Istanbul, and was arrested by Jamal Pasha, the military governor of Syria. He joined the Syrian underground in 1916 and supported the

Arab revolt that was launched against the Ottomans by Sharif Husayn, the Prince of Mecca. In 1919, he funded the revolt of the Syrian coast, launched by Saleh al-Ali, and donated significant sums to other rebels who were fighting the French in Lattakia and Aleppo. In 1920, Barazi became head of the Hama Town Council. He was forced out of office by the French Mandate authorities in 1925 due to his connections with the Syrian revolt in the Arab Mountain. In mid-1925, he became a main donor to the anti-French movement of Fawzi Qawuqji in Hama and delegated his followers to fight and assist in the national uprising against the mandate. The French

Najib al-Barazi.

suppressed the revolt and took vengeance on Barazi for his involvement in its activities by destroying his palace and burning some of his vast plantations.

In October 1927, Najib al-Barazi co-founded the National Bloc with Hashim al-Atasi. It was a coalition of urban notables and politicians who were striving to expel the French from Syria through varied means such as armed resistance and diplomatic efforts. Barazi served as the official representative of Hama at the National Bloc founding conference and was a Bloc candidate for the parliamentary elections of 1932, 1936, and 1943, winning in each round. Najib Agha served as president of its Hama branch until all parties were outlawed in 1963.

During the union years with Egypt (1958-1961), Najib al-Barazi suffered the nationalization of his land and confiscation of his property. Like the French Mandate almost forty years earlier, Barazi was "retired" from political life by the Baath Party in March 1963 and remained in seclusion until his death in 1967.

Sources:

Haffar. Salma. *Lutfi al-Haffar 1885-1968* (1993).

Kayyali, Abd al-Rahman. *Al-Marahil fi al-Intidab al-Faransi 1926-1938* (1958-1960).

Khoury, Philip. *Syria and the French Mandate* (1987).

Khury, Colette. *Awrak Faris al-Khury,* Vol II (1997).

Moubayed, Sami. *The Politics of Damascus 1920-1946* (1999).

Qassab Hasan. Najat. *Saniou al-Jalaa fi Souriyya* (1999).

Barmada, Rashad
(1913-1988)

Rashad Barmada grew up in Aleppo. He studied law at Damascus University and established a legal practice in Aleppo. In 1947, he co-founded the People's Party, a political party that was created to counter and oppose the centralized regime of President Shukri al-Quwatli.

The People's Party accused Quwatli of nepotism, centralized administration, and favoritism toward the people of Damascus. The party was funded and supported by the commercial class in Aleppo and administered by Nazim al-Qudsi and Rushdi al-Kikhiya. Its main objective was to create a healthy democracy in Syria and merge Syria and neighboring Iraq into one state.

In 1947, Barmada became a deputy for Aleppo in the Syrian Parliament. In June 1950, Qudsi became prime minister and appointed him minister of interior. Barmada voiced his opposition to having a military officer serving in cabinet, and called for the resignation of General Fawzi Selu, the minister of defense. He constantly clashed with Selu and tried to prevent him from controlling the gendarmerie, claiming that if he lost, the civilian government would lose all ability to enforce its will throughout the country. When Selu got his way and assumed control of the armed units, Barmada resigned from office in protest. He spoke out against the military regime of President Adib al-Shishakli, who came to power in November 1951, and was rewarded by incarceration at the notorious Mezzeh prison in Damascus. Shishakli ruled Syria with an iron fist, outlawing all political parties and tolerating no opinion other than his own. He ordered Barmada's arrest and closed the People's Party. When Shishakli was overthrown by military coup in February 1954, Rashad Barmada was released from jail and appointed minister of defense in the cabinet of Prime Minister Sa'id al-Ghazzi.

In the second half of the 1950s, Rashad Barmada established himself as a vehement opponent to the socialist policies of President Gamal Abd al-Nasser of Egypt and his meddling in the domestic affairs of Syria. In 1955, Shukri al-Quwatli was reelected president and transformed Syria into an Egyptian satellite. He made friends with Nasser's allies in Eastern Europe and appointed socialist leaders in prominent positions in government. Barmada worked against him and called for a break from Egyptian influence. In 1958, Syria and Egypt merged to form the United Arab Republic (UAR) and Barmada voiced his opposition to the new regime.

Barmada was sidelined during the UAR era and supported the coup d'etat that toppled it in September 1961. He joined a group of disgruntled politicians and drafted the "secession" manifesto, declaring Syria's permanent break from the UAR and accusing Nasser of having established a dictatorship in Syria. He then allied himself with the post-union administration of his long-time friend and party comrade, Nazim al-Qudsi. In December 1961, Barmada became minister of defense in the cabinet of Prime Minister Ma'mun al-Kuzbari, and in March 1962, he became deputy to Prime Minister Bashir al-Azma. He also served as minister of education in the independent cabinet of Khalid al-Azm. From 1961 to 1963, Barmada served as a deputy for Aleppo in parliament.

On March 28, 1962, a coup took place in Syria, launched by Colonel Abd al-Karim al-Nehlawi, who arrested President Qudsi, Prime Minister Ma'ruf al-Dawalibi, and Ma'mun al-Kuzbari, the speaker of parliament. Barmada was spared arrest and served as an intermediary between the arrested politicians and Colonel Nehlawi. When he failed at releasing them, a counter-coup broke out on April 1, launched by officers loyal to the Qudsi government.

In March 1963, the Baath Party came to power in Syria and pledged to restore the UAR. The Baath cracked down on all those who had worked with the anti-union government and arrested Rashad Barmada. The People's Party was dissolved, Barmada's civil rights were terminated, and he was briefly arrested. Thus, Rashad Barmada retired from political life and worked at his legal practice in Aleppo.

Sources:

Azm, Khalid. *Muzakarat Khalid al-Azm* (1973).
Faris, George. *Man Hum fi al-`Alam al-Arabi?* (1957).
Hawrani, Akram. *Muzakarat Akram al-Hawrani* (2000).
Samman, Mutih. *Watan wa Askar* (1995).
Seale, Patrick. *Syria and the French Mandate* (1961).

al-Barudi, Fakhri
(1889-1966)

Fakhri al-Barudi was born in Hama and raised in Damascus. He studied agriculture in Paris and returned to Syria in 1910 to work as a journalist. He founded a low-budget magazine of political satire in Damascus and served as its editor-in-chief until it was forced out of business for financial reasons in 1911. He then began writing for the popular daily, *al-Muqtabas*, run by the veteran journalist, Mohammad Kurd Ali.

Al-Barudi was also a founder of al-Fatat, the leading opposition party in Ottoman Syria. Al-Fatat had originally been established by five Arab activists living in Paris in 1911. The organization called on Arab and Turkish citizens to remain united within the Ottoman framework, but claimed that the Arabs should have equal rights and obligations as their Ottoman counterparts. In 1913, al-Fatat moved its offices to Beirut, and in 1914, its founders opened an office in Damascus to coordinate nationalist activity. In the summer of 1913, the al-Fatat founders called for an Arab Congress in Paris to discuss the deteriorating conditions in the Ottoman Empire. Not wishing to create a permanent rift with authorities in Istanbul, al-Fatat did not call for complete Arab emancipation, but rather, tried to mend relations with the Ottomans. When that failed, they publicly headed the separatist movement, demanding a complete break with Ottomanism in favor of Arabism.

When World War I broke out in 1914, Barudi was conscripted into the Ottoman Army. He fought in the Arabian Desert, was imprisoned by the Allies, then was deported to Cairo in 1917. He managed to escape from his Cairo jail cell and joined the Arab underground, whose leader, Prince Faysal, was also a member of al-Fatat. Barudi fled to the Arabian Desert and enlisted in the Arab Army of Sharif Husayn, the Prince of Mecca, who was leading a military uprising against the Ottoman Empire. After the empire was defeated, Faysal was crowned king of Syria in March 1920. Barudi became personal assistant to the new king. He was then promoted to director of the royal entourage. The French imposed their mandate over Syria in July 1920 and dethroned Faysal. He was exiled to Europe and Barudi fled to Jordan, where he remained until the French issued an amnesty that permitted his return to Syria in 1923.

Fakhri al-Barudi joined the People's Party, the first organized party in French Mandate Syria, and allied himself with its leader, Abd al-Rahman Shahbandar. In 1925, he joined the rebel forces of Sultan al-Atrash in the Arab Mountain and led an armed insurrection in the Ghuta orchards on the outskirts of Damascus. When the revolt was suppressed in 1927, the French exiled him from Syria. He went to Amman and stayed there until a general amnesty allowed him back home in 1928.

Upon Barudi's return, he was voted into a three-month tenure on the Constitutional Assembly that drafted the first republican constitution for Syria. Also in 1928, he joined the National Bloc, the leading anti-French movement that was headed by the veteran nationalist, Hashim al-Atasi. The Bloc was composed of a group of urban notables who sought to end the French Mandate through diplomatic means rather than armed resistance. Barudi ran for parliament on a Bloc ticket in 1928, 1932, 1936, 1943 and 1947, winning in every round with an overwhelming majority. In 1934, he founded the Bureau of National Propaganda, a media outlet for the National Bloc, and was responsible for marketing the Bloc, its cause of independence, and its leaders in Damascus, Aleppo, Lattakia, Homs, and Hama.

In addition to his political activity, Fakhri al-Barudi became a popular social figure in Damascus as well. He was a poet, a songwriter, a patron of the arts, a sports coach, and a dance instructor. During the years of the mandate, Fakhri al-Barudi enjoyed street popularity like no other politician in Syria. He spent most of his time pursuing his artistic interests, fostering the careers of young artists and upgrading Syrian Radio, which he had co-founded in 1943. He also served on the administrative board of the Arab Music Academy, which he had also co-founded in 1928.

Among the artists created and promoted by Barudi was the Syrian artist Sabah Fakhri, whose real name was Sabah Abu Qaws, but who renamed himself "Fakhri" in honor of his patron, Fakhri al-Barudi. From 1946 to 1963, Fakhri al-Barudi's palace in the Qanawat district became a daily meeting point for artists, politicians, and intellectuals. No foreign or Arab head of state would visit normally-conservative Damascus without calling on Fakhri al-Barudi and attending one of his celebrated receptions where dancing until dawn was a common practice. Evening forums would be held nightly, where topics of interest would be discussed in conversations chaired by Barudi himself. The Barudi salons debated politics, religion, and philosophical affairs. The forums, open to all, were coined "Barudian nights."

Fakhri al-Barudi.

Throughout the 1930s and 1940s, Barudi single-handedly commanded the masses in Damascus and was able to mobilize citywide support for all Bloc activities. He was the secret behind the Bloc's success, and served as the link between its leadership and the public. In 1936, protesting French activities, Barudi led a massive demonstration in Damascus, calling for shopkeepers and merchants to strike. Instantaneously, the country's commercial and labor force responded to his request, and by the following week, all other cities shut down in solidarity. Syria went into a general strike for a sixty-day period, forcing the French to give in to Bloc demands and recognize its leaders as the legitimate representatives of the Syrian people.

In 1936, Barudi founded the National Youth, a paramilitary youth force modeled after the Brown Shirts in Germany and the Black Shirts in Italy. The National Youth was created to protect locals from French aggression and dispense propaganda for the National Bloc. Its leaders were a group of young men who sought to introduce the concept of disciplined and armed resistance to occupation. As long as the French were not permitting the creation of a Syrian Army, Barudi claimed, the National Youth would have to serve as an alternative. He believed in the concept of mass politics and created a powerful network of young men to engage in marches, strikes, and rallies in favor of the Bloc. The National Youth stalwarts wore armbands depicting an arm with a torch-bearing hand, not too dissimilar to the infamous swastika promoted by Adolph Hitler in Nazi Germany. Among the party's co-founders were the university professors Ahmad al-Samman and Munir al-Ajlani, and the journalists Munir and Najib al-Rayyes. The National Youth remained an authority among Syrian youth from 1936 to 1946 and was disbanded by its founders when the French evacuated from Syria in 1946.

On May 29, 1945, Fakhri al-Barudi took up arms with the National Youth in fighting off the French bombardment of Damascus and was wounded in combat. When Syria achieved independence in April 1946, President Shukri al-Quwatli rewarded him with the Medal of Honor of the Syrian Republic, Excellence Class, and appointed him honorary general in the newly formed Syrian Army. In 1947, the National Bloc was dissolved and renamed the National Party. It was a party composed of former Bloc members who had a political program to modernize Syria, maintain its democratic system, and shun all Arab attempts at uniting Syria with the neighboring Hashemite governments in Iraq and Jordan. The Hashemites sought a monarchy in Syria while the National Party strove to maintain the republic. One of its founders was Fakhri al-Barudi and its spiritual godfather was Shukri al-Quwatli. Also in 1947, Barudi became director of intelligence in the Presidential Palace and personal advisor to the president. He held this post during the turbulent weeks of the Arab-Israeli War of 1948.

In March 1949, General Husni al-Za'im came to power in Syria and ended the Quwatli regime. Barudi was retired from office by that time, but remained on excellent terms with Syria's new leader. He was also a friend of the officers who ousted Za'im and executed him in August 1949. Barudi remained on good terms with all the leaders who ruled Syria from 1949 to 1963.

In 1958, Barudi opposed the Syrian-Egyptian union that was created by President Gamal Abd al-Nasser of Egypt. Barudi claimed that a poorly planned union would destroy Syria's free-market and multi-party political system. Barudi was the first Syrian citizen to write an open letter to President Nasser and point out boldly that his regime in Syria had become a "dictatorship" due to the police state imposed in Damascus led by Interior Minister Abd al-Hamid Sarraj. Barudi warned Nasser against authoritarianism and added, "the consequences are greater than you can ever imagine." He supported the coup that toppled the union government on September 28, 1961 and praised its mastermind, Colonel Abd al-Karim al-Nehlawi.

In March 1963, the Baath Party came to power in Syria and pledged to restore the Syrian-Egyptian union. The Baath officers ordered the shutdown of Barudi's gatherings. He was arrested and his property confiscated. A few weeks later, Barudi was released from jail and exiled to Lebanon. In 1965, President Amin al-Hafez allowed him back to Syria on the condition that he refrained from any political or public activity. In July 1963, Nasserite Colonel Jassem Alwan attempted to stage a coup to wrest power from the Baath. The Baathist state struck back at the opposition and violently suppressed the attempted coup. In the ensuing confusion, an attempt was made on Barudi's life. He narrowly escaped death and his house was burned by unknown assailants. His most celebrated work, the original three-volume dictionary written out in longhand and covering the history and teachings of Arab music, was destroyed in the rampage.

In 1965, Fakhri al-Barudi declared bankruptcy and moved to Lebanon where he lived off the donations of well-wishers for the remainder of his life. In the memoirs of General Mutih al-Samman, an officer of the pre-Baath era, the general recalls that in 1964 Barudi checked into the American University of Beirut Hospital (AUH), but had no money to pay the hospital bill. Barudi's family asked Samman to approach Lebanese President Fouad Shihab and ask him to request a discount from AUH. Samman requested the assistance of the journalist Kamel Mroweh, publisher of *al-Hayat*, who was close to Shihab, but the latter said that the Lebanese president would not interfere in such a matter. Mroweh raised 5,000 LP from an "unknown" benefactor, but Barudi did not take the money, claiming that another "unnamed" benefactor had sent him the money from Aleppo in recognition for his services to Syria in the 1930s and 1940s.

During a cultural and political career that lasted over fifty years, Fakhri al-Barudi wrote many poems, books, manuscripts, and memoirs. His first set of memoirs, *Muzakarat al-Barudi: Sittoun Aman Tatakalam* (*Barudi's Memoirs: Sixty Years Speak Out*), was published in 1952-1953, while the second, *Khamsoun Aman min Hayat al-Watan* (*Fifty Years of the Homeland's Life*), was published in 1999, nearly forty years after his death.

Sources:

Barudi, Fakhri. *Khamsoun Aman min Hayat al-Watan* (1999).
Barudi, Fakhri. *Muzakarat al-Barudi: Sittoun Aman Tatakalam* (1952-1953).
Faris, George. *Man Hum fi al-`Alam al-Arabi?* (1957).
Haffar, Salma. *Lutfi al-Haffar 1885-1968* (1997).
Itri, Abd al-Ghani. *Hadeeth al-Abqariyyat* (2000).
Kayyali, Abd al-Rahman. *Al-Marahil fi al-Intidab al-Faransi 1926-1938* (1958-1960).
Khoury, Philip. *Syria and the French Mandate* (1987).
Moubayed, Sami. *The Politics of Damascus 1920-1946* (1999).
Qassab Hasan, Najat. *Saniou al-Jalaa fi Souriyya* (1999).

al-Bitar, Salah al-Din
(1912-1980)

Salah al-Din al-Bitar was born and bred in Damascus and studied physics at the Sorbonne in Paris. While in Paris, he was introduced to Michel Aflaq, another

Syrian student, who shared the same views espoused by the French Communist Party. They returned to Syria and began parallel careers as high school teachers at the Tajheez School in Damascus. Aflaq taught history while Bitar taught physics and mathematics. They began to teach socialism to their students and preach the revival of a united Arab world.

In 1946, Bitar and Aflaq founded a newspaper called *al-Baath (Rebirth)* to publicize their views. In April 1947, the two men founded the Baath Party in Damascus, with its trinity: "unity, freedom, and socialism." All the problems Syria was facing, the two men claimed, were the result of two problems: the French occupation of Syria from 1920 to 1946 and the overbearing dominance of the urban notability over the country's social, political, and economic affairs. The peasants should rise up against the landowners, they hypothesized, and regain their rights as free citizens, as should workers in factories, professionals in the civil service, and officers in the armed forces. Once Syria became united, went their thinking, other countries should follow in anticipation of a greater unity for the Arab world as a whole.

Aflaq and Bitar found many students eager to listen, especially those from poor families in the Syrian countryside who were attracted to the two mens' socialist ideas. By the late 1940s, their influence had spread from Damascus to Aleppo, Homs, Hama, as well as the Syrian countryside. Aflaq became the party's mentor and ideologue while Bitar administered its day-to-day affairs.

The Baath Party was persecuted under the military regimes of Husni al-Za'im (March-August 1949) and Adib al-Shishakli (1951-1954). In 1953, Aflaq and Bitar fled to Lebanon to avoid being arrested by President Shishakli. In Beirut, they merged their party with the Arab Socialist Party of Akram al-Hawrani and renamed it the Arab Baath Socialist Party. Hawrani gave Aflaq and Bitar the countrywide appeal that they needed, and Hawrani accounted for the party's popularity within rural districts of Syria. In 1954, following the downfall of Shishakli, Salah al-Bitar ran for parliament and won. The second half of the 1950s witnessed an increased number of youth joining the Baath Party, especially from the Syrian Army. Aflaq and Bitar joined the movement of Arab nationalism headed by President Gamal Abd al-Nasser of Egypt, claiming that it was identical to their Baath Party doctrine.

In 1957, Prime Minister Sabri al-Asali formed a national unity cabinet and appointed Bitar minister of foreign affairs. Bitar actively backed the policies of President Nasser and advocated the merger of Syria and Egypt to form the United Arab Republic (UAR) in 1958. He also supported and took took part in Syria's shift from the US orbit toward an alliance with the USSR. Bitar made friends with socialist leaders from around the world and helped create Syria's image as a Soviet satellite. In January 1958, Bitar presented an official request in the name of the Baath Party to President Nasser asking for the unification of

Egypt and Syria. He then traveled to Cairo to negotiate union details with Nasser. He contacted Damascus and asked for instructions on how to deal with the union issue, but neither President Shukri al-Quwatli nor Prime Minister Sabri al-Asali were willing to commit to a framework, asking him instead to leave it up to Nasser to tailor-make the union as he saw fit. As a result, Bitar simply gave in to Nasser's terms, unable to present any of his own.

When the two countries merged to form the UAR in February 1958, Bitar expected to become vice president of the republic, but instead was appointed minister of culture and national guidance. Akram al-Hawrani, who had also established himself as a staunch Nasserist, became vice president of the republic. The two men became disenchanted with Nasser's rule and were particularly annoyed by the favoritism practiced by Nasser toward Egyptian subjects of the UAR. They voiced their opposition to his dictatorship and resigned from office to join the opposition in 1960.

On September 28, 1961, Bitar supported the military coup that dissolved the UAR and expelled Nasser from Damascus. On October 2, he signed the anti-union manifesto drafted by a group of disgruntled politicians, an action that was to bring him much infamy in future years among conservative members of the Baath who were still pro-Nasser, and an action that would discredit his pan-Arab credentials. The document, handwritten by Bitar, accused Nasser of "distorting the idea of Arab nationalism" and said that during the union years, he had "strangled political and democratic life" in Syria. Immediately, radical elements from the party demanded that Aflaq expel him from the party, accusing him of being an opportunist. After all, here was the creator of union now endorsing its destruction. Bitar remained on cordial relations with the post-union government of President Nazim al-Qudsi, and in 1962, he lobbied for the appointment of several Baath Party members in the cabinet of Prime Minister Bashir al-Azma. During the Qudsi years, however, he remained without any government post.

On March 8, 1963, the Military Committee of the Baath Party came to power in Syria and invited Bitar to assume leadership of the state. Bitar's socialist government lasted from March until November 1963. He created another cabinet from May to October 1964, and a third from January to February 1966. Bitar relied heavily on intellectuals to bolster his image in Syria. He appointed Dr George Toemeh from the American University of Beirut (AUB) as minister of economy, Dr Shaker al-Fahham from Damascus University as minister of education, and the academic, Dr Mohammad al-Fadil, as minister of justice.

Bitar launched a socio-political revolution in Syria, breaking with the past in every possible manner. Bitar's era witnessed the closure of independent newspapers, termination of all political parties other than his own, confiscation of property, redistribution of wealth, and nationalization of private banks and private education institutes. Salah al-Bitar's last cabinet was created on January

1, 1966, and lasted until February 23 of the same year. It was overthrown by a coup launched by Salah Jadid and Air Force Commander Hafez al-Asad, who represented the young and more radical wing of the Baath. Aflaq and Bitar were banished from Syria with orders never to return, and President Amin al-Hafez was arrested.

Bitar fled to Beirut where he briefly resided before moving to Paris. In 1969, a Syrian military court sentenced him to death in absentia on the charge of conspiracy against the regime. From exile, he led a group of banished Baathists in opposing the regime of President Nur al-Din al-Atasi and Salah Jadid. When Hafez al-Asad came to power in 1970, Bitar welcomed his ascent. Asad pardoned Bitar and invited him back to Syria in January 1978. The ex-prime minister complied and visited Damascus that same year. After his visit he returned—disillusioned with the Baathist state in Syria—to Paris and lived in self-imposed exile for the remainder of his life.

Bitar was vocal in his criticism of Baathist Syria's politics. He founded a magazine called *al-Ihiyya'a al-Arabi* (*The Arabic Revival*) to promote his views. Among his published works in the 1970s are *Al-Siyassa al-Arabiyya Bayn al-Mabda' wa al-Tatbiq* (*Arab Politics between Theory and Practice*), published in 1970, and *Maza Ba'ad Gamal Abd al-Nasser?* (*What Comes After Gamal Abd al-Nasser?*), published in 1973.

Salah al-Bitar was assassinated by unknown assailants at his hotel in Paris on July 21, 1980.

Sources:
Batatu, Hanna. *Syria's Peasantry: the Descendants of its Lesser Rural Notables and their Politics* (2000).
Commins, David. *Historical Dictionary of Modern Syria* (1996).
Devlin, John. *The Baath Party: a History from its Origins to 1966* (1976).
Elias, Joseph. *Aflaq wa al-Baath* (*Aflaq and the Baath* (1991).
Hawrani, Akram. *Muzakarat Akram al-Hawrani* (2000).
Moubayed, Sami. *Damascus Between Democracy and Dictatorship* (2000).
Seale, Patrick. *Asad: The Struggle for the Middle East* (1988).
Seale, Patrick. *The Struggle for Syria* (1961).

al-Boukhari, Nasuh
(1881-1961)

Nasuh al-Boukhari grew up in a family of political activists in Damascus. His father was Saleem al-Boukhari, a religious leader who had been arrested by Ottoman authorities for his views in 1915 and his brother, Mahmud, was a national activist who had been executed by the Ottomans in 1916.

Nasuh al-Boukhari studied at the Ottoman Military Academy in Istanbul. He joined the Ottoman Army and held several posts in Mecca and Medina. He was arrested by the Allies in World War I and deported to Siberia. He managed to escape through a secret channel that took him through Manchuria, China, Japan, and crossing the Pacific Ocean all the way to the United States. From San Francisco he traveled to New York City, then Cyprus, finally returning to Istanbul in 1916 after an escape route that took two years to complete.

In October 1918, the Ottoman Empire was defeated and Boukhari allied himself with King Faysal I, the new ruler of Syria. During the Faysal years (1918-1920), Boukhari became commander of Aleppo's military unit, then director of the Bureau of Military Consultation. In January 1920, Faysal appointed him military attaché to Egypt. In July 1920, while he was in Cairo, the French Army occupied Syria and proclaimed the French Mandate.

In December 1920, Nasuh al-Boukhari became minister of military affairs in the pro-French cabinet of Prime Minister Haqqi al-Azm. He retained this post until June 1922. In June 1926, he became minister of agriculture in the pro-French cabinet of Prime Minister Ahmad Nami, holding this post until 1928. In the midst of an on-going cabinet crisis, President Hashim al-Atasi, leader of the nationalist movement, appointed him prime minister on April 5, 1939. He created a cabinet, and appointed himself minister of interior and defense. Boukhari appointed the prominent economist, Khalid al-Azm, minister of foreign affairs, and in a bid to appease the opposition, appointed Hasan al-Hakim, a declared anti-Bloc leader, as minister of education.

Boukhari was given responsibility for holding supplemental talks with the French high commissioner, Gabriel Peaux, aimed at ratifying an independence treaty that Syria had signed in 1936. The agreement affirmed Syria's independence and promised to unite all parts of Syria, including the regions made autonomous in 1920, into one country. The French, however, reneged on the terms of the treaty and demanded that Boukhari relinquish control of the two mountains to France in order to attain immediate independence. The French also demanded that Syria present France with military facilities on its territories, claiming that the outbreak of World War II in Europe required fortification in the Middle East. Boukhari turned down the requests and then, unable to advance talks any further, resigned from office on July 8, 1939.

In August 1943, President Shukri al-Quwatli appointed Boukhari minister of education and acting minister of defense in the cabinet of Prime Minister Saadallah al-Jabiri. He held both posts until November 1944. In 1945-1946, Boukhari campaigned vigorously for the creation of a Syrian Army and advocated the concept of the military draft, where every Syrian aged eighteen or above would be required to undertake military training. His campaign was unpopular and angered many people in Damascus, who lobbied against him and had him voted out of parliament in 1947.

Nasuh al-Boukhari lived in political retirement and died on July 1, 1961.

Sources:

Hakim, Yusuf. *Souriyya wa al-Intidab al-Faransi* (1966).
Khoury, Philip. *Syria and the French Mandate* (1987).
Moubayed, Sami. *The Politics of Damascus 1920-1946* (1999).
Shambrook, Peter. *French Imperialism in Syria* (1999).

Buzo, Ali
(1916-1966)

Ali Buzo was born and raised in Damascus. He studied law at Damascus University. Buzo established a legal practice in Damascus and began work as an attorney in 1945.

Buzo co-founded the People's Party in 1947. This party aimed at maintaining Syria's democratic system, breaking the centralization of power practiced by the politicians of Damascus, and establishing union with neighboring Iraq. It was funded by the Hashemite family in Baghdad and administered by Nazim al-Qudsi and Rushdi al-Kikhiya. In 1948, the party's secretary-general, Rushdi al-Kikhiya, appointed Buzo editor-in-chief of its political daily, *al-Sha`b* (*The People*). Buzo wrote daily articles in *al-Sha`b* accusing the regime of President Shukri al-Quwatli of ignoring the interests of Aleppo and practicing favoritism toward his fellow Damascenes.

In March 1949, Chief of Staff Husni al-Za'im deposed the Quwatli regime, arrested its top figures, and appointed Buzo as his private advisor. Buzo initially supported the coup, believing that Za'im would maintain a democratic system, modernize Syria, and work for the materialization of union with Iraq. When Za'im declared himself military governor of Syria, closed political parties, and threatened to declare war on Iraq, claiming that the Hashemites were out to destroy him, Ali Buzo resigned from office in protest. He shifted into the opposition and hailed the coup that ousted Za'im in August 1949.

Buzo then allied himself with Hashim al-Atasi, Syria's new leader and ally of the People's Party. Buzo served on the Constitutional Assembly in December 1949 and helped draft a new constitution for Syria. In 1950, he became minister of agriculture in the People's Party cabinet of Prime Minister Nazim al-Qudsi. In 1951, President Adib al-Shishakli came to power and outlawed the People's Party, claiming that it was a propaganda machine for the Hashemite kingdoms in Amman and Baghdad. Buzo, as all other members of the party, was summarily arrested and persecuted from 1951 to 1954.

Buzo was released from the Mezzeh prison by the officers who overthrew

Shishakli in February 1954. In March 1954, Atasi returned to the presidency and Buzo became minister of interior under Prime Minister Sabri al-Asali. He held office from March to June 1954, and in October 1954, he became minister of justice under Prime Minister Faris al-Khury. He was also appointed director of media affairs under President Hashim al-Atasi, who ruled from February 1954 to September 1955. When Atasi retired from office, Shukri al-Quwatli replaced him in the presidency.

Wanting to ally himself with the People's Party, Quwatli appointed Buzo as minister of interior under Prime Minister Ghazzi from September 1955 to June 1956. Ali Buzo supported Syria's merger with Egypt in 1958 and became a deputy in the joint Syrian-Egyptian Parliament from 1958 to 1961. When the United Arab Republic (UAR) was dissolved in 1961, Buzo co-founded the Socialist Union with Nihad al-Qasim, a coalition of Arab nationalists who sought to restore the UAR regime.

Ali Buzo retired from political activity in 1963.

Sources:
Azm, Khalid. *Muzakarat Khalid al-Azm* (1973).
Hawrani, Akram. *Muzakarat Akram al-Hawrani* (2000).
Itri, Abd al-Ghani. *Alam wa Mubdioun* (1999).
Seale, Patrick. *The Struggle for Power in Syria* (1961).

al-Dandashi, Abd al-Karim
(1917-?)

Abd al-Karim al-Dandashi was born in the town of Tal Kalakh in the Syrian Midwest. He studied political science and Arabic history at the American University of Beirut (AUB).

While at AUB, Dandashi was influenced by Dr Constantine Zurayk, Arab nationalism's leading philosopher and professor at the Department of History. Dandashi joined a cultural club in AUB called al-Urwa al-Wuthqa (The Indissoluble Bond), created by Dr Zurayk to promote secular and liberal views on Arab nationalism. Dandashi was also a founding member of the League of National Action in Qurnai'l (Mount Lebanon), a movement aimed at uniting Arab intellectuals into one political force that would help liberate the region from European colonialism. The League rose to overnight fame in Syria and Lebanon and called for economic integration of all Arab countries upon the termination of the French Mandate in Syria and Lebanon and the British Mandate in Palestine. The League included promising young men who were to become leaders in Syria. Among its earliest members were the philosopher Zaki al-Arsuzi, the politician Sabri al-Asali, the diplomat Farid Zayn al-Din, and Dr Zurayk.

Dandashi graduated from AUB and began his career as a history teacher in Basra, Iraq in 1939. He taught in Iraq until 1945, when he returned to Syria and joined the Ministry of Foreign Affairs. When independence was achieved in April 1946, he became director of political affairs at the Ministry. One year later, he became secretary of the permanent Syrian mission at the UN headed by Prime Minister Faris al-Khury. Dandashi also became second secretary of the Syrian Embassy in London. In July 1950, he became consul to the Syrian Embassy in Brazil and held this post until January 1951. He then became second secretary to the Syrian Embassy in Turkey and held this post until 1954.

Dandashi was critical of the radical socialist policies of President Gamal Abd al-Nasser of Egypt, and chose to lay low during the Syrian-Egyptian union of 1958, but supported the coup that toppled union in September 1961. In December 1961, he became a deputy in parliament and allied himself with Syria's new president, Nazim al-Qudsi. Among other things, the new leaders of Syria wanted to revoke the socialist measures imposed on her during the union years (1958-1961) and put an end to the meddling of officers in political affairs.

On March 28, 1962, the officers struck back with a coup, launched by Colonel Abd al-Karim al-Nehlawi. Qudsi was arrested, along with all of his ministers and deputies. Dandashi remained in jail until a counter-coup took place on April 2, where he was released along with President Qudsi. On March 8, 1963, the Baath Party came to Syria and deposed the Qudsi government. The Revolutionary Command Council (RCC) pledged to restore the Syrian-Egyptian union and arrested, exiled, or fired all those who had collaborated with Qudsi. The RCC terminated the civil rights of Abd al-Karim al-Dandashi and forced him into political retirement.

Sources:
Barada (March 24, 1963).
Faris, George. *Man Hum fi al-`Alam al-Arabi?* (1957).
Khoury, Philip. *Syria and the French Mandate* (1987).
Samman, Mutih. *Watan wa Askar* (1995).

al-Dandashi, Abd al-Razzaq
(1899-1935)

Abd al-Razzaq al-Dandashi was born into the wealthiest political family in Tal Kalakh, a town in the Syrian interior. He studied law at the University of Belgium and was involved in Arab student politics during his college years. He returned to Syria and opened a legal practice.

In August 1933, Dandashi helped found the League of National Action in Qurnai'l (Mount Lebanon), a movement aimed at uniting Arab intellectuals into one political force that would help liberate the region from European colonialism. The League rose to overnight fame in Syria and Lebanon and called for economic integration of all Arab countries upon the termination of the French and British Mandates. The League included promising young men who were to become leaders in Syria. Among its earliest members were the professor Constantine Zurayk, the philosopher Zaki al-Arsuzi, the politician Sabri al-Asali, and the diplomat Farid Zayn al-Din.

Dandashi served as secretary-general of the League and acquired a vast power base in Syria. He appealed to young lawyers like himself, high school students, university academics, and café intellectuals. Primarily, the League served as an opponent of the National Bloc, the leading anti-French movement in Syria. The Bloc favored honorable cooperation, demanding that emancipation be earned through diplomatic rather than violent resistance, while the League called for a national uprising against the French. Dandashi was an impassioned orator and a hard-line Arab nationalist.

In 1935, Dandashi died at the apex of his career, at the age of thirty-six. An exceptional person, Abd al-Razzaq al-Dandashi met his death under the most unusual circumstances. While riding the train, he looked out the window while passing through a tunnel and his head was smashed into pieces after hitting the tunnel wall.

Sources:
Khoury, Philip. *Syria and the French Mandate* (1987).

al-Dawalibi, Ma'ruf
(1907-2004)

Ma'ruf al-Dawalibi was born in Aleppo to a middle-class mercantile family. He studied journalism and law at Damascus University and obtained a graduate degree in Roman law from the Sorbonne in Paris.

In the 1930s, Dawalibi helped establish a militant youth group in Aleppo, inspired by the rising Fascist movement in Italy. In 1936, he joined the National Bloc, the leading anti-French movement in Syria, but was never an active member of its Aleppo branch during the years of the French Mandate (1920-1946). In 1937, Dawalibi rose to fame in nationalist circles for helping to smuggle Amin al-Husayni, the ex-Mufti of Jerusalem, from Europe to Syria. Dawalibi visited Husayni in prison in Paris and provided him with a disguise and fake passport to make his escape. During World War II, Dawalibi made a name for himself as an ardent supporter of the Nazis and joined several pro-Axis associations in Europe.

In 1947, one year after independence, Dawalibi ran for parliament in Syria, becoming a deputy for Aleppo, and began to teach at Damascus University. He also practiced law and co-founded the People's Party, an organization aimed at maintaining Syria's democratic system, breaking the centralization of power practiced by the politicians of Damascus, and establishing union with neighboring Iraq. It was funded by the Hashemite families in Amman and Baghdad and administered by Nazim al-Qudsi and Rushdi al-Kikhiya, both of whom had been members of the National Bloc with Dawalibi in the 1930s.

In 1949, Dawalibi nominated himself for the Constitutional Assembly and served as a deputy for Aleppo. In December 1949, he became minister of national economy in the People's Party cabinet of Prime Minister Nazim al-Qudsi. Dawalibi allied himself with the Muslim Brotherhood, who were gaining popularity in Syria, and established a reputation for his distrust of the politicians of Damascus. He was also famed for his hostility toward the officers, especially after their blunder in the Arab-Israeli War of 1948.

Dawalibi was elected speaker of parliament from June to November 1951. President Hashim al-Atasi, an ally of the People's Party, asked him to form a cabinet on November 27, 1951. Dawalibi complied and allocated the ministry of defense for himself. Traditionally, that post would have been given to General Fawzi Selu, the right-hand man of Syria's deputy chief of staff, General Adib al-Shishakli. By appointing himself minister of defense, Dawalibi was challenging the authority of General Shishakli, who had long demanded that the portfolio of defense be given to an officer. Shishakli demanded immediate adjustments, but Dawalibi refused to reshuffle. The following night, on November 28, Shishakli arrested Dawalibi, his entire cabinet, and the People's Party founders Nazim al-Qudsi and Rushdi al-Kikhiya. From behind bars, Dawalibi presented his resignation to President Atasi, who also resigned in protest to Shishakli's measures.

In 1952, Dawalibi was released from prison and went to Aleppo, where he joined the opposition to the Shishakli regime, headed by ex-President Atasi. When Shishakli was overthrown in February 1954, Atasi returned to office and appointed Dawalibi as minister of defense in the cabinet of Prime Minister Sabri al-Asali. In his new government office, Dawalibi clashed with the officers and curbed their influence in day-to-day politics. He prevented them from taking part in political decision-making and tried to pass a law forbidding them from becoming members in political parties.

Dawalibi opposed the leadership of President Gamal Abd al-Nasser of Egypt and tried to dismiss Nasserist officers in the armed forces—an act that eventually led to his downfall. Dawalibi accused Nasser of harboring dictatorial ambitions in Syria and warned that Syria's alliance with the socialist leader would lead to trouble. A coalition of Baathist, communist, and Nasserist officers lobbied for Dawalibi's dismissal from office, claiming that he was "an enemy of Arab nationalism," and Dawalibi was forced to step down in 1956. He then became a deputy of Aleppo and lobbied against Nasser from within parliament, voting against the Syrian-Egyptian union in 1958. During the union years (1958-1961), Dawalibi retired from political activity and went into self-imposed exile in Lebanon.

When the union was dissolved in September 1961, the People's Party was voted back into office. Nazim al-Qudsi became president of the republic and Ma'ruf al-Dawalibi became prime minister. He restored all political parties outlawed by Nasser, readopted Syria's 1958 constitution, released all political prisoners, and abolished many of Nasser's socialist measures. Dawalibi formulated a three-year plan to restore nationalized lands to its original owners and accused the officers of wanting to seize power for themselves. In secret, a group of disenchanted officers went to Cairo and offered to topple the Qudsi government and remove Dawalibi from office. They asked for money to stage a coup, but Nasser refused, claiming that this would greatly destabilize Syria.

Ma'ruf al-Dawalibi.

On March 28, 1962, a group of officers tried seizing power in Damascus in a direct response to the prime minister's measures, arresting both Dawalibi and President Qudsi. The coup was headed by Abd al-Karim al-Nehlawi, who resented Dawalibi's officer complex. A counter-coup took place on April 1, launched by loyalists to the existing order, sending Nehlawi into exile and restoring Qudsi and Dawalibi to their posts. To avoid further problems, Dawalibi resigned from office.

On March 8, 1963, the Baath Party came to power in Syria and pledged to restore the union. The Baath arrested all anti-Nasser politicians and sent Ma'ruf al-Dawalibi to the notorious Mezzeh prison. He was accused of having worked against the union government and his civil rights were terminated by the party's Revolutionary Command Council. The Baath Party officers exiled him to Lebanon in the summer of 1963. He remained briefly in Beirut, then moved to Saudi Arabia where he lived until his death on January 15, 2004.

Dawalibi became private advisor to King Saud and held the same posts under his brothers, King Faysal al-Saud, King Khalid, and King Fahd. Among Ma'ruf al-Dawalibi's published works are *Al-Islam wa al-Salam wa al-Mushkilat al-Insaniyya* (*Islam, Peace, and Humanitarian Problems*), published in 1980, and *Al-Dawla wa al-Sulta fi al-Islam* (*The State and Authority in Islam*), published in 1982. His classic work, *Nazarat Islamiyya fi al-Ishtirakiyya al-Thawriyya* (*Islamic Views on Revolutionary Socialism*), was published in 1963.

Sources:
Azm, Khalid. *Muzakarat Khalid al-Azm* (1973).

Babil, Nasuh. *Sahafa wa Siyassa fi Souriyya* (1987).

Hawrani, Akram. *Muzakarat Akram al-Hawrani* (2000).

Itri, Abd al-Ghani. *Alam wa Mubdioun* (1999).

Moubayed, Sami. *Damascus Between Democracy and Dictatorship* (2000).

Rathmell, Andrew. *Secret War in the Middle East* (1995).

Samman, Mutih. *Watan wa Askar* (1995).

Seale, Patrick. *The Struggle for Syria* (1961).

Torrey, Gordon. *Syrian Politics and the Military* (1964).

Zahr al-Din, Abd al-Karim. *Muzakarati an Fatrat al-Infisal fi Souriyya* (1968).

Droubi, Ala al-Din
(d.1920)

Ala al-Din Droubi was born in Homs and studied at the Ottoman Medical Academy in Istanbul. He practiced medicine at the turn of the century and became one of the many doctors of Sultan Abdulhamid II.

When the Ottoman Empire fell in October 1918, Droubi switched his loyalties to the Arab regime that was created in Damascus and became director of the Bureau of Consultation under King Faysal I, the new ruler of Syria. Droubi pledged loyalty to the Hashemite family of Arabia, rose in prominence within Faysal's court, and kept his post without interruption through the years of the Arab government (1918-1920). When the French imposed their mandate on Syria in July 1920, they dethroned Faysal and sent him into exile. Before leaving, Faysal appointed Droubi prime minister on July 25, hoping that he would succeed in upholding the Arab regime.

To Faysal's surprise, however, for the next four weeks the new prime minister proved to be the exact opposite of a reliable resistance leader. Droubi welcomed the mandate system and promised to uphold French interests in Syria. Droubi contacted Faysal while he was leaving the country and informed him that under no circumstances would he be permitted to return. If he should try, Droubi added, then he would be arrested. While making his exodus from Syria, Faysal stopped at a gas station, but the attendant refused to fuel his automobile, claiming that he too had received orders from the prime minister not to offer the ex-king any assistance.

Droubi announced steep taxes on Syrians to help raise money for the French Army and declared that taking up arms against the mandate authority would be considered a crime punishable by death. He ordered a house-to-house search in Syria, confiscated weapons held by private citizens, and canceled the Ministry of Foreign Affairs. France, he announced, would now be responsible for Syria's foreign relations.

Shortly after declaring their mandate, the French transferred the Syrian districts of Baalbak, the Beqqa Valley, Hasbayya, and Rashayya to Lebanon, creating the Christian state of Greater Lebanon in September 1920. Prime Minister Droubi watched in silence, refusing to protest.

On August 21, 1920, less than one month after the proclamation of the French Mandate, Ala al-Din al-Droubi was traveling in Hawran, a district in southern Syria near the Syrian-Jordanian border, when his train was ambushed by supporters of the ex-king, and he was killed in cold blood by men who claimed to be loyalists of Faysal.

Sources:

Hakim, Yusuf. *Souriyya wa al-Ahd al-Faysali* (1986).
Husari, Sati. *Yawm Maysaloun* (1947).
Moubayed, Sami. *The Politics of Damascus 1920-1946* (1999).
Russell, Malcom. *The First Modern Arab State: Syria under Faysal I* (1987).

Farha Bakdash, Wisal
(1932-)

Wisal Farha studied at Damascus University and obtained a diploma in journalism from the University of Moscow in the USSR. She joined the Syrian Communist Party in 1948 and was imprisoned in 1949 for criticizing the military regime of President Husni al-Za'im.

From 1951 to 1954, Farha fled to Lebanon to avoid persecution for her views on the regime of President Adib al-Shishakli. In 1955, one year after Shishakli's fall, she began writing for the party's two newspapers, *Sawt al-Sha`b* (*Voice of the People*) and *al-Noor* (*The Light*). In the second half of the 1950s, she opposed the rising influence of President Gamal Abd al-Nasser of Egypt and Syria's merger with Egypt. During the years of the United Arab Republic (1958-1961), the Communist Party was outlawed and Farha fled to Lebanon to avoid arrest in Syria. She spent the next five years writing articles for Arab newspapers, touring Eastern Europe, and promoting her Marxist views in Damascus.

In 1964, Wisal Farha married Khalid Bakdash, the secretary-general of the Syrian Communist Party, and immediately rose in rank within the party. Bakdash, who had founded the party in 1934, promoted Farha into its Central Committee and brought her into the National Progressive Front (NPF), a pan-socialist coalition operating under the umbrella of the ruling Baath Party. The NPF had been created by Bakdash and President Hafez al-Asad, who came to power in 1970, and it aimed at uniting the socialist parties in Syria into a modern parliamentary bloc. In 1984, Farha became a deputy for Damascus in parliament and was reelected three times in a row on an NPF ticket. When Khalid Bakdash died in 1996, the party chose Farha to succeed him and she was voted into the Central

Committee of the NPF.

In 2000, President Bashar al-Asad authorized NPF parties to establish their own political publications and reactivate themselves into public life. Farha relaunched *Sawt al-Sha`b* in January 2001, forty-four years after the newspaper's initial closure in 1958. As of this writing, Wisal Farha continues to write in *Sawt al-Sha`b* and serve as its editor-in-chief.

Sources:
Al-Bayan (February 14, 2002).
Bawab, Sulayman. *Mawsuat Alam Souriyya fi al-Qarn al-Ishreen,* Vol III (1999).

Faysal I (King Faysal)
(1889-1933)
Alternate spelling: King Faisal I.
Faysal Ibin al-Husayn was born in Mecca and raised in the Arabian Desert and Istanbul. His father was Sharif Husayn, the paramount Arab leader of his genera-tion, who the Ottoman Sultan Abdulhamid II had appointed Prince of Mecca and defender of the Holy Shrines in 1908. Prince Faysal pursued his higher edu-cation in Istanbul and returned to the Hijaz, nominating himself for the Ottoman Parliament as a representative of Jeddah in 1910.

After the outbreak of World War I in August 1914, Husayn began planning for an Arab rebellion against the Ottoman Turks, to be launched in coordination with Great Britain. Husayn sent Faysal to Damascus in January 1915 to contact the political underground and recruit members for the Arab Revolt. Faysal met with the notability of Damascus and joined al-Fatat, the leading anti-Ottoman society in Syria. On June 10, 1916, Sharif Husayn declared an Arab Revolt against the Ottoman Empire, aimed at terminating the empire in all territories occu-pied by native Arabs. The British promised that if Husayn helped the Allies win World War I, they would create an Arab kingdom in the Arabian Desert and Syria (including Palestine and Lebanon), to be ruled by Husayn and his three children, Faysal, Abdullah, and Ali.

Faysal became a commander in the Arab Army and befriended T.E. Lawrence, the British officer who came to Mecca in December 1916 to organize the raids on the Ottoman Army. Faysal's troops were composed of 1,000 Bedouin fighters and 2,500 ex-prisoners of war from the Ottoman Army. His first victory in Aqaba on July 6, 1917, earned him the admiration of both Lawrence and Faysal's own father. Consequently, Husayn appointed Faysal field commander of the Hijaz and made him a general in the Arab Army. Faysal was placed under the command of the British General Edmund Allenby. On September 26, 1918, Faysal led an offen-sive on Damascus and expelled the Ottoman Army, declaring the end of four hundred years of Ottoman influence. He entered the city in triumph on October 1, and established an Arab government based in Damascus under his crown.

The thirty-year-old king worked for a modernized and unified country with a centralized administration and modern infrastructure. Although viewed with scrutiny in conservative districts of Syria for his connections to Great Britain, Faysal managed to garner support from the urban notability in Damascus, Aleppo, Homs, Hama, and Lattakia. He built a power base among the country's youth and urban intelligentsia. He befriended academics and invested heavily in the Arab Medical Academy, which later became Damascus University. He marketed himself as a reformer and tried granting suffrage rights to women, but his decree was vetoed by conservative elements in the Syrian Congress.

In early 1919, Faysal left his young state behind and attended the Paris Peace Conference to decide on the new post-World War I order. In Paris, he lobbied for complete Syrian independence, but discovered that the promises of independence, made during the war to his father, were lies, and that no international endorsement would be made for his state. Rather, Great Britain and France had taken matters into their own hands and carved up the region accordingly, allocating "mandates" for themselves in the Middle East and North Africa. Syria and Lebanon became France's share for the World War I victory, while Palestine and Iraq were given to Great Britain. Faysal was humiliated in France, and the French government refused to recognize him as an official representative of the Arab people.

King Faysal I in Paris in 1919. This photo was taken by the wife of Woodrow Wilson.

On July 14, 1920, the French made their mandatory claims to Syria. Faysal refused to give in and ordered his army to fight the invading French troops at the Maysaloun pass on the Damascus-Beirut highway. On July 24, his army was defeated and the French occupied Damascus, dethroning the king, dissolving his army, and imposing the French Mandate. The ex-king left Syria on August 1, 1920. He headed to Europe and protested the overthrow of his regime to any official willing to listen. He lobbied with Sir Winston Churchill, the newly appointed British colonial secretary, and was appointed king of Iraq in March 1921.

Faysal ruled his kingdom from Baghdad for the next thirteen years, but always lived with the hope of returning to his throne in Syria. In Baghdad, he was surrounded by Syrian officials or Iraqi officials who had held office with him in Damascus. His trusted friend Nuri al-Sa'id became chief of staff of the Iraqi Army and then prime minister, while the scholar Sati al-Husari became minister of education. Husari had been Faysal's education minister in Syria and he created the school curriculum in Iraq, with a strong emphasis on Arab nationalism. In 1925, Faysal financed the People's Party in Damascus headed by his ex-foreign minister, Abd al-Rahman Shahbandar, and worked for independence from the French and union with Faysal's Iraq.

In 1928, Faysal founded another party in Syria, headed by his ex-prime minister, Rida al-Rikabi, called the Monarchist Party. It had one goal: to restore Faysal I as king of Syria. In 1932, when the French considered the idea of recreating the Syrian throne, Faysal hurried to Europe and marketed himself as a suitable candidate, but the French did not welcome his return, claiming that he harbored anti-French views and would obstruct French interests in the Middle East. He then sent his trusted adviser Rustum Haydar to Damascus to meet with Syrian officials, but discovered that their interest in a monarchy was lukewarm. In the 1930s, a group of Syrian leaders emerged in Damascus and promoted themselves as the republican candidates for leadership of Syria, claiming that Faysal had been an "imported" king no longer welcome on the Syrian throne. Faysal's ambitions at regaining the throne failed, however, and he served as king of Iraq from 1921 until his sudden death on September 7, 1933. His son, King Ghazi I, succeeded him in Iraq, and ruled until he was killed in a car accident in 1939. Faysal's line continued to rule Iraq until his grandson, King Faysal II, was slain in a bloody revolution carried out by officers in the Iraqi Army headed by General Abd al-Karim Qasim.

Sources:
Encyclopedia of the Modern Middle East, Vol I (1996). Article by Reeva Simon.
Hakim, Hasan. *Muzakarati: Safahat min Tareekh Souriyya al-Hadeeth* (1965-1966).
Hakim, Yusuf. *Souriyya wa al-Ahd al-Faysali* (1966).
Husari, Sati. *Yawm Maysloun* (1947).
Kedourie, Elie. *England and the Middle East 1914-1921* (1978).
Khoury, Philip. *Syria and the French Mandate* (1987).
Lawrence, T.E. *Seven Pillars of Wisdom* (1935).
Moubayed, Sami. *The Politics of Damascus 1920-1946* (1999).
Qadri, Ahmad. *Muzakarat an Al-Thawra al-Arabiyya al-Kubra* (1956).
Rihani, Amin. *Faysal al-Awal* (1958).
Russell, Malcom. *The First Modern Arab State: Syria under Faysal I* (1987).
Sa'id, Amin. *Al-Thawra al-Arabiyya al-Kubra* (1954).
Simon, Reeva. *Iraq Between the Two World Wars* (1986).
Tlas, Mustapha. *Al-Thawra al-Arabiyya al-Kubra* (1987).

al-Ghanim, Wahib
(1919-2003)

Wahib al-Ghanim was born in the Sanjak of Alexanderetta in northern Syria and studied medicine at the Sorbonne in Paris. He went to Lattakia and opened a private clinic in 1943.

In 1947, Ghanim joined Michel Aflaq and Salah al-Bitar, two schoolteachers who were also recent Paris graduates, and founded the Baath Party. It was a socialist party with an Arab nationalist identity, aimed at unifying the Arab world, liberating it from foreign control, and establishing a democratic and socialist government in Syria. In April 1947, Ghanim co-wrote the party constitution with Aflaq and Bitar, and in 1948 began an active campaign to promote the trinity of "union, freedom, and socialism" within Syrian intellectual circles. Ghanim volunteered for service in the Arab-Israeli War of 1948, and following the defeat of the Syrian Army, took part in demonstrations calling on President Shukri al-Quwatli to resign from office, blaming him for the defeat.

Wahib al-Ghanim was always popular among Baath Party students, but never enjoyed much appeal among urban political elites. In 1947 and 1949, he ran for parliament as a deputy for Lattakia, and lost both elections. To boost his popularity, Dr Ghanim began to hold political meetings at his clinic and gave political lessons for free on Baath Party ideology. From 1951 to 1954, he worked against the military dictatorship of President Adib al-Shishakli and was persecuted for his views.

In February 1955, one year after Shishakli's fall, Ghanim became minister of health in the cabinet of Prime Minister Sabri al-Asali. He became close to the party leader Akram al-Hawrani, and together the two men supported the Syrian-Egyptian union of 1958. Like Hawrani, Ghanim grew disenchanted with union and supported the coup d'etat that toppled it in September 1961. He became a deputy in the first post-union parliament on December 12, 1961.

Ghanim's name was elevated in political circles when the Baath Party came to power in March 1963. He was hailed as a veteran leader by President Hafez al-Asad, who came to power in 1970, and who had been Ghanim's student in the 1940s and 1950s.

Dr Wahib al-Ghanim died in 2003, three years after Asad's own death.

Sources:
Commins, David. *Historical Dictionary of Modern Syria* (1996).
Faris, George. *Man Hum fi al-`Alam al-Arabi?* (1956).
Hawrani, Akram. *Muzakarat Akram al-Hawrani* (2000).

al-Ghazzi, Fawzi
(1891-1929)

Fawzi al-Ghazzi was born in Damascus and studied law in Istanbul. He was conscripted into the Ottoman Army in World War I and served until the Ottoman Empire collapsed in 1918. Ghazzi allied himself with King Faysal I, the new ruler of Syria, and became mayor of Rashayya in 1919. In 1920, Faysal appointed him mayor of Hasbayya. In July 1920, the French proclaimed their mandate on Syria and retired Ghazzi from government service. He became an instructor at the Arab Academy of Law, incorporated into Damascus University in 1923. Four years later, he co-founded the People's Party, the first official party in French Mandate Syria, with its leader, Dr Abd al-Rahman Shahbandar. The party was aimed at terminating the mandate, setting up a British-style democracy, and uniting Syria with the Hashemite governments in Jordan and Iraq.

In 1925, Ghazzi joined the Syrian revolt of the Arab Mountain, co-organized by Shahbandar, and aimed at terminating the mandate by force. The French ordered his arrest, accused him of high treason, and locked him up on Arwad Island, just off the coast of Tartus, in a castle used by the Christian crusaders of the Middle Ages. Ghazzi was brought to trial and sentenced to death, but a general amnesty set him free in January 1927. The pro-French Prime Minister Ahmad Nami appointed the young lawyer Ghazzi as minister of interior in March 1927, but he turned down the post for political reasons, claiming that he could not work with the Nami cabinet, which had been appointed by the French and not elected by the people.

In 1928, Fawzi al-Ghazzi co-founded the National Bloc, the leading anti-French movement in Syria, with a group of urban notables in Beirut. It was a coalition of landowners, lawyers, and merchants who wanted to terminate the mandate system through diplomatic means rather than armed resistance. That same year he ran for parliament on a National Bloc ticket and won with an overwhelming majority. In June 1928, he was elected into the Constitutional Assembly and, after winning a majority vote, appointed chairman. He presided over the drafting of Syria's first republican constitution, which was declined by the mandate authority due to the "anti-French nature" of its 115 articles. Ghazzi met with French officials and lobbied energetically for the constitution. When the talks failed, he mobilized countrywide protests demanding that the proposed constitution be ratified.

In the midst of his diplomatic battle with the French, Ghazzi died in the most unusual circumstances. On July 9, 1929, his wife Latifa al-Yafi poisoned him in order to marry her lover, who ironically was Fawzi al-Ghazzi's young nephew. Ghazzi died at the age of thirty-eight and was buried in Damascus.

Sources:

Babil, Nasuh. *Sahafa wa Siyasa fi Souriyyia* (1987).

Haffar, Salma. *Lutfi al-Haffar 1885-1968* (1997).

Hakim, Yusuf. *Souriyya wa al-Intidab al-Faransi* (1966).

Itri, Abd al-Ghani. *Abqariyyat* (1996).

Kayyali, Abd al-Rahman. *Al-Marahil fi al-Intidab al-Faransi 1926-1938* (1958-1960).

Moubayed, Sami. *The Politics of Damascus 1920-1946* (1999).

al-Ghazzi, Sa'id
(1893-1967)

Sa'id al-Ghazzi was born and raised in Damascus. He studied law at Damascus University and graduated in 1922, beginning his career as an attorney and instructor at the Faculty of Law in Damascus.

In 1928, Ghazzi co-founded the National Bloc, the leading political movement in Syria that aimed at terminating the French Mandate through diplomacy rather than armed resistance. The Bloc was headed by Hashim al-Atasi and included urban notables from Damascus, Aleppo, Homs, Hama, and Lattakia. In 1928, Ghazzi held office for three months on the Constitutional Assembly that drafted the first republican constitution for Syria. In 1936, Prime Minister Ata al-Ayyubi appointed Ghazzi minister of justice in a ten-month caretaker cabinet, created to supervise parliamentary elections. Ghazzi then returned to his legal practice. He made a political comeback in April 1945 as minister of justice, and in December 1946 as minister of finance. In October 1947, one year after independence from the French, Ghazzi became minister of national economy in the cabinet of Prime Minister Jamil Mardam Bey. In 1943-1947 and 1947-1949, Ghazzi served as a deputy for Damascus in parliament.

In 1954, President Hashim al-Atasi called on Sa'id al-Ghazzi to create a nonpartisan government that would supervise parliamentary and presidential elections. Ghazzi formed a cabinet of technocrats on June 19 and managed to supervise the first democratic elections in Syria since 1947. On the day of his appointment, Colonel Mohammad Safa was arrested by government authorities for trying to seize power in Syria with the assistance of Iraq. By all accounts, the elections Ghazzi supervised were honest and efficiently planned. He appointed Ismail Quli, a civil servant with a particularly unblemished record, as minister of interior and As'ad Kourani, a prominent legal mind, as minister of justice and economy. Ghazzi kept the ministry of defense for himself and held office until October 29, 1954.

Due to his total impartiality in the elections, President Shukri al-Quwatli asked Ghazzi to form another cabinet on September 13, 1955. He was charged with keeping the army from meddling in politics, and ending the civilian-military hostility that had developed following the overthrow of Syria's last military regime in 1954. Ghazzi created one of the most well-balanced cabinets in Syrian history, and made his anti-officer views clear by appointing Rashad Barmada, a civilian, in the ministry of defense. Ali Buzo, another declared opponent of the officers, was made minister of interior, while Ma'mun al-Kuzbari, a former ally of the Syrian Army and General Adib al-Shishakli, was moved to the less critical post of minister of education. To market his cabinet, Ghazzi appointed the poet Badawi al-Jabal as minister of state for media affairs.

The new prime minister shifted Syria out of the pro-American orbit and into the Eastern bloc of the Cold War. This policy had been laid out by Prime Minister Sabri al-Asali and was continued by Ghazzi since nobody could stand up to the leftist and Nasserist current that was rock-ing the Arab World in the mid-1950s. During the Ghazzi era, relations between Damascus and Moscow improved significantly. An arms deal was conducted with Czechoslovakia, official recognition was given to Communist China, trade agreements were made with Bulgaria, Romania, and Hungary, and student exchange programs went into effect between Syria and East Germany. It was also marked with a sweeping wave of sympathy and affection for President Gamal Abd al-Nasser of Egypt, who wanted Syria to become pro-Soviet.

Sa'id al-Ghazzi.

At home, Ghazzi proved to be a staunch democrat, shunning all attempts by military officers to inter-vene in political decision-making. The officers lobbied against him and were able to secure his resignation on June 3, 1956. His cab-inet was forced to resign when university students stormed and occupied the Ministry of Economy, to protest against the revision of a ban on wheat shipments to France.

In February 1958, Syria and Egypt merged to form the United Arab Republic (UAR). Sa'id al-Ghazzi declared his opposition the UAR and retired from politi-cal activity in the years 1958-1961. On September 28, 1961, a group of officers toppled the UAR. Ghazzi allied himself with the new leaders of Syria and became a member of parliament in December 1961. Due to his age, he was responsible for opening the first post-Nasser parliament on December 12, 1961. He nomi-nated himself for the post of speaker, and was supported by Muwafaq Assasa, one of the architects of the coup against the UAR, but lost the election to Ma'mun al-Kuzbari. President Nazim al-Qudsi toyed with the idea of appointing him prime minister in 1962, but it never materialized. Sa'id al-Ghazzi remained a member of parliament until the Baath Party came to power in March 1963. He retired from political life in the Baathist era and died on September 18, 1967.

Sources:

Azm, Khalid. *Muzakarat Khalid al-Azm* (1973).
Babil, Nasuh. *Sahafa wa Siyassa fi Souriyya* (1987).
Faris, George. *Man Hum fi al-`Alam al-Arabi?* (1956).
Itri, Abd al-Ghani. *Abqariyyat* (1996).
Seale, Patrick. *The Struggle for Syria* (1961).

al-Hafez, Amin
(1925-)

Amin al-Hafez was born in the city of Aleppo in northern Syria and studied at the Homs Military Academy. As a young officer, he volunteered for service in the Arab-Israeli War of 1948. He took part in a military uprising against General Adib al-Shishakli in 1954 and then allied himself with the movement of Arab nationalism headed by President Gamal Abd al-Nasser of Egypt.

Hafez rose steadily in rank and advocated Syria's merger with Egypt to form the United Arab Republic (UAR) in 1958. During the union years, he became a staff college instructor of military affairs in Cairo. He came in contact with other Syrian officers stationed in Egypt, mainly members of the Baath Party, but kept a distance from them to avoid harassment by Egyptian intelligence. On September 28, 1961, Hafez clashed with the officers in Damascus who dissolved the UAR and criticized the civilian regime of Syria's new president, Nazim al-Qudsi, claiming that it was working against Arab unity. Hafez took part in a military uprising against the new regime in December 1961, but the attempted coup was crushed by units of the Syrian Army loyal to the post-union order. In 1962, Qudsi appointed Hafez military attaché to Argentina, a traditional exile for political troublemakers.

On March 8, 1963, the officers of the Baath Party Hafez had known in Cairo came to power in Syria through a military coup and promised to restore the UAR. The Military Committee, which had orchestrated the putsch, appointed Hafez to the party's National Command and Revolutionary Command Council (RCC). A tough and reliable figure, Hafez also became minister of interior in the cabinet of Prime Minister Salah al-Bitar.

Shortly after the Baath assumed control of the state, its leaders clashed with Nasserist officers in the Syrian Army. Between April 28 and May 2, 1963, over fifty pro-Nasser officers were purged from the armed forces. Mohammad al-Sufi, the minister of defense, and Rashid al-Qutayni, the deputy chief of staff, were also retired from service. Riots broke out in Damascus and Aleppo from May 8-9, and Hafez ordered his police force to break up the marches, leading to the killing of fifty protestors. Jassem Alwan, a Nasserist officer, tried to seize power on July 18, 1963. He launched a daylight assault against the radio station and tried to occupy it. Amin al-Hafez arrived at the scene of the coup, with a submachine gun in hand, and fired at the conspirators. He restored order, dismissing the coup leaders from the army and arresting officers who were sympathetic to Alwan. Hafez replaced Lu'ayy al-Atasi as president of the RCC, hauled the conspirators before military courts, and had them executed.

Amin al-Hafez.

Hafez breached the time-honored tradition of banishment practiced by ex-President Qudsi against Hafez and his comrades when they tried to seize power in December 1961. Hafez's ascent came with the direct backing of Baath Party's founders, Michel Aflaq and Salah al-Bitar, and with the approval of the officers, who since 1963 were the de facto rulers of Syria. In future years, however, his enemies were to argue that his post was ceremonial. After coming to power in 1970, Hafez al-Asad recalled, "he (Hafez) could not transfer a single soldier without our permission."

The era of Amin al-Hafez was marked with trouble from the beginning. To carry out his socialist vision, Hafez launched a sweeping nationalization program, breaking the power of the urban notability by confiscating their land, factories, and companies. This destroyed his image in the eyes of Syria's powerful bourgeoisie families. In January 1965, one hundred companies (employing 12,000 people) were nationalized by the government. State ownership was also extended to electricity, oil distribution, and around 70% of foreign trade. Hafez banned all political newspapers, outlawed all political parties, and arrested many dissidents who were opposed to his rule. In April 1964, the Muslim Brotherhood launched a military uprising in the city of Hama and called for a holy war against the regime. Hafez responded with force, sending planes to attack Brotherhood headquarters and arresting leaders of the Brotherhood.

In January 1965, Amin al-Hafez suffered a humiliating scandal when his personal friend, Elie Cohen (alias Kamel Thabet), turned out to be an Israeli spy working undercover in Damascus. Cohen had befriended Hafez in 1961, while the latter was serving in Argentina. Hafez helped facilitate Cohen's return to Syria, thinking that he was a wealthy Syrian émigré, and introduced him to many senior government officials. When the Baath came to power in 1963, Cohen rose to prominence as an ally of Hafez, who wanted to appoint him minister of state in the cabinet of Prime Minister Salah al-Bitar. In 1964, Hafez took Cohen on a tour of the Syrian-Israeli border and boasted of the latest weapons Syria had purchased from the USSR. The information was secretly transmitted to Israel and presumably resulted in the occupation of the Golan Heights in 1967. The Cohen ordeal tremendously damaged Amin al-Hafez's credibility among Baath Party conservatives. Although Cohen was executed by Amin al-Hafez in 1965, the president was never able to distance himself from the scandal.

By late 1965, internal party strife had alienated Hafez from his former comrades in the armed forces. He was accused of striving to create his own hegemony in the Syrian Army and of wanting to demilitarize Syria. He clashed with two leading officers, Salah Jadid and Air Force Commander Hafez al-Asad, and tried to dismiss them both from the Syrian Army. Asad approached him in late 1965 with the hope of reaching a rapprochement and said, "Abu Abdu (as Amin al-Hafez was popularly called in Syria), we all have confidence in you. Disassociate yourself from the National Command (that was dominated by Michel Aflaq) because it has support neither among the military nor among the civilians. Put your hand in mine and let us act together. They (the civilians) are plotting against you!"

When Hafez refused, Jadid and Asad launched a coup on February 23, 1966, arresting Hafez and sending Bitar and Aflaq into exile. In his final hours in office, the president fought a street war with his enemies, appearing on his office balcony in central Damascus at 5:00 AM, brandishing a machine gun and opening fire on Saleem Hatum and Rifaat al-Asad who had come to arrest him. He was wounded in combat, arrested, and sent to the notorious Mezzeh prison. Asad helped with the hospital expenses of treating Hafez's daughter in France, since she was wounded in the combat, too.

Following the Arab-Israeli War of 1967, Jadid and Asad ordered the release of all political prisoners. Amin al-Hafez was set free on June 9 and exiled to Lebanon. Immediately, he was approached by a group of disgruntled officers who wanted to stage a coup and restore him to power. Hafez sensibly refused, claiming, "I don't want history to say I helped Israel by creating chaos at home." The ex-president fled to Iraq and allied himself with the Iraqi Baathists who had come to power in July 1968. Along with Michel Aflaq, who also fled to Baghdad, Hafez led the opposition to the regime of Salah Jadid from 1967 to 1970. In August 1971, Asad came to power in Syria and sentenced Amin al-Hafez to death in absentia. His sentence was commuted to life imprisonment in November 1971.

Amin al-Hafez allied himself with Iraqi President Saddam Hussein, who came to power in 1979 and treated him as an honored guest throughout the 1970s and 1980s. In 2001, thirty-eight years after his banishment from Syria, Hafez appeared on the Qatar-based Aljazeera news station and recounted his controversial history. Hafez declared himself innocent of any murder charges in 1963 and 1964, claiming that he had not ordered the killing of members of the Muslim Brotherhood or the Nasserist officers in the Syrian Army. He also argued that the Cohen case was a failed mission, stressing that the Israeli spy was arrested before transmitting information of substance to Tel Aviv.

Amin al-Hafez fled Baghdad when the Anglo-American War on Iraq began in March 2003 and returned to live in Syria, under the permission of President Bashar al-Asad, having spent thirty-six years in exile.

Sources:
Al-Hawadeth (November 20, 1970).
Al-Sharq al-Awsat (April 16, 2003).
Al-Watan al-Arabi. Interview with General Amin al-Hafez (June 17, 1988).
Batatu, Hanna. Syria's Peasantry: the Descendants of its Lesser Rural Notables and their Politics (2000).
Encyclopedia of the Modern Middle East, Vol II (1996). Article by Charles U Zenzie.
Seale, Patrick. Asad: Struggle for the Middle East (1988).
Commins, David. Historical Dictionary of Modern Syria (1996).
Devlin, John. The Baath Party: a History from its Origins to 1966 (1976).
Interviews with ex-President Amin al-Hafez on Aljazeera TV (February-May 2001).

al-Haffar, Lutfi
(1891-1968)

Lutfi al-Haffar was born to a family of merchants and raised in Damascus. He studied sociology, literature, and economics with private tutors in Damascus. In his teens, he joined the Arab underground during the final years of the Ottoman Empire, but was not an active member in the anti-Ottoman movement. Rather, he devoted his time to commercial activity.

In 1913, Haffar signed a famed declaration presented to the first Arab Congress in Paris and demanding emancipation from the Ottoman Empire. In 1922, he joined the Damascus Chamber of Commerce and two years later became deputy to the chamber's president, Aref al-Halbuni. In 1923, Haffar attempted to solve the ongoing water shortage in Damascus. The residents of the Syrian capital had relied on the River Barada for both irrigation and drinking water, but the river had insufficient flow for both uses. Haffar took clean drinking water from the Ayn al-Fija spring, on the outskirts of Damascus, and founded the Ayn al-Fija Waterworks Company in 1924. This allowed the water of the Barada to be used strictly for irrigation. The company was an overnight success and earned Haffar widespread acclaim in Syria.

Lutfi al-Haffar then made an alliance with Abd al-Rahman Shahbandar, the nationalist leader who had been working against the French Mandate in Syria. On June 5, 1925, Haffar joined Shahbandar in founding the People's Party, the first political movement in French Mandate Syria. The party, composed of leading statesmen, lawyers, and professors who would later become nationalist leaders in the 1940s, promoted the creation of a constitutional government in a free and unified Syria that would include Palestine, Jordan, and parts of Lebanon.

In 1925, an uprising against the French took place in the Arab Mountain, launched by the Druze chieftain Sultan al-Atrash and funded by the Hashemites. The revolt killed six thousand Syrian citizens and uprooted one fifth of the population. The economy was dislocated, commerce was at a standstill, agricultural production was interrupted, and thousands were reduced to poverty by the destruction of their homes and property.

In October 1925, the French launched the largest of their counter offensives, bombarding Damascus for forty-eight hours to break the Syrian resistance. At this point, Haffar emerged with an appeal to end the revolt and spare the locals more suffering. Haffar headed a group of moderate politicians who demanded an end to armed violence and called for peace talks with the French. Diplomacy, said Haffar, would do more for Syria than armed resistance. In April 1926, Haffar took part in the French-sponsored cabinet of Prime Minister Ahmad Nami, becoming minister of public works and commerce. He resigned in protest to French policies in July 1926, however, and the mandate authority ordered his arrest and transportation to a remote district in northern Syria.

Upon his release in 1928, Lutfi al-Haffar went to Beirut and co-founded the National Bloc, a group of landowners, lawyers, and merchants who were headed by the veteran nationalist Hashim al-Atasi. The National Bloc created a centralized nationalist movement that was to lead Syria for the next two years, calling for diplomatic resistance to occupation. Haffar ran for parliament on a Bloc ticket in 1928, 1932, 1936, and 1943, winning the elections in every round. In 1928, he held office for three months on the Constitutional Assembly that drafted the first republican constitution for Syria.

In 1936, Haffar helped orchestrate a sixty-day strike in Damascus, protesting France's refusal to address the issue of Syrian independence, and was arrested for

Lutfi al-Haffar.

leading demonstrations against the pro-French prime minister, Taj al-Din al-Hasani. In June 1938, the Bloc was elected to office, and Atasi became president of the republic. Haffar became minister of finance in the cabinet of Prime Minister Jamil Mardam Bey. He held office from December 1936 to July 1938. On February 23, 1939, President Atasi asked Haffar to form a government, and he managed to create one that lasted until April 5, 1939. During this time, Haffar served as prime minister and minister of education.

Haffar's years in power were marked by increased

tension with the French and rising discontent among the masses, created by his former ally Abd al-Rahman Shahbandar, who was leading the opposition to the Bloc regime. Shahbandar had returned from twelve years in exile and expected to receive a government post in the Atasi government. When the Bloc left him with nothing, he joined the opposition. In 1940, Shahbandar was killed by agents of France. Four Bloc chiefs, Haffar included, were accused of the murder by a French military tribunal. The ex-prime minister fled to Baghdad and remained in exile until a French court declared him innocent of the charges.

In August 1943, Lutfi al-Haffar ran for parliament on a joint list with Shukri al-Quwatli, the most powerful and popular nationalist in Damascus. When Quwatli was elected president of the republic, he appointed Haffar minister of interior in the cabinet of Prime Minister Saadallah al-Jabiri. Haffar held this post from August 1943 to November 1944. He was given the same post by Prime Minister Faris al-Khury from August to September 1945, and again by Prime Minister Jabiri from September 1945 until independence was achieved in April 1946.

In 1947, one year after independence from the French, the National Bloc was dissolved and renamed the National Party. It was a party composed of former Bloc members who championed a political program of modernizing Syria, maintaining its democratic system, and shunning all Arab attempts at uniting Syria with the neighboring Hashemite governments in Iraq and Jordan. The Hashemites wanted a monarchy in Syria, whereas the National Party wanted to maintain the republic. Haffar became the party's secretary-general, while President Quwatli served as its spiritual godfather.

Haffar became deputy to Prime Minister Jamil Mardam Bey during the Arab-Israeli War of 1948. In March 1949, the Syrian chief of staff, General Husni al-Za'im, came to power in Syria and overthrew the Quwatli regime. Haffar led a parliamentary coalition that remained loyal to ex-President Quwatli and refused to recognize the new leadership. Za'im had Haffar arrested, and he remained in prison until Abd al-Hamid Karameh, the former prime minister of Lebanon, intervened on his behalf and secured his release. He was placed under 24-hour surveillance, however, until the Za'im regime was deposed, also by coup, in August 1949.

In 1955, Lutfi al-Haffar nominated himself for presidential office in Syria, running against the independent Khalid al-Azm. Haffar withdrew his nomination, however, when ex-President Quwatli returned to Syria and renominated himself for the presidency. Haffar received no posts in the new Quwatli administration (1955-1958) and was politically dormant during the years of Syria's union with Egypt (1958-1961). In 1956, however, Quwatli wanted to appoint Haffar prime minister, but his name was vetoed by the Baath Party, which was opposed to his politics.

In 1961, Haffar supported the coup that brought down the union and signed the secession declaration, a document drafted by leading politicians that accused President Gamal Abd al-Nasser of Egypt of being a dictator. In April 1962, Abd al-Karim al-Nehlawi, another military officer, launched a coup and ousted the post-union government of President Nazim al-Qudsi. Nehlawi arrested all leading politicians in Damascus and accused them of shunning the officers and preventing them from assuming their role as decision-makers in Syria. In the manhunt that ensued, Nehlawi arrested Haffar and sent him to the notorious Mezzeh prison in Damascus. Haffar later was released by a group loyal to the post-union order. These officers defied Nehlawi's orders, wrecked his coup, and sent him into exile.

Lutfi al-Haffar retired from politics when the Baath Party came to power in March 1963. In 1998, his daughter, the novelist Salma al-Haffar published his memoirs and private papers in a book entitled, *Lutfi al-Haffar 1891-1968*.

Sources:

Babil, Nasuh. *Sahafa wa Siyasa fi Souriyyia* (1987).
Barudi, Fakhri. *Muzakarat al-Barudi: Sittoun Aman Tatakalam* (1952-1953).
Barudi, Fakhri. *Khamsoun Aman min Hayat al-Watan* (1999).
Commins, David. *Historical Dictionary of Modern Syria* (1996).
Faris, George. *Man Hum fi al-`Alam al-Arabi?* (1957).
Haffar, Lutfi. *Zikrayat* (1954).
Haffar, Salma. *Lutfi al-Haffar 1885-1968* (1997).
Kayyali, Abd al-Rahman. *Al-Marahil fi al-Intidab al-Faransi 1926-1938* (1958-1960).
Khoury, Philip. *Syria and the French Mandate* (1987).
Khury, Colette. *Awrak Faris al-Khury,* Vol II (1997).
Moubayed, Sami. *The Politics of Damascus 1920-1946* (1999).
Qassab Hasan, Najat. *Saniou al-Jalaa fi Souriyya* (1999).
Shambrook, Peter. *French Imperialism in Syria 1927-1936* (1998).

al-Hakim, Hasan
(1886-1988)

Hasan al-Hakim studied at the Academy of Public Administration in Istanbul and graduated in 1908. He returned to Damascus and became director of posts and telegraphs in 1918. During World War I, he joined the Arab underground and allied himself with Sharif Husayn, leader of the Arab Revolt in Mecca against the Ottoman Empire.

When the empire was defeated in October 1918, Hakim became a personal friend of King Faysal, the new ruler of Syria. Faysal appointed him director of the treasury in 1919. Meanwhile, he kept his post as director of posts and telegraphs. In July 1920, the French proclaimed their mandate in Syria, dethroning Faysal and sending both him and Hakim into exile. A French military tribunal sentenced Hakim to death in absentia and he was forced to flee to Amman. Hakim then became minister of finance in the Jordanian cabinet of Prime Minister Rashid Tali'. He also served as a political advisor to Prince Abdullah (Faysal's older brother), the Emir of Transjordan.

Hakim remained a favorite in the Hashemite court of Amman until the French issued a general amnesty that permitted his return to Syria in 1921. He befriended Abd al-Rahman Shahbandar, the former minister of foreign affairs under Faysal, and the two men led the underground resistance to the French occupation in the early 1920s. The French arrested Hakim in 1922 on the charge of meeting with American diplomats and receiving funds from them to topple the mandate regime.

In 1925, Shahbandar founded the People's Party, the first official party in French Mandate Syria, and appointed Hakim as its secretary-general. The party aimed at liberating Syria from the French, establishing a constitutional democracy, and uniting Syria with the Hashemite kingdoms in Baghdad and Amman. The Hashemite royals funded the party and both Shahbandar and Hakim administered its day-to-day affairs. They worked under the guiding influence of Faysal, who by then had become king of Iraq. In 1925, Hakim joined the underground and helped launch a national uprising against the French with the Druze leader Sultan al-Atrash. The revolt, co-planned by Shahbandar, inflicted heavy losses on the French, but was crushed in 1927. Hakim, Shahbandar, and Atrash were sentenced to death and exiled from Syria.

The three leaders fled to Transjordan and Iraq, working with King Faysal and King Abdullah during the late 1920s. In 1931, Hakim went to Palestine and became director of the Arab Bank in Jerusalem. In September 1933, King Faysal died and his successor, King Ghazi I, summoned Hakim to Baghdad and appointed him director of the Agricultural Bank of Iraq. He lived in Baghdad until a national government was created in Syria in 1936, headed by President Hashim al-Atasi, a former prime minister under Faysal. Hakim was invited back to Syria in 1937 and appointed director of Islamic affairs.

Hakim's relationship with the Bloc regime deteriorated when Shahbandar returned to Syria in 1937 and clashed with Prime Minister Jamil Mardam Bey. The latter, fearing Shahbandar's popularity, refused to allow Shahbandar to operate a political party, and Shahbandar in turn accused the prime minister of being a traitor

Hasan al-Hakim.

to Syria. Shahbandar also criticized the Bloc regime for the concessions it had promised France in 1936. Back then, Atasi and Mardam Bey had signed a treaty in Paris, guaranteeing independence for Syria over a twenty-five year period in exchange for military, political, cultural, and economic privileges for France in Syria. Shahbandar headed the opposition to the Treaty of 1936, claiming that it was poorly planned and granted too many concessions to France. Hakim echoed his criticism, and in a bid at silencing his opposition, Prime Minister Nasuhi al-Boukhari appointed Hakim minister in education. He held office from April to July 1939. One year later, however, in July 1940, Shahbandar was killed by agents of France agents in Damascus.

In September 1941, the Bloc regime was replaced by the pro-French administration of President Taj al-Din al-Hasani. The new president, wanting to distance himself from the Bloc, appointed Hakim as prime minister on September 20, 1941. Hakim appointed himself minister of finance and ruled Syria until April 17, 1942. He sought a rapprochement with the National Bloc by appointing three of its members in critical portfolios. Faydi al-Atasi was made minister of education, Mohammad al-Ayesh became minister of economy, and Fayez al-Khury took the position of minister of foreign affairs. During his era, the French declared Syria an independent republic on September 27, but due to the war in Europe, France refused to evacuate their troops from Syrian territory. Hakim clashed with Hasani over the distribution of power and accused the president of marginalizing Hakim's role as prime minister. In April 1942, Hakim resigned from office. In 1947, one year after independence, he ran for parliament on an independent ticket and won. In September 1950, he became minister of state in the cabinet of the pro-Hashemite statesman Nazim al-Qudsi.

Syria then faced a prolonged cabinet crisis when two alternating premiers, Qudsi and Khalid al-Azm, failed to create a suitable government that seemed acceptable to the officers who were the de facto rulers of Syria. As a result, President Atasi, who returned to office in 1949, appointed Hakim prime minister in August 1951. Hakim appeased the officers by appointing General Fawzi Selu as minister of defense and befriended General Adib al-Shishakli, the military strongman of Syria. Economic conditions were dire in the second Hakim cabinet. Unable to improve the economy, Hakim was forced to resign on November 28, 1951. From 1954 to 1958, he served as an independent deputy in the Syrian Parliament. But he resigned from politics when Syria and Egypt merged to form the United Arab Republic (UAR) in 1958, and he spent the remainder of his years writing articles in newspapers and publishing books. In September 1961, he reemerged briefly to support the coup d'etat headed by Colonel Abd al-Karim al-Nehlawi that overthrew union. Hakim joined a group of politicians in Damascus and, due to his age and standing, chaired the meeting that hailed the post-union order and accused President Gamal Abd al-Nasser of Egypt of imposing a dictatorship on

Syria from 1958 to 1961.

Hasan al-Hakim's works include the two-volume autobiography, *Muzakarati: Safahat min Tareekh Souriyya al-Hadeeth* (*My Memoirs: Pages from Syria's Modern History*), published in 1965-1966, and a biography of Dr Shahbandar entitled, *Abd al-Rahman Shahbandar: Hayatuh wa Juhduh* (*His Life and Struggle*), published in 1985.

Sources:

Azm, Khalid. *Muzakarat* (1973).
Commins, David. *Historical Dictionary of Modern Syria* (1996).
Hakim, Hasan. *Muzakarati: Safahat min Tareekh Souriyya al-Hadeeth* (1965-1966).
Itri, Abd al-Ghani. *Abqariyyat wa Alam* (1996).
Kourani, As'ad. *Zikrayat wa Khawater* (2000).
Rathmell, Andrew. *Secret War in the Middle East* (1995).
Seale, Patrick. *The Struggle for Syria* (1961).

al-Hakim, Hikmat (1892-1958): see "Administrators"

Haroun, As'ad
(1903-1968)

As'ad Haroun was born and raised in the coastal city of Lattakia. He studied business administration at the American University of Beirut (AUB) and obtained his graduate degree in political science from the Sorbonne in Paris. His father was Abd al-Wahid Haroun, a veteran statesman who in 1928 had co-founded the National Bloc, the leading anti-French movement.

In 1937, the young Haroun joined the National Youth, a paramilitary youth force modeled after the Brown Shirts in Germany and the Black Shirts in Italy. The goal of the National Youth was to protect locals from French aggression and mobilize popular propaganda for the National Bloc. Its leaders were a group of young men who wanted to introduce the concept of disciplined and armed resistance to occupation. As long as the French were not permitting the creation of a Syrian Army, Haroun claimed, the National Youth would have to serve as an alternative.

Haroun believed in the concept of mass politics and created a powerful network of young men to engage in marches, strikes, and rallies. The National Youth stalwarts wore an armband showing a torch-bearing hand, similar to the infamous swastika promoted by the Nazis in Germany. Among the party's co-founders were the university professors Ahmad al-Samman and Munir al-Ajlani, and the journalists Munir and Najib al-Rayyes. The National Youth remained in charge of Syrian mass politics from 1936 to 1946 and was disbanded by its founders when the French evacuated Syria in 1946. Haroun also became a leader of the Steel Shirts, the National Youth's military branch, and director of its youth affairs and human resources.

In 1937, President Hashim al-Atasi, a leader of the National Bloc, appointed Haroun consul to Baghdad. During World War II, Haroun expressed his support for Nazi Germany and rallied young Syrians under the slogan, "the enemy of my enemy is my friend." Haroun was arrested by the French in 1942 on the charge of harboring Fascist sympathies and imprisoned him in Beirut. In 1943, President Shukri al-Quwatli set him free. In 1946, right after independence from the mandate, Quwatli appointed Haroun ambassador to Iran. He became a deputy for Lattakia in parliament from 1947 to 1949. In September 1955, the independent prime minister, Sa'id al-Ghazzi, appointed Haroun minister of state and director of religious affairs. He resigned from office in May 1956 and in December became minister of health in the cabinet of Prime Minister Sabri al-Asali.

Haroun left office when Syria and Egypt merged to form the United Arab Republic (UAR) in 1958. He took part in the union talks with President Shukri al-Quwatli held in Cairo that resulted in the signing of the union charter on February 1, 1958. Haroun supported the coup that toppled the union on September 28, 1961, and on October 2 he co-authored the secession declaration, a statement criticizing the UAR. The declaration accused Nasser of "distorting the idea of Arab nationalism" and said that during the union years, Nasser had "strangled political and democratic life" in Syria.

As'ad Haroun retired from political activity when the Baath Party came to power in March 1963.

Sources:
Encyclopedia of the Modern Middle East, Vol II (1996). Article by
Charles U Zenzie.
Faris, George. *Man Hum fi al-`Alam al-Arabi?* (1956).
Samman, Mutih. *Watan wa Askar* (1995).
Uthman, Hashem. *Al-Ahzab al-Siyasiyya fi Souriyya: al-Siriyya
wa al-Mu'lana* (2001).

al-Hasani, Taj al-Din
(1885-1943)

Taj al-Din al-Hasani was born and raised in a family of Muslim scholars in Damascus. His father was Bader al-Din al-Hasani, one of the most respected Islamic scholars in the late nineteenth century. The young Hasani studied Islamic theology with his father, and in 1905 became his personal assistant. Like his father, Hasani trained young students of his generation in conduct and thought.

In 1912, Hasani became a member in the committee for school reform, which had been established by the Municipality of Damascus.

In 1916, he became editor-in-chief of *al-Sharq* (*The East*), a daily newspaper published by Jamal Pasha, the Ottoman governor of Syria. Hasani held this job throughout the years of World War I. When the war ended in 1918, Hasani's father delegated him to meet with King Faysal I, the first post-Ottoman ruler of Syria. Hasani's mission was to explain the conditions and needs of the Muslim community in Syria. Faysal was impressed by Hasani's eloquence, and in March 1920, appointed him director of the Royal Palace. Hasani retained this post until the French occupied Syria in July 1920 and dethroned Faysal, setting up their mandate in Syria. Hasani went to Paris and established secret channels with the French, promising them absolute loyalty if they agreed to support his political ambitions. The French government accepted the arrangement and began grooming Hasani for future leadership in Syria.

In 1925, French High Commissioner Maurice Sarrail asked Hasani to form a government during the climax of a national uprising in the Arab Mountain. Hasani failed at creating a suitable composition. He was given another try and succeeded, creating a government of prominent figures on February 15, 1928. With no presidential office in Syria, Hasani was vested with supreme presidential powers, but had to report on all of his actions and decrees to the French high commissioner in Beirut. Hasani's cabinet included the historian and scholar Mohammad Kurd Ali as minister of education, the attorney Sa'id Mahasin as minister of justice, and Jamil al-Ulshi, an Ottoman-trained officer and ex-prime minister, as minister of finance.

The opponents to Hasani's regime were mainly hard-line nationalists critical of the French connections maintained by Ulshi, Mahasin, and Hasani, claiming that they had not contributed to the nationalist movement since the French Mandate was imposed in 1920. In April 1928, Hasani held office for three months on the Constitutional Assembly that drafted the first republican constitution for Syria. Hasani ruled Syria with three different cabinets from February 1928 until November 1934, and his era was infamous for the misuse of public office and gross embezzlement. The opposition, headed by the National Bloc, accused Hasani of tampering with the ballots to secure his election through Interior Minister Sa'id Mahasin. In 1932, Hasani nominated himself for presidential office. The French, who were under mounting nationalist pressure to reform the political system in Syria, distanced themselves from the elections. With no proper French backing, Hasani was defeated at the polls.

Hasani protested to government authorities in Paris, who compensated him with the post of prime minister in the administration of President Mohammad Ali al-Abid. Hasani's fourth cabinet, created on March 17, 1932, provoked strikes and demonstrations in every city across Syria. Armed protestors carried

President Taj al-Din al-Hasani (left) with President Alfred Nakkah of Lebanon in 1941.

slogans accusing Hasani of treason, while many showed up to deride him in public with chants and insults. The National Bloc, Hasani's prime opponent in local politics, staged a countrywide strike that lasted for sixty days, demanding Hasani's resignation and compelling France to seriously address the issue of Syrian independence. During the strike, commercial life was brought to a standstill and hundreds of Syrians were arrested and incarcerated in remote prisons on the Syrian-Turkish border. Hasani arrested many leaders of the National Bloc, including Saadallah al-Jabiri from Aleppo and Fakhri al-Barudi from Damascus. Shukri al-Quwatli and Nasib al-Bakri, two politicians from Damascus, were placed under house arrest. The entire ordeal embarrassed the French and Hasani was dismissed from office on February 24, 1936, and invited the Bloc leaders to independence talks in Paris. When a Franco-Syrian treaty was ready, the Bloc leadership assumed power and Hasani moved into the opposition to the new regime of President Hashim al-Atasi, the leader of the National Bloc.

Ex-Prime Minister Hasani remained on the margins of political life until 1941, when following the Bloc downfall, France's General Charles de Gaulle appointed him president of Syria on September 12, 1941. Hasani was required to contain the nationalist movement and provide funds for France's war effort in Europe. To raise money, President Hasani increased taxes and raised the price of bread, thereby alienating himself throughout the poor districts of Syria. De Gaulle rewarded Hasani's services by officially recognizing Syria's independence on September 27, 1941, and promising complete French evacuation once the war in Europe ended. The French general invalidated a law formulated in the 1920s that divided the Alawite Mountain and the Arab Mountain into independent zones, thereby reincorporating them into the Syrian Republic. France, however, was given the right to retain military bases throughout the country and receive economic, financial, and political privileges in Syria.

Hasani then tried to distance himself from French influence and began befriending members of the National Bloc. He also tried to convince the French to reinstate the democratically elected parliament of 1936-1939, but his efforts proved futile. He died suddenly of a heart attack on January 17, 1943. His son-in-law, Munir al-Ajlani, claims that in his final years, Taj al-Din al-Hasani wanted to distance himself from the French and project the image of a true nationalist, but died before that goal could be accomplished. History has labeled Hasani as one of the greatest collaborators with the French Mandate in Syria. He was the first Syrian president to die while in office.

Sources:
Babil, Nasuh. *Sahafa wa Siyasa fi Souriyya* (1987).
Al-Sharq al-Awsat (September 20, 1998).
Hakim, Hasan. *Muzakarati* (1965).
Hakim, Yusuf. *Souriyya wa al-Intidab al-Faransi* (1966).
Itri, Abd al-Ghani. *Alam wa Mubdioun* (1999).
Khoury, Philip. *Syria and the French Mandate* (1987).
Mardam Bey, Jamil. *Syria's Quest for Independence* (1994).
Moubayed, Sami. *The Politics of Damascus 1920-1946* (1999).
Shambrook, Peter. *French Imperialism in Syria 1927-1936* (1998).
Interview with Dr Munir al-Ajlani (Beirut August 13, 1999; September 9, 1999).

al-Hawrani, Akram
(1912-1996)

Akram al-Hawrani was born and raised in Hama, a city located on the Orontos River. His father, Rashid al-Hawrani, was a second-tier notable who had nominated himself for the Ottoman Parliament in 1908, but was defeated by the aristocrat Khalid al-Barazi. The bitterness of his father's defeat at the hands of an aristocrat had a profound effect on the young Hawrani. He studied law at Damascus University and graduated in 1936. As a college student, he joined the Syrian Social Nationalist Party (SSNP) of Antune Sa'ada, which aimed at uniting Greater Syria.

In 1932, Hawrani tried and failed to assassinate the pro-French prime minister, Subhi Barakat. This brought Hawrani into the limelight of the nationalist movement in Hama. In 1941, he volunteered for service in a military uprising in Iraq led by Rashid Ali al-Kaylani against the British forces stationed in Baghdad. He returned to Syria when the revolt was crushed and joined the National Bloc, the leading anti-French movement in Syria. The National Bloc wanted to end the French Mandate in Syria through diplomatic means rather than armed resistance. Hawrani ran for parliament on a Bloc ticket in 1943 and won with an overwhelming majority. His election was repeated in 1947, 1949, 1954, and 1962.

Once in power, Hawrani began to criticize the National Bloc administration of President Shukri al-Quwatli, arguing that it did not equally represent the people. He accused the Syrian president of harboring dictatorial policies and preached his downfall. A charismatic speaker, Hawrani gathered villagers and rural chiefs around him, enabling him to separate himself from the Bloc ranks and lead what was labeled "the socialist coalition" in parliament. In May 1945, Hawrani used his influence among the peasants to marshal an uprising against the mandate authority in Hama and manage to seize the city's garrison from the French.

In 1946, shortly after independence, Hawrani officially founded the Arab Socialist Party, created on Marxist ideals and centered on his cult personality. He became a savior to the peasant class (which composed two million of Syria's three and one half million inhabitants), encouraging the revolution of the countryside against the town, and single-handedly introduced new terms into Syrian politics like "classless society," "rule of the working class," and "socialism." His "Land Belongs to the Peasant" campaign took Syria by storm, and he was able to encourage villagers in Hama to riot against their landlords, demanding a classless society with equal distribution of wealth.

Prior to Hawrani, these socialist terms were unheard of in Syria. He made them common in his native Hama, the stronghold of landed power and the base for big landowning families like the Barazis, the Azms, and the Kaylanis, who owned ninety-one of the 113 villages in Hama. The city was known for its feudalism and conservatism, and Hawrani shocked it out of its Puritan nature and exposed its leaders to the plight of the countryside. He claimed that the landowners had "stolen" the land from the villagers, and promised his supporters that the land would be restored to them. He turned agitation into violence and encouraged his supporters to burn crops, attack landlords, and make the villages too dangerous for their owners to inhabit.

Hawrani's popularity can be measured through his following in parliament. In 1949, there were six deputies from Hama, with him alone representing the peasants. The rest were from the traditional landowning families. At the next elections in 1954, the situation was reversed—only one landowner won the elections and the remaining six seats for Hama were filled by deputies for the peasantry.

In 1947, Hawrani nominated himself for parliament on an Arab Socialist Party ticket and won with ease. He also fought in the Arab-Israeli War of 1948 as a voluntary recruit with the Raqqa deputy Abd al-Salam al-Ujayli. Thirty deputies had volunteered to fight, but only two showed up for battle. In March 1949, he united his efforts with General Husni al-Za'im and launched the first military coup in the Arab world. The coup was planned by Hawrani and executed by Za'im, and resulted in the overthrow of Quwatli and his National Party from power.

Hawrani became Za'im's advisor and speechwriter. In July 1949, however, after working with the new president for three months, the relationship between the two men faltered. A crisis developed over the political asylum and extradition of Antune Sa'ada, president of the Syrian Social Nationalist Party (SSNP). With a price on his head in Lebanon, Sa'ada had fled to Damascus seeking Za'im's protection. He had tried and failed to topple the Lebanese regime of President

Bshara al-Khury. Za'im and Hawrani welcomed Sa'ada in Syria, having their own reasons to topple the Khury regime. Being a friend of ex-President Quwatli, Khury had refused to recognize Za'im as president of Syria and embarrassed the new Syrian leader in Arab circles. Hawrani was a former member of the SSNP, which called for the unification of Greater Syria, and was a hard-line sympathizer with Sa'ada's efforts. He called on Za'im to welcome Sa'ada and assist in overthrowing the independent governments in Iraq, Jordan, Lebanon, and Palestine in order to unite them with Greater Syria. With no proper explanation, Za'im betrayed Sa'ada on July 8, 1949, and extradited him to Lebanon, where he was executed on the charge of treason. Frustrated, Hawrani began plotting for the overthrow of the regime he had helped create. On August 14, 1949, along with General Sami al-Hinnawi, another SSNP sympathizer, Hawrani succeeded in overthrowing Za'im. The president was arrested and killed by SSNP officers. The military coup was funded by Iraq, carried out by Hinnawi, and planned by Hawrani.

Once rid of Za'im, Hawrani became a deputy for Hama in the Constitutional Assembly that drafted a new constitution for Syria. He also served as minister of agriculture in the all-party government of Prime Minister Hashim al-Atasi. In December 1949, Hawrani became minister of defense in the independent cabinet of Prime Minister Khalid al-Azm. When Atasi was elected president, he faced a cabinet crisis resulting from ideological conflict between the military officers, the de facto rulers of Syria, and the civilian leaders who wanted to curb the influence of the officer class.

In search of a neutral politician on good terms with the officers, Atasi asked Hawrani to form a cabinet on December 21, 1950, but he failed to reach a suitable compromise. Earlier, in December 1949, Hawrani allied himself with General Adib al-Shishakli, Syria's new military strongman, and began plotting for the overthrow of Sami al-Hinnawi and President Hashim al-Atasi. Shishakli was a childhood friend, a former member of the SSNP, and a relative from Hama. They had served together in the Arab-Israeli War of 1948, helped topple the Quwatli regime, and seemingly were the only two conspirators from the Za'im interlude who had survived the coup of 1949. Both he and Hawrani firmly believed in Syria's republican regime and accused Hinnawi of wanting to replace it with a Hashemite monarchy. Both men had no intention of being ruled from Baghdad, and Hawrani made that clear in a speech delivered in parliament in 1950, where he said, "I too stand for Arab unity. But I don't want an English or American Arabism. I believe in Arab socialism, but I reject Communist socialism. I should like to adopt a saying from the French Revolution that describes our situation, Arab unity, what crimes are committed in your name!"

When Shishakli overthrew the Hinnawi regime in December 1949, Hawrani became Shishakli's right-hand man and helped him seize full control of Syria in December 1951. He advised Shishakli to rule Syria through a puppet regime and helped prop up General Fawzi Selu as president of the republic. Shishakli controlled affairs of the state through the less public post of deputy chief of staff. In 1953, however, Shishakli became confident enough to appoint himself president of the republic.

Fearing that Hawrani had become too strong, Shishakli began to curb his influence. He sacked many of Hawrani's loyalists from the Syrian Army and refused to appoint the socialist leader as prime minister. In dismay, Hawrani fled to Lebanon and created the anti-Shishakli movement in exile. In Beirut, he merged his Arab Socialist Party with the Baath Party of Michel Aflaq and formed the Arab Baath Socialist Party. In 1954, Hawrani took part in a national uprising that ousted the Shishakli regime. When Shishakli fled Syria, Hawrani returned to Damascus and allied himself with Syria's new president, Hashim al-Atasi. He ran for parliament and became a deputy for Hama. He also joined the movement of Arab nationalism emerging in the mid-1950s and headed by President Gamal Abd al-Nasser of Egypt. When Shukri al-Quwatli returned to power in

Akram al-Hawrani.

1955, Hawrani supported his candidacy, and the following year supported his friendship with Gamal Abd al-Nasser. By the late 1950s, Hawrani became one of Nasser's most visible and powerful allies in Syria.

On October 14, 1957, Hawrani replaced the anti-Nasser statesman Nazim al-Qudsi as speaker of parliament. He worked relentlessly to promote pro-Egyptian sentiment in Syria and cracked down on all anti-Egyptian views. He allied himself with Chief of Staff Afif al-Bizreh and Director of Intelligence Abd al-Hamid Sarraj, two protégés of Nasser, and the three men transformed Syria into an Egyptian satellite. In 1957-1958, Hawrani headed the Syrian-Egyptian union talks, and when the United Arab Republic (UAR) was created in February 1958, Nasser rewarded his services and made him vice president of the republic.

During the union years (1958-1961), Hawrani's most far-reaching achievement was the land redistribution program he influenced Nasser to implement. Under his advice, Nasser struck at Syria's urban notability in July 1961 and nationalized all vast plantations owned by the landowners of Damascus, Aleppo, Homs, Hama, and Lattakia. Many traditional landowners were bankrupted by Nasser's socialist decrees, but Hawrani called for more socialist legislation, claiming that the land should be owned by the peasant who farmed it, and not by the absentee landlord. In 1960, however, Hawrani became so popular among Syria's peasants that Nasser himself began fearing his influence. He was retired from office and soon shifted into the anti-Nasser bloc. Hawrani supported the coup that toppled the UAR on September 28, 1961, and he allied himself with Abd al-Karim al-Nehlawi, the new military strongman of Syria.

On October 2, Hawrani signed the anti-union manifesto drafted by a group of disenchanted politicians, an action that was to bring Hawrani much trouble in future years among conservative members of the Baath who were still pro-Nasser. The document, handwritten by Bitar, accused Nasser of "distorting the idea of Arab nationalism" and proclaimed that during the union years Nasser had "strangled political and democratic life" in Syria. Now that Syria was rid of him, the document added, "correct socialism" could be implemented. Patrick Seale, author of *The Struggle for Syria*, best describes Hawrani's stance in 1961 saying, "Had he condemned both Nasser and the secessionists, then he might have stood a chance of climbing out of the chaos then engulfing Syria to take power for himself, becoming perhaps a Syrian Castro."

Hawrani's alliance with anti-union statesmen damaged his credibility within traditional Baath Party circles that were still pro-Nasser. He pledged loyalty to Syria's new president, Nazim al-Qudsi, and became a deputy for Hama in the first post-Nasser parliament. So critical was the Baath Party of his policies that Hawrani formally resigned on June 20, 1962, and revived his Arab Socialist Party. Considered an opportunist, however, Hawrani was not appointed minister in the Qudsi administration, but created a large parliamentary bloc around his leadership.

In March 1963, the Military Committee of the Baath Party came to power in Syria and pledged to restore the UAR. The Baath officers cracked down on all anti-Nasser elements and expelled Akram al-Hawrani from the party. Officially, it was declared that his expulsion was due to his alliance with President Nazim al-Qudsi. In reality, however, everyone in the Baath, including Michel Aflaq, feared his influence. If he were to remain in Syria, he would help topple the Baath government once his demands were not fulfilled, just as he had overthrown all leaders that had ruled Syria since 1949. As a result, the Baath Party had Hawrani's civil rights terminated and he was banished from Syria, with orders never to return. Feared by enemy and ally alike, it was to everyone's benefit that Akram al-Hawrani be destroyed. He moved to Iraq and worked with exiled politicians against the regimes of Amin al-Hafez (1963-1966), Nur al-Din al-Atasi (1966-1970), and the government of Hafez al-Asad. In his memoirs, published by his wife after his passing in 1996, Akram al-Hawrani claimed that in 1994, Asad dispatched Chief of Air Force Intelligence Mohammad al-Khuly to invite him back to Syria. He refused, however, and died at the age of eighty-four in Amman.

Akram al-Hawrani contributed heavily to the awakening of rural society in Syria. He was the first politician to grasp the dimension of the peasant problem and use it, or as some would say, abuse it, to create a devoted power base for himself.

Sources:

Azm, Khalid. *Muzakarat* (1973).

Batatu, Hanna. *Syria's Peasantry: the Descendants of its Lesser Rural Notables and their Politics* (2000).

Commins, David. *Historical Dictionary of Modern Syria* (1996).

Diab, Izz al-Din. *Akram al-Hawrani Kama Arifuhu* (1998).

Devlin, John. *The Baath Party: a History from its Origins to 1966* (1976).

Elias, Joseph. *Aflaq wa al-Baath (Aflaq and the Baath)* (1991).

Faris, George. *Man Hum fi al-`Alam al-Arabi?* (1957).

Hamdan, Hamdan. *Akram al-Hawrani: Rajul lil Tareekh* (1996).

Hawrani, Akram. *Muzakarat Akram al-Hawrani* (2000).

Khayyer, Hani. *Akram al-Hawrani* (1996).

Moubayed, Sami. *Damascus Between Democracy and Dictatorship* (2000).

Owens, Jonathan. *Akram al-Hawrani (1948)*.

Samman, Mutih. *Watan wa Askar* (1995).

Seale, Patrick. *Asad: The Struggle for the Middle East* (1988).

Seale, Patrick. *The Struggle for Syria* (1961).

Haydar, Sa'id
(1890-1954)

Sa'id Haydar came from a prominent family in Baalbak, in what is today modern Lebanon, and studied at the Ottoman Law Academy in Istanbul. He returned to Syria in 1914 and opened a legal practice in Damascus. In November 1919, he was elected to the Syrian National Congress (equivalent of a modern parliament) that was delegated to run state affairs in the immediate post-Ottoman era.

Haydar joined the court of King Faysal, the new ruler of Syria, and became his special envoy to Turkey. He made numerous visits to the Turkish national-ist Kemal Ataturk in Anatolia, hoping that Ataturk would support Syria's desire to remain a free country, independent from the influence of Great Britain and France. Haydar lobbied with Turkish authorities, pleading that they use their considerable influence in Europe to help terminate the mandate system that was due to be implemented in Syria.

In July 1920, however, the French proclaimed their mandate over Syria and occupied Damascus, forcing King Faysal and his team into exile. A French military tribunal sentenced Haydar to death in absentia. He lived briefly in Cairo, returning to Syria when the French issued a general amnesty in 1922. In 1923, he was accused of conspiracy against the pro-French prime minister, Haqqi al-Azm, and sentenced to fifteen years in prison. Haydar was jailed for one year, and released in 1924 by Azm's sucessor, Prime Minister Subhi Barakat.

In 1925, Sa'id Haydar joined the Syrian revolt of the Arab Mountain. He took up arms with the revolt commander Sultan al-Atrash and helped coordinate the national uprising in Damascus, Homs, and Hama. Once again, the French sentenced him to death for his actions and he fled to Jordan when the revolt was crushed in 1927. In Amman, he was arrested by British authorities who returned him to Syria. The French brought him to trial on the charge of treason. King Faysal, who by then had become king of Iraq, intervened on Haydar's behalf and secured his release. President Ataturk gave him political asylum in Ankara, where he lived until a general amnesty allowed him back to Syria in 1936.

Haydar became director of the Bureau of Consultation in the administration of President Hashim al-Atasi. He retained his job until President Atasi resigned from office in July 1939. In 1943, Sa'id Haydar nominated himself for parliament but lost the election. In 1949, he was voted into the Constitutional Assembly that drafted a new constitution for Syria. One year later, he became a deputy for Damascus in parliament. But Haydar retired from political life when General Adib al-Shishakli came to power in November 1951 and dissolved the Syrian Parliament.

Sources:
Khury, Colette. *Awrak Faris al-Khury,* Vol I (1989).
Encyclopedia of the Modern Middle East, Vol II (1996). Article by Elizabeth Thompson.
Khoury, Philip. *Syria and the French Mandate* (1987).

Homad, Abd al-Wahab
(1915-2002)

Abd al-Wahab Homad was born and raised in Aleppo and studied criminal law and Arabic literature in Paris. He began as an attorney and professor at Damascus University and co-founded the People's Party in Aleppo in 1947. The party aimed at maintaining Syria's democratic system, breaking the centralization of power practiced by the politicians of Damascus, and establishing union with neighboring Iraq. It was funded by the Hashemite royals in Amman and Baghdad and administered by Nazim al-Qudsi and Rushdi al-Kikhiya, both from Aleppo.

In 1949, Homad nominated himself to the Constitutional Assembly, a body that drafted a new constitution for Syria. In recognition for his role in writing the constitution, President Hashim al-Atasi rewarded Homad with the Medal of Honor of the Syrian Republic, Excellence Class. He also served as a deputy in parliament from 1947 to 1951. In 1951, he became minister of education in the cabinet of Prime Minister Hasan al-Hakim.

Homad launched the first and biggest scholarship program of its kind, sending three hundred Syrian students to Europe and the United States for higher education. He was arrested for his views during the military regime of President Adib al-Shishakli (1951-1954), but was released when Shishakli was toppled in February 1954. He then became minister of finance in the cabinet of Prime Minister Sa'id al-Ghazzi from September 1955 to June 1956. From June to December 1956, Homad served as minister of education under Prime Minister Sabri al-Asali.

In the late 1950s, Abd al-Wahab Homad discarded his pro-Hashemite policies in favor of a pan-Arab approach. He joined the movement of Arab nationalism headed by President Gamal Abd al-Nasser of Egypt and defected from the line of politicians who wanted union with Iraq, preferring union instead with Nasser's Egypt. In February 1958, he supported Syria's union with Egypt to form the United Arab Republic (UAR) and suspended his membership in the People's Party.

During the union years, Nasser outlawed the People's Party and appointed Homad minister of justice. He held this post until the UAR was overthrown by military coup on September 28, 1961. His former ally, Nazim al-Qudsi of the People's Party, became president and Homad worked against him, calling for the restoration of the UAR. In 1962, Homad survived an assassination attempt when unknown assailants planted a bomb in his car. In March 1963, the Baath Party came to power in Syria and pledged to restore the UAR. Briefly, Homad served as minister of finance in the cabinet of Prime Minister Salah al-Bitar.

Homad devoted the remainder of his years to his legal practice and to his teaching career at Damascus University. In 1991, he was voted into the Arab Language Assemblage, the highest international scientific authority in the field of Arab language and literature, and remained an active member, conducting academic research until his death in February 2002.

Sources:
Itri, Abd al-Ghani. *Abqariyyat* (1996).
Hawrani, Akram. *Muzakarat Akram al-Hawrani* (2000).
Samman, Mutih. *Watan wa Askar* (1995).
Interview with Dr Abd al-Wahab Homad (Damascus September 9, 1999).

al-Husari, Sati (1882-1968): see "Educators"

Ilyan, Mikhail
(1880-?)

Born into a wealthy commercial family in Aleppo, Mikhail Ilyan began his career as a businessman, administering his family's various enterprises. In 1928, he co-founded the National Bloc, the leading political movement in Syria, with its president, Hashim al-Atasi.

The Bloc called for the liberation of Syria from French control through diplomatic means rather than armed resistance. Ilyan served on the Bloc's council and donated heavily to its treasury from 1928 to 1939. In 1943, he nominated himself for parliament on a Bloc ticket and won. In 1945, he became minister of foreign affairs in the National Bloc cabinet of Prime Minister Saadallah al-Jabiri. In April 1946, the French evacuated from Syria and the National Bloc was dissolved by its founders.

Ilyan helped establish the National Party and in April 1946 became minister of public works in the first National Party cabinet of Prime Minister Jabiri. But, to protest the "authoritarian" policies of Prime Minister Jamil Mardam Bey, Ilyan resigned from party ranks during the Arab-Israeli War of 1948. In March 1949, the National Party was removed from power by General Husni al-Za'im, who launched a coup d'etat and became president of Syria. Ilyan retired from politics during the four month regime of General Za'im and supported the coup that brought Za'im down in August 1949. Then, Ilyan allied himself with the post-Za'im order and became minister of national economy in the cabinet of Prime Minister Hashim al-Atasi.

From 1950 to 1955, Mikhail Ilyan became a friend of Crown Prince Abd al-Illah of Iraq. It was widely believed that the Iraqi crown prince wanted to appoint Ilyan prime minister of Syria in order to achieve his ambitions of a Syrian-Iraqi union under the Hashemite crown. Ilyan became increasingly alienated by the rising popularity in Syria of President Gamal Abd al-Nasser of Egypt, who threatened the ambitions of the Syrian-Iraqi union. Ilyan joined a group of like-minded politicians who sought to bring down the pro-Nasser and pro-USSR regime of President Shukri al-Quwatli, who had returned to office in 1955.

Along with Ilyan, the conspiracy involved Munir al-Ajlani, a long-time ally of the Hashemites, Sami Kabbara, publisher of the *al-Nidal* newspaper, and Adnan al-Atasi, a founding member of the People's Party. It was planned that a group of armed men, trained in Lebanon (by the anti-Nasser government of Kamil Sham'un), and funded by Hashemite Iraq, would occupy Damascus, dismiss all pro-Nasser officials, and force Quwatli to change his pro-Egypt and pro-USSR policies. (The conspirators had no intention of actually toppling President Quwatli.) Once all Nasserist elements were dismissed, went the plan, Syria would unite with Hashemite Iraq. The plan was funded from Baghdad by Crown Prince Abd al-Illah and Prime Minister Nuri al-Sa'id. But Abd al-Hamid Sarraj, the pro-Nasser director of intelligence, foiled the plot prior to its implementation and had all of its leaders charged with high treason and imprisoned.

Ilyan was sentenced to death in absentia on the charge of conspiring with a foreign country to attack Syria and initiate aggression with the aim of fomenting civil war. Mikhail Ilyan's sentence was commuted to life imprisonment, but he evaded arrest and lived in exile until the Syrian-Egyptian union (created in 1958) was dissolved in 1961.

Sources:

BBC Archives. "The Damascus Trial" February 26, 1957.

Faris, George. *Man Hum fi al-`Alam al-Arabi?* (1957).

al-Jabiri, Ihsan
(1882-?)

Ihsan al-Jabiri was born and raised in Aleppo and studied at the Ottoman Law Academy in Istanbul. He graduated with distinction in 1902 and opened a legal practice in Istanbul. In 1904, he joined the Ottoman civil service.

Jabiri steadily rose in rank and became private secretary to Sultan Abdulhamid II in 1909. The sultan had suffered a sharp cutback in his powers in 1908 when a group of young officers from the Ottoman Army launched a coup, curbing Abdulhamid's powers and forcing him to grant more political freedoms in the Ottoman Empire. Jabiri entered the imperial court just fifteen days before the officers struck at Abdulhamid for a second time and forced him to step down in favor of his brother in 1909. Jabiri kept the same job, however, under Sultan Mohammad Rashad V and retired from service when Syria was liberated from the Ottoman Empire in October 1918.

Jabiri joined the court of King Faysal I, the new ruler of Syria, serving as mayor of Aleppo from 1918 to 1919 and head of the Royal Office from 1919 to 1920. When the French proclaimed their mandate in Syria on July 24, 1920, they dethroned Faysal and sentenced Jabiri to death. But he fled into exile in Switzerland, and while in Geneva, called for an all-Arab congress aimed at defying the colonial ambitions of France and Great Britain in the Middle East. Jabiri chaired the meeting, which came to be known as the Syrian-Palestinian Congress, and served as a board member of the nationalist movement in exile from 1920 to 1925.

The Syrian-Palestinian Congress was vehemently pro-Hashemite, demanding the liberation of all Arab territories once under Ottoman control, and championing the creation of an Arab kingdom to be headed either by King Faysal, or by his older brother, Prince Abdullah of Transjordan. To achieve the goal of Arab unity and emancipation, Jabiri met with David Ben Gurion, leader of the Zionist Agency in Europe, and discussed the possibility of the creation of a Jewish state in Palestine in exchange for Zionist support for the Arab cause. His meeting with Ben Gurion was attended by his ally Prince Shakib Arslan and ended in failure. Jabiri returned to Syria in 1923, but the French forced him to leave once again for helping fund and plan the revolt of 1925.

Jabiri returned to exile, first in Istanbul and then in Geneva, where he remained until the French issued a general amnesty and allowed him to return to Syria in 1936. President Hashim al-Atasi appointed him governor of Lattakia in 1937. Jabiri's tenure was marked with ongoing hostility between the central government in Damascus and the inhabitants of the Syrian coast who wanted to remain autonomous under the French Mandate. Jabiri arrested many leaders of the separatist movement, and when they threatened to assassinate him, he resigned from office and returned to Damascus. He became an advocate of Nazi Germany in World War II and was arrested for his views by the French in 1940. Another amnesty set him free in 1942. Ihsan al-Jabiri did not take part in the final struggle against the French Mandate that ended with independence in April 1946.

Sources:
Azm, Khalid. *Muzakarat* (1973).
Ben Gurion, David. *My Talks with the Arabs.*
Encyclopedia of the Modern Middle East, Vol II (1996). Article by
Charles U Zenzie.
Khoury, Philip. *Syria and the French Mandate* (1987).

al-Jabiri, Saadallah
(1893-1947)

Saadallah al-Jabiri grew up in Aleppo in one of the most prominent landowning families in Syria. He studied law in Istanbul and was conscripted into the Ottoman Army when World War I broke out in August 1914. During the war, Jabiri became a member of al-Fatat, the leading underground movement in Syria working to topple the Ottoman Empire. He remained in the army until the war ended in October 1918 and Syria was liberated from Ottoman control.

Jabiri allied himself with King Faysal I, the new ruler of Syria, and became a deputy for Aleppo in the Syrian National Congress, the equivalent of a modern parliament. In congress, Jabiri joined the Beirut deputy Riyad al-Sulh and lobbied for women's suffrage in Syria. But conservative Muslim deputies vetoed their proposal. Jabiri remained a member of congress from November 1919 to July 1920. In January 1920, he smuggled arms and money to the Aleppine leader, Ibrahim Hananu, who was leading an armed revolt against the French invasion of Syria.

In July 1920, the French occupied Syria, dethroned Faysal and exiled Jabiri to Egypt. He remained in Cairo until the French issued an amnesty and permitted his return in 1922. Once back in Syria, Jabiri founded an underground movement in Aleppo called the Red Hand Society, modeled after the Iron Hand Society, a group operating in Damascus under the leadership of Dr Abd al-Rahman Shahbandar, Faysal's former foreign minister. Jabiri coordinated anti-French activity with

From left to right: Riyad al-Sulh, Hashim al-Atasi, Saadallah al-Jabiri, and Emile Khury, editor-in-chief of the Cairo daily Al-Ahram during the Syrian-Frech independence talks in Paris in 1936.

Shahbandar and supplied arms and funds to Ibrahim Hananu and his forces in the uprising they were leading in northern Syria. Due to his connections to the Hananu Revolt, the French arrested Saadallah al-Jabiri and imprisoned him at the Safita prison, where he remained for six months.

In October 1927, Jabiri co-founded the National Bloc, the leading anti-French movement in Syria, with its president, Hashim al-Atasi. It was a political party aimed at liberating Syria from the French through diplomatic means rather than armed resistance. In 1928, Jabiri held office for three months on the Constitutional Assembly that drafted the first republican constitution for Syria. In 1929, he became deputy to President Atasi in the Permanent Council of the National Bloc.

In 1935, Jabiri joined Bloc leaders in bringing Syria into a sixty-day strike, aimed at pressuring the French to recognize Syria's right to independence. He was briefly detained, then released, but kept under 24-hour surveillance by agents of the mandate authority. The strike disrupted the Syrian economy, led to the killing of hundreds of civilians, and embarrassed France, tarnishing her democratic image in the international community and forcing the French government to give in to the National Bloc.

The French recognized the Bloc leaders as the true representatives of the Syrian people and invited a senior Bloc delegation for independence talks in Paris. In March 1936, Hashim al-Atasi headed the Bloc delegation that included Jabiri, Faris al-Khury, Jamil Mardam Bey, and Riyad al-Sulh. The delegation succeeded in formulating a treaty that guaranteed gradual independence for Syria over a twenty-five-year period. In return, the Bloc leaders promised to grant France a series of military, political, and economic privileges in Syria. They also promised to support France in the Middle East if another deadly war were to break out in Europe. The Bloc returned to Syria in November 1936 and were voted into power with an overwhelming parliamentary majority. Atasi was elected president of the republic and he appointed Saadallah al-Jabiri as minister of interior and foreign affairs in the cabinet of Prime Minister Jamil Mardam Bey.

For the next three years, Jabiri played an instrumental role in diplomatic talks with the French, who broke their promise of moving toward Syrian independence and refused to ratify the treaty of 1936. Jabiri made numerous visits to Paris to secure a compromise with French Prime Minister Leon Blum, but his mission ended in failure. Due to the developing war situation in Europe and the rise to power of Adolph Hitler, the French government would not relinquish its colonies in the Middle East.

During his tenure at the Ministry of Interior, Jabiri was faced with violent protests in the Jazeera region, the Arab Mountain, and the mountains surrounding Lattakia where separatist movements refused to submit to the central government in Damascus and demanded autonomy from the rest of Syria. Jabiri took charge of suppressing the anti-independence movement and arresting many of its leaders. The inhabitants of Jazeera (northeast Syria) responded by kidnapping the governor, Tawfiq Shamiyya, and deporting him to Damascus. In Lattakia, the separatist leaders threatened to assassinate their governor, Ihsan al-Jabiri, and forced him to resign. When the cabinet of Mardam Bey was dissolved in February 1939, Jabiri was ousted from office. In July 1940, three agents of the French murdered Abd al-Rahman Shahbandar, the Bloc's primary opponent, and the mandate regime accused the Bloc leaders of ordering the killing. The French issued a warrant for Jabiri's arrest, forcing him to flee to Iraq where he remained until a court declared him innocent of the charges in 1941.

In 1943, Saadallah al-Jabiri allied himself with the Damascus leader, Shukri al-Quwatli, and ran for parliament on Quwatli's electoral list. When Quwatli became president in August 1943, he delegated Jabiri to form a government. Jabiri created his cabinet on August 19, 1943, and filled all positions with members of the National Bloc. He appointed Jamil Mardam Bey as minister of foreign affairs, Lutfi al-Haffar as minister of interior, and Abd al-Rahman al-Kayyali as minister of defense. Jabiri strengthened Syria's relations with Egypt, Saudi Arabia, and Lebanon, and held independence talks with French officials in Paris. On October 1944, he went to Cairo and laid the foundation of the Arab League with King Farouk of Egypt. On November 14, 1944, Jabiri resigned from office and Quwatli appointed him speaker of parliament.

Annoyed by the Bloc leaders policies and their refusal to grant political and military concessions to France, the French general Charles de Gaulle ordered the bombardment of Damascus on May 29, 1945, and the arrest of President Quwatli, Foreign Minister Mardam Bey, and Speaker Jabiri. French warplanes air raided the Syrian Parliament and French troops stormed Jabiri's office and seized all documents. When they were unable to find him, they set his office ablaze. Jabiri barely escaped death and fled to Lebanon, where he held a press conference and appealed to the international community to intervene and stop the bloodshed in Damascus. Prime Minister Winston Churchill responded to the Syrian plea and sent British troops to implement a cease-fire and administer the final withdrawal of French troops from Syria and Lebanon.

On September 30, 1945, Jabiri was asked to form a second cabinet, charged with negotiating the final details of independence with General de Gaulle. In addition to his duties as prime minister, Quwatli also appointed Jabiri minister of foreign affairs and defense. When the French evacuated Syria in April 1946, Quwatli asked Jabiri to form his third cabinet, the first in post-mandate Syria. Jabiri's government, created on April 24, 1946, lasted until December 27, 1946. It supervised the transfer of all administrative duties from France to Syria, and played an instrumental role in securing a smooth transition for Syria from the mandate era into that of independence. Jabiri's cabinet took over control of public security from France, along with electricity services, telecommunications, radio stations, military bases, airports, and public transport. He authorized the creation of a Syrian Army and donated personal funds for its first shipment of arms from Europe. On July 20, 1947, only one year after independence was achieved, Saadallah al-Jabiri died after a prolonged illness.

Sources:

Babil, Nasuh. *Sahafa wa Siyasa fi Souriyyia* (1987).
Barudi, Fakhri. *Muzakarat al-Barudi: Sittoun Aman Tatakalam* (1952-1953).
Barudi, Fakhri. *Khamsoun Aman min Hayat al-Watan* (1999).
Commins, David. *Historical Dictionary of Modern Syria* (1996).
Faris, George. *Man Hum fi al-`Alam al-Arabi?* (1957).
Haffar, Salma. *Lutfi al-Haffar 1885-1968* (1997).
Kayyali, Abd al-Rahman. *Al-Marahil fi al-Intidab al-Faransi 1926-1938* (1958-1960).
Khoury, Philip. *Syria and the French Mandate* (1987).
Khury, Colette. *Awrak Faris al-Khury,* Vol II (1997).
Moubayed, Sami. *The Politics of Damascus 1920-1946* (1999).
Qassab Hasan, Najat. *Saniou al-Jalaa fi Souriyya* (1999).

Jabri, Rashad
(1910-?)

Rashad Jabri studied business administration at the American University of Beirut (AUB) and obtained his graduate degree at Manchester College in the

United Kingdom. He worked briefly in Cairo, then returned to become manager of the Syrian Oil Company in 1939. He held the post until 1941, when he was appointed manager of the al-Khumasiyya industry group in Damascus. It was a pioneering holding company that specialized in the manufacturing of high quality textiles.

In 1951, President Hashim al-Atasi appointed Jabri governor of Damascus, and in March 1954 he became minister of public works and telecommunications in the cabinet of Prime Minister Sabri al-Asali. He also became a member of parliament in October 1954. He also served as minister of agriculture from June to December 1956 under Prime Minister Asali.

Jabri emerged in the second half of the 1950s as a moderate politician opposed to Syria's alliance with the USSR and Gamal Abd al-Nasser's Egypt. In February 1958, Jabri was opposed to Syria's union with Egypt, but a pro-union majority overruled his voice in parliament. He retired from political activity during the union years (1958-1961), but reemerged on September 28, 1961, as a supporter of the coup that brought down the Nasser government in Syria. Jabri joined a group of politicians on October 2 in drafting a secession declaration, accusing Nasser of imposing a dictatorship on Syria. The document accused Nasser of "distorting the idea of Arab nationalism" and stated that during the union years Nasser had "strangled political and democratic life" in Syria.

Jabri allied himself with the post-Nasser government of President Nazim al-Qudsi and served as a member of parliament in 1961-1963. When the Baath Party came to power in March 1963, they dissolved parliament and pledged to restore the UAR. Jabri was arrested and his civil rights were terminated by the Revolutionary Command Council. Rashad Jabri was released shortly thereafter, however, and devoted the remainder of his years to commercial activity, becoming a board member on the Damascus Chamber of Commerce from 1962 to 1970.

Sources:
Barada (March 24, 1963).
Damascus Chamber of Commerce Member Archive, presented by Dr Abd al-Rahman Attar.
Encyclopedia of the Modern Middle East, Vol II (1996). Article by Charles U Zenzie.
Faris, George. *Man Hum fi al-`Alam al-Arabi?* (1957).

Jadid, Salah
(1926-1993)

Salah Jadid was born in a village next to the coastal town of Jableh. He studied at the Homs Military Academy and joined the Syrian Army in 1946.

Jadid was briefly a member of the Syrian Social National Party (SSNP) in the 1940s but switched loyalties to join the Baath Party of Michel Aflaq and Salah al-Bitar. Salah Jadid remained close to the SSNP because his brother Ghassan was one of the most prominent leaders of the party in Syria. In the 1950s, Jadid became a member in the movement of Arab nationalism headed by President Gamal Abd al-Nasser of Egypt and supported Syria's merger with Egypt to form the United Arab Republic (UAR) in 1958.

During the union years (1958-1961), Jadid was stationed in Cairo. He joined other Baath Party officers and founded the Military Committee in 1959, a secret society aimed solely at protecting the UAR. Its members were Hafez al-Asad, Abd al-Karim al-Jundi, and Mohammad Umran. In September 1961, the UAR was dissolved by coup and a post-union government was created under President Nazim al-Qudsi. Jadid and his comrades were persecuted for their Nasserist loyalties and retired from the Syrian Army. In 1962, they began plotting for Qudsi's downfall. The young party members were influenced by the coup that took place in Iraq on February 8, 1963. This coup was carried out by a group of Baath Party officers, and Jadid hoped that he and his comrades could do the same in Syria.

On March 8, 1963, Jadid launched a coup that ousted the Qudsi government, arresting the president and exiling his prime minister, Khalid al-Azm, to Lebanon. Jadid put on his military uniform and took over the Bureau of Officer Affairs that controlled transfers and promotions in the Syrian Army. At 8:40 AM, the committee issued a decree over the radio reinstating the Baath Party officers into the armed forces. They established a one-party socialist state, ruled by the Baath Party, and declared that their ultimate goal would be to restore the UAR. Along with Asad, Umran, and Jundi, Jadid shared power with Syria's new president, Amin al-Hafez, and his prime minister, Salah al-Bitar. In August 1963, Jadid became chief of staff of the Syrian Army. Michel Aflaq, the party's supreme ideologue, remained secretary-general of the Baath Party.

Shortly after assuming power, President Hafez and Prime Minister Bitar accused Jadid and his comrades of wanting to militarize the regime and reduce them to ceremonial heads of state. Jadid's powers had increased when, in addition to his duties as chief of staff, he became assistant secretary-general of the Regional Command and appointed his friend Yusuf al-Zu'ayyin as prime minister in August 1965. At Officer Affairs, he tailored the Syrian Army to his desire, promoting friends, dismissing enemies, and drafting back into service a large number of reserve officers from the Baath Party who owed him direct allegiance. In the process of dismissals, Jadid retired Mohammad Umran from the Syrian Army and dispatched him to "serve the revolution" as ambassador to Spain. In reality, however, Jadid was banishing one of his most serious rivals from Syria to keep the stage clear for his political ascent.

On February 23, 1966, Jadid joined Air Force Commander Hafez al-Asad and toppled the regime of Amin al-Hafez. They arrested the president and exiled Aflaq and Bitar from Syria, with orders never to return. Asad became minister of defense and Nur al-Din al-Atasi, a veteran civilian Baathist close to Jadid, became president of the republic. Jadid chose for himself the less public post of deputy secretary-general of the Baath Party.

For the next four years, Salah Jadid dictated his own vision over Syria's domestic and foreign

Seated from left to right in 1968: Chief of Staff Mustapha Tlas, Ahmad al-Meer, the Commander of the Golan Heights front, and Salah Jadid.

affairs. He tried to refashion society from top to bottom through all the cabinets that came to power from 1966 to 1970. He packed the armed forces with his supporters and dismissed all opponents from the government, the diplomatic corpse, and the Syrian Army.

On Arab affairs, Syria became increasingly alienated, quarreling with Lebanon, Jordan, Iraq, and Saudi Arabia during the Jadid years. Jadid's only allies in the Arab world were President Gamal Abd al-Nasser and Yasser Arafat, leader of the Palestinian Liberation Organization (PLO). Jadid believed in armed resistance to occupation and extended political support to the PLO and their war on Israel from Jordan. Farouk al-Qaddumi, a founder of the PLO who was based in Damascus during the 1960s, describes the situation during the Jadid years, saying, "Syria was an essential support base for our movement, acting to accommodate a strong current of feeling in favor of the Fedayeen (the Palestinian commandos) among army officers and Baath Party members." Jadid authorized the establishment of training camps for Arafat's Fateh movement, gave much autonomy for the guerrillas, facilitated their raids on Israel from Lebanon, but came short of giving them access to Israel from the Syrian Golan.

In the area of foreign affairs, Salah Jadid allied himself with the USSR. To please them, he appointed Samih Atiyya, a member of the Syrian Communist Party, as minister of telecommunications in the cabinet of Prime Minister Zu'ayyin. He was the first communist to assume a ministerial post in Syria. Jadid then welcomed Khalid Bakdash, the veteran leader of the Communist Party, back to Syria after spending eight years in exile. The Soviets rewarded Jadid with loans, arms, and military experts. The USSR donated heavily to Syrian infrastructure and funded industrial projects and road networks, a dam on the Euphrates River, and the opening of newly discovered oil fields in the northeast.

In 1966, one of Jadid's local allies, Saleem Hatum, tried seizing power in Syria and besieged Atasi and Jadid in the Arab Mountain. His coup was foiled by Defense Minister Asad, however, and Hatum was arrested and shot on Jadid's orders. The new regime ruled Syria through a massive intelligence apparatus where citizens were persecuted for their political views and loyalty to anyone but Jadid became a capital offense, punishable by lengthy imprisonment.

But Jadid suffered a humiliating defeat during the Arab-Israeli War of 1967, when Syria was defeated and Israel occupied the Golan Heights. Following the war, his relationship with Asad became strained. Asad accused him of weakness at the war front and poor leadership in Syria. In September 1968, the conflict between both men erupted when Asad arrested some of Jadid's allies in the army, along with the newspaper editors of *al-Baath* and *al-Thawra* (who were pro-Jadid) and seized the radio and television stations. Asad stopped just short of a complete power takeover, but only wanted to show Jadid the power that Asad wielded.

In November 1970, Jadid called for a Baath Party conference to expel Asad and his ally, Chief of Staff Mustapha Tlas, from party ranks. Asad, however, struck first. He launched his own coup on November 16, 1970, and had both Jadid and President Atasi imprisoned. Asad's overthrow was greatly welcomed by the commercial class in Syria who had been badly affected by Jadid's hard-line socialist policies. The merchants staged joyful parades in Damascus chanting, "We asked God for aid (*al-madad* in Arabic)—he sent us Hafez al-Asad!" Salah Jadid remained in prison until his death in August 1993.

Sources:
Al-Huriyya (January 25, 1968).
Batatu, Hanna. *Syria's Peasantry: the Descendants of its Lesser Rural Notables and their Politics* (2000).
Commins, David. *Historical Dictionary of Modern Syria* (1996).
Razzaz, Munif. *Al-Tajruba al-Murra* (1967).
Seale, Patrick. *Asad: Struggle for the Middle East* (1988).
Tlas, Mustapha. *Mirat Hayati* (1995).

al-Jaza'iri, Sa'id
(1883-1981)

Prince Sa'id al-Jaza'iri studied law in Istanbul and began his career as a judge in the Ottoman courts in Damascus. He belonged to a family of Algerian ancestry and his grandfather was Prince Abd al-Qadir al-Jaza'iri, the Algerian freedom fighter exiled to Syria in the late nineteenth century.

Prince Sa'id took no part in politics during the final years of the Ottoman Empire, but was allied to the Arab Revolt of Sharif Husayn, the Prince of Mecca. When the Ottomans evacuated Syria on September 26, 1918, Jaza'iri created a council of notables that administered state affairs in the immediate post-Ottoman period. He declared himself a self-appointed head of state, charged with heading a preliminary government that would rule Syria while awaiting orders from the Arab Army of Sharif Husayn. Jaza'iri's cabinet included Shukri Pasha al-Ayyubi, the ex-director of the Ottoman Military Academy, Jamil al-Ulshi, a former officer in the Ottoman Army, and the attorney Faris al-Khury. Jaza'iri was voted into the Syrian National Congress, the equivalent of a modern parliament, and appointed head of state from September 26 to October 1, 1918. He confiscated all official Ottoman documents, guarded the treasury, and raised the Hashemite flag over all government buildings.

When the Anglo-Arab armies took over Damascus on October 1, 1918, the British officer T.E. Lawrence forced Prince Sa'id out of office and appointed Faysal, the Arab commander in World War I, as king of Syria. Lawrence claimed that Jaza'iri had no authorization to assume leadership of Syria and exiled him to Europe.

Prince Sa'id spent the next three years in exile, making his peace with the French, who occupied Syria in 1920, and marketing himself as a potential king-in-waiting for Syria. In 1925, an armed uprising took place in the Arab Mountain and the French responded by shelling the Syrian capital. Jaza'iri intervened with French High Commissioner Maurice Sarrail to secure a cease-fire. In 1932, the French considered restoring the monarchy to Syria and appointing Jaza'iri king, but the idea was badly received by the public, and called off altogether by the French government. Jaza'iri spent the 1940s and 1950s running a periodical entitled, *al-Hadara al-Islamiyya (Islamic Civilization)*.

In the final years of the French Mandate, Prince Sa'id's name appeared frequently in local newspapers as an opponent of the National Bloc and an ally of its main rival in Syrian politics, Dr Abd al-Rahman Shahbandar. When Shahbandar was killed by agents of the French in 1940, Prince Sa'id kept a low profile, then reemerged as a critic of the National Bloc regime of President Shukri al-Quwatli. This government lasted from 1943 until 1949. In 1958, Jaza'iri was opposed to union between Syria and Egypt, claiming that the socialist policies of President Gamal Abd al-Nasser would prove disastrous for Syria's economic and political system. On September 28, 1961, Prince Sa'id al-Jaza'iri welcomed the coup that overthrew the union and delivered a speech on Syrian Radio, hailing the officers who expelled Nasser and who would go on to rule Syria from 1961 to 1965.

Sources:

BBC World Service Archives on Syria for September 28-30, 1961.
Khoury, Philip. *Syria and the French Mandate* (1987).
Samman, Mutih. *Watan wa Askar* (1995).
Russell, Malcom. *The First Modern Arab State: Syria under Faysal I* (1987).

al-Jundi, Sami
(1921-1996)

Sami al-Jundi studied dentistry at Damascus University and graduated in 1944. During his college years, he met the political philosopher Zaki al-Arsuzi and was attracted by his socialist doctrine and his calls for Arab nationalism. Jundi was later exposed to other left-wing ideologies and in 1947 joined the Baath Party of Michel Aflaq and Salah al-Bitar.

Jundi was critical of the regimes that ruled Syria in the 1940s and 1950s but joined the movement of Arab nationalism headed by President Gamal Abd al-Nasser of Egypt in the second half of the 1950s. Jundi supported Syria's merger with Egypt to form the United Arab Republic (UAR) in February 1958 and was appointed director of information and propaganda for President Nasser.

In September 1961, a coup toppled the union and brought President Nazim al-Qudsi to power. Jundi was highly critical of the new regime, and as a result, was retired from service. On March 8, 1963, officers from the Baath Party staged a coup that ousted the Qudsi government, pledging to restore the Syrian-Egyptian union. Jundi hailed the coup and became minister of information in the cabinet of Prime Minister Salah al-Bitar. He also became official spokesman for the Revolutionary Command Council (RCC) created in Damascus and modeled on the RCC that Nasser established in Cairo in 1952. In April 1963, Jundi went to Cairo to discuss a new union deal with Nasser. On May 11, 1963, the RCC delegated Jundi to form a cabinet. He was named prime minister but could not compose a suitable government and resigned from office three days later. He became minister of information, culture, and national guidance in the second cabinet of Prime Minister Bitar and held office until November 1963. Jundi's post was renewed by President Amin al-Hafez and he remained a member of government until October 1964. President Hafez then appointed him ambassador to France.

In 1970, Jundi retired from political activity when President Hafez al-Asad came to power. Jundi moved to Beirut, spending his time writing his memoirs and returned to Syria following the Israeli invasion of Lebanon in 1982. In Syria, Sami al-Jundi worked as a dentist and took no part in politics.

Sources:
Razzaz, Munif. *Al-Tajruba al-Murra* (1967).

Tlas, Mustapha. *Mirat Hayati* (1995).

Kabbara, Sami
(1903-1967)

Sami Kabbara was born and raised in Damascus. He studied political science at Montpellier University and returned to Syria in 1932 to serve as secretary-general of parliament in the administration of President Mohammad Ali al-Abid.

In the mid-1930s, Kabbara founded the *al-Nidal* newspaper with Dr Munir al-Ajlani, another French-educated politician who had recently returned to Syria. *Al-Nidal* was a political daily that became famous for spearheading opposition to the regime of President Shukri al-Quwatli from 1943 to 1949. In 1947, Kabbara was voted into parliament on an independent ticket. His election was repeated in 1949 and 1954. In December 1949, he served on the Constitutional Assembly charged with laying out a new constitution for Syria. He spent the 1940s criticizing Quwatli's policies, claiming that the president was unfit for leadership of Syria.

When Quwatli was overthrown by a military coup in 1949 Kabbara supported the change in leadership but refused to work with the military regime of General Husni al-Za'im. He criticized Za'im's dictatorship, leading to the closure of his newspaper. In August 1949, Kabbara backed the coup that brought down the Za'im regime. He became minister of justice and health in the cabinet of Prime Minister Hashim al-Atasi from August to December 1949. He then became minister of interior under Prime Minister Khalid al-Azm, holding office until June 1950. Azm then appointed Kabbara minister of interior for a second time from March to August 1951.

Kabbara criticized the military regime of General Adib al-Shishakli, who came to power in November 1951, and was arrested for his views. When released, he shifted into the opposition headed by former President Atasi and worked with the underground until Shishakli was deposed by military coup in February 1954.

In October 1954, Kabbara nominated himself for the first post-Shishakli parliament but was defeated in the elections. In the second half of the 1950s, however, Kabbara became increasingly alienated from the rising movement of socialism headed by President Gamal Abd al-Nasser of Egypt. Kabbara joined a group of disgruntled politicians seeking to bring down the pro-Nasser and pro-USSR regime of President Shukri al-Quwatli. (See Munir al-Ajlani, page 136.)

But the conspiracy was foiled and all of the plot's leaders, including Kabbara, were imprisoned and charged with high treason. Kabbara was sentenced to death in January 1957 on the charge of plotting with a foreign country to try to create a civil war in Syria. He remained in prison until 1960, then he was moved into house arrest in Alexandria following the merger between Syria and Egypt in 1958.

When the union was dissolved in 1961, Kabbara and his friends were released. In December 1961, he nominated himself for the first post-Nasser parliament, but authorities turned down his nomination, claiming that his court record prevented him from running for public office. Sami Kabbara's career ended when the Baath Party came to power in Syria on March 8, 1963.

Sources:
Azm, Khalid. *Muzakarat* (1973).
BBC Archives. "The Damascus Trial" February 26, 1957.
Moubayed, Sami. *Damascus Between Democracy and Dictatorship* (2000).
Seale, Patrick. *The Struggle for Syria* (1961).
Information supplied by Dr Jamil Kabbara (Damascus April 12, 1999).

al-Kallas, Khalil
(1921-)

Khalil al-Kallas studied law in Beirut, graduating in 1936. He returned to Syria and taught at Damascus University from 1938 to 1954. Meanwhile, he joined the Baath Party of Michel Aflaq and Salah al-Bitar and became an active member in the party's Damascus bureau.

Kallas became an ally of the Baath Party leader Akram al-Hawrani and one of the most prominent figures among Hawrani's followers (who were centered in Hama). Kallas ran for parliament on a Baath Party ticket in 1954 and won. In June 1956, he became minister of national economy in the "national unity" government of Prime Minister Sabri al-Asali. In the second half of the 1950s, Khalil al-Kallas became a member in the movement of Arab nationalism headed by President Gamal Abd al-Nasser of Egypt and supported Syria's merger with Egypt to form the United Arab Republic (UAR) in 1958. He took part in the union talks with President Shukri al-Quwatli held in Cairo, which resulted in the signing of the union charter on February 1, 1958.

During the union years (1958-1961), Khalil al-Kallas served as minister of national economy and commerce. His mentor Hawrani became vice president of the UAR. When the union was dissolved by military coup in September 1961, Hawrani shifted his allegiance to the post-Nasser government of President Nazim al-Qudsi. So did Kallas, who joined a group of politicians in drafting the secession declaration, a handwritten document that accused Nasser of having imposed a dictatorship on Syria. The new Syrian president, Nazem al-Qudsi, appointed Kallas minister of finance in the cabinet of Prime Minister Khalid al-Azm. In July 1962, Syria filed an official complaint against Nasser, claiming that he was interfering in Syria's affairs and trying to get officers in the Syrian Army to rebel against the post-Nasser order. The Arab League called for round table talks between Syria and Egypt, held in the Lebanese town of Shtura on the Syrian-Lebanese border. Qudsi appointed Kallas as deputy chairman of the Syrian delegation to the talks, but they were foiled when the Egyptian team walked out before the Arab League issued a verdict condemning Egypt for her accusations against Syria.

Khalil al-Kallas also served as a member of parliament from 1961 to 1963. He held office from September 1962 until the Military Committee of the Baath Party came to power in March 1963 and pledged to restore the UAR. Kallas was punished for his alliance with the Qudsi government, and along with Hawrani, expelled from the Baath Party. The Revolutionary Command Council (RCC) banished both men from Syria and had their civil rights terminated.

Sources:
Faris, George. *Man Hum fi al-`Alam al-Arabi?* (1957).
Samman, Mutih. *Watan wa Askar* (1995).

al-Kassem, Abdel Raouf
(1932-)

Abdel Raouf al-Kassem was born and raised in Damascus. His father was Sheikh Ata al-Kassem, the Mufti of Bilad al-Sham (which in Ottoman times included present-day Syria, Lebanon, Palestine and Jordan). The young Kassem joined the Baath Party of Michel Aflaq and Salah al-Bitar in 1949 and was active in its student politics until he left for Europe to complete his higher education in 1953. He studied architecture and city planning at the University of Geneva and returned to Syria in April 1963, one month after the Baath Party came to power in Syria.

Kassem became an instructor of fine arts at Damascus University. In 1964, he became dean of the Faculty of Fine Arts. Six years later, he became chairman of the Department of Architecture, and in 1977 was appointed deputy president of Damascus University. In 1977-1978, he served as a visiting lecturer at the University of Geneva, and in 1979 became governor of Damascus.

On December 14, 1980, President Hafez al-Asad appointed Kassem prime minister, granting him more power than any other prime minister since 1970. Asad had known Kassem since 1969, and prior to that Asad had been a student of his older brother, Badih al-Kassem, a veteran Baath Party philosopher. To contain local grievances, Kassem increased wages of the state employees in February 1981, issued laws for price control, and spearheaded the anti-corruption campaign. In his first year in power, he dismissed thirty-seven officials and twenty-four general managers of public sector companies from office, bringing many of them to trial on the charge of corruption.

The Kassem years, however, were some of the hardest Syria had ever known. Products became scarce (in some cases non-existent), regulations crippled

Abdel Raouf al-Kassem.

commerce, the US embargo on Syria made living conditions harsh, and domestic peace was shattered by the violent activities of the Muslim Brotherhood, who were trying to topple the Asad government. Kassem was also faced with a prolonged and costly war in Lebanon, where Syria was engaged in combat with the Israeli Army that had besieged Beirut in 1982. The Kassem cabinet was required to provide welfare to the families of the wounded, compensation for the families of the martyred, and raise funds for a greater war effort in Lebanon. In addition, the government had to provide assistance and work for the 500,000 Lebanese refugees who fled to Syria during the war years. In evaluating his era, Kassem said that he "invested heavily in oil extraction and dam construction, to transform Syria from infertile to fertile soil, and from an oil importing to an oil exporting country."

In November 1983, Asad suffered a heart attack and appointed Kassem to a six-man presidential committee delegated to run state affairs while Asad was recovering. In 1987, Asad relieved Kassem of his duties as prime minister and appointed him president of the National Security Bureau. He had served the longest tenure as prime minister since Syria's independence from France in 1946. He accompanied Asad on several occasions in meetings with US President George Bush in the wake of the Gulf War in 1990, and President Bill Clinton in 1994, 1995, and 2000. Kassem established himself during the talks with the Americans as a hard-liner, refusing normalization with Israel and demanding complete retrieval of the Golan Heights occupied by Israel in June 1967. He claimed that the Baath Party had struggled against Israel in 1948, 1956, and 1967, not for the Golan, but for Palestine as a whole, and he argued that this should remain the case even if the Golan Heights were restored to Syria.

Asad died in June 2000 and Kassem was dismissed from the National Security Bureau by President Bashar al-Asad. In 2003, Abdel Raouf al-Kassem returned to academia, becoming president of the University of Arts and Architecture in Aleppo, one of the many private universities that opened in Syria in the post-Hafez al-Asad era.

Sources:
Seale, Patrick. *Asad: Struggle for the Middle East* (1988).
Interview with Dr Abdel Raouf al-Kassem (Damascus April 6, 2002).

al-Kayyali, Abd al-Rahman
(1887-1969)

Abd al-Rahman al-Kayyali was born to a prominent political family in Aleppo and studied medicine at the American University of Beirut (AUB). He graduated in 1914 and opened a clinic in Aleppo in the wake of World War I, taking no part in politics during the early years of the French Mandate.

In 1928, however, Kayyali co-founded the National Bloc, the leading anti-French movement in Syria, with the Bloc's president, Hashim al-Atasi. The National Bloc was a coalition of urban landowners, politicians, and working professionals focused on liberating Syria from French control through diplomatic means rather than armed resistance. Kayyali ran for parliament on a Bloc ticket twice, in 1936 and 1943, winning both times. In 1928, he held office for three months on the Constitutional Assembly that drafted the first republican constitution for Syria.

In 1935, the National Bloc called for a sixty-day strike to protest France's refusal to address the issue of independence in a "serious manner." Kayyali led the strike in Aleppo and was responsible for citywide demonstrations that eventually resulted in his arrest. The sixty-day strike succeeded in forcing the French to recognize the Bloc's legitimacy, and invite its leaders to Paris for independence talks with French Prime Minister Leon Blum. The talks resulted in a treaty that promised independence over a twenty-five-year period.

When the Bloc leaders returned to Syria in November 1936, they were elected to parliament with an overwhelming majority. Hashim al-Atasi became president of the republic, and he appointed Kayyali as Syria's first non-resident ambassador to the League of Nations. Atasi also made him minister of education and justice in the first Bloc cabinet of Prime Minister Jamil Mardam Bey. Kayyali kept both jobs until Mardam Bey resigned from office in February 1939. In August 1943, following a Bloc comeback, President Shukri al-Quwatli appointed him minister of justice and supply in the cabinet of Prime Minister Saadallah al-Jabiri. Kayyali held this post from August to November 1943. He also served as a deputy in parliament from 1947 to 1949.

In 1947, the National Bloc was dissolved and renamed the National Party. It was a party composed of former Bloc members who had a political program of modernizing Syria, maintaining its democratic system, and shunning all Arab attempts at uniting Syria with the neighboring Hashemite governments in Iraq and Jordan. The Hashemites wanted a monarchy in Syria while the National Party wanted to maintain the republic. Dr Kayyali became president of the National Party in 1948, but real decision-making lay in the hands of its secretary-general, Sabri al-Asali, and its spiritual godfather Shukri al-Quwatli. In 1947, Kayyali became Syria's representative to the General Assembly of the United Nations. He lost his job, however, when a military coup d'etat took place and ousted President

Quwatli from office in March 1949.

Kayyali remained in obscurity from 1950 to 1958 and retired from politics when Syria and Egypt merged to form the United Arab Republic (UAR) in 1958. When a military coup toppled the union in September 1961, Kayyali met with leading notables from Aleppo to support the coup architects in the Syrian Army. He also supported Nazim al-Qudsi, the first post-union president of Syria, who came to power in December 1961. From 1958 to 1960, Abd al-Rahman al-Kayyali published a four-volume history of the French Mandate as seen by the National Bloc in a book entitled, *Al-Marahil fi al-Indtidab al-Faransi wa Nidalina al-Watani* (*Stages of the French Mandate and our Nationalist Struggle*). He died in Aleppo on September 13, 1969.

Sources:

Barudi, Fakhri. *Muzakarat al-Barudi: Sittoun Aman Tatakalam* (1952-1953).

Barudi, Fakhri. *Khamsoun Aman min Hayat al-Watan* (1999).

Faris, George. *Man Hum fi al-Alam al-Arabi?* (1957).

Haffar, Salma. *Lutfi al-Haffar 1885-1968* (1997).

Itri, Abd al-Ghani. *Hadeeth al-Abqariyyat* (2000).

Kayyali, Abd al-Rahman. *Al-Marahil fi al-Intidab al-Faransi 1926-1938* (1958-1960).

Khoury, Philip. *Syria and the French Mandate* (1987).

Qassab Hasan, Najat. *Saniou al-Jalaa fi Souriyya* (1999).

Khaddam, Abd al-Halim
(1930-)

Abd al-Halim Khaddam studied law at Damascus University, and during his studies joined the Baath Party of Michel Aflaq and Salah al-Bitar. While still a university student, he befriended Hafez al-Asad, another young party member serving as an air force pilot. Khaddam spent the 1950s working as an attorney in Lattakia.

In March 1963, the Baath Party came to power in Syria, and Khaddam became governor of Hama, a conservative city in the Syrian heartland overwhelmingly opposed to the regime of President Amin al-Hafez. In April 1964, the Muslim Brotherhood launched a military uprising from Hama, occupying a local mosque and calling for a war against the government. Khaddam tried solving the crisis diplomatically, but when that failed, President Amin al-Hafez ordered an air raid of the mosque under siege and transferred Khaddam to Qunaitra, the central town in the Golan Heights, where he became governor. But Khaddam was forced to flee the town on June 5, 1967, following the Israeli occupation of Qunaitra.

In 1968, President Nur al-Din al-Atasi appointed Khaddam briefly as governor of Damascus, then made him minister of economy in May 1969. When Hafez al-Asad came to power in 1970, Khaddam became minister of foreign affairs and deputy to Prime Minister Abd al-Rahman al-Khlayfawi. He retained both posts under all cabinets in the Asad era until 1984. He also served as a deputy in the first parliament under President Asad from February to December 1971. In November 1983, Asad suffered a heart attack and appointed Khaddam to a six-man presidential committee that oversaw state affairs while Asad recovered from his illness. During the troubled 1980s, along with Information Minister Ahmad Iskandar Ahmad and Defense Minister Mustapha Tlas, Khaddam became one of the three closest officials to the Syrian president. In 1984, Khaddam became vice president of the republic, and continues to hold this post until the time of this writing.

Foreign Minister Khaddam played an instrumental role in bringing Syria out of the global isolation it had experienced during the early Baath years (1963-1970). He strengthened Syria's foreign relations with its Arab neighbors, especially Lebanon, Jordan, Saudi Arabia, and Iraq. In May 1974, he lobbied for opposing the disengagement treaty with Israel (following the Arab-Israeli War of 1973) and prompted Arab leaders to reject Anwar al-Sadat's peace initiative in 1978. He also played an instrumental role in strengthening Syria's relations with Iran following the downfall of Shah Mohammad Reza Pehlavi in February 1979. Khaddam embraced the Islamic Revolution, visited Iran in August 1979, and described the revolution as "the most important event in our contemporary history." He then played an instrumental role in orchestrating Syria's alliance with Ayatollah al-Khomeini, the new leader of Iran.

In April 1975, Khaddam became Asad's special envoy to Beirut, acting as an intermediary between the rival factions in the early months of the Lebanese Civil War. He held the position throughout the late 1980s, growing in influence both in Syrian and in Lebanese political circles. In 1985, he orchestrated the Tripartite Agreement in Syria, convincing the Druze militia leader Walid Jumblatt, the Shiite militia leader Nabih Berri, and the Maronite militia leader Elie Hobeika, to call for a cease-fire and work for a restoration of peace in Lebanon. In October 1989, he helped draft the Taif Accord in Saudi Arabia, a framework agreed to by most Lebanese parties to end the seventeen-year Civil War, and negotiated the surrender of General Michel Aoun, the anti-Syrian prime minister of Lebanon. Khddam also created, along with Asad, the post-war administration of President Elias al-Hrawi and backed the election of Prime Minister Rafic al-Harriri to power both in 1992 and in 2000. Throughout the 1990s, Abd al-Halim Khaddam was popularly labeled the *wali* (governor) of Beirut, in reference to the paramount influence he exercised over Lebanese politics.

Abd al-Halim Khaddam remained in charge of the "Lebanese Portfolio" until 1998, when it was transferred to the president's son, Bashar al-Asad. When Asad died in June 2000, Khaddam became acting president of the republic for an intermediary period that lasted from June 10 to July 17, 2000. During this time, he appointed Bashar al-Asad as commander-in-chief of the Syrian Army and promoted him in military rank. In July 2000, Bashar al-Asad became president and kept Khaddam at his post as vice president. During the first year of the new Asad government, Khaddam's political influence increased tremendously, and he played a crucial role in reaffirming Syria's relations with Lebanon following the September 2000 campaign against Syria launched by the Maronite Patriarch Mar Nasrallah Boutros Sfeir.

In June 2001, Khaddam intervened to solve domestic problems taking place between Lebanon's three leaderships, President Emile Lahhoud, Prime Minister Rafic al-Harriri, and Speaker Nabih Berri. He arbitrated continuously between Lahhoud and Harriri during the years 2000-2002 and opened channels with the Druze leader Walid Jumblatt that were strained following the death of Asad in 2000. In 2003, Abd al-Halim Khaddam published a book on his political views called, *Al-Nizam al-Arabi al-Mouasir* (*The Contemporary Arab Order*).

Abd al-Halim Khaddam resigned from his post as vice-president of the republic in June 2005 at the Baath Party Conference and also left his job as a member of National Command and Central Command of the Baath Party.

Sources:
Khaddam, Abd al-Halim. *Al-Nizam al-Arabi al-Mouasir* (2003).
Seale, Patrick. *Asad: Struggle for the Middle East* (1988).
Interview with Abd al-Halim Khaddam (Damascus November 4, 2002).

al-Khatib, Bahij
(1895-?)

Bahij al-Khatib received his high school education in a village in Mount Lebanon and began his career as an oil merchant in Beirut. When the French Mandate was proclaimed over Syria and Lebanon in July 1920, he joined the civil service in Damascus where he worked until becoming director of police and public security in 1927.

Khatib allied himself to Taj al-Din al-Hasani, France's staunchest ally in Syria, when Hasani became prime minister in February 1928. Khatib mobilized his armed police force to uphold the unpopular regime of Prime Minister Hasani. In 1925, the French had made carrying arms a capital offense, punishable by lengthy imprisonment. The only people permitted to arm themselves were Khatib's forces. They monitored the streets, kept a lookout for anyone criticizing Hasani, and hampered the activity of the National Bloc, the leading anti-French movement in Syria. During the parliamentary elections of 1932, Khatib's forces tampered with the ballots to secure the victory of Prime Minister Hasani. He then ordered the arrest of any National Bloc member who was speaking, demonstrating, or writing against Hasani.

Hasani and Khatib left office when Mohammad Ali al-Abid was elected president in 1932, and they remained in obscurity during the National Bloc regime of President Hashim al-Atasi (1936-1939). In July 1939, President Atasi resigned from office in protest of France's refusal to address the issue of Syrian independence, and he was replaced by Bahij al-Khatib as head of state. Khatib was given presidential powers and created his cabinet on July 9, 1939. In addition to his already broad duties, he made himself minister of interior as well.

In September 1939, France declared war on Nazi Germany to protest the occupation of Poland. Khatib tried to control political activity and prevent the spread of Nazi propaganda in Syria. The concept of "the enemy of my enemy is my friend" was gaining popularity in Syria, and many Syrians wanted Germany to defeat France in the war, thinking that this would make Syrian independence easier to achieve. Khatib closed down cafes playing Hitler's inflammatory speeches, outlawed Hitler's autobiography, *Mein Kamph*, and disbanded pro-Nazi organizations like the Steel Shirts of Munir al-Ajlani modeled after the Brown Shirts in Germany. Khatib turned the life of Syrian citizens into a massive terror campaign. Arbitrary arrests became common, and so did spontaneous house searches with no warrants.

Khatib made it a habit to travel with a large entourage of bodyguards, starting a trend that was to be followed by nearly every Syrian leader after him. At one point, his car was stopped by a group of angry demonstrators who called on him to step down from office. He personally confronted them, took out his gun, and shot down two demonstrators who happened to be university students. He filed legal cases against most National Bloc leaders, accusing them of illegal conduct during the years they served in office (1936-1939), and banished Shukri al-Quwatli, a nationalist leader from Damascus, to Saudi Arabia. An attempt was made on his life shortly after he came to office and he accused the nationalist leaders Nabih and Adil-Azma of wanting to kill him. Khatib had these men arrested, but they were released for lack of evidence.

In July 1940, the nationalist leader Abd al-Rahman Shahbandar was killed by four men working on the French payroll. Glad to see the last of Shahbandar, and wanting to capitalize on the murder, Khatib accused the nationalist leaders Jamil Mardam Bey, Saadallah al-Jabiri, and Lutfi al-Haffar of murdering Shahbandar, their primary opponent. The three men fled to Iraq, but when investigations were made it was revealed that Khatib had personally met with the conspirators right after the murder and ordered them to implicate Mardam Bey, Jabiri, and Haffar, promising them a commuted sentence if they complied. In December 1940, one of the killers said in court that he had been subjected to various methods of torture and then taken to meet Khatib who threatened to kill him if he did not implicate the National Bloc.

Bahij al-Khatib realized that the revelations would destroy his reputation and probably lead to his downfall. To secure his future, he obtained a job as director of the petroleum companies in Syria. On April 1, 1941, Khatib was asked to resign by French General Charles de Gaulle, who promised to grant more political freedoms to Syria. Khatib was replaced by the moderate statesman Khalid al-Azm. In May 1945, the French bombarded Damascus and tried to arrest President Shukri al-Quwatli. Once rid of Quwatli and his comrades, they wanted to appoint Khatib as head of a provisional government. The idea, however, never materialized.

Sources:
Babil, Nasuh. *Sahafa wa Siyassa fi Souriyya* (1987).
Mardam Bey, Jamil. *Syria's Quest for Independence* (1994).

al-Khatib, Zaki
(1887-1961)

Zaki al-Khatib studied law and public administration in Istanbul. From 1907 to 1916 he served in the Ottoman civil service in Damascus. In 1918, he joined the regime of King Faysal I, the post-Ottoman ruler of Syria, and became director of intelligence in Aleppo from 1918 to 1920.

In 1920, the French imposed their mandate over Syria and dethroned Faysal. Unlike many civil servants, Zaki al-Khatib was not dismissed from office, but rather moved to the less important post of director of correspondence in Syria. In 1922, he became director of real estate for Damascus, Aleppo, and the mountains surrounding Lattakia. He resigned in 1927 in disagreement with his French superiors and opened a legal practice in Damascus.

In 1928, Khatib held office for three months on the Constitutional Assembly that drafted the first republican constitution for Syria. In February 1928, he was appointed minister of justice in the cabinet of Prime Minister Taj al-Din al-Hasani. In 1930, Khatib joined the National Bloc, the leading anti-French movement in Syria, and became a ranking member of its Damascus bureau. He nominated himself for parliament on a Bloc ticket in 1932, and again in 1936, winning in both rounds.

Khatib split from the Bloc following its failure to prevent the Turkish annexation of Alexanderetta in 1939 and joined the opposition headed by Dr Abd al-Rahman Shahbandar. Khatib was arrested for his views by Prime Minister Jamil Mardam Bey, a former comrade in the National Bloc. But Khatib was in prison only briefly, and was released by Mardam Bey himself. Then Shahbandar asked Khatib to form a party to serve as a public face for their political activity that would unite all political groups in Syria. Khatib created the Party of National Unity, but the party was never taken seriously by the French or the Syrian public.

When Shahbandar was killed by agents of the French Mandate in 1940, Zaki al-Khatib became a political independent. He served as legal advisor to the Shahbandar family in court in December 1941. Also in 1941, he became minister of justice in the cabinet of Prime Minister Hasan al-Hakim, who was also a former ally of Shahbandar. After independence was achieved in 1946, Khatib joined the People's Party, a coalition of lawyers and landowners who were opposed to the National Bloc regime of President Shukri al-Quwatli.

In 1947, Khatib nominated himself for parliament and once again won with ease, joining the parliamentary opposition to President Quwatli. In December 1949, Khatib became minister of justice under Prime Minister Khalid al-Azm and held his post until June 1950. He then assumed the same post under Prime Minister Nazim al-Qudsi and remained in office until March 1951. In November 1949, he also served on the Constitutional Assembly that drafted a new constitution for Syria.

In September 1950, he once again became a deputy in parliament. In 1951, President Hashim al-Atasi asked Khatib to form a government, but he failed at reaching a suitable alliance with other parties. He retired from politics when General Adib al-Shishakli came to power in November 1951. Zaki al-Khatib died on April 24, 1961.

Sources:
Babil, Nasuh. *Sahafa wa Siyassa fi Souriyya* (1987).
Faris, George. *Man Hum fi al-Alam al-Arabi?* (1957).

al-Khlayfawi, Abd al-Rahman
(1927-)

Abd al-Rahman al-Khlayfawi studied at the Homs Military Academy and received advanced training in France and the USSR. He joined the Baath Party of Michel Aflaq and Salah al-Bitar and pursued a career as a military officer.

When the Baath Party came to power in March 1963, Interior Minister Amin al-Hafez appointed Khlayfawi military commander and governor of Daraa, a town in southern Syria near the Jordanian border. In 1964, he assumed the same duties in Hama, a conservative city in the Syrian interior that was overwhelmingly opposed to the Baath Party government. In 1965, he was transferred to Egypt and appointed to the joint Arab Military Committee, an organ of the Arab League, where he served as director of a security bureau. Right after the Arab-Israeli War of 1967, Khlayfawi was called back to Syria and appointed to a military court charged with bringing officers to justice who had been responsible for the defeat.

Meanwhile, he also served as commander of Armed Forces Administration. From 1967 to 1970, he served as an intermediary between the rival leaders of the Baath and tried to mend relations between Defense Minister Hafez al-Asad and Salah Jadid, who was the de facto ruler of Syria. President Nur al-Din al-Atasi and Jadid considered appointing Khlayfawi prime minister but the idea never got past the drawing board.

On November 16, 1970, Asad came to power in Damascus and arrested both Jadid and Atasi. Asad created a provisional government with himself as prime minister, and appointed Khlayfawi as minister of interior in November 1970. When Asad became president in March 1971, Khlayfawi became his first prime minister. He also served as a deputy in the first parliament under President Asad from February to December 1971. Khlayfawi was a familiar face and a respected officer on good terms with both the old administration of Jadid and the new one of Asad. In addition, he was renowned for his efficiency and financial honesty. Prime Minister Khlayfawi remained in office until December 1972.

From 1972 to 1976, Khlayfawi served as director of the Economic and Financial Bureau at the Regional Command of the Baath Party. In August 1976, Khlayfawi was once again entrusted with the premiership. He clashed from the outset, however, with his interior minister, Adnan al-Dabbagh, and tried to cease the arbitrary arrests that Dabbagh had made common. In addition, Khlayfawi blocked the confiscation of homes and property—a tactic that some officers had used since their early days in power. He made it illegal to arrest a citizen with-out Khlayfawi's personal approval and tried to curb Dabbagh's powers at the Ministry of Interior. He raised wages significantly, combated unemployment, and reshuffled his cabinet posts. Najah al-Attar was the first woman to assume ministerial office in Syria, becoming minister of culture under Khlayfawi. His cabinet took Syria through the most vital years of its intervention in Lebanon, allowed marginal freedom of speech, and garnered general consent.

Despite his personal friendship with President Anwar al-Sadat, built during his service in Cairo, Khlayfawi opposed the Egyptian leader's peace initiative in 1977-1978. At home, Khlayfawi tried to fix the administration and instituted a five-year economic plan to revive the country's stagnated economy. The prime minister made it a habit to make surprise visits to different districts of Syria and show up at government offices to inspect work progress. He also worked to restore respect for one-time politicians who had been sidelined by the Baath Party coup d'etat of 1963. He honored the pre-1963 leaders of Syria, befriended Sabri al-Asali (who had been prime minister in the 1950s), and ordered that retirement wages be paid to the families of those leaders who had admirably served Syria.

Prime Minister Khlayfawi remained in power until March 1978. He remained a member of the Regional Command until 1980. Then he ceased all political activity. He devoted the remainder of his years to agriculture and social issues

Prime Minister Abd al-Rahman al-Khlayfawi (right) with Bader al-Din al-Shallah, President of the Damascus Chamber of Commerce.

and served as chairman of the Syrian Association for Combating Cancer.

Abd al-Rahman al-Khlayfawi collected funds and helped construct a large hospital for cancer patients in Damascus that opened in 2003.

Sources:
Interview with General Abd al-Rahman Khlayfawi (Damascus July 30, 2002).

al-Khury, Faris
(1877-1962)

Faris al-Khury was born in the town of Hasbayya in what is today modern Lebanon. He studied law at the American University of Beirut (AUB) and began his career by teaching at AUB.

In 1908, Khury nominated himself for the Christian seat in the Ottoman Parliament and also served as a translator for the British Consulate in Damascus. During World War I (1914-1918), Khury wrote articles in numerous Arab and Turkish newspapers warning against the increasing number of Jewish immigrants in Palestine. In 1914, he was delegated to an Arab committee charged with meeting the Zionist National Agency. The proposed meeting was scheduled at the summer resort of Brummanah in Mount Lebanon, but was canceled due to the outbreak of World War I in August 1914.

In 1916, Khury joined the Arab underground and pledged support for the Arab Revolt launched from Mecca by Sharif Husayn. His connections with Husayn, the primary nationalist of his era, resulted in his arrest and trial by a military tribunal in Aley. In 1918, the Ottoman Empire was dissolved and Khury allied himself with King Faysal I, the new ruler of Syria. In the interlude between the departure of the Turks and the arrival of the Arab Army (September 26 to October 1), Khury created a preliminary government with a group of notables in Damascus headed by Prince Sa'id al-Jaza'iri.

Khury then became minister of finance in the first post-Ottoman cabinet of Prime Minister Rida Pasha al-Rikabi. His post was renewed by Prime Minister Hashim al-Atasi in May 1920. He held this post until Faysal was dethroned and the French Mandate was proclaimed in July 1920. Khury laid the groundwork for the Syrian Ministry of Finance, created its infrastructure, distributed its administrative duties, formulated its laws, and handpicked its staff. In 1923, he helped co-found Damascus University, and along with a group of veteran educators, translated its entire curriculum from Ottoman Turkish into Arabic.

At an early point in his career, Faris al-Khury befriended Dr Abd al-Rahman Shahbandar, the leading nationalist of his era who had worked with Khury in the Arab underground during World War I and served as minister of foreign affairs under Faysal. In June 1925, Shahbandar and Khury founded the People's Party, the first political movement in French Mandate Syria. Composed of leading statesmen, lawyers, and professors who were to become nationalist leaders in the 1940s, the People's Party promoted the creation of a constitutional government in a free and unified Syria that would include Palestine, Jordan, and parts of Lebanon. The Hashemite family funded the party's activities and King Faysal I, who had now become king of Iraq, served as its spiritual godfather.

In July 1925, Khury and Shahbandar worked with Sultan al-Atrash in the Arab Mountain, organizing an armed uprising against the French. They supplied the Druze fighters with protection and recruited volunteers to take part in combat. The revolt, however, was crushed in 1926, inflicting heavy losses on Syria as a whole and affecting Faris al-Khury deeply. Khury then decided to confront the French through diplomacy and abandon the idea of armed resistance. The revolt, he pointed out, heroic as it was, had cost the lives of six thousand Syrians and resulted in the uprooting of another thousand. Independence, therefore, could not be achieved by armed resistance alone, he argued, but rather it needed diplomatic means as well.

In April 1926, Khury became minister of education in the pro-French cabinet of Prime Minister Ahmad Nami. He accepted office as part of his newfound policy of positive interaction with the French. In July 1926, however, the French dismissed Khury from office and arrested him on the charge of being in contact with the rebel leaders while holding office under the mandate regime. He was incarcerated in a remote detention center in northern Syria.

In 1928, Khury co-founded the National Bloc, a leading nationalist movement with the Bloc's president, Hashim al-Atasi. It was a party which aimed at ending the mandate through diplomatic means rather than armed resistance. Khury laid out the Bloc's constitution and served as dean of its permanent office in Damascus. In 1928, he also served as a member on the Constitutional Assembly that drafted the first republican constitution for Syria. In 1932, he became a member of parliament, running on a National Bloc ticket. His election was repeated in 1936, 1943, and 1947.

In 1935, Khury helped launch a sixty-day strike throughout Syria protesting France's refusal to address Syrian independence in a "serious manner." The French responded by dismissing Khury from his teaching post at Damascus University. The strike dislocated the economy of Syria and led to the death of hundreds of civilians in Damascus, Aleppo, Homs, and Hama. The strike embarrassed the French in the international community and forced them to recognize the Bloc leaders as the legitimate representatives of the Syrian people, inviting them for independence talks in Paris.

In March 1936, Khury was part of a Bloc delegation that journeyed to Paris and conducted six-month talks with French Prime Minister Leon Blum. The Bloc leaders succeeded in formulating a treaty that guaranteed independence over a twenty-five-year period in exchange for military, economic, and political privileges for France in Syria. The Bloc leaders also promised to support France in the Middle East if another deadly war broke out in Europe. The Bloc representatives returned to Syria in September 1936 and were voted into parliament with an overwhelming majority. Atasi became president of the republic and Khury became speaker of parliament on December 21, 1936. When Atasi left office in July 1939, so did Khury, who reverted to his earlier post as an instructor at Damascus University.

In August 1943, Faris al-Khury rose to prominence once again when the National Bloc leader Shukri al-Quwatli was elected president of the republic. Khury became speaker of parliament from August 17, 1943, to October 16, 1944. Quwatli asked him to form a government in November 1944. Khury created a cabinet filled with National Bloc members, appointing former Prime Minister Jamil Mardam Bey as minister of defense, economy, and foreign affairs. The portfolios of interior and education were handled by Khury himself.

The new prime minister journeyed to San Francisco in April 1945 to attend the founding conference of the United Nations. Khury was charged with promoting Syria's cause before world statesmen and meeting with US President Harry Truman for the purpose of pressuring France to evacuate Syria. Khury brought along a team of young diplomats, all in their late twenties who were AUB graduates like himself. Khury and his delegation remained in the USA for six months. The conference was Syria's first venture into the international community as a to-be-independent state of its own, and Khury's visit was the first of its kind by a senior Syrian official to the USA.

In September 1945, Khury once again became speaker of parliament and held

Faris al-Khury.

this post until March 1949. Following independence in April 1946, he became Syria's permanent ambassador to the United Nations. In 1947, Syria was voted into the Security Council for a one-year round and Khury was appointed head of the Syrian Mission to the Security Council. He held this post until the Quwatli regime was overthrown in March 1949.

Syria's new ruler, General Husni al-Za'im, arrested all members of the Quwatli administration but refrained from harming Khury in respect for his elevated standing in political circles and his career as a senior statesman since Ottoman times. Za'im approached the veteran Khury and asked him to form a new cabinet that would administer state affairs with the officers. Khury declined and said, "If I assume government office under your leadership, the first task I would do is to clamp you in chains because your regime is un-constitutional. May God forgive you, you have opened a door on Syria that history will have a difficult time in closing." Looking to the future, Khury was speaking prophetically of the trend of military coups that would rock Syria in future years, totaling fifteen from 1949 to 1982. He retired from political activity during the four month era of Husni al-Za'im and the military regime of General Adib al-Shishakli (1951-1954).

When General Shishakli was overthrown in February 1954, civilian rule was restored to Syria and President Hashim al-Atasi asked Faris al-Khury to form a government on October 29, 1954. He returned to power at a critical stage, when Syria was being pressured to join the Baghdad Pact, an Anglo-American axis aimed at blocking Soviet influence in the Arab world. The pact was also designed to curb the influence of President Gamal Abd al-Nasser of Egypt, who was vehemently pro-USSR. The Syrian public was in favor of Nasser while Khury preferred to join the Baghdad Pact, but he refused to do so for fear of losing popular support at home. He went to Cairo and met with Nasser to discuss the Baghdad Pact. He argued with the Egyptian leader and claimed that Nasser was not a spokesman for the entire Arab world, but only a spokesman for Egypt. Nasser could turn down the offer to join the Baghdad Pact, if he so wished, but he had no right to criticize or pressure pro-Western governments like Jordan, Lebanon, and Syria to adhere to his pro-USSR policy. Khury's open clash with the Egyptian leader led to the eruption of marches and strikes in the streets of Damascus, called for by the socialist Baath Party, asking for Khury's downfall.

On February 13, 1955, Khury was forced to step down due to the pressure of pro-Nasser sentiment throughout Syria. During his final years, he stood by and watched Syria drift into Egypt's orbit, unable to stop it. He was opposed to union in 1958 and was politically finished when Nasser became president of Syria in

1958. He later recalled the ill-fated union and said, "It was done in a minute, in a foolish minute."

Khury lived just long enough to see a group of young officers, headed by Colonel Abd al-Karim al-Nehlawi, overthrow the Nasser government on September 28, 1961, and restore civilian rule to Syria. Syria's new president, Nazim al-Qudsi, was Khury's student at Damascus University and so was the new prime minister, Ma'ruf al-Dawalibi. Khury's son Suhayl became minister of rural affairs in the Dawalibi cabinet. Qudsi and Dawalibi honored the veteran statesman and gave him a presidential funeral upon his death on January 2, 1962.

Faris al-Khury published many political and philosophical works during his lifetime and wrote a lot of romantic verse and political poetry. His granddaughter, the novelist Collette Khury, published his memoirs in 1987 entitled, *Awrak Faris al-Khury (The Papers of Faris al-Khury)*. His other published works include *Rushdat al-Tillab fi al-Sarf wa Nahu al-Lugha al-Othmaniyya (A Student Guide to Conjugation and Grammar of the Ottoman Language)*, published in 1892, *Mujaz fi `Ilm al-Mall (Concise Book in Finance)*, published in 1924, *Usul al-Muhakamat al-Huquqiyya (Origins of Legal Court Cases)*, published in 1936, and a classic Turkish-Persian dictionary published in the final years of the Ottoman Empire.

Sources:

Azm, Khalid. *Muzakarat* (1973).
Babil, Nasuh. *Sahafa wa Siyasa fi Souriyyia* (1987).
Barudi, Fakhri. *Muzakarat al-Barudi: Sittoun Aman Tatakalam* (1952-1953).
Caplan, Neil. *Futile Diplomacy* (1983).
Farhani, Mohammad. *Faris al-Khury wa Ayyam la Tunsa* (1965).
Faris, George. *Man Hum fi al-`Alam al-Arabi?* (1957).
Haffar, Salma. *Lutfi al-Haffar 1885-1968* (1997).
Hakim, Hasan. *Muzakarati* (1965).
Itri, Abd al-Ghani. *Hadeeth al-Abqariyyat* (2000).
Kayyali, Abd al-Rahman. *Al-Marahil fi al-Intidab al-Faransi 1926-1938* (1958-1960).
Khabbaz, Hanna. Haddad, George. *Faris al-Khury Hayatuh wa Asruh* (1952).
Khoury, Philip. *Syria and the French Mandate* (1987).
Khury, Colette. *Awrak Faris al-Khury,* Vol II (1997).
Moubayed, Sami. *Damascus Between Democracy and Dictatorship* (2000).
Moubayed, Sami. *The Politics of Damascus 1920-1946* (1999).
Qassab Hasan, Najat. *Saniou al-Jalaa fi Souriyya* (1999).
Seale, Patrick. *The Struggle for Syria* (1961).
Interview with Colette Khury (Damascus June 21, 2001; September 2, 2001).

al-Kikhiya, Rushdi
(1900-1988)

Rushdi al-Kikhiya was born and raised in Aleppo and studied law at the Sorbonne in Paris. While a student in Paris, the French proclaimed their mandate over Syria in July 1920. Kikhiya returned to Syria in 1922. He apparently opened a law office in Aleppo, yet he forged a career as a politician, not a lawyer.

Kikhiya engaged in anti-French demonstrations and was arrested for his views in 1925. In 1928, he joined the National Bloc, the leading anti-French movement, and rose to become one of its most promising young leaders in the 1930s. The Bloc leaders were dedicated to the liberation of Syria from the French Mandate through diplomatic means rather than armed resistance. In 1936, he ran for parliament on a National Bloc ticket and won.

In 1939, Kikhiya clashed with the Bloc leadership, however, over their failure to prevent Turkey's annexation of the Sanjak of Alexanderetta, territory in northern Syria that had once been part of the Ottoman Empire. Kikhiya accused the Bloc leaders of having given too many concessions to the French in exchange for a treaty of friendship between Damascus and Paris in September 1936. He resigned in protest to the Franco-Syrian alliance and nominated himself for parliament on an independent ticket in 1943, winning with a majority vote in Aleppo. His election was repeated in 1947, 1949, and 1954.

Kikhiya joined Nazim al-Qudsi, also from Aleppo, and campaigned against the election of Shukri al-Quwatli, the National Bloc candidate for the presidency in 1943. Kikhiya accused Quwatli of being too regional in his policies and of favoring Damascenes over Aleppines. Kikhiya wanted to unite Syria with neighboring Iraq while Quwatli was a declared opponent of the Hashemite family that ruled Baghdad. The difference in policies between both men made an alliance between him and Quwatli impossible. Kikhiya's veto was overruled in parliament and Quwatli was elected president in August 1943. Kikhiya then headed the parliamentary opposition to Quwatli, and in August 1947, transformed it into the People's Party.

In March 1949, President Quwatli was deposed by a military coup, launched by his chief of staff, General Husni al-Za'im. Syria's new leader asked Kikhiya to form a cabinet, but he refused, claiming that he could not work with a military regime. As a result, Za'im outlawed his party and placed Kikhiya under house arrest for four months.

Kikhiya supported the coup that ousted Za'im in August 1949 and allied himself with Syria's new leader, President Hashim al-Atasi. Kikhiya became minister of interior in a cabinet headed by Atasi himself that lasted from August to December 1949. Kikhiya then became chairman of the Constitutional Assembly that drafted a new constitution for Syria. In September 1950, he became a deputy for Aleppo and was elected speaker of parliament. His ally, Nazim al-Qudsi, was appointed prime minister, and along with President Atasi, the three men began meeting with Iraqi officials to discuss the Syrian-Iraqi union. Kikhiya met with King Faysal II of Iraq, his Crown Prince Abd al-Illah, and the Iraqi Prime Minister Nuri al-Sa'id, and they decided that union would be for economic, military, and cultural reasons, but two autonomous governments would exist in Damascus and Baghdad.

To prevent the merger from taking place, General Adib al-Shishakli came to power in November 1951 and dismissed Kikhiya and Qudsi from office, leading to the resignation of President Atasi. Shishakli promised to uphold the republic and said that he did not want to be ruled from Baghdad. He outlawed political parties and placed Kikhiya under house arrest for his anti-regime and pro-Hashemite views. Kikhiya joined the underground that was headed by ex-President Atasi and supported the coup that deposed the Shishakli regime in February 1954. Atasi returned to the presidency and asked Kikhiya to form a government, but he refused once again, claiming that so long as the officers had the authority to meddle in his decision-making, then he simply did not want the premiership.

In October 1954, Rushdi al-Kikhiya ran for parliament and won, but he resigned in 1957 to protest Syria's newfound relationship with Egypt. He argued that if union were to materialize, it should be with Iraq and not with Egypt, and claimed that President Gamal Abd al-Nasser had a socialist vision that was inappropriate for Syria's socio-economic structure. Kikhiya was opposed to union in February 1958, and remained an advocate of the Hashemites even after the fall of the Hashemite dynasty in Baghdad in July 1958.

During the union years with Egypt (1958-1961), Kikhiya joined the opposition to the Nasser government and was placed under house arrest in Aleppo. His followers were persecuted by union authorities and his property was confiscated by the nationalization laws of July 1961. Kikhiya backed the coup that ousted Nasser in September 1961 and joined a group of politicians who signed the secession declaration, the document criticizing Nasser's dictatorship and blaming him for the destruction of Syria's democracy and free market

Rushdi al-Kikhiya.

system. A group of deputies, headed by Ma'ruf al-Dawalibi and Sa'id al-Ghazi, asked Kikhiya to nominate himself for the presidency, but he refused yet again, claiming this time that the officers would not let him practice his constitutional powers. Instead, he nominated his friend Nazim al-Qudsi for presidential office in December 1961.

In the book, *The Struggle for Syria*, the author Patrick Seale describes the situation: "He (Kikhiya) was an elegant, cautious, old-world Aleppo notable, honest and widely respected but lacking political daring. He lacked the heart to fight back." This explains why Kikhiya turned down top leadership posts in 1949, 1954, and 1961.

The Military Committee of the Baath Party came to power in March 1963 and pledged to restore the Syrian-Egyptian union. They arrested all politicians who had worked against union and overthrew the government of President Qudsi. The People's Party was outlawed, its newspaper *al-Sha'ab* was closed, and its members were either arrested or sent into exile. Kikhiya spent several months in prison and was then released and exiled to Cyprus where he died in 1988.

Sources:
Azm, Khalid. *Muzakarat* (1973).
Fansa, Bashir. *Al-Naqbat wa al-Mughamarat* (1997).
Hawrani, Akram. *Muzakarat Akram al-Hawrani* (2000).
Itri, Abd al-Ghani. *Abqariyyat* (1996).
Moubayed, Sami. *Damascus Between Democracy and Dictatorship* (2000).
Rathmell, Andrew. *Secret War in the Middle East* (1995).
Seale, Patrick. *The Struggle for Syria* (1965).
Uthman, Hashim. *Al-Ahzab al-Siyasiyya fi Souriyya: al-Siriyya wa al-Mu'lana* (2001).
Interview with Dr Abd al-Wahab Homad (Damascus September 9, 1999).

Kourani, As'ad
(1907-1995)

As'ad Kourani was born in Acre in modern-Palestine and raised in Aleppo. He studied law at Damascus University and opened a legal practice in Aleppo in 1932. In 1945, he became president of the Lawyers' Syndicate in Syria, and one year later, secretary-general of the Ministry of Justice.

In March 1949, the civilian regime of President Shukri al-Quwatli was overthrown by military coup, launched by Chief of Staff Husni al-Za'im. Za'im appointed Kourani as chairman of the Constitutional Assembly, charged with drafting a new republican constitution for Syria. Kourani also became minister of justice and public works, holding office in a cabinet headed by Za'im himself, from April to June 1949. Kourani gave the military regime of Husni al-Za'im the legal image it badly needed to legitimize itself within political circles. Kourani was also behind most of the legal reforms passed during the short-lived Za'im era. Among the fundamental contributions Kourani introduced were the current civic law, punishment law, commercial law, and construction law, all of which are still functioning today, fifty-five years later. Along with Za'im, Kourani also passed a law giving women the right to nominate themselves for public office and vote in parliamentary elections.

When Za'im was toppled by military coup in August 1949, Kourani returned to his legal practice in Aleppo. He made his comeback in June 1954 as minister of justice and economy in the independent cabinet of Prime Minister Sa'id al-Ghazi. In February 1958, Kourani was categorically opposed to Syria's merger with Egypt to form the United Arab Republic (UAR) and was a sharp critic of the socialist measures of President Gamal Abd al-Nasser of Egypt. During the UAR years (1958-1961), he moved into the opposition and declined any public office. He supported the coup that overthrew Nasser in September 1961 and signed the secession declaration, a document drafted by Syrian politicians that accused Nasser of having established a dictatorship and ruining Syria's free market and democratic system. In December 1961, Kourani became a member of parliament. In September 1962, the independent prime minister, Khalid al-Azm, appointed Kourani minister of justice. Azm's health deteriorated sharply while in office, and he appointed Kourani as acting prime minister to oversee state affairs in his absence. Kourani remained acting prime minister until the Baath Party came to power in March 1963 and pledged to restore the UAR.

Kourani willingly retired from politics and spent the remainder of his years at his legal practice in Aleppo. The Revolutionary Command Council (RCC) of the Baathist era terminated his civil rights to punish him for his alliance with the post-Nasser order. As'ad Kourani's memoirs entitled, *Zikrayat wa Khawater* (*Memoirs and Reminiscence*), were published by his son in 2000, five years after his death.

Sources:
Kourani, As'ad. *Zikrayat wa Khawater* (2000).
Zahr al-Din, Abd al-Karim. *Muzakarati an Fatrat al-Infisal fi Souriyya* (1968).

al-Kuzbari, Ma'mun
(1914-1998)

Ma'mun al-Kuzbari studied international law at the University of Lyon and graduated in 1940. He returned to Syria, worked as an attorney, and taught at Damascus University.

In 1953, Kuzbari ran for parliament on an independent ticket and won. He allied himself with President Adib al-Shishakli, who appointed him speaker of parliament on October 24, 1953. Kuzbari was a refined man of letters. Although he had no political background, Kuzbari was nevertheless a well-known figure from a respectable family in Damascus. He gave the military regime of Shishakli the cultured and civilian touch that it needed, and he legitimized Shishakli's image for those skeptics who accused him of relying strictly on officers to administer state affairs. Kuzbari presided over parliamentary affairs and became chairman of the Constitutional Assembly that drafted a new constitution for Syria. Seeing that Kuzbari was well received by the public, Shishakli appointed him vice president and secretary-general of the Arab Liberation Movement (ALM). It was a party created by Shishakli in 1952 that called for land reform, progressive taxation, full employment, a classless society, emancipation of women, and Arab unity. Kuzbari also managed the party's political daily *al-Tahrir al-Arabi*.

In February 1954, a military revolt broke out against President Shishakli and forced him to step down from office. When Shishakli left for Lebanon, Kuzbari called for an emergency session in parliament and appointed himself president on February 25, 1954. He then dismissed all of Shishakli's men from office and filled the bureaucracy with his associates, claiming that it was time to return to civilian rule. In doing so, Kuzbari was trying to exploit his remaining authority under Shishakli, and at the same time, take advantage of his status as a civilian politician. He hoped that the Syrian citizens would support him for being one of them, and that the officers would back him due to his alliance with Shishakli.

Kuzbari issued a presidential address to the Syrian people and asked that they support his leadership and assist in restoring calm to Syria. A group of rebel officers, backed by the civilian Hashim al-Atasi (who had been president before Shishakli came to power in 1951), asked Kuzbari to step down. Atasi came to Damascus in March 1954 and resumed his duties at the presidency. Kuzbari resigned from his self-appointed post but remained in charge of the ALM. In October 1954, Kuzbari became a member of parliament, and in February 1955, was appointed minister of justice in the cabinet of Prime Minister Sabri al-Asali. In September 1955, Kuzbari became minister of education in the independent cabinet of Prime Minister Sa'id al-Ghazzi and kept this post until June 1956. In May 1956, in addition to his cabinet post, Kuzbari also became acting president of Damascus University.

In 1958, Syria and Egypt merged to form the United Arab Republic (UAR). Kuzbari took part in the union talks with President Shukri al-Quwatli that were held in Cairo and resulted in the signing of the union charter on February 1, 1958. Kuzbari refrained from political conduct during the UAR years but endorsed the coup that overthrew the UAR in September 1961, claiming that the regime of President Gamal Abd al-Nasser of Egypt had been a dictatorship. Kuzbari rallied with a group of disgruntled politicians and issued a secession declaration in October 1961, criticizing Nasser and praising the officers who had dissolved the union.

On September 30, 1961, these officers, headed by Kuzbari's cousin, Haydar al-Kuzbari, asked Kuzbari to form the first post-Nasser cabinet. Kuzbari faced great difficulty in convincing the people of his ability to lead since he lacked the charisma and popularity that Nasser had enjoyed. Kuzbari appointed himself minister of defense and foreign affairs and created a cabinet of technocrats, thereby distancing himself from established politicians and political parties in order to avoid creating tension among them. Arguments divided the officers who brought Kuzbari to power, however, and on November 20, 1961, his cousin Haydar was arrested by Abd al-Karim al-Nehlawi, the military strongman of Syria. The following day, Nehlawi forced Prime Minister Kuzbari to resign from office and Izzat al-Nuss, a university professor with no political affiliations, became the new prime minister.

Ma'mun al-Kuzbari.

In December 1961, Kuzbari became a member of parliament and considered nominating himself for presidential office, but his candidacy was vetoed by Nehlawi. Nazim al-Qudsi was elected president instead, and he appointed Kuzbari speaker of parliament on December 12, 1961. On March 28, 1962, Nehlawi tried to seize power in Syria and arrested both Qudsi and Kuzbari, accusing them of wanting to curb his powers and marginalize his role. The coup was foiled by a group of officers who were loyal to the post-union order. They launched a counter-coup against Nehlawi and released Qudsi and Kuzbari from prison. Kuzbari remained at his post in parliament until September 12, 1962.

On March 8, 1963, the Baath Party came to power in Syria and pledged to restore the UAR. They dismissed all anti-Nasser politicians and arrested Ma'mun al-Kuzbari. He served briefly in jail and his civil rights were terminated by the Revolutionary Command Council (RCC). He then moved to France and resided briefly in Paris before setting up permanent residence in Morocco. He taught at Rabat University and moved to Lebanon when the Civil War ended in 1991.

Ma'mun al-Kuzbari died in Beirut in 1998 and was buried in Damascus.

Sources:
Azma, Bashir. *Jeel al-Hazeema Bayn al-Wihda wa al-Infisal* (1991).
Azm, Khalid. *Muzakarat* (1973).
Babil, Nasuh. *Sahafa wa Siyassa fi Souriyya* (1987).
Barada (March 24, 1963).
Hawrani, Akram. *Muzakarat Akram al-Hawrani* (2000).
Moubayed, Sami. *Damascus Between Democracy and Dictatorship* (2000).
Samman, Mutih. *Watan wa Askar* (1995).
Seale, Patrick. *The Struggle for Power in Syria* (1961).
Torrey, Gordon. *Syrian Politics and the Military* (1964).
Zahr al-Din, Abd al-Karim. *Muzakarati an Fatrat al-Infisal fi Souriyya* (1968).

al-Mahayri, Issam
(1918-)

Issam al-Mahayri was born in Damascus and raised in Cairo. He studied law at Damascus University and in 1944 joined the Syrian Social Nationalist Party (SSNP) of Antune Sa'ada.

Mahayri became a dedicated disciple of Sa'ada and preached the doctrine of abolishing imperialism from the region and reuniting the districts of Greater Syria. He was opposed to the artificial boundaries of Lebanon, Iraq, Jordan, and Palestine and advocated that they all unite with modern Syria. He befriended Sa'ada when the latter resided in Damascus in the summer of 1949. In June 1949, Sa'ada tried to seize power in Lebanon and was executed for treason by Prime Minister Riyad al-Sulh. Sa'ada's death left a vacuum in SSNP leadership that was partially filled by Issam al-Mahayri.

In August 1949, Mahayri became a member of the Constitutional Assembly that drafted a new constitution for Syria. In September 1950, he became a deputy in parliament, running on an SSNP ticket. Also in 1950, Mahayri was appointed secretary-general of the SSNP. His political career blossomed when General Adib al-Shishakli, a former member of the SSNP, came to power in November 1951. All parties, except for the SSNP, were outlawed during the Shishakli years. To show his solidarity with the SSNP, Shishakli befriended Mahayri and took him along on official visits as a presidential advisor. From 1951 to 1954, Mahayri became Shishakli's confidant, media advisor, and personal companion. When Shishakli was overthrown by military coup in February 1954, and Hashim al-Atasi took power, Mahayri lost his influence in dictating national Syrian policy. Mahayri nominated himself for the first post-Shishakli parliament in October 1954, but was defeated in the elections.

In April 1954, the SSNP suffered a crippling setback when its president, George Abd al-Masih, ordered the killing of Adnan al-Malki, the deputy chief of staff in the Syrian government. Abd al-Masih was acting on his own to settle a personal score with Malki, and did not consult the party leadership. The entire SSNP leadership, however, suffered from the ordeal. The SSNP was outlawed by President Atasi. Abd al-Masih vanished into exile. And along with his comrades Ghassan Jadid and Juliet al-Meer, Sa'ada's widow, Mahayri was accused of orchestrating the murder. He was brought to trial and sentenced to life imprisonment in 1955.

Mahayri remained in jail until the Baath Party came to power in March 1963 and released all political prisoners. Mahayri ceased all political activity after that, spending the remainder of his years between Beirut and Damascus. Occasionally, he would write articles in the SSNP monthly *al-Binaa* (*Construction*). In July 2001, President Bashar al-Asad authorized the SSNP to resume activity after a forty-six-year ban on the party's conduct. SSNP publications were allowed to be sold on newsstands and SSNP members were allowed to stage public rallies to demonstrate against the atrocities of Israeli Prime Minister Ariel Sharon.

Issam al-Mahayri re-emerged at the age of eighty-three as leader of the SSNP in Syria. In 2003, members of the SSNP were invited by Asad to attend meetings of the National Progressive Front (NPF), a parliamentary coalition of socialist parties that dominate political life in Syria. In May 2004, the SSNP was given a license to operate officially once again, granted by President Bashar al-Asad, after being outlawed since 1955. It joined the NPF and attended the famed Baath Party Conference of June 2005, where the Baath and NPF decided to restore political party life to Syria.

Issam al-Mahayri.

Sources:
Faris, George. *Man Hum fi al-`Alam al-Arabi?* (1957).
Itri, Abd al-Ghani. *Alam wa Mubdioun* (1999).
Moubayed, Sami. *Damascus Between Democracy and Dictatorship* (2000).

Makhous, Ibrahim
(1925-)

Ibrahim Makhous studied medicine at Damascus University and joined the Baath Party of Michel Aflaq and Salah al-Bitar. He was a student volunteer in the Arab-Israeli War of 1948 and served as a volunteer medic in the Algerian Revolution (1952-1962). He returned to Syria and practiced medicine until the Military Committee of the Baath Party came to power in March 1963.

Makhous rallied around the party officers and was appointed minister of health in the cabinet of Prime Minister Salah al-Bitar. Makhous's post was renewed in the cabinet of President Amin al-Hafez from November 1963 to May 1964. In September 1965, Dr Yusuf al-Zu'ayyin, another medical doctor who had served with Makhous in Algeria, became prime minister and appointed Makhous minister of foreign affairs. Makhous was also appointed deputy prime minister and voted into the Regional Command of the Baath Party. President Amin al-Hafez gave Makhous the task of building political bridges between Syria and President Gamal Abd al-Nasser of Egypt.

On February 23, 1966, a coup took place in Syria, launched by Salah Jadid and Hafez al-Asad. Dr Nur al-Din al-Atasi, another doctor who had volunteered in Algeria, was appointed head of state while Zu'ayyin retained his post as prime minister. Makhous allied himself with Jadid and was once again appointed minister of foreign affairs. In comment to the Atasi-Makhous-Zu'ayyin coalition, an editorial in the Beirut daily *L' Orient* said, "Syria is ruled by three doctors. She must be sick."

On June 1, 1967, Ibrahim Makhous warned against the eventual outbreak of war between Syria and Israel. He traveled to Moscow and Europe to call attention to the crisis and garner support for Syria, but he returned home empty-handed. His diplomatic failure that led up to the Arab-Israeli War of 1967 led him to resign from office in January 1968. In March 1968, Makhous was appointed director of the Peasant's Bureau. He hastened the pace of land redistribution throughout Syria, taking property from big landowners and distributing it to farmers. In many cases, he let the farmers choose what lands they wanted him to confiscate.

When President Hafez al-Asad came to power in November 1970, Ibrahim Makhous was relieved of his duties and forced to flee Syria. He took up residence in Algeria to work as a surgeon at the Mustapha Pasha Hospital, where he still resides.

Sources:
Seale, Patrick. *Asad: Struggle for the Middle East* (1988).
Batatu, Hanna. *Syria's Peasantry: the Descendants of its Lesser Rural Notables and their Politics* (2000).

Mardam Bey, Jamil
(1893-1960)

Jamil Mardam Bey was born into a socially prominent family in Damascus. He studied at the School of Political Science in Paris and was a founder of al-Fatat, the leading opposition party in Ottoman Syria.

Al-Fatat was founded by five Arab students living in Paris in 1911. The organization called on Arab and Turkish citizens to remain united within the Ottoman framework, but claimed that the Arabs should have equal rights and obligations as their Ottoman counterparts. In 1913, al-Fatat moved its offices to Beirut. In 1914, its founders opened an office in Damascus to coordinate nationalist activity.

In the summer of 1913, the al-Fatat founders called for an Arab Congress in Paris to discuss the deteriorating living conditions in the Ottoman Empire. Not wishing to create a permanent rift with authorities in Istanbul, the founders did not call for complete Arab emancipation, but rather tried to mend relations with the Ottomans. When that failed, they publicly headed the separatist movement, demanding a complete break with Ottomanism in favor of Arabism.

In 1916, Jamil Mardam Bey joined the Arab Revolt of Sharif Husayn, a military uprising demanding full independence for the Arab provinces in the Ottoman Empire. The Ottomans sentenced Mardam Bey to death in absentia and he fled to Europe where he coordinated nationalist activity between the politicians in exile and the underground in Syria. His comrades were hanged in public in Damascus and Beirut on May 6, 1916.

When the Ottoman Empire was defeated in 1918, Mardam Bey returned to Syria and became private advisor and translator to King Faysal I, the new ruler of Syria. In 1919, he accompanied Faysal to the Paris Peace Conference and became deputy to Foreign Minister Abd al-Rahman Shahbandar. Mardam Bey took part in the diplomatic talks between Syria and the French aimed at preventing the implementation of the French Mandate in the Middle East. Along with Shahbandar, Mardam Bey met with French General Henri Gouraud and tried to reach a compromise, but the talks ended in failure.

On July 24, 1925, the French Army occupied Syria, dethroned Faysal, and sentenced Mardam Bey to death. Mardam Bey fled to Jerusalem and remained there until the mandate authority issued an amnesty and allowed him back to Damascus in 1921. He became a member in the Iron Hand Society, an underground movement headed by Shahbandar. In May 1922, the French accused both him and Shahbandar of meeting in secret with envoys of the US government and striving to topple the French Mandate in Syria. Mandate authorities sentenced Shahbandar to twenty years in prison and banished Mardam Bey to Europe, where he remained until the French issued another amnesty in 1924.

Upon his return to Damascus, Jamil Mardam Bey joined the People's Party, the first modern party in French Mandate Syria. It was headed by Shahbandar and funded by King Faysal I, who by then had become the king of Iraq. The party worked to terminate the mandate and establish an Arab kingdom headed by a member of the Hashemite family—either Faysal or his brother, King Abdullah of Jordan.

In July 1925, the chieftan, Sultan al-Atrash, launched a military uprising against the French from the Arab Mountain. Shahbandar served as the revolt's mastermind and delegated Mardam Bey to channel funds from Amman and to recruit members into the rebel army from Damascus. He also smuggled weapons from Palestine and offered sanctuary to the Druze warriors in the Ghuta orchards that surrounded Damascus. Mardam Bey's orchards in Ghuta, known as Hosh al-Matban, became storehouses for arms and ammunition. In 1927, the revolt was crushed by the French Army and its leaders were sentenced to death, but all of them evaded arrest and fled into exile. Atrash and Shahbandar fled to Amman while Mardam Bey went to Jaffa, but he was arrested by British authorities and extradited to the mandate authority in Syria. For one year, Mardam Bey was imprisoned on Arwad Island on the Syrian coast, but he was released by a general amnesty in 1928.

Mardam Bey then returned to Damascus and helped co-found the National Bloc in October 1927, the leading anti-French movement in Syria. The Bloc was to contest the leadership of Shahbandar and his People's Party in future years.

The party was composed of politicians, landowners, merchants, and lawyers who wanted to terminate the mandate through diplomatic means rather than armed resistance. Hashim al-Atasi, a former prime minister under Faysal, became its president and appointed Mardam Bey as a permanent member of its executive council. Mardam Bey nominated himself on a Bloc ticket for parliament in 1928, 1932, 1936, and 1943, winning in every round. In 1932, he became minister of finance in the cabinet of Prime Minister Haqqi al-Azm

In 1936, Jamil Mardam Bey helped orchestrate a sixty-day strike in Syria where the whole of Syrian society closed down in protest to French policies. The strike turned violent, claimed lives on both sides, and forced the French to acknowledge

Jamil Mardam Bey.

the National Bloc leaders as the true representatives of the Syrian people. A senior Bloc delegation was invited to Paris for independence talks in March-September 1936. Mardam Bey accompanied Hashim al-Atasi to France and was the principal architect of an agreement that guaranteed independence for Syria over a twenty-five-year period. In exchange for independence, the National Bloc agreed to give France numerous political, economic, and military privileges in Syria and support her in the Middle East if another deadly war were to break out in Europe. The Bloc returned to Syria in triumph and Atasi was elected president of the republic. In turn, Atasi called on Jamil Mardam Bey to form a government on December 21, 1936.

The Atasi-Mardam Bey alliance was fraught with problems from the outset. Among other things, they faced disturbances in the Jazeera district of northeast Syria, where locals refused to submit to the new regime and demanded the autonomy that France had granted them in the 1920s. Other problems grew out of domestic opposition to Mardam Bey's former patron, Dr Abd al-Rahman Shahbandar.

After spending twelve years in exile, the veteran nationalist Shahbandar returned to Syria in 1937 and expected to receive a government post in the new administration. Fearing that Shahbandar's popularity would sideline him, Mardam Bey refused to give him a position in the government and tried to control the activities of his former patron. When Shahbandar requested permission to open a political party, Mardam Bey also refused. Shahbandar criticized him, claiming that he was leading a dictatorship in Syria. Mardam Bey responded by placing Shahbandar under house arrest at his summer resort in Bludan. When a bomb exploded in Mardam Bey's car, he immediately accused Shahbandar of the attempted assassination, and ordered the arrest of Shahbandar's right-hand man, Nasuh Babil, owner and publisher of the Damascus daily *al-Ayyam*.

Adding to Mardam Bey's worries was an evolving crisis with France, where the French reneged on the promised treaty, claiming that if war were to break out in Europe they would need to use their Middle Eastern colonies as strategic out-posts. Shahbandar criticized Mardam Bey's inability to get the French to honor the Treaty of 1936. Unable to implement this promised treaty, and facing mount-ing pressure from Shahbandar and the public, Jamil Mardam Bey resigned from office on February 23, 1939.

In July 1940, Abd al-Rahman Shahbandar was murdered in Damascus, and his family accused Jamil Mardam Bey and the two Bloc leaders, Lutfi al-Haffar and Saadallah al-Jabiri, of the assassination. The accusations were backed by Bahij al-Khatib, the new head of state. Ex-Prime Minister Mardam Bey fled to Iraq, where Prime Minister Nuri al-Sa'id gave him political asylum. Mardam Bey was tried in absentia, but was declared innocent of the charges and returned to Syria in 1941.

In 1943, Mardam Bey allied himself with the National Bloc leader, Shukri al-Quwatli, and they ran on a joint list for parliament. When Quwatli was elect-ed president in August 1943, he appointed Mardam Bey as minister of foreign affairs in the National Bloc cabinet of Prime Minister Saadallah al-Jabiri. Quwatli delegated Mardam Bey to help found the Arab League in Cairo in March 1944. Mardam Bey spent the next six years traveling back and forth to Egypt, where he co-authored the constitution of the Arab League and laid out its infrastructure with the league's secretary-general, Abd al-Rahman Azzam.

In November 1944, Jamil Mardam Bey became minister of foreign affairs, economy, defense, and deputy to Prime Minister Faris al-Khury. Mardam Bey held all four positions until August 1945. He led diplomatic talks with the French and tried to secure a treaty, similar to the one of 1936 that guaranteed inde-pendence for Syria. This time, however, he refused to grant any privileges to the French in Syria.

On May 29, 1945, French General Charles de Gaulle ordered an air raid on Damascus and demanded the arrest of President Quwatli, Acting Prime Minister Jamil Mardam Bey, and Saadallah al-Jabiri, the speaker of parliament. All three of them were charged with obstructing French interests in the Middle East. In the Damascus air raid, the French destroyed the Syrian Parliament and the Ministry of Defense. French troops raided Mardam Bey's private office, confiscated all official documents, and burned the office down.

When Syria achieved independence on April 17, 1946, Jamil Mardam Bey began grooming himself for the upcoming elections and had his eyes set on the presidency. In a bid at curbing his influence, President Quwatli appointed him ambassador to Egypt and then Saudi Arabia. In 1947, however, Prime Minister Saadallah al-Jabiri died and left a vacuum at the premiership. Unable to find a suit-able substitute, Quwatli called on Mardam Bey to form a government on October

6, 1947. Mardam Bey created his second cabinet from former members of the National Bloc who had transformed the Bloc into the National Party. Mardam Bey appointed himself minister of foreign affairs and health. When, on May 26, 1948, Defense Minister Ahmad al-Sharabati resigned from office, Mardam Bey took over the Ministry of Defense as well.

Mardam Bey ruled Syria with President Shukri al-Quwatli during the first Arab-Israeli War of 1948. The war defeat damaged Mardam Bey's credibility among conservatives who accused him of poor leadership at the war front. Accusations were fired at him from different opposition parties, including the Baath Party of Michel Aflaq, which claimed that Mardam Bey had profiteered at the army's expense. Mardam Bey was also accused, along with ex-Defense Minister Ahmad al-Sharabati and Finance Minister Wehbi al-Harriri, of having purchased arms at inflated prices and then pocketing the difference. Mardam Bey also clashed with the officers, accusing Chief of Staff Husni al-Za'im of inefficiency in battle and calling for his dismissal from office.

When anti-Mardam Bey riots took over Syria, the prime minister responded with force, declaring martial law, appointing himself military governor, and arresting prominent critics like Michel Aflaq. He then ordered the army to keep order on the streets and had many demonstrators arrested in Damascus and Aleppo. Under advice from President Quwatli, however, Mardam Bey resigned from office on August 22, 1948. He then announced his resignation from political life and warned that ruling Syria would be difficult in the face of the army-civilian divide at home and the Israeli threat on Syria's border.

Jamil Mardam Bey spent the remainder of his years in Egypt, living in self-imposed exile. He was an honored guest at the court of King Farouk, but he also made friends with the officers who came to power in Cairo in July 1952. In 1955, President Gamal Abd al-Nasser asked Mardam Bey to run for presidential office in Syria, claiming that Cairo would support his candidacy, but the ex-prime minister declined the offer for health reasons.

Jamil Mardam Bey died in Cairo in 1960 and was buried in Damascus. In 1994, his daughter Salma Mardam Bey published his handwritten memoirs about the years 1939 to 1945, later translated from French into English and entitled, *Syria's Quest for Independence*. The book was translated into Arabic and published under the title, *Awrak Jamil Mardam Bey* (*Memoirs of Jamil Mardam Bey*).

Sources:
Azm, Khalid. *Muzakarat* (1973).
Babil, Nasuh. *Sahafa wa Siyassa fi Souriyya* (1987).
Barudi, Fakhri. *Muzakarat al-Barudi: Sittoun Aman Tatakalam* (1952-1953).
Barudi, Fakhri. *Khamsoun Aman min Hayat al-Watan* (1999).
Commins, David. *Historical Dictionary of Modern Syria* (1996).

Haffar, Salma. *Lutfi al-Haffar 1885-1968* (1997).

Hawrani, Akram. *Muzakarat Akram al-Hawrani* (2000).

Itri, Abd al-Ghani. *Abqariyyat wa Alam* (1996).

Kayyali, Abd al-Rahman. *Al-Marahil fi al-Intidab al-Faransi 1926-1938* (1958-1960).

Khoury, Philip. *Syria and the French Mandate* (1987).

Mardam Bey, Jamil. *Syria's Quest for Independence* (1994).

Moubayed, Sami. *Damascus Between Democracy and Dictatorship* (2000).

Moubayed, Sami. *The Politics of Damascus 1920-1946* (1999).

Qassab Hasan, Najat. *Saniou al-Jalaa fi Souriyya* (1999).

Shambrook, Peter. *French Imperialism in Syria 1927-1936* (1998).

Seale, Patrick. *The Struggle for Power in Syria* (1961).

Mu'ayyad al-Azm, Badih
(1870-1960)

Badih Mu'ayyad al-Azm studied at the Ottoman Law Academy in Istanbul and graduated in 1895. He began his career at the central Ottoman administration in Istanbul and became manager of legal affairs in the Ottoman Empire in 1898. Six years later, he became a senior government inspector in Mosul, and in 1908 assumed the same job in Istanbul. In 1911, he became a director in the Ottoman Customs Department.

In 1913, Mu'ayyad al-Azm nominated himself for the Ottoman Parliament and became a deputy for Damascus. When the Ottoman Empire was defeated in World War I in October 1918, Mu'ayyad al-Azm was voted into the Syrian National Congress, the equivalent of a modern parliament charged with administering state affairs in the absence of an official government. In March 1920, Mu'ayyad al-Azm became president of the Royal Electoral Committee that crowned Faysal I, the post-Ottoman leader of Arabia, as king of Syria. Mu'ayyad al-Azm also served as advisor to Prime Minister Rida al-Rikabi from October 1918 to January 1920.

The French proclaimed their mandate on Syria in July 1920, and Mu'ayyad al-Azm served as minister of education in the first cabinet under their rule, headed by Prime Minister Ala al-Din al-Droubi. A group of Faysal loyalists killed Droubi in August 1920, and Syria's new prime minister, Jamil al-Ulshi, appointed Mu'ayyad al-Azm minister of justice in September 1920. But Mu'ayyad al-Azm's collaboration with Droubi and Ulshi, two ranking pro-French politicians, damaged his credibility in nationalist circles, and he was accused of being an agent of the French by the National Bloc, the leading anti-French movement in Syria.

In 1923, Mu'ayyad al-Azm ran for parliament on an independent ticket and won. With French backing, he was elected speaker of parliament on November 12,

1923. He presided over a small chamber of thirty deputies and kept his post until July 14, 1925. In 1930, Prime Minister Taj al-Din al-Hasani appointed Mu'ayyad al-Azm minister of economy, agriculture, and public works in a cabinet boycotted by the National Bloc.

In 1932, Badih Mu'ayyad al-Azm served briefly as minister of interior under Hasani before retiring from political activity for good.

Sources:

As'ed, Shakir. *Al-Barlaman al-Souri 1919-2001* (2001).

Faris, George. *Man Hum fi al-`Alam al-Arabi?* (1957).

Shambrook, Peter. *French Imperialism in Syria 1927-1936* (1998).

al-Murshed, Sulayman
(1905-1946)

Born in the Syrian mountain next to the coastal city of Lattakia, Sulayman al-Murshed came from a poor Alawite family of village shepherds. He did not attend school and grew up illiterate, working in the fields until he moved into politics in the 1920s.

In 1923, Murshed played a practical joke on his fellow townsmen, claiming that a divine spirit had entered his soul and was demanding obedience. Gullible and uneducated, the villagers were enchanted. Murshed enjoyed the game and pursued it for the next twenty-four years. He attracted the attention of the French, and by 1930 the mandate authority was sponsoring Murshed's façade. Using French funds, his opponents argued, Murshed would paint himself in phosphorous colors and rise to the mountaintop at night, claiming that he was God. Seeing him glow, his followers would drop to their knees in reverence.

His tricks worked, and by 1928 Murshed was being hailed as *al-Rabb* (the God). He built an empire for himself and married many times, just like the Prophet Mohammad. Murshed created a team of armed followers, levied taxes for his own treasury, and asked locals for their allegiance in exchange for his protection. In the early 1930s, many of those locals who did not give him deference were ostracized or harassed.

In 1936, Sulayman al-Murshed ran for parliament on an independent ticket and won with an overwhelming majority. His election was repeated in 1943. By 1940, his believers were estimated at 50,000 among residents of the mountain. In 1945, he created a small army to topple the anti-French administration of President Shukri al-Quwatli. But the French ended their mandate in Syria in April 1946 and Murshed's influence was greatly reduced by President Quwatli.

On September 6, Murshed tried to collect taxes from a neighboring village, but Adil al-Azma, the governor of Lattakia, prevented him. Threats between

Azma and Murshed escalated into violence, and police forces were dispatched to the mountain to keep order. The forces were commanded by Captain Hrant Bey. Murshed ordered his troops to mobilize in defense. Mushed had inspired his follower to the point that they counted on their espirit des corps and the rightness of their cause to overcome the modern armaments and superior military training of the French.

Sulayman al-Murshed.

Hundreds of Murshed's men were slaughtered in combat. While planning his escape, Murshed shot his wife because she objected to his decision to go to war. He was eventually arrested and brought back to Damascus where a heated debate developed over whether he should be tried for treason or pardoned. Prime Minister Saadallah al-Jabiri wanted appeasement, fearing that killing him would arouse the anger of his followers, while hard-liners like Jamil Mardam Bey and Adil Arslan wanted to end his outrages and have him executed.

A military court sentenced Murshed to death, but President Quwatli refused to sign the execution warrant, claiming that he did not believe in capital punishment and that instead Murshed should spend a lifetime in prison. But Interior Minister Sabri al-Asali had other plans. The minister carried out the execution, thereby surpassing Quwatli's authority, and had Murshed hanged in public at 4:45 AM on December 16, 1946.

As soon as Murshed saw the hangman's noose, he screamed that he was a devout believer and not a heretic, repeating the *shahada* of Islam and claiming that there is only one God and Mohammad is his prophet. Sobbing, Sulayman al-Murshed pleaded that upon his death he be wrapped in the Syrian Flag. He begged Jamil Mardam Bey for forgiveness, but the latter sarcastically replied, "Since when do Gods plead to mortals?"

The US envoy in Syria commented on the event saying, "Vast crowds jostled and fought to get a closer look at the God who proved to be mortal after all. Decent citizens breathe a sigh of relief that the myth of al-Rabb has forever been dispelled and a vicious cancer in the side of the young republic has been neatly removed."

Sources:
Arslan, Adil. *Muzakarat al-Ameer Adil Arslan* (1972).
Landis, Joshua. *Nationalism and the Politics of Za'ama* (1997).
USNA "Gordon Mattison (Damascus) to Secretary of State (February 16, 1947) 890D.00/12-1646.

Nami, Ahmad
(1879-1960)

Prince Ahmad Nami was born and raised in Beirut to an affluent Circassian family related by marriage to Sultan Abdulhamid II. Nami studied at the Ottoman Military Academy and received advanced military training in Paris. In 1900, he married Princess Aisha, the daughter of Sultan Abdulhamid II, and earned the princely title of Damad (which means the son-in-law of the Sultan in Ottoman Turkish). He took no part in local politics and moved into exile in France when Abdulhamid was overthrown in 1909.

Nami remained in Paris until the Ottoman Empire was defeated in October 1918. He returned to Beirut and administered his family enterprises, befriending the French officers who occupied Syria and Lebanon in July 1920. The French delegated him to form a government in Syria, and in the absence of a head of state, Nami was given limited presidential powers. The French charged him with improving economic conditions, fighting unemployment, and suppressing the national uprising that had erupted in the Arab Mountain against the French Mandate in 1925.

Nami created his cabinet on April 26, 1926, and tried to adhere to popular demand by appointing three leaders of the nationalist movement in government posts. The landlord Husni al-Barazi became minister of interior, the attorney Faris al-Khury became minister of education and Lutfi al-Haffar, the deputy president of the Damascus Chamber of Commerce, became minister of commerce. The three men resigned in June 1926, however, to protest French policies toward the nationalist movement, and were promptly arrested by French High Commissioner Henri de Jouvenel. Nami tried to secure their release, but when threatened with a similar fate, he backed down and replaced them with three pro-French politicians.

On economic affairs, Nami used state subsidies to encourage industrial and commercial activity and offered financial assistance to any industrialist wishing to set up a factory in Syria. He also worked relentlessly against the establishment of a separate Lebanon, believing in the need to preserve Syrian unity with its historical boundaries. Nami met with de Jouvenel and proposed that the mandate be replaced with a treaty of friendship between Syria and Lebanon that would last for thirty years. Meanwhile, France would have all the economic, political, and military privileges it wanted in Syria. In exchange, France would grant Syria the right to have a national army, unity of Syrian lands, and entry into the League of Nations. Nami also demanded financial compensation for those citizens whose homes had been destroyed by the fighting of 1925-1927, and he also asked that France issue a general amnesty to permit the return of Syrian exiles.

Although de Jouvenel welcomed Nami's proposal, authorities in Paris did not. In February 1928, the French accused Nami of trying to establish a monarchy in

Syria and appoint himself king. The French objected to Nami's ambitions and removed him from office on February 8, 1928. In 1932, the French reconsidered creating a throne in Syria and appointing Nami king. The idea was poorly planned, however, and never got past the drawing board. Other candidates for the throne included Abbas Hilmi, the ex-Khedive of Egypt, King Abdullah of Jordan, King Ali of the Hijaz, and Faysal al-Saud (the future king of Saudi Arabia).

Ahmad Nami (seated) with his government in 1926.

In 1940, Ahmad Nami became a possible candidate for presidential office, but the National Bloc, the leading anti-French movement in Syria, objected to his leadership. The French considered appointing Nami president and appointing the pro-nationalist notable Khalid al-Azm as prime minister, but National Bloc President Hashim al-Atasi claimed that he would not support Nami's candidacy no matter who his prime minister would be.

Prince Ahmad Nami then retired from public life and moved to Lebanon where he lived until his death in 1960. Occasionally, he would travel to France and serve as a visiting lecturer on history and politics at the Sorbonne in Paris.

Sources:

Hakim, Yusuf. *Souriyya wa al-Intidab al-Faransi* (1966).
Jumaa, Souad and Zaza, Hasan. *Al-Huqumat al-Souriyya fi al-Qarn al-Ishreen* (2001).
Khoury, Philip. *Syria and the French Mandate* (1987).
Moubayed, Sami. *The Politics of Damascus 1920-1946* (1999).
Shambrook, Peter. *French Imperialism in Syria 1927-1936* (1998).

Nehme, Daniel
(1928-2003)

Daniel Nehme came from the Safita district on the Syrian coastline and studied law at Damascus University. In May 1945, he joined the Syrian Communist Party and five years later was put in charge of the party's Safita branch.

In 1949, a military coup took place, bringing the pro-American General Husni al-Za'im to power. Za'im banned the Communist Party and arrested all of its members for their views. Nehme spent the four-month era of President Za'im at the Palmyra prison in the Syrian Desert, only to be released when Za'im was overthrown in August 1949. Nehme was imprisoned for his views once again during the military regime of President Adib al-Shishakli (1951-1954), but resumed political activity in 1954 when civilian rule was restored to Syria.

Nehme worked as an attorney in Damascus and became editor-in-chief of the party's daily newspaper *al-Noor*. In the second half of the 1950s, the Syrian Communist Party was opposed to the rising popularity of President Gamal Abd al-Nasser of Egypt. When the two countries merged to form the United Arab Republic (UAR) in 1958, the new regime dissolved the Communist Party, arrested its leaders, and closed *al-Noor*. Nehme was imprisoned while Khalid Bakdash, the party's secretary-general, was exiled to Eastern Europe.

In March 1963, the Baath Party came to power in Syria and outlawed all parties. Nehme remained on the sidelines of political life until President Hafez al-Asad came to power in November 1970 and relaunched the Communist Party. In the 1970s, Nami served as a liaison officer between Asad and the Communist leaders in Moscow. In 2001, when President Bashar al-Asad permitted political parties to restart their publications, Daniel Nehme reactivated *al-Noor*, forty-three years after its initial banishment. He served as its editor until his death in December 2003.

Sources:
Bawab, Sulayman. *Mawsuat Alam Souriyya fi al-Qarn al-Ishreen*, Vol III (1999).

Qaddur, Nasser
(1932-)

Nasser Qaddur studied at the Homs Military Academy and graduated in 1955. He joined the Baath Party of Michel Aflaq and Salah al-Bitar in 1948 and began his career as an officer in the Syrian Army in 1955.

Qaddur was vehemently in favor of Syria's union with Egypt in 1958. When the two countries merged to form the United Arab Republic (UAR), Qaddur became an officer in the Ministry of Interior and was appointed director of General Intelligence in Syria by President Gamal Abd al-Nasser. Qaddur was only twenty-six years old—the youngest director ever in the history of the Syrian intelligence service. Qaddar tried to uphold the union and was a vehement supporter of President Nasser. A coup overthrew the union government on September 28, 1961, and the coup masterminds relieved Qaddur of his duties and had him arrested for four months.

From 1961 to 1963, Qaddur opposed the anti-Nasser government of President Nazim al-Qudsi and joined a group of like-minded officers in demanding restoration of the UAR. Meanwhile, he held a civilian job at the Bureau of Social

Security. In March 1963, the Baath Party came to power in Syria and Qaddur moved into the Ministry of Foreign Affairs, becoming chargé d'affaires at the Syrian Embassy in Baghdad. His duties included strengthening ties with the newly created Iraqi regime of President Abd al-Salam Aref and monitoring the activities of Hardan al-Takriti, an Iraqi member of the Baath Party. Iraqi authorities accused Qaddar of espionage and arrested him on the Syrian-Iraqi border. He tried to evade arrest by showing his diplomatic identity, but the Iraqi officer scoffed and told him, "We shot Nuri al-Sa'id, what makes you think we will stop from arresting you?" Under orders from Iraqi Chief of Staff Rashed Musleh, however, Qaddar was released but forbidden from reentering Iraq.

In 1964, Qaddur became chargé d'affaires in Libya during the regime of King Ahmad Idris. In 1966, Qaddur was transferred to the Syrian mission in Bonn, Germany. In 1970, Qaddur became director of financial and administrative affairs at the Ministry of Foreign Affairs, and in 1971 President Hafez al-Asad appointed him ambassador to Yugoslavia. Qaddur worked to strengthen Syria's ties with the Tito administration in Belgrade, and kept his post until becoming deputy to Foreign Minister Abd al-Halim Khaddam in 1977.

In 1983, Qaddur nominated himself for the Joint Inspection Unit, an international UN watchdog organization based in Geneva. The unit was composed of two representatives from each continent, and Qaddur was elected by the UN General Assembly as a representative for Asia. In 1986, he became deputy president of the Inspection Unit. In 1987, he was elected president, but declined the post to become minister of state for foreign affairs in the cabinet of Prime Minister Mahmud al-Zu'bi. In December 2001, President Bashar al-Asad created a Ministry of Expatriate Affairs for the government of Prime Minister Mohammad Mustapha Miro. Qaddar became a deputy in parliament in March 2003 and was elected deputy to Speaker Mahmud al-Abrash. In September 2003, Nasser Qaddur was relieved of his duties as minister of expatriate affairs under Prime Minister Mohammad Naji al-Itri.

Sources:
Interview with Nasser Qaddur (Damascus October 21, 2002).

Qanbar, Ahmad
(1900-1971)

Ahmad Qanbar began his career as a political journalist, launching the newspaper *al-Nazir* in Aleppo in 1937. In 1947, he joined the People's Party, a coalition of notables from Aleppo intent on uniting Syria with neighboring Iraq and restoring Aleppo's status as a trade link between Europe and the Far East.

The People's Party was dedicated to the Hashemite cause and funded by the Hashemite families in Baghdad and Amman. From 1947 to 1949, Qanbar became a deputy for Aleppo in parliament. He was highly critical of Chief of Staff Husni al-Za'im during the Arab-Israeli War of 1948, accusing him of poor leadership and corruption, and calling on President Shukri al-Quwatli to dismiss Za'im from office. On March 29, 1949, Za'im seized power in Syria and ordered Qanbar's arrest. He was persecuted for his views during the four-month era of Husni al-Za'im and supported the coup that deposed Za'im's military regime on August 14, 1949.

Then Qanbar allied himself with Syria's new president, Hashim al-Atasi, and became a member of the Constitutional Assembly that drafted a new constitution for Syria. He was also voted into parliament from 1949 to 1951. In September 1950, Qanbar became minister of public works in the cabinet of Prime Minister Nazim al-Qudsi, who was also secretary-general of the People's Party. On November 28, 1951, Qanbar became minister of interior in the cabinet of Prime Minister Ma'ruf al-Dawalibi. The cabinet was dismantled on the day of its creation by General Adib al-Shishakli, another military officer who seized power and arrested Dawalibi and all of his ministers.

Qanbar spent the Shishakli years (1951-1954) between house arrest and prison. But he joined the underground headed by ex-President Atasi and supported the coup that overthrew Shishakli in February 1954. In October 1954, Qanbar became a deputy for Aleppo in the first post-Shishakli parliament. In October 1954, he became minister of interior under Prime Minister Faris al-Khury, and his post was renewed by Prime Minister Sabri al-Asali.

Qanbar resigned from office in 1956 in protest to Prime Minister Asali's radical pro-USSR policy. Qanbar was opposed to an alliance with the USSR and criticized Syria's friendship with the socialist regime of President Gamal Abd al-Nasser of Egypt. He was also highly critical of the pro-Nasser policies in parliament, and accused the deputies of becoming arrogant despots in their defense of Egypt. Qanbar said, "A great reign of terror prevails in the chamber. I stand opposed to this terror and to the government and I challenge it." He voted against the Syrian-Egyptian union in 1958, arguing that union with Iraq would be better for Syria, and retired from public life during the union years (1958-1961).

Qanbar supported the coup that ousted the union government on September 28, 1961, and signed the secession declaration on October 2, a document criticizing Nasser for authoritarian policies during the UAR years and accusing him of having imposed a dictatorship on Syria. The declaration also accused Nasser of "distorting the idea of Arab nationalism" and went on to say that during the union years Nasser had "strangled political and democratic life" in Syria. In December 1961, Qanbar became minister of interior in the cabinet of Prime Minister Bashir al-Azma, and held this post until March 1962. From 1961 to 1963, Qanbar also served as a member of parliament.

Ahmad Qanbar ceased all political activity when the Baath Party came to power in March 1963 and pledged to restore the union. The Revolutionary Command Council (RCC) terminated his civil rights for ten years, but the law was revoked in 1966.

Sources:
Faris, George. *Man Hum fi al-`Alam al-Arabi?* (1957).
Samman, Mutih. *Watan wa Askar* (1995).
Seale, Patrick. *The Struggle for Syria* (1988).

Qannut, Abd al-Ghani
(1925-2001)

Abd al-Ghani Qannut studied at the Homs Military Academy and befriended General Adib al-Shishakli, who emerged as the uncontested military leader of Syria in 1950. Along with Shishakli, Qannut took part in the Arab-Israeli War of 1948.

On July 31, 1950, Qannut was implicated in the assassination of Air Force Commander Mohammad Nasser, a vehement opponent of General Shishakli. Nasser was rushed to hospital where he named Qannut as his assailant before dying. Qannut was arrested and brought to trial, but he was declared innocent and released shortly afterward. He remained loyal to Shishakli and helped him seize power on November 28, 1951. Once firmly in power, Shishakli appointed Qannut deputy to Ibrahim al-Husayni, the director of Syrian Intelligence. Qannut held this post until Shishakli was overthrown by military coup d'etat in February 1954.

In the second half of the 1950s, Qannut became a ranking supporter of President Gamal Abd al-Nasser of Egypt. He joined the officers who went to Cairo in January 1958 to plead for union with Egypt. When the United Arab Republic (UAR) was created, President Nasser appointed Qannut minister of social affairs. He held this post until a military coup overthrew the UAR in September 1961. From 1961 to 1963, Qannut was a member of parliament. In July 1962, Syria filed an official complaint against Nasser, claiming that he was interfering in Syrian affairs and trying to get officers in the Syrian Army to rebel against the post-Nasser order. The Arab League called for round table talks between Syria and Egypt, held in the Lebanese town of Shtura on the Syrian-Lebanese border. Syria's new president, Nazim al-Qudsi, appointed Qannut to the Syrian delegation, but the talks were ruined when the Egyptian team walked out before the Arab League issued a verdict condemning Egypt for her accusations against Syria.

When the Baath Party came to power in March 1963, the Revolutionary Command Council (RCC) terminated Qannut's civil rights to punish him for collaborating with the government of Nazim al-Qudsi. Qannut remained powerless throughout most of the 1960s until he allied himself with Defense Minister Hafez al-Asad, who came to power in November 1970 and appointed Qannut minister of public works. He also served as a deputy in the first parliament under President Asad from February to December 1971. In 1974, Qannut co-founded the National Progressive Front (NPF) with President Asad. The NPF was a parliamentary coalition that united all socialist parties in Syria under the umbrella of the Baath Party. Abd al-Ghani Qannut headed the Arab Socialist Movement, a coalition of hard-line supporters of the late President Nasser, and served as its secretary-general until his death on March 3, 2001.

Sources:
Juma, Sami. *Awrak Min Daftar al-Watan* (2001).

al-Qudsi, Nazim
(1900-1998)

Alternate spelling: Nazim al-Kudsi

Nazim al-Qudsi was born and raised in Aleppo. He obtained his undergraduate degree in law from Damascus University, his MA from the American University of Beirut (AUB), and his PhD from the University of Geneva.

Qudsi returned to Syria in 1935 and joined the National Bloc, the leading anti-French movement, and became one of its most prominent members in Aleppo. The National Bloc was a political organization dedicated to Syrian emancipation from French control through diplomatic means rather than through armed resistance. In 1936, Qudsi ran for parliament on a Bloc ticket and won. But he clashed with the Bloc leadership which failed to prevent the annexation of Alexanderetta to Turkey in 1939, and resigned from Bloc ranks.

Qudsi formed a coalition of Aleppine intellectuals around himself and Rushdi al-Kikhiya, another politician who shared Qudsi's views. The two men nominated themselves for parliament in 1943, winning with ease. They lobbied against the election of National Bloc leader Shukri al-Quwatli as president, but their veto was overruled and Quwatli was voted into office in August 1943. To appease the opposition, the new president appointed Qudsi as Syria's first ambassador to the United States. Qudsi founded the Syrian Embassy in Washington from scratch, and on March 19, 1945, presented his credentials to President Franklin Roosevelt.

In 1947, Qudsi founded the People's Party in Aleppo along with Rushdi al-Kikhiya. The People's Party was an opposition movement to the Quwatli regime and was created to counterbalance the political weight of the National Party, a coalition of politicians from Damascus loyal to Quwatli. The People's Party founders were mainly notables from Aleppo focused on creating union between Syria and Iraq, maintaining a democratic government, and advocating stronger ties with the West. These ideas were supported by the Hashemite royal family in Baghdad. Although primary funding for the party was from Syrian notables, some sources insist that the Hashemite royal family also provided funds.

Nazim al-Qudsi.

In 1947, Qudsi ran for parliament on a party ticket and won. His election was repeated in 1949, 1954, and 1962. He vetoed the reelection of Quwatli as president, but a parliamentary majority overruled his veto. On March 29, 1949, the Quwatli regime was overthrew by a military coup launched by Chief of Staff Husni al-Za'im.

Syria's new ruler asked Qudsi to form a government, but he declined, maintaining that the Za'im regime was unconstitutional and arguing that despite his faults Quwatli was a constitutionally elected president while Za'im's takeover was "illegal." As a result, Za'im had Qudsi arrested and the People's Party was closed. Qudsi was released from jail shortly thereafter and placed under house arrest in Aleppo. He became highly critical of Za'im when the latter closed Syria's border with Jordan and Iraq and threatened to go to war with both countries, accusing them of being agents of Great Britain in the Middle East.

On August 14, 1949, Qudsi supported a coup that overthrew Za'im. The coup was launched by General Sami al-Hinnawi, an old friend of the People's Party and an ally of the Hashemite royals in Baghdad. Hinnawi created a political committee to run state affairs in the absence of an official government and appointed Qudsi to its top leadership. Qudsi also served on the Constitutional Assembly that drafted a new constitution for Syria and became minister of foreign affairs in the first post-Za'im cabinet of Prime Minister Hashim al-Atasi (another ally of the People's Party). Qudsi's ally, Rushdi al-Kikhiya, became minister of interior, and other posts were distributed accordingly to other members of the People's Party.

Qudsi conducted talks with Crown Prince Abd al-Illah of Iraq for creating immediate union between Syria and Iraq, and he made numerous journeys to Baghdad for that purpose. Qudsi formulated an agreement that called for federal union, preserving independent governments in Damascus and Baghdad while coordinating military, economic, social, cultural, and political affairs between the two states. He then went to Cairo and proposed a similar program for all Arab states at the Arab League on January 1, 1951.

To advance union talks, Hashim al-Atasi, who had recently been elected president, called on Qudsi to form a government on December 24, 1949. Qudsi complied, but military officers vetoed his cabinet and he resigned from office five days after coming to power. The officers argued that his government did not include an officer among its midst and that many of its members were declared opponents of officers meddling in political affairs. On June 4, 1950, Qudsi created a new government, less extremist than the first, and was able to secure its approval by appointing General Fawzi Selu as minister of defense. Selu was the right-hand man of General Adib al-Shishakli, the military strongman of Syria. The cabinet existed for ten months, but was unable to take the union issue any further. Qudsi resigned on March 27, 1951. But on October 1, 1951, he was elected speaker of parliament.

Shortly afterward, on November 28, Adib al-Shishakli seized power in Damascus and arrested the entire People's Party leadership, accusing them of wanting to replace Syria's republican regime with a monarchy loyal to Great Britain and Iraq. Shishakli appointed Selu provisional head of state and arrested Qudsi, sending him to Mezzeh prison. Qudsi was released from Mezzeh in January 1952 and placed under house arrest. But he joined the underground and worked in secret against Shishakli, supporting the coup that brought Shishakli down in February 1954.

In October 1954, Nazim al-Qudsi became a deputy in the first post-Shishakli parliament and was elected speaker on October 14, 1954. He tried to regain some of his influence in political circles, but by that time the People's Party had fallen out of favor, and few Syrians advocated union with Iraq anymore. Instead, they wanted union with Egypt under the rising leadership of the young, charismatic Egyptian president, Gamal Abd al-Nasser.

Qudsi tried challenging Nasser's authority, but failed. He preached pro-British and pro-American views at a time when the majority of Syrians had become pro-USSR. He called on Syria to join the Baghdad Pact, an Anglo-American treaty designed to contain the spread of communism. Pro-Nasser newspapers accused Qudsi of working as an agent for the Hashemites. On October 12, 1957, Qudsi resigned from office and was replaced by the pro-Nasser socialist leader, Akram al-Hawrani. Qudsi voted against the Syrian-Egyptian union, and when the two countries merged to form the United Arab Republic (UAR) in 1958, he resigned from public life altogether and retired to Aleppo.

On September 28, 1961, a military coup took place in Syria and toppled the UAR. Qudsi rallied to the support of the coup and nominated himself for the first post-union parliament, becoming a deputy for Aleppo in December 1961. He then ran for presidential office and won, becoming the first post-Nasser leader of Syria on December 12, 1961. As president, Qudsi worked to restore Syria's friendship with the anti-Nasser governments in Jordan, Saudi Arabia, and Lebanon, and build bridges with the United States and Great Britain. The Hashemite family in Baghdad had supported Qudsi's career for the previous thirty years until the monarchy was deposed by a bloody military revolution in July 1958. Qudsi was never on good terms with the new leaders of Iraq, especially the leader of the revolt, General Abd al-Karim Qasim.

The West, particularly US President John Kennedy, welcomed Qudsi's ascent and labeled him a "friend" of the United States. To promote Syria's relationship with Washington, Qudsi appointed Omar Abu Risheh, a renowned poet from Aleppo who like Qudsi was an AUB graduate, as ambassador to the United States in 1961. Qudsi began a massive economic reform program, restoring factories that had been nationalized by Nasser in July 1961 and dismissing all pro-Nasser officials from office. And all officers still loyal to the Egyptian president were discharged from the Syrian Army. Qudsi drafted a new constitution for Syria, restored the outlawed political parties, and received loans from the World Bank for rebuilding Syria's tattered economy.

President Qudsi clashed with the officers that had brought him to power and tried to marginalize their role in political affairs. He appointed Ma'ruf al-Dawalibi, a veteran of the People's Party with declared anti-officer views, as prime minister. Bitter from his experience with the officers since the Shishakli era, Dawalibi began curbing their influence in all state affairs and centralizing power in the hands of Qudsi and the government.

On March 28, 1962, a coup took place in Syria, headed by Colonel Abd al-Karim al-Nehlawi. He arrested Qudsi and Dawalibi, accusing them of misusing their powers and persecuting the officers of the Syrian Army. A countercoup broke out on April 2, led by Chief of Staff Abd al-Karim Zahr al-Din, who ordered all troops to stand by President Qudsi. The army complied, releasing Qudsi from prison and restoring the dissolved parliament. Qudsi refused to arrest or kill Nehlawi, but rather curbed his power by appointing him military attaché to Indonesia—a purely ceremonial post.

Qudsi then tried to appease the officers and the socialists by calling on Bashir al-Azma, a doctor who had been close to Nasser and who held office as minister of health under the UAR, to become prime minister in April 1962. Azma's cabinet included members of the socialist, pro-Nasser Baath Party. Qudsi and Azma dispatched Foreign Minister Adnan al-Azhari to Cairo to mend relations with the Egyptian president. When that failed, however, they filed a complaint to the Arab League, accusing Nasser of wanting to destabilize Syria through interference in Syria's domestic affairs and calling on the army to rebel against the Syrian government.

On March 8, 1963, however, another coup took place in Syria, launched by the Military Committee of the Baath Party. The officers who came to power pledged to restore the UAR and had Qudsi arrested. The Revolutionary Command Council (RCC) stripped Qudsi of his civil rights as a Syrian citizen and banished him from Syria, with orders never to return. Qudsi moved to Europe, then

Lebanon, and finally Jordan where he lived in exile until he died in 1998.

Sources:

Azma, Bashir. *Jeel al-Hazeema Bayn al-Wihda wa al-Infisal* (1991).
Azm, Khalid. *Muzakarat* (1973).
Babil, Nasuh. *Sahafa wa Siyassa fi Souriyya* (1987).
Hawrani, Akram. *Muzakarat Akram al-Hawrani* (2000).
Itri, Abd al-Ghani. *Alam wa Mubdioun* (1999).
Kourani, As'ad. *Zikrayat wa Khawater* (2000).
Moubayed, Sami. *Damascus Between Democracy and Dictatorship* (2000).
Samman, Mutih. *Watan wa Askar* (1995).
Seale, Patrick. *Asad: the Struggle for the Middle East* (1988).
Uthman, Hashim. *Al-Ahzab al-Siyasiyya fi Souriyya: al-Siriyya wa al-Mu'lana* (2001).
Zahr al-Din, Abd al-Karim. *Muzakarati an Fatrat al-Infisal fi Souriyya* (1968).

al-Quwatli, Shukri
(1892-1967)

Shukri al-Quwatli was born and raised in Damascus. He studied political science and public administration at the Muluki Academy in Istanbul and began his career in the Ottoman civil service in Damascus.

Quwatli joined the Arab underground in 1916 and became a founding member of al-Fatat, the leading opposition party in Ottoman Syria. Jamal Pasha, the military governor of Damascus, arrested Quwatli in 1916 on the charge of treason. In jail, Quwatli was tortured and he attempted suicide to stop himself from betraying the names of his fellow rebels in the underground movement. Ahmad Qadri, a fellow inmate who happened to be a practicing doctor, saved his life. When the Ottoman Empire collapsed in October 1918, Quwatli was released from prison and joined the newly created Arab civil service. From 1918 to 1920, he became an assistant to Ala al-Din al-Droubi, the governor of Damascus.

In July 1920, the French occupied Damascus and sentenced Quwatli to death for his anti-colonial activity. Quwatli fled to Germany and became an unofficial spokesman for the Syrian cause, speaking out against the French Mandate and demanding its termination. In 1922, he co-founded the Syrian-Palestinian Congress with a group of exiled nationalists dedicated to liberating the region from foreign control and establishing an Arab kingdom headed by the Hashemite family of Arabia. Particularly involved in the congress was King Faysal I, who had ruled Syria in the post-Ottoman era from 1918 to 1920, and his father Sharif Husayn, leader of the Arab uprising against the Ottoman Turks from 1916 to 1918. The Syrian-Palestinian Congress was headed by Prince Michel Lutfallah, a Lebanese banker, and Abd al-Rahman Shahbandar, a leading politician from the Ottoman era. Both men delegated Quwatli to raise funds for their activities in Europe, the Middle East, and North Africa.

Shukri al-Quwatli.

In July 1925, a military uprising against the French took place in Syria, headed by Sultan al-Atrash. The Syrian-Palestinian Congress hurried to raise funds for the uprising and recruit members into the rebel army. Quwatli toured Europe to raise money, and then went to Saudi Arabia to approach King Abd al-Aziz, an old friend of the Quwatli family. Abd al-Aziz had recently ousted Sharif Husayn from his kingdom in the Arabian Desert, and the Hashemites were infuriated by his friendship with Quwatli.

The congress leaders Shahbandar and Lutfallah asked Quwatli to choose between Husayn and Abd al-Aziz. Quwatli chose Aziz. Quwatli then distanced himself from the Syrian-Palestinian Congress and created a branch for himself that was still loyal to Syrian independence, but which relied on Saudi Arabia for political and financial support. He rallied the support of prominent politicians into his orbit, like Nabih al-Azma, Adil al-Azma, Prince Shakib Arslan, Prince Adil Arslan, and Amin al-Husayni, the Mufti of Jerusalem (an archenemy of the Hashemites). Shahbandar and Lutfallah accused Quwatli of betraying their cause and pocketing funds allocated for the resistance. In turn, Quwatli accused Shahbandar and Lutfallah of being agents of the Hashemites and Great Britain.

Quwatli spent the remainder of the 1920s engaged in a war of words with his former allies. When Shahbandar and Lutfallah, along with Atrash, called off the Syrian Revolt of 1925, Quwatli accused them of cowardice and called on the resistance in Damascus to continue fighting. He returned to Syria when the French issued a general amnesty in 1932 and joined the National Bloc, the leading anti-French movement in Syria, where he allied himself with the Bloc president, Hashim al-Atasi. The Bloc leaders were a combination of landowners, politicians, and lawyers who shared the common goal of seeing Syria free from foreign control. The Bloc brain trust wanted to liberate Syria from the French through diplomatic means rather than armed resistance. Quwatli became a member of the Permanent Office of the National Bloc.

In 1935, the National Bloc called Syria into a sixty-day strike to protest France's refusal to address the issue of Syrian independence in a "serious manner." Quwatli was a prime architect of the sixty-day strike and the French had him arrested for provoking violence against the mandate authority. The strike led to the killing of hundreds of civilians and the destruction of the Syrian economy, thereby embarrassing France and damaging her image in Europe.

In 1936, the French agreed to recognize the Bloc leaders as the legitimate representatives of the Syrian people and invited them for independence talks in Paris. Hashim al-Atasi headed the delegation and appointed Quwatli as acting president of the Bloc. In the absence of the Bloc's top leadership, Quwatli recruited many Damascenes into its ranks, all owing him direct allegiance. Quwatli relied heavily on quarter bosses (the traditional neighborhood strongmen), merchants, and middle-class professionals to market his leadership to the public. In 1936, his ally Amin al-Husayni launched a military uprising against the British and the Zionists in Palestine, inspired by the sixty-day strike in Syria against the French. Quwatli channeled arms, ammunition, and money to Husayni, and invited him to set up base in Damascus.

By the mid-1930s, Shukri al-Quwatli was literally the most popular man in Damascus, counterbalancing the two former city chiefs, Jamil Mardam Bey and Abd al-Rahman Shahbandar. The National Bloc delegation returned to Syria in November 1936, having secured a treaty with France that guaranteed independence over a twenty-five-year period. Quwatli became a deputy in parliament in 1936, running on a Bloc ticket and winning with an overwhelming majority. The Bloc was voted into office and Hashim al-Atasi became president of the republic, and Jamil Mardam Bey became prime minister. Quwatli became minister of finance and national economy in the Mardam Bey cabinet. Quwatli created the Ministry of Defense from scratch (since there had been no such portfolio in Syria).

Within a few months of taking office, however, Quwatli resigned over disagreements with Mardam Bey. Quwatli was opposed to Mardam Bey's willingness to comply with the French over financial concessions in Syria and argued that all financial deals should be made through him in his capacity as minister of finance. Mardam Bey ignored his plea and signed a financial deal with France without referring to Quwatli.

In 1939, Quwatli met with several Nazi officials in Syria and expressed his willingness to become an ally of the Nazis if Adolph Hitler would support the Arab quest for independence. The French responded to Quwatli's pro-German sympathies by exiling him to Saudi Arabia. King Abd al-Aziz lobbied on his behalf with British and French officials and secured his return to Syria in 1941. In return, Quwatli promised to refrain from any anti-French or pro-Nazi activity.

In 1943, having made peace with the French, Quwatli became a member of parliament and nominated himself for presidential office. Quwatli was elected president of the republic on August 17, 1943. He appointed Saadallah al-Jabiri, a notable from Aleppo in the National Bloc, as his first prime minister.

The Quwatli era was marked with an on-going diplomatic campaign for independence carried out by President Quwatli and Prime Minister Jabiri. They demanded immediate and unconditional independence, and refused to grant France any military, political, or economic privileges in Syria. Quwatli rallied support for his cause through US President Franklin Roosevelt and British Prime Minister Winston Churchill. To ally himself with both men, Quwatli declared war on Nazi Germany.

Roosevelt rewarded Syria's alliance by inviting a Syrian delegation to attend the founding conference of the United Nations in San Francisco on March 31, 1945. French President Charles de Gaulle responded to Quwatli's stubbornness by ordering an air raid on Damascus on May 29, 1945. French forces bombed the Syrian capital and tried to arrest Quwatli and his team. Churchill sent a special envoy to Damascus and asked Quwatli to go to Amman until matters settled down with the French, but the Syrian president refused, saying, "I will not leave! I am not Faysal (in reference to the Hashemite King who evacuated Syria to make way for the French in 1920)." Churchill then intervened with de Gaulle to stop the assault and dispatched British troops to Syria to oversee the evacuation of the French Army.

On April 17, 1945, with British support Quwatli was able to declare Syria independent. He presided over a constitutional democracy and multi-party system from 1946 to 1949. The highlight of his foreign policy was the alliance created with King Abd al-Aziz of Saudi Arabia, King Farouk of Egypt, and his longtime friend, President Bshara al-Khury of Lebanon. Quwatli's one enemy was King Abdullah of Jordan, who right after independence issued an appeal to the Syrian people, asking them to topple Quwatli and unite Syria with Jordan under the Hashemite crown. Quwatli responded by forbidding Abdullah entrance into Syria and not opening a Syrian embassy in Amman.

Matters between the two leaders were further strained during the Arab-Israeli War of 1948 when King Abdullah became commander-in-chief of the Arab Army fighting in Palestine. Quwatli accused Abdullah of betraying the Syrian Army in combat. When word of defeat reached Syria, angry protestors took to the streets, accusing the government of weakness and demanding the resignation of Quwatli and his new prime minister, Jamil Mardam Bey. Faced with a near-state of anarchy, Quwatli declared martial law, called in the army to maintain security, and appointed Mardam Bey as military governor of Syria. Mardam Bey arrested dissidents and closed anti-government newspapers, causing so much discontent that Quwatli was forced to dismiss him and appoint Khalid al-Azm as prime minister instead. The new prime minister clashed with the officers of the Syrian Army, accusing them of corruption and bringing many of them to trial on the charge of corruption that led to defeat at the war front.

On March 29, 1949, Chief of Staff Husni al-Za'im seized power in Syria through a military coup d'etat. He arrested Quwatli and Azm, dissolved parliament, and set up a military dictatorship that lasted until August 14, 1949. All of Quwatli's loyalists were persecuted, arrested, or exiled to Lebanon. Quwatli himself was forced to resign from office and exiled to Egypt, where he was treated as an honored guest by King Farouk and by the Free Officers who seized power in Cairo in July 1952. By 1954, Quwatli had befriended the new Egyptian president, Gamal Abd al-Nasser.

In 1955, Shukri al-Quwatli returned to Syria to nominate himself for presidential office. He campaigned against his former prime minister, Khalid al-Azm, and was elected president in August 1955. Quwatli pursued a radical pro-Egyptian foreign policy, believing in Arab nationalism and an alliance with the USSR. He established contacts with Eastern European countries, signed an arms deal with the Soviet Union, and severed his relations with Great Britain and France during the Suez Canal War in Egypt in 1956. Quwatli hurried to Moscow in 1956 to plead with the Russian leader Nikita Khrushev, pleading, "They (Britain, France, and Israel) want to destroy Egypt!" He tried to get the Soviet Army to back Nasser, and sent hundreds of Syrian recruits for combat in the Suez War. Quwatli and Nasser were the only Arab leaders to extend recognition to the communist regime in China.

The world viewed Syria during the second Quwatli presidency as a Soviet satellite, and two CIA attempts were made at toppling his regime in 1956 and 1957, but they both ended in failure. Quwatli's relations with neighboring Arab countries also plummeted and Syria got involved in espionage with Jordan, Lebanon, and Iraq, three regional powers that were opposed to Nasser's leadership.

Nasser pressured Quwatli to keep Abd al-Hamid Sarraj, a ruthless officer who had come to power in 1954, as chief of intelligence, and Afif al-Bizreh, a communist officer, as chief of staff. The two men were responsible for containing all political movements in Syria and arresting or dismissing all anti-Nasser officers in the Syrian Army. Quwatli further allied himself with the Egyptian president by appointing Salah al-Bitar, a socialist leader of the Baath Party, as minister of foreign affairs, and Akram al-Hawrani, another veteran socialist, as speaker of parliament.

In January 1958, Chief of Staff Bizreh headed an officer delegation to Cairo to plead for union with Nasser's Egypt. The officers went to Cairo with no authorization from the president. Quwatli dispatched his foreign minister to Cairo with the same demand, and then headed to Egypt to conduct serious negotiations over the merger of Syria and Egypt. Quwatli created the United Arab Republic (UAR) in February 1958 and resigned from presidential office in Syria to make room for Nasser to become president of both countries. To honor his struggle, Nasser appointed Quwatli "First Arab Citizen."

Shukri al-Quwatli retired from political activity during the union years (1958-1961). He repeatedly clashed with Nasser, however, and accused him of having imposed a dictatorship on Syria. Quwatli was highly critical of the land distribution program and the nationalization of industry that Nasser implemented in July 1961, claiming that this would damage Syria's economy for years to come.

Among those who lost property under the Egyptian socialist measures was Quwatli's son-in-law Fayez al-Ujl. Quwatli considered the nationalization of Ujl's property a personal insult, and criticized Nasser's socialism and the arbitrary arrests that became common in the UAR. He also spoke out against the closure of newspapers and the termination of all political parties.

On September 28, 1961, a group of officers launched a coup that ousted the UAR. Quwatli supported the coup and allied himself to the officer junta that came to power. At first Quwatli refused to comment on the union that he had created. Finally, he was intimidated into speaking by Israeli Radio, which broadcasted a program about him on the day after the secession coup. The Israeli broadcast addressed him, "Have you nothing to say? Many are waiting to hear whether this man still possesses the strength of youth and the courage of men. Get up man, and speak!" Quwatli then gave a televised speech supporting the "secession regime" from Switzerland on October 23, 1961.

This speech, generally overlooked by historians who deal with Shukri al-Quwatli, is expressive of his career and thoughts. In it, Quwatli harshly criticizes Nasser and the UAR, saying, "unity does not mean an act of annexation and the presidential system does not mean the separation of the ruler from the ruled." In the speech, Quwatli looks back at Nasser's record from 1958 to 1961 and says, "my disappointment is great and my amazement greater." He then addresses Egyptian authorities who administered union and calls them "executioners of the people," claiming that "it is this system of rule that struck the foundations of unity. It is the system of rule that has 1,001 spies." He warns, "had they (Nasser and his men), lasted longer, then the entire republic would have been divided." He then addresses the Syrian people directly, saying, "You are responsible for determining your own future. Ranks and titles come and go but you the people are immortal! I have known you for a long time and am certain that you cannot be wrong."

Then, in a moment of introspection, Quwatli expresses for the first time in public a self-evaluation and says, "I was able to serve your struggle as an ordinary citizen and as a struggling soldier more than I was able to serve you when I was president and ruler." He concludes, "The most that one who has worked in the public field as a child, in youth, and in old age can expect is that the ordinary citizen continues to be satisfied with him as a good citizen."

The officers, pleased at Quwatli's remarks, met to discuss the feasibility of tapping him for a fourth term as president. Due to to his age (seventy years), however, the idea never materialized. Some wanted to act as if the UAR had never taken place and restore Quwatli to office to complete what was left of his four-year term when he resigned in 1958.

When the Baath Party came to power in March 1963, Quwatli left Syria and took up residence in Beirut. He suffered a heart attack during the Arab-Israeli War of 1967 when he heard the news of the Syrian defeat and died on June 30,

1967. At first, authorities refused to allow his burial in Damascus but agreed under pressure from King Faysal of Saudi Arabia.

Shukri al-Quwatli received a hero's funeral in Damascus. "Shukri Bey," as he was known in Damascus, is considered by historians, academics, and Syrians in general as one of the most renowned Syrian leaders of the twentieth century.

Sources:

Azm, Khalid. *Muzakarat* (1973).

BBC World Service Archives "Shukri al-Quwatli's Speech" on October 23, 1961.

Faris, George. *Man Hum fi al-`Alam al-Arabi?* (1949).

Gaith, Yusuf. "Shukri al-Quwatli wa dawruh al-Siyasi" (*al-Quds* newspaper 2000).

Haffar, Salma. *Lutfi al-Haffar 1885-1968* (1997).

Halabi, Samir. *Shukri al-Quwatli wa al-Hayat fi Zil al-Mashanik* (2000).

Hawrani, Akram. *Muzakarat Akram al-Hawrani* (2000).

Historians from Syria. *Shukri al-Quwatli* (1948).

Kayyali, Abd al-Rahman. *Al-Marahil fi al-Intidab al-Faransi 1926-1938* (1958-1960).

Khani, Abdullah. *Jihad Shukri al-Quwatli* (2004).

Khoury, Philip. *Syria and the French Mandate* (1987).

Moubayed, Sami. *Damascus Between Democracy and Dictatorship* (2000).

Moubayed, Sami. *Shukri al-Quwatli and the Politics of Urban Notability* (2000).

Moubayed, Sami. *The Politics of Damascus 1920-1946* (1999).

Office of Information. *Al-Za'im al-Ra'is Shukri al-Quwatli* (1943).

Qassab Hasan, Najat. *Saniou al-Jalaa fi Souriyya* (1999).

Quwatli, Shukri. *Shukri al-Quwatli Yuwkhatib Ummatuh* (1970).

Rathmell, Andrew. *Secret War in the Middle East* (1995).

Seale, Patrick. *The Struggle for Power in Syria* (1961).

Torrey, Gordon. *Syrian Politics and the Military* (1964).

Yunis, Abd al-Latif. *Muzakarat Dr Abd al-Latif Yunis* (1992).

Yunis, Abd al-Latif. *Shukri al-Quwatli* (1959).

Interview with Dr Abdullah al-Khani (Damascus July 15, 2003).

Interview with General Suhayl al-Ashi (Damascus July 14, 2003).

Raslan, Mazhar
(1887-1949)

Mazhar Raslan belonged to a prominent landowning family in Homs. After secondary school, he studied public administration at the Muluki Academy in Istanbul. He graduated in 1910 and returned to Syria to administer his family estates during World War I.

Raslan joined the Arab underground working against the Ottoman Empire from 1916 to 1918. In October 1918, the Ottoman Empire was defeated and King Faysal I, commander of the anti-Ottoman revolt, became the new ruler of Syria. Raslan joined Faysal's court and became governor of Salt, a small town located in modern Jordan. In November 1919, Raslan became a member of the Syrian National Congress, the equivalent of a modern parliament created to administer affairs in the post-Ottoman period.

In July 1920, however, the French occupied Syria and imposed their mandate, dethroning Faysal and exiling all those who had supported him. Raslan fled to Amman where he became advisor to Faysal's brother, King Abdullah of Jordan. In August 1921, Abdullah gave Raslan Jordanian citizenship, bestowed upon him the princely title of pasha, and appointed him prime minister of Jordan.

Prime Minister Raslan remained in power from August 1921 until March 1922. In February 1923, he formed another government at Abdullah's request. This government lasted until September 1923. During his tenure as prime minister of Jordan, Mazhar Pasha laid out the modern infrastructure of Amman, constructing hospitals and schools, and relying heavily on Syrian merchants for investment. He packed the Jordanian court with Syrian officials and gave asylum to numerous Syrian fugitives escaping arrest or death in French Mandate Syria.

Raslan returned to Syria in 1925 and helped administer the Syrian revolt of the Arab Mountain launched against the mandate by the Druze leader Sultan Pasha al-Atrash. The French arrested Raslan in 1927 and charged him with high treason. He was released in 1928 when the French pardoned some of the revolt leaders. Raslan then joined the National Bloc, the leading anti-French movement in Syria, and became a prominent leader of its Homs branch. In June 1928, he held office on the Constitutional Assembly that drafted the first republican constitution for Syria. In 1932, he became minister of justice and education in the cabinet of Prime Minister Haqqi al-Azm.

In 1936, the Bloc was voted into office and Syria's new president, Hashim al-Atasi, appointed Raslan governor of Lattakia. From February to April 1939, Raslan held office as minister of interior and defense in the short-lived cabinet of Prime Minister Lutfi al-Haffar. In August 1943, President Shukri al-Quwatli, another Bloc leader, appointed Raslan minister of public works and supply in the cabinet of Prime Minister Saadallah al-Jabiri. Mazhar Raslan also served as a deputy for Homs in parliament from 1932 to 1939 and 1943 to 1949.

Sources:
Babil, Nasuh. *Sahafa wa Siyasa fi Souriyyia* (1987).
Haffar, Salma. *Lutfi al-Haffar 1885-1968* (1997).
Kayyali, Abd al-Rahman. *Al-Marahil fi al-Intidab al-Faransi 1926-1938* (1958-1960).

Khoury, Philip. *Syria and the French Mandate* (1987).

Moubayed, Sami. *The Politics of Damascus 1920-1946* (1999).

Shambrook, Peter. *French Imperialism in Syria 1927-1936* (1998).

Wilson, Mary. *King Abdullah of Jordan* (1989).

al-Razzaz, Munif
(1919-1984)

Munif al-Razzaz was born in Syria and raised in Jordan. He studied law in Amman and joined the Baath Party of Michel Aflaq and Salah al-Bitar in 1950. He co-founded the Jordanian branch of the Baath Party in Amman and promoted his party ideology in Jordanian newspapers.

From 1955 to 1957, the Jordanian Baath were vociferously opposed to the pro-Western views of King Hussein, and using the help of Syrian intelligence, they sought to bring down the Hashemite monarchy. Dr Razzaz spearheaded the anti-Husayn movement and criticized Husayn's adherence to the Baghdad Pact, an Anglo-American agreement created in the 1950s to contain communism in the Middle East. Razzaz also criticized Husayn's animosity with President Gamal Abd al-Nasser of Egypt and was imprisoned in 1956, 1958, 1959, and 1960.

In March 1963, the Baath Party came to power in Syria. In May 1965, its civilian leadership headed by Michel Aflaq clashed with the military officers, the de facto rulers of Syria headed by Chief of Staff Salah Jadid. The officers objected to the leadership of Aflaq, claiming that he was too moderate in his views and wanted to demilitarize Syria. The officers called for the dissolution of the National Command, a party organ that included all of Aflaq's supporters. And Aflaq tried to curb the influence of the Regional Command, another organ that was dominated by the officers.

Aflaq made Razzaz secretary-general of the National Command in January 1966. Razzaz called for an urgent session of the National Command and formed, on paper at least, a new leadership for Syria where Jadid's opponents were promoted in rank. Amin al-Hafez was kept at his post as president, Salah al-Bitar was made prime minister, and Mansur al-Atrash, a civilian Baathist, became president of the Revolutionary Command Council (RCC). Razzaz also created a new assembly that excluded members of the party's Military Committee. Mohammad Umran, an officer who was allied to the civilians, became minister of defense.

On February 21, 1966, Umran assumed his new post at the Ministry of Defense, and the following day the entire political leadership was deposed by a coup led by Jadid and Air Force Commander Hafez al-Asad. The two men dissolved the National Command, arrested President Amin al-Hafez, and ordered the arrest of Razzaz, Atrash, and Umran. Razzaz went into hiding, and from various hiding places in Damascus he issued manifestos calling for a counter-coup against the coup leaders.

In September 1966, Razzaz supported a coup launched by Saleem Hatum, but it ended in failure and Jadid arrested all of its leaders, forcing Razzaz to flee to Lebanon. He retired from political activity when Hafez al-Asad became president of Syria in 1970. President Saddam Hussein of Iraq gave Razzaz political asylum, but due to his views placed him under house arrest in Baghdad, where he died in 1984.

Munif al-Razzaz's most widely acclaimed work is *Al-Tajruba al-Murra* (*The Bitter Experience*), published in Beirut in 1967. Other works include *Makalat fi al-Ishtirakiyya* (*Articles on Socialism*), co-written with Michel Aflaq and the socialist leader Jamal al-Atasi in 1974.

Sources:
Razzaz, Munif. *Al-Tajruba al-Murra* (1967).
Razzaz, Munif. *Durus fi al-Hazeema* (1969).
Razzaz, Munif. *Tatawur Ma'na al-Qawmiyya* (1973).
Seale, Patrick. *Asad: Struggle for the Middle East* (1988).

Rida, Rashid
(1865-1935)

Rashid Rida came from a scholarly family in a village near Tripoli (modern Lebanon). He studied Islam with private tutors and mastered the Arabic language. At a young age, he joined the order of Muslim mystics and devoted himself to spiritual life and ascetic prayer.

Rida's views on Islam and life were completely changed when in 1884 he came across *al-Urwa al-Wuthqa*, a Muslim periodical published by the leading thinker of his generation, Mohammad Abdu. Rida met Abdu in Tripoli and became his student and friend. By the turn of the century, Rida had also become Abdu's public relations director, the guardian of his views, and his official biographer. Some viewed Rida as the spiritual heir to Abdu, similar to how Abdu had been the successor to his master, Jamal al-Din al-Afghani. Rida later recalled how Abdu's writings affected him, saying, "Every edition was like an electric current striking me, giving my soul a shock. My own experience, and that of others, and history, have taught me that no other Arabic discourse in this age or the centuries that preceded it has done what it did in the way of touching the seat of emotion in the heart and persuasion in the mind."

In 1897, Rida went to Cairo to write and preach with Abdu on Islamic revival. One year later, Rida founded his own periodical, *al-Manar*, reflecting Abdu's views on life, politics, and Islam. The publication included articles on Islamic reform, world politics, and different interpretations of the Qur'an. Rida also wrote a book on Mohammad Abdu that has become the single most important source for the history of the Muslim Arab mind in the late nineteenth century.

Rida tackled the question: "Why are the Muslim countries backward in every aspect of civilization?" He argued that if properly understood and fully obeyed, the teachings of Islam would lead to success both in this world and in the next. If the teachings were ignored, however, then barbarism, weakness, and decay would be the result, and this was the condition of the Muslim world in the late nineteenth century Rida argued. He was among the earliest thinkers to actually say that the Muslim world which he inhabited was decaying and needed repair. He noted that Muslims were currently more backward than non-Muslims. This could be seen in the Middle East and North Africa—a comparison between Muslims of the East and Christians of the West was not necessary. In comparing the Arab Muslims with the Christians living among them, Rida added, one can notice the clear difference in education, civilization, strength, and happiness. He founded an office for Muslim missionaries in Egypt in 1912, designed to promote his views, but it only remained active until World War I broke out in 1914.

Like Abdu, Rida was highly critical of the Khedive Abbas Hilmi of Egypt and of his ancestor Mohammad Ali Pasha, the founder of modern Egypt. Rida's views got him into trouble in Egypt and he gave up on politics and shifted instead to Ottoman affairs. Prior to the war, Rida had allied himself with the Party of Decentralization, a Syrian opposition party based in Cairo and headed by Rafic al-Azm. The party called for a break in the centralization of power practiced by the Ottoman Turks in Istanbul and demanded more autonomy for the Arab provinces in the Ottoman Empire.

Rida was not an opponent of the Ottoman Empire in theory, however, believing that it was needed to unify Muslims and protect them against foreign influence. He remained an advocate of the empire until it was defeated in October 1918. He then shifted his allegiance to the post-Ottoman order created by Faysal I, the new ruler of Syria.

Rashid Rida became a deputy for Homs in the Syrian National Congress (the equivalent of a modern parliament) that administered political affairs in post-Ottoman Syria. He was elected president of the congress and kept this post until May 1920.

When the French imposed their mandate over Syria in July 1920, Rida went to Egypt once again to work on *al-Manar*. In 1922, he co-founded the Syrian-Palestinian Congress with a group of exiled nationalists, whose goal was to liberate the region from foreign control and establish an Arab kingdom headed by the Hashemite family of Arabia. Particularly involved in the congress was King Faysal I, who had ruled Syria in the post-Ottoman era from 1918 to 1920, and his father Sharif Husayn, leader of the Arab uprising against the Ottoman Turks from 1916 to 1918. The congress was headed by Prince Michel Lutfallah, a

Lebanese banker, and Abd al-Rahman Shahbandar, a leading politician from the Ottoman era. Rida served as vice president of the congress.

In July 1925, a military uprising broke out against the French from the Arab Mountain in Syria. The congress leaders created political committees to raise arms, funds, and ammunition for the resistance in Syria, and Rida became a member of the Higher Committee of the Great Syrian Revolt in Egypt. In 1926, he allied himself with Shukri al-Quwatli, a young congress member who was distancing himself from the Hashemite family for their connections to Great Britain. When Quwatli had come to Egypt in 1920, Rida had taken him under his wing and introduced him to the different political movements in Egypt.

Rida broke with Shahbandar and Lutfallah in October 1927 and headed (with Quwatli and Prince Shakib Arslan) a faction of the congress in Cairo loyal to Syrian independence but allied to King Abd al-Aziz of Saudi Arabia. Matters erupted between the two groups when Lutfallah and Shahbandar called for a cease-fire in November 1927. Rashid Rida spoke out in favor of Quwatli's argument, claiming that the Hashemites who were protecting Lutfallah and Shahbandar and calling for a cease-fire, were "the worst disaster that has befallen Islam in this age." By relying so much on the British, Rida argued, the two men along with their Hashemite patrons, had paved the way for British occupation of the Middle East and "cheated" the Syrians with false promises of independence.

Shahbandar responded from Amman that Rida and his allies were nothing but "idealists" who had no clue what revolution was really like. There was, he added, an immense military obstacle in keeping the revolt alive, in addition to the fact that funds and morale was running low and could not survive more battles. Rida's allies hurried to defend him and accused Shahbandar of treason, leading Shahbandar to take matters into his own hands and call off the revolt.

Rashid Rida ceased political activity after that, and continued to publish *al-Manar* until his death in 1935. When he died, he was hailed as one of the most important Muslim thinkers of the twentieth century.

Sources:
Center for National History al-Qism al-Khas, Shahbandar File 10/26 (Shahbandar to Hakim April 22, 1927).
Hourani, Albert. *Arabic Thought in the Liberal Age* (1961).
Khoury, Philip. *Syria and the French Mandate* (1987).

al-Rikabi, Rida
(1864-1942)

Rida al-Rikabi studied at the Ottoman Military Academy in Istanbul and began his career as an officer in the Ottoman Empire. He rose to the rank of general in

1901 and was one of the most reliable Arab soldiers serving in the Ottoman Army during World War I. In reward for his services, he was given the princely title of pasha from the Ottoman Sultan.

Rikabi became commander of Ottoman troops in Jerusalem and in 1908 was appointed army commander and mayor of Medina. He then became commander of the Ottoman Army in Baghdad, but was retired by his superiors after World War I began in 1914 for having a "defeatist" attitude. (Rikabi had argued—rightly it turns out—that the Ottoman Army would lose the war.)

Rikabi then joined the rebel army of Sharif Husayn, the Prince of Mecca, who was leading an armed uprising against the Ottoman Empire from the Arabian Desert. Rikabi worked as a mayor of Damascus and advisor to Jamal Pasha, while also working undercover in the Damascus underground.

Faysal I, the new ruler of Syria, appointed Rikabi prime minister and military governor on October 1, 1918. Following the Ottoman evacuation, looting and vandalism took place in Damascus in the absence of a police force to keep order. Rikabi arrested scores of troublemakers and created a public execution arena in Marjeh Square in downtown Damascus, threatening, "I won't be more merciful than the Ottomans!" He had a hard time imposing order on a country liberated after four hundred years of Ottoman control.

The Rikabi government, being the first independent cabinet in Syrian history, led Syria into troubled times, for shortly after its formation, French troops landed on the Syrian coastline in anticipation of proclaiming a French Mandate in Syria. The French Army occupied the coastal city of Lattakia, and on July 14, 1920, presented King Faysal with an ultimatum, demanding that he dissolve his kingdom and authorize the establishment of the French Mandate in Syria and

Rida al-Rikabi.

Lebanon. Rikabi refused to send his troops to war, claiming that they would suffer humiliating defeat.

Rikabi resigned from office in July 1920, weeks before Syria was occupied by France. When the mandate was proclaimed, a French military tribunal sentenced him to death, forcing him to flee to Amman. Rikabi served as military advisor to King Abdullah of Jordan and in March 1922 became the first prime minister of Jordan. In his new post, Rida Pasha relied heavily on Syrian politicians, who like him had been exiled by the French, and he laid the foundations of a modern state in Jordan's tribal society.

In May 1924, Prime Minister Rikabi made his peace with the mandate authority and was welcomed back to Syria. In December 1931, he created the Monarchial Party, a loose coalition of ex-Ottoman officers and statesmen who had held office under Faysal (1918-1920) and demanded Faysal's return to the throne in Syria. Rikabi became a deputy for Damascus in 1932 and nominated himself for presidential office, but was defeated by the independent politician Mohammad Ali al-Abid. When King Faysal died in September 1933, Rida al-Rikabi retired from political life and died in Damascus on May 25, 1942.

Sources:
Husari, Sati. *Yawm Maysloun* (1947).
Khoury, Philip. *Syria and the French Mandate* (1987).
Moubayed, Sami. *The Politics of Damascus 1920-1946* (1999).
Russell, Malcom. *The First Modern Arab State: Syria under Faysal I* (1987).

Sa'ada, Antune
(1904-1949)

Antune Sa'ada was born and raised in Brazil where his father Khalil published an Arabic newspaper. In 1928, Sa'ada moved to his native Duhur Shuwayr village in Mount Lebanon, then took up residence in Damascus and worked as a journalist for Nasuh Babil's daily *al-Ayyam*.

On November 16, 1932, Sa'ada founded a secret society of five intellectuals, bound by an oath of loyalty to himself, called the Syrian Social Nationalist Party (SSNP). The SSNP first flourished among students at the American University of Beirut (AUB) and spread to other intellectual centers in Lebanon and Syria. At first, Sa'ada's audience was a limited number of teachers and students who came to hear him speak over tea at the staff common room at AUB. The SSNP was a radical, secular paramilitary party that believed in the Syrian identity and refused to recognize the current boundaries of the Arab world.

Sa'ada said, "Syria belongs to the Syrians who constitute a nation complete in itself. The Syrian homeland is that geographic environment where the Syrian nation evolved. It has natural boundaries which separate it from other countries extending from the Taurus range in the northwest and Zagros Mountains in the northeast to the Suez Canal and the Red Sea in the south and includes the Sinai Peninsula and the Gulf of Aqaba and from the Syrian Sea (Mediterranean Sea) in the west, including the island of Cyprus to the Arch of the Arabian Desert and the Persian Gulf in the east.

Antune Sa'ada.

This region is also called the Syrian Fertile Crescent with the island of Cyprus being its star."

In 1935, the SSNP emerged from the underground and held its first conference in Beirut, challenging the first Lebanese Republic of President Charles

Debbas by refusing to recognize the country's legitimacy as an independent state, claiming instead that it must merge with Greater Syria. Authorities in Beirut feared Sa'ada's views and ordered his arrest on December 10, 1935. The French Mandate authority brought him to trial and accused him of treason. He boldly countered the French court and said that it was the French who had committed treason against Syria when they signed the Sykes-Picot Agreement in 1916 and carved up the Middle East into mandates for themselves and Great Britain.

The trial brought Sa'ada much publicity, and he spent some time in jail before being released into exile. He went to Europe where he lived during World War II and was often heard broadcasting his views on Radio Berlin and expressing support for the Axis in their war against France and Great Britain.

Sa'ada returned to Beirut on March 3, 1947, having spent nine years in exile, and reactivated his campaign for unity with the Syrian fatherland. His return was facilitated by the Lebanese Druze leader Kamal Jumblatt and Interior Minister Kamil Sham'un, both of whom wanted Sa'ada's political support in the upcoming parliamentary elections. At the airport, Sa'ada gave a provocative speech and called his comrades to arms to topple the regime of President Bshara al-Khury. Sa'ada was highly critical of Khury's plan to amend the constitution to permit his reelection for another term at the presidency, and he was also opposed to the National Pact of confessional coexistence that Khury had conducted in 1943 with his prime minister, Riyad al-Sulh. The confessional coexistence described in the National Pact divided powers in Lebanon among Muslims and Christians, in opposition to the secular nature of the SSNP.

Sa'ada also had an intense dislike for Sulh which dated back to 1935 when Sa'ada had supported Khayr al-Din al-Ahdab, rather than Sulh, as prime minister. Sa'ada also accused Sulh and Khury of working against his Greater Syria project, and they fired back, accusing Sa'ada of wanting to overthrow the government. Sa'ada made his views public when he said that coexistence with Sulh and Khury was impossible, telling the SSNP, "its either them or us."

On June 9, 1949, armed violence broke out in the Jazmatiyya neighborhood in Beirut, where the SSNP printing press was located. Sa'ada's forces clashed with the Phalange Party of Pierre Gemayel, a vanguard of Lebanese independence which had struggled for a Christian-dominated Lebanon and an ally of Lebanese Prime Minister Riyad al-Sulh. Sa'ada accused Gemayel's forces of acting on orders from Prime Minister Sulh and of deliberately killing members of the SSNP. A court headed by Rashid al-Sulh (Riyad's brother) was set up to investigate. The court found the SSNP guilty of the armed violence and the party was shut down. Around seven hundred party members were arrested but escaped to Syria.

Antune Sa'ada arrived in Damascus and was warmly received by Syria's new president, Husni al-Za'im. Both men saw many enemies in the Sulh administration in Lebanon and longed to bring it down. Sa'ada wanted to do so for ideological reasons while Za'im wanted to topple the Sulh cabinet that was hostile to his regime and replace it with a friendly administration. Za'im offered Sa'ada money and 5,000 soldiers to launch an insurrection into Lebanon.

Sa'ada declared Damascus to be the "headquarters of the first popular social revolution," and began his war on Lebanon in July 1949. Sa'ada's men crossed the border with orders to attack government offices and police stations in Beirut, the Shouf, al-Metn, and the Beqqa Valley. But they were immediately apprehended by Lebanese authorities. One group walked straight into an ambush. Another group was disarmed and forced to surrender, while a third group discovered that it had been sent into combat with machine guns that had the wrong caliber ammunition.

Juliet al-Meer, the widow of Antune Saada, was arrested in 1954 after the SSNP assassinated Adnan al-Malki, the deputy chief-of-staff. She was released from jail when the Baath Party came to power in 1963.

To Sa'ada's dismay, a secret deal had been struck between Husni al-Za'im and Riyad al-Sulh, where Za'im would hand over Sa'ada in return for Lebanon's endorsement of the Za'im regime. On July 6, 1949, Za'im delivered Sa'ada to Lebanon, where he was executed by firing squad on July 8.

Sa'ada's legacy continues to live until today, and he is probably one of the most inspiring and charismatic Arab philosophers of the twentieth century. His death in July 1949 led to Husni al-Za'im's own killing in August 1949, and Riyad al-Sulh's assassination in July 1951. In his book, *The Struggle for Syria*, Patrick Seale writes, "Sa'ada inspired devotion as probably no other leader in Arab politics had done. Many who knew him at this time describe him as a sort of intellectual dictator: authoritarian, magnetic, immensely fluent, with a brilliant knowledge of many subjects."

Antune Sa'ada's most famous publication is a philosophical work outlining his policies, written while he was in prison and published in 1938 entitled, *Nushu' al-Umam* (*The Rise of Nations*). His other famous work, *Al-Islam fi Risalatuh al-Masihiyya wa al-Muhamadiyya* (*Islam in its Christian and Muslim Message*), was published in 1945.

Sources:
Fansa, Bashir. *Al-Naqbat wa al-Mughamarat* (1997).
Fansa, Nazir. *137 Yawm Hazzat Souriyya wa al-Watan al-Arabi* (1982).
Moubayed, Sami. *Damascus Between Democracy and Dictatorship* (2000).
Rathmell, Andrew. *Secret War in the Middle East* (1995).

Seale, Patrick. *The Struggle for Syria* (1965).

Sarraj, Abd al-Hamid
(1925-)

Abd al-Hamid Sarraj studied at the Homs Military Academy and began his career as an officer in the French gendarmerie. In 1946, following independence, he joined the Syrian Army and fought in the Arab-Israeli War of 1948.

At the war front Sarraj befriended Chief of Staff General Husni al-Za'im. When the latter came to power in March 1949, he appointed Sarraj as his private bodyguard. Sarraj failed at preventing a coup on August 14, 1949, that led to the capture and killing of General Za'im. Officers close to the Syrian leader accused Sarraj of being involved in the conspiracy against Za'im.

Sarraj allied himself with General Adib al-Shishakli when Shishakli seized power in November 1951, and Sarraj became assistant military attaché to Egypt. When Shishakli was ousted in February 1954, Sarraj shifted his allegiance to Chief of Staff Shawkat Shuqayr, who appointed Sarraj director of the Deuxième Bureau, Syria's central intelligence agency.

In the mid-1950s, Sarraj joined the movement of Arab nationalism headed by President Gamal Abd al-Nasser of Egypt. In April 1954, Colonel Adnan al-Malki, the deputy chief of staff, was assassinated in Damascus by members of the Syrian Social Nationalist Party (SSNP) who were opposed to his pro-Egyptian policies. Sarraj played an instrumental role in investigating the Malki murder and crushing the SSNP. He lobbied to outlaw the party, then arrested all of its principal leaders on the charge of murder. The party leader Issam al-Mahayri was arrested and so was Juliette al-Murr, widow of the party founder Antune Sa'ada. Ghassan Jadid, another leading party member, escaped to Beirut. Sarraj hunted him down and had him assassinated on February 19, 1957.

That same year, Sarraj helped uncover a plot to overthrow the pro-Egyptian regime of President Shukri al-Quwatli. The conspiracy was funded by Iraq and executed by a group of leading politicians from Syria, including Munir al-Ajlani, Hasan al-Atrash, Adnan al-Atasi, and Mikhail Ilyan. Some of these men had been leaders of the nationalist movement against the French occupation of Syria from 1920 to 1946, but to Sarraj they were all traitors. He arrested the conspirators and sentenced them either to death or life imprisonment.

Abd al-Hamid Sarraj's bent for police work, his dominant personality, and his large following among junior officers in the Syrian Army attracted the attention of Gamal Abd al-Nasser in Cairo. Sarraj became Nasser's protégé and "special agent" in Syria. He transformed the Syrian Intelligence Bureau into a massive espionage network that promoted Nasserist propaganda, purged anti-Nasserist elements, and maneuvered Syrian politics in the direction of Nasser's principal ally, the USSR. In 1956, as Egypt was leading its war against Israel, France, and Great Britain, Sarraj ordered the destruction of British pipelines in the Syrian Desert without getting permission from superior officers. And he pressured President Quwatli to banish the British ambassador from Syria.

Sarraj earned a reputation for ruthlessness unmatched in modern Syrian history, and he was accused of dissolving his prisoners in sulfuric acid. By 1957, he was funding and co-planning military coups against Nasser's prime enemies in the Arab world, King Saud of Saudi Arabia, President Kamil Sham'un of Lebanon, Prime Minister

Abd al-Hamid Sarraj.

Nuri al-Sa'id of Iraq, and King Hussein of Jordan. Sarraj repeatedly tried and failed to assassinate all four leaders from 1956 to 1958. President Shukri al-Quwatli and Defense Minister Khalid al-Azm tried to dismiss him from office in 1957, but his officers threatened a military insurrection. Fearing trouble, Quwatli and Azm postponed their decision, then called it off completely.

When Syria and Egypt merged to form the United Arab Republic (UAR) in 1958, Sarraj was the most powerful man in Syria. Nasser appointed him minister of interior in the UAR, giving him unlimited authority in dealing with the Syrian province. From 1958 to 1960, Sarraj's police measures increased dramatically, unintentionally destroying the image of Gamal Abd al-Nasser in Syria. He cracked down on dissent and terminated the Syrian Communist Party as he had done the SSNP. He arrested activists from all parties and closed most newspapers. In 1960, Nasser appointed him president of the Provincial Council, the most powerful state institution in the UAR.

By 1961, Sarraj had grown so powerful that even Nasser began fearing his authority. Nasser relieved him of his duties and appointed him instead vice president of the UAR, a purely ceremonial post. At his new job Sarraj clashed with Nasser's other right-hand man, Abd al-Hakim Amer, and tried to dismiss him from office. Amer was Nasser's best friend, having served with him in the Arab-Israeli War of 1948 and the Free Officer Revolution of 1952. Sarraj thought that Nasser would support him against Amer, but he was mistaken.

Nasser sided with Amer and forced Sarraj to resign on September 26, 1961. His offices were closed, his allies were fired from their posts, and the prisoners he had arrested were set free. A number of notable Syrians objected to his resignation, but the majority of the population was relieved. Among Sarraj's loyalists was the writer Shukri Faysal, the journalist Bakri al-Muradi, the Director of Interior Security Mohammad al-Jarrah, and the attorneys Rashad al-Jannan and Zuhayr al-Midani.

On September 28, 1961, the UAR was dissolved by a military coup led by

Colonel Abd al-Karim al-Nehlawi. The officers who seized power arrested Sarraj and brought him to trial as a war criminal. He escaped in May 1962 and took up residence in Beirut. In 1964, the SSNP tried to kill him, but he fled from Lebanon to Cairo where he made peace with Nasser and set up permanent base in Egypt. He was appointed director of Egyptian social security and remained in Egypt under Anwar al-Sadat (1970-1981) and the current government of President Husni Moubarak. As of 2004, Abd al-Hamid Sarraj still resided in Cairo.

Sources:
Commins, David. *Historical Dictionary of Modern Syria* (1996).
Juma, Sami. *Awrak Min Daftar al-Watan* (2001).
Moubayed, Sami. *Damascus Between Democracy and Dictatorship* (2000).
Seale, Patrick. *The Struggle for the Middle East* (1961).
Zakariya, Ghassan. *Al-Sultan al-Ahmar* (1991).

Selu, Fawzi
(1905-1972)

Fawzi Selu studied at the Homs Military Academy and joined the French-sponsored Troupe Speciales after the French Mandate was implemented in Syria in July 1920. He rose steadily in rank and when Syria achieved independence in April 1946, he became director of the Homs Military Academy.

Selu served as a commanding officer in the Arab-Israeli War of 1948 and befriended Chief of Staff Husni al-Za'im, who upon coming to power in March 1949 appointed Selu military attaché to the Syrian-Israeli armistice talks. Selu became the chief architect of the cease-fire that was signed in July 1949. Selu showed a willingness to reach a comprehensive peace deal with Israel. Za'im asked him to propose a broad agreement with the Jewish State that included the resettlement of Palestinian refugees in Syria, the opening of a Syrian embassy in Tel Aviv, and restoration of Lake Tiberias and Galilee to Syria. The idea was welcomed by Israeli Foreign Minister Moshe Sharett, but it never materialized because Za'im was killed in August 1949. Za'im was replaced by the civilian leader Hashim al-Atasi, who upheld the armistice agreement, but refused to discuss peace with Israel.

Selu then allied himself with General Adib al-Shishakli, who seized power in November 1951 and overthrew the Atasi government. Shishakli had been the de facto ruler of Syria since 1949 and had appointed Selu, a military officer, as minister of defense in the cabinets of Khalid al-Azm, Nazim al-Qudsi, and Hasan al-Hakim, claiming that the portfolio of defense should not be held by a civilian. On November 28, Syria's new prime minister, Ma'ruf al-Dawalibi, created a new cabinet, but did not appoint Selu as minister of defense, maintaining that military officers must stop meddling in political affairs. Shishakli retaliated by arresting Dawalibi and his entire government on November 29.

In protest, Atasi resigned from the presidency and Shishakli appointed Selu, making him president of the republic, prime minister, and chief of staff. Real authority, however, lay in the hands of Shishakli, who gave himself the less public post of deputy chief of staff. The two men ran a police state in Syria, outlawing political parties, arresting opposition figures, and monitoring the lives of civilian leaders. Selu dissolved the existing parliament and terminated Syria's constitution while drafting a new one that gave broader powers to the president. He strengthened Syria's relations with Jordan, and under Shishakli's orders, opened the first Syrian Embassy in Amman and befriended King Talal. He also improved relations with Lebanon, Saudi Arabia, and Egypt.

On July 11, 1953, Shishakli brushed Selu aside and appointed himself president of the republic. General Selu left Syria and took up residence in Riyadh, becoming advisor to King Saud and his brother, King Faysal al-Saud. When Shishakli was overthrown by military coup in February 1954, a military court in Damascus charged Fawzi Selu with corruption, political abuse, and of amending the Syrian Constitution. He was sentenced to death in absentia.

Sources:

Commins, David. *Historical Dictionary of Modern Syria* (1996).
Khayyer, Hani. *Adib al-Shishakli* (1994).
Moubayed, Sami. *Damascus Between Democracy and Dictatorship* (2000).
Rathmell, Andrew. *Secret War in the Middle East* (1995).
Seale, Patrick. *The Struggle for Syria* (1961).
Torrey, Gordon. *Syrian Politics and the Military.*

Shahbandar, Abd al-Rahman
(1879-1940)

Abd al-Rahman Shahbandar studied medicine at the American University of Beirut (AUB) and became a professor at its Faculty of Medicine. He returned to Damascus in 1908 to join the Arab political underground. Meanwhile, he opened a clinic in Damascus and became private physician to Jamal Pasha, the Ottoman military governor of Syria.

In 1913, Shahbandar signed a famed declaration, presented to the first Arab Congress in Paris, demanding emancipation from the Ottoman Empire. In 1914, he was approached by members of the Zionist National Agency to assist in establishing a Zionist state in Palestine. In exchange, the Zionists promised to support the liberation of the Arab world from Ottoman control and the establishment of an independent Arab kingdom. Shahbandar welcomed the idea and wrote extensively in favor of the Jewish proposal, meeting with Zionist leader David Ben Gurion for the purpose.

In 1914, Shahbandar's activities aroused Ottoman suspicion and a warrant was issued for his arrest. He fled to Egypt where he practiced medicine and came into contact with British intellectuals, doctors, and officers. He became vehemently pro-British during World War I and allied himself with the Hashemite family in Arabia who were fighting to topple the Ottoman Empire. In Cairo, Shahbandar became a freemason and befriended leading British statesmen who put him in contact with US President Woodrow Wilson. Shahbandar approached the American president as a spokesman for the Arab world and demanded US support for an Arab world independent from Ottoman influence.

In 1918, the Ottoman Empire was defeated and Shahbandar returned to Syria, becoming minister of foreign affairs in the regime of King Faysal I (1918-1920). He also became Faysal's private envoy, translator, and political consultant. In 1919, Shahbandar joined a group of Arab educators and founded the Arab Academy of Medicine. It was the first independent academic institute in post-Ottoman Syria. Along with a group of doctors, Munif al-Aidi, Rida Sa'id, and Ahmad Hamdi al-Khayyat, Shahbandar translated all medical works from Ottoman Turkish into Arabic, recruited a faculty and staff for the new institute, served on the board of directors, and taught at the faculty. When the French Army took over Syria in July 1920, they sentenced Shahbandar to death for his Hashemite sympathies, forcing him into exile.

From 1920 to 1922, Shahbandar remained in Europe, acting as an unofficial spokesman for the Syrian cause. He visited Western capitals, met with whoever was willing to receive him, and preached Arab unity, Syrian independence, calling for an Arab kingdom under the Hashemite crown. He joined Michel Lutfallah, Faysal's private banker, in forming the Syrian-Palestinian Congress, a coalition of nationalists in exile who were working for the Arab cause. The congress was headed by both men and funded by the Hashemite royals.

In 1922, a general amnesty allowed Shahbandar to return to Damascus where he opened a clinic. He quickly established contacts with American statesmen sympathetic to the Arab cause and held intellectual forums at his home to recruit locals into his political following. Later in the year he was once again arrested, and the French sentenced him to twenty years in prison for his involvement in what was labeled an "American plot" to topple the mandate. A French amnesty set him free in 1923. He returned to his medical practice and eventually became the best-known Syrian physician of his day. He helped found Damascus University, becoming a professor at its Faculty of Medicine.

In June 1925, Abd al-Rahman Shahbandar founded the People's Party, the first political movement in French Mandate Syria. The party promoted the creation of a constitutional government in a free and unified Syria that would include

Palestine, Jordan, and parts of Lebanon. The party was composed of leading statesmen, lawyers, and professors who were to become nationalist leaders in the 1940s.

On July 18, 1925, Shahbandar joined Sultan al-Atrash, another Hashemite protégé, and declared the Syrian revolt of the Arab Mountain, a national uprising against the French launched by the Druze community and funded by the Hashemites. Shahbandar helped fund the rebels, provided them with shelter in Damascus orchards, and called on Damascus fighters to take part in the uprising. He also wrote all revolutionary material dealing with the revolt, was charged with its political communiqués, distributed anti-French pamphlets, and served as speechwriter to Atrash, who became commander-in-chief of the Syrian Resistance. The French sentenced Shahbandar to death on the charge of high treason and he was once again forced into exile, living briefly in Amman, then moving to Europe where he spent the next eleven years in exile. French authorities confiscated his property, arrested his followers, and outlawed his People's Party.

In 1936, the French signed an independence treaty with the National Bloc, the leading anti-French movement that had emerged in Shahbandar's absence. The Bloc leaders were voted into office and promised independence from France over a gradual twenty-five-year period. Shortly after their rise to power in 1936, the French, fearing the outbreak of war in Europe, breached their promises and canceled the treaty. Shahbandar, who had returned home in 1936, grabbed at the opportunity to criticize the Bloc leadership for failing to impose themselves on French circles. He clashed with Prime Minister Jamil Mardam Bey, who had drafted the treaty, and accused him of being a stooge of the French. Mardam Bey snapped back by accusing Shahbandar of being on the British payroll and claiming that he was working to destroy Syria's republican regime and impose a Hashemite monarchy instead. Shahbandar rallied his followers to bring down the Mardam Bey cabinet, and the prime minister responded by having Shahbandar arrested. During the confrontation, a bomb exploded in Mardam Bey's car, and it was widely believed that Shahbandar had planted it. The French persecuted Shahbandar's followers and placed him under 24-hour police surveillance.

In 1939, Shahbandar further clashed with Mardam Bey over the Turkish annexation of the Sanjak of Alexanderetta, territory in northern Syria that had once been part of the Ottoman Empire. When France gave the Sanjak to Turkey, Shahbandar launched a publicity campaign claiming that Mardam Bey was involved in

Abd al-Rahman Shahbandar.

From the collection of Colette Khury.

the deal and had conducted the barter with Turkish President Kemal Ataturk. These aaccusatins led to Mardam Bey's downfall in 1939, whereupon Shahbandar immediately offered himself as a substitute.

In July 1940, however, local agents of the mandate authority assassinated Shahbandar at his clinic in Damascus. To honor his achievements, the Syrians buried him next to the shrine of Saladin, the twelfth century Islamic sultan who fought off the Christian crusaders and recaptured Jerusalem. A French court accused Jamil Mardam Bey of murdering Shahbandar, but he was declared innocent of the charges.

During his lifetime, Abd al-Rahman Shahbandar published several books about nationalism in Syria. The most famous is *Al-Thawra al-Wataniyya al-Souriyya* (*The Syrian National Revolt*), published in Damascus in 1933.

Sources:
Babil, Nasuh. *Sahafa wa Siyasa fi Souriyya* (1987).
Hakim, Hasan. *Muzakarati* (1965).
Hakim, Hasan. *Abd al-Rahman Shahbandar* (1985).
Hakim, Yusuf. *Souriyya wa al-Intidab al-Faransi* (1966).
Hanna, Abdullah. *Abd al-Rahman Shahbandar 1879-1940* (1989).
Itri, Abd al-Ghani. *Abqariyyat* (1996).
Khoury, Philip. *Syria and the French Mandate* (1987).
Mardam Bey, Jamil. *Syria's Quest for Independence* (1994).
Moubayed, Sami. *The Politics of Damascus 1920-1946* (1999).
Saikaly, Samir. *Abd al-Rahman Shahbandar: The Beginings of a Nationalist Career* (1986).
Saikaly, Samir. *Damascus Intellectual Life in the Opening Years of the 20th Century* (1981).
Shahbandar, Abd al-Rahman. *Al-Amal al-Kamila* (1989).
Shahbandar, Abd al-Rahman. *Al-Thawra al-Wataniyya al-Souriyya* (1933).
Shambrook, Peter. *French Imperialism in Syria 1927-1936* (1998).
Interview with Dr Munir al-Ajlani (Beirut August 13, 1999; September 14, 1999).

al-Shara, Farouk
(1938-)

Farouk al-Shara studied English literature at Damascus University, graduating in 1963, and obtained a diploma from the University of London.

Shara began his career in 1963 as manager of Syrian Arab Airlines in Dubai, moving shortly thereafter to the London office where he remained until President Hafez al-Asad appointed him ambassador to Italy in 1976. In 1980, Shara became minister of state for foreign affairs in the cabinet of Prime Minister Abdel Raouf al-Kassem. In 1984, Asad appointed him minister of foreign affairs. Shara helped Asad negotiate Syria's involvement in Operation Desert Storm in 1991, working to liberate Kuwait from Iraq. Following the collapse of the USSR in 1991, Shara was charged with mending Syria's relations with the USA and its allies.

Farouk al-Shara.

On October 30, 1991, Farouk al-Shara journeyed to the Madrid Peace Conference on behalf of Asad. For the next ten years, Shara would remain occupied with the peace process with Israel. For the conference, Shara had prepared a moderate speech with Ambassador Walid al-Moualim but decided to tear it up after hearing a provocative speech by Israeli Prime Minister Yitzhak Shamir. The Israeli premier had accused Syria of being a terrorist state, and Shara responded by rising to the podium and showing a newspaper clipping from 1948 with a picture of Shamir and the word "WANTED" written above it in bold letters. Shara addressed the conference and said, "I will just show you, if I may, an old photograph of Mr Shamir. Why was this picture distributed? Because he was WANTED! He helped, as I recall, in the assassination of Count Bernadotte, the UN mediator in Palestine in 1948. He kills peace mediators!"

Shara then marketed Syria's "land-for-peace" formula and negotiated along the lines of Asad's strategy: peace with Israel in exchange for a return of the Golan Heights occupied by Israel since 1967.

In December 1999, Shara met Israeli Prime Minister Ehud Barak at the White House in Washington, DC. Despite heavy American bargaining, no breakthrough was made in the Syrian-Israeli peace track. Barak and Shara met again in Shepherdstown, West Virginia, but the meeting also ended in failure.

Shara accompanied Asad on all his journeys and was also present at the March 2000 summit in Geneva with US President Bill Clinton. This summit also failed at solving the Syrian-Israeli conflict. In June 2000, Asad died and his son Bashar al-Asad became president of the republic. The new president kept Shara at his post as minister of foreign affairs, and in December 2001 made him deputy to Prime Minister Mohammad Mustapha Miro. Apart from President Asad, Farouk al-Shara is the most well-known Syrian politician in the world.

Sources:
Bawab, Sulayman. *Mawsuat Alam Souriyya fi al-Qarn al-Ishreen,* Vol III (1999).

Bergman, Ahron. Tahri, Jihan. *The Fifty Years War* (1998).
Syrian Arab News Agency (SANA).

al-Sharabati, Ahmad
(1909-1975)

Ahmad al-Sharabati studied engineering at the American University of Beirut
(AUB) and obtained his graduate degree from the Massachusetts Institute of
Technology (MIT). His father, Uthman al-Sharabati, was a prominent merchant
who helped finance the nationalist movement against the French Mandate in the
1920s and 1930s.

The young Sharabati returned to Damascus and ran a tobacco factory, serving
also as an agent for General Motors in Syria. In August 1933, he helped found the
League of National Action in Qurnai'l (Mount Lebanon), a movement designed
to unite Arab intellectuals into one political force that would help liberate the
entire region from European colonialism. The league rose to overnight fame in
Syria and Lebanon and called for economic integration of all Arab countries once
the French and British Mandates were terminated. The league included promising young men who would become future leaders in Syria. Among its earliest
members were the professor Constantine Zurayk, the philosopher Zaki al-Arsuzi,
the politician Sabri al-Asali, and the diplomat Farid Zayn al-Din.

In 1936, Sharabati defected from the League of National Action and joined
the National Bloc, the leading anti-French movement in Syria. The Bloc called
for liberation from the French Mandate through diplomatic means rather than
armed resistance. Sharabati allied himself with the Bloc's leadership in Damascus
and ran for parliament on a Bloc ticket in 1943 and 1947, winning both times.
In March 1945, Prime Minister Faris al-Khury appointed Sharabati minister of
education and national economy. In April 1946, the French Mandate ended in
Syria and Sharabati became minister of defense in the cabinet of the National
Bloc leader Saadallah al-Jabiri. Sharabati allied himself with President Shukri
al-Quwatli (a close friend of his father's), who delegated Sharabati to create the
Syrian Army.

Sharabati knew little to nothing about military affairs and Quwatli gave him
the impossible task of winning the affection of the officers. Rather than delight-
ing in the companionship of Syrian officers who were neither socially refined
nor highly educated, Sharabati preferred mixing with high society, drinking with
foreign dignitaries, and talking politics. He treated the officers badly, and one
officer complained that Sharabati would strike them with his billy-stick at the
war front if they did not jump to their feet and salute him properly. The officer
remarked that, "even Churchill or Clemenceau do not demand similar ceremony
at the war front. This is not military custom."

POLITICIANS

Sharabati had no one to turn to for military advice, since even the most senior officers serving during the mandate had been subordinate to their French counterparts and thus had been left out from any important administrative positions in the French-sponsored Army of the Levant. Also, neither the president nor any members of the National Bloc had any military experience.

Sharabati unwillingly presided over military affairs during the first Arab-Israeli War of 1948 and was accused of profiteering at the army's expense and collaborating with some officers in illegal arms deals. Sharabati was married to a European woman, who many in Syria believed to be a spy, and his business partner was Arif Tutah, a Damascene Jew. His connection to Tutah caused uproar in Syria and the Arab press, and many began calling on Quwatli to dismiss him from office. Sharabati's image was badly affected when an arms shipment headed for Syria ended up in Israel, and he was accused, along with General Fou'ad Mardam Bey, of selling the weapons to the Zionists.

Sharabati resigned from his post on May 26, 1948, thereby unofficially accepting blame for the Arab defeat in the War of 1948, and devoted his time to commercial activity. He was highly critical of the Syrian-Egyptian union created by President Quwatli and President Gamal Abd al-Nasser of Egypt in February 1958. When union was dissolved by military coup on September 28, 1961, Sharabati hailed the coup mastermind, Colonel Abd al-Karim al-Nehlawi. A group of leading politicians assembled at the Sharabati residence on October 2, 1961 and drafted the secession declaration. The document accused Nasser of "distorting the idea of Arab nationalism" and proclaimed that during the union years Nasser had "strangled political and democratic life" in Syria. Ahmad al-Sharabati retired from public life when the Baath Party came to power in March 1963.

Sources:
Arslan, Adil. *Muzakarat al-Ameer Adil Arslan* (1972).
Babil, Nasuh. *Sahafa wa Siyassa fi Souriyya* (1987).
Encyclopedia of the Modern Middle East, Vol III (1996). Entry by Abdul Kareim Rafeq.
Moubayed, Sami. *Damascus Between Democracy and Dictatorship* (2000).
Samman, Mutih. *Watan wa Askar* (1995).
Seale, Patrick. *The Struggle for Syria* (1961).

al-Sharif, Ihsan
(1889-1963)

Ihsan al-Sharif was born and raised in Damascus. As a student, he studied at the elite Maktab Anbar School in Damascus and got into trouble for rebelling against his Ottoman instructors. Along with a group of Arab students, Sharif abducted

333

the Ottoman school principal and was punished with early conscription into the Ottoman Army.

Sharif was highly critical of the Armenian massacre that took place in 1915-1916 and was sentenced to death by Ottoman authorities. Yusuf al-Azma, a prominent officer in the Ottoman Army related to Sharif by marriage, helped Sharif escape and he went to Paris where he studied international law. He returned to Syria when World War I ended in 1918 and opened a legal office in Damascus. He allied himself with Dr Abd al-Rahman Shahbandar, the leading nationalist of his generation who led the resistance against the French Mandate imposed on Syria in July 1920.

In June 1925, Shahbandar and Sharif founded the People's Party, the first political movement in French Mandate Syria. The party promoted the creation of a constitutional government in a free and unified Syria that would include Palestine, Jordan, and parts of Lebanon. The party was composed of leading statesmen, lawyers, and professors who would become nationalist leaders in the 1940s. Shahbandar became president and Sharif became secretary of the party.

On July 18, 1925, Shahbandar and Sharif joined Sultan al-Atrash in the Syrian revolt of the Arab Mountain, a national uprising against the French launched by the Druze community and funded by the Hashemite royals in Amman. Sharif helped fund the rebels and provided them with shelter in the orchards surrounding Damascus. French High Commissioner Maurice Sarrail responded by ordering an air raid on Damascus in October 1925, killing hundreds of civilians and crushing the resistance leadership. Shahbandar fled to Amman, but Sharif was arrested and sent into internal exile on the Arwad Island off the Syrian coast.

Upon his release in 1927, Sharif devoted his life to his legal practice in Damascus. In October 1927, he co-founded the National Bloc with Hashim al-Atasi, a coalition of notables pledged to offer their skill, wealth, and connections to the cause of liberating Syria. The Bloc leaders aspired to liberate Syria through diplomatic

means rather than armed resistance. In 1928, Sharif held office for three months on the Constitutional Assembly that drafted the first republican constitution for Syria. He became a deputy in parliament in 1932, 1936, and 1943. In 1936, Sharif helped orchestrate a sixty-day strike in Damascus to protest France's refusal to address the issue of Syrian independence. In 1944, Shukri al-Quwatli appointed Sharif governor of Aleppo, and in 1946 he was appointed Syrian ambassador to Turkey.

In March 1949, a coup took place in Syria, toppling President Quwatli and bringing Chief of Staff Husni al-Za'im to power. Sharif, a declared opponent

Ihsan al-Sharif.

of officers meddling in political affairs, criticized Za'im's move and refused to congratulate him on assuming the Syrian presidency. Annoyed, Za'im cabled Sharif, asking, "We have not received your congratulations." Sharif responded, "That is because we did not send any." And Za'im wrote back with two words, "You're fired!"

When Za'im was toppled in August 1949, Ihsan al-Sharif founded the Republican Democratic Party in Syria, but it did not last long and was outlawed by General Adib al-Shishakli, who came to power in November 1951. Za'im replaced all political parties with one revolving around his cult figure called the Arab Liberation Movement (ALM).

Sources:
Khoury, Philip. *Syria and the French Mandate* (1987).
Information supplied by Hassan Ihsan al-Sharif (Damascus June 21, 2001).

Shayya, Jamil
(1931-)

Jamil Shayya was born into an influential Druze family in the Shouf district on Mount Lebanon. He studied education at Damascus University and taught at high schools in the Arab Mountain in Syria.

In 1955, Shayya joined the Baath Party of Michel Aflaq and Salah al-Bitar and began to preach Baath rhetoric to his students. He became a member in the movement of Arab nationalism headed by President Gamal Abd al-Nasser of Egypt and supported Syria's merger with Egypt to form the United Arab Republic (UAR) in 1958. In March 1963, the Baath came to power in Syria and Shayya became minister of supply in the cabinet of President Amin al-Hafez (October 1964-September 1965). Shayya held office under President Hafez, but allied himself with the officers who deposed Hafez in February 1966. On March 1, 1966, Prime Minister Yusuf Zu'ayyin appointed Shayya minister of information, culture, national guidance, and acting minister of tourism.

On August 1966, government authorities uncovered a coup attempt in the Arab Mountain and arrested many notables and inhabitants involved with the coup mastermind Saleem Hatum. To calm the Druze citizens angered by the arrests, Shayya went to the Arab Mountain on September 8 with President Nur al-Din al-Atasi and Salah Jadid, the de facto ruler of Syria. They were arrested at gunpoint by Hatum but released by Defense Minister Hafez al-Asad. Shayya then became ambassador to Brazil, and in 1969 President Atasi appointed him ambassador to Italy. In November 1970, Hafez al-Asad came to power and appointed Shayya ambassador to the USSR, where he was charged with serving as a link between Asad and the Kremlin during the Arab-Israeli War of 1973.

Jamil Shayya remained in Moscow until 1975, then was transferred to Damascus to become deputy to Prime Minister Mohammad Ali al-Halabi, holding office until 1980.

Sources:

Batatu, Hanna. *Syria's Peasantry: the Descendants of its Lesser Rural Notables and their Politics* (2000).

Seale, Patrick. *Asad: Struggle for the Middle East* (1988).

al-Shishakli, Adib
(1909-1964)

Adib al-Shishakli was born in the city of Hama in 1909 and studied at the Military Academy in Damascus. In 1936, he joined the Syrian Social Nationalist Party (SSNP), a radical party that hoped to unite all regional territories into Greater Syria. He ceased his SSNP activity in the early 1940s but remained close to its leadership and a believer in its ideology.

Shishakli joined the French-created Troupes Speciales but deserted in May 1945 when France bombarded Damascus. He then took up arms with the Syrian resistance against the French Mandate. When the mandate ended in April 1946, Shishakli enlisted in the newly created Syrian Army. In November 1946, he took part in a military mission in the Alawite Mountain where units of the Syrian Army cracked down on the rebel forces of the pro-French chieftain, Sulayman al-Murshed, and had him arrested.

Shishakli volunteered to help lead the Arab volunteer army during the 1948 war in Palestine. He earned a reputation for being one of the most able and courageous officers in battle. In the first days of May 1948, however, the northern Palestinian city of Safad (now part of Israel) was under attack by Zionist forces and President Quwatli refused to support Shishakli's brigade by sending much needed ammunition and reinforcements. In consequence, Shishakli became disillusioned with Syria's civilian leadership. An embittered Shishakli accused President Shukri al-Quwatli of corruption and poor leadership. Shishakli's headquarters at the war front became a daily gathering place for similarly discontented officers who would listen to the general's caustic denunciations of the civilian regime and his promises of revenge.

Shishakli's views brought him to the attention of Chief of Staff Husni al-Za'im. On March 29, 1949, Shishakli helped Za'im seize power in Syria and topple the regime of President Quwatli, leading an armed battalion to occupy Damascus. But Shishakli quarreled with Za'im's method of rule, claiming that he had alienated Syria in the Arab neighborhood. Shishakli then sought to bring Za'im down.

In July 1949, tensions between Zai'm and Shishakli rose when Za'im extradited

Antune Sa'ada, leader of the SSNP, to Lebanon where he was executed by Prime Minister Riyad al-Sulh. Authorities in Beirut had demanded Sa'ada's extradition, claiming that he had tried to lead a military insurrection against the regime of President Bshara al-Khury. Za'im promised Sa'ada asylum, but then reneged on his promise and handed him to Beirut authorities, who executed Sa'ada on July 8, 1949. On August 6, 1949, Za'im retired Shishakli from the Syrian Army.

Infuriated by the betrayal, Shishakli began plotting revenge with General Sami al-Hinnawi, another sympathizer with the SSNP who was also a one-time member of Za'im's inner circle. On August 14, 1949, the two men launched a coup d'etat, arresting Za'im, then killing him along with his prime minister, Muhsen al-Barazi. Shishakli personally drove Sa'ada's family to a convent for safety following the assassination of Za'im.

Hinnawi called on leading civilian politicians to rule Syria in the post-Za'im era, asserting that he had no personal ambitions for power. He appointed Shishakli commander of the 1st Brigade. Hinnawi's alliance with Shishakli quickly crumbled when Hinnawi declared that he wanted to unite Syria with Iraq and impose a Hashemite monarchy in Damascus. To do so, Hinnawi lobbied for the appointment of Hashim al-Atasi as president and Nazim al-Qudsi as prime minister. Both men were allies of Hashemite Iraq working for the materialization of union.

Shishakli often repeated that he had no intention of being ruled from Baghdad, claiming that Nuri al-Sa'id, the Iraqi prime minister in charge of the union talks, was an agent of the West who wanted to destroy Syria's Arab identity. To counterbalance the union talks, Shishakli went to Saudi Arabia, a declared opponent of the union issue, and secured a six million dollar interest-free loan. Then Shishakli went to Cairo where King Farouk gave him another five million British pounds. This was the price that regional Arab states were willing to pay to keep Syria out of the Hashemite orbit.

Hinnawi began talks with Iraq for unification, and Shishakli responded by launching his own coup on December 19, 1949, and ordering Hinnawi's arrest. Shishakli then declared that he had no further ambitions in Syria except the appointment of Anwar Bannud as chief of staff and Fawzi Selu as minister of defense. Wishing to avoid a confrontation with the army, Atasi complied with his demands. Having Bannud at army headquarters and Selu in government meant that the pro-Iraq movement would always remain under control. With an anti-union soldier like Selu in his cabinet, Prime Minister Qudsi, a pro-Hashemite promoter of a Syria-Iraq union, could do little more than talk about union.

Then, on July 31, 1950, Air Force Commander Mohammad Nasser, Shishakli's most serious political rival, was gunned down in the suburbs of Damascus. As he lay dying, Nasser said that his assailants were Ibrahim al-Husayni and Abd al-Ghani Qannut, two allies of Adib al-Shishakli. In October 1950, an attempt

King Talal of Jordan (left) with President Adib al-Shishakli in 1952.

was made on Shishakli's own life by a terrorist group in Syria that resented his dictatorship. In November 1951, Syria's prime minister, Ma'ruf al-Dawalibi, created a cabinet and filled it with pro-Iraqi politicians. A declared opponent of Shishakli, Dawalibi refused to give the Ministry of Defense to General Selu in deference to Shishakli and his anti-Iraq sentiments as others had done for the previous thirteen months. Dawalibi also insisted that the Gendarmerie (police) be returned to civilian control under the minister of interior.

Shishakli retaliated with force on November 29 (twenty-four hours after the formation of the cabinet), arresting Dawalibi, his entire cabinet, and all pro-Iraqi officials and members of the People's Party. The following day, Shishakli issued a decree dissolving parliament and accepting the resignation of President Hashim al-Atasi. Shishakli terminated Syria's constitution and appointed Selu as head of state "with presidential powers." His tactics were laid out by Akram al-Hawrani, a childhood friend from Hama who had been a member in the SSNP and served with Shishakli in the Arab-Israeli War of 1948.

From 1951 until 1953, Shishakli ruled Syria through the puppet regime of President Fawzi Selu. He believed that nations, like armies, could be run by order and discipline. Shishakli outlawed all political parties, closed many political newspapers, and created his own party in August 1952, naming it the Arab Liberation Movement (ALM). The party was created less than one month after a group of officers had come to power in Egypt, toppling the pro-Western regime of King Farouk.

The Arab masses welcomed the Egyptian Revolution, and Shishakli took great care to model his rhetoric after that of the Free Officers in Cairo. His political program resembled that of Egypt's new president, Mohammad Nagib, and his right-hand man, Colonel Gamal Abd al-Nasser. Shishakli called for land reform, progressive taxation, full employment, a classless society, emancipation of women, and Arab unity. On the last note he elaborated, saying that the Arab nation was "spreading from the Taurus to the Gulf of Basra, and from the Mediterranean Sea to the Atlantic." Echoing the words of the Egyptian Revolution, he said, "Our country is the home of the Arab idea!"

Then, to further portray himself as an extension of the Egyptian Revolution, Shishakli visited Cairo in December 1952, extending full recognition to the Negib regime. Shishakli also severed his relations with Iraq and strengthened those with Jordan, Lebanon, and Saudi Arabia. He ended thirty years of gridlock between

Damascus and Amman by opening a Syrian embassy in Jordan following the assassination of King Abdullah in 1951. Shishakli visited Jordan to congratulate its new monarch, King Talal, and received the king as a a guest of honor in Damascus, becoming the first Jordanian king to visit Syria. Shishakli also allied himself with the United States and Great Britain, and was offered military and financial aid by US President Dwight Eisenhower. Economically, Syria witnessed a boom during the Shishakli years, for he reduced taxes and favored a policy of laissez-faire in commercial conduct.

On July 11, 1953, Adib al-Shishakli called for national elections and nominated himself for the presidency. No one dared run against him and he was elected president of the republic with 99.98% of the vote. That same summer, he drafted a new constitution that has gone down in history as "Shishakli's Constitution." Outlawed political parties began plotting against him, accusing him of becoming an "Arab Caesar." He struck back by arresting scores of politicians, professors, and prominent notables who harbored anti-regime views. At one point, he ordered the army into Damascus University, with orders to arrest students and professors with declared anti-Shishakli views.

Shishakli clashed with Syria's Druze community, whom he accused of trying to topple him, and placed the veteran Druze leader Sultan al-Atrash under house arrest. He then discovered that the Druze were smuggling arms to lead an insurrection against him and struck with force, ordering an air raid on the Arab Mountain. The uprising spread rapidly from the Arab Mountain to Homs, Aleppo, and Lattakia, where officers mutinied against Shishakli and declared war against his regime. Facing an explosive situation, Shishakli resigned from office on February 24, 1954, claiming that he wanted to avoid a civil war, and moved to Beirut. The Lebanese Druze leader Kamal Jumblatt tried to assassinate him, forcing him to move to Riyadh, where King Saud gave him political asylum.

In 1955, the Iraqi government began plotting an insurrection in Syria. Iraq wanted to topple the pro-USSR regime of Shukri al-Quwatli, who had returned to power in 1955, and end Syria's alliance with Gamal Abd al-Nasser of Egypt. Searching for a Syrian to carry out the coup, Iraq found no better candidate than their former enemy, Adib al-Shishakli. They offered to bring him to Baghdad, but he refused, asking them to come to Europe instead. Prime Minister Nuri al-Sa'id dispatched General Ghazi al-Daghastani, the deputy chief of staff of the Iraqi Army, and Burhan al-Din Bashayan, the foreign minister, to meet Shishakli in Switzerland.

Shishakli complied, and went to Lebanon in June 1956, reportedly on a British arms smuggling ship, to seek potential allies who would help him stage a coup. He met with members of the SSNP, who had been outlawed from Syria in 1955 and sought revenge. Ghassan Jadid, a leader of the SSNP, provided Shishakli with a fake passport, a car, bodyguards, and different places of residence to avoid being recognized or tracked by Lebanese authorities or the press. The SSNP members claimed that a coup would only be successful if it led to the assassination of Akram al-Hawrani, Shishakli's former right-hand man, and Abd al-Hamid Sarraj, his former disciple, since they were the leaders of the leftist movement in Syria.

Shishakli declined, saying that he was opposed to targeted assassinations and fearing that this would lead to reprisal attacks against his own family in Hama. An experienced revolutionary, Shishakli could not commit himself to an ill-fated coup attempt that had a high risk of failure. As a result, he left Lebanon and headed once again to Europe, moving to Brazil for permanent residence in 1960.

In January 1957, the attempted coup was uncovered in Syria, and a military tribunal sentenced Shishakli to death in absentia on the charge of treason. He was also accused of conspiring with a foreign country to attack Syria with the aim of fomenting civil war. On September 27, 1964, Adib al-Shishakli was assassinated at his farm in Goias, Brazil, by a Syrian immigrant exacting revenge for the massacre ordered by Shishakli against the Arab Mountain in 1953. Shishakli was only fifty-five years old. Syrian historians have called Shishakli one of the most ruthless and cunning leaders to rule Syria and also one of the ablest politicians in modern Middle East history.

Sources:
Abu Ismail, Nadim. *Min Asrar al-Shishakli* (1954).
BBC Archives. "The Damascus Trial" February 26, 1957.
Khayyer, Hani. *Adib al-Shishakli* (1994).
Moubayed, Sami. *Damascus Between Democracy and Dictatorship* (2000).
Rathmell, Andrew. *Secret War in the Middle East* (1995).
Seale, Patrick. *The Struggle for Syria* (1961).
Torrey, Gordon. *Syrian Politics and the Military* (1964).

al-Siba'i, Mustapha
(1915-1964)

Mustapha al-Siba'i studied Islamic theology at the al-Azhar University in Cairo. During his studies in Egypt he attended the lectures of Sheikh Hasan al-Banna, the charismatic leader of the Egyptian Muslim Brotherhood, and joined the organization in 1930.

Siba'i returned to Syria and taught theology at Damascus University, becoming dean of the Faculty of Theology in 1940. One year later, he founded Shabab Mohammad (Mohammad Youth) in Damascus, a paramilitary group of religious men modeled on the Egyptian Muslim Brotherhood. Shabab Mohammad organized support for any Islamic organization or activity and led parades, strikes, and protests against the French Mandate. The group was allied to the National

Bloc, the leading anti-French movement in Syria headed by Hashim al-Atasi with the goal of ending the mandate through diplomatic means rather than armed resistance.

In 1946, Siba'i worked with Hasan al-Banna on founding the Syrian Muslim Brotherhood. From 1946 to 1957, Siba'i led the Muslim Brotherhood through their most active parliamentary campaigns, spreading propaganda, teaching at high schools, and creating a powerful base of disciples among the conservative families of Damascus, Aleppo, Homs, Hama, and Lattakia. In 1949, Siba'i was voted into the Constitutional Assembly that drafted a new constitution for Syria. He also served as a member of parliament from 1949 until 1951.

Mustapha al-Siba'i was a democrat who aspired to creating an Islamic state in Syria through "evolution" and Islamic awareness, and not revolution. He was opposed to the military regimes of Husni al-Za'im (1949) and Adib al-Shishak-li (1951-1954), and he was a declared opponent of secularist parties like the Baath and Communist Parties. In 1958, he criticized Syria's merger with Egypt to form the United Arab Republic (UAR), claiming that President Gamal Abd al-Nasser would destroy the country's healthy political system and persecute the Brotherhood in Syria like he had done in Egypt in 1954. As Siba'i expected, Nasser outlawed the Muslim Brotherhood when union was created and arrested hundreds of its members throughout Syria and Egypt.

Siba'i joined the underground during the union years (1958-1961) and supported the coup that toppled the UAR on September 28, 1961. He allied himself with President Nazim al-Qudsi, the new leader of Syria, but was persecuted again when the Baath Party came to power in March 1963. The Baath Party pledged to restore the UAR and arrested many politicians who had opposed union. The Revolutionary Command Council (RCC) outlawed the Muslim Brotherhood and banned most of Siba'i's works, sending him into political retirement.

Among Siba'i's published works are *Al-Din wa al-Dawla fi al-Islam* (*Religion and State in Islam*), published in 1954, *Ishtirakiyyat al-Islam* (*The Socialism of Islam*), published in 1960, and *Hakaza Alamatni al-Hayat* (*This is What Life Taught Me*), a collection of his memoirs published posthumously in 1972.

Sources:
Faris, George. *Man Hum fi al-`Alam al-Arabi?* (1957).
Uthman, Hashim. *Al-Ahzab al-Siyasiyya fi Souriyya: al-Siriyya wa al-Mu'lana* (2001).

al-Tabba', Abd al-Hamid
(1900-1950)

Born and raised in Damascus to a family of Islamic scholars, Abd al-Hamid al-Tabba' studied Islam with private tutors and began his career as a merchant in Damascus.

In 1924, Tabba' co-founded the al-Gharra society in Syria with Sheikh Ali al-Daqr. The society was composed of religious men, schoolteachers, and middle-class merchants who were attracted to the principles of Islamic law (Sharia) and wanted to protest French control of the education system in Syria. The leaders of al-Gharra were particularly disturbed by the mixed schools becoming commonplace in Damascus.

Tabba' led a campaign during the 1920s and 1930s against the influx of foreign goods to Syria and the increasingly pro-Western lifestyles that Syrians were leading. He was especially active in the movement that opposed the emancipation of women and criticized the increasingly common practice of unveiling in Damascus, Aleppo, and Lattakia. The swelling number of nightclubs, cinemas, and restaurants that served alcohol was also a concern of Tabba'.

In addition to his political program, Tabba' was also involved in numerous charity organizations during the French Mandate. He donated hefty sums to orphanages, schools, and mosques. He was also active in the nationalist movement and provided funds for the National Bloc, the leading anti-French party in Syria.

In 1943, Tabba' nominated himself for parliament as a deputy for Damascus and won with an overwhelming majority. He allied himself with the National Bloc leader Shukri al-Quwatli, who was elected president in August 1943 and who promised to attend to the numerous social grievances of al-Gharra. Once firmly in power, however, Quwatli proved to be a liberal himself and increased the liberalization of Syrian society, prompting Tabba' to join in an alliance aimed at bringing him down. He criticized Quwatli's liberalism, and his campaign for woman suffrage, claiming that it was demoralizing society.

On May 19, 1944, Tabba' gave a speech at the Tankiz Mosque (headquarters for al-Gharra), denouncing unveiling as immoral and evil. So popular was his speech that it echoed throughout every mosque in Damascus at prayer-time the following Friday. He led a demonstration of three hundred men, protesting a charity ball that was being planned by the Goutte de Lait (Drop of Milk Society) where Muslim women would attend functions unveiled. Tabba' called on the organizer Rafiqa al-Boukhari, the wife of ex-Prime Minister Nasuh al-Boukhari, to cancel the ball. When she refused, Tabba' led the protestors through the streets of Damascus, shouting insults at the government. Overwhelmed, the angry crowd picked up armed supporters, attacked government headquarters in Marjeh Square, and the Goutte de Lait building in the Salhiyya district. They then stormed the Empire Cinema, where a ladies' matinee was showing, stoned its doors, and threatened to attack all the women inside who were unveiled.

In the violence that ensued, police officers were killed and so were young members of al-Gharra. In response, Quwatli jailed Mohammad Ashmar, co-leader of the march, but refrained from arresting Tabba'. Some deputies asked Parliament Speaker Faris al-Khury to lift Tabba's parliamentary immunity and bring him to court on the charge of disturbing civil peace and upsetting order, but Khury refused. The "Islamic opposition" became so powerful that even Tabba' could no longer control it. He called on Quwatli and Khury to quell the demonstrators, and then Tabba' disclaimed responsibility for the mob's actions.

Abd al-Hamid al-Tabba'.

In March 1949, Quwatli was overthrown, but Abd al-Hamid al-Tabba' clashed with his successor Husni al-Za'im. Tabba' criticized Za'im for establishing a secular, military dictatorship, and then Tabba' retired from public life, but his society lived on, and many members went on to create the Syrian Muslim Brotherhood in the 1950s.

Sources:
FO 684 15-1-1 British Security Mission to Political Office (Damascus) May 23, 1944 and May 26, 1944.
Khoury, Philip. *Syria and the French Mandate* (1987).
Thompson, Elizabeth. *Colonial Citizens* (1999).
Information supplied by Karim al-Tabba' (Damascus May 11, 2002).

al-Turk, Riyad
(1930-)

Riyad al-Turk was born in Homs and studied law at Damascus University. He joined the Communist Party of Khalid Bakdash in 1955, establishing himself as a young and enthusiastic politician. He contributed regularly to the party newspaper *al-Nour* and was categorically opposed to the Syrian-Egyptian union in 1958.

When the United Arab Republic (UAR) was created, Bakdash fled to Eastern Europe, and his followers were persecuted in Syria. Turk was arrested with hundreds of other communists, spending most of the union years behind bars, until the union was overthrown by military coup in 1961. The post-union government of Nazim al-Qudsi feared communist influence and so it too did not allow the Communist Party to operate. The ban was extended under the first Baath Party government of President Amin al-Hafez, and lifted when Salah Jadid came to power in February 1966.

Turk argued with Bakdash on the degree of communism needed in Syria, himself being in favor of a Maoist approach. The two men supported Hafez al-Asad's seizure of power in 1970. But in 1972, Bakdash brought the Communist Party into the newly formed National Progressive Front, a coalition of social-ist parties dominated by the Baath. The following year, Turk and his followers left the party, forming the Communist Party Political Bureau. The party was not licensed by the Asad government, but its activities were tolerated until a military uprising broke out in Aleppo in 1979 headed by the Muslim Brotherhood. Turk spoke out in favor of the Brotherhood, and was arrested in Damascus along with his wife on October 28, 1980. His wife, a medical doctor from Homs, was released shortly afterward. But Turk remained in captivity for eighteen years, earning the nickname "Mandela of Syria."

On May 30, 1998, Turk was finally released from prison under orders from President Asad. Turk reportedly agreed to stay away from politics and spend the remainder of his life in peace and quiet. For the next three years, Turk avoided public life and was not harassed by government authorities. On August 15, 2001, however, he appeared on a talk show on the Doha-based Aljazeera TV and spoke very negatively of the Syrian government. He was arrested later that month in the coastal city of Tartus, in a clampdown on ten prominent members of the opposition.

There was much international condemnation of Turk's arrest, and as a result, he was given a public trial, sentenced to five years in prison, then released under orders from Syria's new President Bashar al-Asad in November 2002. Since then, Riyad al-Turk has given up political activity, but he remains the most prominent name among the Syrian opposition, having spent most of his political career behind bars.

Source:
Haddad, Lutfi. *Al-Hiwar al-Mutamaddin* #1146 (Marach 24, 2005).

al-Ulshi, Jamil
(1883-1951)

Jamil al-Ulshi was born and raised in Damascus. He studied at the Ottoman Military Academy in Istanbul and graduated in 1906.

Ulshi joined the Ottoman Army and was arrested in 1915 for his connections to the Arab underground working to overthrow the Ottoman Empire. Ulshi defected from the Ottoman Army in 1917 and joined the troops of Sharif Husayn, who was leading an armed revolt from the Arabian Desert against the Ottomans. When the war ended in 1918, Ulshi served as a member of the six-man com-mittee charged with administering state affairs in the immediate post-Ottoman period. In October 1918, he became private chamberlain to King Faysal I, the new ruler of Syria.

In July 1920, the French Army arrived on the Syrian coast and began advancing on Damascus with the purpose of ousting the Faysal regime and establishing the French Mandate in the Middle East. Faysal delegated Ulshi to meet with General Henri Gouraud of the French Army to negotiate a diplomatic solution to the crisis, but his talks ended in failure. The French occupied Syria on July 25, 1920, and dethroned Faysal.

Unlike many members of the royal entourage who departed Syria with Faysal, Ulshi stayed behind and became minister of defense in the pro-French cabinet of Prime Minister Ala al-Din al-Droubi. Droubi taxed the Syrians heavily and said that any collaboration with Faysal or resistance to the French would be considered a criminal offense, punishable by arrest or heavy fines. But Droubi was assassinated by Faysal loyalists in the southern town of Hawran on August 12, 1920. Thus Ulshi became acting prime minister and created his own government on September 6, 1920, making himself minister of defense. He was accused, among other things, of packing the cabinet with relatives and allying himself with the mandate authority.

The mandate authority annexed the city of Tripoli to Lebanon and Ulshi did nothing to protest the annexation, causing uproar in nationalist circles. Armed revolts broke out in different parts of Syria, protesting the French occupation. The French retaliated with force, arresting leaders of the nationalist uprising and sending many of them into exile. The public was highly critical of Prime Minister Ulshi for doing nothing to stop the arrests. Facing increased alienation in nationalist circles, he resigned from office on November 30, 1920.

Jamil al-Ulshi spent the 1920s watching politics from a distance and playing no role in Syrian affairs. In 1928, however, he became minister of finance in the pro-French cabinet of his longtime friend and neighbor Taj al-Din al-Hasani. Ulshi held this post until August 1930, then retired from politics until Hasani became president of the republic in September 1941. Ulshi served as his political advisor, and in January 1943, Hasani asked him to create a government. In a bid at appeasing the opposition, Ulshi appointed the National Bloc leader Fayez al-Khury as minister of foreign affairs and the famous nationalist poet Khalil Mardam Bey as minister of education. In January 1943, however, Taj al-Din al-Hasani died while in office and Ulshi kept his post as prime minister while serving also as acting president until March 25, 1943.

Ulshi's tenure was marked by public disturbances over the sharp increase in bread prices that he imposed to help pay for France's war effort in Europe. His eagerness to supply money to France caused turmoil throughout Syria, where violent marchers took to the streets, vandalizing government property, attacking officials, and calling for Ulshi's downfall. Jamil al-Ulshi resigned from office and disappeared from public life altogether, spending the remainder of his years in solitude.

Sources:
Hakim, Yusuf. *Souriyya wa al-Ahd al-Faysali*, Beirut (1986).
Husari, Sati. *Yawm Maysaloun* (1947).
Khoury, Philip. *Syria and the French Mandate* (1987).
Moubayed, Sami. *The Politics of Damascus 1920-1946* (1999).
Russell, Malcom. *The First Modern Arab State: Syria under Faysal I* (1987).

Umran, Mohammad
(1922-1972)

Mohammad Umran studied at the Homs Military Academy and joined the Baath Party of Michel Aflaq and Salah al-Bitar in 1947. In 1953, he helped overthrow the military government of General Adib al-Shishakli, which had previously outlawed the Baath and sent its leadership into exile.

While working undercover against Shishakli, Umran became a student of the Baath Party leader Akram al-Hawrani and was highly influenced by his views. Umran also became a fervent supporter of Egypt in the second half of the 1950s and rallied in support of President Gamal Abd al-Nasser. Umran advocated Syria's merger with Egypt to form the United Arab Republic (UAR) in 1958 and allied himself with other Baath officers who shared his pro-Nasser views. In 1960, Umran and the other officers founded the Military Committee of the Baath Party, a secret coalition determined to preserve the UAR and uphold Nasser's views of Arab nationalism. The ages of the coalition members ranged from twenty-eight to thirty-eight, and Umran was the oldest. He was appointed president of the committee and held this post until the Baath came to power in 1963.

In September 1961, a coup dissolved the UAR and the leaders of the new government dismissed most of the officers from Syrian Army. The Military Committee vowed to oppose the post-Nasser government of President Nazim al-Qudsi. The young party members were influenced by the coup that took place in Iraq on February 8, 1963, and which led to the killing of General Abd al-Karim Qasim. The Iraqi coup was carried out by a group of Baath Party officers, and Umran hoped that he and his comrades could do the same thing in Syria.

On March 8, 1963, the Baath officers came to power in Damascus, overthrowing Qudsi and promising to restore the UAR. Umran toppled General Abd al-Karim al-Abid and took over command of the 70th Armoured Brigade at Kisweh, south of Damascus. Back in military uniform after once being fired by Qudsi, Umran was now commander of one of the most strategically placed military units in Syria. The country's new leaders distributed government and military posts to senior party members, and Umran became a deputy to Prime

Minister Salah al-Bitar.

Mohammad Umran befriended two of Syria's top leaders: Michel Aflaq, who was still serving as secretary-general of the Baath Party, and Prime Minister Bitar. Umran's alliance with the civilian leadership alienated him from his previous allies, the members of the Military Committee who began to see him as a threat to their existence. Umran clashed with his former allies, Hafez al-Asad and Salah Jadid, and began lobbying for their dismissal from office.

Threatened with expulsion by his former comrades, Umran publicly shifted into Aflaq's orbit and offered his allegiance to the civilian wing of the Baath Party. In retaliation, the officers stripped him of his military title, expelled him from the Military Committee, and made him ambassador to Spain, the traditional exile for political dissidents.

Aflaq responded to Umran's maltreatment by calling eighty of his followers into conference and passing a law making the Regional Command, dominated by officers, subject to the authority of the civilian National Command, a body under Aflaq's chairmanship. Michel Aflaq added that an officer could not be transferred from his post or dismissed from office without authorization from the civilian leadership. Aflaq was then replaced by Dr Munif al-Razzaz, another civilian Baathist, who created a new pro-Aflaq leadership for Syria. Bitar was reappointed prime minister. Amin al-Hafez was kept as president. Umran became minister of defense. And Mansur al-Atrash, a veteran member of the Baath, was appointed president of a Revolutionary Command Council (RCC) that excluded members of the Military Committee.

Salah Jadid, Umran's chief military rival, rebelled against these orders and arrested a number of Umran's allies in the armed forces. Umran assumed his new duties on February 21, 1966, and carried out his revenge by transferring three of Jadid's best men to remote districts and dismissing a handful of others. He transferred the powerful Ahmad Suwaydani, a powerful Jadid loyalist, from Military Intelligence to a ceremonial post at Officers Administration.

The military wing struck back with a final blow, toppling President Amin al-Hafez, along with the two Baath leaders Aflaq and Bitar, and arresting Mohammad Umran on February 23, 1966. Umran was discharged from the Syrian Army and expelled from the Baath Party. Jadid jailed him in the Mezzeh prison in Damascus where he remained until the Arab-Israeli War of 1967 broke out. To unite Syria in the face of Israeli arms, Jadid ordered the release of all political prisoners. Umran went to Lebanon and supported the coup that ousted Jadid in November 1970 and brought Hafez al-Asad to power.

Four years later, on March 4, 1972, Mohammad Umran was murdered by unknown assailants at his Tripoli residence.

Sources:

Batatu, Hanna. *Syria's Peasantry: the Descendants of its Lesser Rural Notables and their Politics* (2000).

Commins, David. *Historical Dictionary of Modern Syria* (1996).

Seale, Patrick. *Asad Struggle for the Middle East* (1988).

al-Yusuf, Abd al-Rahman
(d.1920)

Abd al-Rahman al-Yusuf studied in Istanbul and grew up in Ottoman luxury. His father had been close to the Ottomans and was appointed Prince of Hajj, a religious post, in the final years of the nineteenth century. The elder Yusuf's duty had been to accompany the Muslim pilgrims from Damascus during their annual pilgrimage to Mecca. Upon the father's death, his son Abd al-Rahman inherited the job and earned the princely title of pasha from Ottoman Sultan Abdulhamid II.

Being a relative of the three leading political families in Damascus, Yusuf's numerous connections to the Azms, the Abids, and Shamdin Agha added to his elevated social and political standing. Abd al-Rahman Pasha was considered the wealthiest man in Damascus. He owned the whole east shore of Lake Tiberias, known as al-Btayha, three villages in the Ghuta orchards surrounding Damascus, five in al-Marj, and twenty-four in the Golan Heights.

In 1908, a coup d'etat took place in Istanbul headed by the Committee for Union and Progress (CUP). The CUP was a coalition of Ottoman officers who longed for domestic reforms and forced Abdulhamid to carry out political changes in the Ottoman Empire. The CUP forced Abdulhamid to lift press censorship, reinstate the constitution of 1876, and dismiss most of his Arab advisors, replacing them with Turkish officials.

Yusuf allied himself with the CUP and managed to keep his post at the imperial court, becoming advisor to the new Sultan Mohammad Rashad V and a member of the Ottoman Parliament. Yusuf severed all relations with his previous friends who had been close to Abdulhamid and who now created the bulk of anti-CUP movement. Among those one-time allies who became archenemies were the ex-deputies Shukri al-Asali and Rushdi al-Sham'a.

In 1912, Yusuf lobbied against the Ottoman Party of Administrative Decentralization based in Cairo and headed by the opposition leader Rafic al-Azm. Yusuf joined a group of other Ottoman aristocrats, including Sami Mardam Bey, Fawzi al-Azm, and Ahmad al-Shama'a, and called on the CUP to silence the opposition with force. Yusuf worked to prevent the holding of a pan-Arab congress in Paris in 1913 and encouraged CUP officers to arrest leading Arab nationalists in 1915-1916.

Yusuf also worked relentlessly against Sharif Husayn, the Prince of Mecca, who was leading an armed uprising against the Ottoman Empire from the Arabian Desert. It was crazy for the people of Damascus, Yusuf said, to abandon the luxuries and privileges of the Ottoman Empire to follow a group of Bedouins allied to Great Britain. It was religiously wrong, he added, to side with a Christian power against the Muslim leaders of the Ottoman Empire. In 1912, Yusuf nominated himself once again for parliament on a CUP ticket, and won with an overwhelming majority.

Abd al-Rahman al-Yusuf.

When the Ottoman Empire was defeated in October 1918, an Arab administration was created in Damascus and headed by Husayn's son, King Faysal I. Yusuf formed the opposition to the post-Ottoman regime and created the National Party to promote his views on Ottomanism. The party achieved limited success during Faysal's era (1918-1920) and died out when the French abolished the Syrian throne in July 1920. During the Faysal interlude, however, Yusuf served as a deputy for Damascus in the Syrian National Congress, the equivalent of a modern parliament that lasted from 1918 to 1920.

Following the occupation of Syria in July 1920, the French forced Faysal into exile and worked with the pro-French prime minister, Dr Ala al-Din al-Droubi, on crushing the resistance in Syria. Yusuf had been close to Droubi since the early 1900s, when the latter had been Sultan Abdulhamid's private doctor. Droubi created a cabinet on July 25 and appointed Yusuf head of the Bureau of Consultation. The two men welcomed the mandate system and promised to curb Faysal's influence in Syria. They taxed locals to help reconstruct Syria and donated personal funds for infrastructure projects, schools, and roads. They informed Faysal that he was no longer welcome in Syria and that he must leave immediately. If he failed to do so, then they would have him arrested and deported.

On August 12, 1920, less than one month after the proclamation of the mandate, a group of men who claimed to be loyalists of Faysal assassinated Ala al-Din Droubi and Abd al-Rahman al-Yusuf in Hawran, a town in southern Syria next to the Jordanian border. Masked men ambushed their entourage and shot them in cold blood.

Sources:

Batatu, Hanna. *Syria's Peasantry: the Descendants of its Lesser Rural Notables and their Politics* (2000).

Hakim, Yusuf. *Souriyya wa al-Ahd al-Faysali*, Beirut (1986).

Husari, Sati. *Yawm Maysaloun*, Beirut (1947).

Khoury, Philip. *Urban Notables and Arab Nationalism* (1983).

Moubayed, Sami. *The Politics of Damascus 1920-1946* (1999).

Russell, Malcom. *The First Modern Arab State: Syria under Faysal I* (1987).

al-Za'im, Husni
(1894-1949)

Husni al-Za'im was born in Aleppo to a Damascene family of Kurdish origin. He served in the Ottoman Army during World War I. In 1918, he joined the Arab underground and became an officer in the Arab Army of Sharif Husayn, the Prince of Mecca.

In 1918, the Ottoman Empire was defeated and Za'im retired from public life. He emerged once again in July 1920, following the French occupation of Syria, as an officer in the French-created Army of the Levant. He underwent military training in France and in 1939 was a supporter of the Nazi regime in Germany. He admired Adolph Hitler and allied himself with the pro-Hitler Vichy regime in France led by Marshal Petain in World War II. In 1941, Za'im fought with the forces of Vichy against the Free French movement of General Charles de Gaulle.

When the Vichy forces were defeated in Syria, de Gaulle ordered Za'im's arrest and he remained in prison until Syria proclaimed independence in April 1946. Using his connections with former Prime Minister Jamil Mardam Bey, Za'im reentered the Syrian Army and became director of police in 1947. One year later, during the Arab-Israeli War of 1948, he was promoted to chief of staff.

The Syrian defeat in Palestine was a blow to the officers in Syria. Za'im blamed President Shukri al-Quwatli for poor management and Quwatli accused Za'im of incompetent command at the war front. Quwatli also accused officers close to Za'im of profiteering at the army's expense and arrested Antune Bustani, the director of supply, and Fou'ad Mardam Bey, bringing both men to trial on the charge of corruption.

Adding to Za'im's fury at Quwatli were the daily attacks made against him and his men in parliament by Faysal al-Asali, a pro-Quwatli deputy who accused the officers of corruption and demanded that Za'im stand trial for misusing his military post. Infuriated by the criticism, Za'im questioned the duties of Defense Minister Khalid al-Azm, who was letting a deputy attack and insult the head of the Syrian Army and get away with it. Azm summoned Za'im for a meeting, left him waiting for hours, then refused to give him an audience. It was rumored in Syria that Azm was planning to relieve Za'im of his duties as chief of staff.

Backed by a group of angry officers, and with CIA assistance from Stephan Meade, the US Military Attaché in Damascus, Husni al-Za'im launched a military coup d'etat on March 29, 1949. (It should be added that Za'im had informed the British of his plans well before the coup. Most likely he had also spoken to the French, but their archives have not been opened to the public, so French foreknowledge cannot be verified.) Za'im arrested Shukri al-Quwatli, Khalid al-Azm, and all other politicians who had been critical of the officers in the Arab-Israeli War of 1948. The outspoken deputy Faysal al-Asali was also arrested and sent to Mezzeh prison.

Za'im dissolved parliament on April 1 and appointed himself head of state. His coup was the first of its kind in the Arab world. General Za'im outlawed all political parties and began searching for potential allies in the Middle East. The governments of Lebanon, Saudi Arabia, and Egypt were too close to ex-President Quwatli and refused to recognize the coup that brought him down. But when Za'im opened negotiations with Iraq, making it seem that he was receptive to the notion of a Syrian-Iraqi union, Saudi Arabia and Egypt quickly reversed their position and offered to recognize Za'im's new government on condition that Quwatli be freed. Za'im complied, releasing the ex-president from prison and exiling him to Egypt.

In response, Cairo and Riyadh officially recognized Za'im's new government. They offered him further political endorsement if he sided with them against the ambitions of the Hashemite kings of Baghdad and Amman who wanted to create a united Arab monarchy under the Hashemite crown. Za'im agreed and severed relations with King Faysal II of Iraq and King Abdullah of Jordan, accusing them of harboring territorial ambitions in Syria. Furthermore, Za'im arrested all Hashemite sympathizers in Syria, charging them with wanting to abolish Syria's republican regime and replace it with a monarchy. Za'im closed the borders with Jordan, mobilized his army on the Iraqi-Syrian border, and threatened at a press conference to "hang King Abdullah at the Marjeh Square in Damascus!" The Saudis and the Egyptians offered financial assistance to Za'im's regime and King Farouk invited him to Cairo on April 21, 1949, receiving him as a guest of honor at Abidin Palace.

Husni al-Za'im.

King Farouk warned Za'im that Great Britain and the USA were disturbed by his strained relations with the Hashemites, their number one allies in the Middle East, and that the two Western democracies might harass him until he changed his course. Za'im laughed and replied, "Then let them, and I will ask for help from the Soviets and let a third World War start from Damascus!"

Domestically, Za'im introduced many reforms, giving women their suffrage rights and improving the conditions at Damascus University. He perceived himself as a modern Ataturk, outlawing the *tarboosh* (fez), claiming that it was part of an outdated Ottoman order, and threatening any Syrian seen in public in his pajamas with arrest and a hefty fine since it was common for many Syrians to promenade in their pajamas in the traditional quarters of town.

Za'im arrested hundreds of politicians and outlawed forty-six newspapers in Syria. He opened secret channels with Israel and tried to negotiate a peace treaty with the young Zionist state. Za'im offered to resettle thousands of Palestinians in Syria (in the remote al-Jazeera region) and open a Syrian embassy in Tel Aviv if the Israelis were willing to secure US funds for Syria and relinquish Lake Tiberias. He even proposed a meeting with Israeli Prime Minister David Ben Gurion, but Ben Gurion refused his request. Ben Gurion's rejection mattered little, however, because Za'im was ousted from office shortly thereafter.

During his short reign of power, Za'im was up to other mischief as well. Sami Jumaa, an officer in the intelligence bureau, accused Za'im of bringing Israeli Foreign Minister Moshe Sharett to Syria for secret talks in Bludan, a summer resort near Damascus. Jumaa claimed that Sharett was disguised as a senior officer in the Syrian Army and that his talks with Za'im did not advance a Syrian-Israeli peace deal.

Za'im's downfall was brought about by his increasing authoritarian rule at home, and his blunder with the President of the Syrian Social Nationalist Party (SSNP) Antune Sa'ada. In June 1949, Sa'ada had taken refuge in Syria to escape a death sentence in Beirut. Za'im received Sa'ada with open arms and promised to support him in overthrowing the Lebanese government of Prime Minister Riyad al-Sulh.

For a long time, Za'im had complained of his strained relations with the leaders of Beirut, who were still allied to ex-President Quwatli. Early on in his regime, the British Foreign Office noted in its dispatch from Damascus, "There is no love lost between Riyad al-Sulh and Za'im, the former being convinced that Za'im is a dangerous madman, while the latter continues to suspect Riyad of intriguing against him." Shortly after coming to power, Za'im told an American diplomat in Damascus, "Lebanon should be part of Syria. With one hundred additional armored trucks, I can take Lebanon."

In April 1949, Za'im received two Lebanese opposition leaders, Kamil Sham'un and Abd al-Hamid Karameh, and encouraged them to use force to topple the cabinet of Riyad al-Sulh. While Sham'un and Karameh refused, Antune Sa'ada was more than willing to comply. In exchange for Za'im's "unlimited support," Sa'ada pledged to set up an SSNP government in Beirut that would support the ambitions of the Syrian leader.

While Sa'ada was preparing for his insurrection, Za'im sealed a secret agreement with Prime Minister Sulh, promising to extradite the SSNP leader in exchange for Lebanese support for his regime. On July 8, as planned, Sa'ada was abducted and handed over to Lebanese authorities, who immediately executed him.

Sa'ada's death infuriated Sami al-Hinnawi, a prominent officer and SSNP loyalist. Hinnawi rallied the support of like-minded officers and overthrew Za'im later that summer. On Hinnawi's orders, Za'im and his prime minister, Muhsen al-Barazi, who had negotiated the deal with Riyad al-Sulh, were arrested and executed by firing squad on August 14, 1949. The coup was funded by the anti-Za'im monarchy in Iraq and carried out by SSNP officers in the Syrian Army. Husni al-Za'im ruled Syria with force for only 137 days.

Sources:
Arslan, Adil. *Muzakarat al-Ameer Adil Arslan an Al-al-Za'im Husni al-Za'im* (1954).
Azm, Khalid. *Muzakarat Khalid al-Azm* (1973).
Commins, David. *Historical Dictionary of Modern Syria*, Lanham (1996).
Copland, Miles. *The Game of Nations.*
Fansa, Bashir. *Al-Naqbat wa al-Mughamarat* (1997).
Fansa, Nazir. *137 Yawm Hazzat Souriyyayya wa al-Watan al-Arabi* (1982).
Hawrani, Akram. *Muzakarat Akram al-Hawrani* (2000).
Ismail, Thuraya. *Myths and Realities* (2002).
Juma, Sami. *Awrak Min Daftar al-Watan* (2001).
Moubayed, Sami. *Damascus Between Democracy and Dictatorship* (2000).
Ouff, Bashir. *Al-Inkilab al-Souri* (1949).
Rathmell, Andrew. *Secret War in the Middle East* (1995).
Samman, Mutih. *Watan wa Askar* (1995).
Seale, Patrick. *The Struggle for Syria* (1961).
Torrey, Gordon. *Syrian Politics and the Military* (1964).
Al-Ayyam, al-Qabas, and *al-Inkilab* (April 1-August 15, 1949).

Zamarayya, Leon
(1904-?)

Leon Zamarayya was born in Aleppo and studied law at Damascus University, graduating in 1929. He opened a legal practice in Aleppo and rose to become president of the Aleppo Lawyers' Syndicate in the 1930s.

In 1946, Zamarayya joined the National Party, a coalition of notables who shared no ideology other than a common desire to maintain Syria's democratic government and confront the territorial ambitions of King Abdullah of Jordan who wanted to annex Syria to his kingdom.

In October 1954, Zamarayya became a deputy in parliament and in February 1955 was appointed minister of finance in the cabinet of Prime Minister Sabri al-Asali, the secretary-general of the National Party.

Zamarayya emerged in the second half of the 1950s as a radical opponent of Syria's alliance with President Gamal Abd al-Nasser of Egypt. He opposed Nasser's socialist views and argued against his alliance with the USSR, claiming that Syria should not pursue Egypt's leftist policies. When Syria and Egypt merged to form the United Arab Republic (UAR) in 1958, Leon Zamarayya resigned from political activity.

On September 28, 1961, Zamarayya supported the officers that came to power in Syria and toppled the UAR. He became minister of finance and supply in the first post-Nasser cabinet of Prime Minister Ma'mun al-Kuzbari and held office until December 1961. He also served as a member of parliament from 1961 to 1963. In 1962, President Nazim al-Qudsi considered appointing Zamarayya prime minister, but his idea was turned down by a strong veto from the armed forces who despised Zamarayya's anti-Nasser policies.

In March 1963, the Baath Party came to power in Syria and pledged to restore the UAR. The Baath Party officers relieved Leon Zamarayya of his duties and terminated his civil rights as a Syrian citizen.

Sources:
Barada (March 24, 1963).
Samman, Mutih. *Watan wa Askar* (1995).

al-Zu'ayyin, Yusuf
(1931-)

Yusuf al-Zu'ayyin was born in Abu Kamal, a frontier town on the Syrian-Iraqi border that lies on the banks of the Euphrates River. He studied medicine at Damascus University and became a voluntary medic in the Algerian Revolution (1954-1962) against the French, serving alongside the resistance forces of Houari Boumedienne.

Zu'ayyin's experience in Algeria came to shape a bulk of his future vision, especially during the Arab-Israeli War of 1967 when he claimed that Israel, like France in Algeria, could be forced to yield by force. He returned to Syria in 1957 and joined the Baath Party of Michel Aflaq and Salah al-Bitar. Zu'ayyin was attracted to the party's socialist views, preaching a classless society, land redistribution, and Arab nationalism.

In March 1963, the Military Committee of the Baath Party came to power in Syria and Zu'ayyin became minister of agricultural reforms in the cabinet of Prime Minister Salah al-Bitar. Zu'ayyin was charged with confiscating land belonging to the urban notability and redistributing it accordingly among farmers. He nationalized the property of many landowners in Damascus, Aleppo,

Homs, Hama, and Lattakia, and gave the farmers the right to farm the land and keep whatever revenue it produced.

For the following three years, internal strife characterized the Baath Party government of President Amin al-Hafez. Two factions developed within the party, one revolving around the president and the party founders Michel Aflaq and Salah al-Bitar, and the other around the military wing of Air Force Commander Hafez al-Asad and Chief of Staff Salah Jadid. Aflaq and Bitar wanted to demilitarize the state while Asad and Jadid wanted to impose a hard-line, pan-Arab, and socialist policy on Syria.

Zu'ayyin allied himself with Jadid, and at the age of thirty-four was appointed prime minister on September 22, 1965. On February 23, 1966, Jadid and Asad seized power in Syria and overthrew the regime of President Amin al-Hafez. Hafez was arrested while Aflaq and Bitar were exiled to Lebanon. Jadid once again appointed Zu'ayyin prime minister in the new government on March 1, 1966. Zu'ayyin appointed Ibrahim Makhous, another doctor, as minister of foreign affairs and Mohammad Rabah al-Tawil, an officer, as minister of interior.

Zu'ayyin moved ahead with his land redistribution program. Considered a fanatical idealist, he tried to refashion society from top to bottom. True to his socialist views, he appeared in France one day for a meeting with President Charles de Gaulle wearing a Mao-style jacket. He was informed that de Gaulle would not receive him until he dressed formally. Zu'ayyin refused, but when de Gaulle remained adamant, he gave up and put on the Western-style suit and tie before entering the Elysee Palace.

Zu'ayyin ruled Syria during the Arab-Israeli War of 1967 and was blamed by Syrians of poor leadership. Facing mounting criticism from a public who blamed him for their dire economic conditions, Zu'ayyin resigned from office on October 28, 1968. When Asad came to power in November 1970, he had Jadid and Zu'ayyin arrested. The ex-prime minister remained in prison until Asad released him in 1981, and Yusuf al-Zu'ayyin took up residence in Hungary.

Sources:
Batatu, Hanna. *Syria's Peasantry: the Descendants of its Lesser Rural Notables and their Politics* (2000).
Seale, Patrick. *Asad: Struggle for the Middle East* (1988).

al-Zu'bi, Mahmud
(1938-2000)

Mahmud al-Zu'bi was born in Hawran, a province next to the Syrian-Jordanian border, and studied agronomy at Cairo University. He returned to Syria in 1963 to become head of the agricultural office in Idlib, a town in northern Syria.

Zu'bi joined the ruling Baath Party and in 1970 became governor of Hama. In 1972, Zu'bi became secretary of the Peasants' Bureau in Damascus, an office created to supervise the redistribution of land and attend to the needs of farmers. Zu'bi became a deputy in the first parliament under President Hafez al-Asad from February to December 1971. In 1973, he became director of development on the dam being constructed on the Euphrates River. In 1976, the Baath Party appointed him chairman of its financial bureau. And in 1980, he became director of the Peasants' Bureau. In November 1981, Asad appointed him speaker of parliament and kept this post until Asad made him prime minister in February 1988. Zu'bi came to office in the midst of public optimism. It was hoped that his cabinet would end the economic stalemate created under his predecessor Abdel Raouf al-Kassem.

In March 2000, Mahmud al-Zu'bi resigned from office. After thirteen years in power, he was unable to solve any of Syria's long-standing economic grievances. Asad expelled him from the Baath Party when it was revealed that Zu'bi had profiteered at the country's expense and used his office to amass a fortune in an airplane deal conducted with two of his ministers in 1996. Asad discharged him from the party's Regional Command and summoned him to court on the charge of corruption. While waiting to appear before court, Zu'bi's property was confiscated and he was placed under house arrest.

It was officially announced that Mahmud al-Zu'bi committed suicide on May 21, 2000, to avoid the humiliation of a court trial.

Sources:
Al-Hayat (May 22, 2000).
As'ed, Shakir. *Al-Barlaman al-Souri fi Tatawurhu al-Tareekhi* (2002).

Air raid on the old city of Damascus by the French, October 18, 1925. This photo shows the ruins of the home of Nasib al-Bakri (1888-1966), a rebel leader from Damascus. The the bombing caused the death of 1,416 people, 336 of whom were women and children.

Twenty years later on May 29, 1945, a French air raid on the Syrian Parliament and on the Citadel killed 660 civilians in addition to police and soldiers.

Bodies of resistance fighters placed on display in Marjeh Square by the French during the insurgency. The entire revolt, which lasted from July 1925 until 1927, led to the death of 6,000 Syrians. Another 1,000 were left homeless.

Syrian students protest the French attack, October 1925.

Damascus women riot in protest against the French attack, 1925.

NATIONAL ACTIVISTS

The people profiled in this chapter took part in national revolts and social movements that affected public life in Syria.

Al-Fatat, the leading opposition party in Ottoman Syria, was established by five Arab activists living in Paris in 1911. The organization called on Arab and Turkish citizens to remain united within the Ottoman framework, but proclaimed that Arabs should have equal rights and obligations. In 1913, al-Fatat moved its offices to Beirut. In 1914, its founders opened an office in Damascus to coordinate nationalist activity.

In the summer of 1913, the al-Fatat founders were called to an Arab congress in Paris to discuss the deteriorating living conditions within the Ottoman Empire. Not wishing to break completely with authorities in Istanbul, they did not call for full Arab emancipation, but tried to mend relations with the Ottomans. When that failed, al-Fatat publicly headed the separatist movement, demanding a complete break.

Fakhri Hasan al-Kharrat, a commander of the Syrian Revolt, was hanged in public in the Marjeh Square (Martyr's Square) in Damascus in October 1925.

Syrian activists, provocateurs, and guerrilla fighters fought the Ottomans during World War I in the rebel Arab Army of Sharif Husayn (1916-1918). Many of them had been in the Ottoman Army and deserted to join the Arab Army, which was fighting from the Arabian Desert (present day Saudi Arabia). After the French took control in 1920, discontent among Syrians built up until, from 1925 to 1927, Syrians launched a guerrilla war under command of the Druze warrior Sultan al-Atrash. In 1936, Syrian guerillas went to Palestine to join an uprising lead by the Palestinian leader Amin al-Husayni against the British Mandate. In 1941, another group of guerillas went to Iraq to join a rebellion against the British. In 1948, many Syrians volunteered for service in the Army of Deliverance, a pan-Arab force created by the Arab League to fight the Israelis in Palestine.

Marjeh Square has been the center of Damascus since the early days of the Ottoman Empire. It was the place that the Ottomans chose to publicly hang national activists on May 6, 1916, earning it the name "Martyr's Square." In 1925-1926, the French adopted the practice of hanging Syrian rebels in Marjeh.

al-Abid, Naziq
(1898-1959)

Naziq al-Abid was born in Damascus to a family of well-to-do merchants. Her father was Mustapha Pasha al-Abid, a Syrian aristocrat and an insider at the court of Sultan Abdulhamid II. Naziq studied literature with private tutors, learned French and German and obtained a BA in agriculture from the Women's College in Istanbul.

Abid began writing articles for local magazines, criticizing the coup that ousted the regime of Sultan Abdulhamid in 1908. She wrote against the Committee for Union and Progress (CUP) which came to power and "militarized" the Ottoman Empire. Abid argued that the CUP should stop distributing senior government offices only to Ottoman officials, but rather divide them equally among Arabs and Turks.

In 1914, Abid established contacts with other like-minded women and created an association advocating women's rights in Syria. Their links to the Syrian nationalist underground provoked Jamal Pasha, the Ottoman military governor of Damascus. Pasha outlawed Abid's activities and sent her into exile. She moved to Cairo and returned to Damascus in October 1918 when the Ottoman Empire was defeated. During the post-Ottoman era, she participated in politics, writing newspaper articles and giving public speeches that demanded equal rights for women, including female suffrage. In 1919, Abid founded Noor al-Fayha (Light of Damascus), the first women's organization in Damascus. That same year, Abid headed a delegation of Syrian women to meet with the American King-Crane Commission dispatched by US President Woodrow Wilson. The job of the commission was to find out what Syrian's thought about the establishment of a French Mandate in the Middle East. Abid took off her veil before the US officials, in a gesture that signaled her desire for a more secular and liberal Syria.

In 1920, Abid founded a magazine bearing the name of her organization, and became its editor-in-chief. In 1921, she founded the Damascene Women's Club. One year later, she founded and became president of the Syrian Red Star. In 1922, she opened the Syrian Red Crescent, modeled on the Red Cross, an international organization dedicated to caring for the sick and wounded in war.

Naziq al-Abid was a close associate and supporter of King Faysal I, who ruled Syria from 1918 to 1920. In July 1920, she volunteered to serve in the Syrian Army and fought in the infamous Battle of Maysaloun on the Damascus-Beirut highway. At Maysaloun, the Syrian Army was defeated and the French occupied Syria. She paraded to battle through the streets of Damascus in full military uniform and unveiled herself before newspaper cameras, causing an uproar in conservative Syrian circles. King Faysal rewarded Abid for her service by naming her an honorary general in the Syrian Army. Newspapers hailed her as the "Joan of Arc of the Arabs" while others compared her to Khawla Bint al-Azhar, an ancient

Arab woman warrior. When the Faysal regime was overthrew, Abid was again exiled from Damascus, taking up residence in Istanbul.

Abid returned to Syria in 1922, gave up politics, and devoted her time to humanitarian and literary activities. In 1924, she founded the Women's Union with Adila Bayhum and the Lebanese women's rights activist, Labiba Thabet. In 1925, Abid took part in the Syrian revolt of the Arab Mountain and led the life of an outlaw, smuggling food and munitions, and caring for the wounded. During the revolt, Abid and Bayhum founded the Damascene Women's Awakening Society. The women organized workshops to offer handicraft training to the displaced and widowed women of rural Syria.

Naziq al-Abid.

They also offered English and sewing lessons, and encouraged women to complete their educations.

In 1927, Abid fled Syria when the French issued a warrant for her arrest. She moved to neighboring Lebanon and married a Beiruti notable, Mohammad Jamil Bayhum, a former deputy in the Syrian National Congress who had lobbied for women's suffrage from 1918 to 1920. Bayhum believed in Abid's cause and financed her projects in Beirut. In 1928, Abid and her husband helped finance and promote a book, *al-Sufur wa al-Hijab (Veiling and Unveiling)*, written by a twenty-year-old woman, Nazira Zayn al-Din.

In 1935, Abid founded the Association for Working Women in Lebanon. The organization lobbied with President Alfred Naccache to adopt laws permitting sick days for women workers, along with maternity leave and equal pay. Following the Arab-Israeli War of 1948, Abid created and chaired the Association for Palestinian Refugee Employment in Beirut, serving as its president until her death in 1959. Naziq al-Abid also helped finance the construction of a hospital for children and served on its board of directors.

Sources:
Bayhum, Mohammad Jamil. *Fatat al-Sharq fi Hadarat al-Gharb* (1952).
Thompson, Elizabeth. *Colonial Citizens* (1999).

al-Aidi, Shawkat
(1897-1926)

Shawkat al-Aidi was born and raised in Damascus. He joined the Ottoman Army and served as a commanding officer until June 1916, when the Arab Revolt against the Ottoman Turks broke out. Aidi deserted the Ottoman Army and joined the rebel Arab Army of Sharif Husayn, the Prince of Mecca.

Aidi fought with Husayn until the defeat of the Ottoman Empire at the end of World War I in October 1918. Aidi then returned to Damascus and joined the Syrian Army created by King Faysal I, Husayn's son, who had become the new ruler of Syria. Faysal appointed Aidi military advisor to the throne in Damascus. In 1919, King Faysal made him commander of the military garrison on the Golan Heights. He took part in the Battle of Maysaloun on July 24, 1920, when the French defeated the Syrian Army.

In 1920, the French Mandate was proclaimed over Syria and Lebanon, forcing Faysal and his entire entourage into exile. Aidi went to Mecca and joined Sharif Husayn, then king of the Hijaz, to serve as his military advisor. In December 1920, King Hussein appointed Aidi commander of the Jeddah garrison.

Then in 1923, Aidi was exiled once again when Prince Abd al-Aziz Ibn Saud of the Nejd toppled the Husayn regime and expelled the king and his military officers. Husayn went into exile in Amman while Aidi chose exile in Baghdad. King Faysal, who had been enthroned in Baghdad, appointed Aidi as his military advisor. Aidi returned to Syria in 1925 and took up arms with Sultan al-Atrash, the veteran Druze leader, in a national uprising against the French.

Shawkat al-Aidi was killed in combat in 1925.

Sources:

Jundi, Adham. *Tareekh al-Thawrat al-Souriyya fi Ahd al-Intidab al-Faransi* (1960).

Murayden, Izzat. *Dr Ahmad Munif al-Aidi* (1996).

Akash, Sa'id
(1892-1941)

Sa'id Akash was born in Dummar, a small mountain town overlooking Damascus. As a youth, Akash worked with his family and received no proper schooling. In 1916, he joined the Arab underground against the Ottoman Empire. Three years later, he launched a revolt in the Barada Valley against the French, who had come to occupy Damascus and impose their mandate on the Middle East.

In July 1920, Akash volunteered for service in the Syrian Army with Defense Minister Yusuf al-Azma. When the army was defeated, Akash fled to the mountains and joined the underground. He coordinated his armed revolt against the French with Ibrahim Hananu, leader of the Aleppo Revolt, and Saleh al-Ali, leader of the Alawite Mountain Revolt. Akash also worked closely with Lebanese nationalist Tawfiq Hawlu Haydar, who was leading a military uprising against the

French in the Beqqa Valley.

Akash's men aided in Haydar's revolt. They attacked Baalbak prison, released its prisoners, and gave them arms to confront the French. Akash also took control of the Damascus-Beirut highway and commanded battles in Qatana, Sabbura, and Nabek, three districts surrounding Damascus.

The French high commissioner, General Henri Gouraud, summoned Akash to a meeting and offered a financial reward if he would give up his arms. Gouraud also offered Akash any military post he desired in French Mandate Syria. Akash turned down the offer and continued to live the life of an outlaw until French Commissioner Maurice Sarrail put a bounty on his head in 1925. Akash then fled to Cairo and lived in exile until 1941 when President Taj al-Din al-Hasani issued a general amnesty and welcomed him back to Syria. Two weeks after his return, however, French agents tracked Sa'id Akash down and assassinated him in Damascus.

Sources:
Jundi, Adham. *Tareekh al-Thawrat al-Souriyya fi Ahd al-Intidab al-Faransi* (1960).
Bawab, Sulayman. *Mawsuat Alam Souriyya fi al-Qarn al-Ishreen,* Vol III (1999).

al-Ali, Saleh
(1884-1950)

Saleh al-Ali was from a prominent rural family in the Alawite Mountain of Syria. The young Ali commanded the personal allegiance of a small group of soldiers, and he emerged as a local chieftain during the final years of the Ottoman Empire.

In 1919, the first French troops arrived on the Syrian coastline to impose their mandate in the Middle East. Funded by twelve village notables, Ali created a small fighting force and engaged the invading troops in combat. His guerrilla army also received funds and support from King Faysal I who was carrying out his own diplomatic war against the French from Damascus. Saleh al-Ali succeeded in forcing a French garrison to disarm and retreat into the heart of the mountain, where they were taken hostage. This assault was one of the first armed operations against the French in all of Syria. It inspired similar attacks all over the mountain, and by July 1920, the region had been partially liberated from French military occupation. The French convened a military tribunal in the coastal city of Lattakia and sentenced Ali to death on the charge of treason.

For the next two years, Ali lived the life of an outlaw, emerging occasionally in disguise to lead attacks against the French. His rebellion came to be known as the "Alawite Revolt." Ali's rebellion was allied with Ibrahim Hananu's uprising in

Aleppo, the revolt in neighboring Tal Kalakh led by the Dandashi tribe, and the uprising in Antioch instigated by Subhi Barakat. Kemal Ataturk, the reformist leader who was based in Anatolia and opposed the French occupation of Syria, channeled arms and money to Ali's revolt. Two Lattakia-based families, the Harouns and Shraytihs, also donated to Ali's movement. The journalist Abd al-Latif Yunis wrote and delivered all of Ali's speeches for the illiterate warlord.

In June 1920, French High Commissioner Henri Gouraud requested a truce with Saleh al-Ali. But King Faysal's minister of war, Yusuf al-Azma, visited Ali in hiding and encouraged him to continue fighting, claiming that the world community was opposed to France's aggression and would not let Paris occupy Damascus. The balance of power in the Alawite Mountain did not begin to shift in favor of the French until Damascus fell to the forces of General Gouraud on July 25, 1920. In January 1921, Ali sent a petition to the League of Nations requesting international intervention on behalf of the Syrians. He cited the fourteen-point peace declaration of US President Woodrow Wilson and demanded that Syria be given the right to self-determination.

The French ignored Ali's petition and mounted a full-fledged offensive against Ali's forces in March 1921. Three French units circled the Alawite Mountain, from Lattakia and Banyas in the west, and from Hama in the east. In October 1921, the French defeated Saleh al-Ali, and his role in the nationalist struggle came to an end. A French court placed a bounty on his life, brought him to trial in absentia, and sentenced him to death. He remained in hiding until the French issued a general amnesty in 1922.

Ali abstained from all political activity until his death in 1950. But when the French evacuated from Syria on April 17, 1946, President Shukri al-Quwatli invited him to attend the Independence Day celebrations in Damascus. This was, Quwatli claimed, a token of appreciation for Ali's struggle against the French when they first came to Syria in 1919.

It was Ali's first public appearance since his 1922 defeat. The politicians who came to power in the 1930s and 1940s had refused to honor him, claiming that he had led his revolt in the 1920s to preserve the autonomy of the Alawite Mountain, and not for the sake of Syrian independence. Having led the diplomatic struggle against the French, these notables claimed that the armed struggle of the 1920s had achieved nothing for Syria.

Quwatli, however, thought otherwise, and saw the need to honor Saleh al-Ali. At the podium, as the crowds were cheering for the aged and ailing warrior, Quwatli said, "Oh Sheikh Saleh, this is your day! It was you who taught us nationalism and you who pushed us to jihad, for you were the first to open fire on the French. This feast is your feast and the party is your party. If we celebrate the evacuation, then we are celebrating you."

Sources:

Jundi, Adham. *Tareekh al-Thawrat al-Souriyya fi Ahd al-Intidab al-Faransi* (1960).

Khoury, Philip. *Syria and the French Mandate* (1987).

Landis, Joshua. *Nationalism and the Politics of Za'ama* (1997).

Yunis, Abd al-Latif. *Muzakarat Dr Abd al-Latif Yunis* (1992).

Yunis, Abd al-Latif. *Thawrat al-Sheikh Saleh al-Ali* (1947).

al-Asali, Shukri
(1868-1916)

Shukri al-Asali was born to a prominent landowning family and raised in Damascus. He studied at the Ottoman Law Academy in Istanbul and began his career as editor of the Arabic daily, *al-Qabas*. He then joined the Arab Renaissance Society founded by the theologian Tahir al-Jaza'iri. The society aimed to promote Arab, rather than Ottoman, nationalism in the Arabic provinces of the Ottoman Empire.

In July 1908, a coup took place in Istanbul and curbed the powers of the Sultan Abdulhamid II. A group of young, hard-line Ottoman officers named the Committee for Union and Progress (CUP) carried out the coup. Asali allied himself with the officers and supported their reform campaign. When they lifted the press censorship that had been imposed under Sultan Abdulhamid, Asali began to more freely express his views on Arab nationalism.

Then, in 1911, the Damascus deputy, Mohammad al-Ajlani, died and Asali nominated himself for the parliamentary by-elections, easily winning due to his alliance with the CUP. Once a member of parliament, however, Asali grew disenchanted with Turkish favoritism and accused the officers of packing the bureaucracy with Ottoman Turks rather than Arabs. He spoke out against a law that the CUP had recently passed that made Turkish the official language of schools, courts, and Arab provinces in the Ottoman Empire. Asali claimed that the law was unjust and needed to be changed. In the chamber, he allied himself with two other like-minded statesmen, Abd al-Hamid al-Zahrawi and Shafiq Mu'ayyad al-Azm. The three clashed with pro-CUP deputies like Abd al-Rahman al-Yusuf and Fawzi al-Azm, two Ottoman-Arab aristocrats who had been close to Abdulhamid before shifting their allegiance to the CUP.

In addition to his parliamentary career, from 1908 to 1914 Asali wrote in *al-Qabas* and tried to encourage young Syrian men to abandon Ottomanism and turn toward Arabism. Moreover, he was able to bring together a cohesive Syrian-Arab opposition to the CUP, both within parliament and among intellectual circles in Damascus. In April 1912, the CUP called for new parliamentary elections, and Asali and other outspoken deputies lost their seats in parliament. Asali and the others accused the authorities of tampering with the ballots, then they allied themselves with the Ottoman Party of Administrative Decentralization, a movement headed by the opposition leader Rafic al-Azm.

Meanwhile, Asali became increasingly preoccupied with the politics of Palestine. He met frequently with members of the Zionist Agency to hear their claims for a national homeland. The Zionist leaders recommended Arab endorsement for a Jewish state in Palestine, and in exchange, promised to support an Arab kingdom in the Middle East once the Ottoman Empire was defeated. Asali turned down the offer but promised to hold another round of talks with Chaim Weizmann, president of the Zionist Agency. The talks were to take place in the mountain resort of Brummanah in the summer of 1914. Due to the outbreak of World War I in August 1914, however, the meeting was postponed, then called off altogether.

In 1915, Asali officially joined the Arab underground against the Ottoman Empire. With Sharif Husayn, the Prince of Mecca, Asali began planning for an armed uprising against the Ottomans. The Arab Revolt was co-planned with Great Britain and aimed at bringing an end to the Ottoman Empire. The revolt was scheduled to be launched on June 10, 1918, but it never came about because Jamal Pasha, the Ottoman governor of Syria, arrested Asali and brought him before a military tribunal in Aley on Mount Lebanon.

Asali was publicly executed on May 6, 1916, in Marjeh Square—the center of Damascus between Souk al-Hamidiyya and the Hijaz Railway Station. Marjeh was sometimes called "Martyr's Square," and for good reason, for that was where Shukri al-Asali was hung and his body left dangling on the scaffold beside a group of twenty-one other activists, including Mahmud al-Boukhari, Omar al-Jaza'iri, Shafiq Mu'ayyad al-Azm, Rafic Sallum, Rushdi al-Sham'a, and Abd al-Hamid al-Zahrawi.

Sources:
Commins, David. *Historical Dictionary of Modern Syria* (1996).
Encyclopedia of the Modern Middle East, Vol I (1996). Article by Charles U. Zenzie.
Khoury, Philip. *Urban Notables and Arab Nationalism* (1983).
Saikaly, Samir. "Damascus Intellectual Life in the Opening Years of the 20th Century," in *Intellectual Life in the Arab East 1890-1939* (1981).
Al-Muqtabas April 6, 1911.
FO 371/1246 file 41662 "Quarterly report on the affairs of Syria for the quarter ended September 30, 1911".

al-Ashmar, Mohammad
(1892-1960)

Mohammad al-Ashmar grew up in the religiously conservative neighborhood of al-Midan in Damascus. He studied with local theologians and devoted his early years to prayer and Islamic studies. When France imposed its mandate over Syria in July 1920, Ashmar joined the rebel forces of Ibrahim Hananu in Aleppo.

In 1922, however, the French crushed the Hananu Revolt, arresting Ashmar and deporting him to the rural town of Hawran in southern Syria. But Ashmar escaped and continued to take part in rebel activities in the Alawite Mountain, prompting the French to put him on the "wanted list" and publish a reward for his capture.

From 1923 to 1925, Ashmar lived in Amman as a political exile. In July 1925, he returned to take part in the uprising of the Arab Mountain, launched by the Druze leader, Sultan al-Atrash, who appointed Ashmar field commander of the Damascus revolt. He channeled funds and arms to the Syrian capital in preparation for a massive operation. The objectives of the operation were nothing less than the seizure of all government buildings and the capture, or killing, of all Frenchmen found inside these buildings.

On October 18, 1925, Ashmar led a group of armed men into the old marketplace, burned down many government buildings, and occupied the Azm Palace, the residence of the French high commissioner. Hundreds of Frenchmen were killed and all French property was confiscated. The high commissioner, Maurice Sarrail, responded by staging an air raid on the capital for the next forty-eight hours, killing nearly 400 civilians. Sarrail ordered that the Damascus rebels be arrested and hung in public. Ashmar escaped and fled once again to Jordan. He remained in Amman and lived under the patronage of King Abdullah until the French issued a general amnesty that allowed Ashmar to return to Syria in 1932.

Back in Syria, Mohammad al-Ashmar led a group of theologians who were calling for the establishment of an Islamic state, governed by the law of Islam and free from all Western influence. In 1936, Ashmar made a brief journey to Palestine and took part in the anti-Zionist battles there. He allied himself with Amin al-Husayni, the Mufti of Jerusalem, and channeled arms from Damascus to the Palestinian rebels. In 1943, Ashmar supported the election of Shukri al-Quwatli, a secular politician, to the Syrian presidency. Ashmar believed that Quwatli would fulfill his campaign promise and grant more freedoms to Muslim groups. Quwatli used Ashmar's allegiance to win votes in the al-Midan neighborhood, where Ashmar was very popular.

Once firmly in power, however, Quwatli withdrew his support of the Islamic groups and abandoned Ashmar. Thus, Islamic leaders in Damascus created a political movement aimed at bringing down the Quwatli regime. They criticized Quwatli's social liberalism and accused him of morally corrupting Syrian society. Among the practices that became commonplace under Quwatli, and were criticized by Ashmar, were the opening of cinemas and cabarets, and the increasing number of women who were unveiling in public.

On May 19, 1944, Ashmar led a parade of religious men through Damascus, attacking any unveiled woman they encountered. The group stoned businesses that employed women and threatened to destroy any theaters that permitted married women to enter with men other than their husbands. Quwatli ordered Ashmar's arrest and incarceration in the Palmyra prison. Ashmar's imprisonment caused uproar in Damascus, promoting more anti-government demonstrations that lasted until May 22. Fearing an explosive situation, Quwatli released Ashmar shortly thereafter.

In December 1944, Ashmar and Quwatli clashed once again when the Syrian government took part in the first Women's Conference in Egypt. Among other things, the conference discussed female suffrage, unveiling, and the right of women to hold government office. Ashmar and leading scholars from all over Syria drafted a petition against the government, saying, "The realization of these women's aspirations would lead to disastrous consequences for the Arab Muslim nation: corruption, loss of energy, of patriotic spirit, and will provoke a dire reaction in Syria."

Ashmar also threatened that anti-government demonstrations similar to the ones of May 1944 would ensue. Quwatli, however, ignored the threats and Ashmar did little to implement them. From here, Ashmar ceased all political activity. It is not clear why. Perhaps he lost faith or he was starting to advance in age. But, whatever the cause of his sudden silence, Mohammad al-Ashmar lived in seclusion in Damascus until his death in 1960.

Sources:
Itri, Abd al-Ghani. *Abqariyyat* (1997).
Jundi, Adham. *Tareekh al-Thawrat al-Souriyya fi Ahd al-Intidab al-Faransi* (1960).
Thompson, Elizabeth. *Colonial Citizens* (1999).

al-Atrash, Abd al-Ghaffar
(d. 1942)
Abd al-Ghaffar al-Atrash was born and raised in the Arab Mountain to the leading Druze family in Syria. In 1914, he joined the Arab underground against the Ottoman Empire. Two years later, Atrash moved to Mecca and enlisted in the Arab Army of Sharif Husayn, who was leading an armed insurrection against the Ottoman Turks in the Arabian Desert.

When the Ottoman Empire was defeated in 1918, Atrash retired to his native village and tended to his family's vast agricultural holdings. Then, in July 1925, he took up arms with his cousin, Sultan al-Atrash, in a national uprising against the French Mandate. Atrash became a commanding officer in Suwayda, the capital of the Arab Mountain. In 1927, the French sentenced him to death on the charge of high treason. He fled to Jordan and became advisor to King Abdullah from 1927 to 1930. He returned to Syria when the French issued a general amnesty in 1932 and befriended Taj al-Din al-Hasani, a politician close to the decision-makers in Paris. In 1936, Atrash clashed with Defense Minister Shukri al-Quwatli, who accused him of having "sold out" to the French and promised to "clamp him in chains" for what he called "treason." The animosity between Atrash and Quwatli remained until Atrash's death in 1942.

Atrash was opposed to the German occupation of France in 1940 and lobbied against the pro-German administration of Marshal Petain in Vichy. He also opposed the pro-German regime in Syria, headed by French High Commissioner Henri Dentz. Atrash made contact with the French resistance, headed by General Charles de Gaulle, and secured Druze backing for the Anglo-French campaign in June 1941, aimed at ousting General Dentz and the pro-Hitler French forces in Syria. In September 1941, Prime Minister Hasan al-Hakim appointed Atrash minister of defense in the pro-de Gaulle cabinet.

Abd al-Ghaffar al-Atrash died while in office in March 1942.

Sources:
Landis, Joshua. *Nationalism and the Politics of Za'ama* (1997).

al-Atrash, Sultan
(1885-1982)

Sultan al-Atrash came from a prominent political family in the Arab Mountain. He studied at the Ottoman Military Academy in Istanbul and graduated with high honors. In 1913, he became *za'im* (chief) of his native community when the Ottoman Turks hung his father.

Atrash was conscripted into the Ottoman Army, but defected from service in 1915 to join the Arab underground which strove to overthrow the Ottoman Empire. He served as a link between the Arab leadership in Mecca and the Druze warriors in the Mountain. From 1916 to 1918, Atrash served as a commanding officer in the Arab Army of Sharif Husayn and engaged in combat with Ottoman troops in the Syrian desert.

In 1918, the Ottoman Empire was defeated in World War I and King Faysal I, leader of the Arab Revolt, became king of Syria. Atrash allied himself to the new king, who rewarded his services with the princely title of pasha. During the Faysal years (1918-1920), Sultan al-Atrash was a close associate of the Hashemite family.

Following the family's expulsion from Syria in 1920, Atrash established himself as an ally of King Abdullah of Jordan. From 1920 to 1925, Atrash lobbied within Druze circles for the creation of an Arab kingdom headed either by Faysal, who became king of Iraq, or his brother King Abdullah.

In 1925, Atrash welcomed to his village two Syrian fugitives who were fleeing the French dragnet. French High Commissioner Maurice Sarrail ordered their extradition and, when Atrash refused, the mandate authority ordered an air raid on the Arab Mountain. Atrash mobilized a defense. After receiving funds from the Hashemite royals in Amman, Atrash declared a national uprising against the French on July 21, 1925, and called it "the Great Syrian Revolt." Atrash appointed himself commander-in-chief of the Syrian Revolt, and appointed Abd al-Rahman Shahbandar, a popular resistance leader from Damascus, as his deputy.

Atrash knew Shahbandar from the Faysal era, when the latter had served as minister of foreign affairs, and the two men shared common political views. They believed that republican governments were a foreign import, preferring instead that Syria adhere to Islamic and Arab traditions through a monarchical system of rule. They also believed in the need for armed rather than diplomatic resistance to occupation.

The revolt continued for two years, stretching from the coast of Syria to the interior, until the rebellion was completely crushed in 1927. The revolt left 6,000 civilians dead and 1,000 homeless. The economy had been completely dislocated, commerce was at a standstill, agricultural production was low, and thousands had been left penniless and unemployed by the destruction of their property and homes.

The French sentenced Atrash to death on the charge of treason. He fled to Amman where, along with Shahbandar, he established a provisional government in exile, with himself as president and Shahbandar as his deputy. King Abdullah treated Atrash as a guest of honor from 1927 until the French permitted his return to Syria in 1937. Upon his return, Atrash received a hero's welcome in Damascus, having spent ten years in exile creating the cornerstone for the Syrian national myth. For children growing up in Syria in the 1920s and 1930s, no name was more popular or familiar than Sultan al-Atrash.

Sultan al-Atrash.

Atrash retired from political activity from 1936 to 1943, but emerged in 1944 as a fervent opponent of the National Bloc administration of President Shukri al-Quwatli, accusing Quwatli of favoritism toward the Damascenes. Atrash was also critical of the regime's attempts to attribute independence (which was finally achieved in April 1946) to the diplomatic struggle that took place in the 1940s and not to the armed resistance of the 1920s. He accused Quwatli and his allies of trying to rewrite Syrian history and attribute all the glories of independence to themselves. To show his resentment, Atrash did not attend the independence day celebrations on April 17, 1946 in Damascus. He also refused any financial reward or political posts offered to him by Quwatli, seeing himself as the "moral consciousness" of the Arab Mountain.

Druze warriors welcome Sultan al-Atrash back to Syria in 1937, after a decade of exile following the 1925-1927 insurgency.

From 1951 to 1954, Atrash clashed with the military regime of President Adib al-Shishakli. He criticized Shishakli for closing newspapers and arresting political activists. He objected to Shishakli's pervasive intelligence agents who closely monitored law-abiding Syrians. He complained about Shishakli's one-party rule. Accusing the Druze of planning against him, Shishakli arrested many of their notables in 1953 (including Atrash's son Mansur) and placed the veteran leader under house arrest in the Mountain. Shortly afterward, Shishakli released Mansur, but still Atrash refused to soften his criticism, saying, "I did not ask him for the freedom of my son. I asked him for the freedom of my country."

Sultan al-Atrash created a national uprising against Shishakli. Atrash served as political chief and Hashim al-Atasi served as political chief. Atrash joined the underground that operated out of Beirut and Baghdad. Several of his men were caught, and one confessed that Atrash had been stockpiling arms in the Arab Mountain. Shishakli ordered an air raid on the Mountain that killed an estimated 600 civilians. In February 1954, Shishakli was overthrown by a military coup and Atrash regained his reputation, not only as a hero of independence, but also as one of the leaders of the struggle for democracy in Syria. In 1966, Mansur al-Atrash became chairman of the Revolutionary Command Council of the Baath Party, following the party's rise to power through a military coup in 1963. The elder Atrash clashed with the regime of Salah Jadid, who came to power in February 1966, overthrew the civilian leaders of the Baath Party, and arrested Mansur. Sultan al-Atrash made peace with the Syrian government in 1970 when Hafez al-Asad came to power and treated him as an honored citizen.

Sources:
Bu'ayni, Hasan Amin. *Sultan Basha al-Atrash* (1985).
Faris, George. *Man Hum fi al-`Alam al-Arabi?* (1957).

Jundi, Adham. *Tareekh al-Thawrat al-Souriyya fi Ahd al-Intidab al-Faransi* (1960).

Landis, Joshua. *Nationalism and the Politics of Za'ama* (1997).

Qassab Hasan, Najat. *Saniou al-Jalaa fi Souriyya* (1999).

Rayyes, Munir. *Al-Kitab al-Zahabi lil Thawrat al-Wataniyya fi al-Sharq al-Arabi* (1966).

Shahbandar, Abd al-Rahman. *Al-Thawra al-Wataniyya al-Souriyya* (1933).

al-Bitar, Omar
(1886-1946)

Omar al-Bitar was born into a family of landowning notables and was raised in Lattakia. In 1919, when French troops landed on the Syrian coast, planning to occupy the entire country and impose their mandate on Syria and Lebanon, Bitar led a voluntary team of young men who sabotaged the French troops.

Becoming the self-appointed commander of the Lattakia resistance, Bitar established contact with Saleh al-Ali, leader of the Alawite Mountain Revolt, and Ibrahim Hananu, leader of the Aleppo Revolt. They coordinated joint attacks on the French within the Syrian interior and along the coast.

Using funds channeled from Turkey, where Turkish nationalist Kemal Ataturk was striving to regain influence over Syria, territory that formerly lay within the Ottoman Empire, Bitar purchased arms and equipment for his men. Within six months, Bitar had expanded his following from 100 volunteers to 2,000 armed men. Historians dubbed Bitar's uprising as the "Lattakia revolt."

When the French proclaimed their mandate over Syria in 1920, they accused Bitar and his allies of murdering French officers, rebelling against the mandate, and receiving funds from a foreign power. The French authorities summoned Bitar to court, but he fled to Turkey instead, where he lived as a guest of Ataturk for the next sixteen years. Meanwhile, back in Syria, a French military tribunal sentenced Bitar to death in absentia.

In 1936, following the election of veteran nationalist Hashim al-Atasi to the Syrian presidency, Bitar returned to Syria. At his arrival, Atasi gave Bitar red carpet treatment, hailing him as a national hero, and receiving him as an honored guest at the Presidential Palace.

Bitar joined the National Bloc, the leading anti-French movement that Atasi himself headed, and took up residence in his native Lattakia. In 1937, however, the French arrested him for instigating violence against the mandate and incarcerated him in the Citadel of Damascus. He was released from the Citadel under pressure from various nationalist groups in Syria but maintained a low profile from 1939 to 1942. He reemerged in 1943 as a candidate for parliament. On May 29, 1945, the French bombarded Damascus and tried to arrest President Shukri al-Quwatli and other leaders of the resistance movement. But Omar al-Bitar managed to escape the French once again. He fled to Turkey where he remained until his death in 1946.

Sources:
Bawab, Sulayman. *Mawsuat Alam Souriyya fi al-Qarn al-Ishreen*, Vol III (1999).
Jundi, Adham. *Tareekh al-Thawrat al-Souriyya fi Ahd al-Intidab al-Faransi* (1960).

al-Boukhari, Mahmud
(1890-1916)

Mahmud al-Boukhari grew up in a traditional family of theologians in Damascus. His father, Saleem al-Boukhari, was a prominent Muslim scholar, while his brother Nasuh was a senior Ottoman officer who became prime minister of Syria in 1939. Mahmud studied with religious tutors in his youth and completed his higher education in law at the Muluki Academy in Istanbul.

Boukhari joined the Ottoman Ministry of Justice in 1910 and held different administrative posts from 1910 to 1914. In 1916, he joined al-Fatat, the leading opposition party in Ottoman Syria, and served as a liaison officer between the underground in Damascus and the rebel Arab Army of Sharif Husayn which was leading an armed uprising against the Ottoman Turks from Mecca. Husayn entrusted Boukhari with smuggling arms, money, and ammunition from Damascus to troops in the Arabian Desert.

Boukhari also established an intellectual forum at his home where discontented intellectuals would lament the overall deterioration of life in the Ottoman Empire. During a poetry recital at his residence, Boukhari recited a political poem accusing the Ottomans of discrimination against their Arab subjects. Unfortunately, Military Governor Jamal Pasha was in attendance at the recital, and Pasha had Boukhari arrested and brought before a military tribunal in Aley (Mount Lebanon) on the charge of treason.

On May 6, 1916, the Ottoman Turks executed Mahmud al-Boukhari in Marjeh Square in Damascus along with a group of other activists. (See the profile of Shukri al-Asali, page 365.)

Sources:
Bawab, Sulayman. *Mawsuat Alam Souriyya fi al-Qarn al-Ishreen*, Vol I (1999).

al-Dandashi, Ali Abd al-Karim
(1910-?)

Ali Abd al-Karim al-Dandashi came from Tal Kalakh, a town in the Syrian Midwest. He studied law at Damascus University. In July 1927, he became a member in the National Bloc, the leading anti-French movement in Syria, and helped found the Syrian Boy Scouts, modeled after the Ottoman Scouts that Tawfiq al-Hibri had established in 1912.

The organization, first called the Ghuta Troops, was co-founded by Ahmad al-Shihabi, a law student from South Lebanon, and Fayez al-Dalati, a law student from Damascus. The National Bloc youth leader, Fakhri al-Barudi, approached the founders and asked that they bring their scouts under his patronage. The founders refused, however, and Barudi created the Umayyad Troops to counter-balance their influence. Barudi said that his troops would become the prototype for the future Syrian Army.

In 1931, the Umayyad Troops ran into political problems and was dissolved by Barudi. Most of its members then transferred to the Ghuta Troops. Dandashi earned international recognition for his Ghuta Troops by taking thirty-five of them to Bulgaria in 1932 to attend the International Boy Scout Conference. With recognition from the International Scouting Council, the Ghuta Troops became the Syrian Boy Scouts and Dandashi became their executive director. In 1933, he had 3,000 troops under his leadership, and by 1935, the number had increased to 15,000. Three years later, he divided the scouts into two divisions: Cub Scouts (for ages 7-12) and Rover Scouts (18 and over), increasing the number of members to 38,000.

In August 1933, Dandashi was a founding member of the League of National Action in Quarna'il (Mount Lebanon), a movement aimed at uniting Arab intel-lectuals into one political force that would help liberate the region from European colonialism. The League, which gained instant fame in Syria and Lebanon, called for economic integration of all Arab countries upon the termination of the French Mandate in Syria and Lebanon and the British Mandate in Palestine. The League included promising young men who were to become future leaders in Syria. Among its earliest members were the professor Constantine Zurayk, the philosopher Zaki al-Arsuzi, the politician Munir al-Ajlani, and the diplomat Farid Zayn al-Din.

In 1941, Dandashi volunteered for service in a military uprising in Iraq led by Rashid Ali al-Kaylani against the British forces stationed in Baghdad. When the revolt was crushed, Dandashi returned to Syria and split his time between the Syrian Boy Scouts and his new job as director of physical education at the Ministry of Education.

In January 1948, he became founder and president of the Syrian Olympic Committee, appointing Syria's tennis champion, Issam al-Inklizi, as his deputy.

That year, Syria participated for the first time in the Olympic Games in London through its diver Zuhayr Shurbaji. Dandashi kept this Olympic Committee post until the Syrian-Egyptian union was created in 1958, after which Vice President Husayn al-Shafii became committee president, and Abd al-Hamid Sarraj, the minister of interior, became the committee's vice president.

Dandashi volunteered for service in the Arab-Israeli War of 1948 and served as a commanding officer in Fawzi al-Qawuqji's Army of Deliverance. In August 1949, Dandashi became a member of the Constitutional Assembly that drafted a new constitution for Syria. In September 1950, he became a deputy in parliament. Ali Abd al-Karim al-Dandashi was reelected for a second term in parliament from 1954 to 1958. The Syrian Boy Scouts continued to operate until the Baath Party came to power in 1963 when they were replaced with the party's Youth of the Revolution.

Sources:
Faris, George. *Man Hum fi al-`Alam al-Arabi?* (1957).

al-Hafez, Amin Lutfi
(1879-1916)

Amin Lutfi al-Hafez studied at the Ottoman Military Academy in Istanbul and graduated in 1900. He enlisted in the Ottoman Army, and in 1908, became commander of the Aleppo garrison. At the same time, Hafez also joined the Arab underground and transferred information on Ottoman military strategy to the rebel Arab leadership in Mecca.

Hafez became a member of al-Fatat, the underground in Damascus, and founded al-Ahd, another early resistance movement in Ottoman Syria. He channeled arms to Sharif Husayn, leader of the Arab Revolt, and formed the nucleus of anti-Ottoman activity in Aleppo. Hafez marketed the Arab cause in the Ottoman Army and facilitated the escape of Arab officers in the Ottoman Army from Istanbul to Mecca.

Hafez's friendship with prominent Arab politicians brought him to the attention of Jamal Pasha, the Ottoman military governor of Syria, who placed him under twenty-four-hour surveillance. When Hafez's connections to the Arab command became apparent, Jamal Pasha arrested him and brought him to trial on the charge of high treason. A military tribunal in Aley sentenced him to death and he was hanged in public at the Marjeh Square in Damascus on May 6, 1916.

Amin Lutfi al-Hafez is famous for slipping the noose around his own neck and leaping off the chair, preferring to end his own life rather than die at the hands of an Ottoman Turk.

STEEL & SILK

Sources:
Bawab, Sulayman. *Mawsuat Alam Souriyya fi al-Qarn al-Ishreen* (1999).
Farfur, Abd al-Latif. *Alam Dimashq* (1987).

Hananu, Ibrahim
(1869-1935)
Alternate spelling: Ibrahim Hanano.
Ibrahim Hananu was born to a prominent family of Kurdish ancestry and raised in Aleppo. He studied at the Ottoman Law Academy and took a job as a civil servant in the Ottoman administration in Aleppo.

In 1918, the Ottoman Empire was defeated and Hananu became a deputy in the Syrian National Congress, the equivalent of a modern parliament that declared independence from the empire and appointed Faysal I as king of Syria. In 1919, Hananu clashed with his colleagues in the congress who advocated diplomatic resistance to the French Army which had landed on the Syrian coast and was preparing to occupy all of Syria. Hananu, however, called for armed resistance. Realizing that his colleagues were ignoring his pleas, Hananu took matters into his own hands, fled into the mountains, and began recruiting young cadets to prepare for an armed revolt.

In 1919, Hananu launched his revolt, bringing Aleppo, Idlib, and Antioch into a coordinated campaign against French forces. Hananu was responsible for the disarmament of many French troops, the destruction of railroad and telegraph lines, the sabotage of tanks, and the foiling of French attacks on Aleppo. The Turkish nationalist Kemal Ataturk supported Hananu with money and arms. In July 1920, Hananu's forces did not exceed 800 men, but by November 1921, they had increased to number 5,000 armed troops. Some were commanded by Turkish officers whom Ataturk had dispatched to aid him.

To break the Hananu revolt, the French High Commissioner Henri Gouraud stationed 5,000 French troops in Aleppo and another 15,000 in its vicinity. In July 1921, Hananu fled Syria into Transjordan, then Palestine. But in Jerusalem, British authorities arrested him and deported him to Syria. He spent six months in jail and was brought before court on March 15, 1922. In a dramatic courtroom defense, Hananu was tried before a military tribunal, and to the surprise of all, found innocent of the charge of treason.

In 1928, Hanunu co-founded the National Bloc with Hashim al-Atasi, becoming a member of its permanent council and chief of its political bureau. The National Bloc was the leading anti-French movement in Syria from 1928 until the French evacuated in 1946. Created out of the defeat of the armed revolts during the 1920s, the Bloc called for confronting the French through diplomatic means rather than armed resistance.

For three months during 1928, Hananu held office on the Constitutional Assembly that drafted the first republican constitution for Syria. In the 1930s, Hananu affirmed his reputation as a hard-liner, refusing to negotiate with the French until they pledged complete, unconditional independence for Syria. He spoke out against collaboration with French authorities and condemned any Syrian politician who was willing to do so.

Ibrahim Hananu.

In 1932, the National Bloc became divided when one of its founders, Jamil Mardam Bey, became a cabinet minister under the pro-French Prime Minister Haqqi al-Azm. An enraged Hananu led a campaign to have Mardam Bey expelled, forcing the minister to resign from office.

In 1935, Ibrahim Hananu died of natural causes in Aleppo. Along with Sultan al-Atrash, leader of the military uprising of 1925, Ibrahim Hananu is considered one of the most celebrated warriors of the resistance against the French Mandate.

Sources:
Babil, Nasuh. *Sahafa wa Siyasa fi Souriyya* (1987).
Itri , Abd al-Ghani. *Abqariyyat wa Alam* (1996).
Jundi, Adham. *Tareekh al-Thawrat al-Souriyya fi Ahd al-Intidab al-Faransi* (1960).
Kayyali, Abd al-Rahman. *Al-Marahil fi al-Intidab al-Faransi 1926-1938* (1958-1960).
Khoury, Philip. *Syria and the French Mandate* (1987).
Moualim, Walid. *Souriyya 1916-1945* (1988).
Qassab Hasan, Najat. *Saniou al-Jalaa fi Souriyya* (1999).
Shambrook, Peter. *French Imperialism in Syria 1927-1936* (1998).

al-Inklizi, Abd al-Wahab
(1878-1916)

Abd al-Wahab al-Inklizi was born in Ghuta—rural Damascus. He studied at the Ottoman Law Academy and graduated in 1900. Inklizi opened a legal practice in Damascus, then joined the Ottoman civil service, becoming mayor of Aleppo in 1909.

In 1913, Inklizi became the government inspector of Beirut. In 1914, he criticized Ottoman involvement in World War I and wrote in several newspapers for Sultan Mohammad Rashad V to refrain from involving the Ottoman Empire in war. If the sultan insisted on war, Inklizi wrote, then the Arab subjects in the empire should not be conscripted into the Ottoman Army since they would be fighting a war that did not concern them. Inklizi also spoke out against the dismissal of Arab officials from government posts and their replacement with Ottoman Turks.

Inklizi campaigned for his beliefs, and in January 1916, joined in the Arab underground. He became a member of al-Fatat and began to distribute anti-Ottoman material in secret. Perhaps as early as 1913, he signed a famed declaration presented to the first Arab Congress in Paris that demanded emancipation from the Ottoman Empire. Inklizi was arrested by Military Governor Jamal Pasha, who accused him of high treason. Inklizi was brought before a military tribunal in Aley on Mount Lebanon. He was declared guilty and hanged in public in Damascus on May 6, 1916.

Abd al-Wahab al-Inklizi left behind two books, *al-Tareekh al-Amm (General History)*, and *Muhadarat fi al-Siyassa, al-Ijtima'iyyat, wa al-Tareekh (Lectures in Politics, Sociology and History)*.

Sources:
Khury, Faris. *Awrak Faris al-Khury* (1989).

Jarbu, Fadlallah
(1913-?)

Fadlallah Jarbu was descended from a prominent political family in the Arab Mountain. In 1944, he inherited the traditional Druze tribal leadership role from his father and led the resistance in his native village against the French Mandate from 1944 to 1946.

The Syrian government hailed Jarbu as one of the many leaders of the nationalist movement when independence was achieved in April 1946. In 1947, Jarbu founded the Arab Party in the Arab Mountain. The organization preached Arab unity and nationalism among the Druze inhabitants of the Mountain. Its spiritual godfather was Prince Hasan al-Atrash, the veteran Druze leader and Jarbu's patron in Syrian politics.

From 1951 to 1953, Fadlallah Jarbu clashed with the military regime of President Adib al-Shishakli. Jarbu called on his Druze supporters to help him bring down the Shishakli regime. Shishakli had seized power in 1951 and clashed with the entire Druze community, accusing them of being agents of the West intent on toppling Syria's republican regime and replacing it with a Hashemite monarchy.

Consequently, Shishakli cracked down on Druze political activists and placed both Fadlallah Jarbu and Hasan al-Atrash under house arrest in the Arab

Mountain. Shishakli ordered a manhunt of all those connected to both men and arrested many members of their immediate families. After he discovered that arms were being smuggled from Baghdad to the Arab Mountain in order to launch an insurrection, Shishakli ordered an air raid on all Druze districts in Syria. In the war that ensued, 600 inhabitants of the Arab Mountain were killed, and Jarbu himself was injured by gunfire. Eventually, Shishakli was ousted and sent into exile in February 1954.

In October 1954, Jarbu ran for the first post-Shishakli parliament and won with an overwhelming majority. In the second half of the 1950s, he became increasingly critical of the pro-USSR policy of President Shukri al-Quwatli and his adherence to President Gamal Abd al-Nasser of Egypt. Jarbu and Atrash criticized Nasser's socialist policies and his alliance with the Eastern Bloc in the Cold War.

Jarbu and Atrash joined a group of like-minded politicians who wanted to overthrow the existing regime and replace it with a moderate government that would curb Egyptian and Soviet influence in Syria. But Abd al-Hamid al-Sarraj, the director of Syrian Intelligence, uncovered the plot. Both Jarbu and Atrash fled Syria, however, before they could be arrested.

Fadlallah Jarbu was charged in absentia with treason and sentenced to fifteen years' imprisonment. He remained in exile and was opposed to the Syrian-Egyptian union of 1958.

Sources:
BBC Archives. "The Damascus Trial" February 26, 1957.
Faris, George. *Man Hum fi al-`Alam al-Arabi?* (1957).

al-Jaza'iri, Omar
(1871-1916)

Omar al-Jaza'iri studied at the Ottoman Law Academy in Istanbul and became an attorney in Damascus in 1895. At the turn of the century, he began writing for pro-Arab newspapers. In 1914, he joined the Arab underground against the Ottoman Empire. The next year he joined al-Ahd, one of the leading opposition parties in Ottoman Syria.

Along with Shukri al-Asali and Abd al-Wahab al-Inklizi, Jaza'iri formed the core of the Arab nationalist movement in Damascus. In 1915, the Hashemite family of Arabia began to plan a rebellion against the Ottoman Turks. Prince Faysal came to Damascus from Mecca to lobby support for his family's uprising. Jaza'iri helped Faysal secure the defection of several high-ranking Arab officers from the Ottoman Army into the rebel Arab Army of Faysal's father, Sharif Husayn.

Jaza'iri's connections to Faysal caught the attention of Jamal Pasha, the military governor of Syria, who then arrested Jaza'iri in January 1916. He was charged with treason and brought before a military tribunal in the mountain resort of Aley and, along with Asali and Inklizi, was sentenced to death. The Ottoman court accused the three men of receiving funds from France and working for the downfall of the Ottoman Empire.

Along with twenty-one other Arab nationalists, Omar al-Jaza'iri was executed in Marjeh Square in Damascus on May 6, 1916. (See Shukri al-Asali, page 365.)

Sources:
Bawab, Sulayman. *Mawsuat Alam Souriyya fi al-Qarn al-Ishreen* (1999).

al-Jaza'iri, Saleem
(1879-1916)

Saleem al-Jaza'iri studied at the Ottoman Military Academy in Istanbul and graduated with honors in 1905. From 1906 to 1914, he taught at the Military Academy. During World War I, Jaza'iri was commissioned into the Ottoman Army, wounded in combat, taken prisoner by the British forces, and transported to Yemen.

In Yemen, Jaza'iri met members of the Arab underground. They influenced him to abandon Ottoman nationalism and join in their call for Arab nationalism against the Ottoman Empire. While in prison, Jaza'iri became a member of al-Fatat, the leading opposition party in Ottoman Syria.

In 1915, the British released Jaza'iri from prison. Jamal Pasha, the Ottoman governor of Syria, had him arrested once again in January 1916 for his membership in the underground and brought him before a military tribunal in the mountain town of Aley. The Ottoman court convicted him of treason and Saleem al-Jaza'iri was executed in public on May 6, 1916, at the Marjeh Square in Damascus.

Sources:
Bawab, Sulayman. *Mawsuat Alam Souriyya fi al-Qarn al-Ishreen* (1999).

al-Jundi, Abd al-Aziz
(1895-1958)

Abd al-Aziz al-Jundi studied at the Ottoman Law Academy in Istanbul, but in 1915, was conscripted into the Ottoman Army before he completed his degree. He served in the 4th Ottoman Army of Jamal Pasha.

In 1916, Pasha delegated Jundi to lead an armed contingent against anti-Ottoman forces in Mecca, where an Arab rebellion was brewing. But rather than suppress the Arab rebels, Jundi joined their ranks and became an officer in the

Arab Army headed by Sharif Husayn, the Prince of Mecca. Infuriated, Jamal Pasha sentenced Jundi to death in absentia on the charge of high treason.

In 1917, Sharif Husayn appointed Jundi director of inspection in the Arab Army. He kept this post until the end of World War I and the collapse of the Ottoman Empire in October 1918. Husayn's son, King Faysal I, became king of Syria and appointed Jundi as a military advisor at the Royal Palace in Syria. Jundi then became commander of the Nabek garrison situated on the outskirts of the capital. In July 1920, the French proclaimed their mandate over Syria, dissolved the Syrian Army, dethroned Faysal, and forced Jundi to abandon his military career.

Jundi returned to civilian life and enrolled at the Arab Academy of Law in Damascus, obtaining his degree in 1923. He worked as an attorney before returning to political activity in 1925. Specifically, he raised funds to support an armed uprising against the French launched by Sultan al-Atrash from the Druze Mountain. Jundi smuggled funds from King Abdullah of Transjordan to the Druze rebels and provided them with sanctuary in the Ghuta suburbs of Damascus. When the French tried to arrest him, Jundi fled to Amman where he became a legal consultant to King Abdullah. He returned to Syria in 1928 after the revolt was suppressed.

Abd al-Aziz al-Jundi spent the next twenty years teaching at local high schools in Damascus.

Sources:
Bawab, Sulayman. *Mawsuat Alam Souriyya fi al-Qarn al-Ishreen* (1999).

al-Kharrat, Hasan
(1861-1925)

Hasan al-Kharrat was born and raised in Damascus. He received no high school education and worked as a night watchman in the Shaghur neighborhood of Damascus. In 1925, the nationalist leader, Abd al-Rahman Shahbandar, commissioned Kharrat to fight in a military uprising against the French Mandate that had been imposed on Syria in 1920.

Kharrat took up arms with the rebels of the Arab Mountain and recruited men from Damascus to join him in the resistance. He rose to prominence in the battles that ensued and led armed bands into Damascus for sabotage attacks on French installations. He disarmed patrols, held their soldiers hostage, and burned down all French buildings in the Shaghur, Souk Saruja, and Jazmatiyya neighborhoods.

On October 18, 1925, Kharrat's troops marched into the Hamidyya Market and occupied the Azm Palace in the heart of the old city, at the time the residence of the French high commissioner, General Maurice Sarrail. In the fight, around 180 soldiers from the French Army were killed. Kharrat ordered his troops to spare no one associated with them. He then sealed off the old city and prevented the entry of French reinforcements.

General Sarrail retaliated with an air raid on the capital, killing 6,000 Syrians during forty-eight hours of bombing. Entire neighborhoods, including mosques and churches, were raised to the ground and hundreds of national leaders were arrested by the French Army. Sporadic fighting continued throughout Damascus and anarchy filled the streets until the French killed Hasan al-Kharrat on October 21, 1925. The French then arrested his son Fakhri, who had also taken part in the revolt, and executed him in public at the Marjeh Square in Damascus.

Sources:
Itri, Abd al-Ghani. *Abqariyyat wa Alam* (1996).
Jundi, Adham. *Tareekh al-Thawrat al-Souriyya fi Ahd al-Intidab al-Faransi* (1960).
Shahbandar, Abd al-Rahman. *Al-Thawra al-Wataniyya al-Souriyya* (1933).

al-Kuttabi, Mekki
(1894-1973)

Mekki al-Kuttabi was born in Morocco and raised in Syria. He studied at Islamic schools and became an instructor at a local mosque in Damascus. With a calm and dominating personality, he established a wide network of students who turned to him for religious guidance and political leadership.

In 1936, Kuttabi founded a militant youth force called Shabab Filastine (Palestine Youth) to fight Zionist immigrants coming from Europe to Palestine. Shahab Filastine waged guerrilla attacks inside Palestine. They attacked Jewish settlements by night, and blew up Jewish businesses, schools, and banks in Jerusalem, Haifa, and Tel Aviv. Kuttabi provided the young men with inspirational leadership and raised funds for their activities from Islamic societies in Damascus and Aleppo. In 1937, the French government, under pressure from London, curbed Kuttabi's activities and placed him under house arrest. The French then apprehended anyone connected to Shabab Filastine and closed the organization's offices in Syria. Due to French pressure, the organization died out completely in 1940.

Following Syria's independence from France in 1946, Mekki al-Kuttabi co-founded the Scientists' Association in Damascus. What started as a conference of Islamic leaders evolved into a coalition of activists and groups that worked to promote Islam as a way of life. The Scientists' Association included leaders from the Muslim Brotherhood of Mustapha al-Siba'i, the al-Gharra Society of Abd al-Hamid al-Tabba`, and the Society of Islamic Urbanization of Mazhar al-Azma. The coalition provided schooling for Muslim students, funded the education of Muslim girls, and served as a charity organization for the city's poor Muslims. In 1947, Kuttabi was elected president of the association and kept this post until his death in 1975.

In 1956, Kuttabi created another group of young militants to fight for the emerging cause of Arab nationalism headed by President Gamal Abd al-Nasser of Egypt. In July 1956, Kuttabi's new troops joined the Egyptian Army in its war against Great Britain, France, and Israel. They donated funds, arms, and volunteers to the Egyptian war effort in the Suez Canal. In 1957, Kuttabi went to Cairo and met Nasser, pledging his support for the Egyptian president. Kuttabi also supported the Syrian-Egyptian union that was created in February 1958.

Mekki al-Kuttabi.

Like most Syrians, however, Mekki al-Kuttabi grew disenchanted with union in 1960 and began to criticize Nasser's authoritarian government. He called for the re-creation of union on a federal basis and founded the National Coalition, a large group of politicians whose goal was the establishment of a broad-based political front in Syria that was interested in both domestic and foreign affairs. The National Coalition was pan-Arab in character and intent on preserving, and at the same time, modifying the existing Syrian-Egyptian union. Among the organization's leaders was former Syrian President Shukri al-Quwatli, who had created union with Nasser in 1958. Quwatli and Kuttabi criticized the closure of political parties, the arrest of political leaders, and the police state that existed under Nasser.

When the union was dissolved by military coup in September 1961, Kuttabi supported the coup, but called for the immediate establishment of a "new union." When it was clear that the majority of Syrians supported the post-union order, Kuttabi threw his support to the post-Nasser leader of Syria, President Nazim al-Qudsi. In March 1963, officers from the Baath Party came to power in Syria and pledged to restore the Syrian-Egyptian union. They punished Kuttabi for his policies by terminating his civil rights and retiring him from political activity.

During the Arab-Israeli War of 1973, Mekki al-Kuttabi launched a humanitarian campaign to help the families of those serving on the front. He donated money to the Syrian Army, collected funds for relief projects, and visited the wounded soldiers in hospitals. He died less than two months later in December 1973.

Sources:

Barada (March 24, 1963).

Itri, Abd al-Ghani. *Hadeeth al-Abqariyyat* (2000).

Ma'mun, Sayf al-Din
(1905-?)

Sayf al-Din Ma'mun studied political science at the American University of Beirut (AUB) and graduated in 1930. On September 9, 1936, he founded a political party in Syria called the National Youth. It was a paramilitary youth force modeled after the Brown Shirts in Germany and the Black Shirts in Italy.

The National Youth was charged with protecting locals from French aggression and mobilizing popular propaganda for the National Bloc. Its leaders were a group of young men who wanted to introduce the concept of disciplined and armed resistance to occupation. As long as the French were not permitting the creation of a Syrian Army, Ma'mun claimed, the National Youth would have to serve as an alternative. He believed in the concept of mass politics and created a powerful network of young men to engage in marches, strikes, and rallies.

The National Youth increasingly assumed a military character (e.g. wearing military uniforms at official functions and engaging in basic military training). They served as an unofficial police force for the National Bloc in the 1930s and 1940s. Among the party's co-founders were the university professors Ahmad al-Samman and Munir al-Ajlani, and the journalists Munir and Najib al-Rayyes. The National Youth remained in charge of Syrian mass politics from 1936 to 1946. Its founders disbanded the group when the French evacuated Syria in 1946.

Ma'mun retired from political life and announced that, "this warrior (in reference to himself) must rest and this knight must finally dismount." In the early 1950s, however, he reactivated his career and joined the Social Cooperative Party of Faysal al-Asali, a populist party modeled after the National Youth. He nominated himself for parliament on a party ticket in 1954 and won.

Sayf al-Din Ma'mun willingly retired from political life when the Baath Party came to power in March 1963.

Sources:
Khoury, Philip. *Syria and the French Mandate* (1987).
Interview with Dr Munir al-Ajlani (Beirut August 13, 1999; September 4, 1999).

Mu'ayyad al-Azm, Nazih
(1890-?)

Nazih Mu'ayyad al-Azm came from a wealthy political family in Damascus. He studied political science at the American University of Beirut (AUB) and returned to Syria in 1913 to administer his family's vast landownings.

When World War I broke out in 1914, Mu'ayyad al-Azm joined the Arab underground and became a member of the Arab Revolt launched by Sharif Husayn from Mecca against the Ottoman Empire. He channeled funds and information from Damascus to the Arabian Desert.

In 1916, Jamal Pasha, the military governor of Syria, convicted and sentenced Mu'ayyad al-Azm to death. He fled to Mecca and served Husayn until the Ottoman Empire was defeated in 1918. Then he returned to Damascus and allied himself with King Faysal I, the new leader of Syria. Mu'ayyad al-Azm's brother-in-law, Abd al-Rahman Shahbandar, became minister of foreign affairs under Faysal. Mu'ayyad al-Azm served as his advisor until the French proclaimed their mandate over Syria in July 1920, dethroning Faysal and sending both Mu'ayyad al-Azm and Shahbandar into exile.

Mu'ayyad al-Azm spent some time in Egypt, then returned to Syria when the French issued an amnesty in 1921. He joined Subhi Barakat, a notable from Antioch, and the two founded the Party of Syrian Unity in 1922. The party endorsed Barakat's leadership in uniting into one republic all Syrian territory that had been divided into city-states by the French in 1920. In June 1925, Shahbandar and Mu'ayyad al-Azm founded the People's Party, the first populist political movement in French Mandate Syria. It promoted the creation of a constitutional government in a free and unified Syria that would include Palestine, Jordan, and parts of Lebanon. The movement was composed of leading statesmen, lawyers, and professors who were to become nationalist Syrian leaders in the 1940s.

One month after the party was founded, a military uprising against the French Mandate took place in the Arab Mountain, headed by the Druze leader Sultan al-Atrash. Shahbandar and Mu'ayyad al-Azm joined the underground and went to the Arab Mountain where they served on Atrash's political committee. They drafted the revolution declarations, helped raise funds from neighboring Arab countries and Syrian émigrés living in Europe, and carried out diplomatic talks with the French.

When the French Army crushed the revolt in 1927, it sentenced all three men to death. Shahbandar fled to Egypt, Atrash went to Jordan, while Mu'ayyad al-Azm went to Palestine. They returned to Syria when the nationalist leader Hashim al-Atasi came to power in 1936 and issued a general amnesty.

In 1940, Shahbandar was assassinated by French agents. Mu'ayyad al-Azm accused his three opponents, Saadallah al-Jabiri, Jamil Mardam Bey, and Lutfi al-Haffar, of having orchestrated the killing. In a highly publicized trial, the three men were declared innocent of the murder. Nazih Mu'ayyad al-Azm retired from political activity in the post-Shahbandar era and continued to live in Syria.

Sources:

Faris, George. *Man Hum fi al-Alam al-Arabi?* (1957).

Hakim, Hasan. *Abd al-Rahman Shahbandar* (1985).

Khoury, Philip. *Syria and the French Mandate* (1987).

Mardam Bey, Jamil. *Syria's Quest for Independence* (1994).

Shahbandar, Abd al-Rahman. *Al-Thawra al-Wataniyya al-Souriyya* (1933).

Mu'ayyad al-Azm, Shafiq
(1861-1916)

Shafiq Mu'ayyad al-Azm was born to one of the most prestigious political families in Ottoman Syria. He studied at the Ottoman Law Academy in Istanbul and graduated in 1885.

Mu'ayyad al-Azm began his career in the customs department of Beirut. In 1896, he moved to the central administration in Istanbul. In 1900, he founded an Arabic newspaper named *al-Ikha' al-Arabi* (*The Arab Brotherhood*). The newspaper preached Arab nationalism instead of Ottomanism and called on all Arabs living in the Ottoman Empire to lobby for more political freedoms and demand political reforms in the Arab provinces of the empire.

In 1908, a coup took place in Istanbul, carried out by the Committee for Union and Progress (CUP). This group of radical, hard-line officers curbed the powers of Sultan Abdulhamid II and forced him to democratize the empire. Mu'ayyad al-Azm supported the CUP when they reinstated the Ottoman Constitution and the parliament that had been dissolved in 1876, and when they lifted the press censorship practiced under the sultan.

Running on a CUP ticket in 1909, Mu'ayyad al-Azm became a deputy in the Ottoman Parliament. He became critical of the CUP's policies, however, when they dismissed many senior Arab officials from their posts and replaced them with Ottoman Turks. Along with deputies Abd al-Hamid al-Zahrawi and Shukri al-Asali, Mu'ayyad al-Azm led a parliamentary opposition movement against the "Turkification" of the Ottoman Empire. In 1912, the CUP called for new parliamentary elections and rigged the ballots, causing the defeat of all three men. Thus, Mu'ayyad al-Azm joined the Arab underground and became a member of al-Fatat. Jamal Pasha, the Ottoman governor of Damascus, arrested him and brought him to the court at Aley on the charge of high treason against the empire. Shafiq Mu'ayyad al-Azm was declared guilty and hanged in Marjeh Square in Damascus on May 6, 1916 along with a group of other activists. (See Shukri al-Asali, page 365.)

Sources:

Khury, Colette. *Awrak Faris al-Khury* (1989).

Khoury, Philip. *Urban Notables and Arab Nationalism* (1983).

Muraywed, Ahmad
(1887-1925)

Ahmad Muraywed was born in al-Qunaitra, the central town of the Golan Heights. He was a co-founder of al-Fatat. In June 1916, he joined the rebel Arab Army of Sharif Husayn, the Prince of Mecca, who was leading an armed uprising against the Ottoman Turks from the Arabian Desert.

Muraywed recruited officers from the Ottoman Army into the Arab Army and served as a commanding officer under Husayn from June 1916 until the Ottoman Empire was defeated in October 1918. After his return to Syria, Muraywed became a deputy in the Syrian National Congress, the equivalent of a modern parliament. The congress crowned Faysal I (Husayn's son) as king of Syria on March 8, 1920. When the French imposed their mandate on the Middle East in July 1920, they dethroned Faysal and dissolved the Syrian Congress.

Muraywed created a small army of voluntary recruits and engaged in combat with the invading French forces in Lattakia. His army then expanded into the Alawite Mountains and the Golan Heights. He sabotaged French tanks and automobiles, and was responsible for the defeat of General Henri Gouraud's top men in sporadic battles in the Golan.

In August 1920, a French military tribunal sentenced Murawyed to death in absentia and forced him to take refuge in Amman. In 1922, he moved to the Arabian Desert and remained in Mecca until the Druze leader, Sultan al-Atrash, launched a military uprising against the French Mandate in July 1925. Ahmad Muraywed returned to Syria to take part in the combat, but French troops apprehended him at his home and murdered him in cold blood.

Sources:
Jundi, Adham. *Tareekh al-Thawrat al-Souriyya fi Ahd al-Intidab al-Faransi* (1960).
Qassab Hasan, Najat. *Saniou al-Jalaa fi Souriyya* (1999).
Ubaydat, Mahmud. *Ahmad Muraywed* (1997).

Qadri, Ahmad
(1893-1958)

Ahmad Qadri studied medicine in Damascus and Istanbul, then pursued his medical training in Paris. He was a co-founder of al-Fatat and an organizer of the first Arab Congress held in Paris in 1913. The Arab Congress called for more freedom in the Arab provinces of the Ottoman Empire.

Shortly after the Arab Congress concluded, Qadri returned to Syria and became a doctor in the Ottoman Army. His connections to the Arab underground led to his arrest. He remained in prison from 1916 until the Ottoman Empire was defeated in 1918. Upon release, Qadri captured the attention of King Faysal I, the new ruler of Syria, and became his private advisor and physician. In 1919, he became a founding father and professor at the Damascus Medical School, later renamed Damascus University. Meanwhile, he also served as a deputy for Damascus on the Syrian National Congress, the equivalent of a modern parliament that administered political affairs in Syria from 1918 to 1920.

In July 1920, the French occupied Syria and sentenced Ahmad Qadri to death. He fled to Europe with Faysal, and in 1922, went to Baghdad when Faysal became king of Iraq. Qadri once again became Faysal's private doctor and political advisor. In 1930, Faysal appointed him consul to Egypt. Faysal died in 1933 and his successor, King Ghazi I, appointed Qadri as Iraqi ambassador to France. In 1936, he became chairman of medical administration in Baghdad, the equivalent of a modern Ministry of Health.

Then, in 1937, President Hashim al-Atasi invited Qadri back to Syria and he complied, returning to work as a practicing doctor and professor at Damascus University. In 1943, President Shukri al-Quwatli appointed him secretary-general of the Ministry of Health. His relation with Quwatli dated back to 1916, when as members of al-Fatat, the two men had been arrested by the Ottoman Turks. In prison, Quwatli attempted suicide and Qadri saved his life.

Qadri remained in office until Shukri al-Quwatli was ousted by General Husni al-Za'im in March 1949. Then he retired from politics. In 1956, he published his memoirs of the Arab Revolt (1916-1918) called, *Muzakarat an Al-Thawra al-Arabiyya al-Kubra (Memoirs on the Great Arab Revolt)*. Ahmad Qadri died in 1958.

Sources:
Qadri, Ahmad. *Muzakarat an Al-Thawra al-Arabiyya al-Kubra* (1956).

Qambaz, Mohammad Saleh
(1887-1925)

Mohammad Saleh Qambaz studied at the Ottoman Medical Academy in Istanbul and graduated in 1910. He opened a clinic in Hama and practiced medicine until World War I broke out in 1914. He was then commissioned into the Ottoman Army as a practicing physician.

Qambaz served in Jerusalem and was wounded by a British attack on Ottoman garrisons in 1917. When the Ottoman Empire was defeated in 1918, he was discharged from service and moved back to Syria where he worked as a doctor from 1918 to 1923. In 1923, Qambaz was voted into the prestigious Arab Language

Assemblage, the highest international scientific authority in the field of Arab language and literature. From 1923 to 1925 he conducted medical research at the Sorbonne in Paris. He returned to Damascus in 1925, just in time to witness the Syrian Revolt of the Arab Mountain.

On October 14, 1925, Mohammad Saleh Qambaz was killed by a French soldier while treating the wounds of three injured men in the streets of Hama.

Sources:
Bawab, Sulayman. *Mawsuat Alam Souriyya fi al-Qarn al-Ishreen,* Vol IV (1999).

al-Qassab, Kamel
(1873-1954)

Kamel al-Qassab was born and raised in Homs, and received his religious training at the Azhar Mosque in Cairo. He was a founder of al-Fatat. In 1914, he was chosen as part of an Arab delegation to meet with the Zionist Agency and hear their claims concerning Palestine.

Qassab had written extensively on the issue of Palestine in several Arabic and Turkish newspapers and sharply criticized Zionist ambitions in the Arab world. He seemed willing, however, to relinquish parts of Palestine to the Jewish settlers in exchange for Zionist support for an independent Arab state. It was agreed that, along with other Arab statesmen, Qassab would meet with Chaim Weizmann, president of the Zionist Agency, for advanced talks in the resort of Brummanah on Mount Lebanon during the summer of 1914. The meeting was postponed, then later canceled altogether due to the outbreak of World War I in August 1914.

In 1914, Kamel al-Qassab founded the Party of Syrian Unity, demanding that the Ottoman Empire give back all of the territories historically known as Greater Syria. Qassab was highly critical of the Ottoman officers who came to power in 1908. He called on them to grant more political freedoms to their Arab subjects. In 1916, the governor of Damascus, Jamal Pasha, ordered Qassab's arrest, forcing him to flee to the Hijaz where he joined the underground movement of Sharif Husayn.

From 1916 to 1918, Qassab served in Mecca as an officer in the Arab Army. In 1918, the Ottomans were defeated and an Arab regime was established under King Faysal I. Qassab spent the Faysal years (1918-1920) as a journalist and teaching at local mosques in Damascus. When the French Army occupied Syria in July 1920, they sentenced Qassab to death for his anti-French views and forced him into exile in Yemen. He became political advisor to Imam Yehia Hamid al-Din, the ruler of Yemen, from 1922 until his return to Syria in 1937.

In March 1922, Kamel al-Qassab once again met with the Zionist leadership in

Cairo. Weizmann proposed that the Arabs support the creation of a Jewish state in Palestine in exchange for Jewish backing of the termination of the European mandates in the Middle East and North Africa, and a promise to invest Jewish money in the education, economy, and infrastructure of the Arab world. Qassab turned down Weizmann's request but continued to meet Zionist leaders, often in secret, during the second half of the 1920s.

After his return to Damascus in 1937, Kamel al-Qassab allied himself with Taj al-Din al-Hasani, the Syrian prime minister famed for his pro-French views. Qassab supported the prime minister, asking him to establish a Muslim government in Syria. Qassab criticized the merchants and landowners who opposed Hasani's alliance with France, saying that they were nothing but "money-grubbing politicians" who wanted to advance their personal interests rather than the national interests of Syria.

When Hasani died in January 1943, Qassab shifted his allegiance to the National Bloc, the leading anti-French movement in Syria. He allied himself with the same "money-grubbing politicians" he had criticized earlier. In August 1943, he lobbied for the election of Shukri al-Quwatli, a landowner from Damascus, as president of the republic. He clashed with Quwatli, however, when the latter encouraged women's emancipation, claiming that this was "morally unacceptable." He also led demonstrations against the unveiling of women, and his followers clashed often with government police.

In 1947, Qassab accused Quwatli of harboring authoritarian ambitions when Quwatli amended the constitution to enable his reelection for a second term as president. Qassab rallied the support of religious leaders during the parliamentary elections of 1947 and claimed that Quwatli loyalists were tampering with the ballots. Qassab declared that the elections were being carried out "in an atmosphere of terror" and called for new elections, but Quwatli ignored him. Kamel al-Qassab ceased all political activity when the Quwatli regime was overthrown by military coup in March 1949.

Sources:
Kawtharani, Wajih. *Wathaiq al-Mutamar al-Arabi al-Awal* (1980).
Khoury, Philip. *Syria and the French Mandate* (1987).
Thompson, Elizabeth. *Colonial Citizens* (1999).

al-Qassam, Izz al-Din
(1883-1935)

Izz al-Din al-Qassam grew up in Jableh, a small village near Lattakia in north Syria. His father was a religious scholar, and Qassam received an Islamic education at the Azhar University in Cairo.

Qassam lived in Egypt for ten years (1896-1906), where his most influential teacher was the charismatic and renowned Islamic philosopher, Mohammad Abdu. During Qassam's studies, the al-Azhar Mosque in Cairo was the center for intellectual activity in the Arab world and the symbol for rebellion against colonial rule in Egypt.

When Italy invaded Libya in 1911, Qassam returned to Syria and began to tour villages and call men to jihad (holy war) against the invaders. He created a voluntary force of 250 men, but Ottoman authorities refused to let them leave for battle, believing that this would damage their relations with Rome.

In 1919, one year after the Ottoman Empire was dissolved in World War I, Qassam joined Omar al-Bitar in leading the resistance to the French troops landing on the Syrian coast. He headed his own resistance to the French Mandate on the north coast, and when the French occupied Syria in July 1920, they sentenced him to death.

Qassam went to Haifa and preached that armed revolt was the only way to emancipate the Middle East from the European mandates. He portrayed the British in Palestine and the French in Syria as the "new Crusaders" and called for a holy war against them. In 1928, he co-founded the Young Muslim Men's Society in Haifa to preach anti-colonial views. He served as its president from 1932 until his death in 1935.

Qassam attracted an immediate audience for his teachings and was particularly popular among the poor that he lived and interacted with daily. He claimed that only the poor would truly fight for liberty since their lives had not yet been distorted by luxuries or influenced by a good education. Once men became dazzled with what the materialistic world had to offer, he argued, they ceased to become freedom fighters. In other words, people who are rich, in good jobs, and educated would be less likely to go to war than those who are uneducated, poor, and miserable. Therefore, Qassam focused his energies on poor farmers and laborers, ex-criminals, and people with past ethical problems, claiming that they had been forced to break the law due to economic pressure and neglect. Qassam argued that these individuals needed the most attention in society.

Qassam established contact with the fascist government in Rome, hoping that Benito Mussolini would finance an uprising against the British and the Zionists in Palestine. When Mussolini declined Qassam's request, the Syrian leader turned to the Nazi regime in Germany. Adolph Hitler also gave him a cold shoulder and forced Qassam to rely on other Arab leaders to assist in his movement. He allied himself with Amin al-Husayni, the Mufti of Jerusalem, who was to make his own high profile visit to Rome and Berlin during World War II to bolster support for the Arab cause in Europe.

In 1930, Qassam secured a fatwa from Badr al-Din al-Hasani, the supreme religious leader in Syria, calling on Muslims to engage in holy war against the colonial powers. Qassam's men engaged in combat with the British troops and the Zionist militias, and inflicted such heavy casualties on both that the mandate authority put a 500 pound reward on his head.

While in combat, Izz al-Din al-Qassam was killed by the British on November 20, 1935. Haifa went on strike when his death became public and other cities in Palestine and Syria did the same hours later. He was buried in Palestine with his comrades who had died in battle, and their coffins were draped with the flags of the three Arab countries that were still independent from colonial-ruled Saudi Arabia, Iraq, and Yemen. In honor of his legacy, the military branch of Hamas, a future resistance movement in Palestine, was named after him in the 1990s. The Qassam Brigade was responsible for dozens of attacks in Israel beginning in 2000 that resulted in the killing of many Israeli troops.

Sources:

Hammudeh, Sameeh. *Al-Wai wa al-Thawra: Dirasa fi Hayat wa Jihad al-Sheikh Izz al-Din al-Qassam* (1986).

Hout, Bayan Nuwayhed. *Al-Sheikh al-Mujahid Izz al-Din al-Qassam fi Tareekh Filastine* (1987).

Jundi, Asem. *Izz al-Din al-Qassam: Riwaya* (1975).

Sayyid, Ahmad Abd al-Aziz. *Izz al-Din al-Qassam 1871-1935: Ra'id al-Nidal al-Qawmi fi Filastine* (1977).

Sharab, Mohammad Hasan. *Izz al-Din al-Qassam: Sheikh al-Mujahidin fi Filastine* (2000).

Salloum, Rafic
(1891-1916)

Rafic Salloum studied Arabic literature at the American University of Beirut (AUB) and graduated in 1913. He returned to his native Homs and worked as a journalist, writing for several newspapers, including *al-Muqtataf, al-Mazhab* and *Lisan al-Arab.* In 1915, he became managing editor of *al-Hadara,* a cultural weekly, and published his first book, *Hayat al-Bilad fi al-Ilm wa al-Iqtisad (The Life of the Country in Science and Economics).*

During World War I, Salloum established close contact with the Arab national-ist Abd al-Hamid al-Zahrawi. They began to preach Arab nationalism rather than Ottomanism. Salloum joined the Arab underground, wrote extensively against the Ottoman Empire under a pen name, and in January 1915, became deputy president of the Arab Literary Club. It was a literary organization politically affil-iated to the Arab underground which served as a network for Arab intellectuals.

In January 1916, Salloum established contact with Sharif Husayn, who was planning a military uprising against the Ottoman Turks from Mecca. Salloum also joined al-Fatat. Jamal Pasha, the Ottoman governor of Damascus, had him arrested and brought to trial on the charge of high treason. On May 6, 1916, Rafic Salloum was hung publicly in Damascus along with a group of other activists. (See Shukri al-Asali, page 365.)

Sources:
Bawab, Sulayman. *Mawsuat Alam Souriyya fi al-Qarn al-Ishreen*, Vol IV (1999).

Shalash, Ramadan
(1869-1946)

Ramadan Shalash studied at the Ottoman Military Academy in Istanbul and joined the Ottoman Army in 1890. He defected from service in 1916 to join Sharif Husayn, leader of the Arab Revolt in Mecca. He served as a commanding officer in the rebel Arab Army and became private chamberlain to Husayn from 1916 to 1918.

When the Ottoman Empire was defeated in 1918, Husayn's son, King Faysal I, became the new ruler of Syria and appointed Shalash as military governor of Raqqa, the area in northern Syria between the Euphrates and Tigris Rivers. Faysal also appointed Shalash to the Higher Military Command Council in Damascus and gave him the princely title of pasha.

In 1920, sporadic violence erupted between Shalash's troops and the British forces stationed in northern Syria. Without referring to the central government in Damascus, Shalash declared war on the British Army, occupied the Dayr al-Zur province, and appointed himself military governor of Northern Syria. King Faysal tried in vain to force his surrender, but Shalash refused to give up his arms. Shalash claimed that he had mutinied against the British Army in Syria and not, as the British tried to picture it, against the Arab kingdom of King Faysal.

On July 25, 1920, the French Army occupied Syria and launched a full-scale war against Ramadan Pasha, forcing him to flee to Amman. The French dismantled the Faysal regime, sent the king into exile, and sentenced Shalash to death in absentia. He remained in Jordan until 1925, acting as military advisor to King Abdullah.

Shalash returned to Syria in July 1925. Under heavy disguise, he went to the Arab Mountain and took up arms with Sultan al-Atrash in a military uprising against the French. On October 18, 1925, he led 400 armed horsemen into Damascus, burning down all French buildings and occupying the Azm Palace, where the French commissioner resided. The French had Shalash arrested and sentenced him to life imprisonment.

In 1936, the nationalist leader Hashim al-Atasi (who had been prime minister under Faysal), came to power and ordered the release of Shalash. In 1941,

Shalash tried creating further disturbances along the Euphrates, similar to those of 1920, and the French arrested him once again. Following independence in April 1946, Ramadan Shalash was released from prison, having spent seventeen years in French custody.

Sources:
Faris, George. *Man Hum fi al-Alam al-Arabi?* (1957).
Khoury, Philip. *Syria and the French Mandate* (1987).

al-Sham'a, Rushdi
(1865-1916)

Rushdi al-Sham'a studied at the Ottoman Academy of Law and began his career as an attorney in Istanbul. In 1900, he began work with his father, Ahmad Pasha al-Sham'a, a prominent notable in the court of Sultan Abdulhamid II.

The Sham'a family was close to the imperial throne. Ahmad Pasha was the only Arab official who had a "hot line" to the sultan through a private telegraph system that linked his office with that of the Abdulhamid II. In 1908, a revolution took place in Istanbul, curbing the sultan's powers and forcing him to democratize the Ottoman Empire. Abdulhamid reinstated the Ottoman Constitution he had voided in 1876 and established an Ottoman Parliament.

Rushdi al-Sham'a welcomed the changes and became a deputy in the new parliament. He allied himself with two outspoken deputies, Shukri al-Asali and Abd al-Wahab al-Inklizi. Together, the three established themselves as the leaders of Arab nationalism in the pre-World War I era.

Then in 1909, a group of officers overthrew Abdulhamid and began to militarize the empire. This military coalition, known as the Committee for Union and Progress (CUP), practiced favoritism and insisted that senior posts in the imperial court be occupied by Ottoman Turks. As a result, the CUP dismissed both Rushdi al-Sham'a and his father from their posts at the sultan's palace. The CUP then further angered the young nationalist by increasing the centralization of power in Istanbul and by making Ottoman Turkish, rather than Arabic, the official language of schools, courts, and government offices in the Arab provinces of the Ottoman Empire.

Rushdi al-Sham'a was highly critical of the new Turkish policies and joined the Party of Administrative Decentralization in 1913. Headed by an Arab nationalist named Rafic al-Azm, the party called for the decentralization of power from Istanbul and demanded greater input for Arab officials in Ottoman decision-making. Sham'a criticized Arab officials who were working with the new regime, including his father who had made peace with the CUP and joined the Damascus Municipal Council.

Ahmad al-Sham'a retaliated by accusing the Party of Decentralization of trea-son and calling on the new Sultan Mohammad Rashad V to outlaw its activities. He was supported in his demands by two Ottoman-Arab notables, Abd al-Rahman al-Yusuf and Sami Mardam Bey. To silence Rushdi al-Sham'a's opposition, the CUP dissolved parliament and called for new elections. Rushdi nominated him-self for office, but the ballots were rigged and he was defeated at the polls.

In 1914, Rushdi al-Sham'a began to write in the pro-Arab daily, *al-Qabas*, run by his former parliamentary ally Shukri al-Asali. In 1916, Sham'a became a member of the Arab underground and joined al-Fatat. Jamal Pasha, the Ottoman governor of Damascus, arrested him and brought him to court in the town of Aley on Mount Lebanon.

On May 6, 1916, Rushdi al-Sham'a was convicted of high treason and hanged in public at Marjeh Square in Damascus along with a group of other activists (See Shukri al-Asali, page 365.)

Sources:

Barudi, Fakhri. *Muzakarat Fakhri al-Barudi,* Vol I (1999).
Khury, Colette. *Awrak Faris al-Khury* (1989).
Khoury, Philip. *Urban Notables and Arab Nationalism* (1983).

al-Shihabi, Aref
(1889-1916)

Born and raised in Damascus, Aref al-Shihabi studied at the Ottoman Law Academy in Istanbul, and during his studies co-founded al-Fatat. Shihabi found-ed *al-Nahda*, a political periodical that called for pan-Arab solidarity in Ottoman Syria.

In 1911, Shihabi launched another weekly, *al-Mufid,* named after a popu-lar newspaper in Beirut that promoted pan-Arab sentiment and criticized the "Turkification" of the Ottoman Empire. Shihabi called on Arab subjects living in the empire to fight for their rights as Ottoman subjects. He criticized Sultan Mohammad Rashad V for replacing Arab officials in the empire with Ottoman Turks. He also spoke out against Turkish as the official language of the Arab prov-inces, where it had replaced Arabic in schools, courts, and the civil service.

Jamal Pasha, the governor of Syria, arrested Shihabi in January 1916 and brought him before a military tribunal in Aley. Aref al-Shihabi was found guilty of high treason against the Ottoman Empire and executed in public on May 6, 1916.

Sources:

Bawab, Sulayman. *Mawsuat Alam Souriyya fi al-Qarn al-Ishreen,* Vol IV (1999).

al-Shishakli, Tawfiq
(1884-1940)

Tawfiq al-Shishakli was born and raised in a prominent, notable family in Hama. He studied at the Ottoman Medical Academy in Istanbul and joined the Ottoman Army as a practicing doctor in 1914.

When World War I broke out in August 1914, Shishakli became a surgeon at the Military Hospital in Medina (in present-day Saudi Arabia). Shishakli joined the Arab underground and became a member of al-Fatat. When the Ottoman Empire was defeated in 1918, he returned to his native Hama and opened a clinic to practice medicine. He played no role in politics during the brief Arab rule (1918-1920), but was persecuted for his anti-colonial history by the French who occupied Syria in July 1920.

In 1925, Shishakli joined a military uprising against the French Mandate in the Arab Mountain, launched by the chieftain Sultan al-Atrash. Shishakli donated money to the Syrian resistance and oversaw the care of those who were wounded in combat. French authorities had him arrested in 1927, and he spent six months in prison on the charge of conspiracy against the mandate authority.

In 1928, Shishakli co-founded the National Bloc with its president Hashim al-Atasi. The National Bloc was the leading anti-French movement in Syria which called for liberation from the mandate through diplomatic means rather than armed resistance. Shishakli nominated himself on a Bloc ticket for parliament in 1928, 1932, and 1936, winning every election. Dr Shishakli became head of the National Bloc office in Hama, but clashed continuously with his Bloc counter-parts in Damascus. He harbored socialist views and wanted to improve the living conditions of rural Syria, while most of his Bloc colleagues, who were wealthy landowners, showed little interest in his political program and the conditions of rural districts. He commanded the poor people in the Hama countryside while his colleague, Najib al-Barazi, took charge of the wealthy, landowning class of Hama.

Shishakli preached a classless society, redistribution of wealth, and social justice twenty years before Gamal Abd al-Nasser of Egypt launched the socialist move-ment in the Arab world. Among his earliest followers was Akram al-Hawrani, a young lawyer who was to become the prime socialist leader of Syria in the 1950s. Shishakli's home became the national gathering for Hama residents, and was called "House of the Nation." In 1935, he co-launched a sixty day strike in Syria to protest France's refusal to address the issue of Syrian independence. The French arrested him for his activities but released him in 1936.

Tawfiq al-Shishakli died in 1940, six years before Syria became independent from the French Mandate.

Sources:

Babil, Nasuh. *Sahafa wa Siyasa fi Souriyya* (1987).

Jundi, Adham. *Tareekh al-Thawrat al-Souriyya fi Ahd al-Intidab al-Faransi* (1960).

Khoury, Philip. *Syria and the French Mandate* (1987).

Shambrook, Peter. *French Imperialism in Syria 1927-1936* (1998).

al-Tintawi, Ali
(1909-1998)

Ali al-Tintawi was born and raised in Damascus. He began his career as a journalist in the popular Damascus daily, *al-Ayyam*, and moved to the Egyptian weekly, *al-Azhar*, in 1931. From 1929 to 1931, he served as president of the Syrian Students Union.

In 1930, Tintawi launched his own Islamic newspaper called *al-Baath (Renaissance)*. It was the first such newspaper in Damascus, but it closed for financial reasons in 1932. In addition to writing, he taught at different high schools in Damascus, Dayr al-Zur, Baghdad, and Beirut.

In the 1930s, Tintawi became a member of the National Bloc, the leading anti-colonial movement that wanted to liberate Syria from the French Mandate through diplomatic means rather than armed resistance. In 1941, Tintawi became a consultant at the Ministry of Justice and a judge in the civil courts in Damascus. He established himself as an Islamic philosopher, preaching a revival of Muslim ideals and the creation of a social system based on moderate Islam. When Syria achieved independence in April 1946, Ali al-Tintawi became an instructor at Damascus University.

In the 1950s, Tintawi joined the movement of Arab nationalism headed by President Gamal Abd al-Nasser of Egypt. Tintawi also backed the Syrian-Egyptian union of 1958. However, he clashed with the union government when Nasser established a dictatorship over Syria. Among other things, Tintawi opposed the closure of newspapers, the termination of political parties, and the arrest of dissidents in Syria. He was also highly critical of Nasser's Interior Minister Abd al-Hamid al-Sarraj, who established a police state in Syria. Tintawi strongly supported the coup d'etat that ousted the union in September 1961. When the Baath Party came to power in 1963, its officers promised to restore the Syrian-Egyptian union and persecute all those who had supported the post-Nasser government of President Nazim al-Qudsi (1961-1963). As a result, Ali al-Tintawi was banished from Syria.

Consequently, Tintawi moved to Mecca, set up base as a religious reformist, and launched a series of television and radio programs aimed at increasing public awareness of Islam. His sermons were very popular. By the mid-1970s, Ali al-Tintawi had become a household name in Saudi Arabia. In 1977, he visited

Damascus briefly, then moved back to Saudi Arabia where he died in 1998.

Ali al-Tintawi wrote fifty books on life, politics, and Islam. His most widely acclaimed works are *Fusul Islamiyya (Islamic Seasons)*, *Ma' al-Nass (With the People)*, *Fi Sabeel al-Islah (In Pursuit of Reform)*, and *Rijal Min al-Tareekh (Men from History)*. He also wrote two bestsellers: *Dimashq*, a story of the social life of Damascus, and his eight-volume *Muzakarat (Memoirs)*.

Sources:
Itri, Abd al-Ghani. *Abqariyyat wa Alam* (1996).

al-Zahrawi, Abd al-Hamid
(1855-1916)

Abd al-Hamid al-Zahrawi was born and raised in Homs. He studied at the Ottoman Law Academy in Istanbul. His writing career began in Damascus where he wrote for several Arab newspapers. His articles appeared frequently in *al-Qabas*, an Arabic political daily run by the outspoken lawyer and journalist Shukri al-Asali.

In 1908, a coup took place in Istanbul and a group of young officers, who called themselves the Committee for Union and Progress (CUP), came to power. The CUP democratized the rigid political system, reestablished an Ottoman Parliament and curbed the powers of Sultan Abdulhamid II.

At first, Zahrawi supported the CUP and was elected into the Ottoman Parliament in 1909 on a CUP ticket. Once firmly in power, however, the CUP dismissed many Arab officials and replaced them with Ottoman Turks. Zahrawi accused them of practicing favoritism and slowly lost faith in the new system. He began to criticize the CUP from within parliament. Along with two other Arab nationalist deputies, Shafiq Mu'ayyad al-Azm and Shukri al-Asali, Zahrawi led

the parliamentary opposition in the Ottoman Empire during the prewar era. In 1912, wanting to get rid of Zahrawi and his allies, the CUP called for new elections and rigged the ballots, causing the defeat of all three men.

In 1913, Zahrawi joined a group of Arab activists in Europe and held the first all-Arab congress in Paris. The congress aimed at uniting the Arab front in the face of increasing Ottoman persecution and centralization of power in the hands of the Turks. Zahrawi chaired the conference and appointed Jamil Mardam Bey, a young Syrian student studying in France, as director of its public relations campaign. Zahrawi gathered an impressive

Abd al-Hamid al-Zahrawi.

circle of young Arab intellectuals around him and demanded more reforms and more political rights for Arabs living in the empire.

When World War I broke out in 1914, Zahrawi called on Sultan Mohammad Rashad V to refrain from involving the Ottoman Army in the conflict. If the Ottomans were to fight, he contended, then the Syrians should not join the Ottoman Army since this was a war that did not concern them. In 1915, Zahrawi joined the Arab underground and became a member of al-Fatat.

Jamal Pasha, the Ottoman military governor, arrested Zahrawi and charged him with conspiring against the Ottoman Empire. He was tried at a military tribunal in the town of Aley in Mount Lebanon and declared guilty of high treason. On May 6, 1916, Abd al-Hamid al-Zahrawi and a group of other activists were executed in Marjeh Square, Damascus. (See profile of Shukri al-Asali, page 365.)

Sources:
Encyclopedia of the Modern Middle East, Vol IV (1996). Article by Charles U. Zenzie.
Khoury, Philip. *Urban Notables and Arab Nationalism* (1983).

The Syrian diplomatic team (drawn from the National Bloc) that engaged in negotiations toward independence at the Quai d'Orsay in Paris in 1936. From left to right: Mustapha al-Shihabi, Faris al-Khury, Hashim al-Atasi, Jamil Mardam Bey, and Edmond Homsi.

Syrian Prime Minister Faris al-Khury with Paul-Henri Spaak, the Prime Minister of Belgium, at the United Nations in 1945. Syria was present at the founding of the UN in San Francisco in April 1945. Khury presented Syria's case for liberation from French occupation. During his six-month-long stay in the US, he met with President Harry Truman and asked him to pressure the French to grant Syrian freedom. Later in the 1940s, Faris al-Khury served as president of the Security Council at the UN when Syria was a rotating council member.

Foreign Minister Jamil Mardam Bey signing the agreement of French evacuation with French officials in April 1946.

Crowds celebrating independence before the Sarail or government headquarters, near Marjeh in Damascus on April 17, 1946. Currently the Ministry of the Interior occupies this location.

DIPLOMATS

The individuals mentioned in this chapter are diplomats who have assumed senior posts at the Syrian Ministry of Foreign Affairs since 1932. Before that, during the early years of the French Mandate (1920-1932), there was no Ministry of Foreign Affairs in Syria. Of all the state institutions, the Ministry of Foreign Affairs was the one to suffer least during the turmoil that rocked Syria in the 1950s and 1960s. Consecutive regimes did not harass, arrest, or fire career diplomats, seeing them as necessary to maintain Syria's international reputation. This was the case even after the Baath Party came to power in 1963.

JAMES HUGH KEELEY JR.
U.S.A. CONSUL 1923-1928
DAMASCUS-SYRIA

Calling card. Note that the face of the kawwas or body guard has been intentionally obscured.

Within Syria, several diplomatic achievements are viewed as milestones. In 1944 Syria co-founded the Arab League in Cairo. In 1945, Syria participated in the founding of the United Nations in San Francisco. In 1946, Syria negotiated an end to the French Mandate. In Syria's relations with the United States, a diplomatic highlight was the negotiated release of US Navy flier Robert O. Goodman, whose plane was downed over Lebanon in 1984. Under President Hafez al-Asad, Syrians took pride in their country's strict adherence to the ceasefire that ended the 1973 war with Israel. Syria's participation in the 1991 Madrid Peace Conference is a benchmark in its relations with Israel.

Abu Risheh, Omar (1908-1990): see "Arts & Letters"

al-Allaf, Mowaffak
(1927-1996)

Mowaffak al-Allaf was born in Damascus and spent parts of his childhood in Haifa, Palestine, where his father worked as a businessman. The British accused Allaf's father of supporting the Palestinian resistance, and the police surrounded Allaf's home to search for weapons. It was the young Allaf's first exposure to diplomacy when, using the English he had learned at school, he negotiated successfully with the British on his father's behalf.

Allaf returned to Syria, studied law at Damascus University, and obtained a diploma in international relations in 1949. He joined the Ministry of Economy, becoming commercial attaché first to Cairo, then to Jeddah during the military regime of President Adib al-Shishakli (1951-1954).

Allaf then joined the Ministry of Foreign Affairs, and from 1954 to 1967 served at different diplomatic posts in Cyprus, Turkey, Switzerland, and Saudi Arabia. In 1968, Allaf became Syria's ambassador to the United Nations in Geneva.

In 1975, President Hafez al-Asad appointed him ambassador to the UN in New York. Allaf remained in that position until 1978 when UN Secretary-General Kurt Waldheim appointed him under secretary-general of the UN in Geneva, the first Arab to attain such a post.

In 1977, President Anwar al-Sadat made his groundbreaking trip to Israel. Fate had it that Allaf was to be the first scheduled speaker at the UN that Monday morning. The Arab world, Syria included, was caught off-guard and slow to issue an official reaction to Sadat's Israeli trip. Allaf requested instructions from Foreign Minister Abd al-Halim Khaddam, trying to reach him by telex, but no response came from a stunned government in Damascus since Syria had not yet decided how to deal with Sadat's Jerusalem visit. Allaf went ahead and wrote his speech, which blasted Sadat. Allaf told his wife that if his speech happened to contradict what Damascus wanted him to say, that his career would be ruined, and he might never be able to return to Syria. But Allaf went ahead and delivered his speech to the UN, becoming the first Arab to harshly criticize Sadat. At 3:00 AM Eastern Standard Time, Foreign Minister Khaddam reached Allaf by phone, "approving" his stance…after the speech had been made.

In April 1982, Waldheim was replaced by the new UN secretary-general, Perez de Cuellar, who appointed Allaf the first director of the UN office in Vienna, a post he held until 1987. In the late 1980s, Allaf helped establish the Austro-Arab Chamber of Commerce by drafting its bylaws and infrastructure. In February 1987, Allaf was rewarded the Grand Decoration of Honor in Gold in Sash for Services to the Republic of Austria from Austrian President Kurt Waldheim. In 1989, Allaf was elected secretary-general of the Chamber of Commerce, a post he held until his death in 1996.

Following the Gulf War in 1991, the United States initiated the Madrid Peace Conference, where the Arab countries agreed to attend round table talks with Israel. Allaf was summoned from Vienna to head the Syrian delegation to Madrid, having been away from the Syrian Foreign Ministry since 1978. At first Allaf refused, then accepted after personally asking President Asad, "Do you give me your word that the red line is the entirety of the occupied Golan Heights, and that there will be no concessions on that point?" Asad answered yes.

Factions within the Syrian Ministry of Foreign Affairs were upset at Allaf's appointment as chief negotiator. Allaf had been away from Syria too long, they maintained. But the real reason for the acrimony was that Allaf was not a Baathist. Yet Asad had his way as usual. Syria took part in the bilateral talks from October 30 to November 3, 1991.

In the 1990s, Allaf became a member of the political committee at the Ministry of Foreign Affairs. The committee included retired officials like General Yusuf Shakkur and Ambassador Rafic Jouejati and served as an advisory team to Foreign Minister Farouk al-Shara.

In 1994, Allaf became head of the Syrian delegation to the Washington peace talks with the Israeli Labor government of Prime Minister Yitzhak Rabin. Allaf negotiated along the land-for-peace formula agreed to at Madrid which called for complete Israeli withdrawal to its pre-1967 borders in exchange for a comprehensive peace deal with Syria. By total withdrawal, Allaf was referring to the Arab territories occupied in the Arab-Israeli War of 1967 including the Syrian Golan Heights. The Israelis, who argued that "full withdrawal" would only be from the occupied Golan Heights, refused to relinquish South Lebanon and rejected the proposal.

The Israelis, annoyed by the eloquence of Allaf, a seasoned Syrian diplomat and expert in international law, complained to US President Bill Clinton, ostensibly arguing that Allaf was not politically powerful enough in Syria to make decisions on his own. Two US secretaries of state, James Baker and Warren Christopher, asked Asad to replace Allaf. But Asad curtly refused, saying that if need be, he would promote Allaf to deputy foreign minister and private advisor to President Asad himself, thereby giving Allaf plenty of power.

Allaf served on the diplomatic team until January 1996 when, under Asad's insistence that a strong Syrian should be at the Arab League, he became assistant to the secretary-general of the Arab League. Six months after his appointment, however, Mowaffak al-Allaf died suddenly on July 4, 1996.

Sources:
Rabinovich, Itamar. *The Brink of Peace* (1997).
The International Who's Who in the Arab World (1987-1988).
Information supplied by Rime Allaf (April 29, 2005).

Antaki, Naim (1903-1971) see "Politicians"

al-Armanazi, Najib
(1897-1968)

Born and raised in Damascus, Najib al-Armanazi studied international law at the Sorbonne in Paris, and joined al-Ahd and al-Fatat, two underground Arab movements operating in Ottoman Syria.

When Armanazi returned to Syria, he worked as a journalist, and in 1920 became secretary of the Syrian National Congress, the equivalent of a modern parliament that was headed by the veteran nationalist leader Hashim al-Atasi. In July 1920, the French Army invaded Syria, overthrew King Faysal I, dissolved the

Syrian Congress, and imposed their mandate in the Middle East.

That year, Armanazi fled to Europe to evade arrest by the French. Armanazi joined the Syrian-Palestinian Congress, a coalition of Arabs in exile working for emancipation of Syria, Lebanon, and Palestine from colonial rule. Along with Abd al-Rahman Shahbandar, Faysal's ex-minister of foreign affairs, Armanazi was a member of the council's Executive Committee. In 1928, a French amnesty allowed Armanazi to return to home, where he joined the National Bloc, the leading anti-French movement in Syria.

In 1932, Syria's first president, Mohammad Ali al-Abid, appointed Armanazi director of the Presidential Office. In 1942, Armanazi became secretary-general of the presidency during the era of President Taj al-Din al-Hasani. Armanazi then joined the Ministry of Foreign Affairs, and in 1944 was a member of the Syrian delegation that created the Arab League in Egypt. In 1945, President Shukri al-Quwatli, a colleague in the National Bloc, appointed Armanazi minister to Great Britain where he played an instrumental role in solidifying the Syrian-British friendship that began to develop toward the end of World War II.

In May 1945, the French bombarded Damascus, and Armanazi called on Prime Minister Winston Churchill to secure British support for a cease-fire. Armanazi remained on good terms with the British until the Arab-Israeli War broke out 1948, when he criticized Great Britain for its unequivocal support for Israel. From 1946 to 1948, Armanazi also served on the Syrian diplomatic delegation to the United Nations. In 1950, President Hashim al-Atasi appointed him ambassador to India. He worked in Delhi for five years, and in January 1956 was reappointed ambassador to Great Britain by the new Syrian president, Shukri al-Quwatli.

During the Suez Canal War of 1956 launched by Great Britain, France, and Israel against Egypt, Armanazi became Syria's link to British Prime Minister Anthony Eden. But Armanazi retired from diplomatic activity during the Syrian-Egyptian union (1958-1961) and spent the remainder of his years writing books.

Armanazi was opposed to the military dictatorship imposed on Syria by President Gamal Abd al-Nasser of Egypt. On September 28, 1961, he supported a coup that dissolved the union, and he signed the secession declaration drafted by anti-union politicians in Damascus on October 2, 1961. The document accused Nasser of "distorting the idea of Arab nationalism," and said that during the union years Nasser had "strangled political and democratic life" in Syria.

Najib al-Armanazi published several books during his life including *Al-Hamla al-Masriyya* (*The Egyptian Campaign*), published in 1922, *Souriyya Min al-Ihtilal Hata al-Istiqlal* (*Syria: From Occupation until Independence*), published in 1953, and his autobiography, *Ashr Sanawat Min al-Diblomasiyya* (*Ten Years of Diplomacy*), published in 1963.

Sources:

Armanazi, Najib. *Ashr Sanawat Min al-Diblomasiyya* (1963).
Faris, George. *Man Hum fi al-Alam al-Arabi?* (1957).
Samman, Mutih. *Watan wa Askar* (1995).

al-Asha, Rafic
(1910-)

Rafic al-Asha was born and raised in Damascus. He studied economics at the American University of Beirut (AUB) and graduated in 1932. One year later, he became an instructor of banking and finance at Baghdad University.

In 1941, Asha returned to Syria and joined the Ministry of Foreign Affairs, becoming chargé d'affaires at the Syrian Embassy in Cairo. In 1945, the United States invited Syria to attend the founding conference of the United Nations in San Francisco. Prime Minister Faris al-Khury handpicked the Syrian team, composed of recent AUB graduates, to promote Syria's cause of independence from the French Mandate before the UN General Assembly.

Asha and his colleagues met with numerous US officials and rallied the support of China, the USSR, and Great Britain. Asha served at the UN office in New York until 1952, when President Adib al-Shishakli appointed him chargé d'affaires and minister plenipotentiary to Washington. Asha retained his post in the United States for the next six years, serving until 1958. Also in 1952, he became alternate governor to the International Bank for Reconstruction and Development (IBRD) at the World Bank. He held the same post in the US during the regimes of Hashim al-Atasi (1954-1955) and Shukri al-Quwatli (1955-1958).

In 1958, Syria and Egypt merged to form the United Arab Republic (UAR), and Asha briefly became president of the Arab League Council in Cairo. President Gamal Abd al-Nasser then appointed Asha UAR representative to the UN General Assembly in New York. When a coup ousted the union in September 1961, Asha returned to Damascus. Syria's new president, Nazim al-Qudsi, appointed Asha ambassador to the USSR, a post he held until 1962 when he became secretary-general of the Ministry of Foreign Affairs.

Asha found his job in Moscow burdensome, however, coming at a time of increased Soviet resentment toward Syria for Qudsi's newfound alliance with the US administration of President John F. Kennedy. In March 1963, the Baath Party came to power in Syria and Asha became representative to the UN office in New York. Rafic al-Asha resigned from his UN post in 1968 and became senior financial advisor to the United Nations Development Program (UNDP).

Sources:
The International Who's Who in the Arab World (1987-1988).

al-Dawoudi, Adib
(1925-2004)

Adib al-Dawoudi was born in Damascus in 1925. He studied international law at Damascus University and obtained his graduate degree from the Sorbonne in Paris in 1949. He joined the Ministry of Foreign Affairs as secretary of the Syrian delegation at the founding conference of the Arab League in Egypt in March 1944.

In 1943-1944, Dawoudi also served as secretary to Foreign Minister Jamil Mardam Bey. In 1945, he became attaché to the Syrian Embassy in France, in charge of consular affairs. While working at the embassy, Dawoudi continued his studies at the Sorbonne. As a career diplomat, he did not take sides in the military-civilian divide that rocked Syria after the Arab-Israeli War of 1948, and was kept at his post in 1949 after a military coup ousted President Shukri al-Quwatli.

In October 1952, President Shishakli appointed Dawoudi director of the Organization of Palestinian Refugee Camps in Syria. Dawoudi was the first senior official to emphasize that Syrians must read the Israeli press and know their enemy. Every morning, the main Israeli daily newspapers would be flown in from Cyprus, then reviewed and translated into Arabic by specialists in Hebrew. A bi-weekly bulletin would then be published by the Refugee Organization in Syria and distributed to ministries, universities, and the armed forces so that Syrians could understand what was being prepared, said, and done in Israel.

When Shishakli was overthrown in 1954, Dawoudi kept his job at the Refugee Organization and worked with Prime Minister Said al-Ghazzi on improving the conditions of the Palestinian refugees by transferring them from the ghettos to organized camps. Along with Ghazzi and Interior Minister Ali Buzo, Dawoudi founded the Yarmouk Refugee Camp in 1957, which became the largest camp in Syria, and currently houses 112,550 Palestinians with the largest number of UNRWA schools.

In 1955, Dawoudi became a consultant to Najib al-Armanazi, the Syrian ambassador to Great Britain. Dawoudi held this post during the gridlock in Syrian-British relations, especially when Syria cut its diplomatic ties to London after the Tripartite Aggression against Egypt in 1956. In 1958, Syria and Egypt merged to form the United Arab Republic (UAR) and President Gamal Abd al-Nasser appointed Dawoudi advisor to the UAR embassy in Pakistan. In 1961, Dawoudi became minister at the Syrian embassy in Czechoslovakia. He also went to the UN as a representative for the UAR to speak out about Palestinian refugee problems in Syria, vigorously defending the right of return of the Palestinians to the occupied territories.

When a coup dissolved the UAR in September 1961, Dawoudi returned to Syria and allied himself with President Nazim al-Qudsi, who appointed him ambassador to India in 1962. In July of that year, Syria filed an official complaint against

Nasser, claiming that he was interfering in Syrian affairs and trying to provoke officers in the Syrian Army to rebel against the post-Nasser order. The Arab League organized round table talks between Syria and Egypt that were held in Shtura, a small Lebanese town near the Syrian border. The Syrian team included Adib al-Dawoudi, who according to the minutes of the meeting, argued brilliantly against Nasser's Egypt. The talks were foiled, however, when the Egyptian team walked out before the Arab League issued a verdict against Egypt.

Adib al-Dawoudi.

In 1964, Dawoudi became assistant secretary-general in the Department of Political Affairs at the Ministry of Foreign Affairs in Damascus. He held this post during the Arab-Israel War of 1967. He also became president of the Syrian Human Rights Delegation to an international conference held in Iran in 1968. In 1969, President Nur al-Din al-Atasi appointed him ambassador to Belgium. He also became non-resident ambassador to Holland and Luxemburg.

In 1974, Dawoudi returned to Syria and became political advisor to President Hafez al-Asad. By doing so, Dawoudi was among the very few men who worked with every regime to rule Syria since 1943. He worked with Asad until 1981, acting at times as his special envoy to foreign capitals, and serving as director of protocol during the president's numerous travels in the 1970s. Dawoudi also served as Asad's aide-de-camp during his meetings with US President Jimmy Carter. In 1979, UN Secretary-General Kurt Waldheim delegated Dawoudi to serve on an international committee created to mediate between the USA and the leaders in Iran, who had taken seventy American diplomats hostage in Tehran on November 4, 1979. The crisis, and Dawoudi's involvement in it, lasted 444 days. When the international committee failed to end the hostage crisis, Waldheim made Dawoudi his personal envoy in UN negotiations with the mullahs of Tehran.

In 1981, Dawoudi became Syria's permanent ambassador to the UN and non-resident ambassador to the Vatican. He held all posts until 1988. He then resigned from the Ministry of Foreign Affairs and became a senior inspector at the UN office in Geneva, becoming director of the eleven-man inspection committee in 1992.

Adib al-Dawoudi spent his retirement in Switzerland, but died in Lebanon in August 2004.

Sources:
Faris, George. *Man Hum fi al-Alam al-Arabi?* (1957).

Itri, Abd al-Ghani. *Hadeeth al-Abqariyyat* (2000).

Droubi, Sami
(1921-1976)

Sami Droubi was born and raised in Homs. He studied philosophy at Cairo University and obtained his graduate degree from Paris, returning to teach at Damascus University in 1948.

Droubi joined the Baath Party of Michel Aflaq and Salah al-Bitar, becoming one of its most influential leaders in the second half of the 1950s. He was persecuted for his views, however, and arrested along with other Baathists during the military regime of President Adib al-Shishakli (1951-1954). Droubi joined the movement of Arab nationalism headed by President Gamal Abd al-Nasser of Egypt. Droubi advocated the creation of a socialist state in Syria, based on the Nasser government in Cairo, that worked for Arab unity and passionately preached Arab nationalism.

In 1958, Syria and Egypt merged to form the United Arab Republic (UAR) and Droubi became director of the Ministry of Culture in the UAR. Droubi established himself during the UAR years (1958-1961) as a philosopher of Arab nationalism and a hard-line loyalist of Nasser. In 1960-1961, Droubi became cultural consultant at the UAR Embassy in Brazil. When a military coup dissolved the UAR in September 1961, Droubi returned to Syria and joined the opposition to the post-Nasser government of President Nazim al-Qudsi. In March 1963, the Military Committee of the Baath Party came to power in Syria, pledging to restore the UAR. Droubi allied himself with the officers who toppled the Qudsi government and became Minister of Education in the first Baath Party cabinet of Prime Minister Salah al-Bitar. Droubi also became a member of the Revolutionary Command Council (RCC). President Amin al-Hafez appointed him ambassador to Morocco in September 1963, and then ambassador to Yugoslavia in December 1964.

When Amin al-Hafez was overthrown in February 1966, Syria's new president, Nur al-Din al-Atasi, appointed Droubi ambassador to Egypt and the Arab League in Cairo on April 16, 1966, a post intended to keep Droubi away from domestic decision-making in Syria. A dedicated Nasserist, Droubi wept while presenting his credentials to President Nasser in Cairo, saying, "It is painful for me to stand before you today as a foreigner, as if I were not in one proud day a citizen of the republic in which you were president."

Droubi had become highly critical of the party leadership for failing on its promise to restore union, and for its arrest of leading Nasserists in the Syrian Army in July 1963. He was also opposed to the banishment of Michel Aflaq and Salah al-Bitar by Baath Party strongman Salah Jadid in February 1966. Droubi's own banishment into the diplomatic service was intended primarily to silence his opposition inside Syria. At his new job in Egypt, he befriended Nasser and increased his involvement in Middle East politics, becoming one of the closest Syrians to the Egyptian leader throughout the 1960s.

In September 1970, Droubi suffered a severe setback to his career when Nasser died of a heart attack in Egypt. Hafez al-Asad, who came to power in Syria two months later, recalled Droubi to Syria, then appointed him ambassador to Spain in November 1971, and the Vatican in October 1973. He remained in the diplomatic service until requesting to return to Syria in October 1975 for "health reasons." On February 12, 1976, Sami Droubi died while translating Leo Tolstoy's *War and Peace*.

Among Droubi's published works is *Ilm al-Nafs wa al-Adab (Psychology and Literature)*, published in Cairo in 1971. He also translated into Arabic the complete works of Russian novelists Fyodor Dostoyevsky and the French philosopher Jean Paul Sartre. In 1956, he wrote *al-Mujaz fi Ilm al-Nafs (Concise in Psychology)* with the Baath Party leader Abdullah Abd al-Daim. Sami Droubi is considered one of the most prominent leaders of the Baath Party and one of the most acclaimed philosophers of Arab nationalism in modern Syria.

Sources:
Droubi, Ihsan Bayyat. *Sami Droubi* (1982).

al-Farra, Jamal
(1911-)

Jamal Farra was born and raised in Damascus. He studied at the Sorbonne in Paris, graduating as a chemical engineer, and joined the Ministry of Education in Syria, becoming its secretary-general from April to August 1949, during the brief four-month era of President Husni al-Za'im.

In 1950, Farra moved to the Ministry of Foreign Affairs and became ambassador to Sweden during the military regime of President Adib al-Shishakli (1951-1954). He also became non-resident ambassador to Norway, Denmark, and Finland. In 1955, President Hashim al-Atasi appointed him ambassador to the German Democratic Republic, and in 1956, Farra became ambassador to the USSR. He also served as non-resident ambassador to Poland.

In 1958, Syria and Egypt merged to form the United Arab Republic (UAR) and President Gamal Abd al-Nasser appointed Farra UAR ambassador to Brazil. He held office until the UAR was dissolved in September 1961. In 1962, Farra published his book, *Dunya al-Mughtaribeen (The World of Émigrés)*, in Beirut, drawing on his encounters with prominent Arabs in the Soviet Union and Western Europe. In October 1962, Jamal al-Farra held office briefly as minister of foreign affairs in the cabinet of Prime Minister Bashir al-Azma. Also in 1962, following the dissolution of the UAR, Syria's new president, Nazim al-Qudsi, appointed Farra ambassador to West Germany, a post he held until the Baath Party came to power in March 1963. The first Baathist president of Syria, Amin al-Hafez, appointed Farra ambassador to Italy. He resigned from office in 1964, however, and retired from diplomatic activity. In 1965, he began writing for the Lebanese weekly *al-Usbu' al-Arabi*.

Jamal Farra also published his autobiography, *Thalath Sanawat fi Bilad Lenin (Three Years in the Land of Lenin)*, drawing on his experiences in Moscow from 1956 to 1958.

Sources:
Faris, George. *Man Hum fi al-Alam al-Arabi?* (1957).
Itri, Abd al-Ghani. *Abqariyyat* (1997).

Jouejati, Rafic
(1922-2003)

Rafic Jouejati was born and raised in Damascus. He studied law at Damascus University and obtained a graduate degree in political economy from the Sorbonne in Paris. He obtained a PhD in political science from the New School for Social Research in New York, as well as a diploma in Public Administration from Princeton University's Woodrow Wilson School of Public and International Affairs. Late in his career, Jouejati also pursued a degree in Comparative Literature from Athens University in Ohio.

Jouejati began his political and diplomatic career at the Syrian Ministry of Economy in the Department of Conflict Resolution and Labor. In 1946, he joined the Ministry of Foreign Affairs and took his first diplomatic post at the Syrian Embassy in Great Britain. He worked with three consecutive ambassadors, Najib al-Armanazi, Edmond Homsi, and Fayez al-Khury. Jouejati returned to Syria in 1952 to serve as the chief of staff for Foreign Minister Khalil Mardam Bey. In 1954, Jouejati was appointed first secretary and chargé d'affaires to the Syrian Embassy in Spain. In 1956, the Ministry of Foreign Affairs appointed him to the Syrian delegation to the UN in New York. In January 1958, Foreign Minister Salah al-Bitar appointed Jouejati chargé d'affaires to Syria's UN presence.

When Syria and Egypt merged to form the United Arab Republic (UAR) in February 1958, Jouejati returned to Syria to assume the post of secretary-general of the Department of Economic Development and Petroleum in Syria. After the 1961 coup ousted the UAR, Jouejati returned to the Ministry of Foreign Affairs, serving briefly under President Nazim al-Qudsi as director of international relations at the Presidential Palace. In 1963, Jouejati became chief of staff for Foreign

Minister Hasan Muraywed. In 1964, he was once again appointed to the Syrian mission to the UN. He held this post until he was appointed director of planning and research, and one year later director of Western European affairs at the Ministry of Foreign Affairs. In July 1981, President Hafez al-Asad appointed Jouejati ambassador to the United States and Canada. Jouejati faced difficult challenges during his tenure as ambassador, faced with the heightened Syrian-American tensions brought about by the Israeli invasion of Lebanon in 1982.

Nonetheless, through skillful diplomacy Jouejati was able to smooth out the rough relationship between Syria and the Reagan administration, and he was instrumental in securing the release of Lt. Robert O. Goodman, a US Navy pilot downed by Syrian anti-aircraft fire in Lebanon. Jouejati ended his tenure as ambassador in 1986 and spent the next four years writing books and articles, and lecturing on politics, diplomacy, and comparative literature at Damascus University. Jouejati also served as a visiting lecturer at Oxford and Cambridge universities in England and the School of Oriental Studies in Munich, Germany.

In 1990, Jouejati became a member of the political committee at the Ministry of Foreign Affairs. In addition, he served as a member of the Syrian delegation at the Madrid Peace Conference in 1991 and a negotiator to the Syria-Israel track of the Middle East peace talks in March 2000. Jouejati's last post was as director of the Academy for Diplomatic Studies in Syria, an institution newly formed by President Bashar al-Asad. Jouejati died in April 2003, before the academy was fully established.

Rafic Jouejati was known for his love of learning and education. His published works include *The ABC of Economic Development, Introduction to Political Science* and *The Quest for Total Peace: The Political Thought of Roger Martin du Gard.*

Sources:
Tishreen (April 20, 2003).
Interview with Dr Rafic Jouejati (March 23, 2003).
Interview (fact check) with Dr Murhaf Jouejati (April 28, 2005).

al-Khani, Abdullah
(1925-)

Abdullah al-Khani came from Damascus, studied political science at the American University of Beirut (AUB), and graduated from Damascus University. He began his career as an attorney in Damascus and an employee at the Presidential Palace, becoming director-general and acting secretary-general from 1949 to 1958.

Al-Khani held office under presidents Husni al-Za'im, Adib al-Shishakli, Hashim al-Atasi, and Shukri al-Quwatli. Khani was very close to Quwatli from 1955 to 1958, serving as his aide-de-camp and confidant. In addition to his duties

Left to right: President Shukri al-Quwatli, Abdullah al-Khani, and President Hashem al-Atasi, at the Syrian parliament during Quwatli's swearing-in ceremony in September 1955.

with the presidents, Khani taught at Damascus University from 1954 to 1958. In February 1958, he took part in union talks between Syria and Egypt that result-ed in the creation of the United Arab Republic (UAR). During the union years, Khani helped merge and modify the Syrian and Egyptian legal systems which were based on the French and British systems respectively.

In 1959, Khani joined the Ministry of Foreign Affairs and in 1967 became permanent representative to the UNESCO office in France. In the 1960s, he drift-ed through diplomatic posts in Brussels, London, Paris, Ankara, and Madrid. In 1969, he returned to Syria and became secretary-general of the Ministry of Foreign Affairs. In December 1972, he became minister of tourism in the cabinet of Prime Minister Mahmud al-Ayyubi. Khani kept this post until August 1976, when he became an assistant to Foreign Minister Abd al-Halim Khaddam. From 1978 to 1981, Khani became ambassador to India and non-resident ambassador to Nepal, Burma, Bangladesh, and Sri Lanka. During this time, he also served as a member and deputy president of the Anti-Discrimination and Protecting Minorities Committee at the UN in Geneva. He resigned from the Ministry of Foreign Affairs in 1981 and became a judge in the International Court of Justice in Holland, where he served until 1985. Khani became an international judge and a member of the constitutional court created in Sarajevo in 1994. In 1996, he became an honorary member of the judiciary committee at the Olympics Games in Atlanta.

During a long career as a diplomat, civil servant, and government minister, Abdullah al-Khani wrote numerous legal and political works. Among his pub-lished books are *Qisat Nazi' al-Silah* (*The Story of Disarmament*), published in 1944, *Al-Nizam al-Dusturi wa al-Idari fi Baritaniyya* (*The Constitutional and Administrative System in Britain*), published in 1953, and *Huquq al-Insan fi al-Aradi al-Muhtalla (Human Rights in the Occupied Territories)*, published in 1980. He wrote a memoir that shed light on his relationship with Shukri al-Quwatli, and in 2003 he wrote a book dedicated to Quwatli called *Jihad Shukri al-Quwatli* that recounted Quwatli's achievement in creating the first and only Arab union in 1958.

Abdullah al-Khani received the Syrian Medal of Honor, Excellence Class, in 1955 and the Egyptian Medal of Honor, Excellence Class, in 1956.

Sources:
Interview with Abdullah al-Khani (May 17, 2002).

al-Khury, Fayez
(1893-1959)

Alternate spellings: Fayiz al-Khury, Fayez al-Khoury, Fayez al-Khuri

Fayez al-Khury studied law briefly at the American University of Beirut (AUB), then completed his degree at the Ottoman Law Academy in Istanbul. While still a student, he was conscripted into the Ottoman Army at the outbreak of World War I in August 1914.

Khury fought with the Ottoman Turks, but joined the Arab underground in Syria. The underground was dedicated to toppling the Ottoman Empire, and Khury was arrested for his views on January 10, 1916, by Jamal Pasha, the military governor of Syria. Khury was deported to the remote town of Aley on Mount Lebanon. But Khury's his brother Faris, a prominent attorney and deputy in the Ottoman Parliament, secured his release from Talaat Pasha, the Ottoman minister of interior.

When World War I ended in 1918, Khury completed his studies and worked as an attorney and an instructor at the Arab Academy of Law in Damascus. He played no role in the early resistance to the French Mandate imposed on Syria in July 1920. In 1927, however, he joined the National Bloc, a leading political movement co-founded by his brother Faris to end the mandate through diplomatic means rather than armed resistance. In 1928, the Khury brothers held office on the Constitutional Assembly that drafted the first republican constitution for Syria. Fayez al-Khury ran for parliament on a Bloc ticket in 1932 and 1936, winning both rounds with a majority vote.

In 1932, Khury suspended his parliamentary activity to protest the French refusal to ratify the Constitution of 1928 due to the "anti-French" nature of its 115 clauses. He returned to parliament, however, under the request of Bloc President Hashim al-Atasi. In 1936, Khury orchestrated a sixty-day strike with the Bloc leaders to protest France's refusal to address the issue of Syrian independence. The mandate authority dismissed him from his teaching post at Damascus University and arrested him on the charge of encouraging civil unrest.

In November 1936, following the strike, the National Bloc was voted into office and Khury's brother Faris became speaker of parliament. Fayez al-Khury became minister of foreign affairs and finance in the cabinet of Prime Minister Lutfi al-Haffar, holding office from February to April 1939. In May 1939, Khury returned to his teaching career and in 1940 became dean of the Faculty of Law at Damascus University.

In September 1941, the French war leader General Charles de Gaulle appointed Taj al-Din al-Hasani, a pro-French statesman, as president of the republic. The Bloc leadership mobilized in opposition to Hasani's regime, refusing to recognize a president appointed by the French and not elected by the people. To appease the Bloc, Hasani appointed Fayez al-Khury minister of foreign affairs in the cabinet of Prime Minister Hasan al-Hakim. Khury held office in the Hakim cabinet from September 1941 to April 1942. When Shukri al-Quwatli, a leader of the National Bloc, became president in August 1943, he appointed Khury ambassador to the USSR. From 1943 to 1946, Khury promoted Syria's cause in the Kremlin and lobbied with Joseph Stalin to support the requests of Damascus, including admittance to the UN, evacuation of French troops, and termination of the French Mandate.

In 1947, one year after independence, President Quwatli appointed Khury ambassador to the United States, a post he held until 1952. He also became a member of Syria's delegation to the UN, chaired by his brother Faris. The Khury brothers remained in the United States during a critical stage of Arab-American relations. They held office in Washington and New York during the Arab-Israeli War of 1948 and tried in vain to elicit support from the international community for maintaining Palestine as an independent Arab state. In 1952, Fayez al-Khury resigned from the Ministry of Foreign Affairs and joined the World Bank in Washington, DC. In September 1956, Quwatli was reelected president and invited Khury back to Syria, subsequently appointing him ambassador to Great Britain.

Fayez al-Khury resigned from political activity when Syria and Egypt merged to form the United Arab Republic (UAR) in February 1958. He died in Damascus on June 27, 1959.

Sources:
Babil, Nasuh. *Sahafa wa Siyassa fi Souriyya* (1987).
Khoury, Philip. *Syria and the French Mandate* (1987).
Khury, Colette. *Awrak Faris al-Khury,* Vol I (1987).

al-Moualim, Walid
(1941-)

Walid al-Moualim studied economics at Cairo University and graduated in 1965. He returned to Syria, became a member of the ruling Baath Party, and joined the Ministry of Foreign Affairs. In 1966, he became attaché to the Syrian Embassy in Morocco and in 1967 attaché to Saudi Arabia.

In 1968, Moualim became third secretary to the Syrian Embassy in Spain. In 1971, he became bureau chief to Foreign Minister Abd al-Halim Khaddam, who appointed him chargé d'affaires to Great Britain. In 1975, President Hafez al-Asad appointed Moualim ambassador to Romania, and in 1981 Moualim returned to Syria and became director of archives at the Ministry of Foreign Affairs. In June 1990, Walid al-Moualim served as Syria's ambassador to the United States. His tenure in Washington was filled with tumultuous events and upheaval.

In August 1990, less than one month after Moualim assumed office as ambassador to the United States, Iraq invaded Kuwait and the US began searching for regional allies to assist in Operation Desert Storm, the campaign to liberate Kuwait. Moualim served as Syria's link to President George Bush Sr and conveyed Syria's desire to take part in Desert Storm.

In October 1991, Moualim rose to prominence once again when he represented Syria at the Madrid Peace Conference, the first time since 1949 that Syria had agreed to attend round table talks with Israel based on the "land for peace" formula. In 1995, President Hafez al-Asad delegated Moualim to attend the Syrian-Israeli peace talks at the White House, conducted by Ambassador Mowaffak al-Allaf. Israeli Prime Minister Yitzhak Rabin conveyed, via Allaf and Moualim, Israel's willingness to relinquish the Golan Heights in exchange for normalization of relations with Damascus. But Israeli religious fundamentalists killed Rabin in November 1996, before a final settlement had been reached with Syria. In 1999, Moualim joined Foreign Minister Farouk al-Shara in his Washington talks with Israeli Prime Minister Ehud Barak, also based on the "land-for-peace" formula, and which also ended in failure.

In 2000, Moualim returned to Damascus and became director of the Ministry of Foreign Affairs. In 2002, President Bashar al-Asad sent Moualim to Washington to meet with American politicians and bridge the gap between Syria and the United States vis-à-vis peace in the Middle East. Along with other diplomats, Moualim tried to explain Syria's policies toward the Palestinian resistance, claiming that it was a legitimate response to occupation, similar to the Free French Movement against the Nazis in World War II. The resistance was by no means "terrorism," as George W. Bush had called it.

In 2004, Moualim became deputy foreign minister to Farouk al-Shara. When Syria renewed the mandate of President Emile Lahhoud in 2004, anti-Syrian sentiment soared in Lebanon. Supported by France and the USA, the UN passed resolution 1559, calling on Syria to end its military presence in Lebanon and stop intervening in Lebanese affairs. Asad appointed Moualim as his special envoy to Lebanon, to mediate between Syria and the Lebanese opposition. Moualim conducted several meetings in Beirut with ex-President Amin Gemayel and Syria's former ally Walid Jumblatt. The mission was disrupted when on February 14, 2005, Lebanon's ex-Prime Minister Rafic al-Harriri was assassinated in Beirut, sparking off more anti-Syrian demonstrations that led to Syria's complete withdrawal from Lebanon, which it had entered in 1976. The Syrian Army left Lebanon on April 26, 2005.

During his career, Walid al-Moualim published two books on modern affairs, *Souriyya 1918-1958: al-Tahaddi wa al-Muwajaha (Syria 1918-1958: Challenges and Confrontation)*, and *Souriyya 1916-1945 (Syria 1916-1945)*.

Sources:
"Profile of Walid al-Moualim," courtesy of the Syrian Ministry of Foreign Affairs (2004).

Nehlawi, Fayez
(1919-)

Fayez al-Nehlawi was born in Damascus and studied law at Damascus University, graduating in 1944. He joined the Ministry of Foreign Affairs and in 1946 was appointed attaché to the Syrian Embassy in Paris.

While in France, Nehlawi studied at the Sorbonne in Paris and obtained his doctoral degree in international law, graduating in 1949. In 1951, Nehlawi became consul to the Syrian mission in Milan, Italy. In 1955, he became secretary to the Syrian Embassy in France. In 1958, Syria and Egypt merged to form the United Arab Republic (UAR) and Nehlawi became consultant and first secretary at the UAR Embassy in Vienna. In 1961, shortly before the UAR was dissolved, he became consultant to the UAR Embassy in Copenhagen.

In March 1963, the Baath Party came to power in Syria and Fayez al-Nehlawi became director of administrative affairs at the Ministry of Foreign Affairs. He was among those who were not retired from office during the Baathist regime because Syria's new leaders knew that they needed capable diplomats to maintain Syria's standing in the international community. In 1965, Nehlawi became director of asian affairs, and in 1966 President Nur al-Din al-Atasi appointed him consul to the Syrian mission in New York. In July 1967, Atasi made Nehlawi minister in Pakistan.

In September 1970, Nehlawi returned to Syria and became director of protocol at the Ministry of Foreign Affairs. He kept this post when Abd al-Halim Khaddam became minister of foreign affairs in November 1970 and worked with Khaddam until President Hafez al-Asad appointed Nehlawi ambassador to Senegal in June 1977. After the Arab-Israeli War of October 1973, Nehlawi worked with Khaddam in the Syrian talks with Henry Kissinger. The US secretary of state came to Syria in January 1974 to lobby for disengagement between the Syrian and Israeli troops in the Golan Heights.

In 1982, Fayez al-Nehlawi received the Medal of Honor and Loyalty of the Syrian Republic. Then he retired from diplomatic service and took up residence in France where (as of this writing) he lives today.

Sources:
Interview with Dr Fayez al-Nehlawi (April 2, 2002).

Qabbani, Nizar (1923-1998) see "Arts & Letters"

Qabbani, Sabah
(1928-)

Born and raised in Damascus, Sabah Qabbani grew up in an atmosphere boiling with anti-colonial activity. His father, Tawfiq Qabbani, was a prominent merchant and member of the National Bloc, a nationalist movement created by Syrian notables in 1928 to end the French Mandate in the Middle East (established in 1920).

Because of his political views, Qabbani's father was frequently arrested by the French and deported to Palmyra prison in the Syrian desert and to another prison in Lebanon, where he developed tuberculosis from his harsh prison conditions. At one point, Tawfiq Qabbani's factory in Damascus was set ablaze by the mandate authority to force him to abandon his anti-French activity, but to no avail. Despite harassment and vandalism, the Qabbani residence in Damascus remained a daily gathering place for the National Bloc during the mandate years (1920-1946). Thus, Sabah Qabbani was raised in a nationalistic and defiant atmosphere, under the towering influence of his father and friends, primary among them being Shukri al-Quwatli, the leader of Damascus who became president of Syria in 1943. Qabbani studied law at Damascus University, and in 1952 obtained a PhD in international law from the Sorbonne in Paris. He returned to Syria and joined the Ministry of Culture, becoming director of Syrian Radio programs in 1953. In 1956, he married the niece of Prime Minister Sa'id al-Ghazzi, a nationalist like his father who had taken part in the anti-colonial movement under the mandate.

Qabbani became famous for spotting artistic talent. He discovered and promoted Abd al-Halim Hafez, the Arab giant of romantic music, realizing Hafez's talent early on and broadcasting his tunes on Syrian Radio. Qabbani also helped promote other stars in Arabic music, like the Lebanese diva Fayruz and the Syrian singers Fayza Ahmad and Najat al-Saghira. Qabbani's love for music and art was influenced by Abu Khalil al-Qabbani, a composer and dramatist and ancestor of Sabah Qabbani, who had created Arabic theater from scratch in the nineteenth century, just like Sabah Qabbani was to create Syrian TV from scratch in the twentieth century.

On July 23, 1960, Qabbani became the first director of newly formed Syrian Television during the Syrian-Egyptian union. He laid the foundations of modern Syrian TV and was responsible for selecting potential talent and hiring young amateurs to put on comedies and dramas. Qabbani hired Doreid Lahham, a university teacher and amateur actor, to perform with the already established star Nihad Quali. Together, the two men became the most popular comedy duo in the Arab world during the second half of the twentieth century, often acknowledging their success to Dr Qabbani.

In 1962, Sabah Qabbani returned to the Ministry of Foreign Affairs and became Syria's consul to New York. On March 8, 1963, he was greatly disillusioned when the Military Committee of the Baath Party came to power in Syria. Qabbani despised the militarization of politics, but stayed at his post in the Ministry of Foreign Affairs, believing that as a career diplomat he was serving in the best interests of Syria, and not the Baathist regime. The new leaders of Syria wanted to fire him, however, along with all other officials of the pre-Baath era, but they needed him in the Foreign Ministry for his diplomatic skills and linguistic abilities.

In 1966, Qabbani became director of press and media at the Ministry of Foreign Affairs. He remained at his post until becoming minister to Indonesia in 1968. He assumed this office under the second Baathist regime of Salah Jadid and Jadid's civilian president, Nur al-Din al-Atasi. Qabbani did not get along with either man, but remained at his post in Indonesia due to his belief that much work was needed to end Syria's political isolation from the rest of the world, especially after the Arab-Israeli War of 1967.

Qabbani then returned to Syria and became director of the European and US desks at the Ministry of Foreign Affairs. He accompanied Foreign Minister Abd al-Halim Khaddam to his talks with Henry Kissinger after the Arab-Israeli War of 1973. Kissinger conducted shuttle diplomacy and visited Syria in January 1974 to secure a disengagement agreement between the Syrian and Israeli armies in the Golan Heights. Qabbani came to the conclusion that Kissinger had Israeli interests at heart when negotiating with Arab parties, merely wishing to divide and weaken them. In reality, Qabbani believed, Kissinger was not interested in peace in the Middle East at all. After the talks, President Hafez al-Asad appointed Qabbani as Syria's ambassador to the United States.

Qabbani was the first Syrian to hold office in Washington since the Arab-Israeli War of 1967. He served as Asad's link to President Jimmy Carter, who conveyed via Qabbani the American desire that Syria follow the peace initiative of Egyptian President Anwar al-Sadat. Syria curtly refused, believing that Damascus was still speaking on the behalf of the Palestinians and could not betray them with a separate peace with Israel. The proposal was flatly turned down by Hafez al-Asad.

Sabah Qabbani retired from diplomatic activity in the early 1980s and devoted his retirement to photography.

Sources:
Itri, Abd al-Ghani. *Alam wa Mubdioun* (1999).

al-Tarazi, Salah al-Din
(1918-1980)

Salah al-Din al-Tarazi studied law at a French academy in Beirut and began his career as an attorney in Damascus. In 1944, Foreign Minister Jamil Mardam Bey appointed him secretary of the Syrian Embassy in Paris.

After two years, Tarazi returned to Syria to teach law at Damascus University. In 1948, he became legal advisor to the Syrian delegation at the United Nations, headed by Prime Minister Faris al-Khury. In 1948, Mardam Bey summoned Tarazi back to Syria and appointed him advisor to the Ministry of Foreign Affairs. In 1949, he became director of administrative and legal affairs at the Ministry of Foreign Affairs. General Husni al-Za'im, who rose to power in March 1949, appointed Tarazi to the Syrian delegation to the UN-sponsored cease-fire talks with Israel. Tarazi was able to negotiate a cease-fire with Israel and reluctantly co-signed an agreement with his Israeli counterparts in July 1949. Before accepting his duties to negotiate an armistice, Tarazi, an Arab nationalist, reportedly wept before his colleagues.

In 1951, President Adib al-Shishakli appointed Salah al-Din al-Tarazi ambassador to the UN, and in 1954 he became consul to Brussels. In 1956, Tarazi became secretary-general of the Foreign Ministry, a position he retained until Syria and Egypt merged to form the United Arab Republic (UAR) in 1958. During the union years with Egypt (1958-1961), Tarazi served as UAR ambassador to Brazil. When the UAR was dissolved in 1961, he resumed his job at the UN, becoming ambassador to the USSR in the 1960s. He then joined the International Court of Justice, serving as a judge until his death in a car accident in 1980.

Sources:
Interview with Dr Rafic Jouejati (March 23, 2003).
Ismail, Thuraya. *Myths and Realities* (2002).

Zayn al-Din, Farid
(1907-?)

Farid Zayn al-Din was born into a Druze family in Mount Lebanon. He studied law at the American University of Beirut (AUB) and obtained a PhD in international law from the Sorbonne in Paris. He also obtained a minor in political science from the University of Berlin.

Zayn al-Din began his career by teaching economics at AUB. In 1929, he met a Palestinian schoolteacher and fellow AUB alumnus, Darwish Miqdadi, and they decided to unite their efforts to form a modern political party that would work against European exploitation of the Arab East. Zayn al-Din and Miqdadi teamed up with Shukri al-Quwatli, another exiled nationalist, and founded the Arab Liberation Society. But it was an amateurish organization that achieved limited success in the Middle East.

In August 1933, along with a group of fifty radical Arab nationalists, Zayn al-Din and Miqdadi founded the League of National Action in the Lebanese Mountain town of Quarna'il. The league was a pioneering organization established by a second generation of Arab politicians whose ages ranged between twenty-five and thirty and whose aim was to rid the Middle East from foreign influence. Unlike other political establishments dominated by landowners and Ottoman-trained politicians, the League of National Action was created by professors, lawyers, and civil servants who were not living off their family estates, but rather leading career-focused lives. All the league members had studied in Europe, the United States, or at American universities in the Middle East. Zayn al-Din administered the league's political affairs and was among its most promising young leaders. Other prominent members of the league included Sabri al-Asali, Zaki al-Arsuzi, Munir al-Ajlani, and Constantine Zurayk. The league achieved high acclaim in 1933, but fizzled with the early death of its charismatic founder and leader Abd al-Razzaq al-Dandashi in 1935. In 1937, Zayn al-Din joined the Ministry of Foreign Affairs, becoming director of its political affairs until 1939. He resigned when Syria was unable to prevent the annexation of the Sanjak of Alexanderetta in 1939, accusing Prime Minister Jamil Mardam Bey of poor leadership. Zayn al-Din allied himself with Shukri al-Quwatli when the latter became president of Syria in 1943. In April 1945, Zayn al-Din became a member of the Syrian delegation to the UN founding conference in the United States.

When Syrian independence was achieved in April 1946, Zayn al-Din became secretary-general of the Ministry of Foreign Affairs. In 1947, Quwatli appointed him ambassador to the USSR, a position he held until 1951. In 1949, Zayn al-Din briefly served as an envoy for President Hashim al-Atasi in union talks between Syria and Iraq. He went to Iraq to negotiate a union arrangement with Crown Prince Abd al-Illah, but the plan never got off the drawing board. He then became Syria's permanent ambassador at the United Nations.

In December 1952, Adib al-Shishakli made Zayn al-Din ambassador to the United States and non-resident ambassador to Mexico. In August 1957, a diplomatic crisis developed between Damascus and Washington over a failed coup planned by the Central Intelligence Agency (CIA). The CIA tried and failed to stage a coup against Shukri al-Quwatli for his alliance with the USSR. As a result, Syria asked US Ambassador James S. Moose to leave Damascus along with architects of the failed coup, Howard Stone, the US military attaché in Syria, Robert Malloy, the second secretary of political affairs, and Francis Jetton, the vice-consul in Damascus. Consequently, Farid Zayn al-Din was recalled back to Syria.

In the second half of the 1950s, Zayn al-Din joined the movement of Arab nationalism headed by President Gamal Abd al-Nasser of Egypt. He lobbied in favor of Syria's union with Egypt, and when the United Arab Republic (UAR) was created in 1958, he became deputy to Foreign Minister Mahmud Fawzi. He resigned from office, however, when the UAR was dissolved in 1961.

From 1961 to 1963, Zayn al-Din worked undercover with a group of politicians to restore the UAR. He traveled to Cairo for secret talks with Nasser, and allied himself with disgruntled officers in the Syrian Army. In March 1962, he worked as a political mastermind behind a coup that toppled President Nazim al-Qudsi, Speaker of Parliament Ma'mun al-Kuzbari, and Prime Minister Ma'ruf al-Dawalibi. The coup was launched by Colonel Abd al-Karim al-Nehlawi who wanted to seize power for himself. But a few days later, a counter-coup led by Chief of Staff Abd al-Karim Zahr al-Din and a group of officers who wanted to preserve the post-union order, ousted Nehlawi and restored the elected leaders to power.

Farid Zayn al-Din quickly reneged on his loyalty to Nehlawi and shifted his allegiance to General Zahr al-Din, a Druze like himself. The two men began plotting for their own coup, scheduled for the first week of March 1963. Zahr al-Din commanded loyalty among Druze officers in the Syrian Army, while Zayn al-Din served as architect of the new coup, laying out its method, objective, and program. Coinciding with Zahr al-Din and Zayn al-Din's ambitions was another coup planned and launched by the Military Committee of the Baath Party. On March 8, 1963, the Baath Party came to power in Syria and dismissed both men from office.

Sources:
Faris, George. *Man Hum fi al-Alam al-Arabi?* (1957).
Khoury, Philip. *Syria and the French Mandate* (1987).
Rathmell, Andrew. *Secret War in the Middle East* (1995).
Samman, Mutih. *Watan wa Askar* (1995).

Zurayk, Constantine (1909-2000) see "Educators"

Women students in the 1940s.

Exam room at the University of Damascus in the 1930s.

EDUCATORS

The educators listed in this chapter helped to create Damascus University or played an instrumental role in establishing Syrian high schools. This chapter also includes individuals who were of paramount influence on their students or who left a mark on the education system and curriculum of other Arab countries.

Damascus University 1925.

During Ottoman times (until 1918), Syrian education consisted of primary and secondary schools reserved primarily for the urban elite. Advanced education in Syria was found in Beirut at the American University of Beirut (AUB) and other institutions with Protestant missionary roots. During the French Mandate (1920-1946), primary and secondary schooling became more widespread in smaller towns and many rural villages. Syrians continued to access higher education in Beirut and also by traveling to the Sorbonne in Paris and other European universities.

Syrian students at Maktab Anbar in 1904. Anbar was the first school to offer a certified baccalaureate (high school) diploma in Syria.

Under the French, education for women became common. University education had begun under the Ottomans and became formalized as the Syrian University under the French in 1923. After the Baath Party came to power (1963 to the present), roads, electricity, and schools became nearly universal in rural areas. The Baath encouraged children of rural families to seek higher education and sponsored the most precocious among them in seeking advanced studies in France. Since World War II, the children of Syria's urban notables have been active in seeking higher education in Beirut, Europe, and the United States. In 2001, for the first time in Syrian history, private universities were authorized by President Bashar al-Asad as part of the the reforms that composed the Damascus Spring.

Note: The Arab Language Assemblage is the highest international scientific authority in the field of Arabic language and literature and was the most prestigious foundation for Arab men of letters in the twentieth century.

Abd al-Daim, Abdullah
(1924-)

Abdullah Abd al-Daim was born in Aleppo and studied philosophy at the University of King Fou'ad I in Cairo, graduating in 1946. He later obtained a PhD in education from the Sorbonne in Paris in 1956.

Abd al-Daim returned to Syria and became a school instructor, first in Homs and then in Damascus. In 1941, while Abd al-Daim was still a student, the views of Arab nationalism espoused by his history teacher at school, Michel Aflaq, profoundly influenced him. He became a member in Aflaq's Baath Party in 1947. In 1948, Abd al-Daim began teaching at Damascus University, and in 1957 became director of education (the equivalent of a modern minister) in Qatar.

When Syria and Egypt merged to form the United Arab Republic (UAR) in 1958, Abd al-Daim returned to Syria and became director of cultural affairs at the Ministry of Culture and National Guidance. He was an ally of the union government created by the Baath Party and by Egyptian President Gamal Abd al-Nasser. In December 1960, Abd al-Daim became chairman of the Education Department at Damascus University. In September 1961, however, a military coup d'etat ousted the union, and the civilian leader Dr Nazim al-Qudsi replaced Nasser as President of the Syrian Republic.

Abd al-Daim voiced his opposition to the Qudsi government. Regardless, he was appointed minister of information in the cabinet of Prime Minister Bashir al-Azma. Abd al-Daim worked as a member of the opposition in government, and he came to believe (with the encouragement of Azma and Qudsi) that the new government would work for the restoration of a "reformed" union between Syria and Egypt.

In government, Abd al-Daim worked relentlessly to promote union propaganda. At a time when television in Syria was just becoming popular, he gave a weekly televised speech calling on Syrians to remain committed to Arab nationalism. Abd al-Daim often said, "In [the] union there were some mistakes, but the secession is an entire mistake." He permitted outlawed Egyptian newspapers, which were pro-union, to sell on Syrian newsstands, including the pro-Gamal Abd al-Nasser daily *al-Ahram*. When an officer in the security bureau banned some of the newspapers he had authorized, Abd al-Daim resigned from office in September 1962.

Then, in March 1963, the Baath Party came to power in Syria, and Abd al-Daim became minister of information in the cabinet of the party co-founder, Salah al-Bitar. Abd al-Daim resigned, however, in protest over the influence and brutality of Saleem Hatum, a senior party officer who directed the broadcasting station in the early years of the Baathist era. Abd al-Daim then became minister of education in January 1966, but served for only one month.

In February 1966, a military coup overthrew the Baath Party government of Michel Aflaq and Salah al-Bitar. The two men were exiled by Syria's military strongman Salah Jadid, and Abd al-Daim chose self-imposed exile in Lebanon, where he taught at the Lebanese University while working with the UNESCO office in Beirut.

In 1975, Abd al-Daim went to the Omani capital of Muscat as part of a joint education project conducted by the World Bank and Oman. In 1976, the UNESCO appointed Abd al-Daim as head of its mission to Nigeria, Togo, and Ghana, three positions he held until 1978. Abd al-Daim then became director of operational projects in the Arab sates and Europe at the UNESCO office in Paris, a post he held until 1985.

Since 1985, Abd al-Daim has devoted his life to research. He has published many books with the Center for Arab Unity Studies in Beirut, where he became a founding member in 1974. Among his published political works are *al-Ishtirakiyya wa al-Dimocratiyya* (*Socialism and Democracy*), published in 1961; *al-Watan al-Arabi wa al-Thawra* (*The Arab World and Revolution*), published after the Baath Party revolt of 1963; and *al-Takhteet al-Ishtiraki* (*Socialist Planning*), published in 1965. Abd al-Daim also co-wrote two high school textbooks in Syria in 1950—one on philosophy, the other on sociology—with the Baath Party intellectuals Sami Droubi and Hafez al-Jamali.

In 2002, Abdullah Abd al-Daim became a founding member of the Center for the Dialogue of Civilizations, an academic foundation that specializes in conducting research, holding debates, and publishing articles on the post-9/11 world after the September 11, 2001, terrorist attacks on Washington, DC, and New York City.

Sources:
Interview with Dr Abdullah Abd al-Daim (February 6, 2003).
Itri, Abd al-Ghani. *Hadeeth al-Abqariyyat* (2000).

al-Aidi, Munif
(1886-1962)

Munif al-Aidi studied at the Ottoman Medical Academy in Istanbul and graduated in 1906. He allied himself with the Arab nationalist movement that emerged in 1913 and signed a famed declaration that demanded emancipation from the Ottoman Empire. The declaration was authored by leading Arab nationalists and presented to the first Arab Congress in Paris.

During World War I (1914-1918), Aidi taught at the Ottoman Academy in Istanbul, but resigned from his teaching post when the Ottoman Empire was defeated in 1918. During the war years, his brother Shawkat al-Aidi, an officer in the Ottoman Army, deserted to join the Arab underground in Mecca, an

Munif al-Aidi.

action that led Ottoman authorities to persecute the Aidi family and banish them to a remote district in the empire.

The Aidi brothers returned to Damascus when the Ottoman Empire was defeated in 1918, with Munif becoming a doctor and Shawkat an officer in the newly created Arab Army. Along with other Ottoman-trained doctors, Munif al-Aidi co-founded the Arab Academy of Medicine in 1919. King Faysal, the new ruler of Syria, promoted the academy as the first independent Arab academic institution in the Middle East. Aidi and other academics translated material from Ottoman Turkish into Arabic and encouraged Syrians to continue their education at home instead of in Cairo, Beirut, or Europe.

The Arab Academy of Medicine eventually expanded to include other departments, including an academy of law and an academy of literature, and was renamed Damascus University in 1923. A team of educators, including Dr Munif al-Aidi, Dr Abd al-Rahman Shahbandar, and Dr Rida al-Sa'id, hired the faculty and staff, translated all works from Ottoman Turkish into Arabic, served on the university's board of directors, and taught at its Faculty of Medicine. Aidi was an instructor of physiology and pediatrics.

In 1928, Munif al-Aidi nominated himself to serve on the Constitutional Assembly, a legal body charged with drafting Syria's first republican constitution. He dropped out of the election, however, and instead supported the candidates of the National Bloc, the leading anti-French movement in Syria, who had been his friends and allies since the early 1920s. In 1935, Aidi called for and chaired the first pan-Arab Medical Conference in Damascus designed to promote the interaction and exchange of medical knowledge throughout the Arab world. The conference was the first of its kind in Syria and drew doctors from all over the Middle East and North Africa.

Aidi's most lasting contribution is the Scientific National Academy, an elite school that he founded in 1907. He served as director of the academy while keeping his post as a professor at Damascus University. His son Adnan pursued a career in academia and also became director of the Scientific National Academy.

Munif al-Aidi wrote many medical books, including *Ilm al-Ghariza al-Physiologia* (*Science of the Physiological Instinct*), published in 1923; *Al-Mujaz fi Amrad al-Atfal* (*Concise in Pediatrics*), published in 1941; and a six-volume work on physiology that was published from 1923 to 1952.

Sources:
Murayden, Izzat. *Dr Ahmad Munif al-Aidi* (1996).

al-Ajlani, Munir (1904-): see "Politicians"

al-Arsuzi, Zaki (1908-1968): see "Politicians"

al-Azm, Abd al-Qadir
(1881-1952)

Abd al-Qadir al-Azm was born and bred in Damascus to one of the most prominent political families in Ottoman Syria. His ancestors had been the eighteenth-century governors of Damascus and were renowned for their wealth and influence in the empire.

In 1914, the young Azm began his career as an official in the civil service, becoming an advisor to Jamal Pasha, the Ottoman governor of Syria. But Azm distanced himself from the Ottoman Turks after they executed leading Arab nationalists in May 1916 and fired many senior members of the Arab community from office, questioning their loyalty to the empire. The Arab officials were replaced by Ottoman Turks—in what became known as "Turkification." In this way many members of the Azm family lost their jobs in the Ottoman government.

In 1916, Azm became a member in the Arab underground movement of Sharif Husayn, the Prince of Mecca. Azm channeled secret information from Jamal Pasha's office to the Arab command in Mecca and reported on the activities of Jamal Pasha to the Arab command. Jamal Pasha became suspicious of Azm's activities and placed him under 24-hour surveillance. When authorities discovered Azm's connection to the rebels, they arrested him and brought him before court on the charge of high treason. Azm was released before standing trial, however, following the Ottoman defeat in World War I in October 1918.

Azm allied himself to King Faysal I, the new ruler of Syria, and became director of political publications at the Royal Palace from 1918 to 1920. During the Faysal interlude, Azm co-founded the Istiqlal Party with a group of young Arab nationalists which included the journalist Sa'id Haydar, the Palestinian statesman Izzat Darwaza, the Lebanese writer As'ad Daghir, and the Syrian notable Shukri al-Quwatli. The Istiqlal Party called for Arab unity and independence and was popular in Palestine, Syria, Lebanon, and Iraq. It was the first modern party in post-Ottoman Syria and was created from the leftovers of pre-war societies such as al-Ahd and al-Fatat. In its two years of active operation (1918-1920), the Istiqlal Party was funded and supported by King Faysal. In 1920, the French Mandate began in Syria and Azm abandoned his allegiance to Faysal, who was toppled by the French Army and exiled to Europe.

In 1921, Azm became chairman of the Academy of Law in Syria which, in 1923, was merged with other departments and renamed Damascus University. From 1923 to 1925, Azm served on the university's board of directors. In 1926,

Azm became minister of finance in the cabinet of Prime Minister Ahmad Nami. Azm resigned from office one year later, however, to protest the arrest of three ministers allied to the nationalist movement fighting against the French. In 1930, Azm became an instructor of finance at Damascus University. Then, in 1936, members of the National Bloc (at that time the leading political movement in Syria) came to power.

Syria's new president, Hashim al-Atasi, appointed Azm president of Damascus University. He held office until 1941 when he allied himself with President Taj al-Din al-Hasani and became president of the Bureau of Consultation. He kept this post during the regime of President Shukri al-Quwatli (1943-1949) and in 1949, three years after Syrian independence was achieved from the French, Syria's new president, Husni al-Za'im, forced Azm to retire from office. He was retired partly because of old age, but mainly because Za'im wanted to rid himself of all officials connected to the deposed leader, Shukri al-Quwatli.

During his career, Abd al-Qadir al-Azm wrote a four-volume work entitled *Ilm al-Iqtisad* (*The Science of Economics*), published over a ten-year span, from 1931 to 1941.

Sources:
Bawab, Sulayman. *Mawsuat Alam Souriyya fi al-Qarn al-Ishreen,* Vol III (1999).
Faris, George. *Man Hum fi al-Watan al-Arabi?* (1957).
Musslih, Mohammad. "The Rise of Local Nationalism" in *The Origins of Arab Nationalism* (1991).

al-Azm, Sadeq
(1934-)

Sadeq al-Azm studied philosophy at the American University in Beirut (AUB) and obtained his MA and PhD in modern European philosophy from Yale University. In 1961, he taught philosophy at Yale and one year later became an instructor at Hunter College in New York.

From 1962 to 1963, Azm taught at Damascus University and then moved to AUB where he taught philosophy until 1968. In 1965, in addition to his job at AUB, Azm taught at the Beirut College for Women (BCW). From 1968 to 1969, Sadeq al-Azm served as assistant professor of philosophy at the University of Jordan. From 1969 to 1976, he became editor of the *Arab Studies Review* and a senior researcher at the Palestine Research Center in Beirut.

While teaching at AUB, Azm's published views raised much controversy that many public and religious establishments considered blasphemous, and he was dismissed from his post in the summer of 1968. For several days thereafter, AUB students went on strike in protest of Azm's firing, including students from the

Medical School, a very rare occurrence in university history.

At the end of 1969, Azm published a collection of essays under the title, *Naqd al-Fikr al-Dini* (*Critique of Religious Thought*), which quickly turned into one of the biggest literary scandals in Arab history. Al-Azm was arrested by the Lebanese authorities for ten days. Then he was tried along with the book's publisher, Bashir al-Daaouk, before the Lebanese court specializing in "printed matter" cases. After a prolonged and sensational trial, the case was dismissed. Before Azm's arrest, Interior Minister Kamal Jumblatt, a philosopher in his own right, invited Azm to his office, debated the work, and promised to be on the side of free expression in Lebanon.

In 1977, Azm returned to Syria and taught at Damascus University until his retirement in 1999. He taught at Princeton University as a visiting professor from 1988 to 1990 and 1991-1992. He was a fellow at the Wissenschaftskollege in Berlin, 1990-1991, and at the Woodrow Wilson International Center for Scholars in Washington, DC, 1992-1993. In 1995, Azm delivered the Karl Jaspers memorial lectures at the University of Oldenburg in Germany. He served as visiting professor at Humbolt University in Berlin in the summer of 1997 and at Hamburg University during the spring semester of 1998. In the summer of 2001, he was resident scholar at the Center for Interdisciplinary Research, Tohoku University, Japan. In 2004, he accepted the position of visiting professor at Antwerp University, Belgium.

He was awarded the Dr Leopold Luckas Prize for 2004 by Tübingen University in Germany and shared the Erasmus Prize (Holland) for 2004 with the Moroccan author and activist Fatima Mernissi and the Iranian philosopher Abdul Karim Soroush.

During his forty-year career in academia, Azm emphasized the history of Western philosophy and wrote extensively on contemporary Arab society, culture, and thought. His most renowned and controversial work, in addition to *Critique of Religious Thought*, is *Salman Rushdie and the Truth of Literature*, published in 1992. It defends the Indian-born author of *The Satanic Verses*, a novel that the Islamic government of Iran considered blasphemous. The mullahs of Tehran had banned Rushdie's book and called for his death, while Azm stood up in his defense, claiming that the work of Rushdi, a secularized Muslim like himself, was a legitimate expression of independent views.

Azm's other classical works include *Self-Criticism After the Defeat* (1968), *Of Love and Arabic Courtly Love* (1968), *Zionism and the Class Struggle* (1975), *Orientalism and Orientalism in Reverse* (1981), and *Beyond the Tabooing Mentality: Reading the Satanic Verses* (1997). Also *The Origins of Kant's Arguments in the Antinomies* (Oxford 1972), *Studies in Modern Western Philosophy* (1979), *Materialism and History: A Defense* (1990), and *Islamic Fundamentalism Reconsidered* (1997).

Sadeq al-Azm established himself forcefully in the Arab world as a thinker not afraid of expressing courageous views that aim at advancing human progress. It is these views, according to Azm, that need to be debated, tried in the court of history using the judgment of the human mind, then either established or discarded.

Although most of Azm's books are banned in the Arab world (except Lebanon), they have all been reprinted in many editions.

Sources:
Information provided by Dr Sadeq al-Azm (November 1, 2001).

Bayhum, Adila
(1900-1975)

Adila Bayhum was born into a prominent family in Beirut. She studied with local tutors and began her career by writing for several Beirut-based Arabic newspapers. She wrote in the popular daily *Fata al-Arabi* (*The Male Arab Youth*) under the pen name al-Fatat al-Arabiyya (The Female Arab Youth).

The nationalist leader Abd al-Ghani al-Arissi, who was martyred by the Ottoman Turks in 1916 and immortalized in Syria thereafter, ran *Fata al-Arabi*. Bayhum criticized the Ottoman Empire and its involvement in World War I. She called attention to the devastating effects of the war through the presentation of shocking statistics. For example, Bayhum documented the astonishing decrease in Beirut's population, from 180,000 in 1914 to 75,000 in 1916. She also publicized the fact that, during the same period, 240,000 soldiers in the Ottoman Army had died of disease, while 250,000 were missing, and a minimum of 325,000 had been killed in combat.

In 1916, the Ottoman Military Governor Jamal Pasha invited a delegation of Arab women to meet him in Damascus and express their grievances. Bayhum demanded the establishment of social security institutions to care for the wounded and the relatives of those who had died or been disabled in the war. Jamal Pasha responded positively to their initiative and established an orphanage in Beirut for Muslim children. Along with two other women, Salma al-Sayyigh and Ibtihaj Qaddura, Bayhum administered the orphanage. In 1918, the same three women founded the Muslim Girls Club (Nadi al-Banat al-Muslimat), which provided library and classroom facilities free of charge to Muslim girls. It offered classes in English and modern handicrafts and organized weekly lectures by poets, novelists, and religious scholars. In 1920, Bayhum became head of the club's handicraft section, employing 1,800 women and donating all of its revenue to charitable organizations in Beirut.

Also in 1920, US President Woodrow Wilson dispatched the King-Crane Commission to meet with Arabs and advise on the feasibility of establishing a

French Mandate in the Middle East. Bayhum headed a delegation of Beiruti women who protested to the US envoys that a French Mandate, or any other mandate in the Arab world, would be totally unacceptable to the inhabitants of the Middle East.

In 1922, Adila Bayhum moved to Damascus and married a Syrian notable from the Jaza'iri family. She established the Women's Union in Syria and served as its president from 1927 until 1967. From 1967 until her death in 1975, she maintained the title of honorary president.

Adila Bayhum.

In 1925, the Druze leader Sultan al-Atrash launched a military revolt against the French Mandate in Syria. Bayhum smuggled food and weapons to the guerrillas hiding in the orchards surrounding Damascus. She also gave lessons in textile and carpet weaving to rural women who had been widowed during the revolt. She also provided the children of the widows with free education and housing.

In 1927, Bayhum co-founded the Damascus Women's Awakening Society "aimed at reviving the female intelligentsia." Her slogan was "first independence, then women's rights." For the next forty years, Adila Bayhum led a campaign for the emancipation of women in Syria, demanding female suffrage and the right to hold public office. Some feminists considered the veil an embodiment of female seclusion. They unveiled and called on other women to remove the veil. Bayhum, however, refused to endorse this campaign.

In 1928, Bayhum established Dawhet al-Adab (Tree of Culture Society) in Damascus. It was a cultural and literary society that founded an all-girls school of the same name in 1929. Over the years, Dawhet al-Adab became one of the finest schools in Damascus. In Bayhum's own words, the school was created "to offer an Arabic education and produce patriotic female citizens."

From 1930 to 1936, Adila Bayhum became involved in the activities of the National Bloc, the leading anti-French organization in Syria, primarily as a fundraiser. Shukri al-Quwatli, Fakhri al-Barudi, and Saadallah al-Jabiri supported her movement in the Central Committee of the National Bloc. In 1938, Bayhum headed the Syrian delegation to the Women's Conference in Egypt. The conference was chaired by Huda Sharawi, leader of the feminist movement in the Middle East and North Africa.

In 1943, Bayhum clashed with the leaders of al-Gharra, an extremist Muslim group, who insisted that she remain at home and eschew public activity, and who claimed it was immoral for women to be taking part in public life. When al-Gharra discovered that many women were planning to attend unveiled a charity ball hosted by Bayhum, they threatened to set fire to the building where the dinner was to be held. In response to the threat, Bayhum ceased donating milk to the city's poor neighborhoods for twenty-four hours. The poor rioted in protest, demonstrating in the streets against al-Gharra and demanding that they permit Bayhum to carry out her duties in peace. The fundamentalists backed down and Bayhum resumed her work, having made all of Syria aware of her cause.

In January 1945, Adila Bayhum led what was at that time the largest women's march in Syrian history. It comprised over five hundred women protesting the French refusal to address the issue of Syrian independence during talks with President Quwatli. French soldiers beat and arrested many of the marchers. In 1946, following independence, President Quwatli honored Bayhum with the Medal of the Syrian Republic, Excellence Class, "in recognition of her services to the nation."

In 1949, Bayhum supported the rise of the reformer, General Husni al-Za'im, to the presidency and beseeched him to devote greater attention to women's rights. Za'im complied and issued a presidential decree allowing females to vote in national elections and to run for public office. Za'im's decree represented a remarkable victory for Bayhum, who began encouraging women through door-to-door house calls to run for parliament.

During the 1950s, Bayhum resumed her humanitarian work throughout Syria and supported the Syrian-Egyptian union from 1958 to 1961. In 1956, President Quwatli declared an "Arms Week" to prepare for an expected war between Egypt and Israel. Quwatli donated a two-month salary for the purpose and so did every citizen in Syria. The Syrian president appointed Bayhum as member of the central committee of "Arms Week," charged with collecting funds from the public. In 1960, President Gamal Abd al-Nasser appointed her chairman of the African-Asian-Arab Women's Association. Due to old age, Bayhum's activities were curtailed during the 1960s.

However, with the onset of the Arab-Israeli war in 1973, the seventy-three-year-old Bayhum resumed her humanitarian activities. She visited Syrian hospitals and comforted troops wounded at the war front. Bayhum's daughter, Amal al-Jaza'iri, continued a career in humanitarian work after her mother and led the feminist movement in Syria in the 1970s.

Adila Bayhum died in Damascus on January 3, 1975.

Sources:
Itri, Abd al-Ghani. *Alam wa Mubdioun* (1999).
Sakakini, Widad. *Sabiqat al-Asr* (1986).
Thompson, Elizabeth. *Colonial Citizens* (1999).

Droubi, Sami (1921-1976): see "Diplomats"

Chahine, Anastas
(1901-1974)

Anastas Chahine studied medicine at Damascus University and continued his medical studies at the Sorbonne in Paris. He returned to Syria in 1928 and became an instructor at Damascus University. (Chahine's father was Nicolas Chahine, an officer in the Ottoman Empire, one of the few Christians to hold such a high rank. Nicolas became director of police during the early years of the French Mandate.)

In 1942, Chahine was promoted to full professor and chairman of the Department of Otolaryngology. He held this post until 1967. In 1949, Chahine was appointed dean of the Medical School and retained his post until 1954. In 1955, he was nominated for the portfolio of health in the cabinet of Prime Minister Sabri al-Asali, but he rejected the offer in order to remain at his teaching post. In 1956, he published a medical book entitled, *Diseases of the Ear, Nose and Throat.*

In center on stairs: President Shukri al-Quwatli on left (saluting) and Anastas Chahine beside him on the right. (Location of photo: the Greek Patriarchate in Damascus in 1956.)

Chahine was also civically involved. He was a member of the Grand Masonic Lodge of Syria, and in 1955 became president of Syria's Rotary Club. Chahine remained a member of both organizations until President Gamal Abd al-Nasser of Egypt outlawed them during the Syrian-Egyptian union in 1958.

Anastas Chahine also devoted much of his time to the affairs of the Greek Orthodox Church in Damascus, where he was a council member until his death in 1974.

Sources:
Faris, George. *Man Hum fi al-Alam al-Arabi?* (1957).
Interview with Dr Nicolas Chahine (February 11, 2001).

al-Fahham, Shaker
(1921-)

Shaker al-Fahham studied Arabic literature at the University of Cairo and began his career in 1946 in Syria as a high school teacher. He was an early member of the Baath Party of Michel Aflaq and Salah al-Bitar. Fahham frequently participated in

Shaker al-Fahham.

student protests against the French Mandate staged by the Baath and often was arrested for his protest activities.

In April 1947, Fahham served as secretary of the party's founding conference in Damascus. In 1958, he returned to Cairo for a graduate degree in Arabic literature and began to teach at Damascus University following the Baath Party's rise to power in March 1963.

In 1964, Syria's new president, Baath Party member Amin al-Hafez, appointed Fahham ambassador to Algeria. In July 1968, President Nur al-Din al-Atasi appointed him president of Damascus University. In November 1970, Hafez al-Asad came to power and appointed Fahham minister of higher education in a cabinet created by Asad himself. Fahham held this post throughout the Asad era, until 1980, serving under Prime Ministers Abd al-Rahman Khlayfawi, Mahmud al-Ayyubi, and Mohammad Ali al-Halabi. Fahham also served as a deputy in the first parliament under President Asad from February to December 1971.

In 1993, Fahham became president of the Arab Language Assemblage. An Iraqi academic committee voted him into the Arab Language Assemblage in Baghdad, and in 1984 he was voted into the Language Assemblage of Jordan. From 1981 to 1994, Fahham also served as director of the *Arab Encyclopedia*, a colossal work on Arabic history published in Damascus. From 1980 to 1994, Fahham also worked as chief editor of *Historical Research*, a periodical published by Damascus University.

In 1988, Fahham was awarded the King Faysal Prize for Literature in Saudi Arabia. His works include many volumes of research on poetry and linguistics. Among Fahham's works are a biography of the late Syrian statesman Mustapha al-Shihabi, published in 1975; *Collection of Andalusia Poetry*, published in 1979; and studies in the poetry of pre-Islamic poet Bashar Bin Burd, published in 1983.

Sources:
Interview with Dr Shaker al-Fahham (March 10, 2002).

al-Hafez, Thuraya
(1911-2000)

Thuraya al-Hafez was born and raised in Damascus. Her father, Amin Lutfi al-Hafez, was an Arab nationalist leader whom the Ottoman Turks arrested and executed in 1916. Thuraya studied at local schools in Damascus, and in 1928 became one of the country's first female elementary school teachers.

With the help of Adila Bayhum, Hafez co-founded the Damascene Women's Awakening Society, a foundation aimed at reviving the female intelligentsia. In the 1930s, Hafez rose to fame as a prominent women's rights activist.

In 1930, Thuraya al-Hafez established the Women's School Alumnae Association aimed at uniting all educated women in one organization. Hafez took part in fundraising for the poor, administering an all-girls high school, and ensuring that children received proper bathing, medical care, and academic attention. She supported the anti-veil movement that took place in Cairo, and called on Syrian women to lift the veil, describing the act of veiling as an obstacle to the emancipation of women.

In May 1942, Hafez clashed with Islamic fundamentalists in Damascus demanding an end to "the excessive liberty of Muslim women." The al-Gharra Society and its founder, Sheikh Abd al-Hamid Tabba, headed the riots and petitions. Hafez responded to their demands by leading a march of one hundred women in the Marjeh Square of downtown Damascus. When the women reached government headquarters, they all collectively lifted their veils in defiance. Years later, Hafez remembered the situation saying, "I stood there and gave a speech in which I asserted that the veil we wore was never mentioned in God's Holy Book or by the Prophet Mohammad." She added, "So as our religion does not ask us to veil ourselves, and expects us to show our faces and be men's equal, we now take the veil off!" The march made headlines in the Arab press and shocked Damascus out of its stuffy Puritanism.

In 1947, Hafez became an instructor of Arabic literature at the prestigious Tajheez School in Damascus. In 1953, during the military regime of Adib al-Shishakli, Thuraya al-Hafez was the first woman to nominate herself for parliament, running on a Women's Union ticket. She lost, however, and accused authorities of tampering with the ballots to please conservative Muslim groups like al-Gharra and the Muslim Brotherhood. She claimed to have received 75% of the votes.

In 1953, Hafez began to write in the Damascus daily newspaper *Barada*, owned by her husband Munir al-Rayyes. She wrote a weekly column on women's affairs until the newspaper ceased to operate in 1963. Also in 1953, Thuraya al-Hafez set up a forum at her home in Damascus. Here intellectuals would meet on a periodic basis to discuss political, philosophical, and social issues. Her salon became an instant success due to the number of prominent male personalities who took part in her debates. Among Hafez's regular guests were the National Bloc leaders Faris al-Khury and Fakhri al-Barudi, and the poet Badawi al-Jabal. Among her prominent female guests were the Palestinian poet Fadwa Tuqan and the Syrian novelist Ghada al-Samman.

The mixed salon of Thuraya al-Hafez was a popular attraction for the Syrian intelligentsia from 1953 until it ceased to operate in 1963 when the Baath Party came to power.

Sources:

Bayhum, Mohammad Jamil. *Fatat al-Sharq fi Hadarat al-Gharb* (1952).

Hafez, Thuraya. *Hafiziyyat* (1980).

Nuwayhed, Nadia. *Nisaa Min Biladi* (2000).

Sakakini, Widad. *Sabiqat al-Asr* (1986).

Thompson, Elizabeth. *Colonial Citizens* (1999).

"Thuraya al-Hafez," a publication of the Women's Union released after Thuraya al-Hafez's death on June 1, 2000.

al-Hawrani, Uthman
(1898-1958)

Uthman al-Hawrani studied in his native Hama, a conservative city on the Orontes River in western Syria. In 1922, he co-founded the Arab Club of Damascus, an organization that conducted cultural activities and promoted anti-colonial opinion from all over the Middle East.

The French, who had occupied Syria in 1920, briefly tolerated the club's activities, yet banned it when the Syrian revolt of the Arab Mountain erupted against the French in 1925. Hawrani went to the Arab Mountain and took up arms with Sultan al-Atrash, leader of the revolt, repelling advancing French forces and leading attacks on mandate offices in Hama. In 1926, a military court sentenced Hawrani to death in absentia, forcing him to flee to Iraq, where he remained briefly before moving to British-occupied Bahrain in 1927.

Hawrani's opinions and his record of nationalist activity attracted the Bahraini government, which appointed him director of education (the equivalent of education minister). Hawrani's task was to lay out the foundations of a modern educational system in the sheikdom. Hawrani held this post from 1927 to 1930. During this time, Hawrani introduced a modern curriculum with courses on Arab nationalism, and he inaugurated the country's first all-girls high school.

Hawrani returned to Syria when the French issued an amnesty in 1931 and began to teach at the Scientific National Academy, a prestigious school run by the veteran educator Munif al-Aidi. Hawrani was accused by the French of plotting the assassination of the pro-French head of state, Bahij al-Khatib, and was arrested in 1940. Hawrani remained in jail for one year until President Taj al-Din al-Hasani released him in 1941. He went to the Arab Mountain, resided there for the next eleven years and taught at local high schools.

In 1952, Uthman al-Hawrani retired and returned to his native Hama, shunning public life for the rest of his days.

Sources:
Itri, Abd al-Ghani. *Alam wa Mubdioun* (1999).

al-Husari, Sati
(1882-1968)

Sati al-Husari was born in Yemen to a family originating from Aleppo in north Syria. He studied at the Sultanate School in Istanbul and began his career as a history schoolteacher in Sana.

In 1905, Husari moved to Damascus to lecture on the rising trend of Arabism, as opposed to the existing Ottomanism. His ideas were new, revolutionary, and attractive to the suppressed Arab population living under the reign of the Ottoman Turks. Husari supported the Committee for Union and Progress (CUP), a secret society that young Ottoman officers established in 1903 to bring reforms to the Ottoman Empire.

In 1908, the CUP staged a coup in Istanbul and curbed the influence of Sultan Abdulhamid II, forcing him to reinstate the constitution of 1876, lift press censorship, and reconvene the Ottoman Parliament that he had dissolved thirty years earlier in 1876. Husari broke with the CUP, however, when its leaders executed several Arab nationalists on the charge of treason in May 1916. The CUP also dissolved parliament, called for elections, then rigged them to secure the defeat of disloyal Arab candidates. The young scholar Husari defended the executed nationalists and the men defeated at the polls, claiming that they were champions of the Arab cause and not traitors, and called for the downfall of the CUP. In July 1916, Sharif Husayn, the Prince of Mecca, launched an Arab military uprising against the Ottoman Empire. The revolt was funded and commanded by the British Army, who were engaged in full-scale combat with the Ottoman Turks in World War I. Husari supported the revolt from its early stage until the empire was defeated in October 1918. He then joined the court of King Faysal I, the new ruler of Syria, who established the first modern Arab state in Damascus from 1918 to 1920. Husari became minister of education in the first post-Ottoman government of Prime Minister Rida al-Rikabi, holding office from March to July 1920.

In November 1918, Sati al-Husari began to translate the school curriculum from Ottoman Turkish into Arabic. He compiled a new series of history textbooks, shifting the emphasis from Ottoman to Arab history.

Sati al-Husari.

Also, he made English, rather than Turkish, a mandatory language in all Syrian schools.

Husari introduced a chapter on Arab nationalism into Syrian textbooks that resembled the revolutionary views later preached by Gamal Abd al-Nasser in the 1950s. Husari referred to countries previously omitted in Arab discourse as part of a single Arab homeland, and encouraged solidarity between Greater Syria and countries like Egypt, Yemen, Libya, and Morocco. Until this time, Arab scholars had limited the Arab "homeland" to the area encompassing the Hijaz, Syria, Lebanon, Palestine, Iraq, and Transjordan.

In addition to his efforts to Arabize the Syrian high school curriculum, Husari was also involved in the "Arabization" of the Ottoman Medical Academy in Damascus. He helped translate its books from Ottoman Turkish into Arabic and served as a founding board member of the Syrian Law Academy. In 1923, the Law Academy merged with the Medical School to form Damascus University.

From 1918 to 1920, a sincere friendship developed between King Faysal I and Sati al-Husari. In 1920, while Faysal was negotiating the conditions defining the French Mandate in Syria, Husari served as a liaison officer with Henri Gouraud, the commander of the French Army in the Middle East. Speaking on the king's behalf, Husari met with Gouraud to negotiate a peaceful solution to the crisis and tried to persuade the French not to occupy all of Syria. Nothing, however, came from his negotiations. Husari, therefore, proposed that the mandate be implemented, but with Faysal retaining his title and some of his powers. Nevertheless, Gouraud once again flatly rejected the proposal.

In July 1920, French forces defeated the Syrian Army in a military clash and sent King Faysal and his top officials, including Husari, into exile in London. Faysal begged his British allies for a crown in Arabia, and Colonial Secretary Winston Churchill agreed, making him king of Iraq in 1922. Husari joined him in Baghdad, becoming the first minister of education in Iraq and private advisor to the Royal Palace.

In Baghdad, Faysal commissioned Husari to create a national elementary and secondary school system. Husari borrowed extensively from the British and translated many works from English and Turkish into Arabic. He authored numerous textbooks on Arab nationalism, making it a core subject in Iraqi schools. In 1924, Husari co-founded Baghdad University and served as dean of its Faculty of Law. He also became director of public education in Iraq in 1925.

Husari remained loyal to Faysal until the king died in 1933, shifting his allegiance thereafter to his son and successor King Ghazi I. When Ghazi died in 1939, Husari clashed with Crown Prince Abd al-Illah, the new de facto ruler of Iraq. Consequently, Husari was relieved of his duties by the new leader of Baghdad. The crown prince personally disliked Husari and opposed his pan-Arab views. In 1941, at the height of World War II, Abd al-Illah accused Husari of plotting an armed insurrection against the British troops stationed in Baghdad. A plot, Abd al-Illah added, supported by the Nazis. Husari's Iraqi passport was confiscated and he was exiled to Lebanon. He briefly lived in Beirut until President Shukri al-Quwatli invited him back to Damascus and delegated him to draft a new curriculum for Syria to replace the one he had originally created when he served as minister in 1919.

For the new curriculum, Husari wanted to place a greater emphasis on Arab history, terminate the French baccalaureate system, and introduce a new core subject called *Qawmiyya* (Nationalism). He tried to introduce an American-style education, eliminating the final exam system as the determining factor for students wanting to pursue their higher education. From this point, Husari claimed, students would graduate from high school based on their academic performance during the previous four years of study, and not on the comprehensive final exam known in French as the baccalaureate. In addition, the French language, previously a mandatory subject starting in elementary school, was reduced to an elective course, and primary emphasis was placed on English. Syrian students rejected the project, however, and it was abolished in 1945. In 1946, Husari made his peace with Iraqi authorities and returned to Baghdad, offering his services once again to the new monarch, King Faysal II.

In August 1949, Sati al-Husari founded and chaired the Center of Arab Studies in Baghdad, an academic institute affiliated with Baghdad University, where he taught Arab nationalism and history for the next ten years. From 1950 onwards, Husari served as a political consultant to King Faysal II and devoted his spare time to writing books on pan-Arabism. He also allied himself with the Syrian Baath Party of Michel Aflaq. The Baath advocated views of Arab nationalism similar to Husari's own and praised the defiant new president of Egypt, Gamal Abd al-Nasser. Husari hailed Nasser's nationalization of the Suez Canal in 1956 and his war against France, Israel, and Great Britain.

In 1958, Husari praised the Syrian-Egyptian union conducted by President Nasser and Shukri al-Quwatli. Husari claimed that only through a comprehensive union could the Arab world defeat the rising threat of Zionism. His hopes were dashed when, in July 1958, a revolution took place in Baghdad. In this coup, a group of officers seized power and killed King Faysal II and Crown Prince Abd al-Illah. Husari was not harmed but relieved from all of his duties and sidelined from public life. Then, in September 1961, the Syrian-Egyptian union, which Husari had enthusiastically supported, was dissolved by a military coup carried out by a group of Syrian officers.

In February 1963, the Baath Party came to power in Iraq, killing the dictator Abd al-Karim Qasim. One month later, officers from the Baath Party seized power in Syria, toppling the post-union government of President Nazim al-Qudsi. Husari embraced both coups, and he was honored by both leaderships in Baghdad and

Damascus as the father of modern Arab nationalism. Baath Party founder Michel Aflaq frequently invited Husari to publish and lecture on his views in Syria, hoping that Husari would have a positive influence on Syrian intellectuals.

Upon Sati al-Husari's death in 1968, Syria and Iraq hailed him as a national hero, and he was buried in Baghdad.

Sources:
Cleveland, William. *A History of the Middle East* (2000).
Husari, Sati. *Yawm Maysloun* (1947).
Itri, Abd al-Ghani. *Alam wa Mubdioun* (1999).
Kayyali, Sami. *Al-Adab al-Arabi al-Mouasir fi Souriyya 1850-1950* (1968).

Jabbour, George
(1938-)

George Jabbour was born in the town of Safita near the Syrian coastline. As a youth he was attracted to the views of Michel Aflaq on Arab nationalism and joined Aflaq's Baath Party in the mid-1950s.

Jabbour studied law and philosophy at Damascus University, graduating with both degrees in 1960. In 1962, he obtained his MA in political science from Colorado University, and after a year began studying international relations at the American University in Washington, DC. Ultimately, he obtained his doctoral degree from American University in Cairo.

Jabbour began his career as a judge in Lattakia upon graduation from university in 1960, then became an official at the International Atomic Energy Agency in Vienna, nominated by Prime Minister Salah al-Bitar, where he worked until 1968. In 1969, Jabbour conducted studies for the Palestine Research Center of the PLO in Beirut.

In February 1970, Jabbour joined the Presidential Palace in Damascus, first as a consultant to President Nur al-Din al-Atasi, and then to President Hafez al-Asad, who seized power in November 1970. During these years, Jabbour also lectured at Damascus University and wrote extensively on Arab nationalism, Syria, and the Arab-Israeli conflict. In 1974, Asad appointed Jabbour director of the Presidential Office of Political Studies. In 1977, Jabbour became a professor and chairperson of the Department of Politics at the Arab League Graduate Institute for Arab Studies in Cairo.

While in Egypt, Jabbour co-founded the Arab Political Science Association. Briefly, in 1976, he became a visiting professor at Oxford and Cambridge University in Great Britain. In 1987, Asad proposed that Jabbour become director of human rights at UNESCO, but UNESCO's director preferred that the post remain occupied by a European. In 1989, Jabbour wrote his classic, *al-Fikr al-Siyasi al-Mouasir fi Souriyya (Contemporary Political Thought in Syria)*, published in London. The book was banned by Syrian authorities, and as a result, Jabbour was transferred from the Presidential Palace to the office of Prime Minister Mahmud al-Zu'bi where he served as an advisor. Since 1990, Jabbour has been a professor of political philosophy at the Graduate Law School of Aleppo University, in addition to teaching at Damascus University.

Jabbour began his literary career by writing an open letter on Palestine to UN Secretary-General Dag Hammarskjold when the latter visited Syria in January 1956. Since that time, Jabbour has continued to write articles, books, and academic research papers. Among his published works are *al-Ahzab al-Siyasiyya al-Arabiyya (Arab Political Parties)*, published in 1974, *Hafez al-Asad wa Qadiyyat Filastine (Hafez al-Asad and the Palestinian Cause)*, published in 1988. His classic, *al-Fikr al-Siyasi al-Mouasir fi Souriyya (Contemporary Political Thought in Syria)*, was banned in 1989, but was later authorized in Syria and is currently taught as part of the required curriculum at Aleppo University.

Among Jabbour's works in English is *Settler Colonialism in Southern Africa and the Middle East*, published in 1970. His other books include two on the UN, five on human rights, and two on intellectual property. In 2002, Jabbour was appointed by the president of the UN Human Rights Commission as the expert from Asia in a five-person committee called the Working Group on People of African Descent. Jabbour's term expires in 2006.

In 2003, George Jabbour became a deputy in the Syrian Parliament of President Bashar al-Asad, running on a Baath Party ticket. In 2004, Jabbour founded and became president of the Syrian-UN Association.

Sources:
Interview with Dr George Jabbour (August 30, 2001).

al-Jamali, Hafez
(1916-2003)

Hafez al-Jamali grew up in Homs, a city in the Syrian interior. He studied philosophy and received his PhD from the Sorbonne in Paris, returning to become an instructor at Damascus University in 1947.

During his early teaching career, Jamali befriended Baath Party founders Michel Aflaq and Salah al-Bitar. The founders were Jamali's former schoolteachers who believed in Arab nationalism and called for the establishment of "unity, freedom, and socialism" in Syria. In 1949, due to his alliance with both men, Syria's military dictator Husni al-Za'im briefly arrested Jamali.

In 1953, Jamali became a member of the Baath Party and began to teach its doctrine to his students. The main theme of his lectures was Arab unity. He was

arrested for his views and Baathist loyalties by the military regime of President
Adib al-Shishakli in 1952. Upon his release from jail, Jamali continued to preach
Arab nationalism and encourage his students to enlist in the Baath Party. He
managed to recruit hundreds of students into the party throughout the 1950s.
Among his prominent students was the officer Ahmad Abd al-Karim and Prime
Ministers Mahmud al-Ayyubi and Abd al-Raouf al-Kassem. In addition to his
teaching career, Jamali wrote for the Beirut newspaper *al-Nida* (*The Appeal*) and
contributed ideological articles to a*l-Baath*, a political daily edited by Aflaq himself. Jamali was very much in favor of the Syrian-Egyptian union of 1958, and an
ardent opponent of the coup that brought it down in 1961.

In March 1963, the Baath Party's Military Committee came to power in Syria,
establishing a socialist state and appointing Salah al-Bitar as prime minister.
Jamali was unfamiliar with the officers who came to power and played no role in
the coup of 1963. He supported them, however, because they pledged to restore
the Syrian-Egyptian union. In 1964, Jamali became ambassador to Sudan during
the presidency of Baath Party strongman General Amin al-Hafez.

In February 1966, a coup took place in Syria, removing Aflaq, Bitar, and General
Hafez from office, and bringing the radical military branch of the Baath, headed
by Salah Jadid, to power. Jamali joined the opposition in condemning the Jadid
regime and remained at his diplomatic post in Khartoum from 1966 to 1969. Due
to his standing as a veteran ideologue, the officers that came to power did not fire
Jamali from his post, nor did they harass him for his critical views.

In 1969, President Nur al-Din al-Atasi appointed Jamali ambassador to Italy.
He kept this post until December 1973, when President Hafez al-Asad summoned
him back to Syria and appointed him minister of education in the cabinet of his
former student Mahmud al-Ayyubi. Jamali held office for nine months and then
resigned in disagreement with government policies. (He was not pleased that he
had become minister in a cabinet headed by one of his former students.) Thus,
Jamali returned to his earlier career as a professor at Damascus University.

Jamali devoted the remainder of his years to writing academic books and contributing articles to the magazine *al-Marifa*. In 1975-1976, he served as president
of the Arab Writers' Union in Syria. During a fifty-year career, Hafez al-Jamali
translated over forty works from French into Arabic, and wrote three books:
Arabi Yufakir (*A Thinking Arab*), *Bayn al-Takhaluf wa al-Hadara* (*Between Non-
civilization and Civilization*), and *Hawl al-Mustaqbal al-Arabi* (*Regarding the Arab
Future*).

Sources:
Interview with Dr Hafez al-Jamali (February 7, 2003).
Itri, Abd al-Ghani. *Alam wa Mubdioun* (1999).

al-Jaza'iri, Tahir
(1852-1920)

Born and raised in Damascus to a family of Algerian origin, Tahir al-Jaza'iri studied with private tutors and developed a special interest in Arabic literature and Islamic studies. In 1878, he became an instructor at a prominent school in Damascus. He quickly earned a reputation for eloquence and political liberalism.

In January 1879, Jaza'iri presented Midhat Pasha, the Ottoman governor of Damascus, with a request to upgrade elementary education throughout the Arab-speaking provinces in the Ottoman Empire. The informal gathering of students at the courtyards of mosques should be replaced, Jaza'iri argued, with formal schools built on government property with a full-paid academic faculty and staff. Midhat Pasha agreed and authorized the creation of the Arab Association, a foundation for academic reform, with Jaza'iri as its president.

On February 5, 1879, Jaza'iri opened his first official school in Damascus and served as its director. The school was launched with a total student enrollment of 116 boys. On February 25, the second school opened with a student enrollment of 106 boys. The following year, Jaza'iri opened a similar all-girls school in Damascus.

In 1880, Sultan Abdulhamid II appointed Jaza'iri inspector of education (with ministerial duties) in the vilayat of Damascus and delegated him to reform the entire high school curriculum of the Arab provinces in the Ottoman Empire. Jaza'iri authored books on Islam and mathematics and made them required reading at schools in Ottoman Syria. In 1882, he set up a state-run publishing house in Damascus called Al-Maktaba al-Zahiriyya to print the new material.

One year later, Jaza'iri founded a branch for his printing press in Jerusalem. Al-Maktaba al-Zahiriyya expanded to include a public library where books, manuscripts, and government documents were located, archived, and made accessible to the public. Jaza'iri became director of the public library as well, procuring the original manuscripts of the private memoirs of leading Arab officials in the Ottoman Empire, like Sulayman Pasha al-Azm and Abdullah Pasha al-Azm. The library also contained Islamic manuscripts and documents stored at the Omayyad Mosque from the days of the Omayyad Dynasty. In 1878, Jaza'iri founded one of the earliest Masonic lodges in Damascus and became its first grand master.

During the late nineteenth century, Tahir al-Jaza'iri earned wide respect and a large audience in Damascus. His most prominent student was Abd al-Rahman Shahbandar, a young student who would become a doctor and the leader of the nationalist movement against the French Mandate in Syria during the 1920s and 1930s. Shahbandar went on to become a legendary name in Syria, and he often attributed his enlightenment regarding Arab nationalism to the teachings of Tahir al-Jaza'iri. Other disciples of Jaza'iri include Shukri al-Asali, Abd al-Hamid al-Zahrawi, and Rushdi al-Sham'a, three politicians arrested for their views and executed in public by Ottoman authorities in 1916. Midhat Pasha, who had backed Jaza'iri's reforms with vigor, died in 1883. Without Pasha to defend him any longer, Jaza'iri was vulnerable to attack from anti-reform hard-liners.

These Ottoman hard-liners lobbied against Jaza'iri at the Imperial Palace in Istanbul, claiming that he was encouraging the Arab provinces in the empire to mutiny against the central Ottoman authority. Jaza'iri must be stopped at any cost, the hard-liners told Abdulhamid, or else the empire's future was in danger. Consequently, Abdulhamid dismissed Jaza'iri, but kept him at his job in the curriculum committee until 1899. Ottoman police then seized anti-Ottoman material at Jaza'iri's home and arrested him on the charge of treason. The charges were dropped, however, under orders from the sultan out of respect for Jaza'iri's earlier services to the empire. Abdulhamid exiled Jaza'iri to Cairo, where he wrote books and worked as a journalist until the Ottoman Empire collapsed in November 1918. Jaza'iri then returned to Syria, receiving a hero's welcome, and offered his services to King Faysal I, the new ruler of Syria, who reappointed him director of Al-Maktaba al-Zahiriyya.

Jaza'iri wrote several books on Arabic literature, including *al-Tafseer al-Kabeer* (*The Great Explanation*), *al-Kafi fi al-Lugha* (*The Complete Work in the Linguistics*), and *al-Jawaher al-Kalamiyya* (*Speaker's Jewels*).

Tahir al-Jaza'iri died on January 5, 1920. One of his most memorable contributions was the co-establishment of the prestigious Arab Language Assemblage in Damascus on June 8, 1919.

Sources:
Hourani, Albert. *Arabic Thought in the Liberal Age* (1961).
Itri , Abd al-Ghani. *Abqariyyat wa Alam* (1996).
Kayyali, Sami. *Al-Adab al-Arabi al-Mouasir fi Souriyya 1850-1950* (1968).
Khatib, Adnan. *Sheikh Tahir al-Jaza'iri* (1971).
Khoury, Philip. *Urban Notables and Arab Nationalism* (1983).
Tishreen (April 2, 2003).

Khater, Murshed
(1888-1962)

Murshed Khater came from the district of al-Shouf, a mixed Maronite-Druze area in Mount Lebanon. He grew up in Beirut and studied at Sagesse High School. In 1911, he obtained a medical degree from a university in Beirut.

In 1915, Khater was commissioned into the Ottoman Army and fought in World War I. The British Army captured and imprisoned him in 1916. After his release, he abandoned the Ottomans and joined the rebel Arab Army fighting with Great Britain and working for termination of the Ottoman Empire.

In 1918, Khater took part in the force that liberated Damascus from Ottoman control and was among the first Arab officers to enter the city on October 1, 1918. He resigned from the Arab Army, and King Faysal I, the new ruler of Syria, delegated him to co-found the Arab Institute of Medicine in 1919. Khater played an instrumental role in "Arabizing" the curriculum and translating all medical works from Ottoman Turkish into Arabic. He also became director of surgery at the Military Hospital in Damascus. In 1923, the Institute of Medicine merged with other academic departments and was renamed Damascus University, and Khater became dean of its Medical School.

Murshed Khater.

Khater taught at the university during the years of the French Mandate (1920-1946) and presided over the publication and editing of *al-Majalla al-Tibbiyya* (*The Medical Magazine*), a periodical issued by Damascus University. In 1947, President Shukri al-Quwatli awarded Khater the highest medal of honor of the Syrian Republic. In 1953, he received the same medal from President Adib al-Shishakli, who had appointed Khater minister of health in 1951. Khater later founded a nursing school in Aleppo, a center for treating tuberculosis in Damascus, and dispatched a number of doctors for advanced training in the United States and Europe.

In 1953, Murshed Khater became president of the annual WHO conference in Geneva. When Shishakli was overthrown in 1954, Khater returned to his teaching post and spent the remainder of his years writing medical books until his death in January 1962. His classic work is the six-volume encyclopedia, *al-Amrad al-Jirahiyya* (*Surgical Disease*).

Sources:
Arab Language Assemblage Magazine (January 2000).
Itri, Abd al-Ghani. *Abqariyyat* (1997).
Photo Credit: *Abqariyyat*, (1997).

al-Khiyyami, Madani
(1913-1997)

Madani al-Khiyyami studied medicine at the American University of Beirut (AUB) and graduated in 1936. He went to Lyon in France, studied cardiology, and returned to Syria in 1938. Khiyyami taught at AUB for one year then became

Madani al-Khiyyami.

an instructor at Damascus University.

During the years of the French Mandate (1920-1946), Khiyyami was encouraged to enter into politics by Abd al-Rahman Shahbandar, the nationalist leader who spearheaded opposition to the French Mandate in Syria. As a student activist, Khiyyami was arrested for his anti-French views in the 1930s. Shahbandar liked him and endorsed him for many reasons, one of which was that both of them had studied at AUB and both were doctors. Khiyyami gave up on politics when Shahbandar was assassinated in 1940. In 1946, Khiyyami founded an intellectual salon to debate philosophical affairs in Damascus with Alice Qandalaft, a pioneer woman who had studied in the US on a scholarship from the American government facilitated by Dr Shahbandar in 1922. Their salon became the gathering place for young ambitious intellectuals who debated politics and philosophy, lamenting Syria's troubled domestic affairs in the 1940s and 1950s. Among the young men to flourish at these salons was Baath Party founder Michel Aflaq.

Following Shahbandar's assassination in 1940, Khiyyami opened a private clinic in Damascus and practiced medicine. In 1949, he became private physician to General Husni al-Za'im, saving him from two heart attacks during his four brief months as president of Syria. In 1951, General Adib al-Shishakli, the new military strongman of Syria, offered Khiyyami the post of minister of health, but he refused, reportedly in protest to Shishakli's military regime. In 1958, Syria and Egypt merged to form the United Arab Republic (UAR). President Gamal Abd al-Nasser offered Khiyyami the same post, but he again refused for reputedly the same reasons. In March 1963, the Baath Party came to power and Prime Minister Salah al-Bitar once again offered him the post of minister of health, but once again Khiyyami rejected the position.

In 1968, Khiyyami became dean of the Medical School, and on August 5, 1971, he became president of Damascus University, a post he held until November 29, 1972. In October 1972, President Hafez al-Asad appointed Khiyyami minister of health in the cabinet of Prime Minister Mahmud al-Ayyubi. Khiyyami also served as a deputy in the first parliament under President Asad from February to December 1971. In August 1976, Prime Minister Abd al-Rahman Khlayfawi renewed Khiyyami's post, as did Prime Minister Mohammad Ali al-Halabi from 1978 to 1980.

Madani al-Khiyyami retired from public office in January 1980 and died on February 20, 1997.

Sources:

Itri, Abd al-Ghani. *Hadeeth an al-Abqariyyat* (2000).

Murad, Fatima
(1910-?)

Fatima Murad was born in Palestine and grew up in Syria. Her father, Sa'id Murad, was a prominent theologian known for his liberal views and his campaign to spread women's rights throughout the Arab world. He was a parliamentary deputy in the first post-Ottoman Parliament from 1918 to 1920, and was the first parliamentarian to demand suffrage for women, yet the conservative majority rejected his request. In 1928, despite tremendous opposition, he enrolled Fatima at Damascus University for a BA in International Law.

Murad attended classes unveiled (a taboo in the 1920s) and was the first woman to receive a law degree in Syria. She graduated in 1932, with a minor degree in economics and finance. From 1933 to 1936, she served as an itinerant instructor, dividing her time between Jerusalem, Beirut, Baghdad, and Damascus.

In 1936, Murad joined the Syrian Committee for the Liberation of Palestine and staged rallies in favor of the Palestinian uprising taking place in Jerusalem. She collected funds for the Jerusalem revolt and organized a demonstration in Damascus attended by other women activists who shouted anti-Zionist slogans and demanded that the Syrian government send voluntary troops to fight in Palestine. That same year, the Mufti of Jerusalem, Amin al-Husayni, appointed Murad as Palestine's representative at the first Women's Conference in Damascus.

In 1946, Syrian Minister of Education Munir al-Ajlani appointed Murad as Syria's representative to the second Women's Conference in Tehran, Iran. Fatima Murad devoted the remainder of her years to academics and established herself as a pioneer of the feminist movement in Syria.

Sources:
Faris, George. *Man Hum fi al-Alam al-Arabi?* (1957).
Thompson, Elizabeth. *Colonial Citizens* (1999).

Murayden, Izzat
(1908-2000)

Izzat Murayden was born and raised in Damascus. He studied at the Arab Medical Academy (renamed Damascus University in 1923) and graduated in 1930. From 1932 to 1934, he underwent training in France, then returned to open a clinic in Damascus. In 1947, Murayden became private physician to President Shukri al-Quwatli and a professor of medicine at Damascus University.

When Quwatli was overthrew by a military coup d'etat in March 1949, Murayden became private physician to Syria's new president, Husni al-Za'im, and to his prime minister, Muhsen al-Barazi. In 1952, Murayden became deputy dean of the Medical School at Damascus University and a member of the National Culture Committee of Syria. In 1957, he became dean of the Medical School and kept this post until 1965.

During Syria's union years with Egypt (1958-1961), Murayden worked as a visiting professor at Cairo University. He retained his teaching post until 1971. Then he retired from academics and devoted the remainder of his years to his medical clinic. In 1982, he published a work called *Dirasat wa Taammulat fi al-Ilm wa al-Tibb wa al-Hayat* (*Studies and Observations in Science, Medicine, and Life*). In 1996, Izzat Murayden wrote a biography of his father-in-law, the veteran educator Munif al-Aidi, a co-founder of Damascus University in 1923.

Sources:
Itri, Abd al-Ghani. *Hadeeth an al-Abqariyyat* (2000).
Murayden, Izzat. *Dr Ahmad Munif al-Aidi* (1996).

Mustapha, Shaker
(1916-1999)

Shaker Mustapha studied history at the University of Fou'ad I in Cairo, graduating in 1945. He moved back to Syria and taught history in Dayr al-Zur, a remote town along the Euphrates River in eastern Syria. He returned to Damascus in 1947 and became secretary-general of Damascus University. He taught at the Department of History and administered the university's day-to-day affairs.

In 1956, Prime Minister Sabri al-Asali appointed Mustapha cultural attaché to Cairo. He held office during the peak of Syria's "honeymoon" with Egypt and promoted Syrian art, novels, and plays within Egyptian intellectual circles. Mustapha organized exhibitions for Syrian artists, arranged for novelists to lecture at Egyptian universities, and invited the Syrian National Theater to perform their productions in Cairo and Alexandria.

In 1957, Mustapha became chargé d'affaires in Sudan and held this post until Syria and Egypt merged to form the United Arab Republic (UAR) in 1958. One year later, President Gamal Abd al-Nasser appointed him UAR ambassador to Cambodia. In October 1961, Nasser made Mustapha UAR consul to Brazil. The UAR was dissolved by military coup in September 1961, but Syria's new president, Nazim al-Qudsi, kept Mustapha at his diplomatic post until 1963.

Mustapha returned to Syria and became secretary-general of the Ministry of Foreign Affairs. He was among the few independents that held senior government posts during the Baath Party government of President Amin al-Hafez, who came to power in March 1963. In 1965, Prime Minister Salah al-Bitar appointed Mustapha minister of information, a position he kept until the Hafez regime was ousted by a coup in February 1966.

Mustapha then retired from his post and moved to the Persian Gulf. In 1966, he co-founded Kuwait University with thirty-one Arab academics. He worked as a professor of history in Kuwait for the next twenty-five years and retired due to old age in 1991.

Many of Shaker Mustapha's academic works became classics in the Arab world. Among his renowned publications are *Souriyya wa Lubnan (Syria and Lebanon)*, published in 1949; *Shaker Mustapha.*
Dawlat Bani Abbas (The Abbasid State), published in 1973; and *Azmat al-Tatawur al-Hadari fi al-Watan al-Arabi (Crisis of Civilization Progress in the Arab World)*, published in 1975.

In 1998, prior to his death, Shaker Mustapha released three works: *Salah al-Din al-Ayyubi (Saladin)*, *Fi al-Tareekh al-Islami (In Islamic History)*, and *Fi al-Tareekh al-Shami (In Damascene History)*.

Sources:
Itri, Abd al-Ghani. *Abqariyyat* (1997).

al-Nuss, Ihsan
(1919-)

Ihsan al-Nuss was born in Damascus, studied ancient Arabic literature at Cairo University, and graduated in 1946. While in Egypt, he wrote his first academic article, "Bayn Voltaire wa al-Jahez" (Between Voltaire and al-Jahez) for *al-Thaqafa* magazine. The article was published in 1941 when Nuss was twenty-two years old.

From 1946 to 1956, Nuss came back to Syria to teach at high schools, then returning to Cairo for his graduate studies in 1956. He obtained an MA in 1959 and a PhD in 1962. In 1963, Nuss began to teach at Damascus University. In 1966, he became a visiting instructor at the University of Algeria where, along with a group of Arab academics, Nuss translated the Algerian curriculum from French into Arabic. He returned to teach in Syria in 1972. In 1978, Nuss became dean of the Faculty of Arts at Damascus University. From 1979 to 1989, he held the position of visiting professor at Kuwait University. In 1987-1988, he served as director of the Arabic Language Department at Kuwait University.

In 1979, Nuss joined the Arab Language Assemblage in Damascus. He conducted research for the institution and became deputy to its president, Shaker al-Fahham, in 1993. Nuss wrote extensively on the Umayyad Dynasty and on Islamic history. Among his published works are *Al-Khataba fi al-Asr al-Umawi* (*Speech in the Omayyad Era*), *Al-Sh'ir al-Siyasi fi al-Asr al-Umawi* (*Political Poetry in the Omayyad Era*), and *Al-Shi'ir al-Ghazali fi al-Asr al-Umawi* (*Romantic Poetry in the Omayyad Era*).

Among Ihsan al-Nuss's academic articles are *Sati al-Husari wa Usul al-Tadris* (*Sati al-Husari and the Origins of Teaching*), published in *al-Ilm al-Arabi* magazine and *Al-Takhtit al-Thaqafi fi al-Watan al-Arabi* (*Cultural Planning in the Arab World*), published in *al-Jihad al-Thaqafi* magazine in Algeria.

Sources:
Interview with Dr Ihsan al-Nuss (March 10, 2002).

al-Qanawati, Abd al-Wahab
(1891-1977)

Abd al-Wahab al-Qanawati studied pharmacy at the Ottoman Medical School in Damascus and graduated in 1911. When World War I broke out in 1914, he joined the Ottoman Army and was appointed to the Ottoman Hospital in Zahle. In 1916, Qanawati moved to Beirut and became a medical instructor at Jesuit University.

When the Ottoman Empire was defeated in 1918, Qanawati returned to Syria to teach at the Arab Institute of Medicine. In 1923, the institute merged with other faculties and was renamed Damascus University. Qanawati joined a group of veteran educators in translating works from Ottoman Turkish into Arabic and formulating a unique curriculum for the new university. The team authored new textbooks, created a modern infrastructure for the university, and taught at the Faculty of Medicine.

In 1920, Abd al-Wahab al-Qanawati joined the politician Lutfi al-Haffar in trying to solve the ongoing water shortage problem in Damascus. The residents of the Syrian capital had relied on the River Barada for both irrigation and drinking, often resulting in severe water shortages. In 1921, Haffar and Qanawati tapped water at the Ayn al-Fija spring on the outskirts of Damascus. They founded the Ayn al-Fija Waterworks Company, bringing drinking water to Damascus and keeping Barada strictly for farming and irrigation purposes. In 1923, Qanawati became a board member of the company while Haffar served as its director. Throughout the first half of the century,

Abd al-Wahab al-Qanawati.

Ayn al-Fija Company was one of the most innovative and financially rewarding enterprises in Damascus.

In 1924, the French Mandate offered Qanawati a scholarship to study at the Sorbonne in Paris, where he obtained his MA in chemistry. A year earlier, Qanawati had founded the first medicine factory in Damascus, the Qanawati Medical Company, which he expanded in 1929 to become a shareholding company for the manufacture of prescription drugs and medical equipment. He also taught at the Faculty of Medicine at Damascus University until 1949. Abd al-Wahab al-Qanawati then retired from academia and continued to work as general director of his pharmaceutical company until his death on June 8, 1977.

Sources:

Faris, George. *Man Hum Fi al-Alam al-Arabi?* (1957).
Itri, Abd al-Ghani. *Hadeeth al-Abqariyyat* (2000).

al-Qanawati, Shawkat
(1904-?)

Shawkat al-Qanawati studied at the Arab Medical Institute in Damascus (renamed Damascus University in 1923) and continued his medical residency in France, graduating in 1928. He returned to Syria in 1930 and began to teach at Damascus University, becoming a full-time professor in 1947.

In 1952, Qanawati became dean of the Medical School. The following year, he was appointed deputy to University President Constantine Zurayk. Qanawati introduced many reforms into the university curriculum and encouraged students from the Arab world to pursue higher education in Syria, rather than in Lebanon, Egypt, or Europe. In June 1955, Qanawati became dean of the Faculty of Medicine for another term. On July 14, 1956, he became president of Damascus University and held office until Syria and Egypt merged to form the United Arab Republic (UAR) in February 1958.

On March 8, 1958, Qanawati left his job as university president and became minister of health in the UAR. He held office in a cabinet headed by UAR President Gamal Abd al-Nasser.

In October 1958, Nasser made him minister of social affairs, a post he kept until the dissolution of the UAR in September 1961. Shawkat al-Qanawati spent the remainder of his years teaching at Damascus University and practicing medicine.

Sources:

Faris, George. *Man Hum fi al-Alam al-Arabi?* (1957).
Samman, Mutih. *Watan wa Askar* (1995).

Sabah, Husni
(1900-1986)

Husni Sabah studied at the Arab Institute of Medicine in Damascus and the University of Lausanne in Switzerland. Upon graduation, he returned to work at the newly created Damascus University in Syria. Sabah taught at the university's medical school, helping to translate the school's medical texts from Ottoman Turkish into Arabic. He also authored many medical textbooks himself and became dean of the Faculty of Medicine in 1938.

In 1941, President Taj al-Din al-Hasani appointed Sabah to the medical staff of the Presidential Palace. One year later, Sabah became private physician to President Hasani. When Hasani died in office in 1943, the new president, Shukri al-Quwatli, retained Sabah in this capacity. Sabah was politically affiliated with the National Bloc, the premier anti-French organization in Syria, and known to be close to its Damascus leadership.

In 1943, Sabah became president of Damascus University, a position he retained until September 1946. He briefly resigned from office, but continued to teach in the Faculty of Medicine. In November 1947, Sabah resumed his duties as university president, once again backed by President Quwatli.

In March 1949, a military coup took place in Syria and Shukri al-Quwatli was relieved of his duties by General Husni al-Za'im. All those who had received presidential endorsement in the 1940s, including Sabah, were fired from their jobs by the new administration. Consequently, Sabah lost his job as university president on May 15, 1949. In September 1955, however, Quwatli was reelected president and decorated Sabah with the Medal of Honor of the Syrian Republic, Excellence Class.

In 1968, a group of veteran Syrian academics elected Sabah as president of the prestigious Arab Language Academy. He presided over the academy's publications and gave periodic lectures at Damascus University until his death in 1986.

Sources:
Arab Language Assemblage Magazine (January 2000).
Faris, George. *Man Hum fi al-Alam al-Arabi?* (1957).
Itri, Abd al-Ghani. *Abqariyyat* (1997).

al-Sabbagh, Faysal
(1919-)

Faysal al-Sabbagh is a Damascene born and bred. He studied medicine at Damascus University and graduated in 1946, continuing his studies at Paris University where he also became assistant professor of neurology.

Then Sabbagh moved to Columbia University in New York where he specialized in neurosurgery. In 1947, he became a resident physician in the Neurological Institute of New York. He returned to Syria in 1949, as the first neuro surgeon in the country, to establish the neurosurgery department in Damascus University's Mouwasat Hospital.

In 1951, Sabbagh became one of the youngest professors in Damascus University, and his popular lectures attracted the largest audience of medical students from all fields. He was the first Syrian to instruct in neurosurgery since the Damascus School of Medicine was founded in 1903. During the years of the French Mandate (1920-1946), the post had been exclusively held by French professors.

From 1973 to 1983, Sabbagh chaired the Internal Medicine department in Damascus University. In the presence of many generations of doctors who had been his students, Sabbagh was honored by Damascus University upon his retirement in 1989 at the age of seventy for "his great contributions to wide-spreading medical science and knowledge." Considered by academics as one of the pioneers in pro-

Faysal al-Sabbagh.

viding medical education in Arabic, Sabbagh supervised the translation of the classic, *Harrison's Principles of Internal Medicine*, and received in 1978 an award from the Union of Arab Scientific Research Councils.

The Arabic edition of *Harrison's Principles of Internal Medicine* became the main medical textbook in universities throughout the Arab world. In addition to various fellowships, Sabbagh was elected to the Arab Medical Board. Sabbagh's influence with the board helped Damascus University's hospital receive certification.

Faysal al-Sabbagh is the author of various medical volumes and academic articles in neurology, neurosurgery, and psychiatry. His textbooks are still used in Damascus University today.

Now at eighty-four, Sabbagh has just completed compiling a reference guide on the history of medicine due to be published in Damascus in 2006. His students and peers affectionately call Faysal al-Sabbagh the "father of neurology" in Syria.

Sources:

Information supplied by Rasha al-Sabbagh Haykal (May 19, 2003).

al-Sabbagh, Layla
(1924-)

Layla al-Sabbagh was born and raised in Damascus. She studied history at the University of Cairo and graduated in 1947. She taught and directed local high schools in Syria and returned to Egypt in 1961 to obtain an MA and PhD in Modern Arab History. She served as an instructor at all-girl schools and was director of the prestigious al-Tajheez al-Thaniya High School from 1954 to 1963.

In 1963, Sabbagh became senior inspector on the subjects of history and geography at the Ministry of Education in Damascus. She worked at the ministry until 1966 when she became a visiting instructor at the University of Algeria. While in Algiers, Sabbagh wrote extensively in academic periodicals on Islamic history and its politics.

Sabbagh returned to Syria in 1968 and worked at the directorate of research at the Ministry of Education. In 1971, she began to teach literature at Damascus University and in 1976 moved to the Department of History. In 1993, she served as a visiting lecturer at the University of al-Ayn in the United Arab Emirates. In 2000, a committee of Arab academics honored Sabbagh by voting her into the Arab Language Assemblage. Sabbagh was the first female member since the group's establishment in 1922.

In her works and lectures, Layla al-Sabbagh focused on the culture, society, and politics of the Ottoman Empire. Among her published works are *Al-Mujtama al-Arabi al-Souri fi Matla' al-Ahd al-Uthmani* (*Syrian Arab Society at the Dawn of the Ottoman Era*), published in 1973, and *Min Alam al-Fikr al-Arabi fi al-Asr al-Uthmani al-Awal* (*Among the Eminent Figures in Arab Thought in the first Ottoman Era*), published in 1986.

Layla al-Sabbagh also wrote extensively on the role of women in Arab society, arts, and literature, including the 1975 book, *Al-Mar'a fi al-Tareekh al-Arabi* (*Women in Arab History*), which discussed the roles of women in the pre-Islamic era. Her other books include *Nisa' wa Rijal fi al-Adab wa al-Siyasa wa Islah al-Mujtama* (*Men and Women in Literature, Politics, and Social Reform*), published in 1995, and *Min al-Adab al-Nisai al-Mouasir al-Arabi wa al-Gharbi* (*From Contemporary Arab and Western Women Literature*), published in 1996.

Sources:
Bawab, Sulayman. *Mawsuat Alam Souriyya fi al-Qarn al-Ishreen,* Vol III (1999).
Interview with Dr Layla al-Sabbagh (July 14, 2002).

al-Sa'id, Rida
(1876-1945)

Rida Sa'id was born and raised in Damascus. He studied at the Ottoman Military Academy in Istanbul and graduated in 1898. In 1900, he became military assistant to the Ottoman General As'ad Pasha.

Sa'id took leave from the Ottoman Army in 1908 to study medicine in Paris where he specialized in ophthalmology. He returned to Syria and reenlisted in the Ottoman Army. He served until 1917 when he was appointed mayor of Damascus. Sa'id established secret channels with the Arab underground based in Mecca, and helped smuggle funds and arms to the resistance in Damascus against the Ottoman Empire.

When the Ottoman Empire collapsed in October 1918, Rida al-Sa'id allied himself with King Faysal I, the new ruler of Syria. Faysal assigned Sa'id the task of expanding the Medical Academy of Damascus established by the Ottomans in 1903. Along with other educators, chief among them Abd al-Rahman Shahbandar, Munif al-Aidi, and Hamdi al-Khayyat, Sa'id translated texts from Ottoman Turkish into Arabic, set up an all-Arab board of directors, and upgraded the curriculum to modern European standards. In 1919, the academy was renamed the Arab Academy of Medicine and Sa'id became a member of its board of directors and a professor on its faculty. Eventually, he became dean of the Faculty of Medicine.

Sa'id, however, clashed with the French who proclaimed their mandate over Syria in July 1920. The mandate authority argued that since there were two prominent medical schools in Lebanon, the American University of Beirut (AUB) and Jesuit University, there would be no need for a medical school in Damascus. The Syrian capital at the time was boiling with anti-French sentiment and had been the center for Arab nationalism in the pre-World War I era. The French feared that a healthy academic environment would transform the university into a breeding ground for dissent against the mandate. Sa'id spearheaded the campaign to preserve the school. After much lobbying, he convinced the French to refrain from closing the academic institution.

In 1923, Sa'id co-founded the first law school in Syria and became president of the Academic Faculties, which he renamed Damascus University on June 11, 1923. In the ensuing years, Sa'id founded the Arab Institute for Education, the Scientific Academy, the Department of Pharmacology, the School of Dentistry, the University Printing Press, and the Arab Directorate of Antiquities. In December 1924, Prime Minister Subhi Barakat appointed Sa'id minister of education.

Rida al-Sa'id.

While in office, Sa'id introduced the present-day form of the baccalaureate exam, based on the French model. He also used government funds to send professors for training in France, Great Britain, and the United States. He resigned from government office, however, in December 1925 in order to resume his duties as president of Damascus University. In 1934, Rida Sa'id's tenure as university president expired, but he continued to teach until his death in 1945.

Sources:
Bawab, Sulayman. *Mawsuat Alam Souriyya fi al-Qarn al-Ishreen,* Vol III (1999).
Farfur, Abd al-Latif. *Alam Dimashq* (1987).
Itri, Abd al-Ghani. *Abqariyyat Min Biladi* (1995).
Murayden, Izzat. *Dr Ahmad Munif al-Aidi* (1996).

Saliba, Jamil
(1902-1976)

Jamil Saliba was born in modern Lebanon and studied psychology at the Sorbonne in Paris, obtaining his graduate degree in 1924, a diploma in law in 1926, and a PhD in 1927. He returned to Syria to teach philosophy at high schools and to found a weekly scientific magazine, *al-Ilm al-Arabi* (*Arab Science*). In 1932, he founded the cultural weekly *al-Thaqafa Magazine* with the poet Khalil Mardam Bey and the communist writer Kamel al-Ayyad.

In 1936, Saliba became director of secondary education in Damascus and held this post until 1944. But back in 1942, a group of veteran academics voted Saliba into the Arab Language Assemblage. In 1945, Saliba served as chairman of the education committee of the Ministry of Education. His goal was to upgrade the quality of Syrian high schools. In 1949, President Husni al-Za'im appointed Saliba secretary-general of the Ministry of Education. The following year, Saliba was appointed dean of the Faculty of Education at Damascus University,

a post he retained until 1964. From March to November 1958, Saliba held office as acting president of Damascus University.

In 1964, Saliba left Syria to take up residence in Beirut where he joined UNESCO, becoming director of its Human Resources Department in Lebanon. He resigned from this post in 1970, but spent the remainder of his years in Beirut, serving in various educational positions at seminars, forums, and universities. He lectured at the Kaslik University, the American University of Beirut (AUB), and at the Lebanese University.

Jamil Saliba.

Jamil Saliba produced numerous academic works

including *Mustaqbal al-Tarbiya fi al-Sharq al-Arabi* (*Future of Education in the Arab East*), published in 1963, and *Itijahat al-Naqd al-Hadeeth fi Souriyya* (*Orientation of Modern Criticism in Syria*), published in 1969. His classic, *Al-Intaj al-Falsafi Khilal al-Ma'at Sana al-Akheera fi al-Alam al-Arabi* (*Philosophical Works of the Past One Hundred Years*), was published in 1962.

Sources:
Itri, Abd al-Ghani. *Abqariyyat* (1997).
Kayyali, Sami. *Al-Adab al-Arabi al-Mouasir fi Souriyya 1850-1950* (1968).

al-Samman, Ahmad
(1907-1968)

Ahmad al-Samman studied criminal law at the Sorbonne in Paris, where he also obtained his MA in sociology and his PhD in political science. He returned to Damascus and practiced law at the prestigious firm of Ihsan al-Sharif.

In 1938, Samman became assistant instructor of law at Damascus University. In 1940, President Taj al-Din al-Hasani appointed Samman to the government's Bureau of Consultation. In 1943, Samman resigned his government post and focused on his teaching career, becoming dean of the faculty of law at Damascus University in 1954.

Ahmad al-Samman.

In December 1954, Ahmad al-Samman served as acting president of the university and held this post until March 1956. In the 1950s, he joined the movement of Arab nationalism headed by President Gamal Abd al-Nasser of Egypt and which advocated the merger of Syria and Egypt into the United Arab Republic (UAR) in 1958. Like most Syrians, however, Samman lost faith in the union and supported the coup that toppled Nasser and the union authority in September 1961.

In November 1961, Prime Minister Izzat al-Nuss appointed Samman as minister of education in one of the first post-UAR cabinets. Samman's tenure was brief, however, lasting for only one month. In January 1962, he became president of Damascus University. He remained a strong supporter of the post-UAR regime until a military coup ousted it in March 1963.

The Military Committee of the Baath Party that came to power cracked down on all anti-Nasser officials in Syria, but due to Samman's elevated reputation, they refrained from harassing him. Samman remained president of the University until January 1964. He then spent the remainder of his years publishing books and legal studies.

Ahmad al-Samman's published works include *Mujaz fi al-Iqtisad al-Siyasi* (*Concise of Political Economy*), published in three volumes from 1943 to 1947, and *Muhadarat fi Iqtisad al-Souri* (*Lectures in Syrian Economics*), published in 1955. In 1964, Samman's daughter Ghada began to teach at the university, and her father supported her academic and literary career.

Following Ahmad al-Samman's death in 1968, Ghada al-Samman became one of the most prominent female novelists in Syria.

Sources:
Damascus University Catalogue (1996).
Faris, George. *Man Hum fi al-Alam al-Arabi?* (1957).
The International Who's Who in the Arab World (1987-1988).
Itri, Abd al-Ghani. *Hadeeth al-Abqariyyat* (2000).
Samman, Mutih. *Watan wa Askar* (1995).

al-Samman, Wajih
(1913-1992)

Wajih al-Samman studied mathematics at the Sorbonne in Paris and completed his graduate studies in electrical engineering at the Higher Institute of Engineering in France. He graduated in 1937 and began to teach mathematics and physics in Syrian high schools, first in Aleppo, then later in Damascus.

In 1946, Samman was appointed instructor at the Faculty of Engineering in Aleppo University, and in 1947 he became dean of the faculty. In 1951, he became director of the National Tramway and Electricity Company, a public sector enterprise. Samman held this position until Syria and Egypt merged to form the United Arab Republic (UAR) in 1958. In 1957, Samman also became president of the Syrian Union of Scientists and editor of the scientific periodical *Risalat al-`Ulum* (*Message of Sciences*). He held this post until the magazine ceased to print in 1964. President Shukri al-Quwatli also appointed Samman deputy president of the Higher Committee for Economic Development in Syria.

In October 1958, President Gamal Abd al-Nasser created the Ministry of Industry for the UAR and appointed Samman minister. He was the first person to assume the portfolio of industry in Syria and Egypt as well. He remained at this post until September 1960 when he resigned to return to his job in academia. From 1961 to 1968, he taught at Damascus University and published scientific works in the *al-`Ulum* (*Science*) magazine in Lebanon.

Then in 1968, a team of Arab academics voted Samman into the prestigious Arab Language Assemblage. He spent his final years translating technical works on electrical engineering into Arabic. His published works include *Qissat al-Zara* (*The Story of the Atom*), published in 1964, and *Jism al-Insan al-Ajeeb*

(*The Miraculous Human Body*), published in 1976. Several of his books became required reading for baccalaureate students in Syria during the late 1940s and 1950s.

Wajih al-Samman died on August 17, 1992.

Sources:
Faris, George. *Man Hum fi al-Alam al-Arabi?* (1957).
Itri, Abd al-Ghani. *Abqariyyat* (1997).

al-Sayyigh, Fayez
(1922-1980)

Fayez al-Sayyigh studied philosophy at the American University of Beirut (AUB) and graduated in 1941. During his studies, he joined the Syrian Social Nationalist Party (SSNP) and wrote many articles on SSNP ideology in academic journals in the Lebanon and the West.

Sayyigh obtained his MA from AUB in 1945 and taught philosophy until 1947. He then went to Georgetown University for a PhD in philosophy, which he obtained in 1950. From 1950 to 1955, Sayyigh divided his time between Damascus University and AUB, serving as a part-time lecturer at both. He also worked at Stanford University in the United States and Oxford University in Great Britain. One of his earliest books, *Arab Unity: Hope and Fulfillment*, was published while he was teaching at AUB in 1955. The following year he published his second book, *Arab Property in Israeli Occupied Territories*. This volume documented all the occupied land, real estate, and institutions that Israel confiscated in 1948.

In 1955, Fayez al-Sayyigh joined the United Nations and was appointed as a consultant to the UN mission in Yemen. In 1958, he published his book, *Communism in Israel*, one of the earliest works dealing with communist ideology in the Zionist State. He worked with the UN until 1959, when he returned to teach at AUB. Also in 1959, he published his classic work, *Do Jews Have a "Divine Right" to Palestine?*

In the 1960s, Sayyigh was close to the Palestinian Liberation Organization (PLO) and its founder Ahmad al-Shuqayri. In 1964, Shuqayri appointed Sayyigh to the Executive Committee of the PLO and made him director of the Palestinian Research Center in Beirut, the headquarters for Palestinian literature and academics in the 1960s. The center held all documents, maps, and legal papers relating to Palestine prior to the creation of Israel in 1948. In 1968, Sayyigh befriended the new PLO Chairman Yasser Arafat and was voted into the Palestinian National Congress in 1971.

Fayez al-Sayyigh remained an academic working for the Palestinian cause until his death in 1980. Two years after his death, the Israeli Army demolished the Palestinian Research Center he had founded during the Israeli occupation of Beirut in 1982.

Sources:
Bawab, Sulayman. *Mawsuat Alam Souriyya fi al-Qarn al-Ishreen,* Vol III (1999).
Who's Who in the Arab World (1988).

al-Sayyigh, Yusuf
(1916-2004)

Yusuf Sayyigh was born and raised in Damascus. He studied business administration at the American University of Beirut (AUB), obtaining his PhD in political economy from John Hopkins University in 1951.

During the Arab-Israeli War of 1948, Sayyigh served on the Arab Higher Committee Fund for Palestine, a fundraising body created by the Arab League. He joined the Faculty of Economics at AUB in 1953, and became director of its Economic Research Institute, serving until 1959. That same year, Sayyigh became a research associate at the Center for International Affairs at Harvard University in Massachusetts. In 1961, Sayyigh resigned from AUB to teach at Princeton University. In 1964, he became a non-resident economic advisor to the Kuwaiti government.

Sayyigh returned to Lebanon in 1971 and befriended Yasser Arafat, the chairman of the Palestinian Liberation Organization (PLO), who had just set up his military base in Lebanon. That same year, Arafat appointed Sayyigh director of the PLO National Fund. In 1974, he became non-resident consultant for the Organization of Petroleum Exporting Countries (OPEC) in Kuwait. Two years later, Sayyigh was named a non-resident advisor to the Arab Fund for Economic and Social Development, a foundation the Arab League administered in Cairo. In 1979, Sayyigh became an economic advisor to the Arab League, a post he held until 1980. From 1980 until 1984, Sayyigh served as a researcher at St Anthony's College, Oxford University. In 1992, one year after the Madrid Peace Conference, Yasser Arafat delegated him to lead the Palestinian delegation to the multilateral peace talks with Israel concerning economic development of the Palestinian Authority (PA).

During the 1960s, Sayyigh wrote extensively on the region's economic conditions. His most widely acclaimed books are *Economics and the Science of Economics in the Arab World,* published in 1964, and *The Israeli Economy,* published in 1966. In 1968, he wrote his political work, *Strategy for the Liberation of Palestine.* Sayyigh also wrote *Economics of the Arab World,* published in 1982. Then in 1990, he wrote a companion piece to his 1966 work on the Israeli economy called *The Arab Economy: Achievements of the Past and Horizons for the Future.*

Yusuf al-Sayyigh died in May 2004.

Sources:

Bawab, Sulayman. *Mawsuat Alam Souriyya fi al-Qarn al-Ishreen,* Vol III (1999).
Who's Who in the Arab World (1988).

Shakhashiro, Omar
(1908-1977)

Omar Shakhashiro studied literature at Damascus University, graduating in 1932. He taught at local high schools in Damascus, and in 1940 received a graduate degree in French literature from the Sorbonne in Paris. Shakhashiro returned to Syria in 1941 where he taught briefly before moving to Switzerland to acquire his doctorate in French literature from the University of Geneva, graduating in 1949.

In September 1950, Shakhashiro became an assistant professor at Damascus University. In May 1955, he was appointed director of secondary education at the Ministry of Education. Seven years later, Shakhashiro became secretary-general of the Ministry of Education. He also taught French at Damascus University and served on the advisory board of the Faculty of Arts.

In the second half of the 1950s, Shakhashiro joined the movement of Arab nationalism headed by President Gamal Abd al-Nasser of Egypt and supported the Syrian-Egyptian union of 1958. He grew disenchanted with the union, however, due to the dictatorship created by Nasser, and supported the coup d'etat that overthrew the United Arab Republic (UAR) in 1961. He allied himself with Nazim al-Qudsi, the new president of Syria, and in April 1962 became minister of culture and national guidance in the cabinet of Prime Minister Bashir al-Azma. Shakhashiro's tenure as minister, however, was short and he resigned from office in September 1962. He returned to his teaching position at Damascus University where he lectured on French literature and history until his retirement in January 1968.

During his career, Shakhashiro translated many classics from French into Arabic and published several of his own works, both fiction and non-fiction. Among Omar Shakhashiro's most acclaimed translations are *Al-Hub wa al-Gharb* (*Love and the West*), *Al-Haraka al-Nisa'iya wa al-Nahda* (*Feminism and the Renaissance*), and *Al-Mu'alim al-Arabi* (*The Arab Teacher*).

Sources:

Bawab, Sulayman. *Mawsuat A`lam Souriyya fi al-Qarn al-Ishreen,* Vol III (1999).
Samman, Mutih. *Watan wa Askar* (1995).

al-Shatti, Ahmad Shawkat
(1900-1979)

Ahmad Shawkat al-Shatti studied at the Arab Medical Academy and graduated in 1921. He continued his medical training at Montpellier University in France.

In 1924, he returned to Damascus to teach at the newly formed Syrian University and became dean of the Medical School. Along with pioneering educators Munif al-Aidi, Rida al-Sa'id, and Abd al-Rahman Shahbandar, Shatti laid the foundation for a modern university. Together they translated works from Ottoman Turkish into Arabic and designed a unique Syrian curriculum based on European standards.

In 1949, Health Minister Sami Kabbara appointed Shatti secretary-general of the Ministry of Health, a post he kept until 1951. In addition to his teaching career, Shatti wrote articles on genetics for Syrian, Lebanese, and Egyptian medical journals.

During a teaching career that spanned more than forty years, Ahmad Shawkat al-Shatti published forty medical books, the most notable among them being *Ibin Sinna wa Azhar Tubbihi Ala al-Tibb fi al-Alam* (*Avicena and Effects of His Medicine on the World*), published in 1962; *Risala fi Taqaddum al-`Ulum al-Tibbiyya fi al-Bilad al-Arabiyya* (*Dissertation in the Progress of Medical Science in the Arab World*), published in 1963; and *Al-Arab wa al-Tibb* (*The Arabs and Medicine*), published in 1970.

Sources:

Bawab, Sulayman. *Mawsuat Alam Souriyya fi al-Qarn al-Ishreen,* Vol III (1999).
Farfur, Abd al-Latif. *Alam Dimashq* (1987).

al-Tarabulsi, Amjad
(1918-2000)

Amjad al-Tarabulsi studied literature at Damascus University and obtained his graduate degree from the Sorbonne in Paris. In 1935, he began teaching Arabic literature at Syrian high schools and writing poetry for several academic journals in Damascus and Beirut.

In 1944, Tarabulsi joined the elite, all-male high school Al-Tajheez and became prominent among Syrian intellectuals. In 1946, he became an instructor in the Department of Arabic Literature at Damascus University. In 1947, Tarabulsi became vice dean of the university's Faculty of Arts. One year later he was promoted to dean of the faculty and made chairman of the Arabic Literature Department.

In the 1950s, Amjad al-Tarabulsi supported Gamal Abd al-Nasser and taught Arab nationalism to his students. Tarabulsi espoused Nasserist views in discussions with Syrian intellectuals and publicly praised the Syrian-Egyptian union that created the United Arab Republic (UAR) in 1958. In recognition of Tarabulsi's support, Nasser appointed him minister of education for the Northern Province (Syria) of the UAR. In 1959, Tarabulsi assumed the same responsibilities in Cairo. In 1960, a committee of veteran Arab academics voted Tarabulsi into the prestigious Arabic Language Assemblage.

Tarabulsi was forced to retire from government office when the UAR dissolved in September 1961. He resumed his teaching at Damascus University. Until his death, he continued to work as a research affiliate of the Arabic Language Assemblage. He also lectured on Arabic literature in Beirut, Cairo, and to the Arab émigré community in Paris. In 1962, he became a professor of Arabic at the King Mohammad V University in Rabbat, Morocco.

Amjad al-Tarabulsi's most famous work is *Nazra Tareekhiyya fi Harakat al-Talif And al-Arab (A Historical View of the Arab Literary Movement)*, published in 1954.

Sources:

Bawab, Sulayman. *Mawsuat A`lam Souriyya fi al-Qarn al-Ishreen,* Vol III (1999).
Faris, George. *Man Hum fi al-Alam al-Arabi?* (1957).
Itri, Abd al-Ghani. *Alam wa Mubdioun* (1999).

Toemeh, George
(1922-2004)

George Toemeh was born and raised in Damascus. He studied philosophy at the American University of Beirut (AUB) and obtained his PhD in economics from Georgetown University in 1951.

Toemeh returned to Syria to join the Ministry of Foreign Affairs, becoming first secretary to the Syrian Embassy in Great Britain from 1944 to 1946, and assuming the same post in Washington, DC, until 1951. A year later, he became director of the Treaties Department at the Foreign Ministry. In 1954, he moved to Lebanon and taught philosophy at AUB. In 1956, Toemeh became dean of student affairs at AUB, serving in this capacity for one year. In 1957, he returned to Syria and became director of research at the Ministry of Foreign Affairs.

Toemeh advocated pan-Arabist views in the late 1950s and endorsed the Arab nationalism of President Gamal Abd al-Nasser of Egypt. In 1958, Toemeh supported the merger of Syria and Egypt to form the United Arab Republic (UAR). During the union years (1958-1961), President Nasser appointed Toemeh UAR consul to the UN office in New York, a post he held until union was dissolved by military coup in September 1961.

In March 1963, the Baath Party came to power in Syria and Prime Minister

Salah al-Bitar summoned Toemeh back to Syria and appointed him minister of economy. Toemeh held this office for eighteen months before resigning to resume his teaching career at AUB. In 1965, Bitar appointed him as Syria's representative to the General Assembly in New York. Toemeh held this post until 1972 when he resigned from the Ministry of Foreign Affairs and returned to Beirut, working for three years at the Institute of Palestinian Studies (IPS) chaired by Dr Constantine Zurayk. In 1975, Toemeh became advisor to the Organization of Arab Petroleum Exporting Countries (OAPEC) and kept this post until 1980.

Toemeh then became a professor at Kuwait University from 1980 to 1988. He returned to Beirut in 1988 and became the first president of Balamand University, an academic institution founded by the Greek Orthodox Patriarch Ignatius IV Hazeem. Toemeh was succeeded at this post two years later by the Lebanese journalist Ghassan Tweini.

Among Toemeh's published works are *Israel and South Africa: the Unholy Alliance*, published in 1973, and *Immigration or Mobilization* on the Arab-American community in the USA, also published in 1973. He received the Medal of Honor of the Syrian Republic twice, once in 1957 from President Shukri al-Quwatli (Second Class), and again in 1968 from President Nur al-Din al-Atasi (Excellence Class).

George Toemeh died in Amman, Jordan, on April 5, 2004.

Sources:
Bawab, Sulayman. *Mawsuat Alam Souriyya fi al-Qarn al-Ishreen*, Vol III (1999).
The International Who's Who in the Arab World (1987-1988).

Zurayk, Constantine
(1909-2000)

Constantine Zurayk was born and bred in Damascus. He studied history at the American University of Beirut (AUB) and graduated in 1928. He then earned an MA in history fromthe University of Chicago in 1929 and a PhD in philosophy from Princeton University in 1930. During his residence in the United States, he began to write articles on the subject of Arab nationalism. He returned to Beirut and spent the next fifteen years teaching Arab history at AUB.

In 1945, President Shukri al-Quwatli appointed Zurayk senior consultant to the Syrian Embassy in the United States. Zurayk also became a member of Syria's permanent mission to the United Nations. During his time in Washington, the French bombarded Damascus, and along with Ambassador Nazim al-Qudsi, Zurayk served as a liaison officer between President Quwatli and US President Harry Truman.

From May 16, 1945 to May 14, 1952, Zurayk served as a professor and president at Damascus University, but he resigned in protest of President Adid al-Shishakli's decision to send the Syrian Army into the campus to arrest dissident students. Zurayk then returned to Beirut and became acting president of AUB until 1954. From 1956 to 1977, Zurayk taught at AUB and served as a visiting professor at Columbia University in 1965 and Georgetown University in 1977.

In 1963, together with Walid Khalidi, Burhan Dajani, and Sami al-Alami, Zurayk founded the Institute for Palestine Studies (IPS) in Beirut. It was a research and publication center that specialized in the Arab-Israeli conflict, its solutions and aftershocks. The IPS concentrated on formulating a comprehensive solution to the question of Palestine, and promoted the popular trend of Arab nationalism. Zurayk served as chairman of IPS from 1963 until 1984, and opened branches for its academic activities in Paris, London, and Washington.

From 1965 to 1970, Zurayk served as president of the International Syndicate of Universities, an institution based in France. At the time of his death in 2000, Zurayk was serving as honorary president of the International Syndicate of Universities as well as the IPS. Zurayk's writings span four decades and focus on the philosophy of Arab history and its effect on politics and society. He authored numerous books in Arabic including *Al-Wa'i al-Qawmi* (*National Consciousness*), published in 1939; *Nahnu wa al-Tareekh* (*Us and History*), published in 1959; and *Nahnu wa al-Mustaqbal* (*Us and the Future*), published in 1980. Zurayk's work also concentrated on the effect of Arab history on modern times.

Constantinze Zurayk.

The Arab defeat in the Arab-Israeli War of 1948 had a monumental impact on Zurayk's career, and he wrote one of the all-time classics on the war entitled, *Ma'na al-Nakba* (*The Meaning of Catastrophe*). He applied the word *nakba* (disaster) to the Arab defeat of 1948. In 1949, he wrote a book on this military loss. Later, he published a second book, *Ma'na Jadid lil Nakba* (*The New Meaning of the Disaster*), after the Arab-Israeli War of 1967. Zurayk argued that the main question that prevails in the Arab world is how to transform Arab society "from an emotional, whimsical, mythological and poetic society into an active, practical, intellectual and scientific society." Throughout his writings, Zurayk never abandoned the hope that he could spread awareness of the unique Arab identity and the need for all Arabs to unite in order to create a strong and respectable Arab world.

During Zurayk's final years, he continued to lecture, publish books, and write articles for Arab newspapers. He had also begun to gather material for a book on character, collecting writings on civic duty, spirituality, ethics, and manners as seen through the eyes of different Arab and Western philosophers. In June 2000,

AUB honored Zurayk for a lifelong career of achievements. One month later, on August 13, 2000, Zurayk died in Beirut. Zurayk was considered one of the most prominent Arab intellectuals of his generation who inspired the modern movement of Arab nationalism. Upon his passing, AUB said of him, "One of the most memorable characteristic about him is that while he was an intellectual and moral giant of his times, he was always kind and humble. He treated students and interns with the same deference and cordiality as he did world leaders."

Constantine Zurayk was hailed throughout the Arab world—in Syria and Lebanon particularly—as one of the most eminent historians and philosophers of the twentieth century.

Sources:

Arab Organization for Education, Culture, and Science. Constantine Zurayk: *Raid al-Fikr al-Qawmi wa al-Aqlaniyya al-Khulukiyya* (1999).

Atiyyieh. *Arab Civilization: Challenges and Responses: Studies in Honor of Constantine Zurayk* (1988).

Sayyigh, Anees. *Constantine Zurayk: 65 Amman Min al-Ata* (1996).

The International Who's Who in the Arab World (1987-1988).

The Daily Star (August 15, 2000).

A copy of the front page of the newspaper Lisan Al-Hal (Beirut) *from* March 2, 1969, *announcing a mini-coup that anticipated the Corrective Movement 18 months later. Title: "White Coup in Syria. Hafez al-Asad Controls the Situation." Subtitle: "The moderate branch of the Baath overcomes the radical leftist one."*

Al-Ayyam (The Days; *copy of a front page above*) *was the leading mass circulation daily newspaper in Syria from 1932 until the Baath shut down independent publications in 1963. This paper was published by Nasuh Babil, the President of the Syrian Syndicate of Journalists. During the 1930s, Al-Ayyam supported the nationalist leader Dr Abd al-Rahman Shahbandar.*

JOURNALISTS

This chapter explores the lives of leading journalists and publishers of political, cultural, and economic periodicals in the first half of the twentieth century. Most worked in Syria prior to the forced closure of independent political newspapers when the Baath Party came to power in 1963. This chapter also sheds light on Syrian journalists who went abroad after 1963 and established leading magazines and newspapers in the Arab world and Europe.

In the early 1800s, following Napoleon's invasion of Egypt in 1798, French, British, and American missionary schools imported printing presses to Beirut and Cairo, developing Arabic typefaces. The printing presses were originally used for religious materials, but also were made available for secular newspapers. A

Al-Inshaa (The Creation) *was founded in Damascus by Wajih al-Haffar in 1936. It supported the National Bloc against the French and, after independence in 1946, supported President Shukri al-Quwatli.*

pool of skilled labor was supplemented by more sophisticated presses. Beirut and Cairo are the center of Arab printing and journalism to the present day. Syrian journalism was influenced by the rising journalistic movement in Egypt and Beirut from the early 1800s. At the turn of the century the Syrian press was uncensored and thriving. In 1910 in Damascus, Mary Ajamy launched the newspaper *al-Arous (The Bride)*, the first women's publication in the Middle East.

The Ottomans persecuted Syrian journalists for their nationalist views and their liberal outlook on society and religion. Yet the persecution only seemed to encourage Syrian writers and publishers—who continued working with vigor unmatched outside of Beirut and Cairo for the better part of the twentieth century. Even during the French Mandate (1920-1946) and under military regimes in 1949, 1951-1954, and 1958-1961, journalism in Syria was essentially free, although with some restrictions. Syria's tradition of energetic journalism came to an abrupt end when all independent newspapers were outlawed by the Baath Party in 1963. In the fall of 2000, under the new president Bashar al-Asad, however, independent newspapers were once

Al-Nasar (Victory) *was founded and published by Wadih Sidawi in Damascus (1943-1963) to commemorate the Allied victories in Europe during World War II. Al-Nasar supported President Shukri al-Quwatli (1943-1949 and 1955-1958).*

After the Peoples' Party was created in 1948, Al-Shaab (The People) began publication in Aleppo. Al-Shaab rose in importance when People's Party leader Nazim al-Qudsi became prime minister (1949-1951) and was elected president (1961-1963). This issue from August 6, 1951 features an interview with Prime Minister Fares al-Khury (pictured).

Al-Iqtisad wa Annaqel (Economy and Transport) is the first independent business monthly in Syria since 1963. An outspoken magazine, it was established in 2004 by Abdul Salam Haykal, a young entrepreneur, who used Business Week as a model. Haykal, a supporter of the reform process in Syria, was also founder of Syria's first PR agency. The publication quickly won public acclaim for criticizing the country's economic stalemate. Specifically it denounced confused government policy toward foreign investment, calcified state-owned industries, inadequacies of the law and courts, impenetrable bureaucracy, the tradition-bound educational system, and endemic corruption.

The weekly newspaper Ad-Domari *(The Lamplighter) was founded by the political cartoonist Ali Farzat and was one of the most visible products of the short-lived Damascus Spring that followed the inauguration of Bashar al-Asad in July 2000. In February 2001, it launched with two independent issues that won public acclaim before government pressure forced compromises in subsequent issues. During twenty-nine months of tortured existence, it earned the scorn of many Syrians for caving in to the censors. At the same time, it provoked the wrath of government for its criticism of administration policies.*

again legalized. One of the first publications to take advantage of this opportunity was Ad-Domari (The Lamplighter) which was published by the political cartoonist Ali Farzat (see Arts & Letters) from February 2001 until it closed under government pressure in July 2003.

Tishreen (October), *Syria's leading Baath Party daily newspaper, was founded the year after the 1973 October War against Israel. Today* Tishreen *is frequently criticized (even by government officials) for its bland content.*

Under Baath rule, Syrian journalists whose work was restricted within Syria were often allowed to get their message to a Syrian audience through a circuitous route. The journalists ran articles in pan-Arab dailies (such as *Al-Hayat*) based in Beirut or London. These publications were then circulated in Syria under the careful eyes of the government-operated distribution agency. Although Baath leaders deprived Syrians of the protection of a free press, they were quick to use the free international press in their own defense. One example is especially colorful: In November 1986 a Syrian agent (who may have been a double agent controlled by the Mossad) was convicted of smuggling a bomb aboard an Israeli airliner at Heathrow. Hafez al-Asad feared military retaliation by Israel, the US, Britain—or all three. He realized that he had no military answer. Yet he did have some secret information given him by his Iranian allies. Asad fed facts about US-Israeli arms sales to Iran to the small Lebanese daily *As-Shira*, sparking the Iran-Contra scandal and successfully deflecting US pressure.

Censorship of the Syrian press under Bashar al-Asad has relaxed more than at any time since 1963. In another sign of change, Syrian journalists writing for publication abroad are monitored but not harassed—even when criticizing the government in harsh terms.

Abd Rabbo, Yasser
(1932-)

Yasser Abd Rabbo was born and raised in Damascus. He studied at the Journalism Academy in Cairo and graduated in 1954. He began writing for the popular Damascus daily *al-Ayyam* in 1955. His mentor was Nasuh Babil, publisher of *al-Ayyam* and president of the Syndicate of Syrian Journalists.

Abd Rabbo wrote for *al-Ayyam* from 1955 to 1958 and became famous in Damascus when he interviewed President Shukri al-Quwatli upon his election to office in September 1955. When Syria and Egypt merged to form the United Arab Republic (UAR) in 1958, Abd Rabbo was critical of the policies of Interior Minister Abd al-Hamid Sarraj. Abd Rabbo fled Syria before Sarraj ordered his

Yasser Abd Rabbo.

arrest and went to Kuwait, where in 1961, he headed a daily called *al-Ra'e al-Am*. In 1965, he went to Lebanon and worked for the daily *al-Kifah*. In 1969, the newspaper publisher, Riyad Taha, sent him to Libya as a correspondent for *al-Kifah*. There, on September 1, 1969, Colonel Mu'ammar al-Qaddafi came to power, toppling the regime of the aged and ailing King Idris. Abd Rabbo hailed the Libyan Revolution and helped promote Qaddafi in the Arab media. He became a media favorite in Tripoli and a frequent guest of the Libyan leader. In October 1969, Abd Rabbo was the first Arab journalist to interview Qaddafi. In September 1970, the name Abd Rabbo was so famous that a Palestinian fugitive, Adib Kirki from Nablus, used it on a fake passport to escape from Jordan to Syria. Since Abd Rabbo had conducted an interview with the late King Hussein of Jordan, the journalist's name was famous in political circles in Amman, ensuring the Palestinian a safe escape route to the Jordanian-Syrian border. Subsequently, the Palestinian exile, who became minister of information under President Yasser Arafat, was also known by the nom de guerre, Yasser Abd Rabbo. When the Palestinian Liberation Organization (PLO) was headquartered in Beirut, it instructed Talal Salman, owner of the Beirut daily, *al-Safir*, to refrain from using the name Adib Kirki and officially replace it with Yasser Abd Rabbo.

In 1974, the real Yasser Abd Rabbo directed the Lebanese weekly *al-Usbu' al-Arabi*. Two years later, in 1976, the journalist Nabil Khury invited Abd Rabbo to Europe to work in the newly established magazine *al-Mustaqbal*. Abd Rabbo worked in *al-Mustaqbal* from its founding in 1976 until it closed for financial reasons in 1989. During this time, he wrote extensively on pan-Arab affairs. He was highly critical of Egyptian President Anwar al-Sadat following his visit to Jerusalem in 1977 and the 1978 signing of the Camp David Peace Accord with Israel. As a result, Sadat forbad Abd Rabbo from entering Egypt.

In 1993, Yasser Abd Rabbo founded his own magazine, a Paris-based monthly publication, *al-Shahr*, where he served as editor-in-chief until his retirement in 1997. His son, Waddah Abd Rabbo, also followed a career in journalism and is currently editor-in-chief of *al-Shahr*.

Sources:
Al-Bayan (February 5, 2003).

Ahmad, Ahmad Iskandar (1944-1983): see "Politicians"

Ajamy, Mary
(1888-1965)

Mary Ajamy was born to a Greek Orthodox family and raised in Damascus. She studied nursing at the American University of Beirut (AUB) and graduated in 1906. During her studies at AUB, Ajamy served as a visiting high school teacher in Zahle. In 1908, she became a teacher in Port Said, Egypt, and in 1909 she moved to Alexandria. She then returned to Syria and began to teach English at the Russian missionary school in Damascus.

Meanwhile, Ajamy served as a freelance journalist for Muhammad Kurd Ali's weekly newspaper, *al-Muqtabas*, writing on various social and political affairs. In 1910, she founded her own journal, *al-`Arus (The Bride)*—the first publication in Syria to advocate women's rights. Ajamy served as editor-in-chief and employed a small number of educated Syrian girls on its editorial board, most of whom wrote under false names to avoid recognition and harassment in their male-dominated society. Ajamy's opening editorial in the first edition of *al-`Arus* became the manifesto for Syria's emerging feminist movement. It read, "To those who believe that in the spirit of women is the strength to kill the germs of corruption, and that in her hand is the weapon to rend the gloom of oppression, and in her mouth the solace to lighten human misery." For the next four years, she raised funds for the journal's publication and turned it into one of the highest quality periodicals in the Arab world.

The journal was an enormous success among Syria's educated elite, especially women. But conservative Muslims fiercely condemned it and demanded its abolition. Her journal ceased publication during World War I (1914-1918), but resumed in 1919. In 1920, religious leaders demanded that Ajamy be brought to court on the charge of promoting heresy for writing an article in favor of civil marriage. During the war, Ajamy had written editorials for the Egyptian newspaper, *al-Ahrar (Free Patriots)*, and *al-Islah (Reform)*, an Arabic newspaper in Buenos Aries. Her opposition to the Ottoman Empire increased when her fiancé, the *al-Arus* correspondent in Beirut, was executed in 1915 for criticizing the military regime of Sultan Mohammad Rashad V.

In 1920, following the collapse of the Ottoman Empire, Ajamy spearheaded the women's rights movement in Damascus, petitioning the Syrian National Congress to grant suffrage to women. She met with King Faysal I, the first post-Ottoman ruler of Syria, for that purpose and wrote extensively on the role of women in rebuilding post-war societies. Also in 1920, Ajamy established the Women's Literary Club with a group of prominent Damascene ladies and founded an intellectual salon at her home. Her forum met on a weekly basis to discuss politics, philosophy, and religious affairs, and was attended by prominent Syrian personalities such as the nationalist leaders Faris al-Khury and Fakhri al-Barudi. Many women were also regular visitors to the salon, engaging in intense and spirited debates with men—up to that time an unheard-of act in Syria. In Ajamy's own words, the forum was aimed at "reviving the female intelligentsia."

From 1918 to 1920, Ajamy headed the Christian Women's Club, an organization with branches in Damascus and Beirut aimed at promoting Arabism among Christians. In the 1920s, Mary Ajamy contributed to *Noor al-Fayha* (*The Light of Damascus*), a newspaper founded in 1919 by Naziq al-Abid, another leader of the feminist movement in Syria. In 1921, Ajamy became director of the Martyr's School in Beirut. She lived in Lebanon for one year, lecturing on women's rights, motherhood, and nation-building. In 1926, having run out of funds, she ceased the publication of *al-`Arus*. In 1940, she became a high school instructor in Iraq, living in Baghdad until the French ended their mandate in Syria in 1946. Ajamy devoted the remainder of her years to charity organizations and died on December 25, 1965.

Among Mary Ajamy's published works are *Al-Majdaliyya al-Hasna'* (*The Beautiful Magdalene*), published in 1913; and *Mukhtarat Min al-Shi'r* (*Selected Poems*), published in 1944.

Sources:
Jeha, Michel. *Mary Ajamy* (2001).
Kayyali, Sami. *Al-Adab al-Arabi al-Mouasir fi Souriyya 1850-1950* (1968).
Sakakini, Widad. *Sabiqat al-Asr* (1986).
Thompson, Elizabeth. *Colonial Citizens* (1999).

al-Armanazi, Ali
(1894-1915)

Ali al-Armanazi was born and raised in Damascus. He studied at the Ottoman Law Academy and established a legal practice in Istanbul. In 1908, a military coup d'etat took place in Istanbul, bringing to power a group of Ottoman officers called the Committee for Union and Progress (CUP). They curbed the powers of Sultan Abdulhamid II, calling for political reforms, and lifted the strict press censorship laws that been in place for thirty years.

As a result, Armanazi established his own newspaper in 1912, called *al-`Asi* (*The Orontos River*). It started out as a pro-CUP publication but became critical of CUP policies when the Ottoman officers forced Abdulhamid II to abdicate in 1909. In 1913, the CUP rigged the parliamentary elections in Istanbul and arrested hundreds of disgruntled subjects for expressing their desire of limited autonomy. Armanazi was particularly critical of Jamal Pasha, the military governor of Syria, who replaced all senior Arab bureaucrats with Ottoman officials and enforced the Ottoman Turkish language at Arabic high schools. By 1914, Armanazi's newspaper had achieved prominence as one of the most outspoken publications in the Ottoman Empire, and was particularly popular in Damascus and Beirut. Often, Armanazi would lament the days of former Sultan Abdulhamid, claiming that he had been more sensitive to Arab needs than the current sultan, Mohammad Rashad V.

In May 1915, Jamal Pasha had Ali al-Armanazi arrested, tried by a military tribunal in Aley on Mount Lebanon, convicted of treason, and executed in Beirut on August 21, 1915.

Sources:

Elias, Joseph. *Tatawur al-Sahafa al-Souriyya fi al-Ahd al-Uthmani* (1972).
Rifaii, Shams al-Din. *Tareekh al-Sahafa al-Souriyya 1800-1947* (1969).
Uthman, Hashim. *Al-Sahafa al-Souriyya: Madiha wa Hadiruha* (1997).

Arna'out, Ma'ruf
(1892-1948)

Ma'ruf Arna'out grew up in Beirut to an Albanian family. He studied at the Ottoman Islamic Academy in Beirut and began his career in 1912 by writing for several Beirut-based newspapers. He published weekly editorials in *al-Balagh* (*The Declaration*) and *al-Ra'e al-Am* (*Public Opinion*). In 1914, he was conscripted into the Ottoman Army at the outbreak of World War I.

Ama'out served in the armed forces during the first two years of the war, then defected into the Arab underground in 1916 and joined the rebel forces of Sharif Husayn, the Prince of Mecca. Arna'out became an officer in Husayn's Arab Army and helped liberate Damascus from Ottoman control in October 1918. That December, he returned to journalism and launched his own newspaper, *al-Istiqlal al-Arabi* (*Arab Independence*). The publication ran short of money and went out of business in 1920. In March 1919, Ama'out wrote the play, *Jamal Pasha al-Saffah* (*Jamal Pasha the Butcher*)—staged and directed by actor and director Abd al-Wahab Abu Saud. It was the first staged political production in Syria, mocking the dictatorship of the Ottoman Empire. In 1920, Ama'out launched *Fata al-Arab* (*Arab Youth*), a four-page political daily that became an instant hit and remained in print until 1948.

In July 1920, France imposed her mandate over Syria, and Arna'out joined the nationalist movement, demanding an end to French influence in the Middle East. In 1928, Arna'out transformed *Fata al-Arab* into a mouthpiece for the National Bloc, the leading anti-French movement in Syria. He called for the liberation of Syria from French control through diplomatic means rather than armed resistance.

In 1930, a committee of veteran Arab academics voted Ama'out into the prestigious Arab Language Assemblage, the highest international scientific authority in the field of Arab language and literature. He remained an active member, conducting research and writing poetry, until his death in 1948.

In 1929, Arna'out published his classic book, *Sayyed Quraysh* (*The Master of Quraysh*). In 1943, he began writing a book called *al-Qahira* (*Cairo*), but died before it was completed. In 1932, Ma'ruf Arna'out published in Beirut his only romantic novel entitled, *Ala Difaf al-Bosfor* (*On the Banks of the Bosfor*).

Sources:
Elias, Joseph. *Tatawur al-Sahafa al-Souriyya fi al-Ahd al-Uthmani* (1972).
Itri, Abd al-Ghani. *Abqariyyat wa Alam* (1996).
Kayyali, Sami. *Al-Adab al-Arabi al-Mouasir fi Souriyya 1850-1950* (1968).
Rifaii, Shams al-Din. *Tareekh al-Sahafa al-Souriyya 1800-1947* (1969).

Babil, Nasuh
(1905-1986)

Nasuh Babil began his career at The Government Publishing Agency in Damascus. He was an early member of the People's Party, the first political machine in Syria led by Dr Abd al-Rahman Shahbandar. The party called for emancipation from French rule imposed on Syria in 1920 and the creation of an Arab kingdom under the Hashemite crown.

In 1932, Babil bought the politically outspoken newspaper, *al-Ayyam* (*The Days*), from its owner Yusuf al-Issa and put Shahbandar in charge. Babil firmly believed in Shahbandar's cause: termination of the French Mandate, strengthened ties with the Hashemite monarchs in Amman and Baghdad, and the creation of a modern, democratic state in Syria based on the British model. From 1936 to 1939, Shahbandar clashed with Prime Minister Jamil Mardam Bey, who refused to grant Shahbandar a permit to operate a political party in Syria. Babil declared a war of words on the Syrian prime minister, accusing him of despotism.

In 1937, masked gunmen tried to assassinate Jamil Mardam Bey. Authorities accused Shahbandar and Babil of attempted murder and ordered their arrest. Investigations proved them innocent, however, and they were released but placed under surveillance. In July 1940, agents of the French Mandate assassinated Shahbandar. Without his leadership, the People's Party crumbled.

Babil, a seasoned journalist, shifted his allegiance to the National Bloc, the leading anti-French movement in Syria that had been Shahbandar's archenemy in the 1930s. Babil became a board member of the National Cement Company and the National Conserves Company (dried fruits and vegetables), two industrial enterprises owned and operated by the National Bloc.

Babil allied himself with Shukri al-Quwatli, the most prominent Bloc leader, who was elected president in the summer of 1943. Through his alliance with

Quwatli, Babil rose to paramount fame in Damascus. With Quwatli's blessing, Babil was voted president of the Syndicate of Syrian Journalists, holding this position from 1943 until 1963. Babil managed to remain on good terms with all of the eight consecutive regimes that came to power during those twenty years. Throughout this period, *al-Ayyam* remained the mass circulation daily of Damascus. In February 1954, Babil teamed up with four leading journalists and created a shareholding company to print Syria's four principal newspapers, *al-Ayyam*, *al-Qabas*, *Alif Ba'*, and *al-Sham*. The journalists pledged to unite their efforts to publish the four newspapers and divide the revenue equally among themselves.

Babil became president of the company's board, but the enterprise operated for less than one year due to disagreements among its founders, and the company was dissolved in November 1954. In 1955, Babil founded the Lion's Club in Syria and became president. In 1956, President Quwatli declared an "Arms Week" to raise funds for arms purchases in preparation for an expected war between Egypt and Israel. Quwatli donated a two-month salary for the purpose and so did Babil. The Syrian president appointed Babil secretary of "Arms Week" and charged him with collecting donations from the public.

In February 1958, Babil supported Syria's merger with Egypt to form the United Arab Republic (UAR), but he quickly lost faith in the union and praised the coup that ended the UAR in September 1961. Babil believed that President Gamal Abd al-Nasser of Egypt mishandled the union by appointing corrupt officials to administer Syria's affairs. Babil joined a group of disenchanted politicians in drafting a declaration that criticized Nasser for having established a dictatorship in Syria. In March 1963, the Military Committee of the Baath Party came to power and pledged to restore the UAR. Babil suffered the termination of his civil rights and the permanent shutdown of *al-Ayyam*. He was also fired from his job as president of the Syndicate of Syrian Journalists and spent the remainder of his years in retirement.

Nasuh Babil's memoirs, *Sahafa wa Siyasa fi Souriyya* (*Journalism and Politics in Syria*), were published in 1987 and became an instant classic on the modern history of Syria.

Sources:

Babil, Nasuh. *Sahafa wa Siyasa fi Souriyyia* (1987).

Barada (March 24, 1963).

Faris, George. *Man Hum Fi al-`Alam al-Arabi* (1957).

Handwritten documents by Nasuh Babil, presented by his son Marwan Babil to the author on May 6, 1999.

Uthman, Hashim. *Al-Sahafa al-Souriyya: Madiha wa Hadiruha* (1997).

Fansa, Nazir
(1918-2005)

Nazir Fansa was born in Aleppo. From 1940 to 1949, he worked as a journalist for the daily newspaper *Alif Ba'e*. (The publication was run by his older brother Bashir Fansa.) In 1949, General Husni al-Za'im, a relative of Fansa's through marriage, came to power and ousted the regime of President Shukri al-Quwatli. Fansa joined Za'im's political office and became his private advisor and bureau chief.

Za'im delegated Fansa to garner support for the new regime, a difficult task since the Za'im regime was seen as illegitimate by most of Syria's Arab neighbors. But, in April 1949, Fansa orchestrated an alliance between Husni al-Za'im and King Farouk of Egypt. He also visited King Abd al-Aziz and secured financial assistance from Saudi Arabia for Syria's new regime. He attempted similar missions in Baghdad and Beirut, both unsuccessful.

In July 1949, Fansa quarreled with Za'im when the latter extradited Antune Sa'ada, the leader of the Syrian Social Nationalist Party (SSNP), from Lebanon. Fansa warned Za'im that Sa'ada's death would bring about his rapid downfall. When Za'im was overthrown and killed in August 1949, Fansa was arrested. But, unlike Za'im, Fansa escaped execution by coming to terms with the coup mastermind, General Sami al-Hinnawi.

In 1950, along with ex-Prime Minister Husni al-Barazi, Nazir Fansa founded the newspaper, *al-Nass (The People)*. In the 1950s, *al-Nass* emerged as a leading anti-communist and pro-American publication, supporting the Baghdad Pact and the Eisenhower Doctrine. Fansa then launched another newspaper called *al-Anbaa (News)*. In 1955, Fansa worked as an intermediary between Chief-of-Staff Shawkat Shuqayr and Dr Fadil al-Jamali, the prime minister of Iraq, who was seeking military allies to topple the pro-Nasser government in Syria. Their alliance collapsed, however, when Shuqayr was replaced as chief of staff by the politically independent General Tawfiq Nizam al-Din. When Syria and Egypt merged to form the United Arab Republic (UAR) in 1958, Fansa went to Tehran to establish the first Arabic speaking newspaper in Iran, also becoming advisor on Arab affairs to Shah Rida Pehlavi. In 1968, the regime of Salah Jadid revoked Fansa's Syrian nationality, only to be restored by President Hafez al-Asad after he came to power in 1970. Shortly before the Iranian Revolution in 1979, Nazir Fansa left Iran for exile in Paris where he wrote books about Syria, including a notable biography of Husni al-Za'im, published in 1982.

Sources:

Fansa, Bashir. *Al-Naqbat wa al-Mughamarat* (1997).
Fansa, Nazir. *137 Yawm Hazzat Souriyya* (1982).

Faris, George. *Man Hum fi al-`Alam al-Arabi?* (1957).
Rathmell, Andrew. *Secret War in the Middle East* (1995).

Faris, George
(1905-?)

George Faris studied engineering at Jesuit University in Beirut and began his career in 1928 teaching French at high schools in Lebanon.

From 1927 to 1929, Faris wrote for the French-speaking dailies *L'Orient* and *La Syrie*. In 1930, he became the advisor on Syrian affairs to the Iranian Consulate in Damascus. In 1936, he ran for parliament as a deputy for Damascus but lost the elections. In 1943, he nominated himself again, but lost again. In 1937, he worked for the Arab News Agency in Syria. From 1939 to 1947, Faris worked as a Damascus correspondent for Reuters News Agency. In 1941, he became secretary of the Syndicate of Syrian Journalists. In December 1945, along with the journalist Munir al-Rayyes, Faris founded the newspaper, *Barada*, and served as its editor until November 1947.

One year later, during the height of the Arab-Israeli War of 1948, Faris launched a pan-Arab newspaper from Damascus called *al-Wihda al-Arabiyya (Arab Unity)*. His newspaper was closed by General Husni al-Za'im, who came to power in March 1949 and outlawed most political publications. In the summer of 1949, Faris founded a French daily in Damascus called *La Voix de Syrie (The Voice of Syria)* and established the Center for Arab and Syrian Studies. The center was a pioneering political research institute aimed at documenting the modern history of Syria from late Ottoman times until the present. The center issued a monthly newsletter of media highlights and another newsletter covering economic developments in Syria.

From 1950 to 1955, George Faris served as secretary at the Iranian Embassy in Damascus. He also published many books, the first being *Damas*, written in French in 1933, and *Man Hum fi al-`Alam al-Arabi? (Who are They in the Arab World?)*, written in two editions, one published in 1949 and the other in 1957.

Sources:
Faris, George. *Man Hum fi al-`Alam al-Arabi?* (1957).

al-Haffar, Wajih
(1912-1969)

Wajih al-Haffar was born and raised in Damascus. He studied law at Jesuit University in Beirut and began his journalistic career in 1932, working for the popular daily *al-Qabas (The Firebrand)*.

In 1936, at the age of twenty-four, Haffar founded his own daily in Damascus, entitled *al-Inshaa (Creation)*. The newspaper was funded and co-administered by his cousin, Lutfi al-Haffar, a prominent politician and member of the National Bloc, the leading anti-French movement in Syria.

Wajih al-Haffar joined his cousin and oriented his newspaper to serve as a propaganda outlet for the Damascus leadership of the National Bloc. In return, the Bloc sponsored *al-Inshaa* throughout the 1930s. In 1939, Lutfi al-Haffar became prime minister of Syria, and *al-Inshaa* was transformed into the official mouthpiece of the Haffar government. In 1943, *al-Inshaa* backed the election of Shukri al-Quwatli as president of Syria. In March 1949, a military coup took place in Damascus, launched by General Husni al-Za'im, who arrested Quwatli and all of his supporters. *Al-Inshaa* was closed and Wajih al-Haffar spent the four months of Za'im's era behind bars. His cousin Lutfi was placed under house arrest.

In August 1949, Za'im was toppled by another coup and Haffar was released by General Sami al-Hinnawi, the new strongman of Syria. In 1951, Haffar was arrested again for defying the regime of President Adib al-Shishakli. In February 1954, he teamed up with four leading journalists and created a shareholding company to print Syria's four principal newspapers, *al-Qabas*, *al-Ayyam*, *Alif Ba'e*, and *al-Sham*. The journalists pledged to unite their efforts to publish the four big newspapers and divide the revenue equally among themselves. Haffar became treasurer of the company, but the enterprise worked for less than one year due to disagreements among its founders. It was dissolved in November 1954.

In March 1963, the Military Committee of the Baath Party came to power, permanently outlawing Haffar's paper and abrogating his civil rights. Wajih al-Haffar fled to Saudi Arabia where he spent the remainder of his years in retirement. He wrote a book, *al-Mamlaka al-Mutahida (The United Kingdom)*, published in 1947; and another, *Al-Dustur wa al-Hukom (Constitution and Government)*, published in 1948.

Sources:
Faris, George. *Man Hum fi al-`Alam al-Arabi?* (1957).
Uthman, Hashim. *Al-Sahafa al-Souriyya: Madiha wa Hadiruha* (1997).

al-Hakim, Nazih
(1921-1993)

Nazih al-Hakim studied law at Damascus University and graduated in 1942. He joined the Ministry of Foreign Affairs and in 1947 became consul to Istanbul. In 1951, his long-time friend, Adib al-Shishakli, came to power in Syria and appointed Hakim as private advisor at the Presidential Palace.

Hakim was responsible for promoting Shishakli's public image, relying on the radio to bring Shishakli's inflammatory speeches into every home across Syria. Hakim designed a media plan that involved plastering the new president's photograph everywhere in Syria's main cities. Shishakli's actions, speeches, and decrees received more publicity than any other leader before him.

In 1952, Hakim published his own pro-Shishakli newspaper, *al-Ra'e al-Am* (*Public Opinion*). This paper closed when Shishakli fell from power in February 1954. The publication was administered by Hakim and two other journalists, Ahmad `Usseh and Qadri al-Qal'aji. The post-Shishakli regime refused to deal with Hakim, for he was too closely associated with the former dictator. This refusal effectively forced him into early retirement.

Hakim moved to Lebanon and then Egypt, becoming a supporter of President Gamal Abd al-Nasser. In 1962, eight years after the Shishakli era, Hakim returned to Syria and established a pro-Nasser newspaper, *al-Wihda al-Arabiyya* (*Arab Unity*). Media officials in Syria accused him of being an agent of Nasser and of receiving funds from Cairo, but he ignored the rumors and continued to defend his pro-Nasser views until the Baath Party came to power in March 1963, when the government closed all political newspapers.

Nazih al-Hakim went to Lebanon, but in 1969, joined the translation department at the United Nations in New York. He died in the United States on November 23, 1993.

Sources:
Itri, Abd al-Ghani. *Abqariyyat wa Alam* (1996).

al-Halabi, Tawfiq
(1887-1926)

Tawfiq al-Halabi was born and raised in Damascus. In 1910, he founded the first satirical publication in Syria, a weekly magazine entitled *al-Rawi* (*The Storyteller*) that was critical of the Ottoman Empire and its treatment of Arab subjects.

Al-Rawi mocked the Ottoman administration and criticized Ottoman intervention in World War I. The Ottomans, Halabi claimed, were forcing the Arabs to fight a war that did not concern them, adding that the central government in Istanbul should cease the conscription of Arab cadets into the Ottoman Army.

In 1913, Halabi signed a famed declaration presented to the first Arab Congress in Paris demanding Syrian emancipation from the Ottoman Empire. In May 1916, he intensified his criticism of Ottoman policies when Jamal Pasha, the military governor of Syria, executed twenty-one leading political activists in Damascus and Beirut. Halabi published a lengthy article accusing the military governor of mass murder and labeling him "Jamal Pasha the Butcher."

Hours after the article was released on May 7—and only twenty-four hours after the Marjeh Square executions—Halabi fled Damascus, joining the rebel army of Prince Faysal in Mecca. He took part in the brewing Arab Revolt against the Ottoman Empire and served as an officer in Faysal's army. Meanwhile, Halabi continued to write articles under pen names for numerous Arab newspapers, reporting on conditions at the war front.

Following the Ottoman defeat in October 1918, Halabi returned to Damascus with Faysal and relaunched *al-Rawi*. He became one of the country's most prominent journalists during the years of Faysal's rule (1918-1920). When the French proclaimed their mandate over Syria in 1920, they sentenced Halabi to death, but he escaped into exile in Jordan.

Halabi lived in Amman for five years, serving as advisor to Faysal's brother, King Abdullah, and returned to Syria in disguise to take part in a military uprising against the French in 1925. The revolt was launched by the Druze leader Sultan al-Atrash and funded by the Hashemite royals in Mecca and Amman. In 1926, Tawfiq al-Halabi died in combat and French soldiers purposely mutilated his corpse.

Sources:
Bawab, Sulayman. *Mawsuat Alam Souriyya fi al-Qarn al-Ishreen,* Vol II (1999).
Elias, Joseph. *Tatawur al-Sahafa al-Souriyya fi al-Ahd al-Uthmani* (1972).
Kawtharani, Wajih. *Wathaiq al-Mutamar al-Arabi al-Awal* (1980).
Rifaii, Shams al-Din. *Tareekh al-Sahafa al-Souriyya 1800-1947* (1969).

Husriyyieh, Izzat
(1914-1975)

Izzat Husriyyieh studied at the Higher Arab Academy for Translation. In 1932, he began to write a weekly column for the daily, *al-Sha'b* (*The People*). One year later, he co-founded the Syrian Labor Union in Damascus and helped establish branches in Aleppo, Homs, and Hama.

In 1936, Husriyyieh allied himself with Dr Abd al-Rahman Shahbandar, leader of the Syrian opposition to the National Bloc regime of President Hashim al-Atasi. Shahbandar and Husriyyieh spoke out against the Franco-Syrian Treaty that Atasi had signed in Paris in 1936 that promised Syrian independence from France over a twenty-five year period.

Husriyyieh argued that the National Bloc had given too many concessions to the French, including the right to maintain military bases in Syria for use in the event of war in Europe. Jamil Mardam Bey, the architect of the 1936 treaty who had become prime minister shortly after that, closed *al-Sha`b* and placed Husriyyieh under 24-hour surveillance. Husriyyieh retaliated by issuing a secret pamphlet entitled *al-Istifham* (*Question Mark*) that criticized the National Bloc and its entire leadership, accusing them of establishing a dictatorship in Syria.

In 1942, following the death of Shahbandar, Husriyyieh joined *al-Istiqlal al-Arabi* (*Arab Independence*), another anti-Bloc publication, and served as its editor-in-chief. In May 1944, Izzat Husriyyieh founded his own evening newspaper in Damascus called *al-'Ilm* (*Science*), becoming editor-in-chief. When the Bloc achieved Syrian independence in 1946, Husriyyieh softened his criticism of them and allied himself with the Bloc's successor, the National Party. From 1944 to 1947, his career was supported by Prime Minister Saadallah

Izzat Husriyyeh.

al-Jabiri, a patron of *al-'Ilm* until his death in 1947. In the 1940s, Husriyyieh wrote for the popular Damascus daily, *al-Qabas* (*The Firebrand*). When Syria and Egypt merged to form the United Arab Republic (UAR) in February 1958, he criticized the military dictatorship of President Gamal Abd al-Nasser and hailed the coup that ousted the union in September 1961. From 1961 to 1963, he allied himself with the post-Nasser government of President Nazim al-Qudsi, who like Husriyyieh, had supported Shahbandar during his youth. In March 1963, the Military Committee of the Baath Party came to power and pledged to restore the UAR. The officers closed Husriyyieh's newspaper, terminated his civil rights, and forced him into retirement.

Husriyyieh remained in Syria and worked until 1970 as a publisher without writing any articles in the press. He also worked with an excavation team to renovate historical sites in Damascus. He co-founded a committee to help protect the old quarters of the Syrian capital and set up another committee to monitor human rights issues in Syrian prisons. Izzat Husriyyieh died in Damascus on November 4, 1975.

Sources:
Faris, George. *Man Hum fi al-'Alam al-Arabi?* (1957).
Itri, Abd al-Ghani. *Alam wa Mubdioun* (1999).
Uthman, Hashim. *Al-Sahafa al-Souriyya: Madiha wa Hadiruha* (1997).

al-Itri, Abd al-Ghani
(1919-2003)

Abd al-Ghani al-Itri began his journalistic career in 1941 by writing for the Cairo-based magazine *al-Risala* (*The Letter*). He submitted articles to the Beiruti periodical, *al-Makshouf* (*The Unrevealed*), and in October 1941 founded his own literary magazine in Damascus called *al-Sabah* (*The Morning*). At the time, he was only twenty-two years old.

Itri attracted other young writers to contribute their work, including the then-young and unknown poet Nizar Qabbani. Within one year of its launch, the magazine started to attract prominent literary names like the poet Shafiq Jabri and the novelist Abd al-Salam al-Ujayli. The publication was closed in 1943 and Itri began work for the journalist Bassim Murad in the Damascus daily, *al-Akhbar* (*The News*). Two years later, in March 1945, Itri established another weekly, entitled *al-Dunya* (*The World*). It was one of the earliest color magazines in Syria. Also in 1945, he took part in literary programs on different Palestinian radio stations in Haifa, Jaffa, and Tel Aviv.

In 1947, Itri became a member of the Damascus-based Syrian Association of Satirists. He managed to remain on cordial terms with all of the consecutive regimes that came to power from 1949 to 1958, yet he spoke out against the Syrian-Egyptian union of Gamal Abd al-Nasser (1958-1961). He was opposed to giving the Egyptians a dominant role in Syrian affairs and criticized the police state that Interior Minister Abd al-Hamid Sarraj created in Syria (with the direct backing of Nasser). As a result, Itri's magazine was closed in 1960, and he was arrested. He spent most of the years of the United Arab Republic (UAR) in prison and was released when the union was dissolved by military coup in 1961.

Itri took a radical anti-union stance in his articles and supported the civilian government of Nazim al-Qudsi (1961-1963) that worked to revoke all of Nasser's measures. In March 1963, *al-Dunya* was once again outlawed, however, when the Baath Party came to power and pledged to restore the UAR. Itri went to Saudi Arabia, serving as editor of official publications issued by the Ministry of Information from 1963 to 1965. He also became a consultant to Jamil Juhaylan, the Saudi minister of information, and wrote for the Saudi newspaper, *al-Nadwa* (*The Synopsis*). Itri returned to Syria in 1968 and began writing books on Damascus, the art of journalism, and a five-part biography, *Abqariyyat* (*Geniuses*). This latter work dealt with Syria civilian leaders who held office prior to the military regime of 1963.

Among the leaders Itri eulogized were former presidents Shukri al-Quwatli and Hashim al-Atasi, and former prime ministers Khalid al-Azm and Sabri al-Asali. In the 1990s, Itri began to lecture in Damascus and write weekly columns for the state-run daily, *Tishreen*. In 2000, under the government of President Bashar al-Asad, Itri applied for a license to relaunch *al-Dunya*. He received "positive indicators" from Information Minister Adnan Umran, and prior to his death in an automobile accident in February 2003, Itri was preparing to restart the magazine forty years after its initial closure.

Among Abd al-Ghani al-Itri's published works are *Adabuna al-Dahek* (*Our Humoristic Literature*), published in 1970; and *'Itirafat Shami Ateek* (*Confessions of a Traditional Damascene*), published in 1998.

Sources:
Faris, George. *Man Hum fi al-Alam al-Arabi?* (1957).
Itri , Abd al-Ghani. *Abqariyyat wa Alam* (1996).
Interview with Abd al-Ghani al-Itri (Damascus August 8, 2001).

Kabbara, Sami (1903-1967): see "Politicians"

Kahaleh, Habib
(1898-1965)

Habib Kahaleh was born in Damascus and studied at the American University of Beirut (AUB). In 1919, at the age of twenty-one, he founded *Souriyya al-Jadida* (*The New Syria*), a political daily that enjoyed modest circulation in Damascus.

Kahaleh was a supporter of the Hashemite family of Arabia and called for the creation of a united Arab world under the crown of either King Husayn of Mecca or his son, King Faysal of Syria. In 1929, following the downfall of both monarchs, Kahaleh transformed his newspaper into the famed weekly magazine, *al-Mudhiq al-Mubki* (*Comic and Tragic*). The magazine consisted of weekly cartoons mocking events and local leaders, both those in the national movement and those working for the French Mandate authority in Syria. Kahaleh drew most of the magazine's cartoons and became famous for his sharp criticism. In 1936, he launched another weekly, *al-Musawwir* (*The Photographer*).

From 1923 to 1925, Kahaleh served as a parliamentary deputy in Damascus. He was closely allied to the National Bloc, the leading anti-French movement in Syria that his in-law, Faris al-Khury, had co-founded in 1928. He was related to Khury by marriage: his daughter had married Khury's son Suhayl. Habib Kahaleh was one of the most prominent and popular journalists in Syria. In June 1930, his magazine was closed for depicting a caricature of pro-French ministers in Syria singing the French national anthem *La Marseillaise* instead of patriotic Syrian songs (the national anthem in Syria had not yet been composed). When he was released from prison three months later, he published another caricature, this time of himself coming out of the grave, with the ministers he had depicted earlier running away in fear and saying, "Oh no, *al-Mudhiq al-Mubki* is back!"

In 1932, *al-Mudhiq al-Mubki* was closed again for criticizing the pro-French administration of Prime Minister Taj al-Din al-Hasani. In 1933, a group of parliamentary deputies filed a lawsuit against Kahaleh for publishing a comical story that had a group of donkeys deciding to become deputies since

Habib Kaheleh.

"among current parliamentarians there are indeed many donkeys!"

In 1947, Habib Kahaleh joined the National Party, a coalition of notables who rallied to create a united front following the end of the French Mandate in April 1946. He ran for parliament on a National Party ticket and won with an overwhelming majority. In 1947, he founded his third publication, a political daily entitled *Dimashq* (*Damascus*).

From 1947 to 1949, Kahaleh served as a deputy in parliament. Due to his popularity, none of Syria's military leaders during the years 1949-1958 dared to close his publications, yet they heavily censored all of his works. But Kahaleh willingly ceased publication to protest the military coup that brought General Husni al-Za'im to power in March 1949. But Kahaleh resumed publication when Za'im was toppled 137 days later, in August 1949. Then, in October 1956, Kahaleh willingly closed down his magazine once again, saying, "I did so at my own free will because I am unable to write what I believe. So, I have broken my pen and retired because the true slave, as Oscar Wilde says, is one who cannot express his views freely."

The closure, Kahaleh claimed, was to protest Syria's alliance with the USSR and the militarization of politics at the hands of officers in the Syrian Army. In 1958, Syria and Egypt merged to form the United Arab Republic (UAR), a union that Kahaleh opposed, arguing that the socialist policies of President Gamal Abd al-Nasser would destroy Syria. When a military coup dissolved the UAR in September 1961, Kahaleh supported the new regime of President Nazim al-Qudsi and on October 7, 1962, *al-Mudhiq al-Mubki* was restored to Syrian newsstands. But, in March 1963, the Military Committee of the Baath Party came to power in Syria and outlawed all political publications. *Al-Mudhiq al-Mubki* continued to print, albeit under heavy censorship.

From 1961 to 1963, government authorities tried to close the Baath party daily, *al-Baath*, but Kahaleh lobbied in the daily's favor with President Qudsi, claiming that in a democratic system, all newspapers, even the leftist ones, should be allowed to express their views. Salah al-Bitar, the party's co-founder, acknowledged Kahaleh's favor and permitted him to keep publishing *al-Mudhik al-Mubki*.

Habib Kahaleh died on December 22, 1965. His son Samir took over as editor-in-chief, working with his cousin, the novelist Colette Khury. All editions from *al-Mudhiq al-Mubki*, however, were sharply edited by the military regime in Damascus. As a result, Samir Kahaleh decided to stop the publication. The last edition was released on May 29, 1966.

Sources:
Itri, Abd al-Ghani. *Abqariyyat wa Alam* (1996).
Interview with Colette Khury (Damascus September 2, 2001).

Interview with Samir Kahaleh (Damascus July 30, 2002).

Uthman, Hashim. *Al-Sahafa al-Souriyya: Madiha wa Hadiruha* (1997).

al-Khatib, Muhib al-Din
(1887-1969)

Muhib al-Din Khatib was born in Damascus and studied at the Ottoman Academy of Law in Istanbul, graduating in 1905. His mentor was the Islamic scholar, Sheikh Tahir al-Jaza'iri. Khatib began his career as a journalist for Turkish newspapers in Damascus and Istanbul.

Khatib was a co-founder of al-Fatat, which was founded in Paris in 1911 and was the most prominent opposition party to the Ottoman Empire in the pre-World War I era. The party called on Arab and Turkish citizens to remain united within the Ottoman framework, but claimed that the Arabs should have equal rights and obligations as their Ottoman counterparts. In 1913, al-Fatat moved its offices to Beirut and in 1914, its founders opened an office in Damascus to coordinate nationalist activity.

In the summer of 1913, the founders of al-Fatat called for an Arab Congress in Paris to discuss the deteriorating standard of living in the Ottoman Empire. Not wishing to create a permanent rift between the nationalist movement and authorities in Istanbul, Khatib and his comrades did not call for complete Arab emancipation from the Ottoman Empire, but rather, tried to mend relations with the Ottomans. When that failed, they publicly headed the separatist movement, demanding a complete break with Ottomanism in favor of Arabism. Jamal Pasha, the military governor of Syria, placed Khatib under house arrest in 1914. In 1917, Khatib joined the rebel army of Sharif Husayn, the Prince of Mecca, who was leading an armed uprising against the Ottoman Empire. While in the service to the Arab rebellion, Khatib founded a political newsletter, *al-Qibla* (*The Minaret*), which publicized the Arab cause in different Arabic-speaking districts of the Ottoman Empire.

In October 1918, the empire was defeated, and Khatib returned to Damascus where he co-founded the first state-owned Arab newspaper in Syria, a*l-Asima* (*The Capital*). Meanwhile, Khatib became an ally of King Faysal I, the new ruler of Syria, who had been a member of al-Fatat from 1915 to 1918. When the French dethroned Faysal in July 1920, setting up a mandate in Syria, Khatib fled to Egypt and joined the nationalist movement in exile, calling for an end to the French Mandate in the Middle East. In Cairo, he published two magazines, *al-Zahra'* (the title is a reference to the daughter of the Prophet Mohammad that can't be translated) and *al-Fatah* (*The Victory*), and contributed articles to the Egyptian daily *al-Azhar*. Muhib al-Din al-Khatib died on December 30, 1969.

Sources:

Itri, Abd al-Ghani. *Hadeeth an al-Abqariyyat* (2000).

Uthman, Hashim. *Al-Sahafa al-Souriyya: Madiha wa Hadiruha* (1997).

Kurd Ali, Mohammad
(1876-1952)

Mohammad Kurd Ali was born and raised in Damascus. He studied Islam with local theologians. His mentor was the renowned scholar Sheikh Tahir al-Jaza'iri. In 1897, Kurd Ali became editor of a political newspaper in Damascus called *al-Sham* (*Damascus*). It was published in Arabic, a journal that supported the domestic and foreign policies of the Ottoman Sultan Abdulhamid II.

Kurd Ali served as editor-in-chief of *al-Sham* until 1900, when he moved to Egypt in search of additional income, Egypt being the intellectual capital of the region. In 1906, Kurd Ali founded his own magazine in Cairo, *al-Muqtataf* (*Anthology*). The publication steered clear of political discourse, concentrating mainly on social and literary topics.

Kurd Ali returned to Damascus in 1908, following the Young Turk Revolution that overthrew the regime of Sultan Abdulhamid II. So Kurd Ali shifted his allegiance from Abdulhamid to the Ottoman officers. He praised the new Turkish administration and called for a state policy based on democracy and an Islamic revival that could adapt to the twentieth century. The Ottoman officers responded promptly to intellectual calls, reinstating the Ottoman constitution that Abdulhamid had nullified in 1876. The Ottoman officers called for parliamentary elections and lifted the press censorship that had been imposed by the regime of the former sultan.

In 1909, Mohammad Kurd Ali founded a newspaper in Damascus, *al-Muqtabas*, that immediately attracted a large audience due to the quality of its articles and topics. Calling for a pan-Islamic campaign to prevent Jews from immigrating to Palestine, Kurd Ali was the first Syrian to deal openly with the issue of Zionism and shed light on the Zionist threat to the future of the Arab world. His newspaper also vehemently supported the Committee of Union and Progress (CUP) that came to power after Abdulhamid in 1908. He remained in charge of *al-Muqtabas* until 1914, when he relinquished control to his brother, Ahmad Kurd Ali, to become editor-in-chief of *al-Sharq* (*The East*), a daily newspaper published by Jamal Pasha, the Ottoman military governor of Syria, who was a leading member of the CUP.

In 1913, the Jewish National Agency (JNA) in Europe proposed a meeting between Zionist and Arab leaders to discuss the issue of Palestine. The meeting was to be held in the mountain resort of Brummanah in present day Lebanon, headed by Chaim Weizmann, president of the JNA. The Arab delegation included Kurd

Ali who, through his articles, had established himself as an expert on Palestine, along with the Syrian leader Abd al-Rahman Shahbandar, the Palestinian nationalist Jamal al-Husayni, and the Palestinian journalists Yusuf al-Issa and Abdullah Mukhlis. The meeting was postponed until August 1914, and then canceled altogether due to the outbreak of World War I on August 2. In March 1922, the Zionist Agency met with Kurd Ali in Egypt, trying to convince him to support a Jewish-Arab alliance against French imperialism in the Middle East. In exchange for Arab support of a Jewish state in Palestine, the Zionists promised to use their considerable influence in Europe to end the French Mandate in Syria and Lebanon (imposed in July 1920). Kurd Ali, however, categorically refused to endorse the project.

Mohammad Kurd Ali.

Kurd Ali's most memorable contribution to Syria was the establishment of the prestigious Arab Language Assemblage in Damascus on June 8, 1919. The organization became the highest international scientific authority in the field of Arab language and literature. In 1920, Kurd Ali was elected permanent president of the organization by a group of veteran Arab academics. In recognition of his services, French High Commissioner Henri Gouraud appointed Kurd Ali minister of education in the cabinet of Prime Minister Jamil al-Ulshi on September 6, 1920.

Kurd Ali accepted this post despite strong reservations in nationalist circles. There were those who argued that under no circumstances should he accept office under the French. He revolutionized the Syrian curriculum, however, introducing French language instruction beginning in grade school, adapting the French baccalaureate system, and concentrating heavily on the humanities for high school students.

In February 1928, Kurd Ali was once again appointed minister of education in the cabinet of Prime Minister Taj al-Din al-Hasani, the most prominent pro-French politician in Syria. He remained in the Hasani cabinet until November 1931 when he left office to return to work in *al-Muqtabas*. He spent the remainder of his years in Damascus working at his newspaper and publishing historical books. Meanwhile, he continued to serve as president of the Arab Language Assemblage until his death on April 2, 1952. Among his most widely acclaimed works are *Gharayeb al-Gharb* (*Peculiarities of the West*), published in 1924; and the six-volume work, *Khutat Dimashq* (*Maps of Damascus*), published 1935.

In 1936, Kurd Ali wrote the two-volume study, *al-Islam wa al-Hadara al-Arabiyya* (*Islam and Arab Civilization*), and in 1952 published a history of Damascus, *Dimashq Madinat al-Sihr wa al-Shi'r* (*Damascus the City of Magic and Poetry*). His memoirs, *Muzakarat*, were published in four volumes over the years 1949-1951. He also wrote a book praising the policies of Prime Minister Taj al-Din al-Hasani called *Thalath Sanawat fi Hikm Souriyya* (*Three Years in the Government of Syria*), published in 1931.

Although he is widely remembered as an excellent historian and scholar, Mohammad Kurd Ali was also one of the most moderate politicians in Syria. Throughout the 1920s and 1930s, he was willing to play politics by the rules of the French, more so than many of his contemporaries. In a career that lasted over fifty years, he played no role in the nationalist movement, either under the Ottomans or the French.

Sources:
Caplan, Neil. *Futile Diplomacy, Vol* I (1983).
Elias, Joseph. *Tatawur al-Sahafa al-Souriyya fi al-Ahd al-Uthmani* (1972).
Itri, Abd al-Ghani. *Hadeeth an al-Abqariyyat* (2000).
Kayyali, Sami. *Al-Adab al-Arabi al-Mouasir fi Souriyya 1850-1950* (1968).
Khoury, Philip. *Syria and the French Mandate* (1987).
Kurd Ali, Mohammad. *Muzakarat* (1949-1951).
Rifaii, Shams al-Din. *Tareekh al-Sahafa al-Souriyya 1800-1947* (1969).
Salama, Fayez. *Alam al-Arab fi al-Siyassa wa al-Adab* (1935).
Uthman, Hashim. *Al-Sahafa al-Souriyya: Madiha wa Hadiruha* (1997).

Murad, Bassim
(1908-1973)

Bassim Murad was born and raised in Damascus. He began his career in 1922 as a journalist, writing for several Damascus-based newspapers, including the popular daily *al-Ayyam*. In 1928, he founded his own cultural weekly, *al-Osbou' al-Musawwar* (*The Photograph Weekly*).

Murad allied himself with the National Bloc, the leading anti-French movement in Syria that wanted to terminate the mandate regime through diplomatic means rather than armed resistance. In 1936, Murad founded the newspaper *al-Akhbar* (*The News*) and supported the election of Hashim al-Atasi, the leader of the Bloc, as president of the republic. The newspaper remained a Bloc mouthpiece until independence was achieved in 1946. After that, Murad became an ally of the National Party and its leader, President Shukri al-Quwatli.

Murad continued to write in *al-Akhbar* until General Husni al-Za'im came to power in March 1949 and closed most political newspapers. He criticized Za'im, claiming that he had established a military dictatorship and praised the coup d'etat that toppled Za'im in August 1949. Hashim al-Atasi, veteran of the nationalist movement, was reelected president, ordering the restoration of *al-Akhbar*.

Murad became a fervent supporter of the young officers who came to power in

Egypt and ousted the Egyptian monarchy in July 1952. He supported the rise of Gamal Abd al-Nasser to pan-Arab leadership and the nationalization of the Suez Canal in 1956. When Syria and Egypt merged in 1958 to form the United Arab Republic (UAR), Murad called on Arabs to follow the Syrian-Egyptian example. His newspaper increased in popularity during the UAR years (1958-1961), but he grew disenchanted with how Egypt was mistreating Syrian citizens of the UAR. As a result, he supported the coup that ousted the UAR and allied himself with the post-union government of President Nazim al-Qudsi.

In March 1963, the Baath Party came to power and pledged to restore the UAR. The Baath Party officers closed *al-Akhbar* and terminated the civil rights of Bassim Murad. He retired from journalism and died in Damascus on December 25, 1973.

Sources:
Faris, George. *Man Hum fi al-`Alam al-Arabi?* (1957).
Information provided by Mr Nazir Sinan (Damascus March 30, 2001).

al-Ouff, Bashir
(1917-1994)

Bashir al-Ouff was born and raised in Damascus. He studied at the Journalism Academy in Cairo and began writing for *al-Ayyam*, the leading Damascus daily, in 1938. In 1943, Ouff became a member of *al-Ayyam's* editorial board. He was also a founding member of the Syrian Boy Scouts and a member of their Central Committee.

In 1945, al-Ouff began to write in *al-Manar* (*The Light*), a political daily issued by the Syrian Muslim Brotherhood. By 1947, Ouff had become the newspaper's editor-in-chief and had risen in prominence within Muslim intellectual circles in Damascus. From 1943 to 1949, the Brotherhood increased in popularity throughout Syria, and *al-Manar* became a success in Damascus. In April 1949, Ouff became an official member of the Brotherhood and was appointed secretary of the Damascus office by the Brotherhood General Supervisor, Mustapha al-Siba'i. In March 1949, General Husni al-Za'im, Syria's first military dictator, came to power and outlawed *al-Manar* for its religious views.

When Za'im was overthrown in August 1949, the newspaper returned to print, but Ouff resigned from its editorial board, and in November 1949, established his own daily, *al-Manar al-Jadid* (*The New Light*). In March 1950, Ouff founded an evening daily called *al-Masa'* (*The Evening*) that circulated briefly, then closed down for financial reasons in 1951.

When General Adib al-Shishakli came to power in 1951, he ordered the merging of two political newspapers into one. On August 25, 1952, *al-Manar al-Jadid* merged with the Damascus daily *Barada* to become *al-Liwaa*. Ouff became editor-in-chief, while Munir al-Rayyes, the owner of *Barada*, became director. When Shishakli was overthrown by military coup in 1954, the two papers split once again, and Bashir al-Ouff resumed publication of his own newspaper.

In February 1954, Ouff teamed up with four leading journalists and created a shareholding company to print Syria's four principal newspapers, *al-Qabas*, *al-Ayyam*, *Alif Ba'e*, and *al-Sham*. The journalists pledged to unite their efforts to publish the four major newspapers and divide the revenue equally among themselves. Ouff became secretary of the board, but the enterprise worked for less than one year, due to disagreements among its founders and was dissolved in November 1954.

In 1958, Syria and Egypt merged to form the United Arab Republic (UAR), and Ouff became a deputy for Damascus in the joint Syrian-Egyptian Parliament. He held office until the UAR was dissolved by coup in September 1961. He resumed journalism in the post-union era (1961-1963), but his newspaper was permanently closed by the Baath government that came to power in March 1963.

The Military Committee of the Baath Party pledged to restore the UAR and punish all those who had collaborated with the post-union government. The officers closed *al-Manar*, terminated Ouff's civil rights, and sent him into exile in Lebanon. He joined the Islamic Boy Scouts in Beirut and wrote for the Lebanese dailies *al-Safir* and *al-Hayat*. In 1980, he moved to Saudi Arabia and taught at King Abd al-Aziz University in Jeddah.

In 1981, Ouff attended the Islamic Conference in Indonesia and was elected into the Higher Committee for Islamic Media. He also wrote many controversial books, including *Ishtirakiyyatuhum wa Islamuna* (*Their Socialism and Our Islam*), and *La Thawriyya la Ishtirakiyya* (*No Revolution and No Socialism*), both of which were published in Beirut in 1968. His other works include *Al-Arab wa Rusia min Khilal al-Ghazu al-Shiyoui li Czechoslovakia* (*The Arabs and Russia through the Communist Invasion of Czechoslovakia*), published in 1969; and *Rasa'il ila Gamal Abd al-Nasser* (*Letters to Gamal Abd al-Nasser*), published in 1973. In 1949, Ouff published his classic, *Al-Inkilab al-Souri* (*The Syrian Coup*), one of the earliest books about the life and career of Syria's first dictator, General Husni al-Za'im, who launched the first coup in the Middle East and ruled Syria for four months in 1949.

Bashir al-Ouff died on July 15, 1994 and was buried in Jeddah, Saudi Arabia.

Sources:
Barada (March 24, 1963).
Faris, George. *Man Hum fi al-`Alam al-Arabi?* (1957).
Itri , Abd al-Ghani. *Abqariyyat wa Alam* (1996).

Qabbani, Sabri
(1908-1973)

Sabri Qabbani studied medicine at Damascus University and graduated with honors in 1931. He began his career as a physician in the Iraqi Army, serving from 1932 to 1941. He returned to Syria to open a clinic in Damascus and in 1948 began to teach at Damascus University.

Qabbani ran for parliament on an independent ticket in 1947 and lost. At this point, he defected from medicine and founded a political daily in Damascus, *al-Nisal* (*The Sword Blade*). He also wrote for the Damascus-daily, *al-Ayyam*.

In the summer of 1949, he served as an intermediary between President Husni al-Za'im and Antune Sa'ada, the Lebanese founder of the Syrian Social Nationalist Party (SSNP). Sa'ada, wanted in Beirut for plotting to overthrow the Lebanese government, was searching for a neighboring country to grant him asylum. Qabbani helped him get in touch with Za'im, who offered Sa'ada sanctuary in Damascus.

Sabri Qabbani.

In July 1949, the Za'im-Sa'ada alliance negotiated by Qabbani was breached on behalf of Lebanese Prime Minister Riyad al-Sulh, and Za'im extradited Sa'ada to Lebanon. On July 8, 1949, Sa'ada was tried for treason, convicted, and executed in Beirut. Subsequently, Sabri al-Qabbani retired from political activity and vowed never to venture into political activity ever again.

In 1947, Qabbani created *Your Doctor Behind the Microphone*, a radio program for Syrian National Radio which quickly became one of the most popular programs in Syria. Dr Qabbani contributed greatly to public recognition of health issues and urged people to conduct periodic check-ups with their family doctor. He warned against curing disease through unprescribed drugs and unlicensed professionals, a common practice in Syria. He also spoke out against religious figures who claimed to have healing powers and urged "every Syrian to find a professional doctor for himself and his family." For those who could not afford to pay for check-ups, he offered to be their family doctor over the radio for free. Receiving calls from the sick all over Syria, he answered questions and suggested medications, a pioneering practice in Syria at the time.

Dr Qabbani became a household name, one who would respond to inquiries about practically everything related to the human body. In 1956, he closed his clinic and spent the remainder of his years practicing medicine over the radio and publishing a monthly periodical, *Tabibak* (*Your Doctor*), a publication that put his radio addresses and diagnoses into print. It was a pioneering medical journal that achieved instant success.

Qabbani died in April 1973, but his publication continues to the present and remains the most prominent magazine of medical journalism in the Middle East. Sabri al-Qabbani published three books during his career: *Al-Ghiza' la al-Daw`a* (*Nutrition…not Medicine*); *Tabibak Ma`k* (*Your Doctor is with You*); and *Hayatuna al-Jinsiyya* (*Our Sexual Life*).

Sources:
Faris, George. *Man Hum fi al-`Alam al-Arabi?* (1957).
Itri , Abd al-Ghani. *Abqariyyat wa Alam* (1996).

al-Qal'aji, Qadri
(1917-1986)

Qadri al-Qal'aji was born and raised in Aleppo, the second largest city in Syria. He dropped out of school in search of an income and began his career in 1940 by writing for two Arab newspapers, the Cairo-based *Hadeeth* and the Beirut weekly *al-Makshouf.*

During World War II (1939-1945), Qal'aji founded the League for Opposing Fascism, a coalition of intellectuals who were bent on "fighting Fascism through the power of the pen." Among the league's co-founders was Omar al-Fakhuri, a member of the prestigious Arab Language Assemblage, Ra'if Khury, an instructor of Arabic literature at Damascus University, and the engineer Antune Thabet. In 1941, Qal'aji co-founded the newspaper *al-Tareeq* (*The Road*) with Omar Fakhuri. Qal'aji served as editor-in-chief until 1952, when he became director of the Press Office for Chief of Staff Adib al-Shishakli. In 1953, when Shishakli became president, he appointed Qal'aji as his private secretary.

The Shishakli years were marked by authoritarian policies, where a one-party state was created, freedom of speech was curtailed, and arbitrary arrests became commonplace. In 1953, Shishakli went to war with the Druze community in Syria, accusing them of trying to topple his regime. He bombarded the Arab Mountain and imprisoned hundreds of its citizens.

In February 1954, Shishakli was ousted by military coup and, along with Qal'aji, fled Syria to neighboring Lebanon. When word reached them that the Lebanese Druze leader, Kamal Jumblatt, was planning to assassinate Shishakli, the former president fled to Saudi Arabia. But Qal'aji remained in Beirut and launched *al-Huriyya* (*Freedom*), the first opposition paper to the post-Shishakli regime of President Hashim al-Atasi. The newspaper became an unofficial mouthpiece for the ex-President Shishakli and covered all of his communiqués and activities from his exile in Saudi Arabia and Europe.

From 1961 to 1963, Qal'aji served as a consultant to the Kuwaiti government. In 1964, he founded a publishing house in Beirut called *Dar al-Kateb al-Arabi*

(*House of the Arab Author*). That same year, Shishakli was assassinated in Brazil, and Qal'aji's political aspirations ended.

Qal'aji spent the remainder of his years in Lebanon, devoting his time to research. Among his publications are *Tajribat Arabi fi al-Hizb al-Shiyou'i* (*The Experience of an Arab in the Communist Party*), published in 1960; *Adwa' ala Tareekh al-Kuwait* (*Elucidation on the History of Kuwait*), published in 1962; and *Thalath Min Alam Al-Huriyya* (*Three Notables of Freedom*), a collection of biographies published in 1967 on the life of the Islamic thinkers Jamal al-Din al-Afghani and Mohammad Abdu, and the Egyptian resistance leader Sa'ad Zaghloul. In 1995, Qadri al-Qal'aji wrote *Alf Layla wa Layla* (*One Thousand and One Nights*), and in 1996 published *Ashar al-Muhakamat fi al-`Alam* (*The Most Famous Trials in the World*).

Sources:
Faris, George. *Man Hum fi al-`Alam al-Arabi?* (1957).
Uthman, Hashim. *Al-Ahzab al-Siyasiyya fi Souriyya: al-Siriyya wa al-Mu'lana* (2001).

Quodama, Ahmad
(1911-1985)

Ahmad Quodama was born and raised in Damascus. He began his journalistic career in 1930 by writing for the popular Damascus daily *al-Ayyam*. In 1931, he founded a political weekly, *al-Sarkha* (*The Shout*), but it closed in 1933 for financial reasons. In 1934, he returned to *al-Ayyam*, becoming editor-in-chief in 1939. In 1940, he moved to *al-Nidal* (*The Struggle*), a publication that was later to serve as the mouthpiece for the opposition to the government of President Shukri al-Quwatli (1943-1949).

Quodama worked with the paper's founder, Sami Kabbara, on promoting opposition to President Quwatli after his election to office in 1943. Quodama and Kabbara accused Quwatli of centralizing power in his own hands and in those Damascenes who supported him. Quodama worked with *al-Nidal* until 1946. In 1947, he became editor-in-chief of *al-Nidal*, and in 1949, became editor-in-chief of the Damascus daily *al-Watan* (*The Homeland*). In 1953, he returned to serve as editor of *al-Ayyam*. In October 1954, Quodama founded a newspaper, *al-Tahrir al-Arabi* (*Arab Liberation*). This publication was accused of loyalty to the military dictatorship of ex-President Adib al-Shishakli, who had ruled Syria from 1951-1954. To distance himself from Shishakli, Quodama renamed the newspaper *al-Balagh* (*The Declaration*). He also established an agricultural weekly in Damascus called *al-Reef* (*The Suburbs*).

When Syria and Egypt merged to form the United Arab Republic (UAR) in

1958, Quodama resigned from *al-Ayyam* and became chief editor of the daily newsletters published by the Ministry of Information, keeping this post until 1968. He then moved to Lebanon and founded the Al-Bayan Publishing House in Beirut, devoting a bulk of his time to administrative duties. In 1971, he joined the research committee of the Islamic Science Encyclopedia in Kuwait. In 1972, he returned to Lebanon to work with the Khayyat Books Establishment in Beirut, a major publishing house, and to write for the weekly, *al-Majalla al-Arabiyya* (*The Arab Magazine*).

Al-Majalla al-Arabiyya was run by the retired Syrian politician, Munir al-Ajlani, a former co-owner of the Damascus daily *al-Nidal*. Among the published books of Ahmad Quodama are *Rijal al-Siyasa fi al-Sharq wa al-Gharb* (*Men of Politics in the East and West*), published in 1939; and the three-volume encyclopedia, *Ma'lim wa Alam fi Bilad al-Arab* (*Landmarks and Notables in Arab Lands*), published in 1965.

Sources:
Faris, George. *Man Hum fi al-`Alam al-Arabi?* (1957).
Itri , Abd al-Ghani. *Abqariyyat wa Alam* (1996).

al-Rayyes, Munir
(1901-1992)

Munir al-Rayyes was born in Damascus and studied literature at Damascus University. In 1919, he became an employee at the Ministry of Education and started to write for the Damascus daily *al-Ayyam* and the Beirut daily *al-Hayat*.

Highly critical of the French Mandate in Syria imposed in 1920, Rayyes called on Syrians to refrain from working with the mandate regime of Prime Minister Haqqi al-Azm. In 1925, he resigned from the Ministry of Education and joined the Syrian rebels in the revolt of the Arab Mountain. Rayyes took up arms with the Druze warlord, Sultan al-Atrash, and led an armed band of young men to fight the French in his native Hama. When the revolt ended in 1927, Rayyes returned to Damascus and continued to write for *al-Hayat*.

In August 1933, along with a group of fifty radical Arab nationalists, Rayyes founded the League of National Action in the Lebanese Mountain town of Quarna'il. The League was a pioneering organization established by a second generation of Arab politicians, aged between twenty-five and thirty, who were intent on ridding the region of foreign influence.

Unlike other political establishments that were dominated by landowners and Ottoman-trained politicians, the League of National Action was composed of professors, lawyers, and civil servants not living off their family estates but rather leading career-focused lives. All of them had studied in Europe, the United States, or American universities in the Middle East. The League of National Action achieved high acclaim in 1933, but died out in 1935 with the early death of its founder and charismatic leader, Abd al-Razzaq al-Dandashi.

In 1936, Rayyes moved to Palestine, joining Amin al-Husayni, the Mufti of Jerusalem, in a military uprising against the Jewish immigrants who were coming to Palestine from Europe. He returned to Syria in 1938 to become director of political affairs at the police department in Damascus.

In 1945, Rayyes founded the newspaper *Barada* and became editor-in-chief. *Barada*, named after the biggest river in Damascus used for drinking and agriculture, established itself as a sharp critic of Prime Minister Jamil Mardam Bey during the Arab-Israeli War of 1948, accusing him and the civilians around him of poor leadership. Rayyes was a good friend, however, of President Shukri al-Quwatli.

Rayyes allied himself with General Husni al-Za'im, who came to power in March 1949, and founded a newspaper to preach pro-Za'im propaganda called *al-Inkilab (The Coup d'Etat)*. The Za'im coup was the first of its kind in the entire Arab world. Rayyes hailed the coup and labeled Za'im "the Ataturk of modern Syria." Among other things, Munir al-Rayyes called for the emancipation of women and supported Za'im's decision to give women the right to vote and nominate themselves for public office. When Za'im was toppled, also by coup in August 1949, Rayyes quickly reneged on his loyalties and shifted his allegiance to the coup mastermind, General Sami al-Hinnawi.

When General Adib al-Shishakli came to power in 1951, he ordered the merging of the two political newspapers into one. On August 25, 1952, *Barada* merged with the Damascus daily *al-Manar al-Jadid* to become *al-Liwaa*. Rayyes served as the new paper's director while Bashir al-Ouff, owner of *al-Manar al-Jadid*, became editor-in-chief. When Shishakli was overthrown by military coup in 1954, the two papers split once again, and Rayyes resumed publication of his own newspaper. During the Shishakli era, Rayyes encouraged his wife, Thuraya al-Hafez, a veteran schoolteacher and women's rights activist, to nominate herself for parliament.

In February 1954, Rayyes teamed up with four leading journalists and created a shareholding company to print Syria's four principal newspapers, *al-Qabas*, *al-Ayyam*, *Alif Ba'*, and *al-Sham*. The journalists pledged to unite their efforts to publish the four big newspapers and divide the revenue equally among themselves. Rayyes became a member of the company's board, but the enterprise lasted less than a year due to disagreements among its founders. In November 1954, the jointly-owned company was dissolved.

Rayyes identified with the Arab nationalist movement of the 1950s. During the Syrian-Egyptian union years (1958-1961), Rayyes became one of the most prominent supporters of President Gamal Abd al-Nasser of Egypt. But, in

September 1961, the union was dissolved by a military coup headed by General Abd al-Karim al-Nehlawi.

Rayyes criticized the post-union government of President Nazim al-Qudsi and wrote extensively against the officer class that ruled with Qudsi from 1961 to 1963. Rayyes remained loyal to President Nasser, whose wife Thuraya became one of the prominent leaders of the Nasserist movement in Damascus. Rayyes allied himself with other members of the Arab nationalist movement and supported the military coup of 1963 that brought the Baath Party to power and promised to restore the union.

Except for *Barada* and their own daily, *al-Baath*, the Baath Party officers outlawed all other publications. Once firmly in power, however, the party closed *Barada* as well. Munir al-Rayyes' most famous published work is a eulogy of the Syrian revolt of 1925 entitled, *Al-Kitab al-Zahabi lil Thawrat al-Wataniyya fi al-Sharq al-Arabi* (*The Golden Book of Nationalist Revolutions in the Arab East*), published in 1966.

Sources:

Azm, Khalid. *Muzakarat,* Vol III (1964).

Faris, George. *Man Hum fi al-`Alam al-Arabi?* (1957).

Itri , Abd al-Ghani. *Abqariyyat wa Alam* (1996).

Rayyes, Munir. *Al-Kitab al-Zahabi lil Thawrat al-Wataniyya fi al-Sharq al-Arabi* (1966).

Uthman, Hashim. *Al-Sahafa al-Souriyya: Madiha wa Hadiruha* (1997).

al-Rayyes, Najib
(1892-1952)

Najib al-Rayyes began his career in 1924 as a freelance journalist for the popular Lebanese daily *al-Hayat.* By the late 1920s, he was writing political editorials for the Syrian newspaper *al-Muqtabas*, published by the veteran journalist Mohammad Kurd Ali.

In September 1928, with Mohammad Kurd Ali's backing, Rayyes founded his own daily modeled on *al-Muqtabas*, which he named *al-Qabas* (*The Firebrand*). The newspaper established a wide readership for supporting the activities of Abd al-Rahman Shahbandar, leader of the nationalist movement in French Mandate Syria. In the 1930s, *al-Qabas*, the official mouthpiece for the national movement, was closed frequently by French Mandate authorities. When French agents killed Shahbandar in 1940, Rayyes shifted his allegiance to the National Bloc of Hashim al-Atasi. Rayyes befriended the Bloc leader Shukri al-Quwatli and ran for parliament on Quwatli's electoral list in 1943, winning with a majority vote. In August 1943, Rayyes supported Quwatli's election as president of Syria and became part of his inner circle of advisors.

Following the French evacuation in 1946, *al-Qabas* became the most popular newspaper in Damascus and the unofficial forum espousing the ideology of the Quwatli regime. Rayyes covered the Arab-Zionist clash in Jerusalem in 1936 and dispatched correspondents to the war front in the first Arab-Israeli War of 1948. Rayyes was highly critical of the officer class in Syria, accusing them of poor leadership and incompetence in military decisions. In March 1949, a military coup took place in Damascus, launched by General Husni al-Za'im, toppling Quwatli and his entire entourage. Za'im ordered the closure of *al-Qabas* and placed Rayyes under 24-hour surveillance.

Najib al-Rayyes.

When Za'im was overthrown in August 1949, the newspaper resumed publication, but closed altogether following the early death of its founder in 1952. Najib al-Rayyes composed a ten-volume autobiography, *Muzakarat* (*Memoirs*), published in Beirut in 1994 and compiled by the novelist Zakariya Tamer. Rayyes' son Riyad continued a journalistic career after his late father's death.

Sources:
Babil, Nasuh. *Sahafa wa Siyassa fi Souriyya* (1987).
Hawrani, Akram. *Muzakarat Akram al-Hawrani* (2000).
Rayyes, Najib. *Muzakarat* (1994).
Itri, Abd al-Ghani. *Abqariyyat Shamiyya* (1995).
Uthman, Hashim. *Al-Sahafa al-Souriyya: Madiha wa Hadiruha* (1997).

al-Rayyes, Riyad
(1937-)

Riyad al-Rayyes studied at Brummanah High School in Lebanon and obtained his university degree in economics from the University of London. His father, Najib al-Rayyes, was a pioneering journalist in Syria who owned the popular Damascus daily *al-Qabas* (*The Firebrand*).

Young Rayyes began his career in 1958 as a journalist and editor of the *Arab Review*, a publication of the Arab student community in the United Kingdom. He returned to the Middle East in 1961 and was a supporter of President Gamal Abd al-Nasser of Egypt. Rayyes went to Beirut and worked for the pro-Nasser daily, *al-Anwar*, run by his father's friend, the journalist Sa'id Frayha. Rayyes then moved to the daily *al-Muharrir* (*The Editor*).

In 1964, Rayyes began to write for the *Sunday Times, Western Mail,* and the

Beirut daily *al-Hayat*. When *al-Hayat*'s founder, Kamel Mroweh, was killed in 1966, Rayyes left *al-Hayat* and went to the popular Lebanese daily, *al-Nahhar*, run by the Lebanese journalist Ghassan Tweini. At the time, Tweini was striving to give his newspaper a pan-Arab image instead of the local Lebanese image it had enjoyed for years. Tweini wanted *al-Nahhar* to replace *al-Hayat* in popularity and reputation throughout the Arab world, and this was done through extensive coverage of Arab affairs. In 1966, Tweini dispatched Rayyes to Yemen to cover the Civil War, where he remained until 1969.

Rayyes then went to Baghdad and reported on the coup that brought President Abd al-Rahman Aref to power in Iraq in 1968, also covering the Soviet invasion of Czechoslovakia in 1969. Two years later, he became consultant to the UNICEF office in Lebanon. In 1976, Ghassan Tweini appointed him managing director of *al-Hayat* Press Services. Also in 1976, Rayyes founded the weekly *al-Manar* (*The Light*) in London, the first Arab weekly published in Europe. In 1979, Rayyes began to write for the Paris-based *al-Mustaqbal Magazine*, run by the Lebanese journalist Nabil Khury. Rayyes remained with *al-Mustaqbal* until 1988.

In 1986, Rayyes founded his own publishing house, Riyad Najib al-Rayyes Books. He became the most reputed Arab publisher on Middle East issues. In 1988, while publishing books in London, Rayyes founded a weekly magazine called *al-Naqid* (*The Critic*), which continued to print until 1995. It was relaunched from Beirut in revised form with the title *al-Nuqqad* (*The Critics*) in 2000.

In 1989, Rayyes established an Arab library in London, located in Knightsbridge, dedicated to marketing Arabic books and literature. In the 1990s, Rayyes divided his time between Lebanon and the United Kingdom, contributing articles frequently to *al-Hayat*. He has also begun preparation for relaunching his father's daily, *al-Qabas*, forty years after its closure.

Rayyes also published numerous books on Arab politics and his experiences as a journalist. In 1986, he wrote his classic, *Jawasees al-Arab: Sira' al-Mukhabarat al-Ajnabiyya* (*Arab Spies: The Clash of Western Intelligence*). Other books include *Al-Khaleej al-Arabi wa Riyah al-Tagheer* (*The Arab Gulf and the Winds of Change*), also published in 1986; and *Al-Arab Wa Jiranuhum* (*The Arabs and their Neighbors*), covering minority rights in the Arab world and published in 1989.

Riyad al-Rayyes' most recent works include *Riyah al-Sumum* (*The Poisonous Winds*), covering the political conditions of Saudi Arabia and the Persian Gulf after the Gulf War of 1991, and *Aktub Ilaykum Bi Ghadab: Kayf Nakul La fi Asr Na'm* (*I Write to You in Fury: How to Say No in the Era of Yes*), published in 1996.

Sources:
Al-Bayan (November 27, 2000).
The International Who's Who in the Arab World (1987-1988).

al-Sawwah, Ahmad Nawras
(1915-1992)

Ahmad Nawras al-Sawwah studied at the Arab Academy of Law and began his career as a high school instructor, moving into journalism in 1944. He was appointed editor-in-chief of the Homs-based newspaper, *al-Souri al-Jadid* (*The New Syrian*), and in 1946 founded his own newspaper in Homs, *al-Ra'e al-Am* (*Public Opinion*).

Sawwah joined the Syrian Social Nationalist Party (SSNP) of Antune Sa'ada, and his newspaper became an outlet for SSNP ideology, calling on Jordan, Iraq, Lebanon, and Palestine to unite into Greater Syria, with Damascus as their capital. In April 1949, *al-Ra'e al-Am* was closed by Syria's first military dictator, General Husni al-Za'im. In August 1949, the newspaper returned to print when Za'im was overthrown by military coup.

In 1951, Sawwah allied himself with President Adib al-Shishakli, a former member of the SSNP, and joined his Arab Liberation Movement (ALM), a party that called for a united Arab world under Shishakli's leadership. The ALM also demanded the emancipation of women, land reform, progressive taxation, health care, and free education. Sawwah continued to write in favor of Shishakli when the latter lost power in February 1954.

In the second half of the 1950s, Sawwah spoke out against President Gamal Abd al-Nasser of Egypt and was opposed to the unification of Syria and Egypt in 1958. When union was dissolved in September 1961, Sawwah ran for parliament and won. He founded the Constitutional Bloc with Hani al-Siba'i, another deputy from Homs, and the two men lobbied against all Nasserist influence in parliament. In March 1963, the Baath Party came to power and pledged to restore the union. The officers who came to power punished all those who worked with the post-union government and terminated the civil rights of Ahmad Nawras al-Sawwah. He retired from public life, but his son, Firas al-Sawwah, became one of Syria's most prominent writers in the Arab world in the 1970s and 1980s.

Sources:
Faris, George. *Man Hum fi al-`Alam al-Arabi?* (1957).
Information provided by Firas al-Sawwah (Homs September 30, 2001).

al-Sharif, Jalal
(1925-1983)

Jalal al-Sharif studied law at Damascus University and graduated in 1938. He began his career while still a student in 1945 by writing for the Beirut-based magazine *Lubnan* (*Lebanon*). In April 1947, he joined the Baath Party of Michel Aflaq and Salah al-Bitar, a left-wing socialist party with pan-Arabist views.

Sharif attracted the attention of Aflaq, who appointed him managing editor of *al-Baath*, the party's official newspaper, in 1954. Sharif kept his post for the following four years and served as personal assistant and advisor to Aflaq during the 1950s. In 1958, Sharif wrote in favor of union between Egypt and Syria and praised the pan-Arab policies of President Gamal Abd al-Nasser of Egypt. When the United Arab Republic (UAR) was created in February 1958, other political parties and most political newspapers were outlawed, forcing Sharif to work as a high school instructor.

Sharif was highly critical of the coup that ousted the union government in September 1961. On March 8, 1963, the Military Committee of the Baath Party came to power in Syria and pledged to restore the UAR. Sharif became director of the Wihda Publishing House in Damascus and resumed his editorial duties in *al-Baath*. In 1964, Aflaq appointed Sharif editor-in-chief of the party's new newspaper *al-Thawra* (*The Revolution*). He also became director of journalist affairs at the Ministry of Information.

Following the Arab-Israeli War of October 1973, Sharif helped establish Syria's third state-run daily *Tishreen* (*October*). He wrote extensively during the following decade and published many books and literary studies. His most widely acclaimed works are *Al-Shi'r al-Arabi Hadeeth* (*Modern Arab Poetry*), published in 1975; *al-Adab Kan Mas'ulan* (*Literature was Responsible*), published in 1978; and *Afkar Filastiniyya* (*Palestinian Thoughts*), published in 1981. He also translated *The Grapes of Wrath* into Arabic in 1951. Jalal al-Sharif died on December 3, 1983.

Sources:
Bawab, Sulayman. *Mawsuat Alam Souriyya fi al-Qarn al-Ishreen*, Vol III (1999).

al-Sidawi, Wadih
(1908-1989)

Wadih al-Sidawi studied international law at the American University of Beirut (AUB) and graduated in 1927. He returned to Damascus and opened a legal practice, writing occasionally for the political daily *Alif Ba'*. In 1934, he devoted himself to journalism, closing his legal practice and becoming editor-in-chief of *Alif Ba'*.

In 1940, Sidawi joined the National Bloc, the leading nationalist movement in Syria, allying himself with its leaders Jamil Mardam Bey and Fakhri al-Barudi. In 1943, Sidawi resigned from the newspaper to launch his own pro-Bloc daily called *al-Nasr* (*Victory*). He chose the name *al-Nasr* to hail the recent Allied victory over the Nazis and the liberation of France from German occupation. The newspaper, which appeared on newsstands during the parliamentary elections of 1943, supported for presidential office the candidacy of Shukri al-Quwatli, a prominent leader from Damascus.

When Quwatli was elected president, *al-Nasr* became one of the most prominent propaganda outlets for the new regime. It acquired a favorable audience within political circles in Damascus. The newspaper was banned when President Quwatli was overthrown by a military coup in 1949. Later, Sidawi was arrested during the military regime of Adib al-Shishakli (1951-1954). Sidawi resumed activity when Quwatli returned to office in 1955 and continued to publish when Syria

Wadih al-Sidawi.

and Egypt merged to form the United Arab Republic (UAR) in 1958. Sidawi criticized the manner in which Egyptian authorities treated their Syrian counterparts and praised the coup that overthrew the union in September 1961. From 1961 to 1963, Sidawi supported the anti-union government of President Nazim al-Qudsi. In March 1963, the Military Committee of the Baath Party came to power in Syria and pledged to restore the UAR. The officers punished all those who had worked with the Qudsi government and closed Sidawi's newspaper. Wadih al-Sidawi's civil rights were terminated, but he evaded arrest by moving to the United Kingdom, where he remained until his death in March 1989.

Sources:
Faris, George. *Man Hum fi al-`Alam al-Arabi?* (1957).
Itri, Abd al-Ghani. *Abqariyyat* (1997).

al-Tighilbi, Nash'at
(1914-1995)

Nash'at al-Tighilbi began his career in 1928 by acting in the first Syrian silent movie, *Taht Sama' Dimashq* (*Under the Sky of Damascus*). In 1932, he began to write for the political daily *al-Istiqlal* (*Independence*). In 1936, he moved to the well-reputed Damascus daily *al-Qabas* (*The Firebrand*), working first as a reporter, then becoming editor-in-chief in 1940. In 1942, Prime Minister Saadallah al-Jabiri appointed Tighilbi director of Syrian National Radio, a pioneering channel that broadcasted news, talk shows, and music to the residents of Damascus. It was the first radio station in Syria.

Tighilbi resigned from office in 1945 to run the daily newspaper *al-Akhbar* (*The News*) with its owner Bassim Murad. In 1947, Nash'at al-Tighilbi founded and headed the Editors' Union in Damascus and launched a second newspaper called

`Asa al-Janna (*The Stick of Heaven*). `Asa al-Janna was a satirical periodical well-received in Syria. It continued publication until 1958.

When Husni al-Za'im came to power in March 1949, he appointed Tighilbi as director of Syrian Radio and editor-in-chief of *al-Jundi* (*The Soldier*), the official publication of the Syrian Army. In July 1949, Za'im decorated Tighilbi with the Medal of Loyalty of the Syrian Republic. He was retired from his post at the radio station when Za'im was toppled by coup in August 1949.

Tighilbi spent the 1950s writing for the Egyptian daily *Akhbar al-Yawm* (*The News of Today*). In March 1963, the Military Committee of the Baath Party came to power in Syria and closed all newspaper offices in Damascus. Nash'at al-Tighilbi went to London where he worked with the Lebanese journalist Saleem al-Luwzi for the Arab magazine *al-Hawadeth* (*Events*), contributing a weekly article until his death in December 1995.

Sources:
Faris, George. *Man Hum fi al-Alam al-Arabi?* (1957).
Itri, Abd al-Ghani. *Abqariyyat* (1997).

al-Tillawi, Sa'id
(1915-1973)

Sa'id al-Tillawi was born and raised in Damascus. He did not attend college, but in 1930 began his career as a freelancing journalist, writing for several Arab newspapers in Damascus, Beirut, and Baghdad. In August 1943, he began to write for *al-Ayyam*, supporting the election of Shukri al-Quwatli to the Syrian presidency. Tillawi's articles caught Quwatli's attention, and he became private advisor to the Presidential Palace in 1944.

In November 1945, Tillawi launched a newspaper called *al-Balad* (*The Country*). In 1947, it was renamed *al-Fayha* (*Damascus*), becoming an official mouthpiece for the Quwatli regime. During this time, Tillawi also served as private secretary to President Quwatli. During the Arab-Israeli War of 1948, *al-Fayha* defended the president against accusations of poor leadership, claiming that the war in Palestine was not lost because Quwatli was weak, but rather because the officers in charge of the Syrian Army were corrupt. Tillawi called on Quwatli to discharge his top officers, including Chief of Staff Husni al-Za'im, accusing them of planning a military takeover of Syria. In March 1949, Za'im came to power in Syria and ordered the arrest of Quwatli and Tillawi. During the four-month era of General Za'im, *al-Fayha* was closed for its pro-Quwatli support. But *al-Fayha* returned to print in 1950 and supported the reelection of Quwatli as president in 1955.

In February 1954, Tillawi teamed up with four leading journalists to create a shareholding company to print Syria's four principal newspapers, *al-Qabas*, *al-Ayyam*, *Alif Ba'*, and *al-Sham*. The journalists pledged to unite their efforts to publish the four big newspapers and divide the revenue equally among themselves. Tillawi became a member of the company's board. But the enterprise operated for less than one year, and was dissolved in November 1954 due to disagreements among its founders. Tillawi supported the Syrian-Egyptian union that Quwatli created with President Gamal Abd al-Nasser of Egypt in 1958. But Tillawi grew disenchanted with union when Nasser established a dictatorship in Syria. As a result, Tillawi

Sa'id al-Tillawi.

supported the coup that ousted union in September 1961. From 1961 to 1963, Tillawi became a deputy for Damascus in parliament and supported the post-union government of President Nazim al-Qudsi. During those years, Tillawi also served as a press consultant to Prime Minister Khalid al-Azm.

In March 1963, the Baath Party came to power in Syria and pledged to restore the UAR. The Military Committee of the Baath outlawed all publications, closed *al-Fayha*, and terminated Tillawi's civil rights. He happened to be in Libya at the time of the coup and was forbidden from returning to Syria. He took asylum in Lebanon, but the administration of President Fou'ad Shihab allowed him to stay on the condition that he refrain from writing or criticizing the government while in Beirut. As a result, Sa'id al-Tillawi retired from journalism. He died on January 6, 1973.

Sources:
Faris, George. *Man Hum fi al-`Alam al-Arabi?* (1957).
Itri, Abd al-Ghani. *Alam wa Mubdioun* (1999).

Usseh, Ahmad
(1915-2005)

Ahmad Usseh began his career as a freelance journalist for the Damascus daily *al-Nasr (Victory)*, run by the journalist Wadih Sidawi. In 1946, Usseh became the editor-in-chief of *al-Nasr*.

Usseh was opposed to President Shukri al-Quwatli, who came to power in 1943. Usseh accused al-Quwatli of nepotism and poor leadership, especially after the Syrian defeat in the Arab-Israeli War of 1948. That year, Usseh joined the People's Party (an Aleppo-based opposition party to Quwatli) and in January 1949 became editor-in-chief of the party's political daily *al-Sha'ab (The People)*.

Usseh initially supported the coup led by Chief-of-Staff General Husni al-Za'im that overthrew Quwatli on March 29, 1949. He quickly lost faith in Za'im, however, due to the dictatorship Za'im imposed on Syria. Za'im responded by banning the People's Party and shutting down *al-Sha'ab*. Usseh supported the coup that ousted Za'im in August 1949 and the restoration of civilian rule under the veteran nationalist President Hashim al-Atasi. In 1950, Atasi appointed Usseh director of Syrian Radio. In 1955, Usseh and Nazih al-Hakim co-founded a daily newspaper called *al-Ra'e al-Aam (Public Opinion)*. The newspaper praised Gamal Abd al-Nasser, who had risen to power in Egypt in 1952. *Al-Ra'e al-Aam* called on Atasi to follow in Egypt's alliance with the USSR.

In July 1956, Usseh launched a city-wide campaign in Damascus in support of Nasser's nationalization of the Suez Canal. Usseh helped raise funds for the Egyptian war effort, recruiting volunteers to fight in the Suez War and writing extensively about Nasser, eulogizing him more than any other Syrian journalist. Initially, Usseh was an ardent supporter of the Syrian-Egyptian union of 1958. Before long, however, he grew disenchanted with the Egyptian leadership of the union. In September 1961, he supported the coup that ousted the United Arab Republic (UAR).

Usseh remained in journalism during the post-Nasser era of President Nazim al-Qudsi (1961-1963), but was forced to retire when the Baath Party came to power. To punish his support of the anti-Nasser movement, the Baath government terminated Usseh's civil rights. Usseh went on to become private advisors to King Hasan II of Morocco and King Faysal of Saudi Arabia. Ahmad Usseh died at the age of ninety in Morocco on February 10, 2005.

Sources:
Faris, George. *Man Hum fi al-`Alam al-Arabi?* (1957).

al-Uthmani, Ragheb
(1898-1963)

Ragheb al-Uthmani was born and raised in the coastal city of Lattakia. He studied Islam at the Omariyyah University in Istanbul and began his career during World War I as a judge in an Islamic court in Lattakia. In 1914, he joined the Arab underground that was working to topple the Ottoman Empire.

In 1916, Jamal Pasha, the military governor of Syria, suspected Uthmani of being a member in the underground and placed him under house arrest in Beirut. In 1918, the Ottoman Empire was defeated, and King Faysal became the new ruler of Syria. Faysal released Uthmani from arrest and appointed him as a judge in Damascus. In January 1920, Uthmani became a judge in Hama, a city in western Syria.

When the French proclaimed their mandate in Syria in July 1920, a French military tribunal sentenced Uthmani to death. His nationalist record with the Ottomans proved that he would cause problems for the French. To escape death, Uthmani fled to Amman and joined the court of Prince Abdullah, the Emir of Transjordan. In 1921, Uthmani became the Islamic judge of Kora and held the same post in the town of Irbid in 1923. In reward for his services to the Hashemite crown, Prince Abdullah appointed him Honorary General in the Jordanian Army. That same year, King Ali of the Hijaz appointed him Honorary General in the Arab Army of Mecca.

In 1925, the French issued a general amnesty, allowing Uthmani to return to Syria. He retired from legal services to establish a daily newspaper in Damascus, *al-Siyassa* (*Politics*). The newspaper promoted the nationalist movement, demanding independence from the French and criticizing the regime of Prime Minister Taj al-Din al-Hasani, the leading pro-French politician in Syria who had come to power in 1928. *Al-Siyassa* accused Hasani of corruption, embezzlement, and nepotism. Hasani's most highly criticized actions were the use of government funds to purchase brand new automobiles for the private use of the ministers and Hasani's payment of all his accumulated private debts (for he had money problems prior to assuming office).

Hasani responded by closing *al-Siyassa* and placing Uthmani under temporary house arrest. In 1941, the French appointed Hasani president of the republic whereupon Uthmani, once again, unleashed a war of words against him. Uthmani called on Hasani to step down because he had been appointed by the French and had not been elected by the Syrian people. In 1946, the mandate ended in Syria, and Uthmani was hailed as a leading journalist in the post-French era. In 1951, he became director of education in the Palestinian refugee camps in Syria. He continued to write in *al-Siyassa* until his death in 1963. Thirty years earlier, in 1933, President Mohammad Ali al-Abid had awarded Ragheb al-Uthmani the Medal of Honor of the Syrian Republic, Excellence Class.

Sources:
Faris, George. *Man Hum fi al-`Alam al-Arabi?* (1957).
Khoury, Philip. *Syria and the French Mandate* (1987).

al-Yazagi, Tawfiq
(1880-1957)

Tawfiq al-Yazagi was born in Safita, a city 120 kilometers from the coastal city of Lattakia. He was raised in Beirut and began his career by teaching at high schools in Homs. In 1901, he launched a political weekly in Tripoli (north Lebanon) called *al-Ajyal* (*Generations*).

Yazagi returned to Beirut in 1914 and began work in two other newspapers, *al-Islah* (*Reform*) and *al-Itihad* (*Unity*). Both newspapers were advocates of the Ottoman Empire, but called on Sultan Mohammad Rashad V to grant more freedom to his Arab subjects. In October 1918, the Ottoman Empire was defeated in World War I, and a new Arab administration was set up in Syria under King Faysal I. In 1919, Yazagi started a Beirut-daily newspaper, *al-Difa'* (*Defense*), which called for the creation of an Arab kingdom in the liberated Arab territories. It also argued that the kingdom should be headed by King Faysal or his father, King Husayn of Mecca. In 1920, the French proclaimed their mandate over Syria, and Faysal was dethroned. Due to his alliance with the now ex-King Faysal, a French military tribunal sentenced Yazagi to death. Yazagi fled to Egypt where he worked in the Cairo daily *al-Balagh* (*The Declaration*).

In 1922, Yazagi became editor-in-chief of the popular Egyptian daily *al-Ahram*. In 1926, he established his own newspaper in Cairo, called *Masir al-Haditha* (*Modern Egypt*). He remained in Egypt throughout the period of the French Mandate, only returning to Syria when the French evacuated in April 1946. In 1948, he became chargé d'affaires to the Syrian Embassy in Brazil. In 1950, President Hashim al-Atasi appointed Yazagi ambassador to Argentina.

In 1954, he became director of the Foreign Ministry's press office in Damascus. In 1957, President Shukri al-Quwatli appointed him chairman of a media delegation created to meet with Chinese President Mao Zedong and boost Syrian-Chinese relations. While in Beijing, Tawfiq al-Yazagi suffered a heart attack and died at the age of seventy-seven.

Sources:
Bawab, Sulayman. *Mawsuat Alam Souriyya fi al-Qarn al-Ishreen* vol V (1999).

Yunis, Abd al-Latif
(1914-)

Abd al-Latif Yunis was born and raised in the Syrian Mountains, near the coastal city of Lattakia. In 1934, he began his career by writing for several newspapers. In 1938, he founded his own political daily in Lattakia entitled *Sawt al-Haq* (*The Voice of Justice*).

Yunis wrote inflammatory articles criticizing the French Mandate that was imposed on Syria in 1920. In 1939, he was arrested for his views by the mandate authority. In 1941, he was highly critical of Taj al-Din al-Hasani, a leading pro-French politician in Syria, who had been appointed president by General Charles de Gaulle. Yunis criticized Hasani, claiming that Hasani had been appointed by the French and not elected by the Syrian people. Yunis called on Hasani to step down from office. In reply, Hasani ordered his arrest, and a military tribunal sentenced Yunis to twenty years of hard labor.

To avoid the sentence, Yunis fled to Baghdad. He lived in Iraq until 1942, where he journeyed back to Aleppo in disguise, only to be apprehended by French police. He served a brief sentence and was released in 1943 by President Shukri al-Quwatli, a leader of the nationalist movement.

In 1947, Yunis nominated himself for parliament but lost. In 1954, he repeated his nomination and won, serving as a deputy until 1958. In 1948, Shukri al-Quwatli delegated Yunis as a spokesman for Syria, charged with touring South America and raising funds for the Arab war against Zionism. In 1954, Yunis became an assistant to Speaker of Parliament Nazim al-Qudsi and deputy president of the Bedouin tribe portfolio in the Syrian Parliament. In 1958, Yunis supported the merger of Syria and Egypt to form the United Arab Republic (UAR) and began to write political commentaries for Syrian Radio. Yunis was a supporter of President Gamal Abd al-Nasser of Egypt and a personal friend of ex-President Shukri al-Quwatli, who had created union in 1958. In 1961, on Quwatli's advice, Nasser made Yunis director of the Arab League office in Argentina. Before assuming his new post, however, a coup d'etat took place on September 28, 1961, dissolving the UAR. Nasser asked Yunis to visit Quwatli in Switzerland—where Quwatli had gone in self-imposed exile—and secure a statement of condemnation of the coup. But Quwatli refused to condemn the coup and instead supported the military move carried out by Colonel Abd al-Karim al-Nehlawi.

Yunis became a member of the first post-Nasser parliament in December 1961 and was voted into the Constitutional Assembly that drafted a new constitution for Syria. In 1963, he was accused of supporting the post-union government of President Nazim al-Qudsi (which he did not) after the Baath Party came to power. In 1964, Yunis joined Quwatli in Switzerland, then went to Brazil where he founded an Arabic newspaper called *al-Anba*. He appointed Nabih Salama, a Syrian journalist like himself, as editor-in-chief and published it in Arabic for the large Arab émigré community in South America.

In 1971, Yunis returned to Syria for a press interview with Syria's new president, Hafez al-Asad. He became a fervant supporter of Asad in the upcoming years and wrote extensively about him in *al-Anba*. Subsequently, Yunis befriended and interviewed Arab leaders, notably President Sulayman Franjiyyieh of Lebanon and Yasser Arafat, chairman of the Palestinian Liberation Organization (PLO). Among Yunis' most celebrated works is a biography of President Shukri al-Quwatli entitled, *Tareekh Umma fi Hayat Rajul* (*History of a Nation in the Life of One Man*), published in Cairo in 1959. Abd al-Latif Yunis' memoirs were published in Damascus in 1992.

Sources:
Faris, George. *Man Hum fi al-`Alam al-Arabi?* (1957).
Yunis, Abd al-Latif. *Muzakarat Dr Abd al-Latif Yunis* (1992).

Faris al-Khury with his granddaughter Colette: the elder statesman and the novelist. Faris encouraged his granddaughter's career, and Colette emerged as the most popular Syrian novelist in the 1950s. Her book Days with Him *was reprinted seven times and sparked a feminist consciousness in Syria in much the same way that* The Feminine Mystique *did in the United States. Years later, Colette Khury also served as a Member of Parliament.*

At the opening of the Fine Arts Club in Syria in 1930. From left to right in front row: the journalist Raghib al-Uthmani, Fakhri al-Barudi, Said al-Ghazzi, Mazhar Pasha Raslan, Lutfi al-Haffar, and Afif al-Sulh.

The Librairie Universelle, a bookstore and hangout for Damascus intellectuals in the early 1920s (still in use).

The Sports Scouts Club in Damascus in 1928, The first official group of musicians, actors, and artists in Syria.

ARTS & LETTERS

The individuals in this chapter shaped the cultural, artistic, and intellectual life of Syria during the twentieth century. (Academics are presented in the Educators chapter.)

Many artists and writers during the French Mandate belonged to the National Bloc—the leading anti-French movement in Syria. The organization was created by a group of urban notables dedicated to ending the French Mandate in Syria (1920-1946) by diplomacy rather than armed resistance.

The Arab Language Assemblage is a scientific foundation for the Arab world's most distinguished men and women of letters. It remains the highest international scientific authority in the field of Arab language and literature worldwide. Syrian Arts that depend on printing are linked to the early printing and publishing capabilities in Beirut that were developed in the early 1800s by missionary schools including the American University of Beirut. Syrian playwrights and stage artists began actively performing in Syria after the fall of the Ottoman Empire in 1918.

Did you know? In Sirocco *(1951) Humphrey Bogart (pictured in movie publicity photos wearing a dark trench coat in the old city of Damascus surrounded by sinister looking Arabs wearing the traditional fez headgear) plays an arms smuggler during the anti-French insurgency of 1925. If Syrian artists played a major role in interpreting Arab and Islamic culture to the West, Western movies including* Lawrence of Arabia *used Syria as a stand-in for the wider Middle East.*

Theater in Syria had been originally introduced in the nineteenth century by the pioneer of Syrian theater, Abu Khalil al-Qabbani. Theatrical life was not active under the French Mandate (1920-1946), only becoming a respected and recognized profession during the late 1950s and early 1960s. Although the Baath Party is often regarded as a tight controller of public expression, under Hafez al-Asad (1970-2000) theater flourished in Damascus (see Doreid Lahham, Mohammad al-Maghut, and in particular, the giant of modern theater, Saadallah Wannus, who revolutionized theater from the 1960s onward).

Art that is displayed as paintings hung on the walls of exhibit halls is a Western form. Any art that depicts the human form is often said to contradict traditional Islamic teaching—which helps to explain traditional Arabic emphasis on calligraphy and geometric or floral design. Syrian consciousness of

A poster for Under the Sky of Damascus, *the first Syrian feature film, 1934.*

painting and sculpture grew during the French Mandate when Syrians learned more about French and other European art. After independence, leading Syrian artists such as Fateh Moudarres studied in France and Rome and brought European methods and philosophy home to Syria. During the years of Baath Party rule (from 1963), sculpture and visual art were encouraged, but overt political content in art was not rewarded. Perhaps because of Syria's proximity to Europe, Syrian artists often seem to lead the Arab world in expressing traditional Arab and Islamic themes within modern artistic formats. The most popular form of Syrian art is television drama. Television was introduced to Syria during the union years with Egypt (1958-1961). By the 1990s, Syrian drama challenged and in some cases surpassed that of Egypt, which had dominated the region from the 1960s.

Abu Risheh, Omar
(1908-1990)

Omar Abu Risheh (poet) was born and raised in Aleppo, a central city in northern Syria. He studied chemistry at the American University of Beirut (AUB) and graduated in 1930. He then studied textile manufacturing for one year at an institute in Manchester, Great Britain.

In 1932, Abu Risheh returned to Aleppo and joined the coalition of Abd al-Rahman Shahbandar, the leading nationalist of his generation, who was then demanding an end to the French Mandate and unification between Syria and the Hashemite kingdoms in Jordan and Iraq. By the late 1930s, Abu Risheh had developed a reputation for political poetry and earned a nationwide audience. He became director of the National Library in Aleppo and wrote in the pro-Shahbandar daily *al-Ayyam*, also becoming a member of its editorial board in 1936. Abu Risheh praised Shahbandar's activities and criticized the National Bloc, a nationalist movement vying with Shahbandar for leadership of Syria. Abu

Omar Abu Risheh.

Risheh was particularly critical of the Bloc leader Jamil Mardam Bey, who became prime minister in 1936 and harassed Shahbandar for his views.

In 1940, agents of the French Mandate assassinated Shahbandar, and Abu Risheh became disenchanted with politics. So Abu Risheh abandoned his political career and devoted his time to writing poetry, which he pursued for the next fifty years, earning fame in literary circles throughout the Arab world. In 1948, he was elected to the prestigious Arab Language Assemblage.

In 1949, Abu Risheh joined the Ministry of Foreign Affairs, becoming minister to Brazil in 1950. He held this post until 1953 when President Adib al-Shishakli appointed him minister to Chile and Argentina. After Syria and Egypt merged to form the United Arab Republic (UAR) in 1958, President Gamal Abd al-Nasser appointed Abu Risheh UAR ambassador to Argentina. In 1959, Nasser transferred him to the UAR embassy in Austria.

In September 1961, the UAR was overthrown by a military coup and Syria's new president, Nazim al-Qudsi, appointed Abu Risheh ambassador to the United States. He held this office during the presidency of John F. Kennedy, who showed more sympathy toward the Arab cause than any US president since Franklin Roosevelt. Kennedy strengthened relations with Syria during the Qudsi presidency through meetings with Abu Risheh from 1962 to 1963.

In 1964, Syrian President Amin al-Hafez appointed Abu Risheh ambassador to New Delhi, and his job was renewed by President Nur al-Din al-Atasi, who came to power in February 1966. In 1970, Abu Risheh retired from the Ministry of Foreign Affairs and took up residence in Beirut. When civil war broke out in April 1975, Abu Risheh left Lebanon for Saudi Arabia. In the 1970s and 1980s, he divided his time between Beirut and Riyadh, returning to Lebanon when civil war ended in 1990. President Elias Hrawi awarded Abu Risheh the Lebanese Medal of Honor for his service to Arabic poetry during his fifty-year poetic career. When he died in 1990 in Jeddah, Saudi Arabia, Abu Risheh was hailed in Arab literary circles as one of the greatest contemporary poets in Syria and the entire Middle East. Among Omar Abu Risheh's published works are *Ghannaytu Ma'tami* (*I Sang my Death Song*), *Mukhtarat* (*Selected Works*), and *Min Wahi al-Mar'a* (*From the Inspiration of a Woman*).

Sources:
Faris, George. *Man Hum fi al-Alam al-Arabi?* (1957).
Kayyali, Sami. *Al-Adab al-Arabi al-Mouasir fi Souriyya 1850-1950* (1968).
Khoury, Philip. *Syria and the French Mandate* (1987).
The International Who's Who in the Arab World (1987-1988).

Abu Saud, Abd al-Wahab
(1897-1955)

Abd al-Wahab Abu Saud (actor) was born in Nablus, in modern Palestine, and grew up in Sidon in Lebanon. He studied at the Sultanate School in Beirut, then went to the al-Azhar University in Cairo to specialize in Islamic science.

While in Egypt, Abu Saud attended plays, befriended many up-and-coming actors and actresses, and studied the modern trends of stage acting. He developed an interest in stage production and dropped out of the Azhar Mosque, the most important school of Islamic science in the Islamic world, and became an actor on the Egyptian stage. After one year on the stage, Abu Saud returned to Syria and taught at high schools in the village of Hasbayya in southern Lebanon.

In 1916, Abu Saud was conscripted into the Ottoman Army to serve in World War I. But due to difficult conditions in the army and the fact that most Arabs felt they were being asked to fight a war that did not concern them, he soon deserted

from the army and spent the remainder of the war in disguise, teaching at high schools in rural districts of Syria. But in October 1918, the Ottoman Empire was defeated. In the absence of the brutal, tyrannical system of government that characterized the empire, a sense of hope and a renewal of intellectual life returned to Syria. No longer needing to worry about being an army deserter, Abu Saud threw off his disguise and took up his theatrical interests once again.

Abd al-Wahab Abu Saud.

In March 1919, Abu Saud produced and starred in Syria's first local play, a political show entitled, *Gamal Basha al-Saffah (Jamal Pasha, the Butcher)*, written by the famous Syrian journalist Ma'ruf al-Arna'out. The play exposed the ruthless regime of the Ottoman military governor, Jamal Pasha, who less than six months earlier had been the military strongman of Damascus. It was a great relief for Syrians, who had been brutally oppressed under Jamal Pasha's reign, to see the military governor mocked on stage. In order to promote the work, King Faysal I and his entire cabinet attended the show and delegated Abu Saud to become "an honest political critic of the Arab Government." For the next two years, Abu Saud staged several political comedies that criticized Prime Minister Rida al-Rikabi and his ministers.

When the French proclaimed their mandate in Syria on July 25, 1920, they issued a warrant for Abu Saud's arrest. He fled to northern Syria and again took up teaching at high schools under a false name. After the French issued a general amnesty in 1923, Abu Saud returned to Damascus and continued writing plays. In 1940, he co-founded the Syrian Academy of Music and Acting. He also served as a drama instructor at the elite high school Maktab Anbar. When the French Army left Syria in April 1946, Abu Saud was considered the most popular playwright and actor in Damascus.

Abu Saud also established himself as a pioneer in art. A prolific painter, his paintings were lively, vibrant compositions reflecting his interests in famous historical battles, Muslim architecture in Europe, and landscapes. He was an innovative painter who employed non-traditional methods of color and line.

In 1951, while attending a rehearsal by his students in Bludan, a summer resort near Damascus, Abd al-Wahab Abu Saud had a stroke and died.

Sources:
Itri, Abd al-Ghani. *Hadeeth al-Abqariyyat* (2000).

Adonis (Ali Ahmad Sa'id)
(1930-)

Ali Ahmad Sa'id (poet) was a product of the Qassabin village in the Syrian Mountains. He grew up in poverty and did not attend school until 1944.

At that time, President Shukri al-Quwatli was touring Syria and met the young Sa'id. At first, the elders of Sa'id's village did not allow him to meet Quwatli, and he had to walk to the president's next stop in Jableh, where the mayor proclaimed, "There is a child who walked a long way to read a poem for you Mr President!"

Sa'id recited his original poem to President Quwatli to welcome him. When Quwatli asked if the boy had a request, Sa'id replied, "I want to go to school!" Thus, President Quwatli sent Sa'id to school in Tartus, and later studied philosophy at Damascus University.

In 1947, at the age of seventeen, Sa'id named himself Adonis after the mythic Greek youth of striking beauty who was claimed by two goddesses, Aphrodite and Persephone. While at the university, Adonis was encouraged by his teacher, Dr Antune Makdasi, to begin writing poetry. Another influence was Nizar Qabbani, a poet (and diplomat) who was winning widespread recognition during these years. As Adonis recalls, "Nizar was all over Damascus, rocking the boat in stagnant waters."

Adonis served as an officer in the Syrian Army in the 1950s, then moved to Beirut to obtain a graduate degree from St. Joseph University. He joined the Syrian Social Nationalist Party (SSNP) of Antune Sa'ada, an organization that called for the unification of Greater Syria. In 1955, Adonis was arrested for his views when the SSNP was outlawed in Syria. He was incarcerated in the Mezzeh prison, where he spent a few months before being released into exile in Lebanon. The city of Beirut was the perfect place for Adonis to live the role of exile. It was a vibrant, cosmopolitan, and inspiring haven for ambitious and outspoken Arab poets.

In 1957, Adonis and Yusuf al-Khal, a Lebanese poet who had just returned from New York, co-founded the literary quarterly *Shi'r* (*Poetry*). Periodically, Adonis wrote for the quarterly, which was dedicated exclusively to poetic modernism. From 1960 to 1961, Adonis went to Paris where, under a grant from the French government, he obtained his graduate degree in literature.

In 1968, Adonis launched the avante garde magazine *Mawaqif* (*Stance*) and served on its editorial board. Born out of the Arab defeat in the Arab-Israeli War of 1967, *Mawaqif* advocated for a better collective future for the Arabs. Adonis's early volumes of poetry include *Dalilia*, published in 1950, *Qasaid ula* (*First*

Poems), published in 1956, and *Awrak fi ar-rih* (*Leaves in the Wind*), published in 1959.

In the 1960s, Adonis participated in the creation of a new form of Arabic poetry characterized by revolution, mysticism, elevated diction, and complex surrealism. His poem, *Aghani Mihyar ad-Dimashqi* (*Songs of Mihyar of Damascus*), published in 1961, is characteristic of this new type of poetry and is considered a turning point in his career. Although his subsequent poetry became richer and more experimental, many critics believe that Adonis never surpassed *Mihyar*.

One of Adonis's masterpieces is the four-hundred-page *Mufrad bi-Sighat al-Jam'* (*Single in the Context of Plural*), a dazzling piece of writing that, due to its complexity, has remained unread by many Arabs. Adonis currently thinks that his most complex work is *al-Kitab* (*The Book*), a six hundred-page work published in three volumes in 1993, 1998, and 2002.

Along with Bader Shaker al-Sayyab, Yusuf al-Khal, Onsi al-Hajj, Mohammad al-Maghout, and Nizar Qabbani, Adonis helped create modernism in Arabic poetry. He combines formal innovations of modernism with the mystical imagery of classical Arabic poetry. His work is complex and difficult for common readers. Describing Adonis, an article in a German magazine once said, "He has evoked the anguish of exile, the spiritual desolation of the Arab world, the intoxicating experiences of madness and erotic bliss, the existential dance of self and the other. But what defines his work, above all, is the force of creative destruction that burns through everything he writes."

Adonis clashed with government authorities in Syria during the 1960s and 1970s. Consequently, he took up permanent residence in Lebanon and received Lebanese citizenship. In 1970, he became an instructor of Arabic literature at the Lebanese University, and in 1976 he worked as a visiting lecturer at Damascus University.

In 1980, Adonis was a visiting professor in the Arabic Language Department at the College de France. When the Israeli Army invaded Lebanon in 1982, Adonis was one of the few intellectuals who refused to leave Beirut. During the war, the rivaling militias in Lebanon deliberately shelled his home. In 1986, he made France his permanent residence.

In 1988, Adonis was nominated for the Nobel Prize that ultimately went to Egyptian novelist Najib Mahfouz. Since then, Adonis has been a permanent candidate for the Nobel Prize for Literature. Throughout the years, he has received many medals and prizes in recognition of his work. In 2001, he was the first Arab poet to be awarded the German Goethe medal, a tribute to his literary creativity. As for his rival Arab poets, Adonis claims that they are "continuing the tradition with a few variations, whereas I am the rupture with the past, I am the one who is revolutionizing the order of things, and that is ultimately what matters."

In 1994, Adonis was expelled from the Arab Writers' League in Syria on the charge of meeting with Israeli intellectuals at a conference in Spain. Many noted Arab intellectuals opposed the expulsion of Adonis, including the late playwright Saadallah Wannus and the novelist Hanna Mina.

In September 2000, Adonis joined a group of intellectuals in drafting an appeal to President Bashar al-Asad entitled, "Declaration of the 99." It called on Bashar al-Asad, who had assumed the presidency in July 2000, to allow more political freedoms, release political prisoners from jail, authorize a free press, and lift martial law.

Adonis has been a critic not only of the Arab world, but of the United States and the West as well. In 1971, he wrote a book, *Qabr min Ajla New York* (A *Tomb for New York*)—the vision of a city in flames. The poem takes the perspective of a person walking through the burned city in search of long-lost American poets and culture. Instead, all he finds is "a cloud necklaced with fire" and "people melting like tears."

The Arab media proclaimed Adonis the poet with a prophetic tone. And, after the September 11th attack on the World Trade Center in New York, his work *Qabr min Ajla New York* became a bestseller. Adonis was once described as having "a wild shock of hair, a grizzled face, clever eyes that always seem to be reaching for their target, and the light step of someone who has been on the move for nearly a half century. Small and excitable, he can shift in a moment from literary theory to literary gossip."

The renowned Arab thinker Edward Sa'id called Adonis "today's most daring and provocative Arab poet." The poet Samuel Hazo, who translated Adonis's collection, *The Pages of Day and Night,* said, "There is Arabic poetry before Adonis, and there is Arabic poetry after Adonis!"

Sources:
Adonis. *An Introduction to Arab Poetics* (1990).
Al-Ahram "A Life on Public View" (January 11, 2001).
The Star "Adonis's innovation strikes chord in Arab literature." (January 6, 2002).
Commins, David. *Historical Dictionary of Modern Syria* (1996).
Encyclopedia of the Modern Middle East, Vol I (1996). Article by Kamal Abu Deeb.
Hazo, Samuel. *The Blood of Adonis* (1971).
Meisami, Julie Scott. Starkey, Paul. *Encyclopedia of Arabic Literature* (1998).
The International Who's Who in the Arab World (1987-1988).
Information supplied by Adonis (Paris March 23, 2003).

al-Aghawany, Salama
(1907-1982)

Salama al-Aghawany (master of monologue) began his writing career in 1927 by founding a political weekly in Damascus called *al-Kurbaj* (*The Whip*).

A satirical paper, *al-Kurbaj* criticized the pro-French regime of Prime Minister Taj al-Din al-Hasani and called for termination of the French Mandate. *Al-Kurbaj* combined political literature with humor, cartoons, and short one-act plays written in the Damascene dialect. In 1929, Prime Minister Hasani closed the magazine and had Aghawany arrested.

Three months later, Aghawany was released and began to record small musical number of political humor. The bulk of his musical criticism concentrated on Hasani and his cronies. His sketches gained widespread appeal in Damascus and turned him into an overnight star. When the nationalist leader Fakhri al-Barudi brought him under his patronage, Aghawany's popularity was further heightened. He received funding from nationalist circles and became a member of the National Bloc, the leading anti-French movement in Syria, of which Barudi was a founding member.

In 1929, French High Commissioner Comte Henri De Martel outlawed the monologues of Aghawany, claiming that they insulted the French Republic. Defying French regulations, Aghawany continued to record his music in secret, but toned down his criticism of pro-French politicians and instead spoke out against social injustice, poverty, and corruption.

The Mandate authority arrested Aghawany in 1930 on the charge of defying orders and banished him to Kabul, Afghanistan, the worst possible exile for a political dissident. When Mohammad Ali al-Abid became president of the republic in 1932, he invited Aghawany back to Syria and allowed him to continue his career. In 1940, however, Aghawany's freedom of speech was sharply curtailed, and he again restricted his art to criticizing social affairs. But, unable to contain his ire, within a year he spoke out against the regime of Prime Minister Bahij al-Khatib, Syria's strongman during World War II. Once again he was arrested and sent into exile, first to Cyprus, then to Greece. President Shukri al-Quwatli issued a general amnesty in 1943 and welcomed Aghawany back to Syria where he continued to perform his music until the mid-1960s.

During the union years between Syria and Egypt (1958-1961), President Gamal Abd al-Nasser awarded Aghawany the Medal of Honor, Excellence Class, of the United Arab Republic (UAR). Despite the honor, Aghawany allied himself with the military coup of 1963 that brought the Baath Party to power. In 1971, he became a deputy in the first parliament under President Hafez al-Asad.

Salama al-Aghawany died in Damascus on August 6, 1982.

Sources:

Al-Baath (April 29, 1995).

Itri, Abd al-Ghani. *Alam wa Mubdioun* (1999).

al-Akkad, Mustapha
(1935-)

Mustapha al-Akkad (film director) was born and raised in Aleppo. He attended the local French school. After independence in 1946, he completed his secondary school education at the American Aleppo College. There Akkad discovered his love of acting in the theater arts classes taught by an American teacher named Douglas Hill. When Akkad was nineteen years old, Hill applied for a scholarship to enable Akkad to attend the Theater Arts Department of the University of California at Los Angeles.

During Akkad's studies at UCLA, the insurgency in Algeria was raging. In Los Angeles, famed director Sam Peckinpah was developing a film on this conflict. Searching for an Arab to assist him, Peckinpah contacted Akkad. When the Algerian revolution ended, the film was dropped, but the bond between Akkad and Peckinpah had been forged. After graduation, Akkad accepted Peckinpah's invitation to assist him at the MGM studio on the movie, *Ride the High Country.*

Later, Akkad moved to the CBS News Department. Under Peckinpah's encouragement, Akkad produced his own show, "As Others See Us." He then formed Akkad International Productions to produce and direct documentaries and feature fil

One of his documentaries, *Caesar's World*, was a hit and was broadcast throughout the United States. The success of *Caesar's World* led to Akkad opening offices for his company in Beirut, London, and Hollywood.

In 1972, Akkad founded Filmco International Production. In 1976, he produced and directed his first blockbuster in the Arab world, *al-Risalah* (*The Message*). The movie's popularity in the Arab world prompted him to film an English version for release in the United States. The film was called *Mohammad: The Messenger of God,* and starred Anthony Quinn as Hamza, the uncle of the Prophet Mohammad, and Lauren Papas as Hind, the wife of Abu Sufyan. It was the first time in movie history that a feature film with popular leading actors dealt with the Muslim community and the beginnings of Islam.

The movie received positive reviews in the United States and opened in 3,000 theaters across the country. Some American Muslims, however, were outraged by the idea of a Hollywood movie on Islam, and at least a few apparently assumed that it was a Jewish attack on their faith. In Washington, DC, a group of Hanafi Muslims stormed the Bnai Brith office building, took twenty-two hostages, and threatened violence unless the film was withdrawn from circulation. Akkad negotiated with the Muslim leader Khalif. "Let me show you the movie," Akkad offered. "If you find it objectionable, I will burn it."

The Muslim leader refused the offer, and Akkad was forced to withdraw the film from circulation. Later the movie was released for a second time. Khalif, however, threatened from his jail cell to burn the theaters where the film was showing, and many potential moviegoers kept away from the film. Although Akkad had carefully solicited the approval of various Islamic authorities before creating the film, it was nevertheless banned in Saudi Arabia and other Arab countries. Eventually, Imam Khomeini approved the film for distribution in Iran, and soon it was widely viewed and widely praised in the Muslim world.

Following the September 11, 2001 attacks on Washington and New York City, the Pentagon purchased many copies of *Messenger of God* to help their troops better understand the Islamic faith in preparation for military duty in the Middle East. The film was also widely sold to American educational institutions. *Messenger of God* probably stands as the most successful Muslim attempt at conveying the truth of Islam to a mass Western audience.

In 1978, Akkad produced *Halloween*, a low-budget horror movie that cost no more than $300,000 to produce. It was an instant success in the US box office. The film was inspired by Alfred Hitchcock's *Psycho* and its leading lady Janet Leigh. Akkad hired Leigh's daughter, Jamie Lee Curtis, to play the lead role, even though Curtis was only seventeen and had little experience in films. In Akkad's own words, *Halloween* was a movie where, "horror is based on suspense—there is nothing of the blood, gore, and special effects." As a result of the movie's success, Akkad went on to produce seven sequels, the last released in the United States in 2002. Akkad increased the budget of his movies from $300,000 to fifteen million for the first sequel released in 1981.

In 1981, Akkad produced and directed *Lion of the Desert*. The movie covered the life and struggle of Libyan nationalist Omar al-Mukhtar, who led an armed revolt against the Italian occupation of Libya, but was executed by Benito Mussolini in 1932. *Lion of the Desert* starred Anthony Quinn as Mukhtar, Oliver Reed as General Gratsiani, the officer in charge of crushing the Libyan revolution, and Rod Steiger as Benito Mussolini.

But the impressive cast was not enough to turn the movie into a blockbuster in the United States. Nevertheless, *Lion of the Desert* appeared many times on national US television and was a hit in the Arab world. The film was later dubbed in Arabic and released in the Islamic world, where it is now a perennial classic.

In 1986, Akkad produced a comedy called *Free Ride*. But the movie had a poor cast and a poorer plot, and it passed by unnoticed in Hollywood. In 1987, Akkad produced another horror movie, *An Appointment with Fear*, but it also flopped. In 2001, Mustapha al-Akkad began preparing for his third epic, *Saladin*, a big-budget Hollywood production starring Sean Connery as the Islamic sultan Saladin.

Sources:

Council on American-Islamic Relations-New York Chapter. Biographies published for 2000-2002.

Davis, Scott C. *Light in the Palace* (2006).

Interview with Mustapha al-Akkad. April 28, 2005.

Asmahan (Amal al-Atrash)
(1912-1944)

Amal al-Atrash (vocalist) was born to a notable family from the Arab Mountain. Her parents divorced in 1924, and she was left in the care of her mother, Princess Alia. In July 1925, the military uprising against the French Mandate in Syria was launched from the Mountain by Atrash's uncle, Sultan al-Atrash.

Many members of the Atrash family fled from Syria to avoid persecution by French authorities. Princess Alia, a singer, went to Egypt where she made records to earn a living. Alia also held monthly gatherings with musicians and friends where she and her children sang.

In the early 1930s, Atrash started working at local nightclubs with her brother, Farid al-Atrash, who played in her back-up orchestra. Wanting a stage presence, Atrash changed her name to Asmahan, a catchy yet classy artistic name, and like Farid became a quick success in Egypt. Asmahan was young and beautiful. She had a strong voice and a confident stage presence. Asmahan attracted the attention of prominent Egyptians such as the musician Mohammad Abd al-Wahab and the banker Talaat Harb, who both endorsed her career. Abd al-Wahab advised her to go into the cinema, a novelty in the Arab world, saying that movies would make her famous. Abd al-Wahab would go on to compose the tune for her operetta, *Majnoun Layla* (*Layla Fanatic*), seen in the film, *Yawm Sa'id* (*Happy Day*). Abd al-Wahab also composed the classic song, *Layali al-Uns fi Vienna* (*Nights of Companionship in Vienna*). She also sang at Mary Mansur's Club with the Qassabji Orchestra.

In 1933, Asmahan quit her career under family pressure and married Prince Hasan al-Atrash, the leading political figure in the Arab Mountain. Hasan al-Atrash, who had been married five times, fell madly in love with Asmahan and agreed to all of her conditions. She refused to wear the veil, for instance, and wanted to live in Damascus

From the collection of Sherifa Zuhur.

Asmahan, at the apex of her career in the early 1940s. A close look at the medalion on her jacket shows that it carries the emblem of the Free French Movement of General Charles de Gaulle.

rather than the Arab Mountain. She also wanted to spend the winters in Cairo. In return, the prince's only condition was that she give up her singing career, which she did.

Asmahan lived with Hasan al-Atrash for six years, but longed for the artistic life she once enjoyed in Egypt. She eventually left Damascus and went to live in Suwayda, the capital of the Arab Mountain. General Gabriel Peaux, the French high commissioner in Syria, met her at Hasan's house in the Druze stronghold and remarked, "She didn't take well to the hardships of Druze life, and tried to create, in sad Suwayda, an Occidental atmosphere.

"Asmahan received us unveiled, in a pleated white gown, speaking a clear, pure French learned in a convent in Egypt. Cocktails were being served in front of a mahogany bar built into the salon of the villa. French officers, sabres in their uniforms, surrounded the Amira (princess) who laughed while drinking a mixture of champagne and whiskey." Intoxicated with Asmahan, the general added, "Eros was a God of Hellenism (in reference to the Greek word meaning culture, grace, and perfection) that Mohammad could not dethrone!"

The rebel in Asmahan overshadowed the prim and proper lady that people expected in a conservative Muslim country like Syria. Asmahan drank much and gambled frequently, at times disgracing her conservative and notable Atrash family. Her family preferred to see Asmahan as a princess rather than the singer that everyone knew and loved. And, despite the Atrash family's attempts at protecting and shielding her from fame, Asmahan eventually began to despise married life. She pressured Hasan al-Atrash into a divorce and returned to Cairo.

By the late 1930s, Asmahan was again performing before international dignitaries and had become popular once again in Egypt. She also developed a romance with Hasanein Pasha, the tutor and chamberlain of King Farouk of Egypt. In 1937, she recorded her first movie song, *Aleik Salat Allah* (*For You is the Prayer of God*), which her brother composed for the film, *Al-Mahfal al-Sharif* (*The Holy Lodge*). In 1940, she recorded her classic operetta, *Majnoun Layla*.

Also in 1940, she made the movie, *Intisar al-Shabab* (*Victory of Youth*), with her brother Farid. The film was directed by the prominent Ahmad Badr Khan, and starred Mary Munir, Thuraya Fakhri, and Anwar Wajdi. Samia Gamal, the dancer and future mistress of Farid, also acted in the movie. *Intisar al-Shabab*, a classic in Egyptian cinema, mirrored real life for Asmahan and Farid al-Atrash. In the movie, Asmahan plays Nadia, a girl who comes with her brother Wahid (Farid) to Egypt in search of fame and stardom. They find employment at a nightclub in Cairo where Nadia becomes popular because of her beauty. When asked to sit down and have a drink with a rich customer (i.e. a prelude to sex—something left unsaid in Arabic cinema), she refuses and is fired by the nightclub manager. The rich man feels sorry for her and guilty for getting her fired. He invites her to sing at his villa, where he proposes marriage. His mother objects to the marriage, saying that she will not have a singer in the family, and forces Nadia to leave the house. She returns to sing with Wahid, who becomes successful in show business (just as Farid did in real life). Once back as a singer, Nadia sings classic tunes like *Ya Badi' al-Ward*, *Idi ala Idak*, and *Kan Andi Amal*. After the movie became a hit, Asmahan made headlines in the Cairo press for her romance with the director Ahmad Badr Khan, and even married him, though briefly, for a grand total of forty days.

Asmahan and her husband, the Druze leader, Prince Hasan al-Atrash. Asmahan used her connections in the Arab Mountain to serve the Allies during World War II and facilitate the entrance of Free French and British Forces to Syria, to defeat the pro-Hitler Vichy regime in Damascus.

In May 1941, Asmahan got involved in politics through her connections with the Allied Forces of World War II striving to liberate Syria from the pro-Vichy regime of General Henri Dentz. Contrary to what was written in many Arabic books, there was no spying involved, but Asmahan was asked to go to Syria on behalf of the Allies to speak with the Druze leaders and obtain a promise from them to help facilitate the entry of the Allied forces into Syria.

The Allies believed that, as a member of the Atrash family, Asmahan would be able to convince prominent Druze leaders like Sultan al-Atrash, Abd al-Ghaffar al-Atrash, and her ex-husband Hasan to resist the Vichy forces that opposed the Allies and prevent reinforcements from coming to the Arab Mountain. Hasan agreed to her request on the condition that she marry him once again, and Asmahan accepted. Some claimed that she was rewarded £40,000 for her service to the Allies, but there is no supporting evidence in any of the sources on her life or in any British documents. Her family later claimed that Asmahan worked with the Allies out of patriotism—she believed that they would advance the cause of Syrian independence.

As planned, the Druze leaders permitted the Allies to move into the Syrian heartland, and they managed to expel the Vichy forces from Syria. While staying at the Orient Palace Hotel in Damascus, Asmahan received anonymous death threats (believed to be pro-Vichy Druze). Disguising herself as a horseman, she escaped by night on horseback, leaving her luggage behind, and rode all the way to the Syrian-Palestinian border. There, using documents given to her by the British, she crossed into Palestine where the Allies protected her. Edward Spears, the British ambassador to Syria, expressed intense admiration for Asmahan saying, "She was and will always be to me one of the most beautiful women I have ever seen. Her eyes were immense, green as the color of the sea you have to cross on the way to paradise." After the invasion, Asmahan returned to Damascus, where she paraded through the streets with her husband Hasan and mingled with General Charles de Gaulle when he visited Syria and promised independence. Hasan was appointed minister of war in the cabinet of Prime Minister Husni al-Barazi in 1942 as a reward for his service. The Free French reneged on their promise to grant independence to Syria, however, and a disgruntled Asmahan shifted her allegiance to the Nazis in revenge. She boarded a train and headed to Ankara, where she hoped to meet with Franz von Papen, Hitler's ambassador to Turkey and master of Nazi espionage in the Middle East. But British officials at the border refused to let her pass, and she was returned to Beirut where she could cause them no harm nor contact the Nazis.

Wanting financial freedom, Asmahan divorced Hasan once again, heading off to Jerusalem. She married Ahmad Salim, an Egyptian, in order to return to Egypt since authorities refused giving her a visa due to her attempted collaboration with the Nazis. Once back in Cairo, she began work on her last film, *Gharam wa Intikam* with Yusuf Wehbi, but died before it was completed. In the film, Asmahan sang her classic, *Layali al-Uns fi Vienna*, composed by Mohammad Abd al-Wahab.

Asmahan died in an accident on July 14, 1944, when her car crashed into a water-filled ditch. As the car careened into the ditch, the driver jumped out. Asmahan tried to grab the wheel but failed to rescue herself or the friend who was with her, and they both drowned. It was generally believed that the accident was no accident: that Asmahan was killed by one of the many enemies that she had made in Egypt during the early war years (1939-1941). Asmahan is still regarded as one of the most celebrated artists of the twentieth century. She is a symbol of glamour and intrigue in the Arab world and a legend in modern Arabic music. Fifty years after her death, the academic Sherifa Zuhur met with Asmahan's brother Fou'ad al-Atrash, and when Zuhur asked him about Asmahan, Fou'ad replied, "You mean you want to talk about the Princess Amal al-Atrash?"

Sources:
Al-Hayat (June 10, 2000).
Jaza'iri, Sa'id. *Asmahan* (1990).
Khalifah, Mohammad Rabi'. *Farid al-Atrash wa Asmahan* (2002).
Zuhur, Sherifa. *Asmahan's Secrets* (2001).

al-Atrash, Farid
(1915-1974)

Farid al-Atrash (vocalist) was born in the Arab Mountain to a family of Druze notables. His parents divorced in 1924, and Farid and his sister, Amal (see the profile of Asmahan), were left in the care of their mother, Princess Alia.

After moving to Cairo, Atrash developed a flare for contemporary Arabic music. He worked as a salesman by day and attended the Egyptian Conservatory of Music by night. He learned to play the *oud* (lute) and progressed quickly on the instrument, even competing with his own mentors, the famed Egyptian musicians Mohammad al-Qassabji and Riyad al-Sunbati. The two men highly recommended Atrash to talent agents, and he began to sing on private radio stations in the 1930s. He then moved to Egyptian Radio and began to perform at nightclubs. By the late 1930s, Atrash was composing

Farid al-Atrash.

and singing his own work as well. Then he also helped boost the career of his sister Asmahan. Atrash composed most of her works and introduced her to the orchestra leader Qassabji, who brought her under his wing and turned her into an overnight star. Atrash then starred with Asmahan in several movies until her early death in 1944.

Throughout the 1940s and 1950s, Farid al-Atrash stood out as a melancholic and heart-broken musician, relying heavily on sad tunes and lyrics to attract an audience. He made numerous movies, like Elvis Presley playing different versions of the same type of character—a sad, lonely, single man singing songs of romance and heartbreak in Egyptian nightclubs. But in real life, Atrash enjoyed the Cairo nightlife, had endless love affairs, and squandered his wealth gambling on race horses.

He found comfort in an affair with Samia Gamal, an Egyptian dancer, and starred with her in a movie in 1947. They made four more movies together, then he distanced himself from Gamal when she was courted by King Farouk of Egypt. The playboy king felt threatened by Atrash's popularity among women and deliberately seduced Gamal to ruin her relationship with Atrash.

Atrash went from one love affair to another, refusing to marry because "marriage kills art." He became the Casanova of Egypt and left behind many heartbroken female singers and actresses. In his own words, he "loved being in love" because it was a prerequisite for a successful career, especially in the music business.

In the late 1940s, Atrash befriended Queen Nariman, the wife of King Farouk, in an attempt to revenge the king's affair with Samia Gamal. In his memoirs, Atrash wrote, "More than once I met King Farouk, who loved the night and spent it in public places in Cairo. He often looked at me with a hate whose source I could never understand. Then the pride of the prince in me would come up, just as it did in my sister Asmahan when she met princesses, and I would pretend I had not seen him and spend my night without one look at his table." The king tried to persecute Atrash for the affair, but he lost power in a military revolution in July 1952.

After the coup, Queen Nariman left Egypt with King Farouk, then returned to Cairo and had a stormy love affair with Atrash, becoming an easy target for the Cairo tabloids. Atrash proposed marriage, but her family refused. Nariman's mother declared that she could not possibly let her daughter, now a former queen, be married to a mere singer. The indictment tormented Atrash and led him to prolonged spells of depression where he declared, "they treated me like a singer and forgot that I am also a prince." From then on, Atrash's noble birth cursed him. In troubled times, he would treat everyone around him with disdain—as if he were a prince whose harsh circumstances had forced him to mix with the masses. Atrash became increasingly preoccupied with his deteriorating health caused by heavy smoking and drinking. He set up residence in both Beirut and Cairo and established himself as one of the big spenders in the Arab world. He opened a gambling parlor in Beirut on the Raouche coast and called it Casino Farid al-Atrash. He also had a love affair with the famed Egyptian star Shadia.

In 1946, Farid al-Atrash put his tune, *al-Rabe' to Um Kalthum,* to the words of the poet Ma'mun al-Shinnawi. The song satisfied Um Kalthum, "The Queen of Arabic Music," something that was not easy to accomplish due to her high expectations, and Um Kalthum began to revise the song with Atrash. But Atrash's competitors intervened and advised her not to work with him because her support would turn him into an overnight star in the Arab world. She agreed and ceased work with Atrash, causing him much grief. At the end of their relationship, he complained that Um Kalthum never sang any of his songs and said, "Why do the years pass and my songs remain far from Um Kalthum? It is a question that haunts me and makes me lose sleep. Um Kalthum has sung the songs of many, and not one of the composers, with the exception of Abd al-Wahab, is more important than me nor do they have a celebrated history of composition as I do!"

In 1948, Atrash also wrote the lyrics and composed a national anthem for Palestine, believing that the Arabs would win the Arab-Israeli War. But upon the creation of Israel and the Arab defeat, Atrash tore up the work and never tried to rewrite it. In the 1960s, he joined Abd al-Halim Hafez, another giant of Arabic music, and began to introduce Western instruments into his work while maintaining the traditional lyrics and beat of Arabic music. Atrash adopted everything from flamenco and tango into his compositions and wrote a great waltz, *Layali al-Uns fi Vienna.* Four of his songs, *Nujum al-Layl* (*The Stars of Night*), *Habib al-Omr* (*Love of My Life*), *Layla,* and *Zemorouda* were recorded by international orchestras in the West. Among his best pieces are *al-Rabe'* (*Spring*), *Nura Nura,* and *Qalbi Wa Miftaho* (*My Heart and its Key*), all of which remain incredibly popular in the Arab world today.

Atrash achieved pan-Arab success as a performer and composer, becoming the "king of oud" and moving on to acting in films like *Lahen al-Kholoud* (*Lyrics of Eternity*) and *Intisar al-Shabab* (*The Victory of Youth*), which he starred in with his sister Asmahan. He battled an artistic war with Abd al-Halim Hafez and scheduled his concerts on the same nights as those of his rival to see which radio stations would broadcast his performances in full-length and ignore those of Hafez.

Atrash was tormented by the fact that he had not received the Medal of Honor in Egypt, certain that the snub was because of his Syrian heritage. He commented in his memoirs, "Egypt hasn't given me its Medal of Honor, although it has given it to many others." That same year, President Gamal Abd al-Nasser had given the medal to Um Kalthum and Mohammad Abd al-Wahab and deliberately passed over Atrash, doubting his loyalty to the Egyptian government after the 1961 breakup of union between Syria and Egypt.

In 1970, shortly before his death, Nasser did award Atrash the Badge of Merit, Excellence Class, but Atrash continued to feel that, despite his popularity in the Egyptian streets, Egyptian authorities had not given him the respect and homage that he deserved for the role he had played in the country's cultural life.

Farid al-Atrash launched a revolution in Arabic music and left an indelible imprint with his profound musical gifts. Holding a record of three hundred composed works and thirty-one films, Atrash is considered one of the four giants of modern Arabic music, rivaled only by Abd al-Halim Hafez, Mohammad Abd al-Wahab, and Um Kalthum. He died in Beirut at age sixty in December 1974 at the height of his career. Thousands of women walked behind his coffin screaming in grief, "You taught us love, Farid!"

Sources:
The Cairo Times (April 21, 2001) "The Crooner Who Died."
Abd al-Wahab, Mohammad. *Farid al-Atrash* (1975).
Khalifah, Mohammad Rabi'. *Farid al-Atrash wa Asmahan* (2002).
Al-Jadid (No. 22; 1998) "Remembering Farid al-Atrash: A Contender in the Age of Giants."

al-Ayyad, Kamel
(1901-1987)

Kamel al-Ayyad (publisher) was born in Tripoli, the capital of Libya, and raised in Aleppo, a major city in northern Syria. He studied history and philosophy at the University of Berlin. After graduating with a PhD in 1929, Ayyad returned to Syria and worked as a journalist for the political daily *al-Ayyam*.

In 1932, Ayyad collaborated with Professor Jamil Saliba and the poet Khalil Mardam Bey to found the literary magazine *al-Thaqafa* (*Culture*) which was popular within intellectual circles. But the magazine was forced to close down one year later for financial reasons.

In 1933, Ayyad joined the two socialist philosophers, Michel Aflaq and Salah al-Bitar, and founded another literary periodical, *al-Tali'a*. The magazine became a pulpit for radical socialist views and a gathering place for future members of the Baath Party, later founded by Aflaq and Bitar. Ayyad worked with both men as a senior editor of *al-Tali'a* and also taught history at Damascus University.

However, in 1936, Ayyad distanced himself from Aflaq and concentrated on his academic career. He clashed with French Mandate officials who accused him of calling on his students to take up arms against the French. As a result, they tried to arrest Ayyad, but he fled to Iraq. In Iraq, he taught at high schools until the French issued a general amnesty in 1943 that allowed him to return to Syria. In 1946, the French Mandate ended in Syria, and Ayyad became a member of the Curriculum Committee. He was charged with designing a post-French education system for Syria. Meanwhile, he taught history at Damascus University until his retirement in 1961.

In 1948, Ayyad, who still harbored socialist views, became president of the Syrian-Soviet Friendship Committee. He made numerous journeys to Moscow, established several student exchange programs with the USSR, and promised to help formulate many long-term economic deals between Damascus and Moscow. When Husni al-Za'im came to power in March 1949, he fired Ayyad from his post for his connections to Michel Aflaq.

Following Za'im's downfall in August 1949, President Hashim al-Atasi restored Ayyad to his post and appointed him director of education in Syria. In 1952, he became a cultural expert and consultant at the Arab League Office in Cairo. In 1958, Ayyad was elected into the prestigious Arab Language Assemblage. He remained an active member, conducting research and writing poetry until his death.

From 1961 to 1967, Ayyad served as a professor at The Jordanian University in Amman. He published many books including *Tareekh al-Sharq al-Quadeem (A History of the Ancient East)*, *Tareekh al-Younan (A History of Cyprus)*, and *Muhimmat al-Jami'a fi al-`Alam al-Arabi (The Role of the League in the Arab World)*. He played an instrumental role in introducing Marxist ideas into Syrian literature, familiarizing readers with terms like "class struggle," "proletariat," and "workers' emancipation."

In 1946, Kamel al-Ayyad wrote his classic, *An Arab Novelist and a Soviet Satellite: Omar Fakhury and Maxim Gorky*.

Sources:
Encyclopedia of the Modern Middle East, Vol I (1996). Article by George Irani.

al-Baba, Anwar
(1925-1992)

Anwar al-Baba (actor) was born and raised in Damascus. He dropped out of school at an early age in order to earn a living. Founding a small amateur theater group in 1937, he performed in a short play called *Ataturk*. In 1938, the group staged *Jarimat al-Aba'* (*Crime of the Fathers*). In 1940, he performed in a third play called *Rasputin*.

In 1943, Baba transformed his theater group into a radio show. He and fifteen actors presented a weekly program on National Syrian Radio. Due to the lack of female actors, however, Baba took on female roles himself and in 1947 created the character Um Kamel. A traditional woman who spoke in a strong, provincial Damascene dialect, Um Kamel was full of humor, superstition, and ignorance. Um Kamel was an instant success, becoming a household name in Damascus, and establishing Baba's fame.

In 1945, Baba began writing a weekly column in the cultural weekly *al-Dunya* called "Um Kamel Speaks to You." In 1960, he moved into television and brought Um Kamel to the screen. Among his movies are *Dima' ala al-Raml* (*Blood on Sand*), *Al-Azwaj wa al-Sayf* (*Husbands and Summer*), and *Imra'a Taskun Liwahdiha* (*A Woman Lives On Her Own*), in which he co-starred with Doreid Lahham. He dressed in black, as many conservative Muslim women did, and appeared on shows with rising actors like Lahham, Nihad Quali, and Mahmud Jabr. When Syria and Egypt merged to form the United Arab Republic in 1958, Anwar al-Baba began to star in Egyptian movies, radio shows, and plays. He remained a popular name in Syria until his death.

Sources:

Itri, Abd al-Ghani. *Abqariyyat* (1997).

al-Barudi, Wajih
(1906-1996)

Wajih al-Barudi (physician, poet) was a native of Hama, a city on the Orontes River, and studied medicine at the American University of Beirut (AUB), graduating in 1932. He opened the first clinic in his native Hama on August 7, 1932 and became the city's only doctor.

Early on during his student days at AUB, Barudi was inspired by Arabic poetry. Along with two other students, Ibrahim Tuqan from Palestine and Hafez Jamil from Iraq, Barudi founded a literary club in 1926 and began writing and reading poetry at student gatherings.

Barudi published his first collection of poems, *Bayni Wa Bayn al-Ghawani* (*Between the Courtesans and Me*), in 1950, and it became an instant bestseller.

Wajih al-Barudi.

The collection contained vivid sexual descriptions and tales of romance, which aroused the jealousy of his wife, who burned Barudi's handwritten manuscripts before they could be published. So Barudi was forced to rewrite the work entirely from memory. His second published work, *Kaza Ana* (*This is Me*, 1971), was also highly controversial. It spoke openly of sexual pleasure and shocked the conservative city of Hama.

In 1994, at the age of eighty-eight, Barudi was a well-known poet when he published his third and final work, *Sayyid al-Oushaq* (*Master of Lovers*). In this collection he dubbed himself "the poet of passion" in comparison to Nizar Qabbani, another famous Syrian poet whom he described as "the poet of romance." Barudi's work is famed for its vivid description of romance, sex, and emotional pleasure. His last work, however, is notable for its melancholy. The death of his wife and three of his eight children had greatly affected him. His depression is clearly reflected in his poetry. Barudi's three works are considered some of the most elaborate modern poetry in twentieth-century Syria. While pursuing his career as a poet, he continued to practice medicine. In 1991, Health Minister Iyad al-Shatti awarded Barudi the Shield of Honor for his medical services to Syria, saying that Barudi was the oldest doctor still practicing medicine. Wajih al-Barudi died on February 11, 1996, and was buried in his native Hama.

Sources:
Itri, Abd al-Ghani. *Abqariyyat wa Alam* (1996).

al-Dayrani, Badawi
(1894-1967)

Badawi al-Dayrani (calligrapher) was born in the village of Darayya on the outskirts of Damascus and studied Arab and Persian calligraphy at an art school in Homs. His mentor was Yusuf Rasa, an Istanbul-based calligrapher who had renovated the Umayyad Mosque in Damascus at the turn of the twentieth century.

Dayrani worked under Rasa's supervision until the latter died in 1915. In 1926, Dayrani opened his own calligraphy school in Damascus. It was the first school of its kind and graduated an entire generation of Syrian artists and calligraphers.

During an artistic career spanning fifty years, Dayrani left behind his hallmark calligraphy on various buildings throughout Damascus, including the Syrian Parliament, which he helped design in its present form, the current Ministry of Justice, and the Ayn al-Fija Waterworks Company in downtown Damascus. Dayrani also worked extensively on mosques, designing and drawing the calligraphy for the Thuraya Mosque and the Mansur Mosque in the conservative al-Midan neighborhood, the Rawda Mosque in Rawda, the Fardoss Mosque on Baghdad Street, and the Saudi Mosque in Beirut.

At the time of his death in July 1967, Badawi al-Dayrani was working on the Ottoman Mosque in the Mayssat neighborhood in Damascus. He was posthumously decorated with the Medal of Honor of the Syrian Republic.

Sources:
Itri, Abd al-Ghani. *Abqariyyat wa Alam* (1996).

Fakhri, Sabah (Sabah Abu Qaws)
(1933-)

Sabah Abu Qaws (vocalist) was born and raised in Aleppo. He studied at the Academy of Arab Music in Aleppo and moved to the Damascus Academy, graduating in 1948.

The nationalist leader Fakhri al-Barudi appreciated Abu Qaws' voice, describing it as "majestic," and took him under his wing, fostering his singing abilities and facilitating his entry into the Syrian Broadcasting Station. Under Barudi's influence, Abu Qaws began recording traditional Aleppine songs and chants, excelling in *muwashahat* (songs from Andalusia). He was influenced by the grand traditions of Arabic song and practiced singing the Arabic *mawal*, a poem delivered in a dramatic tone. In appreciation for his mentor's help, at seventeen the young artist dropped his last name Abu Qaws and renamed himself Sabah Fakhri.

Sabah Fakhri quickly established a wide audience in Damascus and Aleppo, and rose to fame overnight in 1960 when he began appearing on national television. Fakhri concentrated on classical Arabic tunes and traditional Aleppine music, performing all-time classics like *Sayd al-Asari*, *Ya Mal al-Cham*, and *Ib'atli Ghawab*. By the early 1960s, Fakhri had appeared in television comedies starring the Syrian duo of Doreid Lahham and Nihad Quali. He also performed in television programs like *Nagham al-Ams* (*The Tune of Yesterday*) and *al-Wadi al-Kabir* (*The Great Valley*) with the Algerian singer Warda.

Over a fifty-year career, Sabah Fakhri managed to bring Aleppine music into every corner of the Arab world. His performances help to preserve a musical style that is being discarded by a new generation of Arab artists who use techno music

Sabah Fakhri.

and video clips to promote their songs, rather than a strong voice and fine lyrics. Fakhri also established himself as the king of *tarab*, an Arabic term for high quality music that seizes the attention of the music lover. In the 1960s, Fakhri helped co-found the Artist Syndicate in Syria and, in 1990, served as a deputy for Aleppo in parliament. In 1992, he entered the *Guinness Book of World Records* as the first performer to sing nonstop for ten hours.

A journalist who attended a Sabah Fakhri concert at the open air concert stage atop the Citadel of Aleppo, a monument that is the pride of Aleppo and Fakhri's favorite venue, described the concert saying, "Sure enough, down there on the stage, a rather rotund man of somewhat diminutive stature had appeared from nowhere. He stared at the crowd for a while, then strolled slowly toward the musicians, with whom he unhurriedly exchanged a few words. Finally the show seemed about to begin.

"Sabah Fakhri, dressed in a dark suit and tie and looking more like a businessman than my idea of an adulated star, grabbed the old-fashioned microphone, unraveling its cord as he measured his steps around the stage; then, without warning, his voice soared toward the skies. It was strong and pure and very distinctive. There is no way one can ever confuse his voice with anyone else's after hearing him even once. It bestows on listeners one of these rare moments of grace when they are confronted with perfection. The singer, at one with his musicians, was transubstantiated; they formed an uncorrupted composition, an entirely harmonious whole. This kind of music does not touch the intellect, but something far more primordial. It is as pure and nostalgic as the sound of the neigh in the twilight, or a call to prayer at dawn. The concert lasted more than four hours, at the end of which the singer, as if in a trance, began to twirl to the music, faster and faster, not unlike a *zikr* performer, bringing the audience's enthusiasm to a paroxysm."

Sources:
Al-Ahram (November 4, 1999).

Farzat, Ali
(1951-)

Ali Farzat (political cartoonist) was born and raised in Hama, a city on the Orontes River in western Syria. As a child, he demonstrated a flair for drawing and began making small sketches, at first intended for his personal amusement. In 1963, he published his first cartoon on the front page of *al-Ayyam*, shortly before the publication was closed down by the new Baath government. He began his career in 1969 as a political cartoonist for the state-run newspaper *al-Thawra* (*The Revolution*).

In the mid-1970s, Farzat moved to the more outspoken government sponsored newspaper *Tishreen* (*October*) and began to publish caricatures on a daily basis. He criticized bureaucracy, corruption, and hypocrisy in government and among the wealthy elite. His caricatures were scathing but not personal. Farzat depicted types rather than individuals, and his caricatures typically ran without captions. Farzat gave voice to the frustrations of ordinary Syrians living in a security state, yet he also expressed the amusement and horror of world citizens outside the centers of power who gauged the deadly effect of armaments, war, and corporate-inspired environmental degradation.

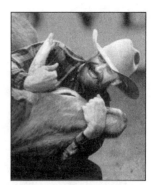

Ali Farzat, a political cartoonist who occasionally competes as a bull wrestler.

In December 2000, Farzat established the first independent newspaper in Syria since the Baath Party came to power in 1963. *Ad-Domari* (*The Lamplighter*) was an effort at political satire similar to the French weekly *Le Canard Enchaine*. The newspaper relied on humorous articles and drawings to shed light on incompetence, embezzlement, and misuse of public office. Farzat hired a staff of renowned critics, such as the comedian Yasser al-Azma and the playwright Mamduh Adwan to help launch the newspaper. As a sign of government approval, the publication was not required to submit its material to censorship prior to publication. *Ad-Domari* published its first issue in February 2001. The entire print run of over 50,000 copies was sold from Damascus newsstands in less than four hours.

Although the details are murky, by the end of February the government apparently pressured Farzat to soften his material—part of a wider effort to keep from losing control of the pro-democracy movement. At this time, Farzat's supporting staff of young, idealistic volunteers quit. In the months that followed, pre-publication censorship for *ad-Domari* was reinstated, and Farzat was required to circulate his publication through the government distribution apparatus. Farzat complained that this system kept his circulation at an artificially low 6,000. Other Syrians attributed the drop in circulation to public disillusionment after Farzat's free editorial policy was curtailed by the government.

In May 2001, Farzat clashed with Prime Minister Mohammad Mustapha Miro, who forced the removal of "Who Put Sticks in the Prime Minister's Chariot?"— an article accusing Miro of mismanagement. Farzat complied, removing the controversial article and instead publishing a blank page that contained only a small drawing of a hand with a pen. In December 2002 Farzat won the prestigious Prince Claus Award from the Hague. To date he has published over 15,000 caricatures in Arab newspapers and in foreign publications such as *Le Monde*. The speed, agility, and ease with which Farzat produces complex and powerful drawings has earned him recognition among his fans as the "Shakespeare of Arab

Political Cartoonists."

Farzat was one of the few public figures in the Arab world to support the removal of Saddam Hussein and, at least tacitly, to support the use of American military power toward this goal. (Farzat's bad blood with Saddam had begun in 1989 when the Iraqi dictator identified himself as the subject of an untitled Farzat caricature. Saddam threatened Farzat's life and barred him from Iraq.) Since then, Farzat has published several dozen anti-Saddam cartoons. In the months leading up to the Iraq War in 2003, both new and old Farzat caricatures ran in Kuwaiti newspapers. Yet the Syrian government strongly condemned the 2003 US-led effort against Saddam. On March 31 and April 1, 2003, the newspaper *Tishreen* denounced Farzat as a money-hungry "foreign" (read: Kuwaiti and American) spy and orchestrated street demonstrations in the plaza near his studio on Pakistan Street in Damascus. Farzat wrote a response, but *Tishreen* refused to run it. Later in the year, Ali Farzat ceased to publish *ad-Domari* for a variety of reasons that included lack of funds, poor readership, and constant clashes with the Syrian censors. By this time, even Syrians sympathetic to the reform movement had tired of Farzat's parodies and longed for straight uncensored news and commentary.

Shortly after his decision to close *ad-Domari*, Ali Farzat's license was revoked by the Syrian government. The final issue, dated July 28, 2003, contained a response to the *Tishreen* attack authored by the human rights lawyer Anwar al-Bunni.

Sources:
Al-Safir (December 16, 1995).
Itri, Abd al-Ghani. *Abqariyyat* (1997).
Tishreen (March 31, 2003; April 1, 2003).
See also:
Davis, Scott C. *The Road from Damascus* (2003) and *Light in the Palace* (2006).
Farzat, Ali. *A Pen of Damascus Steel* (2005).

Fathi, Abd al-Latif
(1916-1986)

Abd al-Latif Fathi (actor), the son of an officer of the Ottoman Army, was born in Damascus to a wealthy family. He studied at Maktab Anbar, the elite school in Damascus, and joined the theater group of Abd al-Wahab Abu Saud in 1927. He was influenced by Abu Saud, the leading actor in Syria, and studied acting through his mentor during the 1930s.

In 1935, Fathi began to work with an Egyptian theatrical group touring Syria that specialized in musical productions. It was here that Fathi learned to direct shows and perform music. In 1936, Fathi co-founded the Music Hall Group with the popular poet Abd al-Ghani Sheikh. One year later, he joined another Egyptian group called the Amin Atallah Group and became an assistant to its director Murad Aslan. Fathi wrote music for the plays and performed short comedy sketches during intermission. In 1939, he became the manager of the Ali al-Ariss Group, one of the leading and biggest theater groups in the Middle East, which specialized in musicals and boasted of a cast of 120 dancers and actors. While working for the group, Fathi wrote the music for the operetta, *Haroun al-Rashid*, about the life of the Abassid caliphate, Sultan Haroun al-Rashid.

As he gained popularity in Syria, Fathi founded his own theater troupe in 1946 and named it Abd al-Latif Fathi Group. It was composed of many actors and actresses, including Ahmad Ayyub, Saad al-Din Baqdunes, Rafic Sibayi, Nour Kayyali, Anwar Murabet, Faten Ahmad, and Claire Sam'an. Fathi's group borrowed heavily from Egyptian theater and performed one-act plays in the Egyptian dialect, the language of Arabic theater at that time.

In 1948, Fathi discarded the Egyptian accent and performed all of his shows in traditional Damascene dialect, claiming that it was improper for Syrians to be speaking an Egyptian accent. The group worked for ten years and achieved unparalleled success, making Fathi the most widely celebrated actor in Syria. He also became the most highly paid star, which enabled him to spend money on wages, production, and scenery. He toured Syria and even performed in rural villages where poor peasants who had little money would pay him with gifts of wheat and other commodities.

In 1956, Fathi founded al-Masrah al-Hurr (The Free Theater) with a group of Syrian actors and worked as an actor, playwright, and director. With this group he stopped making short, one-act plays and turned to longer, more serious shows that aimed at a more sophisticated and educated audience. In 1960 (during the years of the Syrian-Egyptian union), Fathi co-founded the National Theater in Syria, inspired by the National Theater in Egypt. That same year, he became director of Masrah al-Arayyes, the only children's theater in Syria. He hired child entertainment experts from Yugoslavia and Bulgaria, and worked with them to upgrade children's entertainment.

Fathi became director of the People's Theater in Damascus in 1965, and in 1966 produced the classic play, *Azma Asabiyya* (*A Crisis of Nerves*), with Rafic Sibayi and Hala Shawkat. One year later, Fathi directed *Saber Affendi*, a famous play written by Hikmat Muhsen and starring Yasser al-Azma and Muna Wasif. In 1972, Fathi reached nationwide stardom by co-starring in the TV series *Sah al-Nom* with Doreid Lahham and Nihad Quali. In December 1976, he staged William Shakespeare's *King Lear* and was awarded the Medal of Honor of the Syrian Republic, Excellence Class, by President Hafez al-Asad. In an acting career that lasted over fifty years, Abd al-Latif Fathi established himself as the master of Syrian theater and one of the most eloquent stars of television.

Sources:
Olabi, Akram. *Zurafa Dimashq* (1996).

al-Haffar, Salma
(1923-)

Salma al-Haffar (writer) was born and raised in Damascus. She studied diplomacy and public administration at Jesuit University in Beirut and graduated in 1947.

Haffar's father, Lutfi al-Haffar, was a nationalist leader (1920-1946) and served as prime minister in 1939. He encouraged his daughter's writing from her early teens. Haffar's first book, *Yawmiyyat Hala* (*Hala's Dailies*, 1950), described her father's struggle against the French and his exodus from Syria in 1940. In that year, he was accused by the mandate regime of murdering his political rival, Abd al-Rahman Shahbandar. *Yawmiyyat Hala* was an instant bestseller in Damascus, prompting Haffar to write other short stories in Arabic and French in the 1950s. In 1952, Haffar's second book, *Hirman* (*Banishment*), was published in Egypt, and was followed in 1955 by *Zawaya* (*Corners*). In 1961, she wrote *Nisa' Mutafawikat* (*Outstanding Women*) that included a forward by Dr Constantine Zurayk, a renowned academic and one of the greatest philosophers of Arab nationalism.

In 1965, Haffar wrote her best-selling novel, *Aynan min Ishbilia* (*Eyes from Ishbilia*), establishing her reputation as an Arab author. In 1970, Haffar published her autobiography, *Anbar wa Ramad*, and in 1976 wrote a book on the Arab novelist May Ziadeh and her passionate correspondence with the Lebanese poet Gibran Khalil Gibran. Titled *al-Shi'la al-Zarqa* (*The Blue Flame*), the book was published in Syria, and followed Ziadeh and Gibran, two of the greatest poets of all time, as they experienced an ardent love affair through letters alone, never actually meeting each other in person. Their affair has attracted the attention of academics and historians since the early twentieth century. *Al-Shi'la al-Zarqa* was a commercial success and was translated into both English and French in 1996.

In 1986, Haffar published *May Ziadeh wa Alam Asriha* (*May Ziadeh and the Figures of Her Era*), another book on May Ziadeh and her correspondences with other Arab intellectuals from 1912 to 1940. In 1987, Haffar wrote her third book on Ziadeh, a two-volume book entitled, *May Ziadeh wa Ma'sat al-Nubugh* (*May Ziadeh and the Misery of a Genius*). In 1989, Haffar wrote her own memoirs of the Lebanese Civil War entitled, *Al-Hubb B'ad al-Khamseen* (*Love After the Age of Fifty*), and in 1993 her classic, *Basamat Arabiyya wa Dimashqiyya ala al-Andalus* (*Arab and Damascene Fingerprints on Andalus*). In 1998, she published *Lutfi al-Haffar: Hayatuh, Muzakaratuh, wa Asruh* (*Lutfi al-Haffar: His*

Salma al-Haffar.

Life, Memoirs, and Era), the memoirs, correspondences, and achievements of her late father.

Salma al-Haffar has lectured extensively in the Arab world and in Europe about her literary career, and has emerged as one of the most prominent women novelists in Syria. In 1995 she received the King Faysal Award for Arabic Literature.

Sources:
Haffar, Salma. *Lutfi al-Haffar 1885-1968* (1997).
Itri, Abd al-Ghani. *Abqariyyat* (1997).
Nuwayhed, Nadia. *Nisaa Min Biladi* (2000).

Hashim, Labiba
(1880-1952)

Labiba Hashim (journalist) was born in Beirut and studied at the Beirut College for Women (BCW). She wrote for Lebanese newspapers at an early age and studied Arabic literature with private tutors, mainly Ibrahim al-Yazagi. She also studied Persian calligraphy and established herself as a leading and pioneering calligrapher in Syria and Lebanon.

At the turn of the century, Hashim went to Cairo to pursue her literary and journalistic career, writing for the Egyptian magazines *al-Hilal* (*The Crescent*) and *al-Thuraya* (*The Star*). In 1906, she established her own magazine in Cairo called *Fatat al-Sharq* (*Girl of the East*). It was one of the first women's periodicals in the Arab world, and it inspired Mary Ajamy to set up *al-Arous* (*The Bride*) in Damascus in 1910.

In 1909, Hashim sent a long letter to the Ottoman Parliament, outlining her vision for female education in the Middle East and demanding a curriculum change from the new Sultan Mohammad Rashad V. Specifically, she demanded more attention and funds for girls' schools in Syria and Lebanon. She also taught at Egyptian University in 1911 and lectured on the need for better female education in the Ottoman Empire. Inspired by the cultural life of Cairo, her talents flourished. She wrote many poems that were collected by the Lebanese journalist Nicolas al-Baz and published in a book on women's literature in 1919.

Hashim served as editor-in-chief of *Fatat al-Sharq* and employed a large number of young girls as freelancers, editors, and typesetters at her office in Cairo. She would distribute the magazine for free to girls' schools in Egypt, Syria, and Lebanon to encourage girls to read and write poetry, articles, and editorials. Hashim's magazine became very popular among women left behind in their homes during World War I when the region's men were conscripted into the Ottoman Army. She wrote against the war and encouraged the widows of dead soldiers, and the wives and daughters of men serving in the Ottoman Army, to work and provide for their own livelihood. She continued to publish *Fatat al-Sharq* until 1919, one year after World War I ended.

Hashim supported King Faysal I, the new ruler of Syria, who declared himself a supporter of women's rights. In turn, Faysal appointed her inspector of education at the Ministry of Education, accompanied by the scholar Sati al-Husari. Hashim was the first woman to hold a government post in Syria. Along with other women's right activists like Naziq al-Abid, Ibtihaj Qaddura, and Salma Sayyigh, Hashim lobbied heavily for a law granting women their suffrage rights.

In 1921, one year after the French occupied Syria, Labiba Hashim moved to Latin America where she founded another newspaper, *Sharq wa Gharb (East and West)*, in Chile. She worked as its editor until returning to Syria in 1924. Among her most widely acclaimed books was *Qalb Rajul (A Man's Heart)*, published in 1904 and heavily censored in Egypt.

Sources:
Abbud, Khalid. *Nisaa Sha'irat* (2000).
Nuwayhed, Nadia. *Nisaa Min Biladi* (2000).

al-Idilbi, Ulfat
(1912-)

Ulfat al-Idilbi (novelist) was born and raised in Damascus. She began writing while in her teens, and in 1946 published her first masterpiece, *Al-Qarar al-Akheer (The Final Decision)*. In 1947, the BBC Arabic broadcast station chose *Al-Qarar al-Akheer* as the best Arabic storybook of the year.

In 1954, Idilbi published a collection of short stories on the Damascene lifestyle titled, *Qisas Shamiyya (Damascene Stories)*. She wrote about various aspects of life, including dialect, work, and social customs and traditions in Damascus.

Idibli's uncle, the writer Kazem al-Daghastani, brought her under his patronage and introduced her to prominent literary figures in Syria and Lebanon. She attended literary forums in Damascus and was a frequent speaker at the women's rights forum of Thuraya al-Hafez, popular in the 1950s and early 1960s. Idilbi also wrote articles in daily newspapers and appeared at literary salons in Beirut to market her books.

In 1963, making use of her first success, Ulfat al-Idilbi published her second book, *Wada'an Ya Dimashq (Farewell Damascus)*, a bestseller both in Syria and Lebanon. *Wada'an Ya Dimashq* drew the comparison between Damascus in the early years of the century and Damascus in the 1960s, showing how much the city had changed. In 1980, Idibli wrote another bestseller, *Dimashq Ya Basmat al-Hozn (Damascus the Smile of Sadness)*. In 1966, *Dimashq Ya Basmat al-Hozn* was translated into English as *Sabriya*.

Sabriya is the story of a young girl growing up in Damascus in the 1920s. She is tormented by her conservative surroundings and her subordinate role as a woman. She is passionately committed to the nationalist cause, especially when a military uprising breaks out in Syria against the French in 1925. However, she is unable to participate in nationalist activity because of her gender. Her father persecutes her and eventually she commits suicide. Among Idibli's other famed works are *Wa Yadhak al-Shaytan* (*And the Devil Laughs*), published in 1970, *Nazra Fi Adabina al-Sha`bi* (*A Look at Our Common Literature*), and *Hikayat Jaddi* (*My Grandfather's Story*), published in 1991.

Ulfat al-Idilbi has not published many works in recent years due to her advancing years. Nevertheless, she is the most widely celebrated living novelist in Syria.

Sources:
Al-Thaqafa Magazine (November 1993).
Arab Writers' Union. *Tarajim Ada' Itihad al-Kutab al-Arab fi Souriyya wa al-Watan al-Arabi* (2000).
Itri , Abd al-Ghani. *Abqariyyat wa Alam* (1996).
Nuwayhed, Nadia. *Nisaa Min Biladi* (2000).

Ikhlassy, Walid
(1935-)

Walid Ikhlassy (writer) was born in the Sanjak of Alexanderetta, territory in the northern Syria that Turkey later annexed in 1939. Following the annexation of Alexanderetta, Ikhlassy and his family fled to Aleppo, where he grew up. Although he was only thirteen at the time, the Arab-Israeli War of 1948 greatly influenced Ikhlassy's thinking and eventually his writing. The suffering of the Palestinians is a constant theme in his works, and he writes extensively on the Palestinian Diaspora.

Ikhlassy studied agricultural engineering at the University of Alexandria in Egypt and returned to Syria to become a lecturer in the College of Agriculture at Aleppo University. While attending college, he wrote stories. In 1963, he published his first short story collection, *Qisas* (*Stories*). In 1964, he wrote the play, *al-Alam Min Qabl wa Ma Ba'ed* (*The World Before and After*), and in 1970 published another collection of stories, *Zaman al-Hijrat al-Qasira* (*Era of Short Migrations*). Ikhlassy's primary themes were democracy, freedom, responsibility, and alienation from society. Inspired by political events around

Walid Ikhlassy.

him, Ikhlassy wrote about the loss of identity and self, and the failure of human ideals. His writings abandoned the dominant technique of realistic expression in favor of a more surreal and symbolic style. Since the start of his career in 1954, Ikhlassy has published eight collections of short stories translated into English, French, Russian, and Persian. Among his most widely acclaimed works are *Ahzan al-Ramad* (*Sadness of Ashes*), a novel published in Beirut in 1975, and *Sahrat Dimocratiyya ala al-Khashaba* (*An Evening of Democracy on Stage*), a play published in Damascus in 1979. From 1998 to 2002, Walid Ikhlassy served as a member of parliament. In April 2005, President Bashar al-Asad awarded him the Syrian Medal of Honor, Excellence Class.

Sources:
Arab Writers' Union. *Tarajim Ada' Itihad al-Kutab al-Arab fi Souriyya wa al-Watan al-Arabi* (2000).
Encyclopedia of the Modern Middle East, Vol II (1996). Article by Sabah Ghandour.
See also: Davis, Scott C. *Light in the Palace* (2006).

Ismail, Sidqi
(1924-1972)

Sidqi Ismail (novelist) came from Antioch, a town in Alexanderetta, and studied philosophy at Damascus University. In 1947, Ismail joined Michel Aflaq and Salah al-Bitar and founded the Baath Party, a socialist party with an Arab nationalist identity and the goal of unifying the Arab world, liberating it from foreign control, and establishing a democratic system based on socialist views.

In April 1947, Ismail began to write in the party's daily newspaper *al-Baath*. Meanwhile, he taught philosophy at Damascus University. In 1950, he launched a monthly political satirical magazine, *al-Kalb* (*The Dog*), with the Baath Party poet Sulayman al-Issa. Ismail and Issa served as its editors for the next five years. In 1955, Ismail ceased working as a journalist to publish his research on the life of the Tunisian nationalist Mohammad Ali Quabsi. Ismail published his second study, *al-Arab Wa Tajribat al-Ma'sat* (*The Arabs and the Experience of Misery*), in Beirut in 1963.

The 1960s were a literary boom for Ismail, who published a number of his greatest works during that time. He wrote the classic, *Al-Assa* (*The Stick*), a novel set in Syria during the French Mandate (1920-1946) that depicts the misery Syrians experienced. His other masterpiece, *Allah wa al-Faqr* (*God and Poverty*), shows the character of As'ad al-Warrak, a common man plagued by the hardships of life. *Allah wa al-Faqr* was adapted into a television series and was performed on Syrian television in 1960 by TV star Hani al-Rumani. Like the book, the TV series became an instant success.

Among Ismail's other works: *Suqut al-Jamra al-Thalitha* (*Fall of the Heavy Coal*), and *al-Haditha* (*Event*). In 1968, he became secretary of the Higher Council for Art, Literature, and Social Sciences in Syria. One year later, he co-founded the Arab Writers' League in Syria and served as its president until 1971. Sidqi Ismail also worked as editor-in-chief of the cultural publication *al-Mawqif al-Adabi* until his death on September 26, 1972.

Sources:
Arab Writers' Union. *Tarajim Ada' Itihad al-Kutab al-Arab fi Souriyya wa al-Watan al-Arabi* (2000).

al-Issa, Sulayman
(1921-)

Sulayman al-Issa (poet) was born in a village next to Antioch, Turkey. He grew up in Antioch where he took part in anti-French actions in the 1930s. In 1939, he was sentenced to a lengthy prison sentence by a French military court for his protests, but he fled to Baghdad to avoid incarceration.

Issa completed his schooling in Iraq and taught at local high schools, returning to Syria when it achieved independence in April 1946. He taught at Syrian schools and befriended Salah al-Bitar and Michel Aflaq, two schoolteachers who had recently returned from studies in Europe and harbored socialist views and ideas on Arab nationalism. In 1947, Issa joined the Baath Party, a socialist movement founded by Bitar and Aflaq, and Issa helped lay out its ideological structure. The Baath Party was a political organization aimed at achieving the trinity: "unity, freedom, and socialism." The party denounced European imperialism, preached pan-Arabism, and called for a socialist state in Syria. Issa began to write poetry about his nationalist vision and rose to paramount status within party ranks in the 1950s and 1960s. He became the unofficial spokesman for the Baath, promoting its ideology among his students and readers.

In March 1963, the Military Committee of the Baath Party came to power in Syria and included many of Issa's works in the elementary school curriculum. No poet was more familiar to students in Syria from the 1960s to the 1980s. He wrote on Arab inferiority following the Arab-Israeli War of 1967 and praised Hafez al-Asad following the Arab-Israeli War of 1973.

Issa remained a veteran educator and poet, honored and esteemed by Baathists during the thirty-year era of President Asad. In 1991, a committee of veteran Arab academics voted Issa to the prestigious Arab Language Assemblage. As of this writing, Issa has remained an active member, conducting research and writing poetry.

In September 2000, Issa wrote extensively on the Palestinian Intifadah, praising the uprising and calling on Arabs to unite for the recapture of Jerusalem. The works of Sulayman al-Issa include *Ma'al Fajr* (*With the Dawn*), *A'aseer fi Salasel* (*Storms in Chains*), and *Dayaa' al Zohoor* (*The Loss of Flowers*).

Sources:

Arab Writers' Union. *Tarajim Ada' Itihad al-Kutab al-Arab fi Souriyya wa al-Watan al-Arabi* (2000).

Bawab, Sulayman. *Mawsuat Alam Souriyya fi al-Qarn al-Ishreen,* Vol III (1999).

al-Jabal, Badawi
(1905-1981)

Badawi al-Jabal (poet), originally named Mohammad Sulayman al-Ahmad, was born in Difa, a village in the district of Haffa of the Lattakia province. He began his nationalist career at the age of fifteen by joining the forces of Saleh al-Ali in sabotage attacks against the first French forces that landed on the Syrian coast in 1919. Badawi al-Jabal served as a liaison officer between Ali and King Faysal I, the ruler of Syria from 1918 to 1920.

When the Faysal regime was toppled by the French Army in 1920, Badawi al-Jabal was arrested and imprisoned for several months, then released due to his youth. In 1925, he took part in the Syrian revolt of the Arab Mountain, leading a group of rebels in night attacks on French checkpoints. After the French sentenced him to death, he fled to Baghdad, where he he served as a high school teacher of Arabic literature. He returned to Syria in 1936 and enrolled at the Damascus University to study law. The French persecuted him for his earlier anti-colonial activity and arrested him, forcing him to drop out of the university. He spent one year in prison, and upon his release returned to Baghdad to teach Arabic literature.

In 1943, Badawi al-Jabal returned to Syria, joined the National Bloc and allied himself with Shukri al-Quwatli, a member of the Bloc who became president of Syria in August of that year. Also in 1943, Badawi al-Jabal ran for parliament on a Bloc ticket, and won. His election to parliament was repeated in 1947 and 1949. In the post-mandate era, the National Bloc was dissolved by its founders and renamed the National Party. The party was composed of former Bloc members who had a political agenda to modernize Syria, maintain its democratic system, and shun all Arab attempts at uniting Syria with the neighboring Hashemite governments in Iraq and Jordan. The Hashemites wanted a monarchy in Syria while the National Party wanted to maintain the republic. One of its founders and central committee members was Badawi al-Jabal, and its spiritual godfather was Shukri al-Quwatli.

Badawi al-Jabal with a group of Syrian politicians in 1943. Seated from left to right: Fayek al-Nehlawi, Mohammad al- Ayyesh, Speaker of Parliament Faris al-Khury, Sa'id al-Ghazzi, Badawi al-Jabal, and Akram al-Hawrani.

In the early 1940s, Badawi al-Jabal began to write poetry for several literary magazines in Damascus and Beirut. He used the pen name Badawi al-Jabal (Bedouin from the mountain), given to him by Midhat Akkash, the compiler of his poems who ran the newspaper *Alif Ba'e* and published some of Badawi al-Jabal's earliest works. Syrian and Arab literary circles warmly received the young poet and he quickly rose to fame. In no time, he became one of the best-known, yet most dangerous poets of his generation.

Badawi al-Jabal concentrated his work on romantic verse and political criticism. He adhered to the classical school of Arabic poetry, refusing to apply modern words and phrases to his writing. He was transformed into a political poet following the Arab-Israeli War of 1948, when he accused the entire Arab command of poor leadership and of having led the masses into defeat.

When General Husni al-Za'im came to power in Syria in March 1949, he ousted Shukri al-Quwatli and ordered Badawi al-Jabal's arrest. The poet fled to Lebanon where he continued to write against Za'im, eventually returning to Syria when Za'im was killed in August 1949. When Hashim al-Atasi became president of the republic in December 1949, Badawi al-Jabal became a leading publicist for the new government, writing articles in Arabic periodicals praising the new leadership.

From 1951 to 1954, Badawi al-Jabal returned to the underground and worked against the military regime of President Adib al-Shishakli. When Shishakli was overthrown in 1954, Hashim al-Atasi once again became president of Syria and appointed Badawi al-Jabal minister of health in the cabinet of Prime Minister Sabri al-Asali. Badawi al-Jabal held this office from March to June 1954, after which he became minister of health once again in the cabinet of Prime Minister Faris al-Khury (October 1954 to February 1955).

In September 1955, Prime Minister Sa'id al-Ghazzi appointed Badawi al-Jabal minister of state for media affairs and propaganda, a post he held until June 1956. Badawi al-Jabal was critical of the pro-USSR policies of President Shukri al-Quwatli, who returned to power in 1955. He also opposed Syria's alliance with the socialist government of President Gamal Abd al-Nasser of Egypt. In 1956, fearing persecution for his views, Badawi al-Jabal went to Lebanon, then Turkey, then Tunisia, and finally settled in Switzerland for what he claimed was permanent residence. In 1958, Syria and Egypt merged to form the United Arab Republic (UAR). Badawi al-Jabal criticized the union, claiming that it had destroyed Syria's democratic system. He supported the coup of 1961 that overthrew the UAR. Then he returned to Syria in 1962. Badawi al-Jabal no longer took part in politics and devoted the remainder of his years to writing poetry. Among his published classics are *Diwan Badawi al-Jabal*, published in Sidon in 1925, and *Al-A'mal al-Kamila (The Complete Works)*, published in 1978. His poems are mostly nationalistic and patriotic, but he also wrote love poetry.

Sources:
Encyclopedia of the Modern Middle East, Vol I (1996). Article by Charles U. Zenzie.
Kayyali, Sami. *Al-Adab al-Arabi al-Mouasir fi Souriyya 1850-1950* (1968).
Uthman, Hashim. *Badawi al-Jabal* (1998).

al-Jabiri, Shakib
(1912-1996)
Shakib al-Jabiri (writer) was born in Aleppo (not Damascus as some sources say) and studied at the National Academy of Aley and at the Islamic Institute in Beirut, graduating in 1933 with a degree in literature and Islamic studies.

In 1936, Jabiri returned to Damascus and joined the National Bloc. After he participated in anti-French riots, the French Mandate authority banished him from Syria in 1937. Jabiri exiled himself to Geneva and joined the nationalist movement headed by anti-French statesman Prince Shakib Arslan. Jabiri wrote extensively against the mandate while continuing his graduate studies in chemistry at the University of Geneva. Jabiri worked briefly at the League of Nations, then obtained a doctorate degree from the University of Berlin.

In 1937, while in Europe, Jabiri wrote his first novel, *Na'am (Yes)*. In 1939, his second novel, *Qadar Yalhou (Fate that Distracts)* was published in Syria. *Qadar Yalhou* became an instant bestseller. The French granted him amnesty, which allowed him to return to Syria in 1943. The same year, President Shukri al-Quwatli appointed Jabiri director of broadcasting at the newly formed Syrian Radio. Quwatli also appointed him director of propaganda. In 1944,

Jabiri established his own literary magazine, *Alamayn* (*Two Worlds*). He also published a literary periodical at Damascus University, *Asda'* (*Feedback*). In 1946, his third book, *Qaws Qazah* (*Rainbow*) was released, becoming a bestseller throughout the Middle East. Jabiri spent the 1940s teaching and writing while continuing to uphold the Quwatli regime in his articles, speeches, and activity. When Quwatli was ousted in March 1949, Jabiri was retired from his post by Syria's new president, General Husni al-Za'im. In 1952, President Adib al-Shishakli appointed Jabiri ambassador to Iran, and in 1955 he became president of

Shakib al-Jabiri.

the Syrian Syndicate of Arts. Shakib al-Jabiri died in Saudi Arabia on October 13, 1996.

Sources:
Itri, Abd al-Ghani. *Abqariyyat* (1997).

Jabri, Shafiq
(1898-1980)

Shafiq Jabri (poet) was born and raised in Damascus. He was taught literature by private tutors in Jaffa, Alexandria, and Damascus, and began to write for *al-Mazhab* (*The Sect*), a weekly magazine based in Zahle, Mount Lebanon.

Jabri joined the Syrian Ministry of Foreign Affairs in 1918. He became advisor to Foreign Minister Abd al-Rahman Shahbandar, serving until the French proclaimed their mandate in Syria and ousted Shahbandar in July 1920. Jabri then became bureau chief for Education Minister Mohammad Ali al-Abid from 1922 to 1924 and director of the Education Bureau in Damascus.

Meanwhile, Jabri wrote nationalist poetry that was warmly received among the nationalists in Syria, but caused him trouble with the French. A team of veteran Arab academics voted him into the prestigious Arabic Language Assemblage in 1926. He conducted research and published with the Assemblage throughout his life.

In 1930, Jabri became director of a high school in Aley, Mount Lebanon. He praised the National Bloc and wrote extensively on the dedication shown to their cause and the achievements of its leadership. In 1936, Jabri joined the National Youth, a paramilitary movement created by the nationalist leader Fakhri al-Barudi to mobilize the masses into participating in anti-French conduct. Jabri was part of the movement's administrative council, organizing parades, marches, and strikes in favor of the nationalist movement. He also served as director of the Institute of Literature in Damascus and joined the Bloc, becoming an ally of its

Damascus chief Jamil Mardam Bey.

In 1951, Jabri was appointed dean of the Faculty of Education at Damascus University and remained at his post until Syria and Egypt merged to form the United Arab Republic (UAR) in 1958. He was vehemently opposed to the Syrian-Egyptian union and praised the coup that overthrew the UAR in 1961. He allied himself with Syria's new president, Nazim al-Qudsi, and wrote fiery poems criticizing the union government and President Gamal Abd al-Nasser of Egypt.

When the Baath Party came to power in March 1963 and pledged to restore union with Egypt, Jabri retired into seclusion in Bludan, a summer resort in the Syrian mountains. Among his published works are *Bayn al-Bahr wa al-Sahra'* (*Between the Sea and the Desert*), published in 1946, *Ana wa al-Shi'ir* (*Poetry and I*), published in 1959, and *Ard al-Sihr* (*Magical Land*), published in 1962.

Shafiq Jabri wrote two classics: *Al-Anasser al-Nafsiyya fi Siyasat al-Arab* (*Psychological Impacts on Arab Politics*), published in 1945, and his autobiography, *Afkari* (*My Thoughts*), published posthumously in 1998.

Sources:
Itri, Abd al-Ghani. *Hadeeth al-Abqariyyat* (2000).
Kayyali, Sami. *Al-Adab al-Arabi al-Mouasir fi Souriyya 1850-1950* (1968).

Jubran, Mary
(1911-1956)

Mary Jubran (vocalist) was born in Beirut, but raised in Damascus during the early years of World War I. She practiced singing at private gatherings, and in 1924 performed before Salama al-Hijazi, an Egyptian contractor visiting Damascus. Hijazi loved her voice and brought her to Cairo for a one-year singing contract. Jubran was only twelve years old.

In addition to singing in Cairo, Jubran acted on the Egyptian stage with theater star Husayn al-Barbari, often playing minor roles. She returned to Syria when her contract expired in 1925, but was forced to flee when the Syrian Revolt broke out against the French Mandate. Jubran went to Beirut where she performed in local nightclubs, and returned to Syria in 1929 to sing at the Qasr al-Ballour (Glass Palace) nightclub in Qassa, the Christian neighborhood of Damascus.

In 1932, Badia Masabni, an Egyptian dancer, hired Jubran for another contract in Egypt, where as a more mature performer she became a huge success. Her performances had improved and her physical features matured, making her one of the main attractions of Cairo nightlife and earning her the nickname, "Mary the Beautiful." She befriended leading Egyptian composers like Mohammad al-Qassabji, Zakariya Ahmad, and Dawoud Husni. These men had helped elevate the Egyptian diva Um Kalthum to stardom and had previously done wonders for the Syrian singer Asmahan, transforming her into a star in Egypt in the early 1930s. Jubran hoped that they would do the same for her career.

Mary Jubran.

Dawoud composed the music for two of Jubran's classics, *Asl al-Gharam Nazra (Origin of Love is One Glance)*, and *Al-Habib lil Hajr Mayel (The Loved One Wants to Leave)*. Her rapid fame, however, annoyed many well-established Egyptian artists, who began to defame her, claiming that she should return to Syria. They applied pressure on the Egyptian government to extradite her, and when that failed, circulated rumors that tarnished her reputation. In spite of strong pressure to leave, she remained in Egypt until 1937.

When she returned to Syria, Mary Jubran became the number one artist in Damascus. She signed a contract for daily performances at Abbasid Club in Damascus for a staggering salary of 150 gold coins per month. She performed her own songs, but also sang the well-known songs of the Egyptian divas Um Kalthum and Munira al-Mahdiyya. When the Syrian National Radio was established in 1942, Jubran began to perform on radio and recorded her classic song, *Khamrat al-Rabi (Wine of Spring)*.

During the Arab-Israeli War of 1948, Jubran stopped singing romantic verse. Instead, she concentrated on national anthems and lyrics. Among her classics in 1948 were the songs *Dimashq* and *Zanoubia*.

In June 1956, Mary Jubran developed cancer and died at the age of forty-four.

Sources:
Itri, Abd al-Ghani. *Abqariyyat wa Alam* (1996).

Kayyali, Lu'ayy
(1934-1978)

Lu'ayy Kayyali (painter) was born and raised in Aleppo and began to paint landscapes at the age of eighteen. In 1952, he held his first exhibition in Aleppo. He also briefly studied law at Damascus University, but then went to Italy and studied decoration at the Academy of Fine Arts in Rome from 1956 to 1961. He was greatly influenced by the works of Leonardo de Vinci.

Meanwhile, Kayyali began to produce oil paintings and earn artistic awards from Italian art critics. Kayyali combined elegant and classical lines with tightly arrayed compositions that became the hallmark of his works. He painted every day grievances, simple people, and depicted the casual, if sometimes harsh reality of daily life in the Arab world. Most of the people depicted in his paintings had mute, sorrowful faces, along with protruding eyes and long, skinny fingers. Kayyali's paintings expressed how he saw life as filled with misery and sorrow.

Kayyali himself suffered from depression. Believing that art was a reflection of life, Kayyali was obsessed with the tragedy of his own works toward the end of his life. He moved from seeing art as mimicking life to seeing life as a reflection of art. And he became convinced that his life should reflect the sorrow and despair of his art. He considered his personal tragedies and its resulting anguish as a link to universal suffering and a uniting force among people. He said that art needed to depict sorrow at all times so that all people could appreciate it and identify with it.

In 1964, Kayyali began to teach at the College of Fine Arts in Damascus. In 1967, he held his greatest exhibition, "For the Cause," containing paintings about Arabs suffering Israeli aggression, depicted with his signature expressive, skinny fingers. When the Arab-Israeli War took place that year, which lead to a collective Arab defeat, Kayyali was so depressed that he destroyed all of the thirty paintings on display. He resigned from his teaching post and went to Aleppo where he briefly stopped painting. Kayyali fell into a deep depression after the war that was accompanied by heavy drinking, smoking, and dependency on prescription drugs. Meanwhile, in 1970, at the most profound period of his despair, Kayyali began to paint again, and these works are considered some of his finest.

Kayyali painted *The Dama Player* in 1975, which sold at a London auction in 2001 for £25,800. *The Newspaper Boy* sold for £30,400. His paintings, which depicted the poor, always sold for high prices, prompting one journalist to write, "The poor people of Lu'ayy Kayyali live in the homes of the rich and wealthy."

In 1978, Kayyali burned to death in a fire started by his cigarette while he was drunk. Kayyali is one of the most highly acclaimed artists in Syria today. His paintings are rare, expensive, and highly prized. Lu'ayy Kayyali is considered a giant of Syrian art, equaled only by Fateh al-Moudarres.

Sources:
Biographical sketch provided by the Association of Fine Arts in Damascus, Syria.
Maksoud, Saadallah. *Art for All: Dictionary of Contemporary Fine Art in Syria* (2002).
Sotheby's Sale of Art of the Islamic World in May 2001.

Khury, Colette
(1937-)

Colette Khury (novelist) was born in Damascus and studied French literature at Damascus University. She grew up under the influence of her father, the politician Suhayl al-Khury, her journalist uncle Habib Kahaleh, and her grandfather Faris al-Khury, a renowned statesman who led the anti-French movement from 1920 to 1946 and served as prime minister in the 1940s and 1950s.

In 1957, Khury published her first collection of poetry in French, *Vingt Ans* (*Twenty Years*), at the age of twenty. Two years later came her classic work, *Ayyam Ma'ahou* (*Days with Him*), which became a bestseller. Khury's central character in *Ayyam Ma'ahou* was a rebellious Damascene girl who defies the norms of society to attain her professional and romantic dreams—a scenario that conservative people in Damascus viewed with disapproval. Part of the story was based on Khury's real-life early friendship with the Syrian poet Nizar Qabbani.

During the early 1960s, Khury wrote for her uncle's political weekly *al-Mudhik al-Mubki*. She devoted the remainder of her time to writing novels and teaching literature at Damascus University. In March 1963, the Baath Party came to power in Syria and arrested her father for his political views. Khury refused to flee to Lebanon after her father's arrest, as many intellectuals associated with the pre-1963 regime had done. Instead, Khury continued to live and work in Syria. In Khury's own words, she described the situation saying, "In that period, I was facing two difficult situations. Either I become a Syrian living abroad, or a stranger living in Syria. I took the more difficult solution and I stayed." When her uncle Kahaleh died in December 1965, she managed *al-Mudhik al-Mubki* with her cousin Samir Kahaleh until the magazine was closed down by the government in May 1966.

In the early 1980s, Khury began collecting historical documents and information, and published the first part of her grandfather's diary, *Awrak Faris al-Khury* (*The Papers of Faris al-Khury*), in 1989. Her other published works are well-read all over the Arab world and are particularly popular in Damascus. They include *Al-Marhala al-Murra* (*The Bitter Period*), published in 1969, *Wa Marr Sayf* (*And a Summer Passed*), published in 1975, and *Ma'ak Ala Hamish Riwayati* (*With You on the Margins of My Novels*), published in 1986. In 1979, Khury published another classic, *Ayyam Ma' Al-Ayyam* (*Days with the Days*), the story of an upper-class girl from Damascus who falls in love with a poor young man with socialist views. Due to political events, the young lovers are forced to flee Syria. Nonetheless, this girl remains loyal to her country. In

Colette Khury.

this book, Khury tried to show that the notability of Damascus, of which she was a member, had remained loyal to Syria despite the turbulent political conditions they endured.

Two of Khury's other classics are *Da'wa Ila al-Qunaitra* (*Invitation to Qunaitra*), written after the Israeli occupation of the Golan Heights in the Arab-Israeli War of 1967, and *Dimashq Bayti al-Kabir* (*Damascus Is My Big Home*), published in 1969.

From 1990 to 1995, Khury became an independent deputy for Damascus in parliament. One of her novels, *Al-Ayyam al-Mudi'a* (*Bright Days*), which recount-ed the Arab-Israeli War of 1973, became mandatory reading material for eleventh grade students in Syrian high schools.

Colette Khury is one of the most widely read women novelists in Syria and the Arab world.

Sources:
Interview with Colette Khury (June 21, 2001; September 2, 2001).
See also: Davis, Scott C. *Light in the Palace* (2006).

Lahham, Doreid
(1932-)

Doreid Lahham (actor) was born and raised in Damascus. He studied chemistry at Damascus University and became an instructor in the Chemistry Department. Also inspired by theatrical and musical arts, Lahham gave dancing lessons to university students.

In July 1960, Syrian TV director Sabah Qabbani chose Lahham, and several other amateur actors, to star in a television mini-series called *Sahret Dimashq* (*Damascus Evening*). It was one of the earliest shows to be produced, acted, and broadcast on Syrian TV. After gaining popularity as an actor, Lahham resigned from academia to devote his time to acting.

Lahham created an Arabic version of Laurel & Hardy with the well-established theatrical star Nihad Quali, and performed on three television shows that became instant successes throughout the Arab world. Lahham played the role of Ghawar al-Tawsheh, a slapstick clown, rascal, and prankster who resorts to ludicrous pranks in order to attain his desires: a woman he loves, a job, and a chance to sing at a local café. His aspirations are always hampered by Husni al-Burazan, played by Quali, a decent, peaceful, kindhearted man who always puts up with the mad-ness of Ghawar, often resulting in physical, financial, and moral suffering.

"Doreid & Nihad," as they were known, were the stars of a TV series, *Sah al-Nawm (Good Morning)*, in 1971. In this series, Ghawar tries in vain to win the heart of a woman in love with Burazan. A heartbroken Ghawar tries to implicate

Burazan in robbery, tries to bankrupt him, and finally tries to kill him. When all else fails, Ghawar gives his beloved a dose of special medicine that makes her lose her memory and stop loving Burazan. The show was so popular that Lahham produced a sequel in 1973, and made a movie with the same title. The evil yet lovable Ghawar quickly became a household name in Syria and throughout the Arab world.

Doreid Lahham.

Following the Arab defeat in the Arab-Israeli War of 1967, Lahham moved to live theater and applied construc- tive criticism and political satire to his work, abandoning the traditional earlier comedies. He joined Mohammad al-Maghout, a political playwright, and began performing plays that criticized Arab inefficiency, weakness, corruption, and poverty. Lahham's first show, *Masrah al-Shawq (Theater of Thorns)*, consisted of naive, primitive political comedy, but was greatly welcomed by Arab audiences. Authorities in Syria wanted to arrest Lahham for his "hidden meanings." But Syrian Defense Minister Hafez al-Asad refused, claiming that Lahham must be allowed to say what he pleased. Lahham, Quali, and Maghout created an excellent team, dividing the plot, dialogue, and acting among themselves, while making the famed TV director Khaldun al-Maleh the director of all of their plays.

The plays of Doreid Lahham became the only outlet for even marginal politi- cal criticism in the Middle East throughout the 1970s and 1980s. His popularity soared, not only in Syria, but in many other Arab countries as well. He toured the Arab world with several plays. *Day'at Tishreen (October Village)* focused on the Arab-Israeli War of 1973. *Ghorba (Alienation)* addressed Arab emigration to the West. A third play was *Kasak ya Watan (Cheers to the Homeland)*, performed in 1979.

Kasak ya Watan is about Ghawar, an Arab citizen who has great pride in the Arab people but is forced to abandon his nationalist ideals because he is humili- ated in his own country. In Lahham's own words, "It is a play about the death of relations between citizens and their country."

In *Kasak ya Watan*, Ghawar's daughter dies due to hospital negligence. Then Ghawar is forced to sell off his remaining male children to earn a living. Eventually, he is arrested on false charges by his country's intelligence service, and when released sells the medals of his father, a war-hero killed in battle against Israel, to purchase alcohol. Ghawar resorts to drinking heavily, saying that this is the best way for him to forget that he is an Arab living in miserable conditions.

Lahham's next work was *Shaka'ik al-Nu'man (Anemones)*, a sequel to 1974's *Day'at Tishreen*, and his last collaboration with Maghout. In *Shaka'ik al-Nu'man*, Lahham demonstrates that Arabs die just like sea anemones if they are uprooted from their homeland. Lahham calls on Arabs living abroad to return to Syria in order to build a better future for Arab generations to come. The play portrays the confused Arab world Lahham was living in, where the past is mixed with the present, and where the dead talk, interact, and work with the living. Leaders throughout the Arab world received Lahham when he performed each show. He even toured the West, performing to the large Arab émigré communities in North and South America.

In 1976, President Hafez al-Asad decorated Lahham with the Medal of the Syrian Republic, Excellence Class. He was also given medals of recognition by Tunisian President Habib Bourguiba, who gave him the same medal in 1979, and Libyan leader Mu'ammar al-Quaddafi in 1991. Nine years later, Lebanese President Emile Lahhoud awarded Lahham the Order of Merit of the Lebanese Republic in a ceremony held at the American University of Beirut (AUB) and granted through the Syrian Culture Club at AUB.

In the 1980s, having established himself as a revolutionary actor in the Arab world, Lahham presented two political movies: *al-Hudud* (*The Border*) in 1984, and *al-Taqrir* (*The Report*) in 1986. The latter won recognition for Lahham as "the Arab Charlie Chaplin." In 1991, the Arab World Academy in Paris honored him for the two films, producing a one-week festival of his works and declaring him the "best Arab actor" of all time. Throughout the 1990s, Lahham worked alone and presented a variety of works that he wrote, directed, and starred in. In 1992, he performed two more theatrical works without Maghout, Quali, or the director Khaldun al-Maleh. One of them, *Alusfura al-Sa'ida* (*The Happy Bird*), was a children's show. Lahham finally retired from stage acting in 1993, claiming that "the big issues have collapsed" and that Arab audiences were not eager to listen to the type of social problems that he dealt with in the 1970s. His resignation from the theater came immediately after the Arabs began to sign peace deals with Israel, a moment in history that Lahham dreaded. In 1999, Lahham tried to resurrect the character of Ghawar that he had abandoned in the early 1980s when his works became more political than comical. He performed *Awdet Ghawar* (*The Return of Ghawar*), but the work failed to achieve the success Lahham had earned in his earlier comedies.

In 1997, in recognition of his two children's productions, the movie *Kafroun* in 1990 and *Alasfura al-Sa'ida* in 1992, Lahham became the UNICEF representative in Syria for children's affairs. He put on several television series aimed at increasing awareness of the problems of children. Then in 1999, he became UNICEF ambassador for Childhood in the Middle East and North Africa. But in 2004 he left his job at UNICEF after paying a visit to South Lebanon—the districts liberated from Israeli occupation in 2000. At the Lebanese-Israeli border, Lahham gave a press conference criticizing George W. Bush and Ariel Sharon, comparing them to Hitler. The statement was published in Lebanon and republished in Israel, causing Tel Aviv to protest to UNICEF that its goodwill ambassador was using undiplomatic language. UNICEF asked Lahham whether he made the statements that his critics said he made. When Lahham confirmed that he had made those statements, UNICEF sent him a letter thanking him for his service. Lahham considered this letter an indirect message relieving him of his duties at UNICEF.

In 2001, Lahham returned to television work as a talk show host on the Saudi-owned MBC channel. On his talk show, *Ala Mas'uliyati (On My Responsibility),* he conducted political, social, and cultural debates with leading politicians, artists, and intellectuals from the Middle East and North Africa. In 2002, he performed another talk show on MBC called *Alam Doreid (Doreid's World)* where he held lively debates with creative Arab children.

Sources:
Jammal, Farouk. *Doreid Lahham* (2002).
Interview with Doreid Lahham (July 7, 2001).
See also: Davis, Scott C. *Light in the Palace* (2006).

Luka, Iskandar
(1929-)

Iskandar Luka (writer) was born and raised in the province of Alexanderetta. In 1939, the province became part of Turkey as stipulated in the Turkish-French treaty of World War II. In consequence to the treaty, Luka's family was forced to move to Damascus where Luka studied education and psychology at Damascus University. He obtained his graduate and postgraduate studies from Jesuit University in Beirut.

In 1950, Luka began to write for the weekly *al-Alam al-Arabi (The Arab World),* and in 1956 became editor-in-chief of the political daily *al-Jumhour (The Masses).* One year later, Luka joined the *al-Wihda (Union)* daily and wrote articles in favor of President Gamal Abd al-Nasser of Egypt. Luka lobbied for union with Egypt from 1956 to 1958. During the Syrian-Egyptian union (1958-1961), he became director of the press office for President Nasser. Following the dissolution of the United Arab Republic (UAR) in 1961, Luka became director of archives at the Ministry of Information. He held this post from 1962 to 1967. From 1967 to 1971, Luka was director of training personnel at the premiership in Syria. In 1971, he taught Ottoman Turkish at the History Department at Damascus University, and in 1974 began to teach at the Journalism Department. In 1973, he became an advisor in the office of President Hafez al-Asad and continues to hold this office under President Bashar al-Asad.

Luka's first work, *Hubb fi Kanisa (Love in a Church),* was published in 1952, and in 1958 he wrote a play, *Iskandaron* (*Alexanderetta*). He praised the Baath Party revolution of 1963 in his book, *Souriyya wa al-Thawra fi Amiha al-Hadi Ashar* (*Syria and the Revolution in its Eleventh Year*), published in 1974, and compiled a dictionary on the Ottoman Turkish language in 1976. Luka wrote two books on Asad: *Hafez al-Asad: Qiyam Fikriyya wa Insaniyya* (*Hafez al-Asad: Human and Ideological Principles*), published in 1986, and *Sha'b wa Qa'id* (*A People and a Leader*), published in 1992.

Other works of Luka include *Al-Haraka al-Adabiyya fi Dimashq 1800-1918* (*The Literary Movement in Damascus 1800-1918*), published in 1976, and his latest work, *Harb al-Khaleej: Ihtilal wa Tahrir al-Kuwait* (*Gulf War: Invasion and Liberation of Kuwait*), published in Damascus in 1992. Iskandar Luka's last collection of stories, *Awdat Shahine* (*The Return of Shahine*), was published in 1999.

Sources:
Arab Writers' Union. *Tarajim Ada' Itihad al-Kutab al-Arab fi Souriyya wa al-Watan al-Arabi* (2000).
Interview with Dr Iskandar Luka (April 5, 2004).

al-Maghout, Mohammad
(1930-)

Mohammad al-Maghout (playwright) was born and raised in the town of Salamiyya next to Hama, a city on the Orontes River in western Syria. He began his career in 1950 by writing for the periodical *al-Shurta* (*The Police*). In 1955, he began to write for *al-Noor*, the official publication of the Syrian Communist Party.

In 1959, Maghout published his first collection of poems, *Huzn Fi Daw' al-Qambar* (*Sorrow in Moonlight*). In 1960, the regime of President Gamal Abd al-Nasser persecuted Maghout for his political views and ordered his arrest. After his release in 1961, Maghout wrote about the injustice of life, the daily needs of poor citizens, and the ever-present threat of Israel. He wrote with a socialist vision, criticized capitalism and landowners, and advocated for the rights of peasants, workers, and the rural masses. In 1965, he began writing short, one-act plays, claiming that the reasons behind all Arab suffering was fear, hunger, and Israel.

In 1973, Maghout wrote a play on the October War performed by Doreid Lahham and Nihad Quali, two Syrian comedians who were beginning to shine in Arab artistic circles. The play, *Dai'at Tishreen* (*The October Village*), was a political comedy recounting Syria's modern history and covering the years of military revolts, the inefficiency of Arab leaders, and the issue of Palestine and the Arab-Israeli conflict. It indirectly mocked President Gamal Abd al-Nasser of Egypt, showing that when he came to power he had the popularity to achieve victory but misused it, leading the Arabs to defeat in 1967. So successful was the play that Maghout worked with Lahham and Quali once again to produce another show, *Ghorba* (*Alienation*), in 1975. *Ghorba* dealt with the massive Arab emigration to the west in the 1970s. The play is considered a classic of modern Arab theater.

Ghorba was followed by another show in 1978, *Kasak Ya Watan* (*Cheers to the Homeland*), that portrayed current Arab conditions as harsh. The protagonist in *Kasak Ya Watan* is an average Arab citizen who is proud of his heritage. But through poverty, persecution, and defeat, the man is forced into despair, selling his children to earn a few pennies. According to Maghout and Lahham, the play addresses the separation between Arab citizens and their government. The protagonist is arrested by the intelligence service, persecuted by government authorities, and witnesses the death of his daughter due to medical negligence. He is so utterly defeated that he starts to drink heavily in order to forget that he is an Arab. The show ends with Maghout's character making a wistful toast to the homeland, an unforgettable ending that garnered a standing ovation at every performance.

In 1989, Lahham and Maghout mounted their last play together, *Shaka'ik al-Nou'man* (*Anemones*), a sequel to *Dai'at Tishreen*. *Shaka'ik al-Nou'man* focused on an Arab citizen who is released from Israeli prisons after twenty years in captivity and is shocked to see how much the Arab world has changed. He is disgusted by the corruption, the dictatorships, and the poverty around him, and subsequently decides to emigrate to a foreign country. Eventually he discovers that he cannot emigrate since Arabs, Maghout claims, are like anemones, if uprooted they will die. The play ends with a call to Arabs to return to their homeland and help construct a better world for future Arab generations.

After the run of *Shaka'ik al-Nou'man*, the writer and the actor quarreled for professional reasons and ceased collaboration. But the four shows that Maghout produced with Lahham became classics in the Arab world. Both men are household names in Syria.

Mohammed al-Maghout continues to write political works. The most famous of these is *Sa Akhoun Watani* (*I Will Betray My Homeland*), published in 1987.

Sources:
Arab Writers' Union. *Tarajim Ada' Itihad al-Kutab al-Arab fi Souriyya wa al-Watan al-Arabi* (2000).

Makdisi, Antune
(1914-2005)

Antune Makdisi (writer) was born in the town of Yabrud on the outskirts of Homs and studied law in Beirut before completing his graduate studies at Montpellier University in France. He returned to Syria in October 1940 and taught at local high schools in Homs, Hama, and Damascus. He also wrote weekly commentaries on current events and philosophical matters in several newspapers in Damascus and Beirut.

Makdisi joined the Arab Socialist Party of Akram al-Hawrani in the mid-1940s, and personally authored its bylaws and constitution. He became one of the prime young ideologues of socialism in the late 1940s and early 1950s. In 1953, during the military dictatorship of Adib al-Shishakli, Makdisi supported and co-orchestrated the merger between Hawrani's socialist party and the Baath Party of Michel Aflaq,.

In 1961, Makdisi began to teach political science at Damascus University and remained in academia for the next twenty years. One of his most celebrated students was the poet Adonis, who rose to fame in the second half of the twentieth century. When the Baath Party came to power in 1963, Makdisi gave up on politics, arguing against the militarization of Baathism.

In 1965, Makdisi became director of penmanship and translation at the Ministry of Culture. In 2000, he wrote several articles in the Lebanese press that criticized the lack of political freedom in Syria. He also spearheaded the civil society movement following the inauguration of President Bashar al-Asad in July 2000. Specifically, Makdisi demanded that the state lift all emergency laws imposed on Syria after the Baath Party Revolution in 1963. Before the end of the year, he was fired from his post by Culture Minister Maha Qannut, with what Makdisi regarded as little ceremony or respect.

During his long career, Makdisi translated many Western classics into Arabic, including the works of Socrates, Plato, and Karl Marx. He wrote no books, however, adhering to the Socratic view that writing books freezes ideas, while dialogue stimulates them. "I consider the human presence as a journey to discover the world," he once wrote. "It's an endless discovery because the world has no beginning and no end for a human being."

Following his firing in 2000, Antune Makdisi amended his will to stipulate that no state officials be allowed to attend his funeral. So, when he died in January 2005, Makdisi was buried without no government officials in attendance.

Sources
Batatu, Hanna. *Syria's Peasantry: The Descendants of its Lesser Rural Notables and Their Politics* (2000).

Mardam Bey, Khalil
(1898-1959)

Khalil Mardam Bey (poet) studied literature and political science at the University of London and graduated in 1922. He was influenced by the Arab nationalist Abd al-Ghani al-Arissi, who spearheaded the opposition to the Ottoman Empire during World War I.

In 1913, Mardam Bey signed a famed declaration, presented to the first Arab Congress in Paris, demanding emancipation from the Ottoman Empire. As a youth, Mardam Bey was arrested for his allegiance to Arissi in 1914. He began to write nationalist poetry at an early age, beginning when Arissi and his comrades were executed by the Ottoman Turks in May 1916. He supported the Arab underground that declared an uprising against the Ottomans in June 1916 and led to the Ottoman defeat in October 1918.

Mardam Bey served in the government civil service from 1918 to 1920, and founded an intellectual salon at his home in 1921. The salon was attended by leading poets of his generation, including Mary Ajamy, Shafiq Jabri, and Prince Mustapha al-Shihabi. Mardam Bey also wrote nationalist poetry, eulogizing the Syrian revolt of 1925 and the courage of its leaders. His classic poem, *Yawm al-Faza' al-Kabir* (*The Great Day of Terror*), was written when the French bombed Damascus on October 18, 1918.

In 1925, Mardam Bey was voted into the prestigious Arab Language Assemblage. Due to his anti-French views, however, Mardam Bey was forced to flee Syria in 1926 and remain in exile in London until 1929. In 1933, he co-founded the *al-Thaqafa* (*Culture*) magazine with Dr Jamil Saliba, a professor at Damascus University. In April 1942, Prime Minister Husni al-Barazi appointed Mardam Bey minister of education. In January 1943, he was given the same post by Prime Minister Jamil al-Ulshi. In 1949, Mardam Bey served in the same position during the short-lived military regime of President Husni al-Za'im. In 1948, he became a member of the Egyptian Language Academy, and the following year, became a co-founder of the Iraqi Language Academy. When Mohammad Kurd Ali, the founder and president of the Arab Language Assemblage, died in 1952, Mardam Bey succeeded him and remained in charge of the institute's affairs until his own death in 1959.

Khalil Mardam Bey.

In 1953, President Adib al-Shishakli appointed Mardam Bey minister of foreign affairs. He played a crucial role in strengthening Syria's ties with Lebanon and Jordan, two countries that were hostile to the Shishakli regime. During his tenure as minister, Syria opened its first embassy in Amman and eased the tension between Damascus and the Beirut regime of President Kamil Sham'un.

Mardam Bey continued to write poetry even as he served his government. His most renowned and remembered works, however, are the lyrics of the Syrian National Anthem, which he wrote in 1939. Among his written works is *Shu'ara' al-Sham* (*Damascene Poets*), published in 1932. His son, the poet Adnan Mardam Bey, collected, edited, and released many of his father's previously unpublished works including *A'yan al-Qarn al-Thaleth Ashr fi al-Fikr, wa al-Siyasa wa al-Mujtama* (*Notables of the 13th Century in Thought, Politics and Society*), published in 1971, and *Takareer al-Khalil al-Diblomasiyya* (*Khalil's Diplomatic Reports*), published in 1982.

Khalil Mardam Bey died in Damascus on July 21, 1959, and was officially named *Sha'ir al-Sham* (*The Poet of Damascus*).

Sources:
Itri, Abd al-Ghani. *Hadeeth al-Abqariyyat* (2000).
Kayyali, Sami. *Al-Adab al-Arabi al-Mouasir fi Souriyya 1850-1950* (1968).

Mina, Hanna
(1924-)

Hanna Mina (novelist) was born in the coastal city of Lattakia in northern Syria and grew up in the Sanjak of Alexanderetta on the the Syrian-Turkish border. He grew up in poverty and became a communist during his teens.

Mina drifted through several jobs, working as a barber, a bicycle repairman, a pharmacy clerk, and ended up a sailor in 1941. For financial reasons he never went to school, although his mother wanted him to become a priest or police officer. Years later, Mina looked back at his youth and said that he had studied at the "university of black poverty." He added that there are two kinds of poverty: white and black. White poverty was what he was living in now as a professional writer in Syria. Black poverty was how he had lived as a child, "hungry, barefoot, and naked."

Mina started his career by writing letters for his neighbors and getting paid for it. In 1947, he went to Damascus and began writing for the daily newspaper *al-Insha* run by the journalist Wajih al-Haffar. In 1951, Mina became the paper's editor-in-chief and also co-founded the Syrian Writers' Association with the painter Fateh al-Mouderres. Mina was persecuted for his communist views and was frequently arrested during the 1940s, 1950s, and 1960s. In the 1950s, he became a strong supporter of President Gamal Abd al-Nasser of Egypt, who preached a socialist state with a classless society.

Mina wrote about the daily suffering of man, depicting the tumultuous lives of inhabitants of the Syrian coast. Of his thirty novels, eight are about the sea, which he loved during his years as a sailor. He portrayed the complexities of individual life, showing how daily acts can be transformed into heroic ones in the subconscious mind and used to elevate one's perception of life.

Although Mina had no formal education, he became highly regarded in Arab literary circles. In 1985, he wrote his autobiography, *Kayf Hamalt al-Qalam* (*How Did I Carry the Pen?*). Among his best published works are *Al-Thalj Ya'ti Min al-Nafiza* (*The Snow Comes from the Window*, 1969), *Al-Shira' Wa al-Asifa* (*The Mast and the Storm*, 1977), and *Arrabi' wa al-Kharif* (*Spring and Autumn*, 1984).

In the 1990s, Mina's productivity increased threefold. He began producing a novel per year, and all of them became bestsellers in Syria. In 1990, he wrote *Fawq al-Jabal wa Tahet al-Thalj* (*Over the Mountain and Under the Snow*). In 1992 came *Al-Raheel B'ad al-Ghurub* (*Departure After Sunset*). In 1996, Mina wrote *Al-Mar'a Zat al-Thawb al-Aswad* (*The Woman with the Black Robe*). And in 1998, he published his masterpiece, *Al-Rajul Allazi Yakrah Nafsahu* (*The Man Who Hates Himself*).

In 2002, President Bashar al-Asad decorated Mina with the Highest Order of the Syrian Republic in reward for his services to Syrian culture over a fifty-year period. In a rare moment of reflection, Hanna Mina looked back on his career and said that even when he was in his forties, having spent nearly thirty years writing novels, he never imagined that he would become famous in the Arab world. Despite the fame, which he attributed to "pure luck," Mina added, "I have started to hate this melancholic profession and the only way out of it is death. I wanted to meet death but I never did. Death is a coward. For eighty years I have pursued him, but he keeps running away from me."

Sources:
Arab Writers' Union. *Tarajim Ada' Itihad al-Kutab al-Arab fi Souriyya wa al-Watan al-Arabi* (2000).
Interview with Hanna Mina published in Geneva, Switzerland.

al-Moudarres, Fateh
(1922-1999)

Fateh al-Moudarres (painter) came from an affluent, aristocratic family in Aleppo. He studied at the Academy of Fine Arts in Rome and graduated in 1956. During his studies, he painted landscapes and participated in his first art exhibition at the village of Bayt Meri in Mount Lebanon in 1947.

While in Rome, Moudarres met the renowned French playwright Jean Paul Sartre. Sartre admired Moudarres's paintings and his poetry, and the two men became friends. Moudarres spoke to the French existentialist regarding the Arab-Israeli conflict and Palestine, and convinced Sartre that given proper lobbying,

Fateh al-Moudarres.

the atrocities taking place in the Occupied Territories could be stopped. Sartre then wrote extensively against the French government when the Algerian Revolution broke out, claiming that it too was an atrocity against the Arabs. Sartre praised Moudarres with an invitation: "Come to Paris and I will make you famous!" The friendship influenced Moudarres greatly, but it did not make him famous. He declined Sartre's offer and only visited Paris a decade later, after achieving success in the Middle East.

In 1950, Moudarres returned to Syria and held his first independent exhibition in Aleppo. He took part in international exhibitions in Sweden and the United States, and in 1956 became a faculty member of the Academy of Fine Arts at Damascus University. He also established himself as a ranking expressionist, painting traditional Syrian life and depicting ordinary Syrians in their varying moods, customs, and daily expressions. Moudarres became dean of the academy, a post he held until 1993. He devoted the rest of his life to exhibitions in Europe, the United States, and the Middle East. In 1986, he published a collection of short stories, *Awdet al-Nana* (*Return of Mint*). He was better known as a painter, however, than as a short-story writer or poet. Moudarres served as teacher and mentor to Syria's leading artists and was described by critics upon his death in 1999 as "father of the modern art movement in Syria."

Moudarres was a dreamer and a visionary. Villages and nature were two of his favorite subjects, and he strove to depict the soul of Syrians in his paintings through a pallet of browns and reds. Frequently he used his mother, who had profoundly affected his life, as a subject for his paintings. In the 1980s, while meeting an American writer in Syria, Moudarres lectured him on life, beauty, and art. He said, "There must be a bridge from the person within to the beauty of humanity, not ugliness, but the beauty of the soul, the face, life, women, poetry, and science. We call it beaux-arts. One must paint from one's own influence, so that we can enrich the art of the world."

Moreover, added Fateh al-Moudarres, "Art gives humanity a sense of honor."

Sources:
Itri, Abd al-Ghani. *Abqariyyat* (1996).
Maksoud, Saadallah. *Art for All: Dictionary of Contemporary Fine Art in Syria* (2002).
See also: Davis, Scott C. *The Road from Damascus* (2003).

Muhsen, Hikmat
(1910-1968)

Hikmat Muhsen (actor, producer) was born in Istanbul and grew up in Damascus. He received no schooling due to poverty, and began acting in amateur theater at the age of 14. In 1932, he founded his own theater group bearing his name, and joined with the Fine Arts Club of Wasfi al-Maleh in 1936.

Muhsen was admired by the National Bloc leader Fakhri al-Barudi, who encouraged young talent. Muhsen also joined Abd al-Wahab Abu Saud, the leading theater star in Syria in 1937. Muhsen spent the 1940s working on stage in Damascus, performing in colloquial Arabic and often using the traditional Damascene dialect to attract audiences. His theater was not sophisticated, but due to its simplicity attracted a large audience.

Muhsen often portrayed the character of Abu Rushdi, a simple citizen of Damascus who experiences difficulties in life due to poverty, injustice, and day-to-day problems. He teamed up with Anwar al-Baba, another pioneer of Syrian theater, who played the role of Um Kamel. Together, the two men created a comic duo that quickly became popular in Syria.

In 1950, Muhsen moved to the Near East Radio in Palestine and began writing and acting in radio shows as the character Abu Rushdi. One year later, in 1951, Ahmad Usseh, the director of Syrian Radio, hired Muhsen and Baba to produce comedies starring Abu Rushdi and Um Kamel. Muhsen's most widely remembered and acclaimed production was the play, *Saber Affendi* (*Saber Effendi*), produced in 1957.

Muhsen wrote other memorable shows including *Bayt lil Ajar* (*A House for Rent*) in 1960, and *Al-Abb* (*The Father*) in 1966. One year later, Muhsen wrote his classic, *Yawm Min Ayyam al-Thawra al-Souriyya* (*One Day from the Days of the Syrian Revolt*), a musical with a large cast, elaborate stage effects, and finely choreographed dancing. Upon his death in 1968, Hikmat Muhsen was hailed as one of the pioneers of Syrian theater.

Sources:
Olabi, Akram. *Zurafa Dimashq* (1996).

Qabbani, Nizar
(1923-1998)

Nizar Qabbani (poet) was born and raised in Damascus. He studied law at Damascus University and joined the Ministry of Foreign Affairs following his graduation in 1945.

In his early years, Qabbani was influenced by his father Tawfiq Qabbani, a merchant, who had financed the nationalist movement against the French Mandate in Syria from 1920 to 1946. From 1945 to 1948, Qabbani served as Syria's consul in Egypt, and from 1948 to 1952, as consul to Turkey. In 1952, Qabbani was transferred to the Syrian Embassy in London, where he was greatly influenced by European art, culture, and life.

In 1944, while still a university student, Qabbani wrote his first set of love poems, *Qalat Liya al-Samra'* (*The Brunette Said To Me*). A collection of short poems written in simple Arabic, *Qalat Liya al-Samra'* attracted a wide readership in Damascus, especially among teenagers and young lovers. Qabbani used ordinary language in his poetry and concentrated mainly on romantic sentiment and sexual desires. Almost instantaneously he attracted an audience and a large army of critics who called his work blasphemous. From 1944 until his death in 1998, Nizar Qabbani ignored all criticism. Munir al-Ajlani, the minister of education, wrote the introduction to Qabbani's book, affectionately saying, "Nizar, you are certainly something new and strange in our world!"

By the early 1950s, Qabbani's reputation had spread to Lebanon, the cultural center of the Middle East. In 1954, he wrote another classic poem, *Tufulat Nahid* (*The Childhood of a Breast*), which broke all the taboos of Arabic poetry and was highly criticized for its sexual content. In 1955, he performed his first high profile poetry recital at the American University of Beirut (AUB), and one year later he wrote his first political piece, *Khobz, Hashish, wa Qamar* (*Bread, Hashish and a Moon*), that depicted the Arab people as drugged, confused, and destroyed. *Khobz, Hashish, wa Qamar* began a trend in Qabbani's poems that criticized Arab dictatorships. Conservative politicians in Syria severely criticized him. In a heated parliamentary debate, some even recommended his dismissal from the Ministry of Foreign Affairs.

In 1963, Qabbani resigned from the Foreign Ministry to take up residence in Beirut and devote his time to political poetry and romantic verse. In 1966, he wrote the romantic classic, *al-Rasm Bil Kalimat* (*Drawing with Words*). In this work Qabbani abandoned sexual descriptions and wrote about pure love while eulogizing Arab women. After the Arab-Israeli War of 1967, he wrote extensively on the Arab defeat and was highly critical of President Gamal Abd al-Nasser of Egypt for leading the Arabs into a misguided war. In 1967, he wrote his masterpiece, *Hawamesh ala Daftar al-Naksa* (*Margins on the Notebook of Defeat*), a book banned in Egypt. He also wrote another masterpiece, *al-Mumathilun* (*The Actors*), that accused Arab leaders (including Nasser) of being nothing but stage actors who put on performances before the Arab audience.

When Nasser died in September 1970, Qabbani softened his criticism and praised Nasser's nationalism, claiming that "in an age of dwarfs" the only true giant was Nasser. Qabbani composed many poems in homage to Nassar, including *al-Haram al-Rabe'* (*The Fourth Pyramid*). The Egyptian star Um Kalthum sang another classic written by Qabbani on the commemoration of Nasser's birthday following his death.

In 1977, Qabbani was banished once again from Egypt. In his poem, *Min Yawmiyat Bahiya al-Masriyya* (*From the Daily Diary of Bahiya the Egyptian*), he criticized the visit of President Anwar al-Sadat to Israel and accused Sadat of being an agent of Israel who was "mad" and who had "raped" Egypt. Qabbani also clashed with King Hussein of Jordan, accusing him of murdering the Palestinians living in Amman during the Jordanian-Palestinian War of September 1970. Saudi Arabia blacklisted Qabbani for his sexual poetry, claiming that it was immoral for Muslims to read such literature. In 1993, he wrote against Palestinian leader Yasser Arafat, following the signing of the Oslo Peace

Nizar Qabbani.

Accord, accusing him of having conducted "peace of the weak" at a time when what the Arabs needed was "peace of the brave."

Some of Qabbani's most highly controversial works were written in the 1970s including *Qasa'id Mutawahishe* (*Wild Poems*), published in 1970, and *Ash'ar Kharija An al-Qanun* (*Delinquent Poems*), published in 1972. In 1979, he wrote a best-selling poem, *Ashadu an la Imraatan Illa Ante* (*I Swear That There Is No Woman But You*), later performed in song by the Iraqi singer Kazem al-Saher. In the 1980s, Qabbani wrote many political poems collected into anthologies including *Qasa'id Maghdub Alayha* (*Damned Poems*), published in 1986, *Tazawuajtuki Ayatu Hal Huriyya* (*I Married You O Freedom*), *Jumhuriyyat Jununistan* (*The Republic of Crazystan*), published in 1988, and the all-time classic, *al-Kibrit fi Yadi wa Duwaylatikum Min Warak* (*The Matches are in My Hand and Your Small States are from Paper*), published in 1989. Some of Qabbani's works were translated into English while others were performed by leading Arab artists from Egypt, Syria, and Iraq. The Egyptian diva Um Kalthum, the musician Mohammad Abd al-Wahab, and the singers Abd al-Halim Hafez and Kazem al-Saher all performed his poems, as did the Lebanese star Fayruz.

Despite his fame, Qabbani's life was also marked with pain. His sister committed suicide because her family wanted her to marry a man she did not love. His eldest son Tawfiq Qabbani died while studying medicine in Egypt. And his Iraqi wife Balqis al-Rawi was killed during the Civil War in Lebanon in 1981. The death of his sister influenced him to write love poems, while the death of his son led him to write his masterpiece, *Ila al-Ameer al-Dimashqi Tawfiq al-Qabbani* (*To the Damascene Prince Tawfiq al-Qabbani*). To eulogize his wife, a teacher whom he had met at a poetry recital in Baghdad in 1973, he wrote the classic, *Balqis*, widely considered his most complicated and emotional poem. It is also the poem he recited least often on stage, since he frequently cried when delivering it before audiences.

Qabbani wrote extensively on the magic of love and life in Beirut and Damascus, and he lamented the loss of Lebanon during the seventeen-year civil war. For Beirut, he wrote the classic, *Ya Sit al-Dunya Ya Beirut* (*Lady of the World O Beirut*). When the Lebanese Civil War ended in 1991, *Ya Sit al-Dunya Ya Beirut* was adopted as a song lyric by Lebanese singer Majida al-Rumi. Qabbani also wrote extensively about Damascus, making constant reference to its beauty in his poetry and released the volume of poems, *Dimashq Nizar Qabban* (*Nizar Qabbani's Damascus*). Qabbani also praised the Islamic resistance in South Lebanon and the Palestinian Intifadah that broke out in 1987. He claimed that armed resistance was the only way to deal with the Israeli occupation. Qabbani, however, wrote primarily about women and Damascus. In his poems, he often says that he is the savior of women in the twentieth century, encouraging women to free themselves from a male-dominated society and calling on them to love and to live an abundant life.

Qabbani lived in London in self-imposed exile from the early 1980s until his death on April 30, 1998. When he died, Arab leaders whom he had criticized rushed to offer homage. Some tried to pay his hospital bills while others offered airplanes and assistance to the Qabbani family. President Hafez al-Asad named a street in his honor in the Syrian capital, and according to his will, Qabbani was buried in Damascus. Prior to his death, he wrote his last work, *Dimashq Tuhdini Shari'an* (*Damascus Presents Me with a Street*). He received a hero's funeral in Syria, which was transformed into a parade for the people of Damascus. Attended by ten thousand mourners, the funeral was marked by nationalist songs, Damascene traditions, and chants in praise of Qabbani's life. Breaking with a strong—and still current—tradition where Muslim women mourn at home, Qabanni's funeral was the first in Damascus attended by both men and women.

All grieved Nizar Qabbani whom critics hailed as the "Emperor of Arabic Poetry," as opposed to the Egyptian political poet Ahmad Shawqi, who was called the "Prince of Poets."

Sources:
Abu Ali, Nabil. *Nizar Qabbani* (1999).
Abu Sa'id, Reeda. *Bana Jumhuriyyat al-Shi'ri wa Ghadar Malikan* (1998).
Akari, Suzanne. *Nizar Qabbani* (2002).
Kayyali, Sami. *Al-Adab al-Arabi al-Mouasir fi Souriyya 1850-1950* (1968).
Nakib, Mazen. *Nizar Qabbani* (2002).
Nizam al-Din, Irfan. *Akher Kalimat Nizar* (1999).
Qabbani, Nizar. *al-Mar'a fi Shi'ri wa Hayati* (1981).
Qabbani, Nizar. *Arabian Love Poems* (1999).

Qabbani, Nizar. *Qadiyyati Ma' al-Shi'ir* (1973).

Sheikh, Ghareed. *Ayyam Ma' Nizar Qabbani* (2000).

Qassab Hasan, Najat
(1921-1997)

Najat Qassab Hasan (writer, composer) was born and raised in Damascus. He began his public service while a student, by teaching illiterate people in rural villages surrounding Damascus. He then studied law at Damascus University and graduated in 1945. He also joined the Syrian Communist Party and remained a member of its central committee until 1952. Also in that year, he began work as an attorney in Damascus.

Qassab Hasan was particularly interested in social affairs and women's emancipation, writing frequently on both subjects in the Damascus press and lecturing on those issues in Syria and neighboring countries. He also wrote on judicial reform in Syria and published his articles in the daily *al-Ra'e al-Am (Public Opinion)*. In 1952, Qassab Hasan launched the radio program *al-Muwatin wa al-Qanun (The Citizen and Law)* where he answered legal questions asked by his listeners. The show was modeled after another radio program created in 1947 by Dr Sabri Qabbani, who answered medical questions on the radio.

Qassab Hasan's program was an instant success and made him a household name in Damascus. Since he answered legal questions free of charge, the radio show was particularly attractive to people who needed legal advice but could not afford a lawyer. Qassab Hasan talked about reforming the judicial system, giving women more rights, and passing new laws on social security, marriage, divorce, and education. The program continued until 1977. Qassab Hasan's career in journalism began in 1947 when he founded the satirical newspaper *Asa al-Janna (The Stick of Heaven)* with three prominent journalists, Sabri Qabbani, Nash'at Tighilbi, and Abbas al-Hamid. In the 1950s, he founded two satirical periodicals, one called *al-Kazita* that discussed the conditions at the Palace of Justice in Damascus, and the other called *al-Qandil* that focused on the community of novelists in Syria. From 1963 onwards, Qassab Hasan wrote frequently for the two state-run dailies *al-Baath* and *al-Thawra*. He also developed a flare for caricature drawings, and made comical pictures of friends, politicians, artists, and judges. A multi-dimensional intellectual, Qassab Hasan was also interested in oriental music and became director of the Academy of Oriental Music in Syria in 1950. In 1959, during the Syrian-Egyptian union, he founded the Syrian National Theater with leading actors like Nihad Quali and Abd al-Latif Fathi. In 1960, he became director of arts at the Ministry of Culture and National Guidance. He wrote the script for a Syrian movie called *Sha'iq al-Shahina (The Truck Driver)* and wrote children's music for the Kuwaiti TV program *Iftah ya Simsim (Open Sesame)*, an

Arabic version of Sesame Street. In 1962, Najat Qassab Hasan became editor of the monthly publication issued by the Lawyers' Syndicate in Syria.

Qassab Hasan also taught translation at the French Literature Department at Damascus University and translated many works from international literature into Arabic. Among his own publications are *Opera Warda*, published in 1962, *al-Fedayeen Amam Mahkamat Zurich* (*The Fedayen Before the Courts of Zurich*), published in 1970, and *Qisas al-Nass* (*The Stories of People*), published in 1989. In 1988, he wrote the first part of his autobiography, *Hadeeth Dimashqi* (*A Damascene Conversation*), and followed it in 1994 with part two, *Jeel al-Shaja'a* (*The Generation of Courage*). In 1993, he created the radio program, *Rihla fi al-Zakira* (*A Journey through Memory*), a talk show where leading intellectuals, novelists, and writers would engage in debates with him over their careers and literary affairs. In addition to his radio appearances, Qassab Hasan also presented a program on Syrian TV where he debated the relationship between life and law.

Najat Qassab Hasan continued to practice law throughout his life. At the time of his death in 1997, his last book, *Saniou al-Jalaa fi Souriyya* (*Makers of Independence in Syria*), was still in progress. It was published posthumously by his family in 1999.

Sources:
Qassab Hasan, Najat. *Hadeeth Dimashqi* (1988).
Qassab Hasan, Najat. *Jeel al-Shaja'a* (1994).
Information supplied by Mrs Salma Qassab Hasan
and Dr Hanan Qassab Hasan (May 25, 2003).

Quali, Nihad
(1928-1993)

Nihad Quali (producer, actor) was born and raised in Damascus. Upon completing his schooling, he co-founded an amateur theatrical group in 1954 called the Orient Club Theater. The group adapted classic plays and performed them in Damascus for a limited audience. In 1957, the group achieved success when it produced a show, *Lawla al-Nisaa?* (*What If It Were Not for Women?*), written by Quali.

In 1958, Quali wrote and produced another play, *Thaman Al-Huriyya* (*The Price of Freedom*), performed in Cairo shortly after Syria and Egypt merged to form the United Arab Republic (UAR) in 1958. The play was about the Algerian Revolution against the French and was an overwhelming success in the UAR. The following year, the UAR government delegated Quali to establish the National Theater in Syria. Quali complied and established the first group of professional Syrian actors in January 1960. It included names like Abd al-Latif Fathi, Rafic

Sibayi, and Anwar al-Baba, all who had become famous on Syrian radio and theater during the 1940s and 1950s. With them, Quali performed shows like al-*Burjwazi al-Nabeel* (*The Noble Bourgeoisie*) and Fyodor Dostoyevsky's *The Brothers Karamazov*. At about the same time as Syrian TV debuted in Damascus, its director Sabah Qabbani asked Quali to star in a low-budget mini-series with Doreid Lahham, a then-amateur actor, and the professional actor Rafic Sibayi. The show, *Sahrat Dimashq* (*Evening of Damascus*), was an instant hit, leading to two other shows in the early 1960s that became Arabic classics. Under Sabah Qabbani's urging, Quali, Lahham, and Sibayi created a comedy trio that became the most widely acclaimed in Syria.

In 1966, the trio put on their classic TV series, *Maqalib Ghawar* (*The Pranks of Ghawar*). At the time, the show was considered one of the funniest in Syria. The success of *Maqalib Ghawar* prompted them to launch another TV show together, *Hamam al-Hanna* in 1968. Another all-time classic show by Quali and Lahham was *Sah al-Nom* (*Good Morning*), produced as a play in 1971 and adapted into a movie in 1973. A sequel to *Sah al-Nom* made in 1972 is repeated almost every year on Arab satellite TV.

After the Arab-Israeli War of 1967, Quali, Lahham, and Sibayi teamed up in *Masrah al-Shawk* (*Theater of Thorns*), a political comedy criticizing the Arabs after their defeat at the hands of Israel. Nihad Quali and Doreid Lahham eventually parted with Sibayi and established a comic duo modeled after Laurel & Hardy. Quali and Lahham's first movie, *Iqd al-Lulu* (*The Emerald Necklace*), came in 1961 and was adapted from an earlier play. The popular movie co-starred the Syrian singer Fahd Ballan and the Lebanese star Sabah. *Iqd al-Lulu* continued to play in Syrian and Lebanese cinemas for a year and a half, breaking a record in Arab movie history.

Quali and Lahham produced twenty-one other movies. Quali wrote most of them. Often their movies co-starred the leading Egyptian and Lebanese actors and actresses of the time, including the Egyptian comedian Samir Ghanim, the star Nabila Obeid, the singer Shadya, and the Egyptian movie queen Mariyam Fakhr al-Din. Quali created the character Husni al-Bourazan for himself and Ghawar al-Tawsheh for Lahham. These characters made their debut in *Maqalib Ghawar*. Tawsheh, a clown and prankster, always finds himself competing with Bourazan for something—a bride, a job, or money. Often Tawseh outsmarts Bourazan with practical jokes and humorous schemes. In Bourazan, Quali created an evil but adorable character for Lahham (who continues to bask in Ghawar's popularity until the present day). And all of the characters created by Quali have long

Nihad Quali.

outlived him. They are still being played on the stage, in movies, and on TV by a generation of veteran Syrian actors.

Quali and Lahham also collaborated with the political playwright Mohammad al-Maghout. Quali created the characters, Lahham directed, and Maghout wrote the script for two shows that became classics in Arabic theater. In 1974, the three men produced *Dai'at Tishreen* (*October Village*), which eulogized the Arab-Israeli war of 1973, and recounted the coups that rocked Syria in the 1950s, which collectively led to the defeat in 1967. In *Dai'at Tishreen*, Quali plays the roles of the respective leaders of Syria and the Arab world, changing uniforms when he becomes a different character. At one point he indirectly mocks President Gamal Abd al-Nasser of Egypt for his role in the Arab defeat.

In 1976, Quali and Lahham produced *Ghorba* (*Alienation*), a play that dealt with the massive Arab emigration taking place in the 1970s. *Ghorba* covered the Arab condition from the turn of the twentieth century when feudalism was dominant throughout the Middle East. In *Ghorba*, the characters experience feudalism, then socialism, leading up to authoritarianism. Then they are forced to leave their homes in despair and search for a better life in the United States, where they are mistreated and insulted by Westerners. In defeat, they return to their country to help rebuild it, believing that salvation exists only in their own country.

In *Ghorba*, Quali plays the role of a madman obsessed by the dream of purchasing an airline ticket and leaving the Arab world. His character, Abu Risheh, although a lunatic, reflected how many young Arabs felt in the 1970s. *Ghorba* was performed in every Arab country and even toured Europe and the Americas, playing for large Arab émigré communities. Every night for two years, Quali and Lahham would be greeted by a standing ovation from their Arab audiences. In 1977, Quali quarreled with an army officer in a Damascus nightclub and was beat up and left partially paralyzed. He continued to perform *Ghorba* while half-paralyzed, but retired from acting in 1979 due to his deteriorating health. President Hafez al-Asad sent him to the United States for treatment, but he remained ill and was unable to resume his acting. Instead, he began to write short comedies for *Samer*, a children's magazine published in Beirut.

Quali tried acting once more with Lahham in 1991 in the show, *Awdet Doreid wa Nihad* (*The Return of Doreid and Nihad*). However, due to illness he was unable to film the program and died on October 19, 1993. He received a massive funeral in Damascus, where men of letters, arts, and politics came to pay their last respects to Nihad Quali, considered one of the founders of modern theater, television, and cinema in Syria.

Sources:
Itri, Abd al-Ghani. *Abqariyyat* (1997).

Sibayi, Rafic. *Thaman al-Hubb* (1998).

al-Sabban, Rafic
(1931-)

Rafic al-Sabban (director, playwright) was born and raised in Damascus. He studied law in Syria and obtained an MA and PhD in law from the Sorbonne in Paris. During his stay in France, Sabban was interested in the trends in modern European theater, and he studied the classics.

Sabban returned to Syria in 1960 and co-founded the National Theater in Damascus with Syrian actor Nihad Quali. Sabban wrote several plays that Quali starred in, including William Shakespeare's *Julius Caesar*. In 1966, Sabban founded his own theatrical group called Synopsis of Art and Thought, and he became director of cinema affairs in Syria.

Sabban moved to Cairo in 1971 to teach at the Academy of Fine Arts and has remained there ever since, teaching, directing, and writing screenplays and stage productions. Among the published works of Rafic al-Sabban are *Al-Islam wa al-Masrah* (*Islam and the Theater*), *Naqd al-Cinema al-Faransiyya* (*Criticizing the French Cinema*), and *Awrak Majnun* (*Papers of a Madman*).

Sources:
Bawab, Sulayman. *Mawsuat Alam Souriyya fi al-Qarn al-Ishreen*, Vol III (1999).

Sakakini, Widad
(1913-1991)

Widad Sakakini (writer) was born in Sidon (Lebanon) and raised in Beirut. The Lebanese theologian Sheikh Mustapha al-Ghalayini tutored her. She began her career by writing articles for the literary weekly *al-Makshouf* (*The Revealed*).

In 1932, Sakakini married the poet Zaki Mahasin and moved to Syria, where she became a student of the scholar Mohammad Kurd Ali. She wrote for his newspaper *al-Muqtabas* while he worked to enhance her writing skills and promote her literary career. In 1945, Sakakini's first book, *Maraya al-Nass* (*Mirror of the People*), was published and earned limited readership in Beirut. It was popular in Syria, however, because it dealt with the day-to-day affairs of Damascus. Her second book, *al-Hubb al-Muharram* (*Forbidden Love*), was written in 1950 under Kurd Ali's guidance.

In 1955, Sakakini published the novel entitled,

Widad Sakakini.

al-Sitar al-Marfu (*The Raised Curtain*). She then wrote a book on pioneering women: *Nisa' Shaheerat Min al-Sharq wa al-Gharb* (*Famous Women from the East and West,* 1960). In 1970, she published a biography of the pioneering woman poet, May Ziyadeh. In 1978, Sakakini released *Aqwa Min al-Sineen* (*Stronger than the Years*), another bestseller with reflections on her life as a feminist in the Arab world. In 1987, at the age of seventy-four, she published her last book, *Sutur Tatajawab* (*Lines Respond*). During her literary career, Widad Sakakini also wrote extensively for many periodicals including *al-Sabah* (*The Morning*), *al-Dunya* (*The World*), *al-Makshouf* (*The Revealed*), and *al-Thaqafa* (*Culture*).

Sources:
Itri, Abd al-Ghani. *Abqariyyat wa Alam* (1996).
Kayyali, Sami. *Al-Adab al-Arabi al-Mouasir fi Souriyya 1850-1950* (1968).

al-Samman, Ghada
(1942-)

Ghada al-Samman (writer) was born and raised in Damascus. She studied English literature at Damascus University and obtained her graduate degree from the American University of Beirut (AUB). She returned to Damascus in 1964 and began to teach at Damascus University, where her father Ahmad al-Samman was president.

Samman's first book, *Ainaq Quadari* (*Your Eyes are My Destiny*), was published in Beirut in 1962. A romantic work, *Ainaq Quadari* earned her limited success within literary circles in Damascus and Beirut. After she achieved pan-Arab fame, it became popular and was published in nine different editions. In 1976, she published her masterpiece, *Beirut '75,* which spoke of her experience during the early weeks of the Lebanese Civil War. One year later, she produced another book with the same theme, *Qawabis Beirut* (*Beirut Nightmares*), recounting several nightmares she experienced while trapped in her apartment in West Beirut during the bombing of a nearby street. Isolated from humanity, she is trapped in her apartment with thoughts about death, life, love, and friendship as she hears nothing but the sounds of explosions and agony from the streets of Beirut. *Qawabis Beirut* became a classic literary work on the Lebanese Civil War and on the torment experienced by those who lived through it.

By 1980, Samman's reputation had spread throughout the Arab world, and she was being hailed as one of the finest novelists in Syria. On all accounts, she became the most widely read Syrian novelist abroad, and in 1991, her works began to appear in English and French. Among her publications are *La Bahr Fi Beirut* (*No Sea in Beirut*), published in 1963, *A'lant al-Hub Alayk* (*I Declare My Love for You*), published in 1976, and *Laylat Millionaire* (*The Night of a Millionaire*), published in 1986. Her latest work, *Al-Abadiyya Lahzat Hubb* (*Eternity is a Second of Love*), was published in 1999.

Ghada al-Samman currently writes a weekly column for the Lebanese weekly magazine *al-Sayyad* (*The Hunter*).

Sources:
Nuwayhed, Nadia. *Nisaa Min Biladi* (2000).
The International Who's Who in the Arab World (1987-1988).

al-Sawwah, Firas
(1941-)

Firas al-Sawwah (writer) studied economics at Damascus University and obtained his MA in management development in 1966. During the Syrian-Egyptian union (1958-1961), he was imprisoned twice for leading student demonstrations, demanding democracy, and opposing the dictatorship of President Gamal Abd al-Nasser of Egypt.

In 1958, Sawwah began to write articles for *al-Adab* (*Literature*), a literary weekly popular in the Arab world. He was commissioned into the Syrian Army and took part in the Arab-Israeli War of 1967. Seven years later, he volunteered for service in the Arab-Israeli War of 1973 and served in the Golan front as commander of an anti-tank artillery unit. In 1978, he was imprisoned in Damascus for two months on the charge of criticizing the political regime and having sympathies with the outlawed Communist Workers' Party.

In 1976, Sawwah wrote his masterpiece, *Moughamaret al-Aql al-Oula* (*First Adventure of the Mind*), a book showing the unity of man's religion over the ages, with particular emphasis on the continuity of religious ideas between the ancient near-eastern religions and the monotheistic religions of Islam, Christianity, and Judaism. In 1979, Sawwah moved to the Emirates and became director of human resources at a local petroleum company. He worked in Dubai until 1989, but continued to publish books, including his most important work, *Loghuz Ashtar* (*The Riddle of Ashtar*), and an Arabic version of the epic *Gilgamesh*. Prior to Operation Desert Storm in 1990, Sawwah collaborated with a group of other outspoken intellectuals and issued an intellectual petition to President Hafez al-Asad demanding Arab solidarity with Iraq and requesting that Syria not join the US forces. Since then, however, Firas al-Sawwah has devoted his time to research and writing as a freelance scholar. He has published more than ten books, most of which have become bestsellers in the Arab world. He wrote a chapter for *Jerusalem in Ancient History and Tradition*, an English language book compiled by the American scholar Thomas L. Thompson, published in Germany in 2003.

Sources:
Information provided by Firas al-Sawwah (September 30, 2002) and Nawras al-Sawwah (April 11, 2002).

Shaaban, Buthaina
(1953-)

Buthaina Shaaban (writer) was born in Homs and studied English literature at Damascus University. She obtained her graduate and postgraduate degrees at the University of Warwick in the United Kingdom, specializing in European literature.

Shaaban then returned to Syria, wrote articles for Arab and Western newspapers, and began teaching at Damascus University. She specialized in comparative women's literature, and taught the world classics to graduate students in the Literature Department.

Shaaban joined the Arab Writers' Syndicate and became its vice president, also working as managing editor of its publication *al-Adab al-Ajnabi* (*Western Literature*). She wrote extensively on women's rights and living conditions in the Arab world. Her book, *Both Left and Right Handed: Arab Women Talk About their Lives*, was published in the United States in 1993. Two years later, the book was required reading for a course on women and religion at Illinois Wesleyan University.

In Syria, Shaaban wrote a weekly column for the state-run daily *Tishreen*. In the 1990s, she served as private translator to President Hafez al-Asad. Starting in July 2000, she became a private translator to Asad's son, President Bashar al-Asad. In June 2000, Shaaban was voted into the Baath Party Central Committee. In July 2002, Foreign Minister Farouk al-Shara appointed her head of press and public relations at the Ministry of Foreign Affairs, where her role was to defend Syria against accusations made by the United States and Israel that Syria was harboring "terrorist" groups.

Shaaban wrote for several leading English newspapers, including *The International Herald Tribune*, defending the Palestinian organizations stationed in Syria as a national resistance and not as terrorist groups. Her words echoed those of President Bashar al-Asad who drew parallels between the Palestinian resistance stationed in Syria and the French resistance to the Nazis stationed in Great Britain during World War II. She also made several trips to the United States to drum up support for Syria in American political circles.

In April 2003, Shaaban became a prominent spokesperson for Syria after the Anglo-American War on Iraq and the fall of Saddam Hussein. She also vigorously defended Syria against US accusations of harboring terrorist networks and developing so-called weapons of mass destruction. Among her published books are *Al-Sh'ir wa al-Siyasa* (*Poetry and Politics*) and *Al-Nisa' fi al-Mujtama' al-Islami* (*Women in Islamic Society*).

In September 2003, Buthaina Shaaban was appointed minister of expatriate affairs in the cabinet of Prime Minister Naji al-Itri. She continued to act as a spokeswoman for Syria, especially after the Syrian Accountability Act was issued by the Bush administration in December 2003.

Sources:
Bawab, Sulayman. *Mawsuat Alam Souriyya fi al-Qarn al-Ishreen*, Vol III (1999).
The Daily Star (November 8, 2002).

Shora, Naseer
(1920-1992)

Naseer Shora (painter) was born and raised in Damascus. He studied at the Academy of Fine Arts in Rome, but the beginning of World War II in 1939 forced him to transfer to the Higher Institute of Fine Arts in Cairo, where he graduated with high distinction in 1947. He then moved to Europe to study the modern trends in painting, residing briefly in Italy, Germany, and Poland from 1950 to 1955.

Shora returned to his native Damascus in 1955 to begin a career as a professional painter and instructor of painting at the Academy of Fine Arts in Syria. He established his own personal style by painting the Syrian countryside in abstraction to show the beauty in the landscape and the simplicity of rural Syria.

In reward for his services to art, Naseer Shora received the Medal of Honor of the Syrian Republic, Excellence Class. He took part in twenty-one international exhibitions. After his death on November 4, 1992, his wife transformed his workshop into a permanent museum for his works.

Sources:
Itri, Abd al-Ghani. *Abqariyyat* (1997).
Maksoud, Saadallah. *Art for All: Dictionary of Contemporary Fine Art in Syria* (2002).

Sibayi, Rafic
(1930-)

Rafic Sibayi (actor) grew up in poverty in Damascus and had to work to earn a living while studying. He was attracted to acting and singing at an early age, but his family disapproved of the profession. Rather than acceding to their judgement, he dropped out of school to support himself and pursue his career.

Sibayi first performed on stage in 1948. He became friends with Saad al-Din Baqdunes, and the two went to Lattakia on the Syrian coast to perform amateur theater. He then joined a Lebanese theater group headed by the Lebanese actor Ali al-Ariss. At first, Sibayi performed as a singer on stage, seldom taking on any acting roles. But when he moved to al-Masrah al-Hurr (The Free Theater Group) of the well-established Syrian star Abd al-Latif Fathi, Sibayi took an acting part in *al-Qadimun Min Amerika* (*Those Coming from America*) in 1951.

Meanwhile, Sibayi further quarreled with his family and had to change his last name to avoid causing the family any embarrassment. It was a taboo, even among the poor families in Damascus, to be working as an actor, and a particular disgrace to Sibayi's father who also disapproved of Sibayi's marriage to an actress. As a result of family pressure, Rafic Sibayi changed his name briefly to Rafic Sulayman.

Sibayi played the *oud* (lute) and performed folkloric songs in Aleppo in traditional Damascene dialect. He then joined Near East Radio, the most established radio station in the Middle East run by the British government. He originally signed up as a radio announcer, but in 1956 became a radio show actor.

Sibayi worked on a program with Tawfiq Ishaq, a Lebanese Jew, and presented the character of Abu Sayyah, a role that he continues to play. Abu Sayyah was an illiterate *quabaday* (strongman) from the old quarters of Damascus, a man whom people turned to for protection and assistance, a stereotypical character Sibayi had often met as a child. Abu Sayyah was a kindhearted and simple man who spoke in an old-fashioned dialect and was often depicted as the owner of an old-fashioned café. Often, Abu Sayyah would perform songs in Damascene dialect. Sibayi's portrayal of Abu Sayyah as a common man made the character beloved by everyone in Damascus, young and old alike.

Thanks to Abu Sayyah, Rafic Sibayi became a household name in Syria, but he had to leave the Near East Radio station in 1956 when Great Britain declared war on Egypt and Syria severed diplomatic relations with London. Sibayi returned to Syria and briefly worked as an employee at the Central Bank of Aleppo while acting in theater at night. In 1958, Sibayi acted in Abd al-Latif Fathi's play, *Harami Ghasb Anno* (*An Unwilling Thief*), and played the role of Abu Sayyah for the first time on stage in Syria. The play was an instant hit.

In 1960, Sibayi joined the National Theater of Nihad Quali, another well-established stage actor in Syria. Sibayi acted in Fyodor Dostoyevsky's *The Brothers Karamazov* and also adapted the plays by Oscar Wilde for the Syrian stage. He then worked with Hani Snobar, a Palestinian stage director who had just returned from his studies at Yale University. They presented a large stage production, *Abtal Baladna* (*The Heroes of Our Country*), set during the Crusades, with Sibayi playing the leading role of King Louis IX of France.

When Syria and Egypt merged to form the United Arab Republic (UAR) in

1958, Sibayi went to Cairo for a six-month training course in Egyptian theater and worked briefly in Radio Cairo. He joined the Egyptian actor Mohammad Rida, and the two performed a show in their respective dialects to familiarize the people of Egypt and Syria with one another's idioms and ideas.

Rafic Sibayi.

In 1960, Sibayi returned to Syria to co-launch Syrian TV with its director, Dr Sabah Qabbani. Sibayi wrote a TV series, *Qissat Mathal (The Story of a Proverb)*, in which every episode tells the history of a traditional Damascene proverb and explains how the proverb was created. The show was a success, and led to his performance in a TV sketch with Nihad Quali and Doreid Lahham, a rising TV actor. The three were successful, and under Sabah Qabbani's urging, they created a comedy trio that became widely acclaimed in Syria.

The trio performed many short TV sketches in the early 1960s and a play called *Iqd al-Lulu (The Emerald Necklace)*. It was adapted for film, and Sibayi acted in the movie, along with Lahham, Quali, and the singers Fahd Ballan and Sabah. Sibayi also acted with them in a movie, *Gharam Fi Istanbul (Love in Istanbul)*.

After President Amin al-Hafez came to power in 1963, he asked to meet Sibayi because of his role as Abu Sayyah, a character loved by politicians in Syria. President Hafez presented Sibayi with his personal gun as a token of friendship. Sibayi then persuaded Amin al-Hafez to pay more attention to actors in Syria and grant more state funds for their activities, social security, and salaries. President Hafez al-Asad also admired Sibayi and sent him for medical treatment twice in the 1970s and 1980s to London and Czechoslovakia.

In 1966, Sibayi took part, along with Quali and Lahham, in the classic TV series *Maqalib Ghawar (The Pranks of Ghawar)*. The show was considered one of the funniest in Syria and prompted the trio to perform together in another TV show two years later called *Hamam al-Hanna*. After the Arab-Israeli War of 1967, they performed the political comedy, *Masrah al-Shawk (Theater of Thorns)*, criticizing the Arabs after their defeat against Israel. Toward the end of the 1960s, Sibayi quarreled with Lahham and Quali, and they ceased collaboration, though all went on to achieve unprecedented fame in the Middle East in their respective acting roles. In 1982, Sibayi worked once again with Lahham in a TV series called *Wadi al-Misk (Misk Valley)*, written by the famous political playwright Mohammad al-Maghout.

In 1992, Sibayi starred in the classic TV series, *Ayyam Shamiyya (Damascene Days)*, playing the role of *za'im* (chief), who is in charge of his neighborhood's affairs in Ottoman Syria. Among his more recent productions is the play, *Habs al-Ahlam (Prison of Dreams)*, of 1992, and the TV series, *Al-Ayyam al-Mutama-rida (Delinquent Days)*. In 1998, he published his memoirs, *Thaman al-Hubb (The Price of Love)*. In 2004, he made the great TV series *Layali al-Salhiyya (The Nights of Salhiyya)* about life in the Salhiyya neighborhood of Damascus under the Ottoman Empire.

Sources:
Sibayi, Rafic. *Thaman al-Hubb* (1998).

Tahseen Bey, Sa'id
(1904-1985)

Sa'id Tahseen Bey (painter) was a product of Damascus. Although captivated by art from an early age, he never studied art at an academy or university. He started to paint while a teenager. His paintings were characterized by simplistic images, naïve and primitive.

Eventually Tahseen Bey established himself as a painter in Damascus, and in 1934 went to Baghdad to teach elementary school children in rural districts of the Iraqi capital. He was influenced by the anti-colonial sentiment developing against the British forces stationed in Iraq and began to paint works that expressed his views on Arab nationalism. Tahseen Bey painted large pictures from Arab history, with swords, armor, and proud faces of warriors emerging victorious from combat. His paintings were characterized by high drama and Tahseen Bey's faith in ancient Arab history. He also painted abstract ideas like good and evil, freedom and justice, faith and disbelief. Sa'id Tahseen Bey produced over one thousand oil paintings that became prized works in Syria in the second half of the twentieth century. Many of his paintings have been on display in the Presidential Palace in Damascus since the 1940s. Others are located at the Iraqi National Museum in Baghdad. Tahseen Bey co-founded the Arab Association of Fine Arts and served as its president until 1942. In 1982, three years before his death, President Hafez al-Asad awarded him the Medal of Honor of the Syrian Republic, Excellence Class.

Sources:
Faris, George. *Man Hum fi al-Alam al-Arabi?* (1957).
Information from the Association of Fine Arts in Damascus, Syria.
Maksoud, Saadallah. *Art for All: Dictionary of Contemporary Fine Art in Syria* (2002).

Tamer, Zakariya
(1931-)

Zakariya Tamer (novelist) studied at high school, but at the age of thirteen, left school for financial reasons. He drifted from job to job, often working in manual labor, but developed a flare for literature. In 1957, he began to write short stories for publication in literary magazines. He joined the Ministry of Culture in 1963 and became director of composition.

Tamer continued to write for literary periodicals in Damascus and Beirut, and in 1965 became editor of the weekly *al-Mawqif al-Arabi* (*The Arab Stance*). Also in 1965, he joined a group of Syrian authors and founded the Arab Writers' Union in Damascus.

For the remainder of his career, Tamer wrote many children's stories in Syria and became one of the most celebrated children's authors in the Arab world, in addition to his reputation as a novelist. By 2001, he had written a total of seventy-five novels, the most famous of which include *Dimashq al-Harayek* (*Damascus Fires*), published in 1973, *al-Numur fi al-Yawm al-Asher* (*Panthers on the Tenth Day*), published in 1978, and *Sanadhak* (*We Will Laugh*), published in 1998. Two of his popular children's works are *Limaza Sakat al-Nahr* (*Why did the River become Silent?*), published in 1973, and *al-Bayt* (*The House*), published in 1975.

In 1994, Tamer wrote the popular novel, *Nida' Nouh* (*The Call of Noah*). Also in 1994, Tamer collected the articles of the Syrian journalist Najib al-Rayyes and published them in a ten-volume work on Syrian history from World War I until 1946. In 2002, President Bashar al-Asad decorated Zakariya Tamer with the Medal of Honor of the Syrian Republic, Excellence Class.

Sources:
Bawab, Sulayman. *Mawsuat Alam Souriyya fi al-Qarn al-Ishreen*, Vol I (1999).

al-Ujayli, Abd al-Salam
(1918-)

Abd al-Salam al-Ujayli (novelist) was born in the town of Raqqa on the Euphrates River in northern Syria. He studied medicine at Damascus University and graduated in 1945. Ujayli then opened a clinic in his small town and worked as a practicing physician. He was the first doctor in Raqqa.

In 1947, Ujayli became a deputy for Raqqa in parliament. The following year, he wrote his first novel, *Bint al-Sahira* (*Daughter of the Sorceress*), that was well received within literary circles in Syria. From this point on, he simultaneously practiced medicine, wrote, and worked in politics. Ujayli volunteered for service in the Arab-Israeli War of 1948 and spent several months at the war front with Akram al-Hawrani, another parliamentarian from Hama. The war experience and

Abd al-Salam al-Ujayli.

its defeat had a tremendous effect on Ujayli's writings and his nationalist vision, leading him to devote a majority of his novels to the Arab cause. In 1954, he wrote the classic, *Qanadil Ishbilia (Ishbilia Lanterns)*, and in 1958 published his first lengthy novel, *Basima Bayn al-Dumu (She is Smiling Between Tears)*.

In 1962, Ujayli became minister of foreign affairs in the cabinet of Prime Minister Bashir al-Azma, a position he held for three months. He then became minister of information and held this post briefly before retiring from political activity and devoting the remainder of his years to writing and lecturing. In 1992, a team of veteran Arab academics voted him into the prestigious Arab Language Assemblage.

Among Abd al-Salam al-Ujayli's famed works are *al-Da'wa ila al-Safar (An Invitation to Travel)*, published in 1963, *al-Hubb al-Hazeen (The Sad Love)*, published in 1979, and *Ashya' Shakhsiyya (Personal Things)*, published in 1980. In 2002, he published his memoirs covering his career from 1947 to 1963.

Sources:
Itri, Abd al-Ghani. *Abqariyyat wa Alam* (1996).
Kayyali, Sami. *Al-Adab al-Arabi al-Mouasir fi Souriyya 1850-1950* (1968).
Lecture by Dr Abd al-Salam al-Ujayli at AUB May 11, 1998.

al-Wadi, Sulhi
(1935-)

Sulhi al-Wadi (composer, conductor) was born in Baghdad and raised in Damascus. He studied at Victoria College in Alexandria and moved to the Royal Academy of Music in London, where he specialized in composition. Upon his

Sulhi al-Wadi.

return to Damascus in 1961, Wadi founded the Arab Institute of Music and promised to introduce "serious music" into Syrian culture. Wadi served as a conductor and instructor and almost single-handedly taught and nurtured an entire generation of young and talented musicians. In 1962, he became director of the Institute of Music and held this post until 2002.

For four decades, from the 1960s through the 1990s, Sulhi al-Wadi was behind anything that dealt with classical music in Syria, promoting it through newspapers, television, and radio. His style was marked with strong rhythmic accentuation, soaring dramatic melodies, and a touch of Oriental sounds and tunes. He composed various symphonies and borrowed tunes from the Egyptian artist Mohammad Abd al-Wahab, adding a touch of modernity to classical music.

In 1990, Wadi became dean of the Higher Institute of Music. In 1995, he founded the Syrian National Symphonic Orchestra that began to perform operas all over the Arab world. It was the first symphonic orchestra in Syria and quickly gained popularity. Wadi's musicians were an instant success, and today their concerts are annual events in Syria, greatly anticipated within cultural circles. In reward for his contribution to Syria's cultural life and music, President Hafez al-Asad awarded Wadi the Order of Merit of the Syrian Republic, Excellence Class. In 2001, Sulhi al-Wadi suffered a stroke while on stage that left him partially paralyzed. Unfortunately, he continues to suffer limitations that prevent him from conducting, and he has stepped down from the National Symphonic Orchestra.

Sources:
Information supplied by Abd al-Salam Haykal (October 1, 1998).

Wannus, Saadallah
(1941-1999)

Saadallah Wannus (playwright, producer) was born in the village of Husayn al-Bahr, next to the coastal city of Tartus. He grew up under the influence of the Lebanese poet Gibran Khalil Gibran and studied journalism at Cairo University, graduating in 1962.

Wannus contributed literary articles to several journals in Syria and Lebanon and wrote in the Damascus daily newspaper *al-Nasr*. He also contributed one-act plays to the magazine *Adab (Literature)*, which published his first lengthy play, *Jitha ala al-Rasif (Corpse on the Sidewalk)*, in 1964. In 1965, Wannus also published a collection of short poems, *Hakaya Jawkat al-Tamatheel (Story of the Choir of Statues)*. Also that year, Wannus became editor of the cultural section in the state-run daily *al-Baath* and was appointed to the literary board of *al-Mawqif al-Arabi*. In 1966, Wannus published an academic article in the Syrian weekly *al-Mawqif al-Arabi (The Arab Stance)* about the Egyptian playwright Tawfiq al-Hakim and his contributions to the theater of the absurd in Egypt. That same year, Wannus left Syria for Paris to conduct studies on modern European theater. But his endeavor was cut short by the Arab-Israeli War of 1967. The war brought him home and motivated him to produce several works on the bitterness of war and defeat.

In 1968, Wannus wrote his classic, *Haflat Samar Min Ajl 5 Huzayran (Party of Joy for June the Fifth)*, about the Arab defeat in the 1967 War. He also wrote the play *Indama Yal'ab al-Rijal (When Men Play)* for *al-Mawqif al-Arabi*. The defeat of 1967 dominated his work for the remainder of his career, and in 1969 he produced two more political plays, *Ba'iq al-Dibs al-Faqir (Story of the Poor Seller)*, and *Al-Feel Ya Malek al-Zaman (The Elephant O King of all Times)*. Also in 1969, Wannus became director of music and theater in Syria, but resigned four months later, claiming that he was not suited for an administrative job. From 1970 to 1975, Wannus became editor-in-chief of the children's weekly *Usama* and contributed literary articles for the Lebanese daily *al-Safir*. In May 1971, Wannus produced *Haflat Samar Min Ajl 5 Huzayran,* which achieved great success in Damascus. Starting a new policy of openness adopted by the new Syrian president, Hafez al-Asad, the play was welcomed by the new Baathist regime and attended by Prime Minister Abd al-Rahman Khlayfawi. Political criticism was still relatively new and shocking to Syrian society at the time. It became common in Mohammad al-Maghout's works during the late 1970s. But it was Wannus who started the revolutionary trend.

Haflat Samar Min Ajl 5 Huzayran was one of the earliest Syrian plays to tour the Arab world and played in several different countries throughout the 1970s. The play was also translated and published in Spanish, French, and English. In the play, Wannus mocked the Arab-Israeli War of 1967. In one scene, actors dressed in government uniforms appear on a podium and start to repeat official rhetoric regarding the war. Their speeches are interrupted by other actors who are seated in the audience and shout back, "No, that's not what happened!" or "I was there, you are lying, the Israelis took *my* village!"

Saadallah Wannus.

The audience, not aware that the interruptions were made by actors in disguise, would be provoked and take part in the discourse themselves. Every night, the show would cause an uproar, and the audience would have to be restrained from unleashing their anger at the government.

Wannus continued to harbor populist views and was highly critical of the Syrian government when it suppressed freedoms during the bloody clash between Asad and the Muslim Brotherhood in the early 1980s. He went into a depression in 1977 when Anwar al-Sadat of Egypt visited Israel, and once again during the early 1980s when political and economic conditions in Syria became difficult. Both times, Wannus tried to commit suicide. A Marxist at heart, he was also greatly disturbed by the breakup of the USSR in 1991. In 1972, Wannus began to write for the weekly cultural edition of *al-Thawra*. He wrote two plays, *Al-Malik Huwa al-Malik (The King is the King)* and *Sahra Ma' Abi Khalil al-Qabbani (A Night with Abu Khalil al-Qabbani)*. The second play contains a dialogue with Abu al-Khalil, the nineteenth-century founder of modern Syrian theater. His earlier play, *Mughamarat Ra's al-Mamluk Jabir*, was banned in the 1960s, but was allowed in Syria and adapted into a movie in 1974 by Mohammad Shahine.

In 1977, Wannus founded his own literary weekly *al-Hayat al-Masrahiyya* (*Theatrical Life*) and served as its editor-in-chief. He continued to write plays and published several books including, *Bayanat Min Ajl Masrah al-Arabi al-Jadid* (*Declarations of Modern Arab Theater*), published in 1988, and *al-Ightisab* (*Rape*), published in 1989.

Saadallah Wannus was diagnosed in the advanced stages of cancer in 1992. Once ill, his productivity increased, and he quickly wrote three works that later became famous, *Yawm Min Zamanina* (*A Day from Our Times*), *Munamnamat Tareekhiyya* (*Historical*), and *Tuqus al-Isharat wa al-Tahawulat*. In 1994, he clashed with the Arab Writers' Union in Syria. He had co-founded the union in 1965, yet he could not accept the dismissal of the Syrian poet Adonis over the accusation that he had met with Israeli intellectuals at a conference in Spain. Wannus wrote extensively in Adonis's favor in Arabic newspapers.

President Asad offered to provide medical treatment for Wannus in Paris, despite his critical views, and Wannus accepted, traveling to France at the expense of the Syrian Government. He temporarily recovered, yet when his health deteriorated once again in mid-1994, the government refused to support his medical treatment again, apparently due to his defiant nature and critical views. King Hussein of Jordan contacted Wannus and offered to pay for his medical treatment abroad. Egyptian President Husni Moubarak made a similar offer. But Wannus declined. Israeli intellectuals even began a fund-raising campaign for Wannus on Israeli Radio called "A Program of $50,000 for Saadallah Wannus" but he also refused this offer and was treated at his own expense for what remained of his life. In March 1996, the frail Wannus was chosen by the International Academy of Theater to give the UNESCO speech in Beirut. His speech received a standing ovation of well-wishers when he said, "We are bound by hope! What happens today cannot possibly be the end of history." In 1996, he wrote and published *Bilad Adyaq Min al-Hubb* (*Countries Narrower than Love*) and *Malhamat al-Sarab*. His last work, *Al-Ayyam al-Makhmura* (*Drunken Days*), was published in 1997.

In 1999, Saadallah Wannus, celebrated as the greatest Syrian playwright of the twentieth century, died at the age of fifty-five in Syria.

Sources:
Interview with Fayza Jaweesh, the widow of Saadallah Wannus (May 28, 2004).

For Students, Journalists & Researchers

Bibliography

Interviews

Vice-President Abd al-Halim Khaddam (Damascus Nov 4, 2002).

Prime Minister Dr Abdel Raouf al-Kassem (Damascus April 6, 2002).

Prime Minister General Abd al-Rahman al-Khlayfawi (Damascus July 30, 2002).

Dr Shaker al-Fahham (Damascus March 10, 2002).

Dr Abd al-Wahab Homad (Damascus Sept 9, 1999).

Dr Munir al-Ajlani (Beirut August 13, 26, 2000 and Sept 4, 2000).

Dr Haitham Kaylani (Damascus July 2, 2002).

Dr Abdullah Abd al-Daim (Damascus Feb 6, 2003).

Dr Iyad al-Shatti (Damascus July 25, 2001).

Dr Iskandar Luka (Damascus April 5, 2004).

Dr Rana Qabbani (Paris May 8, 2004)*.

Dr Ramez Toemeh (Amman April 4, 2004).

Dr Hafez al-Jamali (Damascus Feb 7, 2003).

Dr Rafiq Jouejati (Damascus March 23, 2003).

Dr Wahid al-Sawwaf (Damascus May 26, 2002).

Dr Layla al-Sabbagh (Damascus July 14, 2002).

Dr Sadeq al-Azm (Damascus Nov 1, 2001)*.

Dr Ihsan al-Nuss (Damascus March 10, 2002).

Mr Abdullah al-Khani (Damascus July 15, 2002).

Mr Nasser Qaddur (Damascus Oct 21, 2002).

Mr Hassan Ihsan al-Sharif (Damascus June 21, 2001).

Mr Mansur Sultan al-Atrash (Damascus Feb 26, 2003).

Mr Adonis (Paris Feb 23, 2003)*.

Mr Abd al-Ghani al-Itri (Damascus August 8, 2001).

Mr Samir Habib Kahaleh (Damascus July 30, 2002).

Mr Doreid Lahham (Damascus July 4, 2001)

Mr Firas al-Sawwah (Homs Sept 30, 2002)*

Mrs Colette Khury (Damascus June 21, 2001 and September 2, 2001).

Mrs Fayzeh Jaweesh (Damascus May 28, 2004).

General Suhayl al-Ashi (Damascus July 15, 2002).

Dr Murhaf Jouejati (fact check) (Washington April 28, 2005).

Mustapha al-Akkad (Los Angeles April 28, 2005)

*Interview through correspondence

Newspapers

Al-Ahram (Cairo)

Al-Ayyam (Damascus)

Al-Baath (Damascus)

Al-Bayyan (Dubai)

Al-Diyyar (Beirut)

Al-Domari (Damascus)

Al-Dustor (Amman)
Al-Hayyat (Beirut) (London)
Al-Inqilab (Damascus)
Al-Iqtisadiyya (Damascus)
Al-Qabas (Damascus)
Al-Safir (Beirut)
Al-Sha`b (Aleppo)
Al-Souri al-Jadid (Homs)
Al-Thawra (Damascus)
Al-Wihda (Damascus)
Alif Bae' (Damascus)
Barada (Damascus)
Dimashq al-Masa' (Damascus)
Jerusalem Post (Jerusalem)
Al-Nahhar (Beirut)
Al-Nidal (Damascus)
Al-Nour (Damascus)
The Daily Star (Beirut)
The Star (Amman)
Lisan al-Hal (Beirut)
L'Orient (Beirut)
Sawt al-Sha`b (Damascus)
Tishreen (Damascus)

Dissertations

Abu al-Shamat, Hania. "Syria: an Improbable Democracy?" MA dissertation. American University of Beirut, 1999.

Atiyah, Najla Wadih. "The Attitude of the Lebanese Sunnis Towards the State of Lebanon." PhD dissertation. University of London, 1973.

Drewry, James. "An Analysis of the 1949 coups d'etat in Syria in Light of Fertile Crescent Unity." American University of Beirut, 1960.

Ismail, Thuraya. "Myths and Realities." MA dissertation. London School of Economics (LSE), 2002.

Landis, Joshua. "Nationalism and the Politics of Za'ma: The Collapse of Republican Syria 1945-1949," PhD dissertation. Princeton University, 1997.

Mufarrij, Fou'ad. "Syria and Lebanon under the French Mandate," MA dissertation. American University of Beirut, 1935.

Nashabi, Hisham. "The Political Parties in Syria 1918-1933," MA dissertation. American University of Beirut, 1952.

Tomeh, Ramez George. "Landowners and Political Power in Damascus 1858-1958," MA dissertation. American University of Beirut, 1977.

Articles

Carlton, Alford. "The Syrian Coup d'Etat of 1949" Middle East Journal, I, 1950.

Saikaly, Samir. "Abd al-Rahman Shahbandar: The Beginnings of a Nationalist Career," published in *Abhath*, a periodical of the American University of Beirut (AUB), Beirut 1986.

Saikaly, Samir. "Damascus Intellectual Life in the Opening Years of the 20th Century," in *Intellectual Life in the Arab East 1890-1939*, Beirut 1981.

Seymour, Martin. "The Dynamics of Power in Syria since the Break with Egypt" Middle East Studies, I, 1970.

Websites / Weblogs

Haykal, Ayman. damascus-online.com.

Landis, Joshua. syriacomment.com.

Moubayed, Sami. syrianhistory.com.

Moubayed, Sami. mideastviews.com.

Books in English

Adonis. *An Introduction to Arab Poetics* (translated by Catherine Cobham), Austin 1990.

Badran, Margot. *Feminism, Islam, and Nation and the Making of Modern Egypt*, Princeton 1998.

Batatu, Hanna. Syria's *Peasantry: the Descendants of Its Lesser Rural Notables and their Politics*, Princeton 1999.

Bregman, Ahron. Tahri, Jihan. *The Fifty Years War: Israel and the Arabs* London 1998.

Cleveland, William. *The Making of an Arab Nationalist*, Princeton 1971.

Cleveland, William. *A History of the Middle East*, Colorado 2000.

Commins, David. *Historical Dictionary of Syria*, Lanham 1996.

Davis, Scott. *The Road through Damascus*, Seattle 2003.

Dawn, Ernest. *From Ottomanism to Arabism: Essays on the Origins of Arab Nationalism*, Illinois 1973.

Devlin, John. *The Baath Party: a History from its Origins to 1966*, Stanford 1976.

Gouraud, Henri. *La France en Syrie*, Corbeil 1922.

Herzo, Samuel. *The Blood of Adonis: Transpositions of Selected Poems of Adonis*, Pittsburgh 1971.

Hinnnebusch, Raymond. *Syria and the Peace Process*, New York 1991.

Khoury, Philip. *Syria and the French Mandate*, Princeton 1987.

Khoury, Philip. *Urban Notables and Arab Nationalism: The Politics of Damascus 1860-1920*, Cambridge 1983.

Kedourie, Elie. *England and the Middle East 1914-1921*, London 1978.

Landis, Joshua: *Democracy in Syria*, London: Palgrave-MacMillan, 2006.

Lawrence, T.E. *Seven Pillars of Wisdom,* London 1935.

Maksoud, Saadallah. *Art for All: Dictionary of Contemporary Fine Art in Syria,* Damascus 2002.

Maoz, Moshe. *Syria under Asad: Domestic Constraints and Regional Tricks,* New York 1986.

Mardam Bey, Salma. *Syria's Quest for Independence,* London 1994.

Meisani, Julie Scott. Starkey, Paul. *Encyclopedia of Arabic Literature,* London 1998.

Moubayed, Sami. The *Politics of Damascus 1920-1946: Urban Notables and the French Mandate,* Damascus 1999.

Moubayed, Sami. *Damascus Between Democracy and Dictatorship,* Lanham 2000.

Ovendale, Richard. *The Middle East since 1914,* Essex 1992.

Qabbani, Nizar. *Arabian Love Songs,* Beirut 1999.

Rabinovich, Itamar. *Brink of Peace,* Princeton 1998.

Rabinovich, Itamar. *Syria under the Baath 1963-1966,* Tel Aviv 1985.

Rabinovich, Itamar. *The Road Not Taken,* New York 1991.

Rathmell, Andrew *Secret War in the Middle East: The Covert Struggle for Syria 1949-1961,.* London 1995.

Russell, Malcolm. *The First Modern Arab State: Syria under Faysal I ,* London 1987.

Saikaly, Samir. "Damascus Intellectual Life in the Opening Years of the 20th Century," in *Intellectual Life in the Arab East 1890-1939,* Beirut 1981.

Shorrock, William. *French Imperialism in the Middle East: The Failure of Policy in Syria and Lebanon 1900-1914,* Madison 1976.

Seale, Patrick. *Abu Nidal: A Gun For Hire,* London 1995.

Seale, Patrick. *Asad: the Struggle for the Middle East,* London 1988.

Seale, Patrick. *The Struggle for Power in Syria,* London 1961

Simon, Reeva. *Iraq Between the Two World Wars,* New York 1986.

Thompson, Elizabeth. *Colonial Citizens,* 1999

Torrey, Gordon. *Syrian Politics and the Military.* Ohio, 1964.

Van Dam, Nikolas. *The Struggle for Power in Syria: Politics and Society under Asad and the Baath Party,* London 1996.

Zamir, Meir. *The Formation of Modern Lebanon,* London 1985.

Ziser, Eyal. *Asad's Legacy,* London 2000.

Zuhur, Sherifa. *Asmahan's Secrets,* London 2001.

Zurayk, Constantine. *Arab Civilization: Challenges and Responses: a study in honor of Constantine Zurayk,* New York 1988.

Books in Arabic

Abaza, Nizar. *Tareekh Ulama Dimashq fi al-Qarn al-Rabi Ashr al-Hijri (History of the Scientists of Damascus in the Fourth Century after Hijra*), Damascus 1986.

Abd Allah, Omar. *The Islamist Struggle in Syria,* Berkeley 1983.

Abd al-Karim, Ahmad. *Hasad* (Harvest), Damascus 1994.

Abd al-Wahab, Mohammad. *Farid al-Atrash: Bayn al-Fann wa al-Hayat (Farid al-Atrash: Between Art and Life*), Cairo 1975.

Abdullah, King of Jordan. *Muzakarat (Memoirs)*, New York 1950.

Abu Ali, Nabil. *Nizar Qabbani: Sha'ir al-Mar'a wa al-Siyassa (Nizar Qabbani: The Poet of Women and Politics*), Cairo 1999.

Abu Assaf, Amin. *Muzakarat,* Damascus 1990.

Abu Ismail, Nadim. *Min Asrar al-Shishakli (From the Secrets of Shishakli*), Beirut 1954.

Adil, Fou'ad. *Qissat Souriyya bayn al-Intidab wa al-Inqilab 1942-1962 (The story of Syria between the mandate and the coup d'etat*), Damascus 2001.

Abu Mansur, Fadlallah. *Aasir Dimashq (Damascus Storms*), Beirut 1959.

Abu Sa'id, Reeda. *Bana Jumhuriyyat al-Shi'ir wa Ghadar Malikan (He Created the Kingdom of Poetry and Left it as a King*), Beirut 1998.

Aflaq, Michel. Atasi, Jamal. Razzaz, Munif. *Makalat fi al-Ishtirakiyya (Articles on Socialism*),

Aflaq, Michel. *Ma'rakat al-Masir al-Wahid (Battle for One Destiny*), Beirut 1958.

Ajlani, Munir. *Difa' al-Doctor Munir al-Ajlani Amam al-Mahkama al-Askariyya fi Dimashq (Defense of Dr Munir al-Ajlani before the Military Court in Damascus*), Damascus 1957.

Akari, Suzanne. *Nizar Qabbani,* Beirut 2002.

Allaf, Ahmad Hilmi. *Dimashq fi Matla' al-Qarn al-Ishreen (Damascus at the Beginning of the 20th Century*), Damascus 1976.

Arab Organization for Education, Culture, and Science. *Constantine Zurayk: Ra'id al-Fikr al-Qawmi wa al-Aqlaniyya al-Khulukiyya (Constantine Zurayk: Pioneer of Nationalist Thought and Behavioural Rationel*), Tunis 1999.

Arab Writers' Union. *Tarajim Ada' Itihad al-Kuttab al-Arab fi Souriyya wa al-Watan al-Arabi (Biographies of the Members of the Arab Writers' Union in Syria and the Arab World*), Damascus 2000.

Armanazi, Najib. *Muhadarat An Souriyya Min al-Ihtilal Hatta al-Jala (Lectures on Syria from Occupation until Evacuation*), Cairo 1953.

Arslan, Adil. *Muzakarat al-Ameer Adil Arslan (Memoirs of Prince Adil Arslan*), 3 volumes 1972.

Arsuzi, Zaki. *Mashakiluna al-Qawmiyya (Our Nationalist Problems*), Damascus 1958.

Ashi, Suhayl. *Fajr al-Istiqlal fi Souriyya (Dawn of Independence in Syria*), Beirut 1999.

Awad, Walid. *Ashab al-Fakhama Ru'asa' Lubnan (Their Excellencies Presidents of Lebanon*), Beirut 2002.

Azm, Abd al-Qadir. *Al-Usra al-Azmiyya* (*The Azm Family*). Damascus 1951.

Azm, Khalid. *Muzakarat Khalid al-Azm* (*Memoirs of Khalid al-Azm*), 3-volumes, Beirut 1973.

Babil. Nasuh. *Sahafa wa Siyyasa fi Souriyya* (*Journalism and Politics in Syria*), London 1988.

Barudi, Fakhri. *Muzakarat al-Barudi* (*Barudi's Memoirs*), 2-volumes, Beirut 1951.

Bawab, Sulayman. *Mawsuat Alam Souriyya fi al-Qarn al-Ishreen* (*Encyclopedia of Syrian figures in the twentieth century*), 5-volumes, Damascus 1999.

Bayhum, Mohammad Jamil. *Fatat al-Sharq fi Hadarat al-Gharb* (*Girl of the East in Western Civilizations*), Beirut 1952.

Bizreh, Afif. *Al-Nasseriyya fi Jumlat al-Istimar al-Hadeeth* (*Nasserism in the Line of Modern Imperialism*), Damascus 1962.

Bu'ayni, Hasan Amin. *Sultan Basha al-Atrash: Masirat Qa'id fi Tareekh Umma* (*Sultan Pasha al-Atrash: the Struggle of a Leader in the History of a Nation*), Damascus 1985.

Dahhan, Sami. *Mohammad Kurd Ali: Hayatuhu wa Atharuhu* (*Mohammad Kurd Ali: His Life and Legacy*), Damascus 1955.

Dayeh, Jean. *Ghassan Jadid,* London 1990.

Droubi, Ihsan Bayyat. *Sami Droubi,* Damascus 1982.

Elias, Joseph. *Aflaq wa al-Baath* (*Aflaq and the Baath*), Beirut 1991.

Elias, Joseph. *Tatawur al-Sahafa al-Souriyya fi al-Ahd al-Uthmani* (*Progress of Syrian Journalism in the Ottoman Era*), Beirut 1972.

Faris, George. *Man Humm Fi al-Alam al-Arabi?* (*Who are they in the Arab World?*), Damascus 1957.

Farfur, Mohammad Saleh. *Alam Dimashq fi al-Qarn al-Rabe' Ashr lil Hijra* (*Damascus Notables in the 14th Century after Hijra*), Damascus 1987.

Farhani, Mohammad. *Faris al-Khury wa Ayyam la Tunsa* (*Faris al-Khury and Unforgettable Days*), Beirut 1965.

Hafez, Thuraya. *Hafiziyyat,* Damascus 1980.

Haffar, Lutfi. *Zikrayat* (*Memories*) 2-volumes, Damascus 1954.

Haffar, Salma. *Lutfi al-Haffar 1891-1968,* London 1997.

Hakim, Da'd. *Awrak wa Muzakarat Fakhri al-Barudi* (*Papers and Memoirs of Fakhri al-Barudi*), 2-volumes, Damascus 1999.

Hakim, Hasan. *Abd al-Rahman Shahbandar: Hayatuh wa Juhduh* (*Abd al-Rahman Shahbandar: His Life and Struggle*), Damascus 1989.

Hakim, Yusuf. *Souriyya wa al-Ahd al-Faysali* (*Syria and the Faysalian Era*), Beirut 1966.

Hakim, Yusuf. *Souriyya wa al-Intidab al-Faransi* (*Syria and the French Mandate*), Beirut 1966.

Hammudeh, Sameeh. *Al-Wai wa al-Thawra: Dirasa fi Hayat wa Jihad al-Sheikh*

Izz al-Din al-Qassam (*Conciousness and Revolution: A Study in the Life and Struggle of Sheikh Izz al-Din al-Qassam*), Amman 1986.

Hanna, Abdullah. *Abd al-Rahman Shahbandar 1879-1940,* Damascus 1989.

Hawrani, Akram. *Muzakarat Akram al-Hawrani* (*Memoirs of Akram al-Hawrani*), 3-volumes, Cairo 2000.

Hout, Bayan Nuwayhed. *Al-Sheikh al-Mujahid Izz al-Din al-Qassam fi Tareekh Filastine* (*The Struggling Leader Izz al-Din al-Qassam in the History of Palestine*), Beirut 1987.

Husari, Sati. *Yawm Maysaloun* (*The Day of Maysaloun*), Beirut 1947.

Itri, Abd al-Ghani *Abqariyyat Chamiyya* (*Damascene Geniuses*), Damascus 1986.

Itri, Abd al-Ghani *Abqariyyat Min Biladi* (*Geniuses from my Country*), Damascus 1995.

Itri, Abd al-Ghani *Abqariyyat wa al-Alam* (*Geniuses and Notables*), Damascus 1996.

Itri, Abd al-Ghani *Abqariyyat* (*Geniuses*), Damascus 1997.

Itri, Abd al-Ghani *Hadeeth an al-Abqariyyat* (*Talk About Geniuses*), Damascus 2000.

Jammal, Farouk. *Doreid Lahham: Mishwar al-Umr* (*Doreid Lahham: the Lifelong Journey*), Beirut 2002.

Jaza'iri, Sa'id. *Asmahan,* London 1990.

Jaza'iri, Sa'id. *Muzakarat al-Amir Sa'id al-Jaza'iri* (*Memoirs of Prince Sa'id al-Jaza'iri*), Algiers 1968.

Jeha, Michel. *Mary Ajamy,* London 2001.

Juma, Sami. *Awraq Min Daftar al-Watan* (*Papers from the Nation's Notebook*), Damascus 2001.

Jundi, Adham. *Alam al-Adab wa al-Fan* (*Eminent Personalities in Literature and the Arts*), 2-volumes, Damascus 1954-1958.

Jundi, Adham. *Shuhada al-Harb al-Alamiyya al-Kubra* (*Martyrs of the World War*), Damascus 1960.

Jundi, Adham. *Tareekh al-Thawrat al-Souriyya fi Ahd al-Intidab al-Faransi* (*History of Syrian Revolts in the Era of the French Mandate*), Damascus 1960.

Jundi, Asem. *Izz al-Din al-Qassam: Riwaya Tareekhiyya* (*Izz al-Din al-Qassam: A Historical Novel*), Beirut 1975.

Jurdi al-Nuwayhed, Nadia. *Nisa'a Min Biladi* (*Women from my country*), Beirut 2000.

Kayyali, Abd al-Rahman. *Al-Marahil fi al-Intidab al-Faransi wa Nidaluna al-Watani 1926-1939* (*Stages in the French Mandate and our Nationalist Struggle*), 4-volumes, Aleppo 1958-1960.

Karkout, Zoukan, *Aflaq: Al-Kitabat al-Ula ma Dirasa Jadida Li Sirat Hayatihi* (*Aflaq: The Early Writings with a New Study of His Life Story*), Beirut 1993.

Kayyali, Nizar, *Dirasa fi Tareekh Souriyya al-Siyyasi al-Mu'assir* (*Study in Syria's*

Contemporary Political History), Damascus 1997.

Kayyali, Sami. *Al-Adab al-Arabi al-Muassir fi Souriyya 1850-1950 (Contemporary Arab Literature in Syria)*, Cairo 1968.

Kawtharani, Wajih. *Wathaiq al-Mutamar al-Arabi al-Awal (The First Arab Congress)*, Beirut 1980.

Khabbaz, Hanna. Haddad, George. *Faris al-Khury: Hayatuh wa Asruh (Faris al-Khury: His Life and Era)*, Damascus 1952.

Khalidi, Ghassan. *Al-Hizb al-Qawmi wa Qadiyyat al-Malki: Hakika Amm Itiham (The Nationalist Party and the Malki Case: Truth or Accusation)*, Beirut 2000.

Khalifah, Mohammad Rabi'. *Farid al-Atrash wa Asmahan: Hayatuhuma wa Aghanihuma (Farid al-Atrash and Ashaman: Their Life and Songs)*, Beirut 2002.

Khani, Abdullah. *Jihad Shukri al-Quwatli*, Beirut 2003.

Khatib, Ahmad. *Sheikh Tahir al-Jaza'iri*, Cairo 1971.

Khayyer, Hani, *Adib al-Shishakli al-Bidaya wa al-Nihaya (Adib al-Shishakli: The beginning and the end)*, Damascus 1994.

Kurd Ali, Mohammad. *Muzakarat (Memoirs)*, Damascus 1949-1951.

Madani, Sulayman. *Ha'ula Hakamu Souriyya (They Ruled Syria)*, Damascus 1998

Malek, Hanna. *Muzakarat Hanna Malek* (forthcomming)

Mardini, Zuhayr. *Al-Ustaz: Qissat Hayat Michel Aflaq (The Teacher: The Biography of Michel Aflaq)*, London 1988.

Marouf, Mohammad. *Ayyam Ishtuha 1949-1969 (Days that I Lived 1949-1969)*, Beirut 2003.

Moualim, Walid. *Souriyya 1918-1958: Al-Tahadi wa al-Muwajaha (Syria 1918-1958: Challenge and Confrontation)*, Damascus 1985

Nakib, Mazen. *Nizar Qabbani: Sha'ir al-Hubb wa al-Watan (Nizar Qabbani: the Poet of Love and the Homeland)*, Damascus 2002.

Nizam al-Din, Irfan. *Akher Kalimat Nizar (The Last Words of Nizar)*, Beirut 1999.

Omari, Subhi. *Awraq al-Thawra al-Arabiyya (Papers of the Arab Revolt)*, 1991.

Qabbani, Nizar. *al-Mar'a fi Shi'ri wa Hayati (The Woman in my Poetry and Life)*, Beirut 1-981.

Qabbani, Nizar. *Qadiyati Ma' al-Shi'ir (My Story with Poetry)*, Beirut 1973.

Qadri, Ahmad. *Muzakarat an al-Thawra al-Arabiyya al-Kubra (Memoirs of the Grear Arab Revolt)*, Damascus 1956.

Qasmiyyah, Khayriyyah. *Muzakarat Fawzi al-Qawuqji (Memoirs of Fawzi al-Qawuqji)*, Beirut 1975.

Qasmiyyah, Khayriyyah. *Muzakarat Muhsen al-Barazi (Memoirs of Muhsen al-Barazi)*, Damascus 1994.

Qasmiyyah, Khayriyyah. *Al-Ra'el al-Arabi al-Awal: Awrak Nabih wa Adil al-Azma*

(*The First Arab Generation: The Papers of Nabih and Adil al-Azma*), Damascus 1990.

Qassab Hasan, Najat. *Saniou al-Jalaa fi Souriyya* (*The Makers of Independence in Syria*), Damascus 1999.

Quwatli, Shukri. *Majmu'at Makalat* (*Collection of Speeches*), Damascus 1957.

Quwatli, Shukri. *Shukri al-Quwatli Yukhatib Ummatuh* (*Shukri al-Quwatli Speaks to His People*), Beirut 1970.

Rihani, Amin. *Faysal al-Awal* (*Faysal the First*), Beirut 1958.

Rifaii, Shams al-Din. *Tareekh al-Sahafa al-Souriyya 1800-1947* (*History of Syrian Journalism 1800-1947*), 2-volumes, Cairo 1969.

Sa'id, Amin. *Al-Thawra al-Arabiyya al-Kubra* (*The Great Arab Revolt*), 3-volumes, Cairo 1954.

Salama, Fayez. *Alam al-Arab fi al-Siyassa wa al-Adab* (*Arab Notables in Politics and Literature*), Damascus 1935.

Samman, Mutih. *Watan wa Askar* (*Homeland and Soldiers*), Damascus 1995.

Sayyed, Ahmad Abd al-Aziz. *Izz al-Din al-Qassam 1871-1935: Ra'id al-Nidal al-Qawmi fi Filastine* (*Izz al-Din al-Qassam 1871-1935: Pioneer of Nationalist Struggle in Palestine*), Kuwait 1977.

Sayyigh, Anees. *Constantine Zurayk: 65 Amman Min al-Ata* (*Constantine Zurayk: 65 Years of Giving*), Beirut 1996.

Sharab, Mohammad Hasan. *Izz al-Din al-Qassam: Sheikh al-Mujahidin fi Filastine* (*Izz al-Din al-Qassam: the Leader of Strugglers in Palestine*), Damascus 2000.

Sheikh, Ghareed. *Ayyam ma Nizar Qabbani* (*Days with Nizar Qabbani*), Beirut 2000.

Sibayi, Rafiq. *Thaman al-Hubb* (*Price of Freedom*), Damascus 1998.

Sulh, Hilal. *Rajul wa Quadiyya* (*A Man and a Cause*), Beirut 1996.

Sultan, Ali. *Tareekh Souriyya 1908-1918* (*Syria's History 1908-1918*), Damascus 1987.

Syrian Team of Historians. *Hayyatuna al-Niyyabiyya* (*Our Parliamentary Life*), Damascus 1962.

Tlas, Mustapha. *Mir'at Hayyati* (*Mirror of My Life*), Damascus 1991

Tlas, Mustapha. *Mir'at Hayyati: al-Zilzal 1968-1978* (*Mirror of My Life: the Earthquake 1968-1978*), Damascus 2002.

Ubaydat, Mahmud. *Ahmad Muraywed,* London 1997.

Uthman, Hashim. *Al-Ahzab al-Siyasiyyieh fi Souriyya: al-Siriyya wa al-Mu'lana* (*Political Parties in Syria: Secret and Public*), Beirut 2001.

Uthman, Hashim. *Al-Sahafa al-Souriyya: Madiha wa Hadiruha* (1997)

Uthman, Hashim. *Badawi al-Jabal,* Beirut 1998.

Yunis, Abd al-Latiff. *Mzakarat Dr Abd al-Latiff Yunis* (*Memoirs of Dr Abd al-Latiff Yunis*), Damascus 1992.

Yunis, Abd al-Latiff. *Shukri al-Quwatli: Tareekh Umma fi Hayat Rajjul* (*Shukri al-Quwatli: History of a Nation in the Life of One Man*), Cairo 1959.

Zahr al-Din, Abd al-Karim. *Muzakarati An Fatrat al-Infisal fi Souriyya* (*My Memoirs on the Secession Period in Syria*), Beirut 1968.

Zakariya, Ghassan. *Al-Sultan al-Ahmar* (*The Red Sultan*), London 1991.

Zaydan, Nemeh. *Alamuna al-Arabi* (*Our Arab World*), Beirut 1956.

Zaytun, Nazir. *Al-Shaheedan al-Zahrawi wa Salloum* (*The Martyrs Zahrawi and Salloum*), Damascus 1961.

Zirikli, Khayr al-Din. *Al-Alam: Qamus tarajim li ashar al-rijal wa al-nisa' min al-arab wa al-musta'ribin wa al-mustashriqin* (*Eminent Personalities: A biographical dictionary of noted men and women among the Arabs, the Arabists, and the Orientalists*), 10-volumes. Cairo 1954-1957.

Photo Credits

SH (www.syrianhistory.com).

SM (personal archive of Sami Moubayed).

Name in Bold (subject of photo).

Name after colon (photo graciously provided courtesy of this individual).

Photo essays on page one and at the opening of Officers, Politicians, National Activists, Educators, Arts & Letters are SH unless noted.

COVER

Asmahan: Amer Bader Hassoun, *The Book of Syria,* (2000).

The National Bloc in 1932 with Faris al-Khury and Hashim al-Atasi: SH

Hafez al-Asad & other government officials: Abdel Raouf al-Kassem.

FRONT MATTER

Naqiz al-Abd: SM.

Faris al-Khury: Mrs Colette Khury.

Husni al-Za'im: Mrs Niveen al-Za'im.

Hafez al-Asad: SM.

OFFICERS

Air Force, first graduating class: General Wadih al-Muqabari and Michel Arcouche.

General Wadih al-Muqabari: General Wadih al-Muqabari and Michel Archouche.

Yusuf al-Azma: Amer Bader Hassoun, *The Book of Syria,* (2000).

Sami al-Hinnawi: SM.

Ghassan Jadid: Mohammad Ma'ruf, *Ayyam Ishtuha,* (2003).

Mohammad al-Khuly: Mr Sinan al-Khuly.

Haydar al-Kuzbari: Courtesy of Mr Yasser al-Kuzbari.

Adnan al-Malki: SM.

Abd al-Karim al-Nehlawi: SH.

Mustapha Tlas: Courtesy of Mr Firas Tlas.

ADMINISTRATORS

Riverside Cafe: Camille Otrakji.

Ahmad Izzat al-Abid: Courtesy of Mr Abd al-Ghani al-Itri.

Nicolas Chahine: Courtesy of Dr Nicolas Chahine.

Hanna Malek: Courtesy of Dr Nicolas hahine.

Fayek al-Nehlawi: Courtesy of Ms Mayssa Nehlawi.

Bader al-Din al-Shallah: Bader al-Din al-Shallah *Lil Tarekh wa al-Zikra* (1991).

Izzat Tarabulsi: Mr Adnan al-Tarabishi.

POLITICIANS
Jamal Pasha: Mrs Colette Khury.
Mohammad Ali al-Abid: Mr Abd al-Ghani al-Itri.
Michel Aflaq: SM.
Munir al-Ajlani: Dr Munir al-Ajlani.
Sabri al-Asali: Mr Abd al-Ghani al-Itri.
Bashar al-Asad: SM.
Hafez al-Asad: SM.
Adnan al-Atasi: Mr Ridwan al-Atasi.
Hashim al-Atasi: Mr Ridwan al-Atasi.
Nur al-Din al-Atasi: Mrs Salma Hasibi al-Atasi.
Mansur al-Atrash: Souad Jumaa. Hasan Zaza, *Al-Huqumat al-Souriyya* (2001).
Ata al-Ayyubi: Mr Abd al-Ghani al-Itri.
Haqi al-Azm: Amer Bader Hasoun, *The Book of Syria,* (2000).
Khalid al-Azm: SM.
Bashir al-Azma: Mr Abd al-Ghani al-Itri.
Subhi Barakat: Souad Jumaa. Hasan Zaza *Al-Huqumat al-Souriyya* (2001).
Husni al-Barazi: Mr Samir al-Barazi.
Muhsen al-Barazi: Mr Samir al-Barazi.
Najib al-Barazi: Mr Samir al-Barazi.
Fakhri al-Barudi: Mr Ridwan al-Atasi.
Ma'ruf al-Dawalibi: Mr Ridwan al-Atasi.
King Faysal I: Brigid Keenan, *Damascus,* (2000).
Sa'id al-Ghazzi: Mr Ghazi al-Ghazzi.
Amin al-Hafez: SH.
Lutfi al-Haffar: SH.
Hasan al-Hakim: Mr Abd al-Ghani al-Itri.
Taj al-Din al-Hasani: Walid Awad *Ashab al-Fakhama Ru'asa' Lubnan* (2002).
Akram al-Hawrani: Souad Jumaa. Hasan Zaza *Al-Huqumat al-Souriyya* (2001).
Saadallah al-Jabiri: Ghassan Tweini *Kitab al-Istiqlal* (2000).
Salah Jadid: SH.
Abd al-Halim Khaddam: Mrs Najat Murqabi Khaddam.
Abdel Raouf al-Kassem: Dr Abdel Raouf al-Kassem.
Abd al-Rahman Khlayfawi: Bader al-Din al-Shallah *Lil Tareekh wa al-Zikra* (1991).
Faris al-Khury: Mrs Colette Khury.
Rushdi al-Kikhiya: Mr Abd al-Ghani al-Itri.
Ma'mun al-Kuzbari: Mr Abd al-Ghani al-Itri.
Issam al-Mahayri: Mr Abd al-Ghani al-Itri.
Jamil Mardam Bey: Mr Adnan al-Olabi.

Juliet al-Meer (wife of Antun Sa'ada): SH.
Sulayman al-Murshed: Mohammad Ma'ruf *Ayyam Ishtuha* (2003).
Ahmad Nami: SM.
Nazim al-Qudsi: Mr Abd al-Ghani al-Itri.
Shukri al-Quwatli: SM.
Rida al-Rikabi: Mr Abd al-Ghani al-Itri
Antun Sa'ada: SM.
Abd al-Hamid Sarraj: Mohammad Ma'ruf *Ayyam Ishtuha* (2003).
Farouk al-Shara: SM.
Ihsan al-Sharif: Mr Hassan al-Sharif.
Abd al-Rahman al-Shahbandar: Mrs Colette Khury.
Adib al-Shishakli: SM.
Abd al-Hamid al-Tabba': Mr Kareem Tabba.
Abd al-Rahman al-Yusuf: Brigid Keenan *Damascus,* (2000).
Husni al-Za'im: Mrs Niveen al-Za'im.

NATIONAL ACTIVISTS
Naziq al-Abid: Mr Abd al-Ghani al-Itri
Sultan al-Atrash: Mr Abd al-Ghani al-Itri
Ibrahim Hananu: Amer Bader Hassoun *The Book of Syria* (2000)
Mekki al-Kuttabi: Mr Abd al-Ghani al-Itri
Abd al-Hamid al-Zahrawi: Mrs Colette Khury

DIPLOMATS
Faris al-Khury: Mrs Colette Khury.
Dinner Party: SM.
James Hugh Keeley, Jr: Camille Otrakji.
Adib al-Dawoudi: Mr Abd al-Ghani al-Itri.
Abdullah al-Khani: Mr Ridwan al-Atasi.

EDUCATORS
Munif al-Aidi: Ms Lamia al-Aidi.
Adila Bayhum: Mr Abd al-Ghani al-Itri.
Anastas Chahine: Dr Nicolas Chahine.
Faysal al-Sabbagh: Mrs Rasha al-Sabbagh Haykal.
Shaker al-Fahham: Mr Abd al-Ghani al-Itri.
Sati al-Husari: SM.
Murshed Khater: Mr Abd al-Ghani al-Itri.
Madani al-Khiyyami: Mr Abd al-Ghani al-Itri.
Shaker Mustapha: Mr Abd al-Ghani al-Itri.
Abd al-Wahab al-Qanawati: Mr Abd al-Ghani al-Itri.

Rida al-Sa'id: Amer Bader Hassoun *The Book of Syria* (2000).
Jamil Saliba: Mr Abd al-Ghani al-Itri.
Ahmad al-Samman: Mr Abd al-Ghani al-Itri.
Constantine Zurayk: Mr Karam Nashar.

JOURNALISTS
Yasser Abd Rabbo: Mr Sahban Abd Rabbo.
Izzat Husriyyieh: Mr Abd al-Ghani al-Itri.
Habib Kahaleh: Mr Abd al-Ghani al-Itri.
Mohammad Kurd Ali: Mr Karam Nashar.
Sabri Qabbani: Mr Abd al-Ghani al-Itri.
Najib al-Rayyes: Mr Karam Nashar.
Sami al-Sham'a: Mr Abd al-Ghani al-Itri.
Wadih Sidawi: Mr Abd al-Ghani al-Itri.
Sa'id Tillawi: Mr Abd al-Ghani al-Itri.

ARTS & LETTERS
Faris al-Khury & Colette Khury: Mrs Colette Khury.
Omar Abu Risheh: Mr Karam Nashar.
Abd al-Wahab Abu Saud: Mr Abd al-Ghani al-Itri.
Asmahan: (2 photos) Sherifa Zuhur, *Asmahan's Secrets,* (2001).
Farid al-Atrash: Amer Bader Hassoun, *The Book of Syria,* (2000).
Badawi al-Jabal: Mrs Colette Khury.
Wajih al-Barudi: Mr Abd al-Ghani al-Itri.
Sabah Fakhri: Mr Abdul Salam Haykal.
Ali Farzat: Mr Ali Farzat.
Salma al-Haffar: Mr Abd al-Ghani al-Itri.
Walid Iklhassy: Mr Scott C. Davis.
Shakib al-Jabiri: Mr Abd al-Ghani al-Itri.
Mary Jubran: Mr Abd al-Ghani al-Itri.
Sami al-Kayyali: Mr Abd al-Ghani al-Itri.
Colette Khury: Mr Scott C. Davis.
Doreid Lahham: Mr Scott C. Davis.
Khalil Mardam Bey: Mr Abd al-Ghani al-Itri.
Fateh al-Moudarres: Mr Abd al-Ghani al-Itri.
Nizar Qabbani: Mr Karam Nashar.
Nihad Quali: Mr Abd al-Ghani al-Itri.
Widad Sakakini: Mr Abd al-Ghani al-Itri.
Rafiq Sibayi: Rafiq Sibayi *Thaman al-Hubb,* (1998).
Sulhi al-Wadi: Mr Abdul Salam Haykal.
Saadallah Wannus: Mrs Dima Wannus.

Historical Information

Syria has had six constitutions in its modern history, the most recent drafted by President Hafez al-Asad in 1973. The first constitution defined a constitutional monarchy for Syria and was created in 1920, four months before the French Mandate was implemented in Syria. It never materialized, however, due to the French occupation of Syria and the toppling of King Faysal I. The second, being the first republican constitution, was drafted in 1928 by a constitutional assembly headed by the attorney Fawzi al-Ghazzi. The third was issued in 1950, after the fall of Syria's first military regime. In 1953, Syria's second military leader General Adib al-Shishakli issued the fourth constitution, calling for direct elections by the people for the presidency and not, as had been done earlier, through Parliament. The fifth constitution was created by President Gamal Abd al-Nasser of Egypt during the Syrian-Egyptian union of 1958-1961.

Suffrage: Universal, age 18 and above. Women were given the right to vote in 1949, and the bill for women suffrage was presented in the Syrian National Congress (parliament) as early as 1919. It never materialized in 1919 because France occupied Syria in July 1920 and dissolved the Syrian Parliament.

Heads of State
King Faysal I (Oct 1918-July 1920).
Mohammad Ali al-Abid (July 1932-Sept 1936).
Hashim al-Atasi (December 1936-July 1939).
Taj al-Din al-Hasani (Sept 1941-Jan 1943).
Jamil al-Ulshi (acting) (Jan 1943-March 1943).
Shukri al-Quwatli (August 1943-August 1947).
Shukri al-Quwatli 2nd term (August 1947-March 1949).
Husni al-Za'im (March 1949-August 1949).
Hashim al-Atasi (December 1949-Nov 1951).
Fawzi Selu (Nov 1951-July 1953).
Adib al-Shishakli (July 1953-Feb 1954).
Ma'mun al-Kuzbari (Feb 26-28, 1954).
Hashim al-Atasi (March 1954-Sept 1955).
Shukri al-Quwatli (Sept 1955-Feb 1958).
Gamal Abd al-Nasser (Feb 1958-Sept 1961).
Nazim al-Qudsi (December 1961-March 1963).
Lu'ayy al-Atasi (March 1963-July 1963).
Amin al-Hafez (July 1963-Feb 1966).
Nur al-Din al-Atasi (Feb 1966-Nov 1970).

Ahmad al-Khatib (Nov 1970-March 1971).
Hafez al-Asad (March 1971-June 2000).
Abd al-Halim Khaddam (acting) (June 2000-July 2000).
Bashar al-Asad (July 2000-present).

Prime Ministers
Rida al-Rikabi (Oct 1918-Jan 1920)
Crown Prince Zayd (Jan-March 1920)
Rida al-Rikabi (March-May 1920)
Hashim al-Atasi (May-July 1920)
Ala al-Din Droubi (July-August 1920)
Jamil al-Ulshi (Sept-Nov 1920)
Haqqi al-Azm (Dec 1920-June 1922)
Subhi Barakat (June 1922-Dec 1925)
Ahmad Nami (April 1926-Feb 1928)
Taj al-Din al-Hasani (Feb 1928-Nov 1931)
Haqqi al-Azm (June 1932-March 1934)
Taj al-Din al-Hasani (March 1934-Feb 1936)
Ata al-Ayyubi (Feb-Dec 1936)
Jamil Mardam Bey (Dec 1936-Feb 1939)
Lutfi al-Haffar (Feb-April 1939)
Nasuh al-Boukhari (April-May 1939)
Bahij al-Khatib (July 1939-April 1941)
Khalid al-Azm (April-Sept 1941)
Hasan al-Hakim (Sept 1941-April 1942)
Husni al-Barazi (April 1942-Jan 1943)
Jamil al-Ulshi (Jan-March 1943)
Ata al-Ayyubi (March-August 1943)
Saadallah al-Jabiri (August 1943-Nov 1944)
Faris al-Khury (Nov 1944-Sept 1945
Saadallah al-Jabiri (Sept 1945-Dec 1946)
Jamil Mardam Bey (December 1946-Dec 1948)
Khalid al-Azm (December 1948-March 1949)
Husni al-Za'im (March-June 1949)
Muhsen al-Barazi (June-August 1949)
Hashim al-Atasi (August-Dec 1949)
Nazim al-Qudsi (December 24-27, 1949)
Khalid al-Azm (December 1949-June 1950)
Nazim al-Qudsi (June 1950-March 1951)
Khalid al-Azm (March-August 1951)
Hasan al-Hakim (August-Nov 1951)

Ma'ruf al-Dawalibi (Nov 28-29, 1951)
Fawzi Selu (December 1951-July 1953)
Adib al-Shishakli (July 1953-Feb 1954)
Sabri al-Asali (March-June 1954)
Sa'id al-Ghazzi (June-Oct 1954)
Faris al-Khury (Oct 1954-Feb 1955)
Sabri al-Asali (Feb-Sept 1955)
Sa'id al-Ghazzi (Sept 1955-June 1956)
Sabri al-Asali (June 1956-Feb 1958)
Gamal Abd al-Nasser (Feb 1958-Sept 1961)
Ma'mun al-Kuzbari (Sept-Nov 1961)
Izzat al-Nuss (Nov-Dec 1961)
Ma'ruf al-Dawalibi (Dec 1961-March 1962)
Bashir al-Azma (April-Sept 1962)
Khalid al-Azm (Sept 1962-March 1963)
Salah al-Din al-Bitar (March-Nov 1963)
Amin al-Hafez (Nov 1963-May 1964)
Salah al-Din al-Bitar (May-Oct 1964)
Amin al-Hafez (Oct 1964-Sept 1965)
Yusuf al-Zu'ayyin (Sept-Dec 1965)
Salah al-Din al-Bitar (Jan-Feb 1966)
Yusuf al-Zu'ayyin (Feb 1966-Oct 1968)
Nur al-Din al-Atasi (Oct 1968-Nov 1970)
Hafez al-Asad (Nov 1970-March 1971)
Abd al-Rahman Khlayfawi (April 1971-Dec 1972)
Mahmud al-Ayyubi (December 1972-August 1976)
Abd al-Rahman Khlayfawi (August 1976-March 1978)
Mohammad Ali al-Halabi (March 1978-Jan 1980)
Abdel Raouf al-Kassem (Jan 1980-Nov 1987)
Mahmud al-Zu'bi (Nov 1987-March 2000)
Mohammad Mustapha Miro (March 2000-Sept 2003)
Mohammad Naji al-Itri (Sept 2003-present)

Ministers of Foreign Affairs
Awni Abd al-Hadi (March-May 1920).
Abd al-Rahman Shahbandar (May-July 1920).
Ala al-Din Droubi (July-August 1920).
The French Mandate canceled the Ministry of Foreign Affairs from Sept 1920 to
     Dec 1936.
Saadallah al-Jabiri (Dec 1936-Feb 1939).
Fayez al-Khury (Feb-April 1939).

Khalid al-Azm (April-May 1939).

The French Mandate canceled the Ministry of Foreign Affairs once again, from May 1939 to Sept 1941.

Fayez al-Khury (Sept 1941-March 1943).

Naim Antaki (March-August 1943).

Jamil Mardam Bey (August 1943-August 1945).

Mikha'il Ilyan (August-Sept 1945).

Saadallah al-Jabiri (Sept 1945-Dec 1946).

Naim Antaki (December 1946-Oct 1947).

Jamil Mardam Bey (Oct 1947-August 1948).

Muhsen al-Barazi (August-Dec 1948).

Khalid al-Azm (December 1948-March 1949).

Adil Arslan (April-June 1949).

Muhsen al-Barazi (June-August 1949).

Nazim al-Qudsi (August-Dec 1949).

Khalid al-Azm (December 1949-June 1950).

Nazim al-Qudsi (June 1950-Nov 1951).

Zafer al-Rifaii (June 1952-July 1953).

Khalil Mardam Bey (July 1953-Feb 1954).Faydi al-Atasi (March-June 1954).

Izzat Saqqal (June-Oct 1954).

Faydi al-Atasi (Oct 1954-Feb 1955).

Khalid al-Azm (Feb-Sept 1955).

Said al-Ghazzi (Sept 1955-June 1956).

Salah al-Din al-Bitar (June 1956-Feb 1958).

Mahmud Fawzi (March 1958-Sept 1961).

Ma'mun al-Kuzbari (Sept-Nov 1961).

Izzat al-Nuss (Nov-Dec 1961).

Ma'ruf al-Dawalibi (Dec 1961-March 1962).

Adnan al-Azhari (April-Sept 1962).

As'ad Mahasin (Sept 1962-March 1963).

Salah al-Din al-Bitar (March-Nov 1963).

Hassan Muraywed (Nov 1963-May 1964).

Abd al-Khaliq al-Naqishbindi (May 1964-Sept 1965).

Ibrahim Makhous (Sept 1965-Jan 1966).

Salah al-Din al-Bitar (Jan-Feb 1966).

Ibrahim Makhous (March 1966-Oct 1968).

Mustapha al-Sayyid (Oct 1968-Nov 1970).

Abd al-Halim Khaddam (Nov 1970-March 1984).

Farouk al-Shara (March 1984-present).

Timeline

1908. July. The Committee for Union and Progress (CUP) seized power in Istanbul and forced Sultan Abdulhamid II to restore parliament and the constitution which he had abrogated in 1876. There was much pleasure in Damascus because Abdulhamid II had imposed a terrible dictatorship on the Syrians. Journalism and freedom of speech flourished under the early months of CUP rule.

1909. The CUP forced Abdulhamid II to abdicate in favor of his brother Sultan Mohammad Rashad V. A process known as Turkification then began. Ottoman Turkish replaced Arabic as the language of the Arab provinces in the Empire, and all senior Arab officials were discharged and replaced by Ottoman Turks.

1910. Mary Ajamy, a nursing graduate from AUB, launched the first women's magazine in the Middle East, called al-`Arus (The Bride).

1911. Al-Fatat was founded in Paris by a group of Arab activists, demanding more rights for the Arab provinces in the Ottoman Empire. It mushroomed to become the single-most important opposition party in Ottoman Syria. One of the founders was Jamil Mardam Bey, a future Prime Minister of Syria.

1913. The CUP rigged the parliamentary elections to oust the Arab deputies from the Ottoman Parliament. Many of the ousted deputies were members of al-Fatat.

1913. Al-Fatat held the first Arab Congress in Paris. It was co-planned by Jamil Mardam Bey and chaired by Abd al-Hamid al-Zahrawi, an Arab deputy in the Ottoman Parliament. Ottoman authorities forbade their citizens from attending the conference, accusing its founders of treason against the Empire.

1914. August. World War I broke out in Europe.

1915. August 15. Jamal Pasha, the Ottoman Governor of Syria, executed many Arab nationalists in Beirut, accusing them of treason against the Empire. Most were members of al-Fatat.

1916. May 6. Jamal Pasha executed twenty-one Arab nationalists in Damascus, mostly from al-Fatat, who were former deputies in the Ottoman Parliament. The execution fueled dramatic anti-Ottoman sentiment in Syria. Most prominent among the executed leaders were Shukri al-Asali, Abd al-Wahab al-Inklizi, Abd al-Hamid al-Zahrawi, Omar Hamad, and Rafiq Sallum.

1916. May. The Sykes-Picot Agreement was signed between Great Britain and France, dividing the Middle East into mandates for the Great Powers. A mandate over Syria and Lebanon is given to France.

1916. June 10. Sharif Husayn of Mecca launched an Arab Revolt from the Arabian Desert against the Ottoman Empire. His rebel army was aided by the British Army officer, T.E. Lawrence.

1917. November 2. The British Government issued the Balfour Declaration, promising the Jews an independent state in Palestine. At the time, the population of Palestine was 700,000, of which 574,000 were Muslims, 74,000 were Christians, and 56,000 were Jews.

1917. December. British troops invade Palestine, in coordination with the rebel Arab Army of Sharif Husayn, and capture Jerusalem. The Ottoman Army in Jerusalem surrendered to General Edmund Allenby. This raised the moral of the Arab rebels and hundreds of volunteers from Syria join the Arab Revolt.

1918. September 26. The last Ottoman troops were evacuated from Syria. An interim government was created in Damascus, headed by the Algerian notable Prince Sa'id al-Jaza'iri.

1918. October 1. The Arab Army entered Damascus, under the command of Prince Faysal, the son of Husayn who was a member of al-Fatat. An Arab Government was established in Damascus, headed by Faysal and the first post-Ottoman Prime Minister of Syria, Rida Pasha al-Rikabi.

1918. November 11. End of World War I.

1919. January 1. Faysal traveled to France to attend the Paris Peace Conference and demanded international recognition for Syria's independence.

1919. February 5. The Istiqlal Party was founded in Damascus. It was the first official party in post-Ottoman Syria, headed by Shukri al-Quwatli, Riyad al-Sulh, Saadallah al-Jabiri, and Adil Arslan. It began as pro-Hashemite, demanding a Hashemite crown in the Arab World.

1919. May. Salih al-Ali, a chieftain from the Alawite Mountain, declared a military uprising against the first French troops to land on the Syrian coast.

1919. June. The first parliamentary elections took place in post-Ottoman Syria.

1920. March 8. The Syrian National Congress (parliament), headed by Hashim al-Atasi, crowned Faysal I as King of Syria. The new king was 32-years old.

1920. March 9. Great Britain denounced the crowning of Faysal as king, saying that his regime was unconstitutional and contradicted the interests of France in the Middle East.

1920. April 26. The San Remo Conference legitimized the French Mandate over Syria and Lebanon.

1920. July 14. The French High Commissioner in Syria, General Henri Gouraud, presented his ultimatum to King Faysal, asking him to dissolve the Arab kingdom, dissolve the Syrian Army, and peacefully accept the French

Mandate in Syria, or face the consequences of war. Faysal refused to step down.

1920. July 21-24. Sati al-Husari, the Minister of Education, attempted to negotiate a peaceful solution to the crisis between Syria and France. His efforts were in vain.

1920. July 24. The Syrian Army fought the battle of Maysaloun and was defeated by the French Army. The Minister of War General Yusuf al-Azma (36-years) was killed in combat.

1920. July. Ibrahim Hananu launched a revolt against the French in all of northern Syria, coined "The Aleppo Revolt."

1920. August 1. King Faysal I left Syria for Haifa with orders never to return from General Gouraud. The Syrian Army was dissolved and the Syrian throne abolished.

1920. August 21. Syria's new Prime Minister Ala al-Din Droubi and Abd al-Rahman Pasha al-Yusuf, head of the Shura Council, were murdered in Hawran by loyalists to Faysal. They were accused of collaborating with the mandate regime.

1920. August. The French split Lebanon from Syria. The new state of Lebanon included the one-time Syrian towns and cities of Beirut, Tripoli, Sidon, Tyre, Rashayya, Hasbayya, and Baalbak, and the Beqqa Valley.

1920. September 1. The French created the State of Aleppo, which included the Sanjak of Alexanderetta. It was governed by Kamil al-Qudsi.

1920. September 3. The French created the State of Damascus, governed by Haqqi al-Azm, the State of the Druze Mountain, governed by Salim al-Atrash, and the State of the Alawite Mountain, governed by the mandate regime.

1921. June. The Syrian-Palestinian Congress was founded in Geneva by a group of Syrian exiles, including Abd al-Rahman Shabbandar, Michel Lutfallah, and Shukri al-Quwatli. It aimed at liberating the Middle East from European colonialism.

1921. June. The Alawite Mountain Revolt of Salih al-Ali was crushed by the French. Ali retired to his native village giving up political activity.

1921. July. The Aleppo Revolt of Ibrahim Hananu was crushed by the French, forcing Hananu to flee to Jordan.

1921. August. Ibrahim Hananu, leader of the Aleppo Revolt, was captured in Palestine and extradited to Syria where he was tried for treason. He was declared not guilty by a French Military Court.

1921. August 23. Faysal I, the ex-king of Syria, became king of Iraq. He continued to dream of ruling Syria until his death in 1933.

1922. June 22. The Syrian Federal Council was created by the French Mandate regime, unifying the states of Damascus, Aleppo, and the Alawite Mountain.

The Council was headed by the Antioch notable, Subhi Barakat.

1922. June 24. The League of Nations recognized the French Mandate in Syria.

1922. July 25. Jamal Pasha, the ex-Ottoman Governor of Syria, was assassinated by an Armenian in Tiflis, a town in Russian Caucasia. There was much joy in Syria since Jamal Pasha, known as "Jamal Pasha the Butcher," was universally hated for having so much Arab blood on his hands during World War I.

1923. July 11. The Syrian University was established in Damascus, headed by its first president, Dr Rida Sa'id.

1924. October 28. The Communist Party was founded in Beirut.

1925. April 8. Lord James Balfour arrived in Damascus and was welcomed by unprecedented violence in the Syrian capital. Preachers at the Umayyad Mosque demanded his assassination. He then fled to Palestine.

1925. June 5. The People's Party was founded in Damascus, headed by Dr Abd al-Rahman Shahbandar, the ex-Minister of Foreign Affairs under Faysal. The party aims were liberation from foreign rule, a constitutional monarchy headed by the Hashemite crown, and modeled after Great Britain.

1925. July 21. Sultan al-Atrash declared a military uprising against the French Army from the Druze Mountain. The revolt was co-planned by Dr Shahbandar.

1925. October 18. The French Army conducted air raids against Damascus for 48-hours.

1926. May. The French Army conducted more air raids against the Midan neighborhood of Damascus, inflicting heavy casualties and killing 200 civilians.

1927. October 25. The National Bloc was founded in Beirut by Hashim al-Atasi after the Great Syrian Revolt of Sultan al-Atrash was crushed by the Mandate. It aimed at liberating Syria through diplomatic means rather than armed resistance.

1928. February. Taj al-Din al-Hasani was appointed Prime Minister of Syria. He was brought to power by the Mandate authority and was greatly despised in nationalist circles.

1928. April. A constitutional assembly, headed by the attorney Fawzi al-Ghazzi and ex-Prime Minister Hashim al-Atasi, was elected to create the first republican constitution for Syria. It was packed with members of the National Bloc.

1932. July 11. The Syrian Republic was created with Mohammad Ali al-Abid as the first President of Syria. He appointed Haqqi al-Azm, a notable from Damascus, as the first prime minister of republican Syria.

1932. November 4. The National Bloc held its first official meeting in Homs. Hashim al-Atasi was elected president, to govern the party's affairs with a permanent council that included Saadallah al-Jabiri, Shukri al-Quwatli, Jamil Mardam Bey, Faris al-Khury, and Ibrahim Hananu.

1932. November 16. The Syrian Social Nationalist Party (SSNP) was founded in Beirut by Antune Sa'ada. It aimed at the unification of Greater Syria. The party was to become immensely popular in Syria in later years.

1932. December. A new Syrian Flag was created, and it remained in use until the Syrian-Egyptian Union of 1958. The flag was restored briefly in 1961-1963. The flag had three bars: green, white, black; with two red stars in the middle.

1933. August 20. The League of National Action was founded in the village of Qarna'il in Mount Lebanon. It was created by a second-generation of Arab notables who wanted to free the Middle East from influence of the Great Powers. Among its founders were Constantine Zurayk, Zaki al-Arsuzi, and Sabri al-Asali.

1933. September 7. King Faysal I died in Switzerland at the age of 45. His successor, King Ghazzi I, declared that he has no territorial ambitions in Syria.

1933. November 25. The National Bloc boycotted Parliament to voice its objection of a proposed Franco-Syrian Treaty of Friendship. In response, the French Mandate regime dissolved Syria's first republican Parliament.

1935. November 18. Ibrahim Hananu, leader of the Aleppo Revolt, died of natural causes in Aleppo, igniting country-wide demonstrations against the French. He was 66.

1936. February. The National Bloc led a 60-day strike in Syria protesting France's abrogation of its constitution. The strike destroyed the Syrian economy and caused the death of hundreds. France was embarrassed in front of the international community and forced to receive a delegation from the National Bloc in Paris to discuss Syrian independence.

1936. March. The National Bloc traveled to France for independence talks, headed by Hashim al-Atasi.

1936. April. An uprising against the Jewish immigrants coming from Europe broke out in Palestine, headed by Amin al-Husayni, the Mufti of Jerusalem. The uprising was funded and supported by the nationalist Shukri al-Quwatli. Many Syrian volunteers followed Fawzi al-Qawiqji, a leader of the Syrian Revolt of 1925, to Palestine, to fight with Husayni.

1936. July 16. Eliahu Epstein, the director of Arab Affairs at the Jewish National Agency, travelled to Damascus to discuss Syrian-Jewish collaboration with the National Bloc leader Fakhri al-Barudi. He offered to help terminate the mandate if the Syrians agree to a Jewish state in Palestine, but Barudi refused his offer.

1936. August 1-9. Epstein returned to Damascus, heading a team of Zionist statesmen, to discuss collaboration with Shukri al-Quwatli. They met many times over a 9-day period, but failed to reach an agreement.

1936. September 9. The National Bloc signed a treaty with France guaranteeing independence over a 25-year period. In exchange, the Bloc leaders pledged French use of their air space and territory if war were to break out in Europe. It also allowed France to keep military bases in Syria. Mohammad Ali-Abid resigned and Hashim al-Atasi was elected the second president of Syria on December 21, 1936. He was 63.

1937. April. Dr Abd al-Rahman Shahbandar returned to Syria, having spent over 10-years in exile, and spearheaded the opposition to the National Bloc regime and the Treaty of 1936.

1937. June. Jamil Mardam Bey barely escaped an assassination attempt, when explosives were placed in his car. He accused Shahbandar of masterminding the plot and placed him under house-arrest.

1939. June 23. The Sanjak of Alexanderetta was annexed to Turkey as a result of a deal concluded between Ankara and Paris.

1939. July 7. President Hashim al-Atasi resigned from office in protest over the annexation, ending the first National Bloc regime (1936-1939).

1939. September 3. France and Great Britain declared war on Nazi Germany, igniting World War II.

1940. June 14. Syria came under the jurisdiction of occupied France and the pro-Nazi regime of Marshal Petain in Vichy. Paris fell to the Nazis. General Henri Dentz became the new Vichy High Commissioner of Syria and Lebanon.

1940. July 6. Dr Abd al-Rahman Shahbandar was assassinated at his clinic in Damascus by agents of the French Mandate.

1941. June 21. The Vichy forces in Syria were defeated by Free French forces loyal to General Charles de Gaulle. The Free French remained in Syria until April 1946.

1941. October. General Charles de Gaulle asked Hashim al-Atasi to resume his duties as president, but Atasi declined. He is asked once again in 1943 but he also refused.

1941. September 12. General Charles de Gaulle appointed Taj al-Din al-Hasani as President of Syria, who ruled with no parliament until World War II ended in Europe.

1941. September 27. General de Gaulle declared the independence of Syria but refused to evacuate his troops until the end of World War II. The Alawite and Druze Mountains, autonomous since 1920, were re-incorporated into the Syrian Republic.

1943. January 17. President Taj al-Din al-Hasani died while in office at the age of 58. Jamil al-Ulshi served as Acting President until March 1943.

1943. July. The National Bloc won an overwhelming majority in the parliamentary elections. The leftist candidates in Damascus, Michel Aflaq and Khalid Bakdash of the Communist Party, were defeated at the polls.

1943. August 7. Shukri al-Quwatli of the National Bloc was elected President of Syria with a 122-vote majority in Parliament. He was 51.

1943. September 21. Bshara al-Khury, a staunch ally of Syria, became president of Lebanon. Along with his Prime Minister Riyad al-Sulh, Khury coordinated all future foreign policy, vis-à-vis the French Mandate, with Syria.

1943. November 8. The French Mandate regime arrested Bshara al-Khury and Riyad al-Sulh, causing uproar and fueling anti-French demonstrations in Syria. The French began to plan for the similar arrest of President Quwatli. The Lebanese statesmen were released on November 22, 1943.

1944. July. Joseph Stalin of the USSR extended Soviet recognition to the Quwatli regime in Syria, also recognizing Syria's independence from France.

1944. September. US President Franklin Roosevelt extended recognition to the Quwatli regime in Syria.

1944. December. French was dropped from school curriculums in Syria.

1945. January 1. The Druze Mountain was reincorporated into Syria.

1945. February 13. President Quwatli met British Prime Minister Winston Churchill in Egypt, and the later promised to support Syria's aspirations for independence.

1945. February 18. The "republic's eagle" was created as the national emblem of Syria.

1945. February 26. Shukri al-Quwatli declared war on Nazi Germany, bringing Syria into World War II.

1945. March 22. The Arab League was founded in Egypt with Syria as a founding member.

1945. April 25. Prime Minister Faris al-Khury went to the USA to attend the founding conference of the United Nations in San Francisco. Syria's admittance to the UN, facilitated by President Roosevelt, was considered a testimony by the world community of its right to independence from the French Mandate.

1945. May 29. The French Army conducted air raids against Damascus for the second time, destroying the Citadel of Damascus, and the Syrian Parliament. The French failed to arrest President Quwatli and his top officials. Around 660 civilians were killed. The assault was halted by Sir Winston Churchill.

1945. August 1. France ended its control of the Syrian armed forces and Quwatli created the Syrian Army, proclaiming the day a national holiday.

1946. April 17. The last French troops left Syria and Shukri al-Quwatli declared Independence Day.

1946. May 18. A pan-Arab conference was held in the summer resort of Bludan, near Damascus. The Arab Summit was hosted by Quwatli to discuss the situation in Palestine.

1946. December 16. Sulayman al-Murshed, the Alawite chieftain who claimed to have divine powers and who tried to lead a French-funded revolt against Quwatli, was executed in Damascus.

1947. February 3. Syrian Radio commenced its first broadcast with the famed line: "This is Damascus!"

1947. March 29. The National Party was founded in Damascus by President Shukri al-Quwatli. It mirrored the socio-political interests of the Damascus notability.

1947. April 7. The Baath Party was founded in Damascus by Michel Aflaq and Salah al-Bitar. It mirrored the socio-political interests of rural Syria, emphasizing on Arab nationalism and socialism.

1947. May-June. An uprising occurred in the Druze Mountain against the Atrash family headed by a group of notables from the Mountain who wanted to break Atrash control over the Druze community. It was funded by Shukri al-Quwatli.

1947. November 29. The UN declared the Partition Plan for Palestine, causing violent demonstrations in Syria.

1947. June 20. Prime Minister Saadallah al-Jabiri died of natural causes in Aleppo. Jabiri's death sparked a rivalry over power between Damascus and Aleppo. As the supreme leader of Aleppo, he had refused to let its notables engage in conflict with the Damascenes. He was given presidential honors for his nationalism under the mandate. He was 54.

1947. November. Prime Minister Jamil Mardam Bey presented a bill to Parliament demanding an amendment to article 68 of the Constitution to enable the election of a president for two consecutive terms. This enabled the re-election of Quwatli for another 5-year term as president.

1948. April 9. Zionist militias in Palestine conducted a massacre in the village of Dayr Yassin, in the western suburb of Jerusalem, killing 245 civilians. The massacre was headed by Menahim Begin, the future prime minister of Israel, and infuriated public opinion in the Arab World. Massive riots broke out in Damascus, demanding that Syria go to war in Palestine.

1948. April 18. Shukri al-Quwatli was elected president for another 5-year term.

1948. May 14. David Ben Gurion declared the creation of the State of Israel.

1948. May 15. The Syrian Army went to war in Palestine and was defeated.

1948. May 25. Ahmad al-Sharabati, the Minister of Defense, resigned from his job, accepting blame for defeat at the warfront. Chief-of-Staff Abdullah Atfeh also resigned and was replaced by General Husni al-Za'im.

1948. June 10. The UN forced Quwatli to accept a cease-fire in Palestine.

1948. August. The People's Party was founded in Aleppo by two lawyers, Nazim al-Qudsi and Rushdi al-Kikhiya. It aimed at challenging Quwatli's policies, and breaking the centralization of power in the hands of Quwatli and his men.

1949. March 29. The Chief of Staff General Husni al-Za'im seized power in Syria and arrested Shukri al-Quwatli and his Prime Minister Khalid al-Azm. He accused them of the poor leadership that resulted in defeat at the warfront.

1949. April 1. Husni al-Za'im dissolved Parliament.

1949. July 8. Husni al-Za'im extradited Antune Sa'ada of the SSNP to Lebanon, where he was executed for treason by Prime Minister Sulh. The case drew international publicity that embarrassed Za'im who had first promised Sa'ada asylum in Syria and then made a secret deal with Riyad al-Sulh that sent Sa'ada to his death.

1949. July 12. Syria signed an armistice agreement with Israel. Za'im has several officials negotiate a peace deal in secret with Israeli Prime Minister Moshe Sharett. It never materialized.

1949. July 25. General Husni al-Za'im held a plebiscite and was elected president with 99.9% of the votes.

1949. August 14. President Husni al-Za'im was overthrown and killed by a military coup, along with his Prime Minster Muhsen al-Barazi. The coup was carried out by Za'im's friend, General Sami al-Hinnawi and officers from the SSNP. Hashim al-Atasi became prime minister, restoring civilian rule to Syria.

1949. October 5. Prince Abd al-Illah, the Regent of Iraq, arrived in Syria for federal union talks between Syria and Iraq. He reached a preliminary agreement with Atasi.

1949. November 15. An assembly (114 seats) was elected to draft a new constitution for Syria. The People's Party of Aleppo won a majority and its leader Rushdi al-Kikhiya became President of the Constitutional Assembly. Michel Aflaq of the Baath Party ran for office but was defeated at the polls.

1949. December 14. Hashim al-Atasi was elected Head of State. He was 76.

1949. December 19. General Adib al-Shishakli launched the third coup of 1949, arresting Chief of Staff Sami al-Hinnawi but keeping Atasi at his post.

1949. December 29. Michel Aflaq declared that his Baath Party's new motto would be to achieve the trinity of "Unity, Freedom, and Socialism."

1950. January 29. Parliament negotiated amending a clause in the Syrian Constitution that specifies Islam as the official religion of the President of the Republic. The proposed amendment was to make the post available for all Syrians, particularly Syrian Christians. It never materialized.

1950. March 14. Prime Minister Khalid al-Azm ordered a famed economic closure of the Syrian-Lebanese border, to prevent Lebanese goods from competing with Syrian goods.

1950. July 31. General Mohammad Nasser, the Commander of the Syrian Air Force, who contested Shishakli for power in the Syrian Army, was murdered near Damascus by two pro-Shishakli officers.

1950. September 7. Hashim al-Atasi was elected President of Syria.

1950. October 31. General Sami al-Hinnawi was murdered in exile in Beirut by Hersho al-Barazi, a native of Hama who was taking revenge for the killing of his cousin, Dr Muhsen al-Barazi, in 1949.

1951. July 16. Riyad al-Sulh, ex-Prime Minister of Lebanon, was gunned down by the SSNP in Amman for the execution of Antune Sa'ada.

1951. July 20. King Abdullah of Jordan, who for long had his eyes set on a throne in Syria, was assassinated in Jerusalem. He was succeeded by his son, King Talal, who claimed to have no territorial ambitions in Syria.

1951. November 29. General Adib al-Shishakli launched his second coup, arrested Prime Minister Ma'ruf al-Dawalibi, and forced President Atasi to resign. He propped up General Fawzi Selu as President of Syria. He dissolved Parliament and outlawed all political parties and newspapers.

1952. January 30. Shishakli issued law # 96, distributing government-owned land to the farmers.

1952. January. The Baath Party of Michel Aflaq began to criticize the Shishakli regime. Shishakli responded by closing down their daily al-Baath. The Baath Party leaders, Aflaq, Salah al-Bitar, and Akram al-Hawrani, all fled to Lebanon in February 1952.

1952. March. Shishakli made a ground-breaking visit to Jordan and was warmly received by King Talal. He broke the gridlock in Syrian-Jordanian relations that existed since 1943.

1952. April. Shishakli outlawed all political parties in Syria.

1952. July 23. The Free Officers of the Egyptian Army seized power in Cairo, toppling King Farouk I. The coup leaders were General Mohammad Negiub and Colonel Gamal Abd al-Nasser. The coup was warmly welcomed in Syria and embraced by Shishakli, who went to Egypt to congratulate the revolutionary leaders in December 1952.

1952. August 11. King Talal of Jordan, one of Shishakli's strongest allies, abdicated in favor of his son King Husayn. The boy-king funded an uprising in Syria against Shishakli, allying himself with the Druze opposition, and continued to interfere in Syrian affairs until his death in 1999.

1952. August 25. Adib al-Shishakli created and headed the Arab Liberation Movement (ALM). It was a progressive party with pan-Arabist and socialist views, calling for Arab unity, women's rights, and gradual democracy for the Middle East. It became the only party in Syria.

1952. December. The Baath Party merged with the Arab Socialist Party of Akram al-Hawrani, becoming the Arab Baath Socialist Party.

1953. January 4. Akram al-Hawrani called on all Syrians, from his exile in Beirut, to rise against the regime of General Shishakli.

1953. June. Shishakli asked Lebanese President Kamil Sham'un to extradite Aflaq, Bitar, and Hawrani. They were forced to leave Lebanon and take up residence in Italy.

1953. July 4. Hashim al-Atasi chaired the first public opposition meeting to the Shishakli regime, held at his residence in Homs. He called for a united front to bring down the dictator.

1953. July 11. Adib al-Shishakli became president of Syria, replacing the puppet regime of General Fawzi Selu that he had set up in 1951. He won the plebiscite with 99.98% of the votes.

1953. October 24. Shishakli drafted his own constitution, and created a Parliament of 83-members, all pledging loyalty to him.

1954. January. A uprising against Shishakli occurred in the Druze Mountain. It was funded and supported by King Husayn of Jordan. Shishakli responded by launching air raids against the Druze Mountain and placing hundreds of dissidents behind bars. He placed two of the revolt commanders, Sultan al-Atrash and Hashim al-Atasi, under house-arrest. Approximately 600 people were killed in the Druze Mountain.

1954. February 1. Iraq called for an Arab League Summit to discuss the bloody events in Syria. Shishakli responded by ordering the Iraqi Military Attaché to immediately leave Syria. On February 6, he closed Syria's border with Lebanon.

1954. February 24. Adib al-Shishakli resigned from the presidency, saying that he wanted to avoid civil war in Syria. He fled to Lebanon, then Saudi Arabia, and then moved to a permanent residence in South America.

1954. March 1. The democratic regime of the civilian President Hashim al-Atasi restored the constitution, parliament, and government that was in power prior to the Shishakli interlude (1951-1954). Al-Atasi claimed that it is the constitutional regime of Syria. Atasi was 81.

1954. April 9. A group of Syrian notables went to Egypt, demanding the return of ex-President Shukri al-Quwatli. Al-Quwatli complied and ended his exile since 1949, returning to Syria on August 7, 1954.

1954. Sept 24-25. Parliamentary elections were held for the first post-Shishakli Parliament. The Baath Party emerged victorious, as did the Communist Party, whose leader Khalid Bakdash became the first Communist in an Arab Parliament.

1955. February 24. The Baghdad Pact was signed by Iraq, Turkey, Pakistan, Iran, and Great Britain to control communist influence in the Middle East. Syria refused to join the Baghdad Pact, as did Gamal Abd al-Nasser.

1955. April 22. Adnan al-Malki, the deputy Chief of Staff of the Syrian Army, was assassinated in Damascus while attending a football match. The SSNP was accused of the murder and outlawed by Prime Minister Sabri al-Asali.

1955. September 5. Shukri al-Quwatli was re-elected President of Syria, for the third time in his career. He ran against the independent Khalid al-Azm and received 91 votes to Azm's 41. Quwatli was 63.

1955. December 11. Israel attacked Syrian posts on Lake Tiberias.

1956. July 26. Gamal Abd al-Nasser nationalized the Suez Canal, creating shock-waves throughout the Arab World, and gaining unmatched popularity in Syria. President Quwatli responded by expelling the British and French Ambassadors from Syria. His intelligence service destroyed the British pipelines running through the Syrian Desert in November 1956. Quwatli traveled to the USSR to elicit support for Nasser's Egypt.

1956. October. The "Tripartite Aggression" began against Egypt. Great Britain, France, and Israel declared war on Nasser, but the war was stopped by US President Dwight Eisenhower.

1956. November 23. Abd al-Hamid Sarraj uncovered "the Iraqi Plot" in Syria, that aimed at toppling the pro-USSR and pro-Egypt regime in Syria. The plan was to arrest and execute those responsible for Syria's social-ist orientation: Abd al-Hamid Sarraj, Afif al-Bizreh, Khalid Bakdash, and Akram al-Hawrani. Sarraj arrested the plot masterminds, Munir al-Ajlani and Adnan al-Atasi, and issued arrest warrants for Ghassan Jadid and ex-President Adib al-Shishakli. The arrested politicians, all being promi-nent ministers and deputies, were brought before a military tribunal in January 1957, headed by General Afif al-Bizreh. They were declared guilty of treason for receiving funds from Iraq to launch a coup in Syria. Ajlani was sentenced to life imprisonment and Atasi was sentenced to death, but his sentence was commuted to life imprisonment. All of them remained in jail until the Syrian-Egyptian union was dissolved in 1961. The "Iraqi Plot" verdicts were the beginning of the end of the rule of the notables in Syria.

1957. February 19. Ghassan Jadid, a prominent member of the SSNP, was assas-sinated in Beirut by an agent of Abd al-Hamid al-Sarraj, the director of Syrian Intelligence.

1957. March. President Quwatli tried to fire Abd al-Hamid Sarraj but was threat-ened with a coup d'etat by Baath Party officers in the Syrian Army. As a result, he abandoned his plan.

1957. August 18. Syrian intelligence declared that it uncovered a CIA plot to launch a coup in Syria, to be carried out by "Damascene officers" in the

Syrian Army. Syria responded by expelling three US diplomats from Damascus, including Ambassador Moose, and recalling its Ambassador, Farid Zayn al-Din, from Washington.

1957. October. Akram al-Hawrani, a leader of the Baath Party, became Speaker of Parliament. This was the highest post to date given to a socialist in Syria. A communist, Afif al-Bizreh, became Chief-of-Staff of the Syrian Army.

1958. January 12. A group of 14 Syrian officers, headed by Chief-of-Staff Afif al-Bizreh, travelled to Cairo by night, with no authorization from the President, to demand union with Gamal Abd al-Nasser's Egypt.

1958. February 22. Syria and Egypt merged to form the United Arab Republic (UAR). Shukri al-Quwatli willingly resigned from the presidency and Nasser became President of the UAR.

1958. July 14. A bloody revolution toppled the Hashemite monarchy in Iraq, killing King Faysal II and his Prime Minister Nuri al-Sa'id. General Abd al-Karim Qasim became President of Iraq. He allied himself with the UAR.

1958. July 15. President Kamil Sham'un of Lebanon requested US military assistance to defend his own regime in Beirut against an uprising similar to the one in Iraq. He had been facing violence for some months, led by Muslim leaders Sa'eb Salam and Rashid Karameh, who were funded and supported by Syria to transform Lebanon into an Egyptian satellite. He refused, igniting the first civil war in which Syria tried and failed to topple him on several occasions in 1956-1958.

1958. September. Nasser introduced socialist measures to break the landowning notability in Syria, limiting individual holdings to 80 hectares (200 acres) of irrigated and 300 hectares (750 acres) of non-irrigated land.

1959. February 23. Nasser began to symbolically re-distribute land in Syria, giving it to the peasants, marking the socialist revolution.

1960. The Military Committee of the Baath Party was created by a group of officers from the Syrian Army stationed in Egypt. Its sole aim was to preserve the UAR. Its founders were Hafez al-Asad, Salah Jadid, Mohammad Umran, Ahmad al-Meer, and Abd al-Karim al-Jundi.

1960. July 23. Syrian Television was launched in Damascus by its first director, Dr Sabah Qabbani.

1960. December 6. Ex-President Hashim al-Atasi died in Homs at the age of 87.

1961. July. Nasser advanced his socialist program in Syria, nationalizing private industry and the banking sector.

1961. September 28. A coup headed by Colonel Abd al-Karim al-Nehlawi ousted the UAR regime. It was funded by the mercantile class in Damascus and

Aleppo and supported by Nasser's rivals in Arab politics, mainly King Husayn of Jordan and King Saud of Saudi Arabia. A civilian regime was created in Syria, headed by Dr Nazim al-Qudsi.

1961. October 10. US President John F. Kennedy extended recognition to the post-Nasser order in Syria.

1962. January 16. Syria's new Prime Minister Ma'ruf al-Dawalibi created a committee to study revoking all socialist laws imposed on Syria by Nasser in 1958-1961, placing emphasis on restoring land to their rightful owners. On February 18, Dawalibi restored 32 factories to their rightful owners. He demanded that Nasser return to Syria all arms, tanks, and assets left behind from the union era, but Nasser refused.

1962. March 28. Nehlawi launched a second coup, arresting President Qudsi and his Prime Minister Ma'ruf al-Dawalibi.

1962. April 2. General Abd al-Karim Zahr al-Din, the Chief-of-Staff, rebelled against Nehlawi's orders, releasing the President and Prime Minister and discharging Nehlawi from the Syrian Army.

1962. May 5. Syria's ex-Director of Intelligence Abd al-Hamid Sarraj escaped from the Mezzeh Prison and fled to Egypt to avoid being tried as a war criminal in Syria. During the union years, Sarraj arrested hundreds of Syrians for their political views, and eliminated many of them during interrogation under torture. A military tribunal in Syria had brought 240 war crimes against Sarraj.

1963. February 8. Baath Party officers seized power in Iraq, killing General Abd al-Karim Qasim. Abd al-Salam Arif becomes president of Iraq.

1963. March 8. The Military Committee of the Baath Party seized power in Syria, arresting the President, exiling his new Prime Minister Khalid al-Azm, dissolving Parliament, outlawing 17 newspapers, nationalizing banks, and pledging to restore the UAR. Leading figures from the pre-1963 era, including Qudsi and Azm, were deprived of their civil rights. On March 23, General Lu'ayy al-Atasi was appointed President of the Revolutionary Command Council (RCC).

1963. April. The Military Committee of the Baath Party argued with pro-Nasser officers in the Syrian Army, discharging many of them from office, including Defense Minister Mohammad al-Sufi.

1963. May 3. The state nationalized the banking sector in Syria.

1963. July 8. The new Defense Minister Ziyad al-Harriri, a pro-Nasser officer who had co-planned and orchestrated the seizure of power on March 8, 1963, was fired from his job while on a visit to Algeria. Leading pro-Nasser figures were sacked by the Baath Party. Harriri was replaced by Amin al-Hafez.

1963. July 18. Officers loyal to Gamal Abd al-Nasser, headed by Colonel Jassem

Alwan, tried to seize power in Syria. Alwan escaped to Egypt and 19 of his men were executed for treason in Syria. This prompted Nasser to declare that the leaders of Syria are "Fascists" and say "No union with the Baathists!"

1963. July 24. Lu'ayy al-Atasi resigned as head of state and is replaced by General Amin al-Hafez.

1963. November 3. Amin al-Hafez created a new oath for officers in the Syrian Army, where they were required, before graduation, to pledge to work for the Baath Party trinity of "Unity, Freedom, and Socialism."

1963. November 12. Salah Jadid became Chief-of-Staff of the Syrian Army.

1964. April 15. The Muslim Brotherhood called for a war against the Baath Party regime of President Amin al-Hafez. He responded by launching air raids against a mosque where they were located, killing hundreds.

1964. September 27. Adib al-Shishakli was assassinated in Brazil by Nawaf Ghazal, a Druze immigrant who was taking revenge for those Druze massacred by Shishakli when he was president in 1953.

1965. January 1. Outbreak of the "Palestinian Revolution" headed by Yasser Arafat and his guerilla movement Fateh. The revolution, and Arafat, were endorsed and funded by Air Force Commander Hafez al-Asad and Chief of Staff Salah Jadid. They set up base in Syria where they received funds and military camps from the leaders of Syria.

1965. January. President Amin al-Hafez nationalized 111 companies (employing 12,000 people). State ownership was also extended to electricity, oil distribution, and around 70% of foreign trade. Aflaq praised the nationalization program in an interview with the Beirut daily al-Ahrar.

1965. January 8. Military courts were created by President Amin al-Hafez to bring opponents of socialism to justice. On January 24, the business community in Damascus went on strike to protest his measures. All of Damascus was shut down in protest to the socialist measures.

1965. February 18. Ex-Prime Minister Khalid al-Azm died in exile in Beirut.

1965. March. The state nationalized all oil companies in Syria.

1965. May 3. The state nationalized the cotton and wool industry in Syria.

1965. May 8. Elie Cohen, an Israeli spy operating in Syria, was executed in public by the Syrian government. His case, one of the most famous in espionage, greatly embarrassed President Amin al-Hafez, who was his friend, and who had toyed with the idea of making him a minister in 1964.

1965. June 24. The Syrian Arab News Agency (SANA) was founded in Syria.

1965. June 29. President Amin al-Hafez greatly angered the US administration of President Lyndon B. Johnson by exchanging ambassadors with Fidel Castro's Cuba. Hafez explained it as part of Syria's plan to ally with the socialist world against US imperialism.

1965. August 9. Freemasonry was outlawed in Syria.

1966. February 23. Hafez al-Asad and Salah Jadid seized power in Syria, toppling the first Baath regime. President Amin al-Hafez was arrested, while Baath Party founders Salah al-Bitar and Michel Aflaq were exiled, with orders never to return. Jadid and Asad appointed the civilian Nur al-Din al-Atasi as President of Syria and Secretary-General of the Baath Party.

1965. April 13. The new leaders of Syria permitted Khalid Bakdash, leader of the Communist Party, to return to Syria after having been in exile since 1958.

1967. April 7. Israel conducted an air raid over Syria, aimed at provoking the Syrian leadership into going to war. The raid was repeated on April 12.

1967. June 5. Outbreak of the second Arab-Israeli War, led by Gamal Abd al-Nasser. The Arab armies were collectively defeated, and Israel occupied the Golan Heights, the West Bank, Gaza Strip, the Sinai Peninsula and all of Jerusalem. UN Resolution 242 was passed, demanding restoration of the occupied West Bank and Gaza. Approximately 250,000 more Palestinians fled to neighboring Syria, Jordan, and Lebanon.

1967. June 9. Nasser resigned from the presidency in Egypt, taking complete blame for the defeat. His resignation was rejected by the Arab masses, and especially in Syria, the masses poured out, demanding that he stay in power and lead them to victory.

1967. June 18. President Nur al-Din al-Atasi went to New York to address the General Assembly of the UN on Syria's crisis with Israel. It was the first appearance for a Syrian President at the UN.

1967. June 30. Ex-President Shukri al-Quwatli died in exile in Beirut at the age of 75.

1969. February 25-28. Asad launched a mini-coup, arresting some of Jadid's loyalists, including editors of al-Thawra and al-Baath newspapers, to prove to Jadid that he was the one controlling Syria.

1969. September 9. The state nationalized private education in Syria.

1969. March 2. Abd al-Karim al-Jundi, the director of Syrian Intelligence, commited suicide in Damascus. He was one of the officers who launched the Baath Party Revolution of March 8, 1963.

1970. September. Outbreak of violence in Jordan between the PLO and King Husayn. Asad refused to engage his troops in combat with either party.

1970. September 28. President Gamal Abd al-Nasser of Egypt died in Cairo at the age of 52. The grief in the Arab World was unparalled.

1970. November 16. Hafez al-Asad seized power in Syria, launching a "correction movement" and arrested President Nur al-Din al-Atasi and Salah Jadid. He propped up Ahmad al-Khatib, a civilian, as president, and making himself Prime Minister. He restored parliamentary life to Syria, renaming it the People's Assembly and created its first chamber with state-appointed officials.

1971. March 13. Asad released a new constitution for Syria, which made the Baath Party the ruling party of the state and society. The constitution remains in effect today.

1972. March 4. Mohammad Umran, the ex-Syrian Minister of Defense, was murdered at his residence in Tripoli, Lebanon. He co-foundered the Military Committee of the Baath Party, which seized power in 1963, but had a falling out with Jadid in 1966.

1973. October 6. Hafez al-Asad and Anwar al-Sadat launched the third Arab-Israeli War, coined by history as "the October War." Syria retrieved al-Qunaytra, the principal town in the Golan Heights, and Egypt retrieved the Sinai Peninsula.

1974. May. Syria signed a disengagement treaty with Israel.

1975. April 13. Outbreak of civil war in Lebanon.

1976. May 31. The Syrian Army entered Lebanon responding to pleas of Lebanese Christians. The decision was reached after lengthy meetings between Asad and the two leading Christian figures in Lebanon, ex-President Kamil Sham'un and Pierre Gemayel. Syria engaged in military operations against the Palestinian Liberation Organization (PLO) of Yasser Arafat, aimed at ending the civil war.

1977. November. Anwar al-Sadat made a groundbreaking visit to Jerusalem.

1978. September. Anwar al-Sadat signed the Camp David Peace Agreement with Israel. He was accused of treason by President Asad and Syria severed diplomatic relations with Egypt.

1979. February. A revolution overthrew Shah Mohammad Reza Pehlavi in Iran, bringing Ayatollah al-Khomeini to power in Tehran. The revolution was greatly welcomed by Asad.

1979. July 16. Saddam Husayn seized power in Iraq.

1980. July 21. Salah al-Bitar, the co-founder of the Baath Party, was assassinated while exiled in Paris, France.

1980. September. Saddam Husayn began a long, bloody, and costly war with Iran that Asad denounced, claiming that it was diverting Arab attention from war with Israel.

1981. October 6. President Anwar al-Sadat of Egypt was assassinated while celebrating the Arab-Israeli War of 1973. There was rejoicing in Syria since he was considered a "traitor" according to official discourse, for having conclude a peace treaty with Israel.

1982. February. The Syrian Army went to war in Hama against the Muslim Brotherhood, who were calling for a holy war against the Baathists. The military uprising against the regime was crushed by force, and the armed forces pledged unwavering loyalty to Hafez al-Asad.

1982. June 6. Ariel Sharon invaded Lebanon and battled both the PLO and the Syrian Army.

1982. September 14. Bashir Gemayel, the president-elect of Lebanon, was assassinated in Beirut. He was an archenemy of Syria because he facilitated the occupation of Beirut by Ariel Sharon in June to expel the Syrian Army and the PLO. Accusations were made against Syria.

1982. September 16. Maronite militias, avenging the killing of Bashir Gemayel, entered the Sabra and Shatila refugee camps and slaughtered thousands of Palestinian civilians. The massacre was committed by the troops of Elie Hobeika, under the watchful eye of Ariel Sharon.

1983. May 17. Lebanese President Amin Gemayel negoitated a peace treaty with Israel, infuriating Hafez al-Asad, who joined ranks with rivaling Lebanese militias to bring it down. He succeeded in foiling the May 17 Agreement.

1983. November. President Asad suffered a heart attack, arousing the presidential ambitions of his brother, Rifaat al-Asad.

1984. March 30. Rifaat al-Asad ordered his troops into the Syrian capital, attempting a coup d'etat against the President. He was confronted by Asad's allies, Defense Minister Mustapha Tlas, Chief of Staff Hikmat Shihabi, and the generals, Ali Haydar and Ali Duba. The coup was foiled, through the intervention of Hafez al-Asad, who reached a compromise with his brother.

1984. May 28. Rifaat al-Asad was banished from Syria.

1985. August. Israel created the "Iron First Policy" against Palestinians living in the Occupied Territories. Defense Minister Yitzhak Rabin ordered troops to demolish homes, arrest and deport Palestinians, and "break bones" of those who resisted Israel.

1985. December 28. Vice-President Abd al-Halim Khaddam brokered the Tripartite Agreement between warring Lebanese militias, hoping that it would help end the civil war, and foil the May 17 Agreement.

1986. February 4. Israel forced a jet carrying Abdullah al-Ahmar, the deputy Secretary-General of the Baath Party, to land in Israel. Syria protested to the United Nations, and as a result Ahmar was freed.

1986. April. British police foiled an attempt to blow up an Israeli airplane at Heathrow Airport in London. The plot was to have been carried out by Nizar Hindawi, a Jordanian, under directives of Mohammad al-Khuly, the Commander of Air Force Intelligence. The Hindawi Affair embarrassed Syria in the world community, and led to the sacking of Khuly by Asad. As a result, Prime Minister Margaret Thatcher severed diplomatic relations with Damascus and they were not resumed until after Syria took part in Operation Desert Storm to liberate Kuwait in 1991.

1987. December 7. The first intifada broke out in the occupied Palestinian territories, causing uproar in the Arab World and attracting worldwide attention. The stone-throwers became a symbol for rebellion and Arab pride, and were eulogized in Syria by government and public alike.

1989. March. General Michel Aoun, the ex-Army Commander and current Prime Minister of Lebanon, staged a war against the Syrian Army in Lebanon.

1989. June 4. Michel Aflaq died in exile in Baghdad at the age of 88.

1989. October. Syria created the Taif Accord in Saudi Arabia, bringing an end to the Lebanese Civil War.

1990. August 2. Saddam Husayn invaded and occupied Kuwait.

1990. October. General Aoun was defeated in Beirut by the Syrian Army, enabling the civilian leader, Elias Hrawi (backed by Asad) to assume his responsibilities as President of Lebanon, a post to which he was elected in November 1989. Syria's victory was endorsed by the USA as a reward for joining the US-headed coalition to liberate Kuwait from the Iraqi Army.

1991. January. Syria joined the USA in Operation Desert Storm, with an international coalition created to liberate Kuwait.

1991. October. Asad sent a senior delegation to the Madrid Peace Conference, held under the auspices of the USA, where Syria agreed, for the first time since 1949, to have round table talks with Israel.

1991. December 25. The USSR, Syria's strategic ally since 1956, collapsed, prompting Asad to open channels with the USA.

1992. August. Syrian-Israeli peace talks began at the State Department in Washington. Syria was represented by Ambassador Muwafaq al-Allaf and Israel by Itamar Rabinovich.

1993. September 13. Yasser Arafat signed a peace deal with Israel at the White House. The Oslo Accord was highly criticized by Syria and Asad accused Arafat of having divided the Arab World by conducting a separate peace with Israel. Arafat was elected first President of Palestine in January 1996.

1994. January 21. Basil al-Asad, the eldest son of Hafez al-Asad, died in a car accident in Damascus. Hafez al-Asad was never the same without him.

1994. October. King Husayn signed a peace agreement with Israel. Again, it was highly criticized by Syria.

1994. December. Chief-of-Staff Hikmat Shihabi met for more US-sponsored peace talks with Israeli Chief-of-Staff Ehud Barak.

1995. November. Israeli Prime Minister Yitzhak Rabin was assassinated in Israel.

1998. April 30. Nizar Qabbani, Syria's leading poet, died at 75 in self-imposed exile in London. He was mourned like no other poet in Syrian history.

1999. February 9. King Husein died in Amman, Jordan, having ruled for 47-

years marked by animosity towards Syria. President Asad attended the funeral in a gesture of goodwill towards the new king, Abdullah II.

1999. December. The last round of high-profile talks between Syria and Israel took place at the White House, hosted by US President Bill Clinton. Attending were Foreign Minister Farouk al-Shara and Israeli Prime Minister Ehud Barak; but both men failed to reach a suitable agreement that would return Israel to its pre-June 4, 1967 borders.

2000. March. Asad held a highly publicized meeting with US President Bill Clinton in Geneva, aimed at resolving the Syrian-Israeli gridlock. The Geneva Conference failed, and Asad refused to normalize relations with Israel before the Golan Heights were returned to Syria according to the pre-June 4, 1967 borders.

2000. May 21. Ex-Prime Minister Mahmud al-Zu'bi commited suicide in Damascus to avoid being tried for corruption. He was discharged from office by Asad in March 2000 after spending 13-years in power in which he greatly misused public office.

2000. May 24. Israel withdrew from occupied South Lebanon. The resistance of Hizbullah, supported by Syria, declared victory over Israel, and this was largely attributed to Asad's unwavering support for the Lebanese resistance since 1978.

2000. June 10. Hafez al-Asad died in Syria at the age of 70.

2000. July 17. Bashar al-Asad was sworn-in as President of Syria. He was the youngest president to date in Syrian history.

2000. August. President Asad authorized private schools and universities to open in Syria, breaking the state monopoly over education, in place since 1963.

2000. September 28. Another intifadah broke out in the Occupied Territories, due to a provocative visit by Ariel Sharon to the al-Aqsa Mosque in Jerusalem.

2000. December 2. President Asad authorized private banks, breaking the state monopoly over the banking sector, in place since 1963.

2001. February. Ariel Sharon became Prime Minister of Israel.

2001. May. Pope John Paul II made a historic visit to Syria.

2001. September. President Asad authorized private newspapers, breaking the state monopoly over political publications, in place since 1963.

2001. September 11. The Saudi-born terrorist Osama Bin Laden and his al-Qaeda network launched two massive attacks on New York and Washington, DC, targeting the World Trade Center and the Pentagon. President George W. Bush pledged a war against international terror, and Syria promised to take part in an international offensive against terrorism.

2001. December. Asad created the Ministry of Expatriate Affairs to bridge the gap between Syrian expatriates and their country. The first minister was Nasser Qaddur, and he was replaced in September 2003 by Dr Buthaina Shaaban.

2003. March. The USA began its war on the Baathist regime of Saddam Husayn in Iraq. The war was criticized throughout the world and Syria voiced its strong opposition at the UN.

2003. April 9. The Baath Party regime in Iraq was defeated by US-led forces.

2003. October 6. Israeli Prime Minister Ariel Sharon attacked the Syrian heartland, bombing a Palestinian refugee camp that he claims, was used as a military base for Islamic Jihad, a faction of the resistance based in Syria. Damascus filed a complaint against Israeli aggression at the UN.

2003. December 12. President Bush signed the Syrian Accountability Act. The Act called on Syria to withdraw from Lebanon, cease its alleged weapons of mass destruction program, and stop supporting the Hizbullah resistance in South Lebanon. It also called on Syria to expel the Palestinian resistance residing on its territory, mainly Hamas and Islamic Jihad.

2003. December 13. Ex-President Saddam Husayn was arrested in Iraq by the US Army. He will stand trial as a war criminal.

2004. March 12. Kurdish unrest occurred in Syria, accompanied by acts of violence and vandalism, unprecedented in Syria and generally believed to be triggered by the USA to add further pressure on Syria.

2004. April. Syria suffered from a terrorist attack in Damascus, where a group of Islamic fundamentalists attacked and destroyed a UN building in the Mezzeh neighborhood.

2004. May. The Syrian Accountability Act was put into effect against Syria.

2004. October. Syria broke a long friendship with France by insisting on renewing the mandate of President Emile Lahhoud in Lebanon, defying public opinion in Lebanon. A bitter French President Jacque Chirac allied himself with President George Bush, and the two men pushed for UN Resolution 1559, calling on Syria to withdraw from Lebanon, and disarm Hizbullah. Syria insisted on renewing the term of President Lahhoud, leading to the resignation of Prime Minister Rafiq al-Harriri. He was replaced by the pro-Syrian Prime Minister Omar Karameh.

2004. December. US pressure on Damascus increased, and the USA accused Syria of supporting the military insurrection in Iraq. Iraq's new President, Prime Minister, and Minister of Defense accused Syria of supporting the rebels in Baghdad.

2004. November. Yasser Arafat, Syria's long-time foe, died in a Paris hospital. Asad attended his funeral, and turned a new page in Syrian-Palestinian relations with Mahmud Abbas, the new Palestinian President.

2005. February 15. Ex-Prime Minister Rafiq al-Harriri of Lebanon was killed in a massive explosion in Beirut. The Lebanese opposition, along with France and the USA, blamed Syria for his death, claiming that as its patron, it did not provide Lebanon with adequate security. All sides pressured Damascus to withdraw from Lebanon. Syria responded by redeploying its troops to the Beqqa Valley, as dictated by the Taif Accord of 1989. On March 5, 2005, Asad gave a groundbreaking speech to Parliament, declaring the withdrawal of his troops to the Syrian side of the Syrian-Lebanese border. Bush reacted to the Harriri assassination by withdrawing his Ambassador, Margaret Scobey, from Damascus.

2005. April 26. The Syrian Army withdraws completely from Lebanon, a country it had entered during the civil war in 1976. By doing so, Syria completed its requirements from UN Resolution 1559. The remaining clause, article 3, calls for the disarmament of Hizbullah, the resistance that is supported by Iran and Syria. The Damascus regime refuses to interfere, claiming that what remains of 1559 is a pure domestic Lebanese issue.

2005. May 7. General Michel Aoun, the former prime minister and army commander of Lebanon, returns after spending 14 years in exile. During his exile, he had been one of the loudest opponents of Syria. After his return, he ends his criticism of Syria and claims that Syria is no longer responsible for Lebanese domestics.

2005. June 6-9. The Baath Party Conference is held in Syria. It is the first since Bashar al-Asad became president in July 2000. The conference comes out with notable changes and reforms. Many of Syria's long-time officials, some in power since 1963, step down from political party life. These include Vice-Presidents Abd al-Halim Khaddam and Zuhayr Masharka, Assistant Baath Party Secretary General Abdullah al-Ahmar, and Defense Minister Mustapha Tlas. The conference also authorizes the creation of a multiparty system in Syria and new parties are not required to join the National Progressive Front (NPF), the parliamentary coalition of socialist parties headed by the Baath since the early 1970s.

2005. July. A group of gunmen are apprehended on Mount Qassiun overlooking Damascus. There is much shooting and several injuries. Weeks later, another terrorist network is apprehended on the Syrian-Lebanese border and a third is captured before sending a three-year old girl with explosives into the crowded Palace of Justice in Damascus.

Sami Moubayed is an author and political analyst specializing in modern Syria, Lebanon, and Palestine. He is a native of Damascus, Syria. Moubayed studied political science at the American University of Beirut and earned a PhD in Middle East Studies from the University of Exeter. He is the author of two previous books on Syria: *The Politics of Damascus 1920-1946* (1998) and *Damascus Between Democracy and Dictatorship 1948-1958* (2000). Moubayed's articles on modern Middle East affairs have appeared in regional and international newspapers including *al-Ahram* (Cairo), *Gulf News* (Dubai), *The Daily Star* (Beirut), *Washington Report on Middle East Affairs* (Washington, DC), and *Asia Times* (Hong Kong). He is founder of the website Syrianhistory.com, the first online museum of Syrian history. He is co-founder of the Syrian Young Enterpreneurs Association (SYEA).

Moubayed is one of just a few Syrians who devotes himself to explaining the Arab perspective to a Western audience. For more: www.mideastviews.com.